Onward to

VICTORY

For Pat,

Go Irish.

Best wishes,

Murray Sperber

10/30/98

MURRAY
SPERBER

Onward to

VICTORY

THE
CRISES
THAT
SHAPED
COLLEGE
SPORTS

HENRY HOLT AND COMPANY

NEW YORK

Henry Holt and Company, Inc./*Publishers since 1866*
115 West 18th Street/New York, New York 10011

Henry Holt ® is a registered trademark of Henry Holt and Company

Published in Canada by Fitzhenry & Whiteside Ltd.,
195 Allstate Parkway, Markham, Ontario L3R 4T8.

Library of Congress Cataloging-in-Publication Data
Sperber, Murray.
Onward to victory : the crises that shaped college sports /
by Murray Sperber.—1st ed.
p.   cm.
Includes index.
ISBN 0-8050-3865-5 (alk. paper)
1. College sports—United States—History.   I. Title.
GV351.S646   1998
796.04′3′0973—dc21   98-17436

Henry Holt books are available for special promotions
and premiums. For details contact: Director, Special Markets.

First Edition 1998

Designed by Victoria Hartman

Printed in the United States of America
All first editions are printed on acid-free paper. ∞
1   3   5   7   9   10   8   6   4   2

For my father
Lawrence Lazarus Sperber
1905–1996
whose gift of optimism sustains me.

Contents

Part 6: *Recovering from the Scandals: Media-Made College Sports*

Preface

This book began as a study of the historic fight between the critics of big-time college sports, mainly academics such as myself, versus its proponents—athletic directors, coaches, and their outside allies, particularly their media supporters. In my book *College Sports Inc.: The Athletic Department vs. the University* (1990), I had participated in the conflict, and subsequently I wanted to understand its roots and context.

After reading the record carefully, and writing one sports history book, I concluded that most contemporary critics have trouble admitting an important truth (I certainly did until I moved from the present era and its disputes to a larger perspective on the situation): big-time college sports has won its struggle with its opponents, annihilating their demands, notably de-emphasis, and long ago moved from a reformable state to its currently entrenched and gargantuan form. The title *Onward to Victory* indicates, and material in this book analyzes, the key phase of that journey.

Battles between the proponents of big-time college sports and their faculty adversaries occurred throughout the twentieth century. Trying to tell the entire story would force a writer to skim the surface, presenting a very superficial account. But how to emphasize important details and still remain cogent and coherent? The answer came while attempting to order the research files for this book. One fact kept recurring, astounding me, demanding explanation: *no* other American institution has experienced greater crises and scandals than big-time college sports, and yet it has not only survived all of them but thrived. Moreover, the problems never end—and they never dent the public's and the media's love for the games and their participants. Why?

To answer this question, I focused on the most crisis-filled and scandal-ridden period in the history of intercollegiate athletics: the financial and manpower failures during the Depression and World War II, and then the horrendous basketball fixing and football cheating scandals of the postwar years. Not only were these events fascinating and illuminating in themselves, but they also shaped the entire subsequent history of intercollegiate athletics, particularly the form of the modern National Collegiate Athletic Association (NCAA), the relations between athletic departments and the media, and the latter's representations of college teams, athletes, and coaches. To comprehend big-time college sports during this period—the 1930s through the 1950s—is to understand its amazing power and popularity, a force that propelled it into the present era and moves it into the next century. Hence the subtitle, *The Crises That Shaped College Sports.*

How did college sports survive its worst crises and scandals, and evolve into its modern form? The short answer is that the media and the fans saved it, and the NCAA papered over the systemic failures. Moreover, as this book makes clear, at one point the academic opponents of big-time college sports came close to achieving their major objective: permanent de-emphasis. However, because the media promoted college sports so well, because the fans loved it and their favorite teams so fervently, and because the NCAA cleverly used the situation for its own ends, the games went on despite the massive problems. The media and the NCAA acted out of self-interest, but what was in it for the fans? Why did they care so much?

After *College Sports Inc.,* I wrote a book, *Shake Down the Thunder: The Creation of Notre Dame Football* (1993), that examined the University of Notre Dame, a school with athletic teams beloved by more Americans and for more generations than any other in the country. That study helped me understand the historic popularity of college sports, the appeal of its star athletes and coaches, and the role the media played in promoting them. I discussed those topics in that work, but I analyze them in much greater depth in this one.

As part of my work for *Shake Down the Thunder,* I read the correspondence of Knute Rockne, approximately 14,500 items, none of them previously examined by a professional researcher, as well as the correspondence between Rockne's widow and officials of the University of Notre Dame, and both parties with Warner Brothers, the Hollywood film studio that made the famous movie *Knute Rockne—All-American. Shake Down the Thunder* described those negotiations but did not discuss the impact of the Rockne movie upon Americans in the 1940s, or how that film forever changed the media portrayal of college sports. That discussion forms the opening section of *Onward to Victory.* Not only did Knute Rockne and his Fighting Irish play a crucial role in establishing the original popularity of college football, but the Hollywood image of Rockne and Notre Dame helped maintain the sport's appeal during the crisis years and beyond, contributing many essential elements to the ideology of modern college sports, including the "student-athlete" metaphor and the coach-as-culture-hero. Therefore this book pays particular attention to the media depictions of Rockne and Notre Dame as well as the historical reality (as best we can ascertain it) of the man, his successors, like Frank Leahy, and his university.

At first glance, it seems illogical that a survey of college sports catastrophes should feature a school that totally avoided them, but closer analysis reveals that Notre Dame played a key part in the battle of public opinion and, as a result of its victories, it helped big-time college sports stay afloat, and gain its modern shape. As the sports maxim explains, "The best defense is a good offense," and, during the crises and scandals, ND's image and its reality often kept the opponents of intercollegiate athletics off the scoreboard.

A note about the title: it is a phrase from the "Notre Dame Victory March," but because that song is so well known, inevitably, previous authors have used *Onward to Victory* as a book title, among them James Armstrong, the first director of the Notre Dame alumni association, for his long-out-of-print work on that group's initial period. Considering the differences between his subject and mine, I do not believe that the similarity of titles will cause confusion for any reader. In addition, the Library of Congress Catalog cites other works with the same title, but all of them so obscure as to not merit mention here.

A word of caution to those college sports fans who assume that the title *Onward to Victory* indicates a triumphal tome, the kind that the NCAA and allied journalists crank out. This book does not belong to that species. *Onward to Victory* presents intercollegiate athletics within the wider context of American social history, and also focuses on the beyond-the-game issues and dealings that shaped the college sports enterprise. In the entire book, no athlete makes a glorious run in a bowl game, but the reader will discover how and why various New Year's Day contests came about, how much money changed hands, and why the media portrayed the games in certain ways as opposed to adhering to the reality of the events.

Notre Dame fans, because of that school's commendable conduct during the crisis-and-scandal years, will probably enjoy the story—although I want to emphasize that I did not set out to write a pro–Notre Dame book, nor do I believe that I have written one. I analyzed documents and incidents as honestly and clearly as I could, and if the results of that analysis show Notre Dame mainly in a positive light, so be it. Similarly, if the analysis places institutions like the NCAA, as well as various individuals, in an unfavorable light, I assure readers that I did not make up the negative facts, that I am quoting from the historical record, and that the footnotes in the back of the book offer full citations of my sources—as they do for the positive material.

A personal disclaimer: I am not a Notre Dame fan—as a graduate of Purdue University and the University of California, Berkeley, I long ago attached my loyalties to those schools. I realize that some college sports fans and members of the media detest the Fighting Irish, absolutely certain that they can do no right, and contemptuous of any author who points out anything positive about them and their history. The anti–Notre Dame fans find their mirror image in rabid ND fanatics. Frankly, I have zero personal sympathy for both groups—however, as a professional researcher, I am fascinated by their attitudes and behavior, and I discuss these at length in this book.

All of which connects to my final point: everyone harbors biases, but authors must acknowledge and deal appropriately with theirs. I, personally, regret the triumph of big-time college sports but, as a serious researcher, I cannot dispute that reality or fail to explore the reasons for it. While reading the historical background for this project I sympathized with the academic critics of big-time college sports, but in writing the book, my disappointment with their failure to achieve reform is far less important than trying to explain what happened and why.

In the end, for the book, my professional expertise matters much more than my personal feelings, and, if I have succeeded in presenting the historical record fairly and clearly, readers will be able to make up their own minds as to the ultimate meaning of the events discussed in *Onward to Victory.*

Acknowledgments

Many people helped me with this book. Foremost were my friend and agent John Wright and my sympathetic editors, Bill Strachan, Darcy Tromanhauser, and David Sobel. John has helped me with many books, and the journey of this one, full of Sturm und Drang, demonstrated his winning wire-to-wire character (to draw metaphors from his two favorite pastimes, Wagner and OTB). Bill made possible my previous books on college sports and helped enormously with this one. When he left Henry Holt and Company to become president of Columbia University Press, Darcy Tromanhauser ably continued the editorial work, and when she departed, David Sobel kindly took in my orphaned book. Unlike many editors with a foundling on their desk, David treated this book with kindness and kept me on schedule.

I am also very grateful to the many persons whom I interviewed for this project. First on the list is the late Edward "Moose" Krause, longtime athletic director at the University of Notre Dame. I was very fortunate to speak with Mr. Krause during the summers of 1991 and 1992; not only was he kind and patient with me, but also argumentative and very funny—frankly, I learned more from our "heated discussions" and his ribald anecdotes than from the times when he lapsed into the "official line." I deeply regret that he cannot see his comments and my thanks in print. In addition, my friend and fellow sports author, John Kryk, conducted extensive interviews with Mr. Krause in the early 1990s, and I thank John for kindly sharing his transcripts with me, and also allowing me to quote from unpublished portions of them.

Many other interviewees helped me with this project. Whether they spoke on or off the record, they were invariably generous with their time and observations. I was able to fit only a small fraction of their words and names into the final text, but they all greatly contributed to my knowledge of college sports, and I thank them. The list of people with whom I discussed aspects of this project is long, but I must single out former Associated Press reporter Jim Beach; former executive vice-president of Notre Dame, Father Edmund P. Joyce; Notre Dame vice-president Richard W. Conklin; and former sports information director, Roger Valdiseri, for their special help. Finally, I must offer very overdue thanks to the late Gordon Graham, longtime sports editor of the *Lafayette (Indiana) Journal & Courier*, for the wonderful interviews he provided many years ago, and his help with my senior project at Purdue (I am pleased that I can finally place some of his wisdom in print).

Over the years I have done research in many archives on this continent and abroad. In all of that time, I have never encountered more accommodating and conscientious archivists than at the University of Notre Dame: I must thank them collectively and individually. Head archivist Dr. Wendy Clauson Schlereth always displayed sympathy and good humor when confronting my time-consuming requests—she made this book and the previous one possible, and helped me complete them on schedule. Charles Lamb, in charge of the University of Notre Dame graphics collection, helped me find many wonderful items in the Notre Dame football game program collection, and in the films and tapes of college football games, as well as photos for this book; in addition, Charles provided ongoing insight into the psychology of Fighting Irish fans and the Notre Dame football phenomenon. Associate archivist Peter Lysy, a true detective, helped me find many important documents in the archives; his assistant Matthew Steffens also helped locate documents and freely offered his advice, whether requested or not; associate archivist William Kevin Cawley solved various computer problems for me; Sharon Sumpter always fulfilled my e-mail requests promptly, firing off faxes of needed material; and Angie Kindig, Marlene Wasikowski, and Delores Fain aided me in many different ways. Finally, thanks to Beth Lamb for the many excellent dinners and the Minnesotan viewpoint on Notre Dame.

I am also grateful to George Rugg, curator of the Joyce Sports Research Collection at the University of Notre Dame. In my search for football game programs from schools across the country, George provided valuable help, not only in locating the programs but also in helping me interpret their iconography. In addition, he helped me make sense of the first decade of *Sport* magazine and shared with me the joy of finding photos and articles on such seminal figures as Walt Dropo, Sam Jethroe, and Fern Flaman.

I must also thank the employees at the Motion Picture, Broadcasting, and Sound Division of the Library of Congress in Washington, D.C. I spent a very profitable summer viewing a large number of their holdings of college sports movies—many of these films are only available in their collection—and listening to some of their recordings. Being able to understand and write about these movies and radio broadcasts on the basis of firsthand viewing and listening added an important dimension to this book. In addition, the archives of the American Council on Education made available important documents on the ACE's failed reform attempt, and I must thank the ACE librarians, particularly Jill Bogard in the D.C. office, for their help. Making my research in "The District" possible was my friend and D.C. landlord, Paul Strohm, and my colleague, Aaron Baker of Arizona State University.

At my own school—Indiana University, Bloomington—many persons aided me with this project: in the main library, Ann Bristow, head of the Reference Department, and her extraordinary assistant Dave Frasier—an expert on everything from celebrity suicides to minor league hockey; also thanks to Christine Brancolini and Colleen Talty of Media/Reserve Services; Marty Sorury and Diana Hanson in Microfilm Services; and Keith Welch in Library Services. In the English department, I received assistance from many people, most notably the chair, Ken Johnston, and staff members Reba Amerson, June Hacker, Linda Goodwin, and Will Murphy, as well as faculty members Don Gray, Susan Gubar, Jim Naremore, David Nordloh, Scott Sanders, and Albert Wertheim. In addition, special thanks to my former student interns James Bridgeman III, Paul DeBlase, Matt Komen, Courtney Rabada, Jonathan Richardson, and Gene Spielvogel, who, during the years I spent on this book, helped make my courses run more efficiently.

At my publisher, Henry Holt and Company, many people helped with this book and my previous ones, and I appreciate the time and effort they extended on my behalf. At the top of the list, Robin Jones, and formerly with Holt, Lottchen Shivers, and Julie Williams; copy editor Susanna Sturgis; editorial assistant Alessandra Bocco; and production editor Kathleen Fridella.

Finally, I am forever indebted to my wife, Aneta, for her love, strength, and good advice; in addition, her wonderful indifference to college sports puts my obsession into sane perspective. I am equally indebted to my daughter Gigi and my foster daughters Jayme and Logan, for their constant patience and understanding, as well as their willingness to sit with me during late-night dinners and early-morning breakfasts. As Gigi, currently an "archi" (architectural student) at Rice University, has discovered, professional writers are not the only ones who have to work under "killer deadlines" and put their social lives on hold for periods of time.

Lastly, I acknowledge my eternal debt to my late son, Oliver, who was so inspiring in life and whose memory keeps me company during the long hours in the library and in front of the computer. Ollie taught me the difference between the trivial and the important, and how sports should be fun and games. To treat sports with deadly seriousness is to ruin them, and to profane the reality of life and death.

Introduction

At various points during the telecast of a college sports game, why do the players' major fields of study flash onto the screen? That information tells viewers nothing about the game, but the TV producers always provide the information as part of their presentation of intercollegiate athletics. Why do the announcers always talk about "all the fine young men"—and, now, also "all the exemplary young women"—in the contests? What the athletes do outside the game is basically irrelevant to the outcome of the match, but apparently essential to the broadcast. These elements of the media coverage of college sports, as well as many others, seem such a permanent part of the TV landscape that viewers take them for granted, like the topography of their own backyards, almost assuming that divine providence put them there.

This mystified view of sports began long ago. The most famous American sportswriter of the first half of this century, Grantland Rice, once exclaimed, "Just what odd turn of evolution brought forward so many outstanding [sports] stars in" the 1920s? "There is no answer to this mystery . . . it must be listed as something that just happened beyond rhyme, reason, or the Milky Way. All that we know is that this Golden Age offered a flame that lit up the sporting skies and covered the world." For Rice, mystification ruled the universe, to be expressed in romantic language that obliterated all inquiry. But human activities do not exist in a baffling void, and researchers can offer plausible explanations for most occurrences, including the emergence of star athletes in the 1920s, and the boxes on TV screens identifying the players' majors. (The NCAA and member schools insist that TV producers put them there to promote the PR line that college sports participants are authentic student-athletes, not professionals wearing varsity uniforms.)

An excellent way to outline the actual history of college sports, from the first decades of this century to its modern form, is to examine the most famous prose and verse lines written by Grantland Rice, and the public reactions to them. These passages also help explain how Notre Dame football achieved its great fame and power, and came to occupy so much of America's consciousness about college sports. Moreover, they indicate why the Fighting Irish require such careful scrutiny and so many chapters in any chronicle on intercollegiate athletics, including this book.

> Outlined against a blue, gray October sky, the Four Horsemen rode again. In dramatic lore, they are known as Famine, Pestilence, Destruction and Death. These are only aliases. Their real names are Stuhldreher, Miller, Crowley, and Layden.

Grantland Rice wrote these lines during halftime of the 1924 Notre Dame–Army game at the Polo Grounds in New York City. A Notre Dame press assistant had suggested the Four Horsemen metaphor to him, prompting Rice to compose what became the single most famous passage in American sports journalism, words that changed the style of sportswriting and catapulted their author to the very top of his profession. Rice's dramatic approach—nicknamed "Gee-Whiz" sportswriting—depicted athletes in the most glorious terms; it greatly pleased the public, spawned countless imitators, and dominated the descriptions of intercollegiate athletics and other sports for a generation. In addition, when radio became popular in the late 1920s, broadcasters adopted the "Gee-Whiz" style, often describing games and players in a breathless, hyperbolic manner.

At the core of Grantland Rice's portrayal of college sports were the Notre Dame Fighting Irish and their coach, Knute Rockne. During Rice's long career, whenever he named the "outstanding" football stars of the "Golden Age," he always listed Rockne and the Four Horsemen first, thus reinforcing Notre Dame's importance in college sports history. Was the emergence of these stars a mystery? Robert Lipsyte, a sports journalist of a later generation, disagreed, explaining:

> The so-called Golden Age of Sports . . . was really the Golden Age of Sportswriting. The glories of the Babe . . . and the Four Horsemen were tunes composed on portable typewriters by gifted, ambitious, often cynical men . . . The Golden Age sportswriters hyped the country's post–World War I sports boom, rode the gravy train and then, for the good of the game, maintained the myths and legends as the country slid into a [1930s] bust."

Indeed, American spectator sports, particularly major league baseball and intercollegiate football, exploded in popularity during the 1920s because of the country's unprecedented economic prosperity. Increasing numbers of

Americans acquired disposable income and the leisure time in which to spend it; among other activities, they bought tickets to college sports events to see the media-created stars. Compared to other decades during the first half of the century, the 1920s seemed a Golden Age.

Elmer Layden, one of the Four Horsemen, later marveled at Grantland Rice's ability to transform this Notre Dame backfield, a quick but limited quartet, into the most celebrated in football history: "Even by 1924 standards, we were small," averaging less than 160 pounds. "By today's [1969] standards, we were almost midgets. We'd probably have trouble getting on most of today's college teams as student managers." With his typewriter, Rice proved that words are more powerful than the most bruising football "hit," and that words can manufacture versions of events more pleasing to many people than accurate reports on what actually occurred.

When the United States entered the Great Depression of the 1930s, Grantland Rice and his colleagues continued to promote college football— and their own careers—and they kept the Fighting Irish at center stage. The University of Notre Dame reciprocated by cultivating the sporting press, and the radio networks—the school allowed the latter to broadcast ND games for free, building Notre Dame's already huge fan following into the single largest in the country. Thus, when a Hollywood studio in the late 1930s decided to make the first major biographical film about a football hero—biopics were a popular movie form of the period—it chose Knute Rockne, knowing that the immense number of Fighting Irish rooters guaranteed break-even box office. In fact, *Knute Rockne—All-American* became a great hit, significantly increasing the cultural importance of Notre Dame football, and giving it a crucial role in the future of intercollegiate athletics.

■   ■   ■

Grantland Rice's most acclaimed prose passage—the Four Horsemen lead— captured the public's desire for college sports heroes; his most famous lines of verse—the conclusion of his poem "Alumnus Football"—expressed the way Americans wanted their heroes to play the games. Tracking his couplet from its creation in the 1900s through the century provides valuable information on the changing public reactions to college sports, the initial acceptance of a traditional ideal evolving into rejection in the modern era:

> *When the One Great Scorer comes to write against your name—*
> *He marks—not that you won or lost—but how you played the game.*

In these lines, Rice echoed the nineteenth-century British and American "amateur sportsman's" credo, i.e., that ethical conduct and effort during a sporting event were more important than winning. The concept originated with the British aristocracy—they won at birth—and their American counterparts accepted and helped promulgate it. The sports aspect was only one part of this gentleman's code, but it attracted attention because it directly opposed other values in United States society, particularly "striving to get ahead by any means." Grantland Rice, an early-twentieth-century graduate of a southern gentleman's school, Vanderbilt University, not only articulated the sentiment in the vernacular of American sports (marking on a baseball scorecard), but also gave it a religious dimension: The Lord will judge your conduct in athletics and all other endeavors. Nonetheless, in his life and career, Rice was extremely ambitious, even ruthless at times, hungry to win in the sportswriting profession.

During the first four decades of the twentieth century, some participants in American college sports followed Rice's dictum, but many did not, cheating in a large variety of ways. Yet in public utterances almost all subscribed to the credo, as did most fans and media members. A famous incident in 1940 illustrated the general acceptance and power of the how-you-play-the-game maxim: the Cornell football team, on course for the national championship, won a late-season game because the referee miscounted the downs, with the Big Red scoring and winning on a fifth down. However, when post-game films indicated the referee's error, Cornell officials renounced the victory and, in effect, the national championship. The team captain and many players quoted Rice's verse as justification for accepting the loss. Moreover, the media and most college football fans, including Cornell's, approved this gesture.

In retrospect, Cornell's action symbolizes one of the last great moments of old-fashioned intercollegiate athletics. When, the following year, America entered World War II, the country and its institutions began to change radically. College sports, particularly football, had long connected to the military, with such terms as platoons, formations, linemen in the trenches, etc., descended from World War I; from World War II came blitz, bomb, and many other concepts and terms. But the latter war also introduced such new links between war and sports as the Allies' demand of "unconditional surrender" applied to opponents on the playing field.

A famous college football coach expressed the new mood in a 1943 piece in a national magazine, "Sport for Sport's Sake Is Now Out." He condemned the traditional approach to athletics: "During the plush years of the '20s and through the fumbling '30s, we got too much of It-matters-not-who-won-or-lost, it's-how-you-played-the-game . . . that approach doesn't win football games—or wars either." The coach then repudiated Rice's dictum with his own formula for victory: "Just two simple rules: 1. You've got to be tough. 2. You've got to win."

World War II also put a greater emphasis on the college coach as leader, the guiding force directing his men to victory. The media had long equated coaches with military officers and, during the war, it reworked and amplified this linkage in many films and print pieces. The new officer-coaches possessed strategic creativity, concern for their "boys," and a passion to win. The wartime depictions changed the public perception of college coaches as well as the latter's self-image. Gone were the gentlemanly types sitting patiently on the sidelines; now "head men" commanded their troops to victory.

In the postwar era, many coaches also became athletic directors (ADs) and brought their new attitudes to the job. A 1950 article in the *Saturday Evening Post* noted that intercollegiate athletics had become a big business, and the "idea, of course, is to get the dough. The well-known quatrain of Noble Purpose has been cynically paraphrased" by big-time coaches and ADs to "And when the One Great Scorer comes / To write beside your name / It's not whether you won or lost / But how many paid to see the game."

But to attract the maximum number of fans, athletic programs had to produce winning teams; as a result, many coaches cheated in the recruiting and retention of athletes to build winners, and a huge "black market" in football and basketball players developed, cash payments to athletes escalating at an amazing rate (participants and the press even used the phrase "black market"). In addition, in the 1940s, with the invention of point-spread betting, college sports attracted massive amounts of gambling money, leading to the basketball fixing scandals of the late 1940s and early 1950s. All of these events mocked Grantland Rice's high-minded sentiments, upsetting many sports fans and members of the media.

During this period, some universities and colleges tried to adhere to the old-fashioned code. Refusing to compete in the black market, many small schools dropped out of big-time college sports, ratcheting their athletic programs down to the club level. And the Ivy League universities—founders of major intercollegiate athletics—de-emphasized, never to return to the top rank. However, a few institutions—most prominently the University of Notre Dame, because of its religious and academic traditions, as well as its unique advantages in recruiting—continued to uphold the college sports ideals, and still played at the highest level.

For proponents of the old values, the football bowl games—over forty a year existed in the postwar era—embodied many of the evils of the new form of intercollegiate athletics: the bowls occurred far from the natural campus settings for college sports; they were highly commercial and run by professional promoters; they required a large amount of extra training and travel for the student players involved; and they caused such ancillary problems as gambling and ticket-scalping frauds. For these reasons, a few universities, notably Notre Dame, refused all bowl invitations—and the large payouts from them—but most schools in big-time college sports embraced the year-end events. In addition, the NCAA, a small and weak organization up to the late 1940s, gained its first success and power by imposing its cartel rules upon the bowls.

Another corrupt college sports practice perfected in this period was the creation of special hideaway curriculums in which to shelter academically inept athletes. Again, some schools refused to sanction these "Mickey Mouse" courses, particularly small colleges and the Ivy League universities. Moreover, Notre Dame not only rejected this gimmick but insisted that all of its athletes obtain a 77 percent grade point average to participate in intercollegiate sports. (Regular ND students only needed 70 percent to remain in "good academic standing.") The Catholic school also allowed outside investigators to inspect the academic files of its varsity athletes, and no examiner ever reported any fudging of the 77 percent rule.

As a result of Notre Dame's adherence to traditional college sports values, and its ability to compete at the highest national level, during the late 1940s and early 1950s, as corruption spread and scandals occurred, the media increasingly focused on the Fighting Irish as an exemplar in intercollegiate athletics. In addition, for many Americans, the film *Knute Rockne—All-American,* still popular at the end of the decade, expressed the cherished college sports ideals, especially its portrayal of Rockne as a true scholar-athlete, a man who could have been a great chemist if he had not become a great sports figure.

In the early 1950s, the NCAA, in a publicity campaign to combat the scandals and also to counter court rulings that college athletes were professionals, put its PR twist on the Rockne portrait, inventing the term "student-athlete" and ordering all members to use it henceforth. (A direct line exists from this NCAA action to the boxes on the TV screens announcing the players' major fields of study.)

Nevertheless, big-time college sports could not return to the Rockne era, and a famous incident in 1953 both changed the public perception of Notre Dame and provided a last hurrah for Grantland Rice's famous dictum. In a late-season game against Iowa, the Fighting Irish faked a number of injuries to stop the clock, scoring key TDs and tieing the match as a result. (During this period, the rules and TV stoppages did not provide an abundance of time-outs, thus most teams resorted to "feigned injuries" to halt the clock.) Iowa coach Forest Evashevski—although he often used the same strategy—mocked Notre Dame's violation of "sportsmanlike conduct" with his version of Grantland Rice's famous lines: "When the One Great Scorer comes to write against our name, / He won't write whether we won or lost, / But how we got gypped at Notre Dame." Evashevski also called the ND players "the Fainting Irish," giving the incident its permanent nickname.

Then Grantland Rice put his imprimatur on the criticism of Notre Dame, commenting that "I consider it [Notre Dame's fake injuries] a complete violation of the spirit and ethics of the game and was sorry to see Notre Dame, *of all teams,* using this method." For all of the real and phony indignation at the ND tactic, the old-time values were waning, and could not endure much longer in mid-century America, with its increasing business competition, labor strife, and racial tensions. Similarly, the NCAA's revival of one-platoon football in 1953—the association's attempt to erase the scandal years and connect the "Grand Old Game" to its supposedly spotless past—soon withered away, permanently replaced by unlimited substitution and many platoons and special units, more in tune with modern American culture.

The final rewording of Grantland Rice's dictum began to appear in the media in the late 1950s. In a national magazine story on college football coach "Big Jim" Tatum, notorious for breaking the rules to produce winning teams, the writer inquired, "Is winning over-emphasized in the bigtime [college] game?" The coach replied, "I don't think winning is the most important thing. I think it is the only thing." Tatum's sarcasm succeeded because it played off of Grantland Rice's line, "He writes—*not that you won or lost.*" Without Rice's prior comment, and the public's longtime endorsement of it, Tatum's version would not have provoked knowing smiles or eventually entered the American vocabulary. (Most authorities attribute this quote to Vince Lombardi, but Big Jim expressed this sentiment years before Lombardi's variation appeared.)

Grantland Rice's verse had proclaimed that ethical conduct and effort were more important in sports than victory. Tatum, Lombardi, and many other Americans, including Richard Nixon (who often quoted the new version), turned the traditional idea upside down, parodying it with their declaration that "winning is the only thing" in sports and life, ethics and effort counting for nothing if victory is not achieved.

The increasing popularity and acceptance of this attitude measures the distance from the old-fashioned college sports world and the modern one, as well as the unbridgeable gulf between them. Humor often maps the route that a society travels; if a parody of a once revered belief prompts smiles, the old values are passing, new ones replacing them.

Not all Americans enjoyed the joke—some still treasured Rice's verse and sentiments—but "winning is the only thing" provided a banner for modern college sports, held aloft during the final decades of the century by many coaches and athletes. Moreover, a revealing parallel to Cornell's "fifth down" victory in 1940 occurred fifty years later: the University of Colorado, in contention for the 1990 national football championship, won a game on a fifth-down play, again caused by referee error. This time, the school did not forfeit the win, but instead counted it proudly as part of the Buffaloes' national championship season. And, in a final irony, in 1990, Colorado also won the annual Grantland Rice Trophy, awarded by the Football Writers Association of America to the best team in college football. This gesture buried Rice's aphorism in a deep grave, irrelevant to modern college sports, the media, and the vast majority of fans.

Author's Note:
A Definition of the Term "Classical"

In this book, the reader will find the terms "classical" and "classic" used frequently, particularly in regard to a certain kind of American movie and the period in which it was made. Film scholars, critics, and many movie fans now refer to the years from the mid-1930s to the mid-1950s—the heyday of the Hollywood studio system—as the *classical* era of American cinema. The late century television cable channels dedicated to these motion pictures also employ the term: American Movie Classics and Turner Classic Movies. In addition, the Classic Sports Network shows films and tapes of sporting events from those years. The expression has become so ubiquitous that the current symbol for "Classic Coca-Cola" is a green five-cent Coke bottle, Coke's main container from the mid-1930s through the mid-1950s.

Some film scholars also maintain that *classical* American films include many elements similar to the *classic* art of ancient Greece and Rome, and this connection validates the adjective "classical" for these movies. This argument seems correct; however, in *Onward to Victory,* to avoid confusion, "classical" and "classic" refer only to certain kinds of American films and other cultural products, not to the art of antiquity. The main text of this book provides full definitions and discussions of twentieth-century *classics.*

Part 1

Knute Rockne— All-American:

American Myths and College Sports

1

Knute Rockne Becomes Myth

The movies are furnishing the nation with a common body of knowledge. What the classics once were in that respect, what the Bible once was, the cinema has become for the average man. Here are stories, names, phrases, points of view which are common national property. The man in Cedar Creek, Maine, and the man in Cedar Creek, Oregon, see the same movie in the same week.

—Sociologist Margaret Thorp, 1939.

D r. Thorp worked at a time when movies were America's favorite leisure pastime, when a large majority of Americans spent at least one afternoon or evening a week in a movie theater, and many went more often. Ticket sales averaged ninety to a hundred million per week in the late 1930s and early 1940s. Her research indicated that film images and stories profoundly influenced moviegoers, with viewers often reacting to the screen behavior of popular actors by imitating it. When Clark Gable revealed in a 1934 film that he did not wear an undershirt, the sales of men's undershirts plummeted, effectively ending their general production.

American mass culture had existed before the 1930s, but during that decade the film industry gave it an immediacy and uniformity previously unknown; this period began the age in which we still live, television and other media building upon the film production system. Movies became the common experience shared by most Americans. Subsequently, even such rebels against mainstream society as the founders of the Beat Generation acknowledged Hollywood's power during the classical studio period: "Moviegoing in the 1930s and early 1940s . . . gave us all a fantasy life in common from which we are still dragging up the images that obsess us" (John Clellon Holmes, the Tom Saybrook character in Jack Kerouac's *On the Road*).

> You'll probably argue with me but I think that the most important movie ever made was *Knute Rockne—All-American*. Certainly in terms of what I love and spent my life doing—college sports. I'm prejudiced, of course, I played for the man and it's about my school . . .
>
> But for college sports and American life, it's the most important picture because it set up the ideal for coaches and players. People forget that college sports was in bad shape before that movie came out . . .
>
> —Edward "Moose" Krause, former Notre Dame athlete,
> coach, and athletic director, in a 1991 interview.

Most film critics would give the Greatest Movie Award to a picture made during the same period as *Knute Rockne—All-American:* Orson Welles's *Citizen Kane*. Without question, from an aesthetic point of view, *Citizen Kane* is far superior to the football biopic. However, in terms of affecting American culture and leaving a permanent imprint upon an important part of it—intercollegiate athletics—Moose Krause's favorite picture deserves full accolades.

Great films use and illustrate great myths: *Citizen Kane*, the rise and fall of a monarch; *Knute Rockne—All-American,* the immigrant and Horatio Alger sagas. Unlike most outstanding films, however, *Knute Rockne* also began a number of important myths and aided the career of a politician who, immersing himself in the old and new myths of the movie, became one of the most popular American presidents of the twentieth century.

■   ■   ■

> LARS ROCKNE:
> I like what I hear about America. It's a new country, full of new life and opportunities for a working man like me. (He glances toward a small, sturdy four-year-old boy who has sauntered into the open shop, eating an apple.)
> But mainly I want those things for my children.
>
> —The opening scene in the shooting script and film,
> *Knute Rockne—All-American*, 1940.

The movie begins in Voss, Norway, the country village where the Rockne family lived at the end of the last century. Knute's father, Lars, announces to three village elders that he plans to go to America. They are skeptical, but he articulates the credo of generations of immigrants, emphasizing the newness of America—as opposed to the quaint street scenes and cottages of Voss in the *old* country. Most of all he wants to emigrate for his children. He calls over young Knute: "I want Knute here, and his sisters, to start their lives on an equal basis with all other children, and they can only do that in America."

This scene fades out and, in the script, the direction for the FADE IN reads, "Over a background-effect of the Atlantic Ocean, blending into the skyline of New York, then Chicago, as those cities appeared in the 1890s, we superimpose [the following words.]" However, in the actual movie, before the city scenes appear we see a long take of the Statue of Liberty and hear many choruses of "America the Beautiful." Then the message scrolls:

> AMONG MILLIONS LIKE THEMSELVES, SIMPLE, HARD-WORKING PEOPLE
> FROM THE OLD COUNTRIES, FOLLOWING THE NEW ROAD OF EQUALITY
> AND OPPORTUNITY WHICH LED TO AMERICA, THE ROCKNE FAMILY
> SETTLED IN CHICAGO . . .

The filmmakers added the extra patriotic touches not from worry that the audience would fail to get the message, but because they enjoyed presenting the national icon and hymn, saw them as crucial to telling the story, and unabashedly celebrated them. In large part because of this film, Knute Rockne's story so came to exemplify the American immigrant saga that *Life Magazine* in its 1976 "Special Bicentennial Issue" proclaimed him, along with Andrew Carnegie and Albert Einstein, the three most important immigrants in the nation's history.

The opening of the film and every subsequent scene connects directly to the title *Knute Rockne—All-American.* Although referring to Rockne's selection as a player on the 1913 All-America squad (third team), the title's emphasis is less on sports than on the coach's qualities as an *All-American,* a man for All Americans, representing the country's deepest hopes and dreams. Forties audiences loved the overt patriotism, accepted the portrayal of Rockne's life, and were deeply moved by the film's final scenes of his tragic death and funeral.

Subsequently, *Knute Rockne—All-American* transcended its Hollywood origins and became not only the most important college sports movie in film history but also part of the nation's political mythos; the actor who played Rockne's great halfback, George Gipp, took on the character's nickname and used his cinematic dying words—"Win one for the Gipper"—as his political slogan for successful gubernatorial and presidential campaigns.

Ronald Reagan also added to the myths. After recovering from the assassination attempt in 1981, his first major address was at the University of Notre Dame, and instead of the planned, prepared talk on administration policy, he spoke at length and in his own words about the film, particularly its meaning for him and his vision of America. Some analysts consider this the moment when the public embraced Reagan as an authentically "heroic character," fully fused with the heroic Gipp and Rockne. The president began his talk with the themes that he loved: "First, Knute Rockne as a boy came to America with his parents from Norway. And in the few years it took him to grow up to college age, he became an All-American in a game that is still to this day uniquely American."

Reagan's next line paraphrases one of Rockne's key speeches in the movie and also illustrates how the film helped to raise Rockne's profession, sports coaching, from a sweaty occupation to a Noble Calling: "As a coach, he did more than teach young men how to play a game. He believed truly that the noblest work of man was building the character of man." The film, the first major portrait and glorification of a college coach, deeply influenced public attitudes about this profession in its time and ever since.

In addition, President Reagan discussed the University of Notre Dame, praising its historic independence and religious values. The *New York Times* noted that "Mr. Reagan's dying words in the film, 'Win one for the Gipper,' provided a political slogan for him, a battle cry for this university, and a strong bond between Notre Dame and Mr. Reagan."

Thus *Knute Rockne—All-American,* a film that is neither great art nor accurate history, became part of the national legend, its importance far transcending its grainy black-and-white images, bad sound, and period acting. Through an amazing process, it fused its biographical subjects and themes with core American myths.

■　■　■

> Rockne stands squarely at the center of America's myth about itself. He deeply believed in that myth, that only in America could an immigrant child be launched within a life's span into the nation's collective unconscious.
>
> —Sports historian Michael Steele, 1983.

Myths are the stories that a society tells itself about itself, helping to unify, celebrate, and distinguish it from neighbors and enemies. Historically, myths were passed on as folktales but, in the age of industrialism, with the population moving from villages like Voss to cities like Chicago, mechanical storytellers replaced human ones, first with the dime novel, then the movies, radio, and, eventually, television.

At the turn of the century, the Horatio Alger stories dominated popular fiction; Rockne himself later commented, "As a boy I read the Horatio Alger works and found them very interesting. They created a fine impression and stimulated ambition." These stories relate the tale of the poor boy who through pluck and hard work achieves fame and fortune. Generations of young Americans cast themselves in this role, and many immigrants came to America to attempt to live it. Not surprisingly, those who fulfilled the dream often described their lives in terms of the Alger formula, including Knute Rockne.

The famous coach frequently pointed to the distance between his hard-scrabble childhood on Logan Square in Chicago and his later prosperity. *Knute Rockne—All-American* plugs him into this paradigm, and one of its earliest scenes shows the young Rockne toiling at the Chicago post office in order to save money for college. The script directions read: "Flashing scenes that convey the busy, swarming atmosphere of a great city's post office at work, and the long hard labor of Rockne's practical education."

Horatio Alger Jr.'s stories and the American tradition of the self-made hero not only influenced a generation of readers but also other authors, notably the writers of sports fiction for young males. In the early twentieth century, Edward Stratemeyer, the promoter of the best-selling Baseball Joe series, and Gilbert Patten, the creator of the popular Frank Merriwell stories, read deeply and borrowed constantly from the Alger parables, in the process creating the athlete-hero, a new ideal for American youth. The best study of this phenomenon notes that in the juvenile sports novels, especially the Merriwell stories, "the athlete-hero's career follows a nearly identical pattern" to the Alger paradigm, "with the single substitution of athletic triumphs for wealth as the success goal."

In the first decades of the century, young sports fans ingested the athlete-hero ideal by reading Frank Merriwell novels and similar stories. By the 1920s, Hollywood began producing silent film forms of this hero for moviegoers. In the 1930s Depression, when many Americans were skeptical of traditional pieties, the fictional athlete-hero languished or sometimes was mocked in stories and films. But in 1940, on the eve of a vast patriotic crusade, Hollywood presented the athlete-hero in a fresh and more persuasive manner, one intended to unify a population of diverse origins.

■　■　■

FATHER:
Knute, where have you been and what have you been doing?

KNUTE:
(eagerly)
Outside, playing the most wonderful game in the world. It's called football!

MOTHER:
(leans forward)
Your nose is bleeding!

KNUTE:
(wipes it with a napkin and looks at the blood with interest)
Somebody stepped on it. I guess that's part of the game.

(This is too much for Papa Rockne. He shoves back his chair and bawls Knute out in a torrent of Norwegian, very angry and stern.)

KNUTE:
(when his father pauses for breath)
Oh, papa, don't talk Norwegian. Talk American. We're all Americans now.
(he looks around proudly, his dirty face beaming)
Specially me. I'm left end.

(Mother and sisters begin to laugh—then father laughs—then Knute. With the whole family laughing at Knute's earnestness, we [cut to next scene])

—From the shooting script and film,
Knute Rockne—All-American, 1940.

This exchange climaxes the movie's second scene. When the parents are not speaking Norwegian, they pronounce English with heavy accents. However, Knute and his sisters already talk Hollywood "American," i.e., neutral middle-class English. The emphasis in the scene is on the "melting-pot" myth, with sports as the means of Knute's integration into American society.

In historical fact, from the nineteenth century on, many immigrants entered the American mainstream through sports, first in boxing with Irish, Jewish, and Italian fighters and champions, then baseball with its legion of ethnic players, and finally, in the first decades of this century, intercollegiate athletics. The epitome of the "melting-pot" dynamic in college sports—one beloved by the media and all immigrant groups—was the University of Notre Dame's Fighting Irish football teams, featuring not only players of Irish descent but also many of Polish, Italian, Slavic, and even Jewish heritage. The main promoter of Notre Dame football was the Scandinavian immigrant Knute Rockne, and this movie codified his great achievement.

The filmmakers plug young Rockne into the athlete-hero paradigm and begin the first sports scene with him watching older boys play sandlot football. He wants to join them, but the largest boy tells him, "Naw, you're too little . . . G'wan, get outta the way!" Knute persists and the script directs the other boys to "look at him again, now very annoyed at the 'runt's' interruption."

The young Knute keeps trying to get into the game but the script directs the other boys to regard him with "disgust for an undersized runt." He is the archetypal underdog. Eventually, because one team is losing by thirty points, its captain allows him to join. On the first play, Knute successfully tackles a bigger boy but is "knocked out cold." The other boys worry that they have seriously injured him, but Knute struggles to his feet, ready for more. With this, he earns the praise of the older boys, their leader telling him, "Kid— you've got spunk, you're all right," and he asks his name. With the reply, "Knute Rockne," we know that our hero has begun to acquire fame and that his life trajectory is moving up.

After *Knute Rockne—All-American* established this scene for the cinema, many sports films used it; indeed, the opening of a 1990s homage to Notre Dame football, *Rudy,* lovingly replicated the entire sequence, even on a Chicago area sandlot. Another mythic element of the scene that is frequently repeated is the ethnic and racial mix of the sandlot teams. The boys represent various immigrant groups, and the ball carrier whom Knute tackles is African American. By depicting him as an important player, the film gives a positive signal about racial integration in America.

In the history of race relations, college sports played a pioneering role and, when combined with Hollywood's approval, advanced racial integration. In 1940, few areas of American life were integrated, but one prominent exception was college sports, particularly on the West Coast. During this period in Los Angeles, Jackie Robinson and his brother Mack as well as other African Americans starred in various sports at UCLA. *Knute Rockne—All-American* suggested that the athlete-hero can come from the lowest economic strata and can even be black. This proposition later became an essential part of the mythos of intercollegiate athletics, one cherished to this day.

In *Knute Rockne—All-American,* the sandlot sequence and the family dinner offer the only glimpse of the hero's childhood in America. However, not only is its content crucial for the athlete-hero legend but so is its form. Anthropologists describe myths as "ritual condensations whereby human experience is quite literally condensed into patterns," and this helps explain the simplicity of the film's story line, the quick and easy plot resolutions, and the larger-than-life qualities of the hero and all other characters.

In 1940, movie audiences did not question the exceptional personality of the hero and those around him. Conditioned by a decade of popular biographical films, moviegoers tended to believe that these movies were accurate accounts of their subjects' lives, and that 1930s biopic heroes like Emile Zola and Madame Curie were extraordinary humans, always exhibiting larger-than-life qualities. *Knute Rockne—All-American* benefited from the audience's fondness for the biopic form. Thus, audience approval continued as the happy scenes of Rockne's childhood faded into the next one: a montage of six years of the hero's life in shots of him working at the Chicago post office, accompanied by a loud sound track of "America the Beautiful."

The years pass by on the dates of canceled stamps; the face on all of the stamps is George Washington's. The apparent message: Rockne's story connects to Washington's, and to the most profound myths of the United States of America.

■   ■   ■

CALLAHAN:
[the president of Notre Dame turns to the adult Rockne]
You've made a fine record in the past three years. Honor Man in your class and next fall you'll be captain of the football team.

ROCKNE:
(embarrassed)
Thank you, father.

CALLAHAN:
Doctor Nieuwland here tells me you've got the best brain for chemistry of any man in the class.

—From the shooting script and film of
Knute Rockne—All-American, 1940.

This exchange occurs in the first major scene of Rockne at Notre Dame. After leaving Chicago, the film shows its hero arriving on campus, briefly meeting his freshman roommate and stating that his first priority is education—although he might try out for football. Then, the script instructs, "TIME LAPSE DEVICE for passing of 3 years" into the scene at the president's office. Father Callahan (a fictional amalgam of a number of Notre Dame presidents during Rockne's ND career), and Father Nieuwland (a famous chemist at the school) ask Rockne to work as a summer research assistant in chemistry. Nieuwland tells the future coach, "I could make a first-class scientist of you inside of ten years." But Rockne declines, explaining that he plans to spend the summer working as a lifeguard in Cedar Point, Ohio. Father Callahan ends the scene with, "I don't suppose that you and Dorais [Rockne's roommate and the quarterback on the football team] would be taking a football along to Cedar Point, by any chance?"

The placement of the encounter in the president's office—before any scenes of Rockne playing football—underscores the academic aspect of the hero's career. In addition, the scene connects to and reinforces subsequent meetings involving the hero, Callahan, and Nieuwland. The day of Rockne's graduation, the chemist offers him a position as a full-time assistant. The young man agrees but asks if he can also help football coach Jesse Harper with the team; Nieuwland objects vehemently, but Callahan mediates and allows him to take both jobs. Finally, after scenes of Rockne teaching college chemistry and verbally jousting with Nieuwland in the chemistry lab, the hero discusses his future with President Callahan. He tells the Notre Dame administrator that he is "at a crossroads," that he has to decide between chemistry and coaching football, and he leans toward the latter. Callahan assures him that coaching, working with young men, is a high calling.

These scenes are remarkable for a number of reasons: none of them were in the original film script; they generated one of the core myths of modern college sports; and, in terms of the historical facts of Rockne's life, they are total fabrications. The scenes exist thanks to Rockne's widow, Bonnie. During the 1939–40 production of the movie, she demanded that Warner Brothers, the studio making the film, construct a fictitious portrait of her husband's academic career. According to the copyright laws of the era, as Rockne's principal heir, she "owned" his life and had the right to approve or veto all books and films about it. The studio had to comply with her requests.

Bonnie acted mainly out of personal motives, but her insistence that Rockne be portrayed as a brilliant scholar-athlete both connected to the basic mythology of college sports and created an important innovation. Because she forced the filmmakers to emphasize this aspect of the biography, ironically, Warners made a much more important film than it originally intended. Instead of a standard potboiler about an athlete-hero, the studio produced the first serious cinematic portrait of a scholar-athlete. In so doing, the filmmakers helped imprint this model on the American public and shaped the future of intercollegiate athletics.

The portrait of Knute Rockne as a scholar-athlete originates in a classic maxim of western civilization: *mens sana in corpore sano,* a sound mind in a sound body. British and American educators in the nineteenth century, with their love of ancient cultures, acted upon this dictum by introducing sports into school curriculums. At that time, when both American higher education and intercollegiate athletics were casual endeavors, actual students played college sports. However, toward the end of the nineteenth century, two conflicting trends occurred: colleges and universities began to raise their academic standards, and the proponents of college sports increasingly demanded winning teams, athletes who could perform at the highest possible level and beat their opponents. The search for authentic scholar-athletes began.

As the opposing trends accelerated in the early twentieth century, finding young men who combined athletic excellence and academic competence became increasingly difficult, and led many college coaches to include non-students—"ringers" and "tramp athletes"—on their teams. This situation bothered university authorities, especially faculty at the better academic schools, but it did not deter the promoters of college sports, particularly the popular press.

Sportswriters, as well as authors of sports novels, maintained that scholar-athletes existed; Gilbert Patten, the creator of Frank Merriwell, explained that the stories "give me the opportunity to preach—by [literary] example—the doctrine of a clean mind in a clean and healthy body." Frank Merriwell at prep school and Yale was not an outstanding student—he feared being called a "grind"—but he was a competent one, even able to win academic prizes if the circumstances demanded.

> Now, Mrs. Rockne and myself will never be satisfied with this picture unless you develop the intellectual side of Rockne. If Rockne had not devoted his life to coaching, wherein he became famous, but had devoted it to chemistry, he would be an equally noted scientist.
>
> —Vitus Jones, attorney for Bonnie Rockne,
> to Warner Brothers, 1939.

In 1939, as Warner Brothers sent Bonnie Rockne drafts of the script for approval, she objected to many things, particularly the lack of emphasis on Rockne as a brilliant science student. The studio had to accommodate her demands, and the main scriptwriter, having heard of chemistry professor Nieuwland (the inventor of synthetic rubber), asked Notre Dame for details about his career. With this information, the scriptwriter fabricated the scenes involving Nieuwland as well as the Callahan-Rockne discussions on whether the young man should become a chemist or a football coach.

The historical Rockne, as his voluminous papers reveal, faced no such dilemma: he loved athletics and always wanted to coach them. That he was an extremely bright man and graduated *magna cum laude* from Notre Dame in pharmacy, not chemistry, is indisputable. However, his daily correspondence indicates that sports was the passion of his life, the impetus for his attending Notre Dame—some of his high school track teammates convinced him to join them on the ND track-and-field squad—and the driving force of his college and adult years. In fact, after graduation, Rockne applied for coaching jobs at other schools, and the ND president wrote letters of recommendation for him; in them, the Notre Dame official praised the young man's "qualifications as a foot-ball expert" and his moral character, but never mentioned his potential as a scientist or even a college chemistry teacher.

Part of Bonnie's motives for the academic portrait resulted from the differences in her and Knute's backgrounds: she came from a well-mannered middle-class family, while he hailed from rough-and-tumble Logan Square in Chicago, his college roommate describing him as a "not very genteel character . . . a very rugged character." During their first years of marriage, in addition to working at Notre Dame, Rockne also inhabited the violent world of semipro football, practicing during the week and playing on Sundays all over the Midwest. He also hung out in South Bend at Hullie and Mike's pool hall and betting parlor. Bonnie abhorred this part of her husband's life and later tried to expunge it from the historical record, replacing it with, as she insisted to Warners, a portrait of a man of "scholarly attainment . . . a lover of good books . . . a man who loved good pictures, good shows, a scholar." For the film, she demanded and received scenes of his academic career at Notre Dame.

The final word on the accuracy of the film depiction belongs to Jesse Harper, head football coach at Notre Dame when Rockne was captain of the team, and the man for whom Rockne worked as an assistant. In 1940, when informed of the film scenes concerning his protege's hiring, Harper commented: "I do not know whether they [Warners] wish too much accuracy but Rock was hired at Notre Dame primarily as the head track coach and assistant football coach. Father John Cavanaugh," the ND president at the time, "decided to have him teach chemistry" in the ND prep school, not the college, "because he would not have enough to do assisting in football and coaching track. What a change in" Rockne in the "twenty-seven years" from the actual events to the film's version of them.

Thus from Bonnie Rockne's mix of personal motives and legal power came the legend that her husband would have become a great chemist if he had not chosen to coach football. Most importantly, she sparked a major innovation in the media portrayal of the college sports hero: the great athlete and competent student was no longer sufficient. For true heroism he had to be like Rockne and excel in all activities, be both a superb athlete and a brilliant student. He had to aspire to be Number One across the board.

In his history of sports literature, Michael Oriard explains that the athlete-hero is "more important as an ideal than as an actual person." Thus, the cinematic version of Knute Rockne is far more significant than the actual historical figure—indeed, our interest at the end of the twentieth century in the real person is a result of the power of the ideal version. Moreover, the main reason for comparing the real to the ideal man is to understand the creation of the ideal. To explore the disjunctures between Rockne's actual life (as best we can ascertain it) and the Hollywood version is an attempt to comprehend the power of the ideal, why it has influenced so many people so deeply and for so many years.

In the same way, even though Father Callahan did not exist and the Notre Dame president of the time, Father John W. Cavanaugh, never spoke to Rockne about choosing either chemistry or coaching as his life's work, this scene in the film is exceptionally powerful. The excellent character actor Donald Crisp played the ND president and, in sympathetic but authoritative tones, advised the young man, "Anyone who follows the truth in his heart never makes a mistake." In the land of opportunity, the country of the lone hero, this advice reverberates as ultimate truth. Callahan then says, "I've watched your work with these boys these past few years and I've seen the splendid results." This places coaching on the same level as teaching, the athletic field on a par with the classroom. Finally, the priest sanctifies the coaching profession—"You're helping mankind and anyone who helps mankind helps God"—thus connecting coaching to religion, to the Supreme Being.

Since 1940, many athletic coaches have quoted this speech and pointed to Knute Rockne as their inspiration. Professor Oriard, who played football at Notre Dame and in the National Football League, explains that the "ideal of the athlete-hero is the rationalization for such organizations as the National Collegiate Athletic Association . . . for the inclusion of athletics in school programs at all levels, and for the hiring of public relations specialists by professional and college athletic teams." He adds, "Perhaps most significant, the athlete-hero is the dominant image in the mind of every father who encourages his son to play . . . football" and other collegiate sports.

For a huge number of Americans, this ideal—with Knute Rockne as the historical prototype—remains real to this day; some, like NCAA officials, both believe it and cynically manipulate it, but a majority of sports fans accept it sincerely, treating it as a cultural and even a religious truth. Not surprisingly, in 1994, the *National Review* placed *Knute Rockne—All-American* on its list of the "Best Conservative Movies" ever made, its criteria for selection being "movies about God and country, tradition and family . . . individual achievement and the American Dream."

2

George Gipp Becomes Myth

The life of Knute Rockne is its own dedication to the Youth of America and to the finest ideals of courage, character, and sportsmanship for all the world.

Knute Rockne was a great and vital force in moulding the spirit of modern America through the millions of young men and boys who loved and respected him and who today are living by the high standards he taught.

—From the on-screen dedication at the beginning of the film, *Knute Rockne—All-American,* 1940.

After reading the first draft of the script, Bonnie Rockne felt not only that the planned film neglected the academic dimension of her husband's life but that "the picture . . . was [supposed] to be an inspiration to young men" and failed in this regard. The scriptwriters responded with major revisions, including the above dedication; as with the scholar-athlete insertions, the additions for Coach Rockne and his "moulding the spirit" of young men helped transform the film from an ordinary sports potboiler into the first major cinematic portrait of a college coach.

In the movie, before the initial scenes of Rockne coaching on the Notre Dame practice field, we see him at home as a loving father to his young son, Billy. He plays with the boy, entertains him, sings to him, and totally fulfills the Hollywood icon of devoted father. Then six Notre Dame football players appear, just returned from summer vacation. Rockne greets them warmly and acts as their surrogate father, feeding them, playing with them, showing them some new football formations, then talking seriously to them. He calls them his "boys" and treats them as larger and older versions of his sons.

College sports coaches have long taken a fatherly interest in their players—the historical Rockne was very paternal toward his athletes, and his coaching rival, Glenn Warner, was nicknamed "Pop"—but this movie set in stone the coach-as-father-figure, an image that greatly helped college sports during its coming crises.

After feeding and playing with his ND boys, Rockne discusses Notre Dame's prospects for the season, emphasizing the tough schedule and his desperate need for "a halfback who can carry the mail, a big fast boy who can run, pass, and kick like—say, Jim Thorpe." One of the players replies, "A guy like that would never come to a little school like Notre Dame." But Rockne is optimistic and says that he's always "praying—and if I ever *do* find a boy like that . . ." The camera highlights his face as he looks upward, indicating the limitless possibilities for his team with such a leader; significantly, in the final cut of the film, "praying" replaced the verb in the script, "hoping."

The next scene occurs on the Notre Dame practice field, where, away from the football squad, a young man, dressed neatly in a tie and sweater, casually plays baseball catch. A football rolls his way; effortlessly he kicks it back, booming it far beyond the field. This attracts Rockne's attention, and he and we discover that the handsome young man is George Gipp. In addition to kicking, he is an extraordinary runner—after putting on a football uniform, he easily weaves through the entire varsity.

An analysis of Hollywood movies in this period suggests that the "classical narrative film unrolls before us as if we were in charge; we seem to be organizing the world we see. It goes the way we want it to; we have the illusion that we have created a world and that it is under our control." Rockne, our hero, prays for a great player: "the sort of fellow I'm looking for only comes along once or twice in a coach's lifetime." And, sure enough, George Gipp appears.

After the practice field triumph, the script orders a montage of "increasing crowds at the games as Gipp and Notre Dame move rapidly from victory to victory, these stock action shots selected for their thrills." The film uses actual Notre Dame game footage, but, interestingly, it is from the 1940 era, with helmets, uniforms, football formations, and stadiums much more advanced than in the 1916–1920 period when Gipp played. Undoubtedly moviegoers, particularly sports fans, noticed this discrepancy, but probably it did not bother them: the Rockne film was a product of 1940 America, and audiences felt extremely comfortable within that world; in addition, the film's lack of historical realism helped viewers identify with the heroes, slipping more easily into their football uniforms.

Another device used in this film and typical of Hollywood in this period, according to a critic, is the "classical editing style, allowing us to see through the eyes of a character in the point-of-view shot, permitting a strong identification with the characters on the screen. In a sense we 'become' the hero, take on the well-defined attributes of the powerful, dynamic, resourceful protagonist." During Rockne's first encounter with Gipp, we see the player through the eyes of the coach: he and we see Gipp playing catch, kicking the ball, then up close as Rockne talks to him. The most famous point-of-view shot in the sequence follows: the camera and coach look down at Gipp in uniform as, according to the script, he "reclines on one elbow on the grass, casually indifferent to the whole proceeding."

Gipp has "attitude," but we know that the cinematic hero, Coach Rockne, will mold him into a great player and a great man. After the montage of Notre Dame and Gipp's football success, the film reveals a well-dressed George, cap in hand, visiting his coach's house, extremely polite to Bonnie and wonderfully kind to young Billy Rockne. The coach has so succeeded in shaping Gipp's character that Bonnie tells him, "Knute and I often talk about you, George. We'd like for our two boys to grow up and be like you, some day." Ronald Reagan played Gipp perfectly for the Hollywood classical cinema, and later, during his political career, he capitalized on this idealized image of the Notre Dame player. Reagan's Gipp embodied the American virtues that the politician cherished and constantly invoked.

During the real George Gipp's lifetime, parents did not want their children to emulate him—except his extraordinary athletic feats. By all accounts, Gipp was a great natural athlete although an undisciplined one: he generally skipped practice. Off the field during his college years, he often lived in the best hotel in South Bend and worked as a high-stakes card player and pool shark, for a time as the "house player" at Hullie and Mike's. Moreover, he was hardly a regular college student: two years of his Notre Dame academic transcript are blank. Some of the reality of Gipp's life was known to the Warners's scriptwriters—they used the 1930 *Collier's* magazine excerpts from Rockne's *Autobiography* for their script, even quoting lines from it, and the *Collier's* pieces discussed Gipp's pool playing, illustrating it with a large silhouette drawing of him late at night with a cue stick.

But Warner Brothers could not portray the historical George Gipp. His wayward character and questionable morality would have totally contradicted all the rules of classical film. The most that the scriptwriters could reveal was a bit of "attitude," and this is merely putty for Rockne to mold into solid character. Because in classic films, the audience instantly recognized heroes by their iconography—Gipp dresses neatly, his hair always trim—moviegoers knew that his "attitude" would soon vanish. Finally, in Hollywood movies like *Knute Rockne—All-American,* an appearance by a character resembling the real George Gipp would have been as strange and upsetting to American moviegoers in the late 1930s and early 1940s as listening to a radio broadcast about an invasion of New Jersey by Martians.

GIPP:
(he stares ahead of him for a moment in silence)
He [Rockne] has given us something they don't teach you in schools—something clean and strong inside—not just courage, but a right way of living that none of us will ever forget . . .

—From the shooting script and film,
Knute Rockne—All-American, 1940.

Ronald Reagan's Gipp tells this to Bonnie Rockne; after the film's release, Reagan would often speak at Notre Dame alumni functions and recite various speeches from the movie. Next to the Gipper's deathbed soliloquy, these were the most requested lines, poignant to audiences because of Rockne's own early and tragic death.

Pat O'Brien, the actor who played Rockne, had an equally active postrelease speaking career, for over forty years reciting the coach's film words at innumerable public gatherings. Again, next to the "Win One for the Gipper" pep talk, the most requested passages concerned the coach's comments on molding character, especially the lecture near the end of the movie when Rockne, accompanied by some coaching colleagues, addresses a Congressional-like committee and, at the climax, pronounces: "We [coaches] believe the finest work of man is building the character of man. We have tried to build courage and initiative, tolerance and persistence—without which the most educated brain in the head of man is not worth very much." Reagan also frequently used these lines in campaign and presidential addresses, at times assuming the character of the coach as well as that of the Gipper.

With *Knute Rockne—All-American,* Hollywood constructed the icon of the college coach that has served Rockne's profession exceptionally well: the molder of character and the architect of victory. And because winning is so important in the American mythos, the winningest coaches are usually considered the greatest builders of character. Knute Rockne, to this day the coach with the best won-lost record in big-time college football, along with his image as character builder, became the apotheosis of his profession, the symbol of the perfect mentor.

In the 1920s, when sportswriters began to write about the "moral function" of coaches, a former Notre Dame press assistant quoted the response of Rockne and some of his colleagues: "You're a great coach when your team wins every game. But when you drop four or five, you make 'em believe the main idea is to build character." However, after *Knute Rockne—All-American,* coaches had to win *and* build character. Subsequently, many young men entered college sports with the Rockne ideal in mind, and when they became coaches they tried to construct winning teams as well as teach their players ethical behavior. Some coaches were sincere and even succeeded in these two—often contradictory—goals; however, many failed to win and/or to impart positive values.

But the media have long loved the Rockne icon and the public has fully embraced it; as a result, for many years Americans have regarded successful college coaches as special, authentic figures. Even in late twentieth-century America, a cynical public often views prominent coaches as the embodiments of success and wisdom, much more credible than any politician, entertainer, or other well-known professional. For many Americans, men like John Thompson, Rick Pitino, and Lou Holtz function as modern oracles, speaking to large audiences about the basics of winning and ethics, writing books, making motivational tapes, endorsing products, and reaping huge incomes from these business activities.

■　■　■

ST. JOSEPH'S HOSPITAL

GIPP'S ROOM

As the camera continues in slow, unbroken advance toward the bed upon which George Gipp is dying, Father Callahan, after finishing the Last Rites, leads the boy's grief-stricken mother gently away to the far side of the room, leaving Rockne standing beside the bed, looking down at Gipp's white face.

—From the shooting script and film,
Knute Rockne—All-American, 1940.

In the movie, when Gipp was at Rockne's house, talking to Bonnie and playing with Billy, he began coughing, at first politely but then with less control. When the coach returned home, after examining the player's throat, he rushed him to the hospital. A fever chart illustrated Gipp's decline, and after the priest administered the Last Rites, the iconography of the very pale face on the pillow indicated to the audience that death was imminent. His coach stands at his bedside and informs him that a telegram has just arrived, naming him first team "All-American"; announcing this honor in this situation connects to the film's title, signifying that the player's life and death has meaning for *all* Americans.

Then Ronald Reagan utters his most famous movie speech—indeed, a speech much better known than any of his political utterances. He begins, "I've got to go, Rock, but it's all right, I'm not afraid"—the athlete-hero does not fear death. "Rock, some day when the team's up against it, the breaks are beating the boys"—even at the moment of death, he wants to inspire his teammates.

Interestingly, Reagan's words here are an improvement on the script's: he changed "Sometimes, Rock" to "Rock, some day," and dropped the vague phrase, "when things are wrong and . . ." The actor's instinctive sense of drama and word cadence improved upon the original, providing a better lead into "Ask them to go in there with all they've got and win just one for the Gipper. I don't know where I'll be then, Rock—but I'll know about it—and I'll be happy." The young Gipp closes his eyes and dies at the height of his athletic abilities, after receiving the greatest accolade of his life, All-America honors.

After witnessing his greatest player's demise, Rockne leaves the hospital and goes home. When he enters, the sound track plays a slow, funereal version of the "Notre Dame Victory March," including a male chorus in the background. Rockne and the audience gaze at the chair in which Gipp had recently sat. The coach sits in it and stares into the fire, confronting death and, because we know how his story ends, foreshadowing his own death. His wife enters and wants to comfort him, possibly share her grief about George's death, but she looks at her husband and hesitates—as a 1940s model wife, she knows that dealing with death, especially the passing of a sports hero, is man's work. Bonnie withdraws from the room; the hymnlike version of the Notre Dame song continues.

Audiences immediately recognized that Gipp's deathbed scene and its aftermath was a special movie moment. Warners "sneak-previewed" the picture in a small California town, and the producer remarked that "the entire sequence of Gipp was one of the highlights of the picture. When he died I don't believe there was a dry eye in the theatre. 90% of the preview cards . . . commented on Reagan's performance" in this scene. A history of the period notes that soon "tears gushed in theaters across the land and Reagan, at 29, was a 'B' actor no more."

Hollywood films, particularly in the classical studio era, frequently depicted the death of a hero in religious terms; *Knute Rockne—All-American* used actual religious ceremonies for Gipp's death and, more elaborately, for Rockne's at the end of the movie. Some observers maintained that many moviegoers in the 1930s and 1940s attended theaters in a religious manner, going to the movies on Saturdays and then to church on Sundays, gaining similar satisfactions from both activities.

Other commentators, however, point to the similarities of religion and sports, dismissing the connection to entertainment; theologian Michael Novak argues that "sports owe more to the ritual grammar of religion than to the laws and forms of entertainment. Millions become involved in the rituals of sport to a depth of seriousness never elicited by entertainment." The cinematic death of George Gipp refutes this assertion: it is at the nexus of entertainment, sports, and religion, its power derived from a synergy of all three. Removing any of the three elements reduces the whole to almost zero.

George Gipp was a truly great athlete who led the Notre Dame football team to its first national championship; he played for America's most famous Catholic university, and some of its priests attended his deathbed; Hollywood made a classical period film with Gipp portrayed as an athlete-hero and rendered his final request, enveloped in religion, the movie's most memorable speech. Remove any of these elements and the power of the Gipp myth deflates. However, build upon these elements, link them to the deepest American myths, and the cornerstone of a brilliant political career moves into place. These elements proved so potent that the Reagan/Gipper political trajectory, starting on the soundstage at Warners, ended in the White House.

Ronald Reagan was always aware of the powerful mix of entertainment, sports, and religion, and he used it throughout his political career, never more effectively than with the Gipper icon. He had years of training as an entertainer; he authentically loved sports, not only as a young athlete but also as a sports announcer and an actor espousing the athlete-hero ideal, and because of his Irish-Catholic father, he easily attached himself to the University of Notre Dame. An aide said of Reagan's trips to ND, "He's going home. In his heart, that's where he thinks he went to school." This mixture was crucial to his successful wooing of middle-class and working-class Democrats, millions of them Catholic, who crossed party lines and voted for him for president. Using and sincerely believing in the Gipper symbol and the conservative values of Hollywood classical movies like *Knute Rockne—All-American,* he convinced this bloc of voters that he shared their vision of America, and in return the "Reagan Democrats" provided him with his margins of victory.

Appropriately, Reagan's last official act in the White House, in January 1989, was a presidential salute to the Notre Dame national championship team of 1988. He welcomed them by remarking that "near the top of the list" of his life "experiences" was his "association with the University of Notre Dame and its legendary hero, Knute Rockne." He then gave his version of the coach's philosophy, ending with a powerful image, both celebrating the Notre Dame championship team and connecting to his most famous movie role: "Right now, I can't help but think that somewhere, far away, there's a fellow with a big grin and a whole lot of pride in his school. And he might be thinking to himself that maybe you won another one for the Gipper." And the subtext: the heavenly Gipper is also proud of his namesake and the conclusion of his two-term presidency.

■   ■   ■

The story in the [South Bend] pool halls from Gipp's pals was that George got so drunk one night, he passed out in the snow and they found him the next morning. That's how he got the pneumonia that killed him.

—Moe Aranson, a South Bend resident
during the Gipp era, 1991.

Reagan's Gipper long ago transcended the actual athlete, but again the disjuncture between the legend and the historical facts reveals a great deal about American popular culture, its values as well as what it chooses to ignore. Knute Rockne did not discover his star player coughing in his living room and rush him to the hospital; the most reliable accounts indicate that Gipp's dissipation in November 1920 led to his fatal illness. (One of the player's closest friends also told an eyewitness story consistent with the South Bend pool hall reports.) Obviously, scenes of Gipp "passed out in the snow" do not belong in the tale of the ideal athlete-hero.

As for his famous last words to Rockne, when George Gipp died in December 1920, no one mentioned the "Win One for the Gipper" request—indeed, no one called Gipp by that nickname, nor did he ever use it for himself. Moreover, Knute Rockne was not at the deathbed, but, after giving no hint of the last request for eight years, he related a version of it in November 1928 in the locker room at halftime of the Notre Dame–Army contest in New York. However, the context of Rockne's highly dramatic and usually fabricated pep talks, as well as his desire to salvage his worst season by winning the Big Game, raises further doubts about the authenticity of Gipp's final utterance. (For a detailed analysis of this question, including the reasons for disputing the genuineness of Gipp's request, see Chapters 15, 26, and 28 in *Shake Down the Thunder: The Creation of Notre Dame Football*.)

The famous speech—the words mainly used in the film—first appeared in Rockne's *Autobiography*, published in 1930 and authored by ghostwriter John B. Kennedy. The scriptwriters at Warners cribbed Kennedy's version, and Ronald Reagan made some changes in delivering it. Certainly Gipp's request was at odds with his character in life, one wit remarking that "it would have been much more like him to ask Rock to put down a bet for him some day when the Irish were a sure thing."

But the reality of George Gipp's life was far from the scriptwriters' minds when they typed the screenplay at Warners. The player did not need any family members to inflate his image. The athlete-hero myth sat waiting for them to fit an idealized Gipper into its formulaic framework. Thus, when the cinematic Rockne invokes the player's deathbed request at halftime of the 1928 Notre Dame–Army game, the audience understands the cues and expects the team to go out in the second half and triumph. And when the Notre Dame player scores the go-ahead touchdown, yelling, "That's one for the Gipper," viewers appreciate and identify with Rockne's skyward look, communicating with Gipp in heaven. (The actual game unfolded in a very different way; moreover, none of Gipp's contemporaries expected him to join the heavenly choir.)

The 1928 game sequence brought a neat closure to the Gipper sequence in the film. Moviegoers in this period demanded satisfactory resolutions, from the cliché happy ending of hero and heroine going off into the sunset to the Gipper-inspired victory within the larger Rockne biopic. Ronald Reagan recognized this as a contract player at Warners, terming the role "a nearly perfect part from an actor's standpoint . . . A great entrance, an action middle, and a death scene to finish up."

The screenwriters of *Knute Rockne—All-American* knew that Gipp's demise, with its tear-jerking appeal based on the fact that he died young, required more closure beyond the deathbed scene. Hence the placement in the film of Rockne's locker-room invocation of Gipp's last wish, with the script turning this into one of the movie's climactic moments, along with the Notre Dame team's glorious fulfillment of the request (as opposed to the events of the actual game, well known to the scriptwriters).

Rockne's death posed a similar problem for the screenwriters. When he died in a plane crash, he was relatively young (forty-three), and his death violated the natural order of his life; thus the screen portrayal needed careful resolution, a way for the audience to deal with it and to leave the theater satisfied.

The film depicted his final trip from Florida to the West Coast—characteristically implying that he made the trip to help out "the boys" whereas he actually went to sign an extremely lucrative movie contract—and after boarding his last flight and waving good-bye through the window, the plane crashes in Kansas. Then a montage of newspaper headlines and telephone switchboard operators inform incredulous callers that Rockne is dead. In historical fact, his death shocked millions of people and their first reaction was disbelief—in large part because he was at the top of his coaching powers, having just won a national championship. Ronald Reagan, a young man in 1931, considered him "a living legend," and later paraphrased the eulogies of the time: "No man connected with football has ever achieved the stature or occupied the singular niche in the nation that he [Rockne] carved out for himself, not just in sport, but in our entire social structure."

Wisely the movie does not end with the plane going down and/or a hokey scene of the coach ascending through the clouds to heaven—a popular Hollywood trope in the 1930s and 1940s. Instead, because Warners knew that audiences demanded full resolution, the studio included a lengthy funeral scene in the cathedral-like church on the Notre Dame campus. Just as funeral rites are important for the family and friends of every deceased person, the screenwriters realized that the community of Hollywood moviegoers demanded a similar ritual for Rockne's passing, and they provided it.

One of the central characteristics of classical Hollywood cinema was the traditional plots of clearly delineated beginnings, middles, and ends. Such plots descended from Greek drama and, when effective, contained a large portion of catharsis for the viewers. *Knute Rockne—All-American* fulfilled these plot requirements to perfection, beginning with the hero's earliest years, taking him through the great triumphs of his life, then ending with a long, cathartic funeral and eulogy. (A year later, *Pride of the Yankees* offered a similar plot and, in a wonderfully cathartic moment, hero Lou Gehrig delivered his own funeral eulogy in Yankee Stadium: "Today, I am the luckiest man in the world . . . ," et cetera.)

The Rockne film reproduced the actual funeral service in Notre Dame Church, a full high mass, a large choir singing the Latin prayers, and the fictional president of Notre Dame, Father Callahan, praising the deceased in the screenwriters' words as well as passages from the actual eulogy given by the ND president of the time. Father Callahan also mentioned the national broadcast of the funeral by the major radio networks and the massive press coverage; this was historically accurate, and many members of the film audience would remember it. For these moviegoers as well as the ones who had heard the stories of the aftermath of Rockne's death, the funeral scenes provided an extra catharsis, the sense of seeing well-known events and reliving initial emotions. In the same way, *Pride of the Yankees* used Gehrig's farewell speech and the location where he spoke it to maximum affect, re-creating the ghostly, echoing effect that most radio listeners and movie newsreel viewers remembered so vividly.

After the film funeral, a ghostly Rockne appears, moving along the outside wall of Notre Dame Stadium. Then comes a shot of the football field within, with an announcer intoning, "And from that field at Notre Dame, the spirit of Knute Rockne is reborn in those who have kept their pledge to carry on for him. Today in every corner of this country, they are teaching his standards of clean sportsmanship and right living to hundreds of American youths. For these are Rockne's boys . . ."

This fulfilled Bonnie Rockne's request for "the picture" to be "an inspiration to young men"; the conclusion also listed the many Rockne players who went into coaching. Thus, the hero, in ghostly form, becomes the deity of college coaches, not only the motivator of his actual "boys" but, more importantly, the metaphorical inspiration for millions of young men who internalized the Hollywood version of his biography.

■　■　■

> Today we see an America ready to compete, anxious to compete . . .
> What is propelling our country forward? That fundamental element
> of the American character that no tyranny and few of our competitors
> can ever hope to match. Knute Rockne knew and appreciated it—the
> creative genius and omnipresent optimism of our people.
>
> —President Ronald Reagan, March 1988.

The coach's story did not end with the final frame of *Knute Rockne—All-American*, nor, unlike most biopics of the period, did the hero freeze-frame in public consciousness. The coach's life became a protean force, constantly shaped and reconstructed by sports media, athletic coaches, and politicians. Thus, in March 1988, to mark the one-hundredth anniversary of Rockne's birth, the president of the United States visited the University of Notre Dame to unveil a postage stamp with a portrait of the coach upon it. The event was conducted with the appropriate amount of entertainment: a number of huge movie screens showed clips from *Knute Rockne—All-American;* at the line in the eulogy where Father Callahan says, "Ask the president of the United States," the band broke into "Hail to the Chief" and Ronald Reagan entered. Behind the speaker's lectern hung a huge banner, "Notre Dame Welcomes the Gipper." In his address, the president revisited some of Rockne's sports triumphs; he also spoke in detail about religion, the spiritual quality of Notre Dame, and his belief that "Knute Rockne did more spiritual good than a thousand preachers. His career was a sermon in right living" (another line from the film's dedication).

Historian Garry Wills noted that throughout Reagan's political career, he not only portrayed himself as the Gipper but also as Rockne, that in essence his political addresses, particularly as president, were locker-room speeches to the nation, invoking the past, explaining the present, and challenging Americans to go out there and win the future. The March 1988 talk at Notre Dame contained such pep-talk lines as "I happen to have always believed in the American people. Don't sell them short. Given the proper tools, and a level playing ground, our workers can outproduce and outcompete anyone, anywhere."

The Notre Dame audience appreciated the speech, particularly its invocation of the traditional sports ideals—hard work and fair competition on a level playing field—and applauded enthusiastically. The audience also enjoyed the clips from *Knute Rockne—All-American,* and some members attended a screening of the film on campus later that day. However, for most of these moviegoers, the movie mainly existed in a vacuum, an artifact from an earlier age. Many viewers enjoyed it, but few comprehended the era in which it was made. Most importantly, they were not aware of its significance in the history of college sports, or the fact that when Warner Brothers produced it, many Americans did not regard intercollegiate athletics with the reverence or awe that later audiences brought to the film.

In the 1930s and early 1940s, the image of college sports was very much in flux, the traditional athlete-hero competing with other figures, some of them frivolous but many distinctly negative. College athletes and coaches were still far from the sacrosanct status they attained in the wake of *Knute Rockne— All-American.* An examination of college sports films before the release of the Rockne biopic contains surprises, none more startling than the many Hollywood pictures portraying intercollegiate athletics in negative terms.

Part 2

The
Best Defense
Is a
Good Offense

3

Hollywood and the Critics of College Sports

I remember when I was a student at Notre Dame starting in 1930, and also throughout the thirties, that not everyone loved college sports like they later did. There were lots of critics . . . there was the famous Carnegie report, and in the Depression lots of schools lost money on college sports. Did you know that Purdue dropped most of its teams, except football and basketball of course . . . I even remember, I couldn't tell you their names, some Hollywood pictures that knocked college football. And plenty of writers who did. The Rockne movie changed all that.

—Edward "Moose" Krause, former Notre Dame athlete, coach, and athletic director, in a 1991 interview.

The image of college sports and coaches imprinted upon the American public by *Knute Rockne—All-American* gave many sports fans in later decades the impression that the history of intercollegiate athletics was an unbroken series of triumphs from the 1920s, the era of Rockne's Fighting Irish teams, to the 1940s and beyond. In reality, during the early decades of big-time college sports, opponents within higher education and the media vigorously attacked the entire college sports enterprise; indeed, in the 1920s and 1930s, the adversaries mounted serious reform and abolition campaigns, attempting to turn the public against big-time college football. To understand the crucial role that classical films like *Knute Rockne—All-American* played in the subsequent public approval of intercollegiate athletics, and how these images later helped college sports survive its worst crises and scandals, it is necessary to examine the opponents of college sports, their arguments, and how the media presented their points of view.

29

■ ■ ■

The question is not so much whether athletics in their present form should be fostered by the university, but how fully can a university that fosters professional athletics discharge its primary [educational] function?

—Henry S. Pritchett, director of the Carnegie Foundation for the Advancement of Higher Education, 1929.

Throughout the 1920s, as the popularity of college football exploded, many schools built large stadiums to accommodate their expanding football programs as well as their sports-loving students, alumni, and fans. The media, including Hollywood silent movies, mainly glorified this expansion, as well as the football hero; however, criticism of college sports also increased at this time.

Within the academy, many faculty members and administrators attacked the "rampant commercialism" of college football, the cutthroat recruiting of athletes, the growing number of sham courses to keep players in school, and the increasing importance and high pay of coaches. The Carnegie Foundation for the Advancement of Higher Education decided to investigate the situation and, in 1924, launched a massive five-year investigation of college sports in all parts of the United States and Canada. In 1929, it published a comprehensive and scathing report. The fallout from this document settled over intercollegiate athletics for the next decade, contributing to press and public skepticism about college sports as well as Hollywood's spurt of anticollege football films.

The Carnegie authors exhaustively documented the well-known abuses in recruiting and illegal payments to athletes, and blamed coaches and their alumni supporters for these violations of the amateur code. In addition, they deplored coaches' high salaries, particularly at a time when faculty were so poorly paid, as well as coaches' training methods, labeling them "professional drill-masters" obsessed with producing winning teams.

In an important section called "The Press and College Athletics," the authors of the Carnegie study condemned the many newspapers that treated college sports as if it were the main purpose of the university. The report also complained about the negative effect of the "Gee-Whiz" sportswriters, personified by Grantland Rice, with their infinite enthusiasm for and promotion of college football, its coaches, and players. During the 1920s, Paul Gallico was one of Rice's main disciples; later he confessed to "spinning a daily tale in the most florid and exciting prose that I could muster, part of the great bally-hoo, member of the great gullibles, swallower of my own bait. I belonged to that category of sportswriters known as the 'Gee-Whizzers.' "

"Gee-Whiz" sports journalism connected directly to athlete-hero juvenile fiction—some writers worked in both fields—and its product, in its simplest form, was the journalistic equivalent of Hollywood's primitive college football films. However, masters like Grantland Rice produced more sophisticated versions of the athlete-hero myth, and their best work, such as the famous "Four Horsemen" piece, foreshadowed classical films like *Knute Rockne— All-American.*

In the 1920s, the "Gee-Whiz" school also spawned its antithesis, the "Aw-Nuts" men, led by Rice's fellow columnist on the *New York Herald-Tribune,* W. O. McGeehan, and enlisting such sportswriters-turned-general-pundits as Damon Runyon, Heywood Broun, and Westbrook Pegler. In a column three days after Rice's Four Horsemen article, McGeehan mocked the "Gee-Whizzers" and the social context in which they operated: "The average reader of the sporting pages is as sentimental as a seminary girl. You cannot tell the persons hungry for their daily heroes that a certain champion did not buy his mother a home out of his first earnings but instead lost the money shooting craps."

In 1929, the "Aw-Nuts" writers welcomed the Carnegie Foundation's report on intercollegiate athletics—the "Gee-Whizzers" either ignored or dismissed it. The report confirmed with hundreds of pages of data what the "Aw-Nuts" skeptics had long argued: college football was a huge commercial enterprise and its famous coaches, including Knute Rockne, were among the greatest self-promoters and buccaneers of the 1920s. The "Aw-Nuts" writers kept the issue of commercialism and corruption in intercollegiate athletics alive during the 1930s, preparing the public for further Carnegie "Bulletins" as well as Hollywood depictions of their criticisms of college sports.

■   ■   ■

FRANK [a student and the college president's son—played by Zeppo Marx]:
A college needs something else besides education. And what this college needs is a good football team, and you can't have a good football team unless you have good players.

WAGSTAFF [the college president and Frank's father—played by Groucho Marx]:
My boy, I think you've got something there, and I'll wait outside until you clean it up. I know it's dangerous but I'm going to ask you one more question. Where do you get good football players?

FRANK:
Well, in a speakeasy down . . .

WAGSTAFF:
Are you suggesting that I, the president of Huxley College, go to a speakeasy—without even giving me the address?

FRANK:

It's at 42 Elm Street, but you can't go there. It's unethical. It isn't right for a college to buy football players.

WAGSTAFF:

It isn't, eh? Well, I'll nip that in the bud. How about coming along and having a nip yourself. Or better still, you wait here.

FRANK:
Anything further, Father . . .

WAGSTAFF:
In a speakeasy? Isn't that against the law, selling football players in a speakeasy?

FRANK:
Dad, two of the greatest football players in the country hang out in a speakeasy.

—From the film *Horse Feathers,* 1932.

In the 1930s, the Marx Brothers, aided by such brilliant writers as S. J. Perelman, produced a long series of comic hits. Their physical antics and zany humor entertained audiences, delighted critics, and aroused the anger of various establishment figures as well as the Legion of Decency censors.

Horse Feathers was the Marx Brothers' most direct social statement, a nonstop mockery of higher education, athlete-heroes, and the pieties of inter-collegiate athletics as established by the "Gee-Whiz" sportswriters. Not only do "two of the greatest football players in the country hang out in a speakeasy," but they sell their services to Huxley College's main rival, Darwin, and thus move the comic plot along. President Wagstaff goes to the speakeasy, mistakes the Chico and Harpo characters for the two football players, and hires them for Huxley.

Once converted to the pro-football position, in all senses of the term, Wagstaff asks his faculty, "Where would this college be without football? Have we got a stadium?" When the professors answer affirmatively, Wagstaff inquires, "Have we got a college?" Again they reply "Yes," but Wagstaff brings the economic reality of the Depression to the discussion: "Well, we can't support both. Tomorrow we start tearing down the college," including the dorms. The faculty protest and ask where the students will sleep. "Where they always sleep," the president retorts. "In the classroom."

Nothing was sacred to the Marx brothers or to their writers. The college president exhibits his football boosterism by announcing, "We're neglecting football for education," and he vows to end that misplaced emphasis. Wagstaff builds up the football team but, for the Big Game, they seem no match for powerful Darwin—until Chico and Harpo take over the contest by putting multiple footballs in play, hiding them under uniforms, and using a huge rubber band as well as a garbage can turned into a chariot to score points. They bewilder the opposition and help Huxley triumph; its president is vindicated.

Finally, the film—described by a 1990s documentary on football movies as an idiosyncratic early attack on college sports, a product of the Marx Brothers' "private agenda" on the subject—appears, in historical context, directly connected to the "Aw-Nuts" sportswriters' cynicism about college football as well as the Carnegie Foundation report on corruption in college sports and higher education. Certainly scriptwriter S. J. Perelman, a Brown University student in the 1920s and a voracious reader of newspapers, knew the issues and saw them as a target for cynical humor. Moreover, the social criticism of *Horse Feathers* was not unique in this period of Hollywood history; the studios produced a surprising number of movies critical of college sports both before and after the Marx Brothers trashed the academy and its athlete-heroes.

> [In *Touchdown*] Richard Arlen is Dan Curtis, a college football coach and former All-American who'll stop at nothing to bring his team victory. He loses everyone's respect after he sends an injured player into the fray—winning the game, but putting the young man into the hospital as a result. Dastardly Dan is later shown to have reformed, however, when he resists temptation to make a lad with a brain concussion play in a crucial game. He forfeits victory on the field, but comes out on top in the "how to make friends and influence people" department.
>
> —Film historian Jeffrey H. Wallenfeldt, 1989.

As various motion pictures, including some starring Red Grange, offered a cinematic version of the "Gee-Whiz" view of college sports, *Touchdown* (1931) provided the "Aw-Nuts" equivalent. Adapted from the novel *Stadium* (1931) by Francis Wallace, a Notre Dame graduate and former Rockne press assistant, *Touchdown* portrayed football coaches in the most negative terms. Wallace based his portrait on the famous Jock Sutherland, the ruthless head coach at the University of Pittsburgh, and the stadium of the title was the huge white elephant of a structure that the school built for its football program in the late 1920s and, during the Depression, had trouble financing. But, even in a primitive "Aw-Nuts" film, the main character cannot continue his bad deeds forever, and the coach in *Touchdown* eventually sees the light.

He loses the Big Game by not playing the injured star, but he wins in the Greater-Game-of-Life.

Francis Wallace's Hollywood career illustrates the crosscurrents and tensions within American culture at this time concerning big-time college sports. In his books, he provided readers with lightly fictionalized behind-the-scenes accounts of college football, including Rockne and the Notre Dame program (*Huddle,* 1930). Hollywood rendered *Stadium* fairly accurately; however, in 1932, it turned the realism of *Huddle* into a sappy football vehicle for former silent screen star Ramon Novarro. Then, in 1936, it twisted a Wallace story about gamblers trying to fix a team by tampering with the college admissions process into a flaccid, wandering movie, *The Big Game,* with a predictable happy ending: the good-guy football players, including the first Heisman Trophy winner, Jay Berwanger, winning the Big Game.

That same year, another studio turned Wallace's *O'Reilly of Notre Dame* (1932) into *Rose Bowl,* obliterating the class and religious conflict between the two main characters—Paddy, the poor Irish battler, and Ossie, the rich WASP kid—and producing, according to one critic, "a totally routine college grid film." Audiences reacted negatively to the Hollywood distortions of Wallace's books, probably less because of their "Aw-Nuts" origins than the incoherent and banal "Gee-Whiz" elements.

Nor did audiences react enthusiastically to straight "Gee-Whiz" college football movies, including *The Spirit of Notre Dame* (1931), a primitive forerunner of *Knute Rockne—All-American.* Based loosely on Rockne's life, the coach overcomes various obstacles to lead his players to great football triumphs. Even Notre Dame fans and officials disliked the movie, the president of the school informing the producer that "little of [the real] Notre Dame appeared in the picture."

The Spirit of Notre Dame did employ some of Rockne's former players, including the Four Horsemen, for the football sequences, and according to one film historian, it also contained "a rare scene" for the 1920s and 1930s: "football players actually attending class." The ND administrators had suggested this segment; however, not until *Knute Rockne—All-American* fully established the scholar-athlete trope did a classroom scene become a requirement for college sports movies as well as press profiles of collegiate athletes.

Finally, *The Spirit of Notre Dame* and similar "Gee-Whiz" college football films failed because of their primitive plots, characterization, and overall implausibility. Early 1930s audiences were more sophisticated than their silent-movie predecessors, and the Depression was "wising them up" on many subjects, including intercollegiate athletics.

In 1933, Warners released *College Coach,* an "Aw-Nuts" critique of college football with Pat O'Brien in the title role, foreshadowing his *Knute Rockne—All-American* appearance—except he played this coach much closer to the historical Rockne than to the fictional Saint Knute. He is cynical about big-time college sports, he demands absolute obedience from his players, but he is sympathetic to their personal problems. However, the film deteriorates into come-from-behind-last-minute heroics in the Big Game, ending happily for the good guys, including a kinder and more mellow coach.

That same year, Universal made an "Aw-Nuts" college football picture without the usual concession of a "Gee-Whiz" conclusion. *Saturday's Millions* referred to the huge amount of money that some schools were supposedly making from their football programs, and the athlete-hero, played by Robert Young, shows contempt for the fans and their childish behavior. In addition, he actually works his way through college, refusing under-the-table money, and he romances a coed who has no enthusiasm for football or its heroes. The ending is a true surprise: on the goal line in the last minute of the Big Game, the hero fumbles the ball, losing the match. And this action wins the girl!

Most reviewers disliked this movie, and box office receipts were poor. Nor did inferior production values and mediocre acting enhance its appeal, but among "Aw-Nuts" films, it marked a turn toward a more thorough skepticism about college sports. This view matched the Carnegie Foundation's 1930s "Bulletins" as well as the continuing comments of the "Aw-Nuts" journalists, including Paul Gallico, who had joined them.

In its studies, the Carnegie Foundation argued that the economic depression would reform college sports more quickly than university administrators ever would, and the early 1930s "Bulletins" cited the general decline in football gate receipts as well as the number of schools dropping the sport and/or other college sports. *Saturday's Millions* missed the mark with its title: millions of Americans still loved college football, but they were not paying millions to see it, in part because they had much less disposable income than before. In the 1930s, very few schools sold out their home games, even Notre Dame and the University of Southern California played a number of their annual contests in half-empty stadiums, and both schools often had low attendance for games against less well known opponents. This decline in gate receipts was as threatening to intercollegiate athletics as any series of Hollywood films, and it also made positive publicity for college sports increasingly imperative.

> MGM films always emphasized strong characterization within a unique kind of setting, and by approaching and developing its subject matter from a more psychological perspective than that of the usual military school movie, *Navy Blue and Gold* enjoyed healthy box office returns.
>
> —Cultural historian Wiley Umphlett, 1984.

As they have rescued so many individuals and institutions in American history, the military academies came to the aid of intercollegiate athletics in the

1930s. In an exception to the general decline in attendance, the annual Army–Navy games always sold out huge stadiums, attracting mammoth newspaper coverage. In addition, the yearly Army–Notre Dame contest consistently filled Yankee Stadium in New York, and the Navy–Notre Dame games did excellently in Baltimore and Cleveland; these series also received fulsome press and radio treatments. The military academies, with their tradition of patriotism and integrity, also helped Hollywood portray intercollegiate athletics in a positive manner. Indeed, the first college sports film that clearly moved from primitive form and approached classical status was MGM's *Navy Blue and Gold* (1937), starring the young Jimmy Stewart.

The plot creaks a bit, particularly the ending where the hero rushes into the locker room at halftime during the Big Game against Army, suits up, and scores the winning touchdown. But the characterization is much sharper than in primitive football movies, and the production values are high. MGM always prided itself on having the highest production standards in Hollywood, and the studio gave *Navy Blue and Gold* a first-class treatment.

The film connected to the primitive military academy movies of the 1930s, particularly the ones stressing sports, like *Hold 'Em Navy*, also released in 1937. But unlike those crank-'em-out screen fillers, usually kept to about sixty minutes in running time, *Navy Blue and Gold* directly anticipated the classical period in sports films. Audiences responded to it as did Hollywood insiders like Frank Capra, who noted, "I had seen Jimmy Stewart play a sensitive heart-grabbing role in *Navy Blue and Gold*," and, on the basis of this, cast him in the lead roles of *You Can't Take It with You* (1938) and *Mr. Smith Goes to Washington* (1939). Their association resulted in the magnum opus of Hollywood classical films, *It's a Wonderful Life* (1947).

In the 1930s, studios also turned out "college life" movies, mainly lightweight comedies with plots and characters connected to college football. Often the sports elements were dumped into other cinematic structures: *Pigskin Parade* (1936) plugged the game into musical comedy; *The Gladiator* (1938) and *$1000 a Touchdown* (1939) were Joe E. Brown slapstick vehicles (he also made a similar series of 1930s baseball farces); and in *70,000 Witnesses* (1932), a murder occurred during a college football game, involving various players in the crime. All of these films and many similar ones about college football were mixed-genre movies, not only combining indigestible elements from other Hollywood genre streams but also mixing primitive and classical forms. They more or less entertained moviegoers and sometimes broke even at the box office, but they did not fully satisfy audiences and move into the major revenue leagues.

Only when the Hollywood studios started producing such pure classical sports films as *Knute Rockne—All-American* and *Pride of the Yankees* did they provide moviegoers with truly satisfying experiences, and reap huge box office dividends. Audiences loved the order and consistency of these classic films, and they responded to them with multiple viewings, establishing these pictures as box office champions. The classical historical drama *Gone with the Wind* set a box office record upon release in 1939 and still holds the all-time Number One position for net receipts adjusted for inflation.

In the late 1930s, however, Hollywood had not quite finished with the "Aw-Nuts" football films. Fox made *Hold That Co-ed* (1938), an excellent satire of the Hold-'Em pictures as well as the underside of college sports, with John Barrymore as a state governor who hitches his political future to the public university's football team. Clearly mocking Governor Huey Long's construction of the Louisiana State University football program and stadium—like Long, Barrymore sits on the players' bench during games and gives orders to the coaches—the film sneers at the "boosters" of big-time college football. Of course, everything comes down to the Big Game against State U's rival, but *Hold That Co-ed* ends with a major surprise: a female player leads State U to victory! The film apparently confused audiences—it also contained standard song-and-dance numbers as well as scenes of students rioting and attacking the police—and did poorly at the box office.

Hollywood produced a few more "Aw-Nuts" college football movies, all of them more somber and coherent than *Hold That Co-ed,* but none box office "boffo." *Saturday's Heroes* (1937) attacked the hypocrisy of "football factory" schools and their sham academic courses for athletes; *Hero for a Day* (1939) depicted a former college gridiron star, semiliterate and working as a night watchman; and *Yesterday's Heroes* (1940) showed how football ruined the main character's opportunity to excel in school and life.

Most of the themes in these "Aw-Nuts" movies appeared in the newspapers and magazines of the time. Robert Hutchins, the president of the University of Chicago, attracted ongoing attention with his winding down of the famous football program at his school (a founding member of the Big Ten), and he contributed to the attention with articles in such mass circulation magazines as the *Saturday Evening Post.* Hutchins mocked the proponents of big-time college football and their most cherished beliefs, including their maxim that athletes were ideal role models for young people: "Since this country needs brains more than brawn at the moment, proposing football heroes as models for the rising generation can hardly have a beneficial effect on the national future."

A few other educators joined Hutchins's campaign, and some professional writers, including Francis Wallace, wrote about the corruption in big-time college football. In addition, Paul Gallico, in a series of articles collected in his 1938 book, *Farewell to Sport,* repented having helped promote what he now termed a "national disgrace": "College football today is one of the last great strongholds of genuine old-fashioned American hypocrisy. During Prohibition, naturally, it ran second, but with the coming of repeal . . . it easily took the lead."

. . .

Many 1990s viewers of *Knute Rockne—All-American* wonder why, at a crucial point in the movie—after the "Gipper" speech at the Army game and before the coach's final plane trip—the film focuses on a lengthy Congressional-like hearing on intercollegiate athletics. To later generations of college sports fans, Rockne's exuberant defense of football and the coaching profession seem self-evident truths. However, in the late 1930s and early 1940s, the debate on intercollegiate athletics was real, and important enough for the scriptwriters to create a scene that never occurred, and to have their fictional Rockne speak words that the real one never uttered.

(SUPERIMPOSE NEWSPAPERS from various large cities, with the BOLD HEADLINES that blazoned the start of the most sensational investigation ever known in the world of sport:)

FOOTBALL SCANDAL ATTACKED BY NATION'S EDUCATORS

Cry of Professionalism Raised by College Authorities

FOOTBALL CALLED STRONGHOLD OF HYPOCRISY!

Cadman Committee Investigating Game as "$50,000,000 Racket"

—From the shooting script and film of
Knute Rockne—All-American, 1940.

In the film, a number of famous football coaches, including Amos Alonzo Stagg of the University of Chicago (who was eased out by Hutchins) and Pop Warner, visit Rockne at Notre Dame, urging him to go east with them and act as their spokesman at the committee hearing. The coaches played themselves in the film, but, at that point, accuracy stopped. No formal hearing into intercollegiate athletics ever occurred during Rockne's lifetime, although the Carnegie Foundation did send field investigators to examine the athletic and academic books of hundreds of schools, including Notre Dame. Thus, no one ever visited Rockne to urge him to attend a nonexistent hearing; moreover, the ND coach's actual response to the Carnegie report, including the charge of overcommercialism, was directly opposite the coach's position in the film:

COACH ROCKNE FINDS FOOTBALL NOT COMMERCIALIZED ENOUGH

Knute Rockne, here [Buffalo, N.Y.] to speak at the annual Canisius College football dinner, said in an interview today that he did not believe college football was over-commercialized. He went even so far as to say that "it is not commercialized enough."

—Associated Press report, December 17, 1930.

From the publication of the Carnegie report in 1929 until his death, Rockne repeated and elaborated upon his opposition to the reform of college sports, particularly his belief that schools should pay their coaches *more*, not less, as many educators suggested. However, in the film, the coaches' argument that convinces Rockne to go is "We're not asking you [to do] this for ourselves [and our profession], Rock. It's for the boys—millions of 'em. It's *their* game we're fighting for." Warners's main screenwriter for this movie, Robert Buckner, described his sense of how the coach, at the hearing, should "defend the game of football to which he has devoted his life . . . It is a very dramatic scene and I know it will play well."

Apparently 1940 audiences enjoyed the scene, so much so that at its conclusion, when Rockne converts the committee skeptics and routs the reformers, many moviegoers burst into applause. Film reviewers also responded positively to the scene and saw it as a key part of the Rockne saga. The *Variety* critic felt that the coach's speech—particularly the long passages on the meaning of football for young men—underlined "the theme of Rockne's whole purpose in life, moulding boys under his care to become good Americans who are conscious of their responsibilities and opportunities." This writer also saw the film as "inspirational and dramatic," concluding, "It's an inspirational reminder of what this country stands for. And decidedly timely."

Other reviewers echoed this theme, including Bosley Crowther of the *New York Times:* "This glowing, heroic account of the great coach's life and noble works will be much more than entertainment. It will be an effective inspiration." And former president Gerald Ford, an All-American at Michigan in the 1930s, remembered his reaction upon first viewing the film: "*Knute Rockne—All-American* was one of the great inspirational movies."

Warners focused on the *New York Times* critic's "much more than entertainment . . . an effective inspiration" line for their newspaper and billboard advertising of the picture. Additionally, because of the excellent box office reception for the movie as well as its longevity—Warners kept it in release throughout the 1940s—the public began to respond to the film's concept of a football coach as classical hero.

The success of *Knute Rockne—All-American* also ended the film industry's flirtation with "Aw-Nuts" criticism of college sports. In addition, as successful films frequently did, the movie codified Hollywood's position on an issue, in this case placing the motion picture industry squarely behind intercollegiate athletics. Bosley Crowther had glimpsed the future: with this film, Hollywood began to treat college sports and its coaches with "reverential respect and intimations of immortality," and this attitude directly shaped the way Americans felt about intercollegiate athletics, greatly aiding college sports and individual coaches during the coming crises and scandals.

Yet the power of the movie results, in large part, from its connection to other Hollywood films of the time. *Knute Rockne—All-American* forever changed the media depiction of college sports, but it would have altered nothing without its links to the main cinematic currents of its era: Hollywood's classical genre period.

4

Hollywood and *Knute Rockne—*
All-American

Our shared knowledge of the rules of any film genre enables us to understand and evaluate individual genre films, just as our shared knowledge of English grammar enables me to write this sentence and you to interpret it.

—Film historian Thomas Schatz, 1981.

Moviegoers in the late 1930s and early 1940s became increasingly conservative in their tastes, favoring films with recognizable plots, characters, themes, and iconography, all reflecting the beliefs they shared with each other and Hollywood. American movies became very similar in structure, so much alike that film scholars now use the concept of genre to analyze these films. (The term has migrated from academic language to the general vocabulary in such phrases as "generic products.")

Genre films are a communal experience, and many social factors created Hollywood's classical genre cinema—most importantly, the waning of the Depression with the Roosevelt Administration's stabilization of the economy. This aided film industry and consumer finances, causing the studios and moviegoers to feel increasingly optimistic about their situations and the country's. Some 1930s pictures had contained direct or implicit criticisms of American society but, by 1940, these critiques, including "Aw-Nuts" views of college sports, started to vanish from the screen. Instead, films that openly and sincerely celebrated American life appeared, pleasing moviegoers and establishing the sunniest period of the Hollywood cinema.

By 1940, an unwritten agreement had evolved between the major studios and moviegoers: the latter paid their money at the box office in return for seeing certain kinds of movies on the screen inside. When the films satisfied audience expectations, box office receipts reflected it: such movies as *Knute Rockne—All-American* and *Pride of the Yankees* did extremely well. However, when pictures like the mixed-genre films confused audiences, or deviated significantly from the norm, they almost always failed; the brilliant and innovative *Citizen Kane,* with its ironic stance on the "American Dream," is the prime example.

By 1940, the conventions of Hollywood films had reached the point where, according to film historians, they attained a classical form: this "stage embodies such classical ideals as balance, richness, and poise, the genre's values are assured and widely shared by the audience." Moreover, "like all classical art," these films are "basically conservative, both aesthetically and politically"; their fixed form stands in opposition "to experimentation, novelty, or the tampering with the given order of things."

Some critics regarded classical genre films as escapist in nature, providing moviegoers with an opportunity to depart mentally from their daily situation for a few hours—at this time, most Americans led rather hard and humdrum lives. The escapist element centered on the larger-than-life characters and the unrealistic plots, full of coincidences and tidy closures. In addition, the "non-present" settings of many of these movies—the idealized version of the past in the biopics, westerns, and historical dramas, as well as the artificial and stylized worlds of the musicals and gangster pictures—contributed to the escapism. Thus, many 1940s viewers of *Knute Rockne—All-American* easily departed to Warners's imaginary 1910s and 1920s, identifying with the athlete-hero Rockne, slipping into his player's uniform and coaching garb, participating in his heroism for the ninety-six minutes of the film and their aftermath.

Other critics, however, argued that Hollywood genre films, particularly in this period, "helped the public define and make sense of the rapidly evolving social reality" in the United States. Certainly *Knute Rockne—All-American* and *Pride of the Yankees,* which portrayed immigrant children becoming full-fledged Americans through sports, gave one clear definition of a cultural experience, and undoubtedly aided some viewers in their adaptation to American life as well as others in their response to immigrants.

Finally, because of the complexity of human nature, classical movies probably provided audiences with both escapist entertainment *and* socialization cues. Audiences believed that George Gipp died thinking of future Notre Dame players, and that Knute Rockne gave up his life for his "boys." Similarly, during the first year of America's entry into World War II, moviegoers wept when a dying Lou Gehrig—the *Pride* not only of his team but *of all Yankees*—affirms, "People say that I've had a bad break, but today I consider myself the luckiest man on the face of the earth" for the opportunity to live in this great country, play a great sport, and give his life to it. His heroic wife and parents listen and fully support him, never railing against an unjust fate. These scenes confirmed for many viewers, at an unconscious even more than a conscious level, that they should become heroes like Lou Gehrig and his family; that going to war or supporting the fighting men in World War II, possibly losing one's life or having a loved one killed, was not only admirable, but a worthy sacrifice, noble and patriotic. They too could become the Pride of the Yankees, of all Americans.

> By the time *Knute Rockne—All-American* came out in 1940, the college football film was tired [and still in its primitive form] . . . *Knute Rockne—All-American* breathed new life into football films, inspiring such biographical films as *The Iron Major* [1943], *Spirit of Stanford* [1942], and *Spirit of West Point* [1947].

> —Film historians Harvey Marc Zucker and
> Lawrence J. Babich, 1987.

Knute Rockne—All-American not only moved college football films to their mature and classical form but, by attracting significant audience approval, prompted Hollywood studios to make other college football biopics. The first one into production was *Harmon of Michigan* (1941), with 1940 Heisman Trophy winner Tom Harmon playing the title role. The film used some biographical facts layered over with a standard athlete-hero plot: a football star's ego overinflates; as a young coach, he commits a series of unheroic acts; an old coach helps him understand his ethical errors; and Harmon ends up a mature and "authentic hero."

Harmon of Michigan succeeded because of high production standards, the competent acting of the lead, and its evocation of the college football athlete-hero. The photography, including newsreel shots of Harmon in action, is effective and, on the sound track, the Michigan fight song, "Hail to the Victors," plays a role analogous to that of the "Notre Dame Victory March" in *Knute Rockne—All-American.*

The success of the Harmon film led its studio, Columbia, to produce the *Spirit of Stanford* the following year. Starring Stanford All-American Frankie Albert, the movie blended autobiographical facts with classic tropes: Albert, with an inflated ego, decides to quit school early and turn pro, but an ill roommate convinces him to stay with the college team and help them win the Big Game. Supposedly, much of this occurred in Albert's life, and the movie neatly plugged these facts into the classical form. (The negative depiction of professional football—still very minor league compared to the college game—also indicated the low opinion that Hollywood and audiences had for the NFL in this period.)

Later in 1942, Columbia again employed the football hero formula in *Smith of Minnesota* with Bruce Smith, a recent All-American halfback at the University of Minnesota, portraying himself. Because of American mobilization for the war in Europe and the Pacific, the studio added extra dollops of patriotism. In its ads for the film, Columbia equated football and the military: "Watch a typical kid learn the kind of real-life heroism the Axis is learning to fear. It's a real-life heart-filled drama of today. Have a seat on the 50-yard line for the thrill-packed drama of a great All-American."

The real Bruce Smith was too modest for the inflated-ego trope; instead the film has a journalist probe Smith's motivations for playing and excelling in sports. The writer discovers that Smith's father, a Minnesota player in a famous 1910 loss to Michigan, inspired Bruce; the film also recreated key plays from that 1910 game. The movie ends with Smith enlisting in the Navy.

Again, the studio pleased moviegoers with a tidy classical football film and reaped excellent box office receipts. Years later, Donald Gray, a critic of American culture, recalled the impact that these college football movies had on him and others growing up at this time: "I remember sitting in the theater in my Chicago neighborhood watching *Smith of Minnesota* over and over, and then playing sandlot football, trying to be like Bruce Smith. I assume that millions of other young men were doing the same thing—that was the power of those films, and the importance of Hollywood in this period. We were naive and innocent, and Hollywood spoke to us directly."

Smith of Minnesota also moved classic sports movies toward a new phase, combining the athlete-hero tropes with the military hero ones (see page 128). But, just as important at this time, classical film tropes were mutating into other media forms, particularly in the press and on radio. During the era that Hollywood dominated American media, sportswriters and broadcasters regularly incorporated successful movie formulas into their work, and the public responded positively.

■   ■   ■

The phone rang in the hallway off the living room of the house at 820 Chestnut Street in Waban, Massachusetts. Floss was upstairs tucking Sue and Flossie in. Frankie the Third was in his pajamas, ready for bed after a goodnight huddle with his dad. The phone bell tinkled again. Probably it was Charley O'Rourke, or maybe those folks from Norwalk, where he was due to speak at the banquet for Mickey Connolly. He stepped into the hall and picked up the phone.

"Mr. Frank Leahy?" queried an operator in crisp tones.

"Yes, this is Frank Leahy."

"I have a long-distance phone call for you," the operator replied . . .

—Sportswriters Arch Ward and Charles Bartlett, 1944.

The phone call led directly to Frank Leahy, at Boston College at the time, becoming head football coach at Notre Dame in 1941. The book *Frank Leahy & the Fighting Irish* began with the above passage; the phone call scene apparently appealed to readers, and many subsequent works on college sports and on Notre Dame reprinted it. (*Chicago Tribune* sports editor Arch Ward is listed as the sole author of the Leahy book; however, Dave Condon, a longtime *Tribune* sportswriter, attributed most of it to "the ghostly typewriter of Charles Bartlett," Ward's assistant at the *Tribune.*)

The setting and plot of this scene were lifted from Hollywood's classical cinema: while attentive parents put their sweet children to bed, an unexpected phone call triggers the action; the hero wonders who's calling, then the terse voice of the long-distance operator escalates the drama. The tropes of Hollywood films had so permeated American culture that journalists, particularly sportswriters, used them in supposedly factual accounts, and readers accepted them as authentic reports. However, an informed 1990s reader questions the Ward/Bartlett version and sources: neither was ever in Leahy's Boston-area home, but they later became friendly with the coach and his family; they learned about the phone call to Leahy that night, but how could they have recorded the latter's thoughts as the phone rang or known the operator's tone of voice? The best explanation for the passage is that ghostwriter Bartlett took the outline details from Ward and plugged them into the Hollywood metaphors.

Forties audiences, including sports fans, so loved classical films that the press and radio often presented players and coaches as if their lives existed within those movies. After *Knute Rockne—All-American,* the media placed the University of Notre Dame and its football program squarely within this cinematic mode, regularly employing movie tropes to depict Fighting Irish players and coaches. Hence the phone call scene for the hiring of Frank Leahy.

But sportswriters and broadcasters extended the classical formula beyond Notre Dame. Soon after *Knute Rockne—All-American* appeared, they began to apply some of the film's tropes to college sports heroes at other schools: if the boy was a good student, they offered a Rockne-like scholar-athlete tale with a photograph and/or description of the athlete-hero in class and/or a comment from one of his teachers; if a "late bloomer," they pointed to Rockne's years at Notre Dame as an "older student"; if from a poor economic background, they used the Rockne/Alger parable of how the athlete-hero "lifted himself up by his bootstraps" . . . and so forth. (In later eras, these stories migrated to television, recycled as up-close-and-personal tales, with their structure and content remarkably intact from their classical origins.)

In addition, after the appearance of the Rockne biopic, the press and radio began supplying audiences with parallel narratives about coaches: if he acted as a father figure to one or more of his players, he became a Rockne molder-of-men; if he did charity work for a youth group or helped out at the YMCA, he was a Rockne inspiration-to-youth; if active in his church and/or a civic group, he proved that coaching was more than a sweaty job, it was a Noble Calling; if . . .

Another subject for generic tales was the team, the group-hero. Before World War II, these narratives were rarer than the stories about athletes and coaches, but the war accelerated the importance of group-heroes, making them the dominant college sports tale for a time. If the team had overcome problems with individual members—injuries, inflated egos, dropouts—it became a harmonious squadron, worthy of flying the colors of its school and fans. If the team had blended players from different ethnic, religious, and socioeconomic origins, it became an American melting pot; sportswriters often focused on the Notre Dame rosters with athletes from various back-grounds, not only Irish Catholics but also the sons of Polish coal miners, Ital-ian street vendors, Protestant accountants, and Jewish lawyers. If the team mastered difficult plays and beat opponents through excellent execution, it became "a well-oiled machine," reminiscent of great units like the "Four Horsemen and Seven Mules" and their mastery of the "Notre Dame Shift" (depicted in the Rockne movie). During World War II, the smoothly func-tioning college football team became a role model, often cited in Hollywood war movies and political speeches as the ideal for soldiers in combat as well as civilians on the homefront to emulate (see pages 121–22 and 126–36).

> We viewers will give ourselves over to the narrative effortlessly and unconsciously, identifying with characters and undergoing vicarious experiences in a willing suspension of disbelief that can be sustained for hours on end.
>
> —Film historian Thomas Schatz, 1983.

This critic wrote about Hollywood fiction films and how moviegoers, as they viewed them, immersed themselves in the stories, ignoring the fact that they were watching mechanically produced images on a screen. It was even easier for sports fans to believe the press and radio narratives about athlete-heroes, coaches, and teams: these reports involved real persons at existing institutions playing or coaching actual contests. However, these tales were no more authentic than the movie fictions; the sports media imposed formulaic fables upon the athletes, coaches, and events to produce a Hollywood effect.

In the primitive period of sports media, one size tale fit all participants and games; in their 1940s classical form, narratives came in a number of sizes and permutations, but the complexity of the form did not render the stories more real, did not portray the subjects with greater accuracy. When viewers cried at the death of Gipp, the actual event in the hospital in 1920 did not induce the tears—it was the media's storytelling of the incident that caused the weeping as well as the earlier cheering for the hero's triumphs. However, the difference between the media's stories—in addition to the movie, many radio programs, newspaper and magazine articles, even comic books related the Gipp deathbed scene—and the reality of the player's demise, as revealed by the historical record, indicates the disjuncture between the classic narrative and, as best we can ascertain them, the actual person and events.

Yet, in the 1940s, the public adored the classical stories and had little interest in the facts of history. Moreover, the media loved telling the stories and did not probe the strata of facts beneath them. Finally, just as these tales departed from authentic people and institutions, the sports themselves began to take on classical genre forms and appeal to fans for many of the same reasons that the fans treasured the media fables.

5

College Sports as Classical Genre

Bound by a strict set of conventions, tacitly agreed upon by [producer] and audience, [college sports] provides the experience of an ordered world and is an essentially classical structure predicated upon the principles of a classical genre world view . . . [College sports] is a paradigm of ritual and order . . . a classical mode in which imitation not of life but of conventions is of paramount importance.

—Film historian Thomas Sobchack, 1975.

Substituting the term "college sports" for "classical film" in the above quotation demonstrates how well the concept of genre applies to intercollegiate athletics, particularly in its 1940s form. Just as Hollywood movies of the classical period provided audiences with clearly ordered experiences and a sense of community, by the 1940s, college sports began to supply its fans with similar pleasures, and continued to do so during the following decades. Confirmation of the appropriateness of using the term "classical" for college sports in this period also comes from the name of a 1990s cable TV channel that shows films and tapes of athletic events of earlier eras: the *Classic Sports Network.*

In the first decades of the twentieth century, college football attracted a large following, but other than the mixed population of students and alumni, the vast majority of fans were adult males—photos of crowds show seas of men's hats and suits—and press coverage emphasized the athlete-hero, often in super-macho terms. However, just as classical films of the 1930s and 1940s depended upon the shared values of a large and diverse audience, college football during those years started to transcend its adult male fan base and become family-oriented. In the 1940s, for many Americans, the cultural experience of college sports began to involve the entire family: parents took children to games; families listened to their favorite teams on the radio; and families often read, in communal fashion, the accounts of games in the Sunday papers. In addition, fans learned the rules of the college football genre and the conventions surrounding particular teams as thoroughly as moviegoers mastered the rules of their favorite film forms.

Like the set structure and content of classical films, the conservative form and content of college football appealed to its fans. By 1940, the sport had also acquired enough history and lore that supporters could cherish and try to "conserve" it. *Knute Rockne—All-American* played a major role in this process: it celebrated and idealized football's past, sanctifying Hollywood's fictional treatment of college sports history. Subsequently, many journalists and popular radio announcers used this approach for innumerable articles and on-air segments on past heroes and events in college sports.

The classical form of college football also clearly distinguished it from professional football, at that time still in its primitive period. (The NFL was so unstable that in 1943, because of economic problems caused by the war, the Philadelphia Eagles and the Pittsburgh Steelers merged as one team, the Pitt-Phil Steagles.) Fans appreciated the conservative nature of college sports, and, unlike professional sports franchises that frequently folded or left abruptly for greener-money pastures elsewhere, college sports teams remained rooted at their schools. This conservativism greatly helped intercollegiate athletics in later eras, including the present one.

■　　■　　■

An analysis of college sports as classical genre can proceed along the same lines that critics use for films in this period: setting, iconography, plot, character, and themes. Setting for college sports was instantly recognizable and reassuring to the fans. By the 1940s, the ideal setting had evolved to its classic form: the large football stadium on an autumn afternoon, the basketball arena on a winter night; the crowds with their mix of ages, many spectators wearing the colors of the competing schools; the cheerleaders and marching and/or pep bands, and so on.

The iconography of college sports events not only extended to the colors— home team and opposition—worn by rooters but, even more importantly, to the costumes of the bands, the cheerleaders, the game officials, and the uniforms of the players. For University of Illinois fans, the orange-and-blue uniforms on their favorites had become as instantly recognizable and meaningful as the trenchcoats worn by detectives in mystery movies; similarly, the gold football helmets of the Fighting Irish meant as much to Notre Dame fans as any sheriff's white hat did to a moviegoer.

Iconography included music, and no sporting event employed music more continually and effectively than an intercollegiate athletic contest. The bands played fight songs and school anthems; large numbers of people in the crowd stood spontaneously and sang. The music at college sports events connected to the history, and the fans relished it. (In later eras, traditional college sports music would contrast with the artificial cacophony at professional sports events.)

> It is a closed world. There is little room in [college sports] for ambiguity anywhere—in characters, plots, or iconography . . . The most important single aspect of [college sports] that gives it this compact sense of shape is the plot [the form of the game].
>
> —Film historian Thomas Sobchack, 1975.

By the 1940s, the rules of the games were as obvious and well defined as the rules of any movie Western. Sometimes the players and/or coaches disputed the officials' interpretations of the rules, but never the existence of the rule book or the fact that the head official was the final arbiter. Moreover, as in Hollywood movies, the dramatic shape of college sports events—the plot—progressed neatly and inexorably.

Conclusions were clear; one team almost always won. For fans the result was cathartic—the best catharsis was if their team won, but there was a sense of closure even in a loss. The only ambiguous result was the occasional tie; however, in the early history of basketball, the rulemakers added overtime to prevent ties and, in football, tinkered with the rules to render them unlikely.

A college sports plot also contained an elaborate set of variations. Games fascinated fans because they combined simplicity and closure with a sense of complexity and open-endedness. Fans knew that probably one team would win a specific contest, but they did not know which team; each game appeared the same *and* different. Fans could summon enormous energy and emotion for many similar but apparently unique events. And after the game, part of the fans' pleasure was to measure how that contest succeeded or failed compared to other contemporary games, and also to others in the history of the sport. (In later eras, many fans continued to enjoy college sports as a classical genre, and even in the present period, middle-aged and older rooters tend to regard it in those terms. Moreover, younger fans, despite their hip skepticism and MTV sensibilities, appreciate many of the traditional elements of college sports.)

IN VIEW OF THE CONCLUSIONS REACHED BY THE OFFICIALS THAT THE CORNELL TOUCHDOWN WAS SCORED ON A FIFTH DOWN, CORNELL

RELINQUISHES CLAIM TO THE VICTORY AND EXTENDS CONGRATULA-
TIONS TO DARTMOUTH.

—Telegram from Cornell University athletic director James
Lynah to Dartmouth College officials, November 13, 1940.

I ACCEPT THE FINAL CONCLUSIONS OF THE OFFICIALS AND WITHOUT
RESERVATION CONCEDE THE VICTORY TO DARTMOUTH . . . WITH HEARTY
CONGRATULATIONS TO YOU AND THE GALLANT DARTMOUTH TEAM.

—Telegram from Cornell University coach Carl Snavely
to Dartmouth College officials, November 13, 1940.

A famous 1940 incident illustrates how the classical form of college football applied to actual contests. During this period, Ivy League schools still
competed for the national football championship. By November 1940, Cornell had won all of its season games and, after beating Ohio State, went to
Dartmouth with an excellent shot at the Number One place in the polls (the
Big Red had finished fourth in 1939). However, underdog Dartmouth held a
3-0 lead into the final minute. With Cornell near the Indians' goal line, Dartmouth held on four consecutive downs. But the scoreboard keeper and the
referee became confused, both claiming that only three downs had occurred.
The ref gave Cornell a fifth down, the Big Red scored, made the extra point,
and the game ended, Cornell elated with the 7-3 win. The visitors left behind
a scene of chaos, some Dartmouth fans celebrating a victory (they began after
the fourth down), others protesting the defeat. Dartmouth officials rushed
from the sidelines, reporters from the pressbox, some yelling at the game officials, all demanding explanations and clarifications.

The following Monday, the movie newsreel films unequivocally proved
that the referee had given Cornell a fifth down. The ref apologized, but he, as
well as the head of the Eastern Intercollegiate Association, to which the
schools belonged, said that they could not change the 7-3 score; the ref's
game ruling had to stand. At this point, the Cornell athletic director and
coach waived the victory and their hopes of a national championship. The
Cornell players were also gracious, the team captain quoting Grantland Rice's
famous couplet as justification for conceding the loss:

When the One Great Scorer comes to write against your name—
He marks—not that you won or lost—but how you played the game.

The press and the public applauded Cornell's gesture. Not only did it terminate the unsettling confusion at the end of the game—the newsreels showed
the head linesman warning the ref that he was giving Cornell a fifth down, and

the Dartmouth captain protesting before the extra down—but it also short-circuited any media condemnation of the referee and the chaotic result.

Cornell did not have to give up the victory, but within the terms of classical college football, its concession seemed absolutely correct, the true sportsman's gesture. Moreover, Carl Snavely, the Big Red's hard-driving coach, also conducted himself the way the public and the media wanted coaches to act: very much within the *Knute Rockne—All-American* mode.

Explaining Cornell's attitude, Mort Landsberg, the Big Red's star player, remarked that although "we wanted to win the game and the national championship in the worst way," the team endorsed the actions of their coach and the Cornell AD. Landsberg, a great runner whom Dartmouth had stopped twice at the goal line on the final drive, added that "it would've been wrong to win by breaking the rules." The media commentary at the time fully endorsed this classical ideal. (A strikingly similar incident occurred fifty years later during Colorado's successful drive for a national championship. However, this time, after winning the game on the fifth down, Colorado refused to give back the victory. In not forfeiting the game, head coach Bill McCartney argued that "only the Lord can judge me, and I'm confident He will find that we did the right thing.")

> Classical . . . characters are certainly far superior to us in what they can do . . . they are unlimited as far as action. They can do what we would like to be able to do.
>
> —Film historian Thomas Sobchack, 1975.

Public approval of the Cornell men's actions after the 1940 Dartmouth game connected directly to the way the media had started to cast college athletes, coaches, and teams as role models. In addition, during this period, athletes and coaches began to regard themselves as role models and to act accordingly—one of the reasons the Cornell men graciously gave up the victory. The process originated in the athlete-hero popular fiction of the early twentieth century; however, during those eras, simple hero-worship was much more prevalent than the more complicated activity of role modeling: "Say it ain't so, Joe" was the cry of a worshiper seeing his idol shattered. In addition, because the "Gee-Whiz" media often portrayed sports in a simplistic manner, many star athletes and coaches did not take the heroic depictions seriously, assuming no obligation to be role models. Shoeless Joe Jackson and George Gipp were oblivious to the concept; Red Grange ignored it, quitting college to make money barnstorming with pro teams; and most coaches, including Knute Rockne and Pop Warner, scoffed at it.

But in the late 1930s and early 1940s, Hollywood and the sports media evolved the images of athletes and coaches from their primitive to their classical form. Fans loved the fuller, more complex stories. Not only could they still marvel at and identify with the on-field feats of athletes and coaches, but now they could turn the objects of their affections into role models, and this became part of their enjoyment of the college sports genre. Films like *Knute Rockne—All-American* moved athlete-heroes into the classical period, but they remained enshrined there thanks to the sporting press.

> I won't deny that the heavy majority of sportswriters, myself in-cluded . . . [were] guilty of puffing up the people they wrote about. I remember one time when Stanley Woodward [sports editor of the *New York Herald-Tribune*], my beloved leader, was on the point of sending me a wire . . . saying, "Will you stop Godding up those ball players?"

—Sports columnist Red Smith, discussing a 1946 incident.

Journalists began to ballyhoo college athletes and coaches in the late nine-teenth century, and men like Grantland Rice played a key part in football's explosion of popularity in the 1920s by performing such promotional feats as transforming a backfield averaging 158 pounds into the Four Horsemen of the Apocalypse. Rice's "Aw-Nuts" rivals often derided him; in part, it was honest criticism, but they also harbored some jealousy at his increasing annual income. One contemporary recalled how "one time we were kidding Grant Rice about him making heroes out of the Four Horsemen, and what-not, and he said, 'Well, I'll tell you. When athletes are no longer heroes to you anymore, it's time to stop writing sports.' " By all accounts, Rice's hero wor-ship was genuine. His readers sensed his sincerity and rewarded it by making him the most popular sportswriter in America for a generation.

During the "Gee-Whiz" and the classical periods, the national writers cre-ated the literary modes and tropes for print coverage of college sports, spawn-ing innumerable regional and local imitators. But the bottom of the pyramid—the hundreds of beat reporters covering university teams through-out the country—was even more important in establishing and maintaining the college sports genre. Local reporters performed the crucial function of explaining the rules and conventions of the genre for new fans, and polishing the traditions for the already converted. Fans read the famous columnists for an overview and for comments on important games and heroes; however, they fed upon the local coverage of their favorite teams and players. The national writers were the dessert for their sports pages meal, but the "beat guys" provided the meat-and-potatoes.

For their part, athletes and coaches increasingly enjoyed being portrayed in heroic terms, and they encouraged this coverage. Not surprisingly, they also disliked the few writers who pointed out their flaws, athletic and human, and frequently they boycotted them; for this reason, the handful of "Aw-Nuts" men were columnists, who never had to enter the locker room and encounter the wrath of players or team administrators.

Reinforcing the tendency of the sporting press to glorify athletes and coaches were the practical circumstances of most sports reporters' jobs, particularly those working in university towns and on regional newspapers. From early in the century, when college sports was a relatively new phenomenon competing with other activities for the public's leisure dollar, athletic directors and coaches wanted their events fully publicized. Because newspapers often "boosted" various aspects of community life, coaches and ADs sought and soon received the same "boost" for their events, with local sports reporters acting as "barkers." In the 1920s, these practical imperatives combined neatly with the "Gee-Whiz" writing style to produce "sports scribes" who, in essence, functioned as publicists for athletic departments, always promoting, never criticizing a school's athletic program, its players and administrators. With the coming of the classical era in college sports, these writers effortlessly plugged teams and personalities into the appropriate literary narratives, relishing the new forms—as, by all accounts, did their readers.

Indeed, the special bond between local sports reporters and fans during the classical era resulted from the fact that a majority of these writers were die-hard fans who loved their favorite teams, athletes, and coaches as much as the rooters did. This bond spread and perpetuated the shared values of the college sports genre. The phenomenon continues to this day in college towns where local sportswriters function as part of the "athletic department's team," constantly promoting its events and personnel.

Significantly, the main attacks upon partisan sportswriters came from fellow journalists and academics, not from fans. The detractors charged that the booster reporters presented their portraits of heroes and their game stories as if these narratives were accurate accounts of reality. One critic suggested that writers who "Godded up" athletes should label their work as propaganda, then *caveat emptor* would apply: readers could accept or reject these fables, but no one could object to the misrepresentation. But classical writers refused to do this, in some cases claiming objectivity but displaying self-delusion, and in many others exhibiting cynicism because they knew the "inside story" on various athletes and coaches and would never print it.

Unlike the critics, however, readers rarely complained about the subjectivity of sportswriters—either they did not notice it or they were aware of it and approved. For readers, partisan reporting was an essential part of the college sports genre: reading the biased pre-game and post-game stories was almost as important as rooting during the contests. Readers cherished the classic profiles of their favorite coaches and players in the same way that movie audiences loved Hollywood's portraits of Rockne and other college sports heroes.

Sometime in the early 1940s after the Rockne picture came out, Notre Dame football got bigger than it had ever been before. Since the 1920s, we always had lots of fans around the country, the Subway Alumni and all that, but after the movie, it just seemed to explode . . . I was living in Massachusetts at the time [coaching at Holy Cross], and so I could see it happen in another part of the country. And it was amazing to behold.

—Edward "Moose" Krause, former Notre Dame athlete, coach, and athletic director, in an interview, 1991.

After the release of *Knute Rockne—All-American*, the press began to portray Notre Dame coaches and players as the classical ideal, and fans reciprocated, snapping up the editions of national and regional publications containing the tales of the Fighting Irish. As the popularity of the movie grew, Warners keeping it in semipermanent release, the process speeded up; readers, not only Notre Dame supporters but college sports fans in general, enjoyed the classical profiles of Notre Dame players and coaches, and the press, realizing that it could sell more magazines and newspapers with ND articles than with pieces on any other college program, published ever more Fighting Irish features. Before the Rockne biopic, Notre Dame was one of the most popular college football teams in the country; after the movie, it lapped all others. It received unprecedented attention, its image becoming an essential part of the classical sports genre.

Thus the Rockne biopic positioned Notre Dame as the most prominent football program in America, and the school's administrators decided to capitalize on this situation, not only for financial reasons—receipts from football games were an important source of revenue for the relatively poor Catholic institution—but also as a means of creating goodwill for the University of Notre Dame, as well as for American Catholics in general. To achieve these goals, the priests in charge of Notre Dame realized that Fighting Irish football had to fulfill the classical ideals in fact, as well as in media fiction.

During the coming decade, this policy, combined with the media and fan adoration of Rockne's school, helped Notre Dame attain its objectives. Even more importantly, it helped intercollegiate athletics survive during the worst crises and scandals in college sports history. At first glance, it seems illogical that a study of catastrophes should feature a school that flew far above them, but upon investigation, it turns out that Notre Dame played a crucial role in the battle of public opinion and, as a result of its victories, in keeping big-time college sports afloat. As the sports maxim decrees, "The best defense is a good offense," and, during the crises and scandals, ND's classic ideal as embodied in its "Fortress Notre Dame" defense often kept the opponents of intercollegiate athletics off the scoreboard.

6

The Fighting Irish as Classical Ideal

After graduation, Rock remained at Notre Dame as a graduate assistant in chemistry. In accepting the post, he attached the stipulation that he be allowed to assist Jess Harper in coaching the football team.

—Notre Dame sports publicity director Joe Petritz, 1941.

After the release of *Knute Rockne—All-American,* the Notre Dame athletic department replied to questions about the coach's life with a biographical statement written by the sports publicity director. This document, used by ND for the next two decades, followed the movie scene by scene, never deviating from the portrait created by Warner Brothers and Bonnie Rockne, and including John B. Kennedy's "Win One for the Gipper" and other speeches. Thus, Notre Dame officially closed the loop on the coach's life, sanctioning the film version as "The True Story of Knute Rockne"—a frequent title on press reprints of this handout.

In the early 1940s, however, many people still at the University of Notre Dame remembered the coach well, and privately they acknowledged the film's inaccuracies and inventions. Nevertheless, as its popularity increased, the movie possessed a life of its own, so powerful that the ND administrators decided to keep their criticisms of it to themselves, and to endorse the cinematic version of Rockne's life. Indeed, the classical ideals espoused by the film neatly tied into their own aspirations for ND football. At this juncture in the history of the University of Notre Dame, sports fantasy and reality merged, beginning the transformation of Fighting Irish football into its classical phase.

I first came to Notre Dame in the 1920s, and it was far different from the way the Rockne movie made it out to be. So was Rockne . . . When I later joined the [Congregatio a Sancta Cruce] order, I heard stories about how Father Walsh, the school president through most of the twenties, fought with the coach about player eligibility and things like that . . . When people congratulate us on how we've run our football program, they should thank Father Walsh, and then Father O'Hara, a lot more than Knute Rockne, the real Rockne that is.

—Father Charles Carey, in an interview, 1996.

The sources of the 1940s conjunction of Hollywood fiction and Notre Dame fact originated in the triumphs and problems that Fighting Irish football had created for the Catholic school since its initial national popularity in the 1920s. As soon as Rockne's squads began beating teams from universities with much larger enrollments, opponents and their fans accused Notre Dame of cheating, hiring nonstudents—including, according to one false but widely published report, a convict from Leavenworth Prison in Kansas—to play for the Fighting Irish. Throughout the 1920s and into the 1930s, the presidents of Notre Dame spent many hours refuting these charges as well as those of the Carnegie Foundation and the "Aw-Nuts" reporters. In fact, Rockne did cut corners in his recruiting and support of athletes, frequently arguing with ND administrators about these issues, but, as the 1929 Carnegie report indicated, his opponents, particularly the Big Ten football programs, regularly committed much more serious infractions. In addition, in a famous article, "Aw-Nuts" columnist W. O. McGeehan, who had traveled to Notre Dame "to investigate the rumor that there was a university located there," reported that the school "is no place of mystery and no football recruiting camp, but just an American university with some fine traditions and some very human American undergraduates."

A crucial event in the history of Notre Dame athletics occurred in the early 1930s when Father John O'Hara became a top executive of the university and rewrote its "Athletic Constitution." Previous administrators had mainly reacted to attacks on the school's athletic program; O'Hara decided on a well-publicized offensive, one that would gain the moral high ground and make Notre Dame cleaner in deed, as well as in word, than all other universities in big-time college sports. A key element in his strategy was the fact that, unlike his administrative predecessors, he did not have to deal with the original "power coach," Knute Rockne, recently deceased; O'Hara could order his athletic director and coaches to carry out his directives, and they would; his authoritarian style was reinforced by the hierarchical nature of his institution. O'Hara's plan was simple: on the ethical heights he would construct "Fortress Notre Dame" and render it impervious to the charges and rumors that had long plagued the Catholic school.

Therefore, in 1934, when the NCAA wrote a code of conduct that discouraged all forms of recruiting except coaches' visits to athletes who had written to them first, O'Hara went one better. He forbade his coaches from leaving campus to meet even legitimate recruits; all prospects had to visit Notre Dame of their own volition and expense and meet ND coaches in the athletic department offices. The NCAA code was purely advisory, since the association lacked an enforcement procedure. Most schools ignored it—but Father O'Hara warned his coaches that he would fire them if they violated his rules.

Similarly, whereas regular Notre Dame students needed a 70 percent average to pass their courses and graduate, O'Hara mandated a 77 percent average for all intercollegiate athletes. At a time when the University of Chicago's Robert Hutchins was gaining public attention by condemning the "sham courses" for college athletes, O'Hara initiated his 77 percent rule, challenging other universities to go beyond their PR claims about educating athletes and institute similar regulations. He also offered to open Notre Dame's academic records so that officials from other schools could examine his rules in action, i.e., Fighting Irish athletes attaining their 77 percent averages in legitimate courses.

O'Hara also reinforced the most reformist elements of Notre Dame's ongoing athletic policy: after its Rose Bowl appearance in 1925, the school had agreed to go along with the Big Ten ban on participation in bowl games. The rationale was that bowls made the football season too long for scholar-athletes and greatly contributed to the commercialization of college sports. In the 1930s, as the Cotton, Sugar, and Orange Bowls joined the Rose Bowl as New Year's Day games, Notre Dame turned down repeated invitations and offers of significant amounts of money to play in bowls.

In the late 1930s, however, the Big Ten began wavering and began the negotiations, interrupted by World War II, that led eventually to the conference's annual participation in the Rose Bowl. O'Hara and his successors remained firm in their bowl game ban. For example, in 1941, ND vice president John J. Cavanaugh reiterated the policy in a letter to a member of the Sugar Bowl committee: "A postseason game draws the football season out over a large part of the regular academic year" and, after the "strenuous . . . regular schedule," the players must focus on their studies. This position connected directly to the classical ideal of the scholar-athlete, and undoubtedly the movie depiction of Rockne as a serious chemistry student reinforced the Notre Dame administrators' resolve.

In this letter, Vice President Cavanaugh also noted that the large payouts from bowl games would help Notre Dame, "but much as we need money and could use it here, it does not seem to us best for the boys [on the football team] and for the University to try to procure it in such a way. So far as we can see, a postseason game would be played at the sacrifice of many values, physical and academic, which properly belong to the students participating in football." Like the men at Cornell in 1940 when they relinquished the win over Dartmouth, officials at Notre Dame truly believed in the classical ideal of intercollegiate athletics. But even more than their colleagues in Ithaca, the ND administrators' decisions cost their school a large amount of revenue—an estimated $250,000 a year during this period, at a time when Notre Dame's total endowment was only $1 million.

When Father O'Hara instituted the "Fortress Notre Dame" policy, and when his successors reaffirmed it, they also acted out of religious and social impulses. In the 1920s, as the school's prefect of religion, O'Hara had promoted the Fighting Irish with evangelical fervor, frequently stating that "Notre Dame football is a spiritual service because it is played for the honor and glory of God and of his Blessed Mother." O'Hara believed that the purpose of ND "victories [was] to acquaint the public with the ideals that dominate" the Catholic school. However, gridiron wins were not an end in themselves; they must also aid and never tarnish Notre Dame's religious reputation. If the university adhered to this mandate, increasing numbers of Catholic Americans would support the school, many would send their boys to play for the Fighting Irish, and Notre Dame would achieve success both on the field and in public esteem.

O'Hara's "Fortress Notre Dame" policy worked well throughout his presidency in the 1930s. ND alumni and fans, at first skeptical, came to take great pride in it: for Catholic America, the school's clean *and* winning athletic program represented a religious and social triumph. When O'Hara's vice president, Father Hugh O'Donnell, became head of the school in 1940, he continued the strategy. Then the film *Knute Rockne—All-American* not only set the policy in stone but also made it important to non-Catholics: Notre Dame players had to be athlete-heroes and excellent students, like Rockne as an undergraduate, and ND coaches had to be innovative, inspirational, and win within the rules, like the cinematic Rockne. For millions of Americans, the Fighting Irish as classical ideal became an essential part of the college sports genre. The movie, however, produced one ironic side effect: it turned the famous coach, rather than the Congregatio a Sancta Cruce (C.S.C.) priests, into the originator of the totally-clean-program edict.

> From the twenties on, Notre Dame always had great press relations, and don't let anyone kid you otherwise, they worked hard at it. Not only did they constantly attract national writers to campus, but they treated regional and local guys really well . . . [As a result] the *Chicago Tribune* was totally in ND's pocket, and the Indiana papers were the same way—except for mine, and that's because we love Purdue.
>
> —Gordon Graham, longtime sports editor of the
> *Lafayette (Indiana) Journal & Courier*, 1961.

The University of Notre Dame had long cultivated the press, and reaped a bountiful harvest. In the 1920s, as a way of countering anti-Catholic prejudice in the country, ND officials answered all reporters' questions at length and also agreed to almost all requests for interviews. In addition, Rockne was adept at massaging journalistic egos and befriending the most influential sportswriters of the time, particularly Grantland Rice and his prominent "Gee-Whiz" associates. But the coach's awareness of the importance of the press went beyond personal contacts; when he participated in the construction of Notre Dame Stadium in 1930, he insisted upon a very large press box at a good angle from the field. A journalism professor later remarked that "the press box at South Bend always struck me as architecturally out of proportion to the structure around it. This distention of scale might be thought of as a fitting symbol of the prominence of publicists and journalists in the making of the fabulous legends of Notre Dame football."

During his administration in the 1930s, Father O'Hara continued the open-door PR policy, frequently inviting prominent journalists, especially from the sporting press, to his school. In October 1934, he wrote Grantland Rice, "I enjoyed that hour with you [in New York] immensely the other night," and he looked forward to seeing him at Notre Dame: "Our [student] journalists have had the benefits of talks by several sportswriters this fall and I certainly hope that you can join this special staff some time at your convenience." In addition, in an internal memo, O'Hara proposed "some recognition . . . given each year to an outstanding sports writer who has defended Notre Dame." He was too canny to give a public "award" because it "would be misinterpreted as the purchase price of a favorable attitude," but he approved sending invitations "to the [ND annual] football banquet" to various writers and feting them there.

When Fathers O'Donnell and Cavanaugh moved to the top positions at the university in 1940, they continued O'Hara's approach to the sporting press, often extending invitations to the "Dean of American Sportswriting," Grantland Rice, and including in their letters such comments as, "You know, dear Grant, that we at Notre Dame always cherish your special, long-standing friendship for Notre Dame." The ND officials saw Rice's 1940s work—his writing had evolved to a classical phase—as the press equivalent of *Knute Rockne—All-American*, and they understood the value of these ideal versions of Notre Dame football history. Because the public so loved the classical stories, because the tales created so much goodwill for the Catholic university, the ND administrators wanted the press to perpetuate them.

For Notre Dame, a key spinner of the Rockne mythology—one even more assiduous than Rice—was the coach's first press assistant, Arch Ward, subsequently the longtime sports editor of the *Chicago Tribune*. According to

Ward's biographer, like Grantland Rice, "Arch genuinely admired the heroes he and his staff wrote about. He believed in them." In private, however, Ward separated the "real heroes"—those who measured up to his expectations—from the "phonies," those athletes about whom he knew less-than-noble truths. Nevertheless, Ward would never expose the "bums," and whenever a *Tribune* writer suggested some "in-depth journalism" on one, Ward vetoed it, not wanting to "tamper with durable [classical] illusions" and spoil readers' love of sports heroes.

Because Arch Ward never saw anything phony about his alma mater, Notre Dame, its players and coaches, he brought devotion and love to his promotion of Fighting Irish football as the classic ideal. During his years at the *Chicago Tribune,* it had the largest weekday circulation of any American newspaper, serving as its city's and the Midwest's morning journal at a time when that region was America's most important agricultural and industrial area. The effect of Ward's work on behalf of Fighting Irish football was profound.

> Arch [Ward] told me one day that anyone could easily arouse him to anger by poking fun at the three great devotions of his life: his [Catholic] religion, his school, or his paper . . .
>
> Since the days of Rockne, everyone who has directed athletics at Notre Dame has depended upon the sure wisdom of Ward . . . [as well as] his courageous support.
>
> —From Notre Dame president Theodore Hesburgh's eulogy for Ward, 1955.

Ward's biographer, Thomas Littleton, neatly summed up the sportswriter's relationship with his alma mater: "Forever after" his student years at the school, "he would proudly refer to himself as a 'Notre Dame man' "; moreover, "the journalism that Ward practiced had as its chief objective the glorification of a man [Rockne] and an institution," Notre Dame. Ward attended the school for three semesters in 1920–21, and spent most of his time working as Rockne's press assistant, learning how to promote college football and the Fighting Irish. Then Ward entered sports journalism full time. As a young reporter at the *Chicago Tribune,* he maneuvered his way into the plum assignment of covering Notre Dame football games, always describing them from a partisan ND viewpoint.

Within a decade, he obtained the sports editor's job, and throughout the 1930s, he assigned himself to cover all Notre Dame home games. In addition, Ward usually arrived on campus the day before the match to attend the Friday evening pep rally and other festivities. Soon, because of his growing celebrity as well as his speaking ability, he became a regular toastmaster at ND football dinners and a speaker at the pre-game rallies. In 1937, the Notre

Dame alumni magazine noted that at the post-season banquet for the team, "Arch Ward . . . sports editor of the *Chicago Tribune*, jokingly introduced himself as *head coach at Notre Dame*."

At times, especially during the down periods for the Fighting Irish in the post-Rockne 1930s, Arch Ward went beyond the joking stage and gave advice to Notre Dame administrators as if he were a qualified head coach. Unlike other ND alums who wrote frequently to the Golden Dome about football, receiving polite but short notes in return, the school's administrators always listened carefully to Ward, replying at length to his suggestions, also granting him extensive private meetings whenever he requested them. His biographer noted that "Arch Ward enjoyed unprecedented access, influence, and what Chicagoans call 'clout' in the athletic affairs of the University of Notre Dame."

In return, the sports editor of the *Chicago Tribune* used his important position to promote Notre Dame sports programs. He directed his staff to write positively, indeed glowingly, about Fighting Irish athletes and coaches, always to portray Notre Dame as the classical ideal in intercollegiate athletics. The results appeared almost daily in his "Wake of the News"—the paper's main sports column—and throughout the *Tribune*'s sports pages. Because staff members often ghostwrote his column, they became particularly adept at imitating their boss's praise of his alma mater.

In addition, Ward performed many private tasks for the University of Notre Dame. In late 1940, he helped President O'Donnell and Vice President Cavanaugh ease out head coach Elmer Layden by arranging for the National Football League to offer him its open commissionership at a salary considerably above his Notre Dame pay. Ward's intervention created a situation where the coach—one of the Four Horsemen—resigned and left his alma mater amid good feelings; without Ward's maneuvering, the stubborn Layden, reluctant to quit, might have caused an embarrassing incident.

Before Frank Leahy's appointment as Layden's successor, Arch Ward did not know him well—Leahy had coached on the East Coast for almost a decade, far from Ward's midwestern orbit—but he immediately liked the new coach, especially his connection to Rockne as a player and student assistant. For his part, Leahy was fully aware of Ward's eminence and treated him accordingly, frequently visiting him in Chicago and entertaining him there as well as at Notre Dame. After the 1941 season, the coach sent a note to his immediate boss, Vice President Cavanaugh, explaining the "expense account voucher for my recent entertainment of Mr. & Mrs. Arch Ward and their son." Leahy admitted that "the figure in the voucher may seem rather high. I took the Wards to dinner at the hotel [in Chicago], and after the game we went to the Chez Paree," the fanciest nightclub in the city. The Notre Dame administrators were famous for their parsimoniousness—one joke was that ND officials "throw nickels around as if they are manhole covers"—but Leahy pointed out, "The sum may seem large, but I think it is money well invested because of the countless courtesies extended to the University by Arch Ward."

In promoting the Notre Dame image, Ward was not only important in his own right but also as a key figure in a network of other pro-ND writers. At the *Tribune,* he employed, among other Notre Dame alums, George Strickler, Bill Fay, and Dave Condon, and, as the most important sports editor in Chicago, he helped the careers of such ND grads as Jim Gallagher, Jim Kearns, and Bill Moloney on other dailies in the city. The Chicago ND writers connected to other Notre Dame men on other midwestern papers—like William "Billy" Fox of the *Indianapolis News*—and beyond them to many journalists around the country, some Catholic but others just fans of the Fighting Irish; all took their cues from the *Chicago Tribune's* coverage of their favorite college football team.

The exemplar of the nonalumni group, and the second most important sports columnist and editor in the Midwest, was Warren Brown. A veteran journalist and a Catholic, Brown had covered the Fighting Irish in the 1920s for the *Chicago Herald & Examiner,* became friendly with Rockne, and, after the coach's death, wrote a worshipful and commercially successful biography of him. In the 1930s, Brown was close to Rockne's coaching successors, and the ND administrators regularly consulted him, like Ward, about athletic matters. An excellent after-dinner speaker, Brown also acted as the toastmaster at many ND banquets; in that capacity, he connected to and hosted during their campus visits such important pro-ND writers who weren't alumni as Frank Graham and Bill Corum, stars of New York sportswriting in the 1930s and 1940s.

In 1941, when Marshall Field started a new paper in Chicago—the forerunner of the *Sun-Times*—various Notre Dame officials wrote to him and his top staff wishing them good luck, and stating their enthusiasm for the appointment of Warren Brown as sports editor. Frank Leahy noted, "From my playing days here at Notre Dame until the present, I have with thousands of others admired Warren Brown as one of America's foremost experts in sports . . . I can speak highly of his character, spirit of fair play, and keen insight." Leahy did not add, "and his devotion to Notre Dame athletics and its coaches," but the phrase would have been totally accurate. Warren Brown almost equaled Arch Ward in his love for and glowing portrayals of the Fighting Irish.

Beyond the Midwest, many prominent journalists belonged to the Notre Dame network. Francis Wallace had succeeded Arch Ward as Rockne's student press assistant, and although Wallace dearly loved the coach, his writing tended toward "Aw-Nuts." By the 1940s, he had become a regular contributor to important national magazines like the *Saturday Evening Post,* and from that position, he often viewed big-time college sports skeptically—but never his alma mater, which he always promoted as the classic ideal. He also coined the phrase "the Notre Dame Writers' Network," frequently convening informal meetings of its members the evening before Fighting Irish games.

Like Ward and Wallace, Red Smith had attended ND in the early 1920s, but Smith never worked for Rockne or was inspired by Grantland Rice. (Smith wondered, in print, about the Four Horsemen lead: since Rice had been in an upstairs pressbox, "At what angle had he watched the game to see the Notre Dame backfield outlined against the sky?") During his long career, Red Smith aspired to independence in thought and writing style, but he also acknowledged the pervasive power of the classical mode and of his alma mater; he always treated Fighting Irish football kindly.

More important than Smith or Wallace, because he wrote the prestigious "Sports of The Times" column for the *New York Times,* was Arthur Daley, another member in good standing of the Fighting Irish network. A colleague at the *Times* later commented that "Daley sprang full-blown from the brow of Grantland Rice. In the manner of Rice, Arthur was determinedly sunny, rarely wrote about people he didn't like." Daley was also Irish Catholic, and although not a Notre Dame alumnus, he considered the Fighting Irish and their coaches, particularly Rockne and Leahy, as the ideal of "collegiate helmsmen."

In 1942, Arthur Daley began writing the "Sports of The Times" column; in 1956, he won the first Pulitzer Prize awarded for sports journalism, and, until his death in 1974, he continued at his desk at the *Times.* From the most prestigious position in American sportswriting, Daley relentlessly pushed his classical view of intercollegiate athletics. His work became particularly important during the crisis years of the 1940s and the scandals of the early 1950s; in that dark time he often invoked the Rockne/Fighting Irish ideal (see pages 303–4).

As Grantland Rice affected a generation of sports reporters in the 1920s and 1930s, Arthur Daley influenced sportswriters in the 1940s and 1950s, especially in their classical coverage of college sports. And, as with Rice, huge numbers of readers appreciated the work of Daley and his colleagues; according to Daley's son, no less a sports fan than President John F. Kennedy "once asked to meet him, and took him along in a motorcade, talking sports. Later Kennedy sent a photo inscribed 'from an avid reader.' "

Nevertheless, listing the sportswriters on the Notre Dame network only provides a scorecard for observing their work on behalf of Fighting Irish football. The actual contests occurred in newspaper offices around the country, and were connected to the main building at the University of Notre Dame (the famous Golden Dome) as well as to the offices of various intercollegiate athletic officials. Fortunately, some of the participants preserved the paper trails, and these documents provide an insight into how the Notre Dame network worked on a daily basis, as well as the distance between these writers' private discussions about college sports and their print portrayals of it.

This separation emphasizes the disjuncture between the reality of intercollegiate athletics and the classical pictures of it. The Rockne movie had provided an excellent illustration of this issue—material history versus classic mystification. The film presents press infatuation with Notre Dame football as a sudden whirring of newspaper printing machines and a spewing of front-page headlines about Fighting Irish victories. But this depiction was totally mystified. Instead of allowing the audience to view the work of Rockne's press assistants and the coach's shrewd handling of journalists, as well as other factors involved in Notre Dame's original football fame, the filmmakers have the Fighting Irish explode into media consciousness as, in Grantland Rice's words, "something that just happened beyond rhyme, reason, or the Milky Way."

However, in nonmystified but much more interesting material history, the network of ND journalists promoted Fighting Irish football in a variety of all-too-human ways, including attacks upon their school's enemies, notably those in the Big Ten conference.

■   ■   ■

We want the help of all of our friends in the administration of Big Ten athletics, but we would rather the sports writers would *tell us* [the commissioner's office] the facts regarding wrongdoing on the part of our Conference men *instead of telling the public about it.* I refer specifically to Billy Fox, Arch Ward, Francis Wallace, and some of the other fine [Notre Dame] men who have written recently about athletics in the Big Ten Conference.

—Big Ten commissioner John L. Griffith to Notre Dame
vice president John J. Cavanaugh, December 1941.

John Griffith's complaint to Father Cavanaugh concerned some sportswriters' breach of normal procedures "regarding wrongdoing" in the Big Ten. The commissioner expected journalists to tell him about infractions, then he would quietly caution the schools involved, asking them to desist (because he lacked any enforcement power, they rarely did); in this way, he would try to keep the lid on "wrongdoing" in his conference. Above all, he did not want the press informing the public about the negative side of college sports; he believed that sportswriters should "boost" intercollegiate athletics at all times, never "knock" it.

Griffith had used this procedure from the day he became the Big Ten's first commissioner in 1923, also employing it when he simultaneously headed the NCAA in the 1930s. The writers about whom he complained—Fox, Ward, and Wallace—were all prominent members of the Notre Dame journalists' network, and the commissioner hoped that the school's vice president would prevail upon them to maintain public silence regarding problems in Big Ten athletics.

The context of this letter included many years of ill will between Notre Dame and various Big Ten institutions. Up to the mid-1920s, the Catholic school had tried a number of times to gain admission to the conference but had always been rebuffed, mainly on account of religious prejudice. Subsequently, even after Notre Dame chose an independent course, many Big Ten schools shunned it, refusing to schedule football games against the Fighting Irish. Out of public view, Big Ten coaches accused Notre Dame of illegal recruiting, and in return, Fighting Irish partisans hunted out Big Ten infractions. (The ND presidential papers in the 1930s contain many letters from alumni with this information.) Father O'Hara's "Fortress Notre Dame" policy did not end the Big Ten accusations, although it rendered them increasingly unsubstantiated.

In 1941, Big Ten coaches and athletic directors worried about the increasing popularity of Fighting Irish football as a result of the Rockne movie, as well as Frank Leahy's new coaching regime. The Big Ten, as the dominant conference in this period, enjoyed regional and national attention—among other athlete-heroes, Harmon of Michigan and Smith of Minnesota came from its ranks—and, not surprisingly, it did not want to lose any power, glory, or fans to an ascendant Notre Dame.

The specific incident that prompted Griffith's letter to Cavanaugh was both trivial and typical of the ongoing behind-the-scenes skirmishes between the Big Ten and Notre Dame. During the summer of 1941, Frank Leahy had put some of his players through conditioning workouts. He did not run full practices— summer drills were not allowed in this period, but several Big Ten coaches heard about the ND workouts, inflated the evidence to "full-scale two-a-days for the entire team," and complained to Griffith, and then to their press allies. The controversy remained private until a number of writers on the ND network heard about it and decided upon a preemptive strike against the Big Ten.

William Fox, the sports editor of the *Indianapolis News,* mentioned in a column that Tom Harmon of Michigan had lived in "luxurious accommodations" during his years at Ann Arbor; Francis Wallace, in a magazine article, discussed Ohio State's ability to obtain well-paying jobs for its football players as pages in the Ohio legislature in Columbus; and Arch Ward, in a "Wake of the News" column, filled in the spaces between some of his dots . . . he loved three-dot ellipses . . . with some veiled comments about Big Ten recruiting irregularities. The Notre Dame men did not consider these remarks as attacks on college sports, or even as examples of "Aw-Nuts" journalism, but merely as strategic moves to aid their alma mater. Nevertheless, their comments tarnished the classical aura within which the Big Ten schools tried to wrap their athletic programs.

These breaches of the traditional facade bothered Griffith, and he complained to Cavanaugh, also sending a copy of his letter to Arch Ward. The *Chicago Tribune* editor angrily answered the commissioner: "I have leveled no specific charges at any Big Ten university or any individual in the conference. There are two reasons for this; (1) I probably am not as good a sports editor as I should be and (2) I have too deep an interest in the welfare of athletics in this section [of the country]. You commend me for not printing information" in the past. "Don't you think I also deserve a hand for my failure to mention"—he then listed various violations recently committed by Big Ten athletic departments as well as Griffith's cover-up of them, and concluded, "Some of the most widely known men in THE TRIBUNE organization are unable to understand my reluctance to print the facts."

Ward's modesty about his abilities and his allusion to *Tribune* pressure were smokescreens, verbal indications of his outrage. Probably no one at the *Tribune* wanted him to print the truth about Big Ten cheating, and, as he made clear to Griffith, even if they had, his view of college sports prevented him from doing so. However, he intended to show Griffith the extent of his anger about the attacks on Frank Leahy, as well as his detailed knowledge of Big Ten "wrongdoing" and Griffith's cover-ups.

A true Chicagoan, Ward never hesitated to use his clout. He wanted an end to the Big Ten rumors about Leahy and, soon enough, they stopped. As sports editor of the Midwest's main newspaper, he knew that he had to promote Big Ten athletics. Early in his letter to Griffith, he stated, "I yield to nobody, not even the commissioner of athletics, in my loyalty to Western Conference [the old name of the Big Ten] football. Several of the athletic directors and coaches are my staunchest friends." However, he added, almost tongue-in-cheek, "I have no apologies for any little support I may have rendered through the years to Notre Dame."

Arch Ward also informed the administrators of Notre Dame of his dustup with Griffith, sending copies of all the correspondence to them. In addition, he suggested that they speak to Frank Leahy about the summer workouts. For Ward, Notre Dame football had to be "like Caesar's wife, above suspicion." The ND administrators shared this point of view and, in fact, had investigated the rumors of full-scale summer practices, finding them to be mainly smoke. Nevertheless, as a result of this incident, they decided to set out very clear guidelines for their AD and coach in a "Memorandum of the Conference . . . Between Father O'Donnell, President of the University, and Mr. Frank Leahy, Director of Athletics."

This document pledged absolute adherence to Father O'Hara's rewritten "Constitution for Intercollegiate Athletics"; moreover, "victories or winning teams are to be sought only in accordance with the Constitution, policies, practices, and the principles of true sportsmanship." Then, unlike other schools with high-minded but vague athletic policies, the memo articulated a long list of "specific points" for Notre Dame's AD and coaches to follow, including a prohibition on summer workouts.

President O'Donnell, like his predecessors, eyed warily the two-edged sword of Fighting Irish football fame. When the school's program stayed within the prescribed rules, it performed "an apostolate for the working of incalculable good." However, if any coach ever deviated because of a desire to win at all costs, he would bring immeasurable harm upon "Our Lady's School." As importantly, now that Fighting Irish football had entered its classical phase, it had to adhere to the ideals espoused by *Knute Rockne—All-American.*

Frank Leahy agreed to the "Memorandum," and no record exists as to his private thoughts about it. However, like his mentor Rockne, Leahy was a perfectionist who hated to lose. In addition, he had a clear memory of the historical Rockne, and the latter's less-than-classical recruiting and coaching methods. Leahy also realized that saints do not win college football championships. Yet, the sports media constantly portrayed the young ND coach as St. Knute's heir, demanding that he live up to the movie ideal as well as Rockne's real ability to win games and national titles.

As Leahy succeeded in balancing these contrary tasks throughout the 1940s, the media focused increasingly on him, lifting him from the coaching ranks and transforming him into a major national figure. Examining the media portraits of Frank Leahy juxtaposed with his real actions is an important chapter of this story.

7

"Rockne Picked Him": Frank Leahy

Only two decades ago people from the realm of entertainment played a very negligible role in the biographical material [in popular magazines]. They form now, numerically, the first group [of subjects]. While we have not found a single figure from the world of sports in our earlier samples . . . we find them now close to the top of the favorite selections.

—Sociologist Leo Lowenthal, 1944.

Lowenthal, one of the first academics to study American popular culture, examined the biographical articles published in the *Saturday Evening Post* and *Collier's* magazines in 1940 and 1941. Lowenthal's insights describe how and why the media elevated the Notre Dame coach to special hero status, as well as how this new phenomenon later turned Frank Leahy into the first modern celebrity coach.

In a pretelevision age, popular weekly magazines had huge circulations and functioned as primary sources of information and entertainment for middle-class Americans. The *Saturday Evening Post* and *Collier's* had provided these services since the turn of the century, and Lowenthal compared their biographies in the period before World War I to the 1940–41 years, discovering that the number of portraits of political figures had declined by 40 percent and those of businessmen and professionals by 30 percent, whereas profiles of entertainers, including sports personalities, had doubled. Moreover, the earlier era "treated [entertainers] as an embellishment of the national scene," while now they "represent a special phenomenon that demands almost undivided attention."

Shaping this development was the explosion in popularity of Hollywood movies and of spectator sports, particularly baseball and college football, that followed World War I. Lowenthal indicated how "the heroes of the past, idols of production," like industrial magnates, had given way to "idols of consumption . . . related to the sphere of leisure time," notably film and athletic heroes. He described the language of the newer biographies as "undiscriminating superlatives," with "the heroes themselves, their accomplishments and experiences, their friends and acquaintances characterized as unique beings and events." He did not link this style to classical films or, for the depictions of athlete-heroes, to classical sportswriting, but these influences obviously applied.

Lowenthal analyzed a year's run of biographies, and on his list of subjects no college coach appeared. But soon after his sample ended, the *Saturday Evening Post* published "Rockne Picked Him," a long biography of Frank Leahy by Tim Cohane, a young classical-style sportswriter, adept with cinematic and popular magazine tropes. From his title to his final phrase, Cohane's premise was that Frank Leahy was totally "unique" and his core group of "friends and acquaintances," Knute Rockne and the Fighting Irish, were equally notable.

Like Hollywood genre movies, the magazine articles asked their audience to respond in a number of prescribed ways: to admire and identify with the hero, regard the hero as a role model, and learn from his/her experiences. Cohane began the Leahy portrait with "Maybe you don't believe in silver linings. Maybe nothing can convince you a disaster can be a blessing in disguise? All right, but before you shut your mind to silver linings and blessings in disguise, take time out for a look at the case of Leahy of Notre Dame."

Innumerable classical films employ this trope. The plot of *It's a Wonderful Life* begins with George Bailey (Jimmy Stewart) encountering a series of awful events, but eventually he—and we—discover that the current setbacks as well as earlier ones in his life were "blessings in disguise." In Frank Leahy's case, according to Cohane, the "disaster" was a severe football injury during his junior year at Notre Dame. After the season, because Rockne was going to the Mayo Clinic for a personal checkup, he took along Leahy to have the player's injury examined (it did end his career). Rockne shared his train compartment and hospital room with the young man, supposedly imparting crucial football wisdom during the journey and, according to the author, symbolically passing the Notre Dame coaching torch to him. Throughout "Rockne Picked Him," Cohane discussed other apparently negative events in Leahy's life that possessed "silver linings," and, at the end, he lovingly repeated the Mayo Clinic tale.

This author also applied a full complement of "undiscriminating superlatives" to Frank Leahy, transforming him into a paragon of all virtues and talents: "a zealot on the football field, serious in the classroom, and quietly devout." (Father Charles Carey, a Notre Dame classmate of Leahy's, later indicated that the future ND coach was indeed a football "zealot," but also an "indifferent student," and "very loudly devout.") Lowenthal pointed out that in these portraits the "use of the superlative is reinforced by frequent references to an assortment of mythical and historical associations"; Cohane filled the Leahy piece with them, including many standard American legends, some from Hollywood Westerns of this period. He quoted Earl Walsh, the football coach who discovered the young Leahy in South Dakota: " 'The night I arrived there [in Leahy's hometown] . . . the Indians were in from their reservation to stage a dance in celebration of the crops. They were well-feathered and well-painted, and some of them were well-oiled [drunk].' " It " 'was quite a town. A fellow was naked if he didn't wear a gun.' " According to historical records as well as Father Carey, the coach's hometown and family circumstances were far from colorful, consisting mainly of dirt, poverty, and hardships—"The Leahys lived in a tent for years, suffering through the winters, the father couldn't really provide for the family"—and the Indians in the region existed in a pitiful state. But these biographical details would not have pleased the readers of the 1941 *Saturday Evening Post* profile.

Cohane's superlatives connect to "mythical and historical associations" in both an overt and, at times, an almost subliminal manner. "Frank Merriwell at Yale had nothing on Frank Leahy," nor did Horatio Alger: as an undergrad, Leahy worked one summer with a construction crew, "lifting asbestos blocks, mixing cement, hauling 100-pound cans of cement up thirty-yard pulleys"— the labor that built America—and he returned to Notre Dame "weighing 178 [pounds]. They'll tell you that is small for a tackle [Leahy's position]. Well, Dempsey was 183 at Toledo in 1919." Forties readers would know that the great Jack Dempsey had won the heavyweight title that day in Toledo against a much heavier opponent. Consciously and unconsciously, they would associate Frank Leahy with the legendary 1920s boxing champion.

Cohane then described the trajectory of Leahy's success after the "disaster" of his knee injury. Because he could no longer play, Rockne hired him as a student aide for his senior year, afterward helping him obtain assistant coaching jobs, first at Georgetown, and then under one of the Four Horsemen, Jim Crowley, at Michigan State. Leahy moved with Crowley to Fordham where, as line coach, he molded the famous "Seven Blocks of Granite" (including Vince Lombardi and Alex Wojciechowicz). Also at Fordham, he became friendly with a student press assistant named Tim Cohane and a graduate of the school, Arthur Daley of the *New York Times*. After Fordham, in Leahy's first head coaching job, he transformed the previously grounded Boston College Eagles into Sugar Bowl champs with a high national ranking.

Lowenthal's term of "undiscriminating" for the "superlatives" in the magazine biographies was apt; not only did writers apply them constantly to their heroes, but often to an absurd degree. For example, in New England after the 1941 Sugar Bowl victory, "Leahy's popularity reached John L. Sullivan proportions"—meaning that of the "Boston Strongman" during his long reign as heavyweight champion and as America's first sports hero.

At times with this classical sportswriter, who was typical of the species, language disconnected from meaning; in the desire to pile on the superlatives, the author detached the narrative from the truth. Cohane claimed that Leahy's Boston College athletes totally believed in him, and the coach "backed up his words [to them] by fighting to protect his players and their interests at all times." Yet in a famous incident before the 1941 Sugar Bowl in New Orleans, Leahy did not suit up his best running back, Lou Montgomery, an African American, because he had decided to comply with the South's Jim Crow laws, forbidding blacks to play on the same fields as whites.

The incident created a major controversy. American liberals opposed northern universities acquiescing to segregation, and one of the best Boston College players, Mike Holovak, later condemned the fact that Montgomery "couldn't play [solely] because he was a Negro. This was in 1941. January 1. A whole world was going to war. And we quit on a big battle. We—as players—should have refused to play" in the Sugar Bowl.

Not a hint of this incident appeared in the *Saturday Evening Post* article on Leahy—even though it had occurred only ten months before. In a sense, to stay within the classic mode, author and reader agreed to a literary lobotomy, banishing all distasteful events from the story. Only comforting anecdotes could exist in a classical sports tale, and anything negative had to possess a positive result, hence the ongoing theme and conclusion, "If it had not been for that disaster [the knee injury], Frank Leahy would not be the new head coach and athletic director at Notre Dame today."

■ ■ ■

> Knute Rockne was Notre Dame's secular saint and he literally singled Leahy out as a disciple. It could only happen in a 1940s movie or at Notre Dame where fiction and reality sometimes merge.

> —Leahy biographer Wells Twombley, 1974.

When Notre Dame hired Leahy in February 1941, the media fell upon the Rockne connection, portraying ND's appointment of Leahy as part of a Hollywood film drama. Twombley described a favorite press trope: during the trip to the Mayo Clinic, "the great coach himself seemed to be reaching out and symbolically anointing" Leahy as his heir.

In fact, Knute Rockne reached out and helped many of his players; calling them his "boys," he pulled all available strings for them, always writing glowing—often prevaricating—letters of recommendation for them, particularly for coaching jobs. By 1940, Rockne's "boys" occupied important coaching positions throughout college football; *Knute Rockne—All-American* concluding with a long list of them and their schools. Thus when Elmer Layden resigned from Notre Dame, the media's roster of replacement candidates contained many Rockne players, including two of the other Four Horsemen, Jim Crowley and Harry Stuhldreher.

Undoubtedly, if Notre Dame had chosen not Leahy but one of the other Rockne "boys"—"Buck" Shaw from the Gipp era teams was a leading contender—the media would have plugged in the appropriate narrative for him—how, for instance, in 1920, Buck had prodded his teammate the Gipper into playing the best football of his career, how an appreciative Rock had later rewarded Buck by recommending him for the best head coaching jobs available, and so on. The stories about Buck or any other Rockne "boy" would connect to football history but contain no more final authenticity than the Leahy tales: in Rockne's correspondence as well as his discussions with friends, even during his serious illnesses, he never designated a specific successor. The 1940s media portrayed the selection of Leahy as predestined, almost divine; however, the only inevitable element in Leahy's ascension to Rockne's job was the classical form of the stories describing it.

At a distance from the media's version of events was the reality behind the selection, as indicated by the Notre Dame presidential papers of the time and later. The ND administrators chose Leahy for pragmatic, not mystical, reasons. Vice President John J. Cavanaugh had followed his career, visiting him on the practice fields at Michigan State and Fordham, noting that players listened much more attentively to him than they did to head coach Jim Crowley. Then, after the 1940 season, the ND vice president secretly sent an assistant football coach, Chet Grant, to the Sugar Bowl to scout the BC head man. Grant reported that the Leahy-trained squad "outsmarted, outcharged, outstayed probably the best team in the country [Number One–ranked Tennessee] . . . *The guy is there*"—at the top of the coaching profession— "*John—believe me, he is there* [Grant's emphasis]." This recommendation confirmed Cavanaugh's sense that Leahy was the best man for the job, and he recommended his appointment to President O'Donnell, who agreed.

The press, even Arch Ward, knew nothing about the ND administrators' maneuvers, and when sports reporters described the hiring with the "Rockne Picked Him" narrative, Fathers O'Donnell and Cavanaugh went along with it, characteristically preferring the classical tale to accounts of their behind-the-scenes activities. Even more deeply buried was an unpleasant dispute with Leahy's former employer, Boston College: a few days before Notre Dame offered him the job, he had signed a five-year contract with BC. His acceptance of the ND job enraged the BC authorities, and they privately protested in every way possible, even complaining to the head of the Society of Jesus in Rome about ND's "raid on our coaching staff"—as a Jesuit institution, BC had much more clout in the Vatican than did Notre Dame, a school belonging to the small C.S.C. order. But Notre Dame would not back down, pointing out Leahy's "alma mater clause" in his Boston agreement—he could break his BC contract at any time if his alma mater offered him its head coaching job.

When Leahy arrived at Notre Dame to sign his contract, Arch Ward described the scene: "Frank Leahy, a true Fighting Irishman, had come home." At a huge campus rally, the students chanted a favorite Notre Dame cheer: "He's a man! He's a man! He's a real Notre Dame man!" After Leahy's first season as head coach of the Fighting Irish, the fan accolades and the media praise grew louder.

THE STORY OF FRANK LEAHY— A CHIP OFF THE OLD ROCK

They said there would never be another Rockne, but when Leahy's victorious team marched through Arizona, Indiana, Georgia Tech, Carnegie Tech, and Illinois, they began to change their song. When the rain and mud grounded the Notre Dame passing attack [in the Army game], the experts were willing to concede that not even Rockne could have saved a scoreless tie against Army. The New Rockne chant became louder as the Irish sank the Navy, out-pointed Northwestern and defeated Southern California.

After the final game, there were alumni in the dressing room shouting, "Our search for another Rockne has ended. We've got his prize pupil."

—*Chicago Times* sportswriter J. Ray Hunt, November 1941.

For all of the huzzahs about Leahy being Knute Incarnate—and the movie portrait had influenced even the ND alums who had known "Rock" personally—in historical fact, Frank Leahy was much further from the cinematic St. Knute and closer to the actual Rockne than the media or the public ever realized. Rockne had been a perfectionist, believing in well-drilled troops playing tough, relentless football—Leahy himself once stayed in a game with a broken arm—but, in 1941, the new ND head man installed a more demanding regimen than his predecessor ever considered, including appointing a ferocious assistant coach, Joe McArdle, to run practices. Players nicknamed McArdle "Captain Bligh" after the crazed and dictatorial sea captain of *Mutiny on the Bounty*—even football players lived within Hollywood films in this period.

One of Leahy's favorite maxims was "Perfection is the residue of hard work." As a confirmed perfectionist, he drove himself and all about him to work hard, then harder, and he never felt that his team's preparations for a game were sufficient. Often practices were so exhausting and the contact so jarring that players would drop, gasping for breath, only to have the head man and/or McArdle tell them to get up immediately and repeat the play or drill. Leahy was also one of the first coaches to use game films as a primary teaching instrument, lengthening his players' days with evening film sessions.

The coach's own days were full. In addition to supervising practice field activities and frequent conferences with his assistants, he met daily with the beat writers covering the team as well as the visiting regional and national reporters. An ND athletic department handout on his regular work schedule began with him rising before dawn, and "usually leaving the office about 10 P.M." In fact, during the football season, he placed a cot in his office and usually slept there. His family stayed in Long Beach, Indiana, thirty-five miles from Notre Dame, and during the fall he only visited them on Saturday nights after home games; however, many media stories on him, particularly those in national magazines, featured photos of the handsome coach with his pretty wife, Flossie, and their young children at home—the perfect classical Hollywood family.

In 1941, the most difficult and hectic part of Frank Leahy's season occurred when he took his team to New York to play the annual game against Army at Yankee Stadium. Since the early 1920s, when Notre Dame persuaded Army to move the series from West Point to New York City, this annual match had become a premier event on the American sports calendar, surpassed only by the World Series. The ballyhoo surrounding the game as well as the sell-out crowds at Yankee Stadium continued even during the worst years of the Depression. Tickets were always hard to obtain, and the media covered all aspects of the event in extraordinary detail. The public loved the game, and starting in the late 1920s, *all* of the major radio networks carried it live. On the Saturday afternoon in the autumn when the Fighting Irish encountered the Army, a significant percentage of the American population left work early or ceased other activities to listen to the play-by-play.

Then, in the early 1940s, *Knute Rockne—All-American* added to the game's glamour by depicting past ND-Army contests as special, magical events; after all, Rockne's "Win One for the Gipper" speech was set at the 1928 ND-Army game, and the first meeting between the schools in 1913 was seen as the highlight of Rockne's playing career, particularly his supposed invention of the forward pass to win that contest for Notre Dame. After the film's release, when an ND quarterback threw a key pass during the Army game, the announcer frequently mentioned that he was using the "Rockne invention." (In fact, a St. Louis University coach had pioneered the pass tactic in 1906, and in 1913 ND head coach Jesse Harper had introduced it into the Fighting Irish attack—but classical films insisted that their heroes accomplish great deeds, such as creating a crucial football weapon, despite historical evidence to the contrary.)

For the 1941 ND-Army game, President O'Donnell and Vice President Cavanaugh received numerous requests for tickets, including from Hollywood notables like Spencer Tracy and Pat O'Brien, as well as important religious and political leaders like Cardinal Spellman and Ambassador Joseph P. Kennedy. The ND officials responded to the requests positively. President O'Donnell obtained a large box for Kennedy "and your dear ones . . . I am happy to honor the mother and father of such wonderful children . . . I express the hope that the Kennedy family can join in singing the 'Victory March' after the Army game."

By all accounts, Frank Leahy performed well at the many public functions, including network radio broadcasts, surrounding the New York game. His public appearances as Boston College coach had not prepared him for occasions on the national stage; however, he discovered that even famous and important Americans held sports heroes in awe, and simply by being Notre Dame head coach and Knute Rockne's heir, he impressed most people whom he encountered. In 1941, Leahy also realized that if he dressed and groomed himself well—he began wearing tailored pin-striped suits and combing his dark hair fashionably—his natural handsomeness combined with his sports celebrity would please the media and the fans. Confirmation of Leahy's success came in letters to the Golden Dome; replying to one from an important ND alumnus, President O'Donnell wrote, "Your personal endorsement of Frank Leahy warms my heart. He is a true Notre Dame man, and an excellent representative both on and off the field."

Leahy never exhibited Knute Rockne's speaking wit or energy, nor the inspirational flourishes, but the younger man learned to project a corporate executive's demeanor that, as it turned out, was much more appropriate to 1940s America than any imitation of Rockne's Horatio Alger persona would have been. Particularly in the postwar era, Leahy came to exemplify the new CEOs of American business—entertainment, no longer "an embellishment of the national scene," had moved to its core, with coaching as a central metaphor for business management—and the most important news magazines of the period, *Life, Time,* and *Newsweek,* placed him on their covers. For many Notre Dame football fans, Leahy was always the heir of the 1920s Rockne, but for the general public, he became—with his handsome, well-tailored appearance, and his great winning teams—an icon of the 1940s.

How sports figures like Frank Leahy achieved their prominence in American society, how college football coaches became more important to the public than the presidents of their universities or the actual CEOs of major corporations is a phenomenon worth examining. One point of departure, often overlooked by researchers a half century later, is the importance of radio during the 1940s.

While in New York for the 1941 ND-Army game, Frank Leahy spent time with various sports broadcasters for the major radio networks. Considering Leahy's ultrabusy schedule, these often lengthy meetings seem odd until one realizes that this was "the Golden Age of American Radio," and that these announcers had millions of daily listeners, tens of millions on autumn Saturdays when they did the play-by-play of major college football matchups, particularly Notre Dame Fighting Irish games.

8

The Golden Age of Sports Radio

Radio, which began to have an impact on sports in the 1920s but did not reach its apogee until the 1940s and 1950s, brought a totally new experience of sports to the fan. Now the fan did not have to await his morning newspaper; he instantly shared the drama transpiring on the playing field. Rather than witness the event live or reading about it the fan heard the mellow-voiced radio announcer describe the drama. While remaining loyal to the basic facts, the announcers could add drama by resorting to hyperbole or altering the rhythm and inflection of their deliveries. Radio inspired the imagination.

—Sports historian Benjamin Rader, 1984.

For sports fans during the early era of radio, the new medium did not replace the newspaper accounts of their favorite athletic events but supplemented them, adding to the total experience, enabling fans to live within an even larger and better furnished sports world than before. Many of the early radio sports announcers came from journalism and brought their "Gee-Whiz" attitudes with them. Ronald Reagan was typical: an athlete in high school and college, he covered sports as a young newspaper reporter and then, in 1932, obtained a job at a radio station in Davenport, Iowa, broadcasting University of Iowa football games. He succeeded so well that he soon moved to WHO, a major "50,000-watter" in Des Moines, working as its main sports announcer until, during a West Coast trip for his station, he obtained a movie studio contract and remained in Hollywood. Even as a successful actor, like many other film stars, he frequently participated in network radio broadcasts, part of the symbiosis between Hollywood and radio in the pretelevision era.

From the beginning of commercial radio in the early 1920s, the medium's romance with sports flourished. Among the very first radio broadcasts that attracted public attention was the Dempsey-Carpentier heavyweight championship fight in 1921. The next year, New York stations began to broadcast college football games from the Polo Grounds, and throughout the decade, as radio gained popularity, stations around the country carried increasing numbers of college football games, including the Rose Bowl on January 1, 1927—the first coast-to-coast transmission of any program.

In a memoir, Ronald Reagan mentioned his admiration in the 1920s for "a little band of [radio] pioneers" who became "as famous as the great teams and athletes they described: Graham MacNamee, Ted Husing, and Pat Flanagan." This first generation of sports announcers not only created a new occupation but also the style in which to do it. Graham MacNamee possessed a resonant voice and an enthusiasm for sports; his excitement often exceeded the actual events occurring before his eyes, but, because it was radio, listeners could not dispute his play-by-play narratives. The "Aw-Nuts" author Ring Lardner, after sitting next to him at a World Series game in 1925, declared that "the Washington Senators and the New York Giants must have played a double-header this afternoon—the game I saw and the game Graham MacNamee announced."

In his college football broadcasts, MacNamee would sometimes frenetically describe the run of a particular player only to discover that he had identified the wrong man, but, the medium being radio, he had a simple solution: his ballcarrier would lateral to the actual runner. After he worked the coast-to-coast 1927 Rose Bowl game in his usual hyperbolic style, some "Aw-Nuts" writers and a number of nonsports journalists criticized his dramatic narrative of the contest, pointing out that Alabama and Stanford, with ineffective running attacks, had provided almost no action and a sluggish 7-7 tie. MacNamee refused to apologize, arguing that his job was to make sports events thrilling for listeners, and that the positive reactions to his narratives by the public and commercial sponsors confirmed the wisdom of his approach.

MacNamee's response to critics underlines the core issue in the American broadcasting of sports and all other events. In the early 1920s, in its first deliberations about radio, Congress decided that the medium should sustain itself privately, without any government support and only distant regulation. As a result, private entrepreneurs set up radio stations, covering their expenses by selling air time to advertisers, and soon the stations with the most popular programs began to make handsome profits. Thus was born the First Commandment of Broadcasting in the United States:

stations must seek the largest possible audiences to generate the maximum profits for their owners. For sports events, Graham MacNamee and his colleagues quickly proved that entertaining, at times semifictional broadcasts gained many more listeners than did objective accounts of often boring contests; some stations tried the "factual approach" and failed to draw listeners. (In Britain, the government set up an opposite model for broadcasting: it established a public entity, the British Broadcasting Corporation, supported it through a tax system, and did not permit any advertising. As a result, for generations, British sports announcers were accurate, impartial, and unexciting.)

The American tradition of radio as entertainment, not public service, also influenced the early sponsors and promoters of sports events. Advertisers wanted announcers like MacNamee who attracted large audiences; they told station owners to hire him or his imitators. Promoters like baseball commissioner Judge Landis, who was in charge of the World Series broadcasting contracts, liked the "Gee-Whiz" announcers, and also demanded that they never speak negatively about any aspect of the game. When the popular Ted Husing questioned some umpiring decisions during his broadcast of a 1933 World Series game, Landis refused to allow him to work another World Series contest—ever.

But Husing's criticism was not an attempt at objective reporting, merely part of his ongoing appetite for center stage and his belief that a star announcer transcended the event he broadcast. Husing dominated 1930s sports radio and often promoted games that he covered. In 1936, the fledgling Orange Bowl sought national attention and *paid* Husing and CBS to broadcast the contest—he was also director of sports for CBS. Husing so liked the arrangement and the Miami revelry that, according to a longtime Orange Bowl executive, "From then on he helped us make it a truly great event. He helped us get good teams. For years he rode in the parade," and, throughout his play-by-play broadcasts, he praised the Orange Bowl Festival, urging listeners to visit Miami for it and the game. With his steady promotional drumbeat, Ted Husing transformed an obscure event into one of the premier New Year's Day bowls.

Broadcasters, even more than sportswriters, "boosted" the events they described. American sports radio had no history of impartial reporting. As one observer indicated, the promoters of sports events, including colleges and universities, "never perceived broadcasters as journalists. The first obligation of play-by-play men, as they saw it, was to promote, not report, the sport."

■ ■ ■

Reagan [as a sports announcer] was attuned to his audience's needs. That was the condition of his success. He addressed them in the name of a reality (there was a ball game being played somewhere) but of a reality about which nice discriminations were not to be made.

—Historian Garry Wills, 1987.

In the first decades of radio, instead of airing expensive live broadcasts of distant games, many stations bought cheap and efficient telegraph transmissions. A telegraph operator at the game transmitted a shorthand version of the event to various radio stations, where a studio announcer translated the messages into exciting and lengthy play-by-play narratives, pretending to be at the ballpark or stadium, even creating studio noises to imitate the sounds of the sport, e.g., thumping a fist into a leather wallet to simulate a football punt.

Ronald Reagan was a master of sports radio illusion, particularly for major league baseball and distant college football games (he did the Iowa Hawkeyes live). Listeners knew when Reagan and other broadcasters re-created games—studio sound effects had a hollow quality—but the fans did not object. They much preferred the breathless inventions to dry recitations, with their long pauses between telegraph messages; stations tried unadorned versions of telegraphed games, but listeners complained. Fans demanded dramatic sports narratives. One commentator explained that "people expected colorful and edifying anecdotes, earthy homilies enlivened by conflict. People wanted mythical figures," so 1930s sports broadcasters filled the air with them, often, like the classical sportswriters, coming "to believe in the mythical figures." These announcers also helped move sports broadcasting from its "Gee-Whiz" early stage to its classic "Golden Age" form.

During games, the station received such terse telegraph messages as 1/10/C26 RUSH PEARSON GAINS 2 RT (OLSEN)—code for first down, ten yards to go; Colorado, with the ball on its 26-yard line, tries a rushing play with Pearson going right, gaining two yards, and being tackled by Olsen. The broadcasters embellished the action by adding blockers and other tacklers to the two-yard gain and, during the long wait for the next message, they fabricated stories about the athletes, the coaches, the teams, the crowd, the history of the sport, and so on. For Ronald Reagan, the transition from on-air sports storyteller, to actor in the Gipper role, to political raconteur with parables about the cinematic Rockne was natural and seamless.

For 1930s and 1940s fans, radio enhanced the mythical dimension of sports. Listeners could not see such heroes as "Dizzy" and "Daffy" Dean, with ugly brown tobacco juice and spittle seeping from their mouths, scratching frequently at various parts of their bodies; the audience could only visualize the Deans in the broadcasters' terms, "fun-loving, good ol' country boys." When announcers lauded Fordham's "Seven Blocks of Granite," listeners imagined huge, hulking linemen, not the under-200-pound, ethnic street toughs of Rose Hill. (Publicists at Fordham in the 1920s conceived the nickname for an earlier group of linemen at the school, but the sporting press and public did not accept it; in 1936, Tim Cohane tried it again and the phrase caught on. So much for the "instant immortality" of famous sports nicknames!)

By the 1930s, in addition to all of the other constraints upon sports announcers, the nature of their employment ensured that "Aw-Nuts" comments would never pass their lips. When baseball broadcasts became popular, major and minor league teams sold their radio rights to stations, but, increasingly, they demanded input on the selection of announcers; the latter were station employees, but the clubs wanted to approve them. (This later evolved into teams selecting and, eventually, directly employing the announcers.) Not surprisingly, in the 1930s, radio stations and teams chose broadcasters like Mel Allen, whose signature phrase, "How about that, everybody," expressed his enthusiastic and uncritical love for the game.

Later in the decade, when major radio stations began to broadcast away as well as home baseball games and to send their regular announcers on the road with the clubs, they set in cement the subjective bond between announcers and teams. Like the beat sportswriters, the broadcasters traveled with the team, became close to the players and team officials, and also depended upon them for statistics and information as well as pre-game, post-game, and other interviews; therefore, the announcers never uttered a critical word into their microphones, even when one was appropriate. (A generation later, the constraints on broadcasters became even firmer with the frequent hiring of ex-athletes as "color commentators": like all members of the clubhouse, they hated "Aw-Nuts" reporting and would never criticize their former colleagues.)

The broadcasting of college sports began somewhat differently from that of professional baseball but soon paralleled it, particularly in the relationship between announcers and athletic departments. In the 1920s, mainly to publicize their teams, most colleges allowed radio stations to broadcast their football games free of charge. By the end of the decade, however, universities with popular teams in major population areas, notably the Ivy League schools in the Northeast, began to sell their broadcast rights to the highest bidders. Because the broadcasts only involved a few home games a year, the schools allowed the radio stations to use their own announcers—mainly men in the MacNamee mold.

In the 1930s, some popular teams—especially Notre Dame, Army, and Navy—continued to give away their rights; Notre Dame wanted to reach as many fans as possible, and the military academies, owned by the American people, worried that selling their broadcast rights to private companies would prompt criticism. In addition, universities in areas where college football had not yet taken firm hold, particularly in parts of the South, Southwest, and West, also welcomed all broadcasters without charge. This strategy paid significant dividends: Notre Dame and the military academies became truly national teams with huge followings, and the schools in less populous regions reached many more fans than previously, building much larger and firmer fan bases upon which to erect new stadiums and bigger football programs.

In the 1930s, because Big Ten football was well established, some conference members started selling their radio rights. In addition, because basketball was a popular sport in the Midwest, Big Ten universities encouraged broadcasts of those games. Regional and local stations carried the state school's football and basketball games, often with the same announcer doing both sports. Usually the radio station hired these men, but frequently they were graduates of the schools whose games they broadcast, and invariably they were close to the current coaches and players. Moreover, some announcers, like Purdue's Johnny Decamp, were employees of their universities, working for their school in various jobs when not broadcasting games. Throughout the Big Ten conference and other leagues, the announcing style was strictly partisan, but the fans approved of it; for example, in Florida, they wanted Otis Boggs to describe his and their beloved Gators in the most biased terms.

In helping popularize the college teams in their home states, these radio broadcasters also built large personal followings, which were reinforced by their frequent appearances at booster luncheons and dinners. In the 1940s and subsequent decades, University of Michigan football announcer Bob Ufer became famous for his "MEESH-E-GAN" cheers, performing them on-air as well as at public functions. Very few radio station owners, university officials, or fans wanted impartial reports on a school's football and basketball programs, so these broadcasters and their successors spent innumerable hours promoting big-time college sports, contributing to the public's classical genre love of intercollegiate athletics. To this day, many Michigan rooters become misty-eyed when recalling Bob Ufer's play-by-play of Wolverine games, as fans of other schools do about their announcers.

> They came from every corner of the Republic to say farewell to Knute Rockne. His devoted boys who had played on his teams carried him to his grave. In a cemetery, not far from the Campus of the great University which nurtured him, Knute Rockne sleeps his eternal sleep.
>
> The Golden Dome of Notre Dame still glistens in the sun and if old sentimental football men gaze at it real long and hard, they may hear the spirit of the Bald Eagle [Rockne] whispering an old familiar battle cry, "Fight to win boys, fight to win!"
>
> —Sports announcer Bill Stern, 1944.

The most successful sports broadcaster of the late 1930s and throughout the 1940s was Bill Stern, play-by-play announcer for national college football games as well as the voice of the most popular network sports show, *The Colgate [Palmolive] Sports Newsreel*—the source of the Rockne story above. Because Stern worked during the "Golden Age of Radio"—when network radio rivaled Hollywood as the most popular entertainment medium in the country—his audience and earning power far surpassed those of all previous sports commentators. On nights when Americans did not go to the movies, they listened to the radio, including Stern's program and such popular sports serials as *Jack Armstrong—All-American Boy.* Stern's *Newsreel* consistently gained the second highest rating for a network talk show, behind only Walter Winchell's broadcasts and eclipsing all competing sports programs.

Stern's style, particularly on *Newsreel*, went beyond hyperbole into realms of pure fantasy. He told stories about athlete-heroes, or famous Americans with real or imagined-by-Stern connections to sports; in addition, he gently interviewed sports-world personalities. He loved classical biopics and appeared in a number of them, including *Pride of the Yankees;* he conceived the idea for his Colgate show from these movies, noting in his memoir that in motion pictures about "people whose stories lack dramatic elements, the scenarios are 'dressed up' to provide a punch. This is done constantly and with unrestrained imagination . . . I proceeded to use those same techniques" for radio broadcasts.

Previous radio sports programs had aimed mainly at a young male audience. Stern believed that applying the Hollywood biopic formula to sports heroes would propel his program out of this ghetto, therefore he wanted his "stories set to music, and fableized and dramatized so that they would appeal to the housewife as well as the sports-hungry husband," and also "capture" their children. He favored tales about legendary figures like Knute Rockne, and among his many fables on the ND coach, he ended one—music swelling—with the "whispering" Golden Dome: "Fight to win boys, fight to win!"

He also embraced "Rockne's heir," Frank Leahy, interviewing him whenever possible and also frequently telling the trip-with-Rockne-to-the-Mayo-Clinic anecdote and other Leahy stories. Unlike many of Stern's interviewees, Leahy never toadied to him. This created cool relations between the two men, but the broadcaster understood his audience's appetite for tales of the Fighting Irish, and he put his egotism on hold to pump out the ND material.

Serious journalists shook their pens at Stern's view of sports, but listeners and Colgate Palmolive embraced him. The acerbic radio critic of the *New York Herald-Tribune,* John Crosby, described *Newsreel* as Stern's "world of sportsdom, where every man is a Frank Merriwell, every touchdown an epic feat of arms, and coincidence stretches like a rubber band to fit every conceivable situation." Unlike Crosby, most sports reporters never attacked Stern in print; nevertheless, they grumbled about him privately. Crosby remarked that "you can start an argument in any saloon where sportswriters congregate by picking out any Stern story as the weirdest he has ever [told]," whereupon every "scribe" in the place will immediately offer a different candidate for the title. This discrepancy between the sporting press's public silence and their private comments was typical of the age, as was the print blackout on Stern's dependence on ghostwriters and, later in the 1940s, on prescription drugs.

But radio listeners loved his work, keeping his *Newsreel* atop the ratings charts and demanding that he broadcast the most important college football games. For fans during this era, Bill Stern's view of athletes and coaches was an important part of their enjoyment of intercollegiate athletics. As one sports historian noted: "The world of sports [at that time] embodied a set of values and aspirations that shaped the lives of millions of Americans." Thus, 1940s sports radio, particularly the narratives of Bill Stern and his imitators, functioned for fans in the same way that Hollywood sports films did, articulating and reinforcing the shared values. Predictably, Bill Stern's listeners not only revered his stories about Knute Rockne and Notre Dame football history but also enjoyed his play-by-play of contemporary Fighting Irish games. However, to understand how these broadcasts became the most popular in the country, it is necessary to briefly outline their history.

■　■　■

After a lengthy discussion . . . it was decided not to commercialize our broadcasting rights for the fall season . . . [our decision] will enable all our friends and admirers throughout the country to enjoy each game, and at the same time save us the embarrassment that might follow from an over-emphasis on the commercialization of football.

—Letter from the Notre Dame Faculty Board in
Control of Athletics to Frank C. Barton,
New York advertising executive, May 1937.

From the beginning of commercial radio in the 1920s, in order to reach as many Fighting Irish fans around the country as possible, Notre Dame allowed radio stations and networks to broadcast its games free of charge. The school stipulated, however, that the games air without commercials: broadcasters could do promotional spots for their own programs but they could not advertise any products. As the Fighting Irish broadcasts grew in popularity during the 1920s and 1930s, many stations as well as the national networks tried to persuade Notre Dame to allow commercials and to accept payment for their radio rights; in addition, at various times, each of the national networks tried to buy exclusive rights to the games with the stipulation that Notre Dame allow them to run ads during the broadcasts. The school refused to change its policy; in 1937, President O'Hara estimated that the ongoing refusal "had cost Notre Dame approximately $1 million" since the broadcasts began (the cost of its most expensive campus building project during this era). Moreover, "no other school in the country . . . has the first-come-first-served policy in vogue at Notre Dame," i.e., to admit as many radio broadcasters as the stadium facilities could accommodate.

This policy provided the Fighting Irish with the largest radio audience of any college football team in America and, as significantly, it greatly enlarged the ND fan base in a number of key demographic areas. Rockne had wanted his squads to become "Catholic America's team"—for that reason he refused to split Catholic loyalties by playing fellow parochial schools—and he believed that radio would allow millions of Catholics, particularly the new working-class fans, to root for Notre Dame against Protestant schools like Northwestern and public universities like Nebraska. (The first radio broadcast of an ND game was the contest against the Cornhuskers in 1924.)

Rockne also realized that radio would help popularize his team among those sports fans who love winners. He cynically called them "front-runners" but, as a 1920s promoter, he knew that many fans flocked to winners and he positioned his Fighting Irish to reap the benefits and dollars from this phenomenon. Again he was prescient: from the 1920s through the following decades, these rooters, including many famous celebrities, embraced such clubs as the New York Yankees and the Notre Dame Fighting Irish during their long winning periods, glamorizing the teams, making their games seem special and important to sports fans as well as to the general public. This glamour also helped persuade Warner Brothers to make the film *Knute Rockne—All-American*.

In the 1930s, the pressure on Notre Dame to sell its radio rights to a single network and/or a single sponsor increased—the reason New York advertising executive Frank C. Barton, a founder of the important BBDO advertising agency, wrote to the school in 1937, prompting the reply quoted on page 85— but Father O'Hara continued to refuse for the traditional reasons, and also because he saw the broadcasts as part of the religious mission of Fighting Irish football. Thanks to his policy, the benefits to his university kept multiplying: large numbers of Catholic families, as well as some non-Catholics, not only adopted the Fighting Irish as their team but also Notre Dame as their "school." Many of these families wanted their sons to attend ND; in addition, if any of these young men showed promise as football players, particularly in the parochial school system, parents and clergy urged them to play for Notre Dame, often informing the university about them.

The radio broadcasts helped football recruiting in another, even more powerful way: many young men grew up listening to Fighting Irish games, identifying with the team, choosing certain players as heroes, and dreaming of playing for Notre Dame one day. As Bill Stern and other announcers constantly proved, radio inspired the imagination more than any other broadcast medium. After years of Fighting Irish broadcasts, many young men, when offered the opportunity to put on the blue-and-gold uniform, could not resist. It fulfilled their childhood dreams. Many ND players of the 1940s describe their decision to attend Notre Dame in these terms, linking it to their memories of listening to ND games.

■ ■ ■

Sports reporting tends to lack detachment, objectivity, distance. Other journalists take pride in controlling their reactions even to violent crimes or natural disasters. Sportscasters are encouraged to lose their equanimity over a right hook or a forty-yard run.

—Historian Garry Wills, 1987.

Even though none of the play-by-play announcers of Notre Dame games in the 1930s and early 1940s had attended the school, they tended to broadcast ND games from a gung-ho Fighting Irish viewpoint. Problems occurred when Notre Dame played other teams with national followings, particularly the military academies. For these contests, Bill Stern was the master, able to broadcast with such enthusiasm for the "Great game of football," for the "Great players and coaches on both sides," and for the "Great individual plays," that he pleased fans of the competing schools as well as less partisan listeners. Stern offered the broadcast equivalent of classical movies, with his dramatic game plots, characters, and themes sparking the imagination of his huge audience. And after the release of *Knute Rockne—All-American,* he always tied his commentary of Fighting Irish games to that film, constantly invoking parallels between scenes in the movie and the action unfolding on the field.

However, before college football fans could fully enjoy the classical form of their sport, World War II intervened. Suddenly, on December 7, 1941, the country was at war. The attack on Pearl Harbor surprised Americans, abruptly rousing them from their long isolationist sleep. Some commentators had predicted U.S. participation in the war in Europe, which had begun in 1939, but most Americans discounted the possibility. Overnight, that forecast and much more came true—war not only in Europe but also in the Pacific.

The all-consuming nature of the world war caused massive dislocations in all areas of American society. Because college men were at the prime age for military service, the war totally disrupted university life and, along with it, intercollegiate athletics. The disruption even changed the structure of college sports, threatening their classical ideals in the most profound way.

How intercollegiate athletics responded to the crises created by World War II is an important chapter in its history. In addition, those crises not only led to the postwar scandals but also supplied some of the solutions to them—indeed, the war years provided much of the ideology for the future of big-time college sports. Hence the importance of examining this little known and even less discussed period in college sports history.

Part 3

World War II: The Deterioration of College Sports

9

Snafus

Just after Pearl Harbor, there was a feeling that all sports were facing a near collapse. Instead of any such debacle taking place . . . games have proven more popular than ever. And the leader is sure to be [college] football, which includes body contact, speed, power, durability and quick thinking under heavy pressure.

Those happen to be the ingredients that are badly needed now, and they constitute one of the reasons why football has the strong backing of the War Department.

—Sportswriter Grantland Rice, September 1942.

In his annual preview of college football for *Collier's*, Grantland Rice exhibited his usual optimism, albeit in a subdued manner. He acknowledged the war and suggested how college football, in its classical form, could help the military, but he quickly went on to predict the best teams and the All-American players for the coming season. (Since Rice selected one of the principal All-America teams, his forecasts often came true.)

By the early 1940s, American media provided fans with a very complete sports world, one separate and distinct from all other spheres. Fans loved the fullness and insularity of this world, but, as World War II proved, the media had created an illusion and external events did intrude upon athletics. However, the sports media, particularly leaders like Grantland Rice, and the fans, as well as the sports establishment, had difficulty acknowledging the new and changed circumstances. Big Ten commissioner John Griffith provided a striking example of the sports world's initial denial when, on December 9, 1941, he complained to Notre Dame vice president Cavanaugh about the anti–Big

Ten remarks of Arch Ward and other ND alumni writers: in his long letter, he never mentioned the December 7 bombing of Pearl Harbor or suggested that the war might affect intercollegiate athletics.

Later that month, in an event considered aberrant at the time but, in retrospect, a foreshadowing of the following years, the Rose Bowl committee moved the 1942 New Year's game from Pasadena, California, to Durham, North Carolina. An Army general in California, arguing that large, scheduled gatherings of Americans provided the Japanese with excellent bombing targets, ordered the cancellation of all sports events on the West Coast. In the shock and paranoia after Pearl Harbor, few Californians questioned whether the general had the power to cancel public assemblies or whether the Japanese air force had the capability of bombing the West Coast (military experts considered it implausible). Before Pearl Harbor, the Rose Bowl committee had invited Oregon State and Duke; after the Army general's edict, the Duke authorities suggested the move to their campus stadium.

College football fans in other parts of the country thought that Californians had lost their sanity—in addition, the East-West Shrine game moved from San Francisco to New Orleans. Moreover, the Rose Bowl shift as well as the missed trip to California so upset the Duke team that they voted 25 to 2 against playing the rescheduled game, even though they would have gained home field and home fan advantage. Duke coach Wallace Wade urged the players to agree to the change, but they still voted against it; finally, only the promise of a long Christmas vacation and two weeks without practice obtained a 15 to 12 vote in favor of playing.

Oregon State won the game 20-16, but the low attendance suggested the coming problems in college sports. The incident also illustrated the nature of football at this time: teams were much smaller and closer, players had a decisive voice on participating in bowl games, preparations for bowls were not full-time endeavors, nor was everything sacrificed on the altar of athletic victory.

> Cities leveled by devastating bombing raids . . . huge ships going down in powerful sea battles . . . entire squadrons of planes shot from the air . . . invasions . . . retreats . . . captured and tortured GI's . . . death marches . . .
>
> —Historians Bill Cromartie and Jody Brown, 1989
> (ellipsis in original).

From 1939 on, Americans had watched the war in Europe and the battles in the Pacific between the Allies and the Japanese, but they had not comprehended the difficulty of actually fighting a world war. The U.S. government began registering men for the draft in 1940, inducting some in 1941, but when Congress declared war immediately after Pearl Harbor, the country was not prepared to engage the well-organized Axis powers, nor did it move straight ahead to the all-out struggle.

The government gave mixed signals: it drafted many more men than before but also gave deferments to college students to finish their degree programs; President Roosevelt personally encouraged the continuation of spectator sports for reasons of public morale, but he would not permit deferments for professional athletes; and the government instituted travel restrictions to save gasoline and facilitate troop movements, but it did not discourage fans from going to see their favorite college teams, if they could arrange transportation.

For the 1942 season, college sports officials responded to the war situation by carrying on as usual—recruiting players, scheduling and playing games, and making few accommodations to the changing realities. Only the University of Hawaii dropped its football program; most schools added a game or two against the newly formed teams on military bases. National champion Ohio State started its season against Fort Knox, Kentucky, and ended against Iowa Pre-Flight, a naval air training base, with a full schedule of Big Ten opponents in between. Other big-time football programs also continued playing, including intersectional games that required travel. One author summed up the situation: "Bold front page headlines screaming the war's horrible news became a daily part of American life throughout all of 1942 . . . But as they say in the business, 'The Show Must Go On,' and, brother, Notre Dame–USC is show biz. When the Irish come to town, any town, the people flock to see 'em." More than 95,000 people attended the 1942 game at the Los Angeles Coliseum—the West Coast fear of Japanese bombing raids having abated.

Nevertheless, because some of the older college players had enlisted, the war began to affect team lineups: sophomores gained starting berths and, in some of the minor conferences, freshmen participated in NCAA varsity football for the first time in decades. "But," as Francis Wallace pointed out in the *Saturday Evening Post*, "the Big Ten, Pacific Coast" Conference, and major independents like Notre Dame "are definitely opposed" to freshmen on the varsity, arguing that first-year college students need time to adjust to the academic side of university life and that freshmen lack the physical and mental maturity to scrimmage and play against older collegians. In other words, the traditional scholar-athlete model prevailed at these schools, but, as World War II changed many aspects of American life, it began the erosion of various classical sports ideals, including keeping freshmen off the varsity.

Because of the war, the recruiting of good athletes—always a test of the standards of intercollegiate athletics—escalated. Wallace noted that "with fewer prize" players on the varsity, "the pursuit [of prospects] has been intense. And there's more fat on the pigskin for a wily shopper [recruit] than ever before." Much of the fat came from a relatively new recruiting ploy:

athletic scholarships. A number of years before, two of the weakest conferences, the Southeastern and the Southern, had instituted athletic grants to gain a recruiting advantage over the big-time football powers, and in 1942 other conferences became interested in this tactic.

For many decades in college sports, athletic scholarships had been taboo, considered by most proponents and all critics as play-for-pay, a total violation of the amateur ideal. Only desperate coaches and schools had endorsed these grants, the Southerners claiming that they needed them to lure talent from other regions, particularly football-rich Northern states. The NCAA disapproved but had no power to enforce its displeasure, and the advocates of athletic scholarships justified them with "this is a free country. A coach should be allowed to get his talent wherever he can"—in the subtext, in any way that he can.

In the early 1940s, Father Hugh O'Donnell, the president of Notre Dame, led the traditionalists, stating: "Intercollegiate football today is suffering from a very cankerous sore—subsidization," in the form of "athletic scholarships" and under-the-table cash. It "cheapens the personality of a young man, puts him on the slave block to the highest bidder and handicaps him educationally. It must be stopped before it becomes widespread . . . it is time to call a halt, a quick halt, before real professionalism takes hold." Father O'Donnell, the starting center on the 1915 Notre Dame varsity, believed in the scholar-athlete ideal, and as an administrator, he tried to enforce it at his school; in the 1920s, he expelled a number of Rockne's best players for academic and disciplinary violations. For O'Donnell, athletic scholarships—payment-in-kind to induce athletes to play sports for a school—completely contradicted his own life as well as his vision of college sports at Notre Dame and in the United States.

Father O'Donnell also invoked the film *Knute Rockne—All-American* to bolster his position against athletic scholarships: the cinematic Rockne had come to Notre Dame to study; later, when he participated in intercollegiate athletics, he played for the love of sports and alma mater, not for money. O'Donnell's public denunciations of athletic scholarships separated Notre Dame from an increasing number of schools and, for the media and fans, reinforced the image of the Fighting Irish as the classical ideal. (Like many ND officials of this era, Father O'Donnell forgot about the Rockne whom he had known personally, and he embraced the cinematic version. But the St. Knute statue was much more useful for the campaign against athletic scholarships than was the actual man who, on occasion, advocated them publicly and, in his final years, attempted to establish them at Notre Dame.)

In 1942, a major beneficiary of the sporting press's classical treatment of Notre Dame was the school's newest football star, quarterback Angelo Bertelli. In an article for *Collier's* magazine, ND alumnus Bill Fay wrote:

"Here is the bare outline of a story that would have kept Horatio Alger writing for 300 pages." Bertelli's parents, poor Italian immigrants, had come to the New World, toiled long hours, and prospered in Springfield, Massachusetts. Bertelli also worked hard on his studies and on his sports. An excellent passer at Notre Dame, he "toughened his right arm" by laboring "all summer long" as an industrial painter, also practicing his passing every day with ND varsity end George Murphy. The author then employed a beloved Hollywood trope: "Two other Notre Dame greats, Gus Dorais and Knute Rockne, back in 1913 did the same thing when they spent the summer as lifeguards at Cedar Point, Ohio" and "invented" the forward pass.

In elaborate detail, Fay described Bertelli's triumphs during the 1942 season. The author's only concession to the war that was going on outside the world of college football was the title "Football Bombadier" and a mention near the end about Bertelli's enlistment in the U.S. Marine Reserve, "which means that Angelo will complete his college career before going into active service and therefore will be on hand" for the 1943 season. Bertelli won the Heisman Trophy that year.

> After this rendition of the facts by Mr. Leahy, frank discussion took place. Both Colonel Counts and Colonel Fenton [of the West Point Athletics Board], and also [football] Coach Blaik, felt that since the Army offered an outstanding opportunity to a boy to get a commission and to follow the military profession and in consideration of the fact that Army, because of the difficulty of getting suitable [football] material, had in the past been beaten frequently by Notre Dame, Notre Dame in this case [the recruiting of Johnny Lujack] acted in an unsportsmanlike way. Both of these Colonels, together with Colonel Jones [Army AD] and Coach Blaik, felt that when a boy is offered an appointment to the United States Military Academy, no persuasion should be used to keep him from accepting such an appointment. On the contrary, they felt that an institution such as Notre Dame and all the persons representing it, should do their utmost to encourage such a boy to accept such an appointment.
>
> —"Confidential Report of Visit by Father John Cavanaugh
> and Mr. Frank Leahy to United States
> Military Academy, West Point, on July 1, 1942."

Father John Cavanaugh and Frank Leahy visited West Point to discuss the contentious recruiting of Johnny Lujack, a great high school athlete (and eventual Heisman Trophy winner), and the player's rejection of an appointment to West Point in favor of admission to Notre Dame for the fall of 1942. In spite of the war, Army continued to recruit football players. Ironically, as the above report indicated, the military academy seemed less concerned with fighting the war than with using it as a means to assemble a football team to beat Notre Dame; the Army officials suggested that it was unpatriotic for ND to interfere with West Point appointments of football recruits. Driving the Army's point of view was Army coach Earl Blaik, and although he did not prevail in the Lujack case, he soon assembled the most powerful football team in the country, retooling his heavy-handed argument here into a more classical line to justify his work.

Blaik's great rival, both for Lujack, and throughout the 1940s, was Frank Leahy. In obtaining this high school star, however, the ND coach had mainly benefited from normal Fighting Irish recruiting: Lujack later explained that as "a kid in Connellsville, Pennsylvania, listening to all the Notre Dame games on the radio," he rooted for the school; then, as a high school senior, an ND "Subway Alumnus," Harry Opperman, took him to visit the campus and to meet Leahy. Without Lujack's requesting it, his congressman had appointed him to West Point—many members of Congress functioned as Army's equivalent of "Subway Alumni"—and although the athlete was flattered, he preferred Notre Dame because "like dozens of fellows before and after me, a boyhood dream was about to come true": the opportunity of playing for the Fighting Irish. But Earl Blaik, as obsessive as Leahy about winning at recruiting and everything else, complained so loudly to the West Point brass that they asked Vice President Cavanaugh and his coach to travel to the academy to discuss the situation. The ND officials came and held their ground in the Lujack case, but their departure did not close the controversy; it resurfaced during subsequent disputes between the two most important football programs and coaches of the 1940s.

Blaik and Leahy began to dominate college football during the 1941 season— appropriately, their teams played to a 0-0 tie in that year's ND-Army game— but their detractors claimed that, after Pearl Harbor, so many excellent coaches volunteered for the service that the Army and ND head men lacked coaching competition. (Blaik was already in the military, and, at this time, Leahy was classified 4-F for medical and family reasons.) However, tracing the enlistment of their competitors reveals where those coaches went, and the fact that some did coach against Blaik and/or Leahy during the war years, often with much better teams than before. In late 1941 and 1942, many coaches enlisted, mainly because they realized that, unlike college students, they would not receive deferments; moreover, if they entered the military early in the war, they might be able to coach the teams springing up on military bases. Indeed, in early 1942, the head of the navy's sports program, speaking at a joint meeting of the NCAA and the American Football Coaches Association, urged coaches to join his service and obtain wartime jobs in their football specialties. The media portrayed the coach volunteers in classical terms, part of their Rockne-like patriotism—and, no doubt, some did enlist for patriotic reasons. However, as tough-minded men in a ruthless profession, many signed up for practical career purposes. And some soon faced Blaik and/or Leahy.

The exodus so depleted the college coaching ranks that unusual, even comical situations occurred. For instance, after the 1941 season, the University of Washington fired assistant coach Ralph "Pest" Welch, an old Rockne crony, only to rehire him a few months later—because he was too old for the draft—as head man! However, as the country fully mobilized, the comical aspects of college sports soon disappeared, giving way to much more serious situations, including a threat to the very existence of intercollegiate athletics.

■   ■   ■

I'm convinced that the [college] physical education directors want to get rid of coaches in all [intercollegiate] sports, build themselves up and have their [recreational] programs accepted by all. What good is it to have muscles developed if a boy loses the desire for competition. *When I take part in a sport, I want to win and kick the brains out of the other fellow.* I'm not content to play *with* someone. I want to play *against* them.

—Columbia University football coach Lou Little,
January 1943.

In 1943, as America moved toward full participation in World War II, various university administrators questioned their schools' abilities to continue regular intercollegiate athletic programs, particularly big-time college football. Then, for fans, the unthinkable began to occur: many universities put their football programs in mothballs for the duration of the war. Starting with the *A*'s, Alabama, Arizona, Arizona State, and Auburn dropped out of big-time football after the 1942 season; in the *B*'s, Baylor and Brigham Young; and so on through the alphabet. Institutions in sparse population areas and/or with transportation problems were the first to go.

These events terrorized the college sports establishment, particularly football coaches, and they fought back, trying to justify the need for all schools to continue their intercollegiate sports programs and for the American people to support them. Columbia University coach Lou Little, in New York and with access to the national media, led the campaign, drawing upon his experiences as a soldier in World War I to validate college football during this second world conflict.

In interviews with friendly sportswriters as well as in signed articles in national magazines, Little argued for smash-face football: in 1917 and 1918, the American Expeditionary Force in Europe had prepared for battle against "Coach Hindenburg's outfit" by playing brutal football games in training camps. This was "the toughest football played anywhere . . . We were rough; we had developed a destructive manner of thinking and doing," and now, in the early 1940s, the country needed this football ferocity to fight the Axis powers.

Little titled one piece "Sport for Sport's Sake Is Now Out," and he condemned the gentlemanly approach to athletics: "During the plush years of the '20s and through the fumbling '30s, we got too much of It-matters-not-who-won-or-lost, it's-how-you-played-the game . . . that approach doesn't win football games—or wars either." Little then repudiated Grantland Rice's dictum with his own formula for victory: "Just two simple rules: 1. You've got to be tough. 2. You've got to win." (Predictably, when directing perpetually losing Columbia teams later in his career, Little reversed his position and embraced Rice's aphorism, presenting himself—and being accepted by the media—as "Sweet Lou.")

In 1943, other coaches echoed Little's theme of smash-face football as the best preparation for war, but schools continued to drop their intercollegiate football teams. Apparently, Little's argument was too primitive; he failed to understand that with military machines around the world smashing many faces and whole bodies in much more permanent ways than football ever did, most Americans did not want college football represented his way; they cherished *Knute Rockne—All-American* and other classic portrayals of the sport. Probably the blood-and-guts line drew nods of approval at coaches' meetings but this position did not convince the U.S. public.

The 1943 crisis in college sports also drew comments from the longtime critics of intercollegiate athletics, not only the remnants of the "Aw-Nuts" writers—they endorsed the de-escalation but predicted football's comeback after the war—but also more intellectual critics like John R. Tunis. A distinguished sportsman and author—he wrote many popular novels about athletics—Tunis had long preached the gospel of amateur college sports for authentic college students. Throughout the 1920s, he attacked the "hippodroming" of big-time intercollegiate athletics; in the 1930s, he hoped that the Depression would bring de-emphasis; and, in the spring of 1943, writing in *Harper's Magazine*, he called for the reversion of college sports "to an earlier phase." According to Tunis, because of the war, universities had started to return intercollegiate athletics to actual students, and "at last American colleges are forced to admit their responsibility, not to furnish week-end circuses for exhilarated" fans and the media, "but to provide for the physical as well as intellectual well-being of the students."

Unlike the cynical "Aw-Nuts" writers, Tunis was so upbeat about the current situation that he predicted continued de-emphasis after the war: "Many colleges and universities will be unable to afford professionalized athletics"—he hated the athletic scholarship vogue—"and many [schools] who have dropped the system will not want to return to it because it concentrates on the few [elite intercollegiate athletes] at the expense of the many" students.

The contrasting and conflicting attitudes of coach Lou Little and critic John Tunis illustrate the increasing chaos in American college sports during the first years after America's entry into World War II. Events had overtaken both proponents and opponents, and neither side could find stable ground. The middle, where the sports programs of schools like Notre Dame and Michigan still existed, was somewhat firmer—the radio coverage of their 1942 football game attracted a huge audience, and attendance was excellent—but administrators at those schools and others worried about the rapidly changing world outside of and within their universities.

The Big Ten schools and Notre Dame tried to adhere to the classic ideals, and, after the 1942 season, they emphatically turned down all invitations to bowl games, but because of increasing travel restrictions, these refusals were less meaningful than they had been. On January 1, 1943, the major bowl games took place in their usual locations, including Pasadena, California, but the government allowed only the participating teams to travel to the bowl sites; for example, Tennessee played Tulsa in the Sugar Bowl, but their fans stayed home, as did the supporters of other bowl teams. A Los Angeles sportswriter noted that "for the first time in years, the home folks" could get tickets to the Rose Bowl, but the absence of tourists dampened the festivities.

After this football season, with declining attendance and diminishing media attention—because of wartime shortages, newspapers printed smaller editions, often shrinking their sports sections—observers could almost literally hear the air going out of college football. Faced with the most serious crisis in its history, the proponents of college sports responded in a number of ways; some—like Lou Little's blood-and-guts offense—failed to work, but others proved more successful, particularly when aligned with the classical ideals.

■　　■　　■

ROCKNE:
They say the Battle of Waterloo was won on the playing fields of Eton, well, if they've got to have their wars, perhaps some day we'll be able to say that America's were won on our football fields.

—From the original script of the film,
Knute Rockne—All-American, 1940.

Before and during World War II, many college sports supporters adhered to the belief that victory in war originated in athletic success. Like the Hollywood Rockne, generations of Britons and Americans cited the supposed

Waterloo-Eton connection; in fact, organized sports at Eton and other British public schools began a generation *after* the Battle of Waterloo. Nevertheless, this maxim sanctioned and promoted school games as preparation for military service as well as for the struggle of civilian life.

As various sports evolved into the twentieth century, the military connection grew deeper in obvious and subtle ways. Much of the terminology and thinking of sports, particularly American football, derived from the military: recruits, platoons, offensive and defensive formations, drills, field generals, linemen in the trenches, and so on; from the World War II period came blitz, red dog, aerial attack, and bomb, among many terms. But the military influence upon athletics goes so deep that even sports fans are unaware of some of its specifics: for example, trophies derive from military plunder, symbols of conquest. From ancient times to the GIs who brought home German helmets and Japanese swords at the end of World War II, to the winner of the Minnesota-Michigan football game that took home the Little Brown Jug each year, trophies have signified victory both on the battlefield and the playing field.

During the first phase of World War II, college sports proponents employed many of the traditional sports-and-war metaphors to justify intercollegiate athletics to an increasingly distracted public. The final Notre Dame game of 1942 illustrated the shifting fortunes of big-time college sports, and the publicists' problems and attempts to solve them. ND encountered the Great Lakes Naval Station, an outstanding service team composed of former All-Americans, including Bruce Smith, but the attendance for this contest at Chicago's Soldier Field, which was easily accessible by trolley car and other public transportation, was only 19,225—in contrast to 119,000 at the previous meeting of Notre Dame and the Naval Academy at the same location. The problem for the promoters of the ND–Great Lakes contest was that college football fans, even the huge number of Fighting Irish supporters in the Chicago area, would not accept a service team as an appropriate opponent for their collegiate heroes. The week before the Soldier Field game, USC-ND had drawn 95,000 at the Los Angeles Coliseum, but that contest was clearly within the classical football mode. The Fighting Irish versus an all-star team of nonstudents violated the ideal.

The publicists for the Notre Dame–Great Lakes Naval Station game approached their problem in the same direct way that the naval destroyer on the cover of the game program—beneath the banner HERE COMES THE NAVY—appeared headed for battle. The newspaper advertising for the event urged fans to attend as a patriotic duty, and the game program contained many articles and advertisements on the theme of sports and war. In the longest piece, "Athletics and War," a Navy officer quoted the argument of old-time coach James Conzelman: " 'It is body contact sports alone that breed a familiarity with violence. War is violence' "—and so is football.

Again, like Lou Little, the proponents of college sports did not yet have it right—too few fans responded to this appeal—but, as the war continued, the advocates tried other arguments. The blood-and-guts line diminished, replaced by more subtle themes, particularly the stress on athletic teamwork and competition as preparation for military success. Moreover, college football game programs, like the Notre Dame–Great Lakes Naval Station 1942 one, provide excellent examples of the different publicity campaigns. Not only do the programs contain many articles on the subject of athletics and war, but their text and the graphic material, including advertisements, also reveal how the promoters of college sports tried to defend their dwindling turf and survive the crisis.

Indeed, much of the core ideology of intercollegiate athletics first appeared in football game programs. These documents provide extraordinary and previously unexamined evidence on how the promoters of college sports presented their product to the public and how—particularly during crisis periods—they responded to adversity, altering their message and, at times, even their product. However, to understand the function of the game programs during World War II and in the postwar era, a brief explanation of their history and their link to the ideology of college sports is necessary.

10

Programs as Propaganda

I've seen some very old football programs and they were printed locally. Then for a long time, in the forties and fifties, like other schools, we worked with a company in New York on them, particularly for the cover drawings and the national ads . . .

People really do read and collect them . . . It's important that a university clearly present itself as well as its athletic program in them.

—Notre Dame vice president Richard W. Conklin, 1991.

The modern form of college game programs began in the 1920s. During that decade and the one following, most schools produced their own programs in conjunction with local printers and advertisers. For these publications, the host school's publicity director gathered the players' rosters, solicited material from booster sportswriters and from local photographers and graphic artists, then shepherded the booklet through production and sale.

Then athletic departments began to hire their own publicists, who compiled the football program; in the case of Notre Dame and many other schools, the SPD (sports publicity director) sent the edited articles and ads to the athletic director and athletic board for approval before taking them to the printer. This process ensured that the game programs presented the university and its college sports teams in the most favorable way. The only objective information in the publications were the numbers of the players' uniforms; weights and heights were often exaggerated to trick the opposition.

At many schools, the program's front cover became its most important feature. In an age when magazines like the *Saturday Evening Post* and *Collier's* were powerful national institutions with famous illustrators like Norman Rockwell drawing their weekly covers, college game programs assumed a comparable significance for sports fans, with local and regional artists seeking the cover assignments. In addition, just as the illustrations on the national magazines provide a door into the culture of their period—the iconography reflecting and cueing the values of mainstream society—football game programs offer insights into American attitudes on intercollegiate athletics.

A survey of the game programs from most schools participating in college football in this century reveals the changing values and styles over the decades. The 1920s covers often portrayed the sport in terms of the country's booming industrialism and the athlete-heroes like those of Hollywood's silent movies. As one example, for the 1928 USC-ND program cover, the illustrator placed a football player heroically struggling out of a tackler's grasp, against the background of the new, mammoth Soldier Field.

In the 1930s, the Great Depression made the business boom as well as the sentimental drama irrelevant, and a much harder edged graphic style became popular; the illustrations on pulp crime magazine covers exemplified this fashion, and the college program artists imitated it. This approach also connected to the macho ethos of 1930s football; the mostly male spectators relished the ferocity of the sport as well as vivid representations of its brutality. In a typical cover of the period, for the 1937 Case College (Ohio) against Carroll College (Ohio) game, the artist depicted a side view of a ballcarrier, his left knee smashing into the face of a helmetless defender. This was literally smash-face football, and other artists pictured similarly violent scenes and players. In the early 1940s, however, mainly because of the popularity of *Knute Rockne—All-American* and other classic Hollywood football films, as well as America's entry into a truly savage war, the covers portraying football brutality gave way to other images, often mass-produced and appealing to a more diverse audience than before.

In the transition of football programs from the 1930s to the 1940s, as with other products moving from local to national manufacture, a number of New York public relations companies began to dominate the game program market. In contrast to the local, often drab publications, these companies created attractive multicolored volumes, and also provided schools with extra revenue from the sale of the back covers and the middle pages to national advertisers; thus many colleges and universities switched to the New York "package deals," contracting for an entire season of programs. Well before the first game, the company sent out a package of about ten separate programs, and the school chose covers for four or five home games as well as articles from national sportswriters. The company also left many blank pages for which athletic departments could solicit local advertising and place team photos and features, but the final product was much slicker and more colorful—in a predominantly black-and-white media age—than the 1930s publications.

Madison Avenue's Don Spencer Agency pioneered this system in the late 1930s, and came to monopolize the field for the next two decades. After World War II, approximately 80 percent of all schools in big-time college football bought game program material from Spencer; the remainder, primarily West Coast universities, used regional or local companies. Because of the Spencer influence, college football programs became much more uniform, and the cultural impact of their graphic material and articles increased enormously. At the peak of their popularity, on any given autumn Saturday, millions of Americans saw a particular program cover, and a smaller but significant number read the pieces by the sportswriters. During a whole season, at least fifteen million fans encountered the Spencer covers, ads, and articles; moreover, as a Notre Dame official remarked in the 1940s, "Fans take these game programs away from the stadium with them, and preserve them as a precious souvenir of their visit to" ND and other college campuses. Thus, the drawings and texts truly affected American attitudes on intercollegiate athletics during this crucial period of its history.

The Spencer Agency's main cover artist from the 1930s through the 1950s was H. Alonzo Keller. A disciple of Norman Rockwell, in the 1930s Keller imitated the master's sentimental style and was out of step with the predominantly male football audience. However, with the war, Keller changed his "H. Alonzo" signature to "Lon," and also followed Rockwell into the latter's "cheerful patriotic" period. Just as his mentor attracted widespread attention and approval with such upbeat *Saturday Evening Post* illustrations as "Rosie the Riveter," Keller used a similar style to produce many of the most popular football program covers during World War II.

In 1943, he drew two smiling, round-faced, helmeted GIs for the Army–Notre Dame match. Keller provided spaces on their helmets for the names of the individual schools as well as an open area above their heads for the two school insignias. He inserted the ND and Army names and crests in the appropriate places but, when other universities adopted the cover, the Spencer people airbrushed out the Army–Notre Dame material and substituted the schools *du jour*. Only the helmeted, smiling GIs were national.

Spencer had other illustrators, less skillful than Keller, who experimented with patriotic themes as early as the 1941 season; one artist depicted a quarterback superimposed upon a huge American flag. The agency recycled these first patriotic covers during later war years: the Wisconsin–Notre Dame game of 1943, among many others, utilized the same QB and flag cover. Another of the agency's popular covers, introduced in 1941 and then repeated throughout the war, was of a quarterback literally wrapped in Old Glory. Lon Keller also used American flags on his covers. Imposed against one, he placed an

Army infantryman, left arm extended like a quarterback, right hand about to toss a grenade—then to cement the equation of military heroism with college football, directly beneath the soldier he put a QB with the same face and pose, about to launch a pass. Keller's drawings represent the classical form of program cover art; their imagery and equation of sports and patriotism is similar to movies like *Smith of Minnesota*, as well as other Hollywood war/football pictures (see pages 44 and 126–36).

Keller's single most popular image, repeated throughout the war and then recycled into the Cold War, depicted a fighter pilot gazing upward into the sky; below him is a scene of football action, often featuring a QB studying the sky. The upward gaze signified air attack, the willingness to encounter danger, and the determination to see it through. It also suggested a silent prayer to the Almighty. The message: fighter pilots acquire their mindset from playing football. Significantly, Keller always stylized the scenes of football action with the illustrator's equivalent of slow-motion photography: even when linemen move toward the erect QB, they seem to float. As filmmakers know, "slo-mo" renders violence almost aesthetically pleasing, as opposed to the ferocity of real-time football hits.

Lon Keller's depictions paralleled the United States government's move away from bloodthirsty propaganda. By 1943, the War Department had realized that with Americans engaged in a savage war, emphasizing brutality was counterproductive—it demoralized the participants and, to an even greater degree, their families at home. Keller applied this principle to college football and its fans. The military censored blood-and-gore passages from war correspondents' dispatches, and the War Department, after commissioning realistic documentaries from major filmmakers like John Huston, refused to release them because of their gruesome combat scenes. Similarly, Lon Keller, in his wartime drawings, denatured football violence, stylizing it into cooler images.

To gauge the impact of Keller's program covers, a 1990s viewer has to imagine encountering them in a pretelevision age, a period with much less visual pollution than today. In addition, during the early 1940s, Americans saw vivid color reproductions mainly in national magazines and an occasional color movie; thus the program cover images affected viewers more directly and stayed with them much longer than did visual material in later eras. Finally, because most spectators took the programs home, treating them reverently, often examining them later, the visual linkage of college sports and patriotism helped shape public opinion about intercollegiate athletics.

From this genesis of images and ideas evolved—later in the war and with the aid of Hollywood and the press—a more sophisticated relationship between intercollegiate athletics and patriotism, an association that served college sports exceptionally well at the time and for many subsequent decades.

[The quote in large letters stands against a photo of a cloud-filled sky. Below the quote, the viewer sees the back of a football player's helmet, shoulders, and his upraised right hand gripping a Spalding football, ready to throw it into the sky. The Spalding football is the most prominent object in the photograph.]

"WE'RE SHOOTING TO WIN!" is the . . . One thought in the mind of every American soldier and civilian, paratrooper and pre-flight cadet toughening up with sports.

—To back up this purpose *Spalding's* first aim is the continued production of war material and athletic equipment to keep fighters and workers fit at A.G. Spalding & Bros., Division of Spalding Sales Corporation.

"SPALDING

SETS THE PACE IN SPORTS."

—Spalding advertisement in college football programs and national magazines, 1943–1944.

During the wartime crisis in intercollegiate athletics, many corporations with the greatest economic stake in college sports attached their advertising campaigns to the sports-as-preparation-for-war theme. In addition to the "WE'RE SHOOTING TO WIN!" promo, Spalding frequently ran an ad with two large photos: on the right diagonal, American dive bombers; on the left, a scene of football field action; and above them the large legend: "NEXT WEEK THEY PLAY TOKIO [sic]."

As in the photo of the passing QB, Spalding and other advertisers used generic football photographs to appeal to fans—in this period, sports photography featured athletes in heroic poses, such as quarterbacks launching winning passes, and runners eluding final tacklers. Because cameras as well as color film stock could not yet capture split-second action, photographers usually posed athletes or shot them in standard action sequences, for instance running in the open field. Just as language produces verbal styles and clichés, so does photography: the posed shots during this period—the airborne QB flinging a jump pass—now seem odd and dated but, considering their frequency at the time, contemporary sports fans obviously enjoyed them.

Spalding and other sporting goods manufacturers placed their sports-and-war ads not only in college football programs but also in national magazines. Companies in other industries, particularly armaments, also employed college football imagery in their advertising campaigns, including in game programs. Wright Aircraft Engines featured one of its fighter planes superimposed on a passing QB with the large-letter caption: "FOR SLASHING AERIAL ATTACK," and in smaller letters at the bottom, "Wright Cyclones powers the air arms of our fighting forces."

During the war, the tobacco industry also tied some of its advertising to college sports; not only did it show young, healthy people consuming its product, but it also connected smoking to sports and patriotism. Tobacco companies started to feature healthy collegians in magazine ads in the 1930s. At the end of the decade, the cigarette manufacturers began purchasing the key locations in college football programs for their ads: the middle section—the most viewed pages because they contained the players' numbers—and the back cover—fans tended to wrap the programs from the outside in when they took them home as mementos.

Although the irrefutable scientific studies on the lethalness of smoking came many years later, Americans had long known about its dangers—popular turn-of-the-century nicknames for cigarettes were "coffin nails" and "death sticks"—and from the first decades of the twentieth century, the tobacco industry counterattacked with ads featuring athletes, movie stars, and handsome models smoking its products. In a typical wartime ad campaign placed in football game publications by the Spencer Agency, Liggett and Myers depicted a healthy collegian in an Army Reserve uniform bicycling across the middle pages of the program, his left hand gripping the handlebars and a cigarette, his girlfriend behind him on the back seat of his tandem bike. "CHESTERFIELD," in large type, fills the upper half of the page; the team rosters are in tiny print within the wheels of the bicycle. Not only does the Army uniform indicate patriotism but, because of the gas shortage, so does the bike, and the young couple—she also holds a cigarette—conveys health and sexuality.

The volume and slickness of cigarette advertising in this period, as well as its ubiquity, helps to explain the increasing American addiction to nicotine in the 1940s. Significantly, neither the promoters of college sports nor any individual school objected to the cigarette ads or even to the prominence of the brand logos relative to the roster information. The money from the tobacco industry was already so large and its support of college sports so important, particularly during the difficult wartime period, that higher education authorities not only failed to question the ethics of tobacco industry advertising, but actively solicited it for many campus publications, especially student newspapers and magazines, traditionally underwritten by the school but willingly shifted to commercial advertisers. Meanwhile, university researchers had started to study the medical effects of smoking, and the scientific journals as well as some national magazines, particularly *Reader's Digest,* carried the early and generally negative findings. Thus, in the 1940s, most university administrators knew the dangers of smoking, but in part because of the tobacco industry money for college sports and student publications, they did not act upon their knowledge.

In addition to the national and local advertising pages, every football program contained graphic material provided by the individual schools. For their 1943 game, Army and Notre Dame supplied head shots of their starting players, and the program designer placed strips of these alongside map drawings of Western Europe; on each page, a white arrow angles in from a different direction, pointing to one map spot, the target for a bombing raid: Berlin. World War II propaganda was all-pervasive. Attending a college football game in this period was less a diversion from everyday life than a reminder and reinforcement of America's campaign against the Axis.

For its 1942 home programs, Notre Dame featured a page on the "Mid-shipmen's School"—the Naval training program placed at the university for the war. The photos show the trainees marching past various campus sites, including the recently built Rockne Memorial Gymnasium; the text explains, "A group of trainees pass before the fieldhouse erected in memory of the ideals, teachings, and the victorious accomplishments of Knute Rockne." Thus, the total war effort pushed everything in American society—from used tin cans to Knute Rockne—into the war machine, converting all of it into a shape useful for the fight against the Axis.

■   ■   ■

HITLER DIDN'T PLAY FOOTBALL

The quarterback calls the signals—but it's the team that wins the game. It's the will-to-win of each man, in the line or backfield, that decides who wins or loses. The Nazi youth grew up with compulsory *gymnastiks* instead of competitive sports. This made muscles, sure— but somewhere along the way he forgot how to think for himself. The Nazis couldn't understand that competition and cooperation aren't necessarily opposites. The American youth plays all the better as part of a team because of the individual struggle he had in making the team. Hitler still can't figure out how a highly competitive American business system could team up overnight to overwhelm his goose-stepping mechanical men with the mightiest flood of production in history. But then—Hitler never played football.

—Text of advertisement for McCormick & Co.
in Notre Dame–Navy game program, November 1943.

The visuals for this ad, a series of small military flags, were much less important than the prominently situated text. Composed by an advertising copywriter, the text related how the competitive but cooperative nature of American sports—much preferable to noncompetitive *gymnastiks*—have positioned the United States to triumph over the Nazis. Hitler's failure was not that he overextended his armies by invading both western and eastern Europe, as military analysts at the time and since indicated, but that he "never played football." In retrospect, the text appears too simplistic, but from this argument, with the aid of Hollywood, evolved much more sophisticated war and college sports propaganda.

During the first phase of America's entry into the war, War Department propagandists also experimented with the teamwork-and-brains theme, particularly in the publicity for officer training schools. For the 1942 Army–Notre Dame game, the War Department had West Point host a national radio broadcast, with the emphasis on the academic achievements of the schools and, according to the broadcast coordinator, "the contribution of football to our national preparedness" for the war.

The drumbeat of the sports-and-war metaphors continued as the nation moved toward all-out fighting. When the director of the FBI, J. Edgar Hoover, addressed the 1942 Notre Dame graduating class, he paid homage to the school's football tradition and noted that "red-blooded Americanism, typified by the valorous men of Notre Dame," particularly on the football field, "will not permit our nation to bow in defeat. True defense of democracy comes from unity of mind, soul, and body." Ironically, soon after Hoover made this speech, the United States military began to dismantle many of the classical aspects of big-time college sports, confusing the public and undercutting the effect of the sports-and-war metaphors.

11

The Military vs. College Sports

DROPPING SERVICE TEAMS

Dave Walsh, sports columnist of the *Chicago Herald-American,* writes that a number of college authorities in the midwest are peeved at both the Great Lakes [Naval Station] and Iowa [Pre-Flight] Seahawks for their tactics in pouring it on [college] opponents, both in football and basketball, and [Walsh] says a number of these schools are flatly refusing to have any more to do with those two service teams. He adds that those two service schools, loaded with experienced athletes, many of whom are former professionals, also played a lot of exceedingly rough and, at times, dirty football and basketball.

—Associated Press item, April 1944.

During World War II, into the void left by colleges and universities dropping out of intercollegiate athletics came military training schools and bases. Paul Brown, after coaching Ohio State to a national championship in 1942, went to the Great Lakes Naval Station outside of Chicago and assembled an amazing team. Ray Eliot, the longtime coach at the University of Illinois, commented that Brown "must have stopped every monster of 270 pounds that came into the Naval Station and put a football suit on him . . . All-Pro tackles, All-American, All-This and All-That. We had a kid from our school on that Great Lakes team, an All-American tackle, and he was playing *third* team there."

Brown and other military base coaches recruited actively, assuring many college and pro players that if they enlisted at the coach's installation, the recruit would have at least one season of football, possibly more. Missouri's Don Faurot joined Iowa Pre-Flight, located on the campus of the University of Iowa, and built his innovative split-T offense around Dick Todd of the Washington Redskins and other pro players; then his team mowed down the college opposition. Although as patriotic as other Americans, football fans disliked the dominating military crews, particularly when the older, often rougher players overwhelmed beloved college teams. At the University of Iowa, even though the money from the Pre-Flight facility on campus allowed the school to continue its college sports program, many Hawkeye rooters booed Iowa Pre-Flight when it pounded the UI boys 25-0 in 1943, and 30-6 the following year.

Even more disturbing to the fans were college players switching schools to enter a military training program at a rival university, then immediately suiting up for that college team. In the Big Ten, Michigan, Purdue, and Northwestern had training programs on their campuses and created powerhouse teams of regular student players *and* trainees. The other conference schools lacked similar military connections, and soon outstanding players started moving to Michigan, Purdue, and Northwestern—players like All-Americans Elroy "Crazylegs" Hirsch (Wisconsin to Michigan) and Alex Agase (Illinois to Purdue). One commentator called it "the battle between the Haves and Have-Nots," the latter group fielding teams from a pool of students too young for the draft or rejected as physically unfit.

Rumors circulated that coaches at the Have schools, with the cooperation of the local military commanders, lured players from the Have-Nots, and college sports fans grew increasingly unhappy with the situation. Players jumping from team to team violated the classical nature of intercollegiate athletics; fans were loyal to their favorite teams, and they expected scholar-athletes to show the same allegiance. Thus, when Minnesota rooters watched or listened to their squad's 1943 game against Northwestern, they were outraged to find eight Gophers from the 1942 team in the NU lineup—they also disliked the fact that Minnesota did not flatten the Wildcats as they had the previous year but struggled to a tie.

Similar lineup switches occurred around the country, and fans wrote to newspapers about how "team hopping . . . desecrated the great game of collegiate football," whereas it mainly violated the fans' sense of their favorite sport during its classical phase. (For the first decades of college football, "tramp" and "gypsy" athletes were common, i.e., players traveling about, selling their athletic services to willing coaches, then moving to another school and a better offer the next season.)

In 1943, the Have-Not schools in major conferences became so desperate for players that they prevailed upon their league authorities and the NCAA to suspend the longtime ban on freshmen participation in varsity sports, and allow them to suit up; some smaller conferences had permitted this the previous year. Grantland Rice, ever the optimist, tried to put the best face on the situation; his *Collier's* All-America team for 1943 included transfers, but he added that "the glory of the 1943 season really belongs to the outmanned, overpowered, outclassed, trampled-into-the-dirt kids who gave everything they had against impossible odds to keep the game going along."

The artists at the Don Spencer Agency in New York also attempted to put a positive spin on the youth movement in college football. As the war progressed, the generic athletes on the football program covers maintained heroic poses but became younger and pudgier. Lon Keller contributed a very popular drawing of a rosy-cheeked, almost cherubic runner, cradling a football, bursting through a sheet of United States Savings Bonds. Among many schools using this cover, the University of Cincinnati in 1945 selected it for its contest against Baldwin-Wallace (Ohio), assigning it, with no apparent irony and a large banner on the program, to its annual "High School Day" game.

Some Have-Not schools liked the freshmen eligible rule—in 1943, Indiana University fans rooted for freshman Bob "Hunchy" Hoernschemeyer as he led the Big Ten in total yardage—but opposition from the football traditionalists continued. In a column in the *Chicago Tribune*, Arch Ward argued that sitting out the freshmen season "gives a young man entering college a year to get rooted in academic life without distractions," and in a private response to Ward's column, ND vice president Cavanaugh added that excluding freshmen from the varsity also helps "to prevent even more unethical proselytizing [recruiting]" from occurring.

As Cavanaugh suggested, the wartime football player shortage had spurred recruiters to newer and more creative ways around the rules. In addition, more conferences joined the Southern ones in allowing open recruiting and athletic scholarships. In 1944, the Big Six, forerunner of the Big Eight, permitted athletic grants for the first time, and coaches in other leagues lobbied for them, setting the stage for a major postwar controversy.

During the war, however, the single most important change in college football, the one that most shaped the future of the sport, occurred in the player substitution rules. Until 1942, coaches could insert players into a contest in a very limited manner; for instance, a player leaving the field could not return until the following quarter. Because of the wartime shortage of athletes, conferences increasingly moved to versions of unlimited substitution, and the most imaginative coaches, led by Michigan's Fritz Crisler, began to experiment with two-platoon football. According to Crisler, "Coaches had long known that some boys were better offensive players than defensive, and vice versa," but the tradition of the all-around athlete as well as the macho history of the sport helped one-platoon football prevail until the war. Then, because teaching complete offenses and defenses to very young and/or physically weak players became too difficult for many coaches, and even those like

Crisler who had access to military trainees had problems imparting their systems to men who were with them for only one season, experiments with two-platoon football began.

The results were significant. The coaches who experimented usually won more games than those who stayed with the one-platoon systems, and most fans and the media hated the innovations. Crisler's teams overachieved, whereas the one-platoon coaches tended to sink. According to one commentator, Minnesota's Bernie Bierman, a very successful head man in the 1930s, "failed to adjust to meet the changes made in the game by rules liberalization, especially in free substitution," and his Gophers played less than Golden ball, even against teams without military trainees on their rosters.

The fans and many sportswriters railed against unlimited substitution, condemning its emphasis on specialists. The traditionalists cherished the "sixty-minute hero," and they also criticized two-platoon as "a coach's game," with the sideline strategists dictating every play and moving players like pawns on a chessboard, rather than allowing the athletes on the field to call the plays, competing mentally as well as physically. Two-platoon clearly violated the classic ideals, but the major debate on this issue occurred after the war. The wartime skirmishes foreshadowed the battle ahead and the changing nature of college sports, as well as public attitudes toward it.

> The football season of 1943 was a helter-skelter affair. It was full of action, color, massacre, raw courage, stars who came and left. Great teams in football history fell far back. Unknowns, with their Navy trainees, moved upward . . .
>
> —Grantland Rice, December 1943.

Of all sportswriters, Rice had most exalted the traditions of college football, and had helped instill in the fans a love of the major rivalries, famous coaches, and star players. Beneath the brave surface of the above passage was the upheaval in his favorite sport: the service teams often "massacre[d]" the college boys; star athletes wandered about, great teams disappeared, and "unknowns," like Great Lakes and Iowa Pre-Flight, "with their Navy trainees" suddenly triumphed. Never before had Rice applied the adjective "helter-skelter" to his adored college football, nor was disorganization the way for the sport to win the hearts and minds of Americans.

Reading the 1943 "Final Grid Ratings" is a disorienting experience, almost like entering an alternate reality. Dr. E. E. Litkenhous of the University of Illinois, using a mathematical formula similar to those employed by later computer ratings services, had assembled his rankings since the 1920s. In 1943, his top four teams—Notre Dame, Michigan, Northwestern, Duke— seemed relatively normal for the era, but then Iowa Pre-Flight (5), Great

Lakes Naval Station (7), and Memphis Naval Training (10) appeared. More disorienting was Southwestern Louisiana State (12), 176th Infantry (14), Fort Riley (15), Del Monte Pre-Flight (20), Camp Grant (22), and Marquette (23). But the truly bizarre occurred in subsequent clusters: from 37 through 40 sat Tulane, Camp Lejeune, Oberlin, and Georgia Pre-Flight. Oberlin at 39! Then in a group from 130 through 135: Fort Douglas, Rensselaer Polytech, Blackland Army Air Force, Nebraska, Ohio Wesleyan, Presbyterian. The University of Nebraska Cornhuskers at 133!

The football world made little sense to fans in 1943, and the final game of the season, the usually glorious Rose Bowl, only added to the confusion. USC, with military trainees on campus, had a respectable squad, and won the PCC title, but travel restrictions eliminated many first-class opponents from making the trip to Pasadena. Fans wanted the Notre Dame Fighting Irish to travel west (the ND-USC series was in abeyance), but even after the War Department consented to the Irish going by train to California, the ND administrators held firm to the school's longtime ban on bowl appearances, pointing out the amount of class time the athletes would miss.

Thus, for the Rose Bowl, the University of Washington, after a four-game season against mainly Northwest military bases, traveled down the coast to encounter USC. The Huskies featured a number of freshmen, including one who had played his last high school game in Tacoma in November 1943, entered the university as a second semester student, and suited up on January 1, 1944.

The pre-game sale for the game was so bad that some USC players, including QB Jim Hardy, could not sell their allotment of tickets privately before New Year's Day (selling tickets for pocket money was a longtime perk for Trojan athletes). When the Rose Bowl gates opened, Hardy stood at the main one, hawking his tickets; however, some members of the USC athletic department spotted him and told head coach Jeff Cravath, who refused to start Hardy in the game. But Cravath inserted him in the second quarter, and the QB led Southern California to victory. Cravath subsequently proclaimed Hardy "the grandest quarterback I ever coached. And I mean more as a gentleman than as a player." The press did not reveal the ticket-selling incident, portraying the player as his coach did, in purely classical terms.

■　■　■

> The only thing that a lot of fans had to hold onto during the war years were the great Army and Navy teams, and our [Notre Dame] games. We had huge radio coverage and everyone could hear us everywhere, even overseas . . .
>
> Also Michigan helped a lot, and when they played us, it was terrific. We hadn't played them in years, but Elmer Layden arranged the forties' games and they turned out great, especially the one there [in

Ann Arbor] in '43 when we packed the place and won. It was No. 1 versus No. 2 in the polls, first time that ever happened. There was more buildup for that game than any other during the war.

—Edward "Moose" Krause, 1991.

Before the 1943 season began, many schools, including Notre Dame, had to cancel games with opponents beyond their region, hence the hiatus in the ND-USC series. However, Notre Dame, with help from the War Department, preserved its annual meetings with Army and Navy, and added contests against Iowa Pre-Flight and Great Lakes Naval Station. In addition, the Irish had a visit to Ann Arbor on their schedule. For the media and millions of fans, that game awakened memories of the classical era.

The 1943 Notre Dame team featured good, young players, and one Naval trainee starter; the school had a naval facility on campus, and although ND administrators refused to allow Leahy to aggressively recruit athletes from other universities, he did pick up a few former Big Ten players. The Fighting Irish easily won their opening games, setting up the contest against the University of Michigan as a Big Game. The teams had not played in Ann Arbor since 1909—mainly because of the anti-Catholicism of Michigan's longtime coach and AD, Fielding Yost—and the media trumpeted the ND visit as "an historic meeting between two great college football schools," ignoring the nonstudents on both teams. The game temporarily allowed college football fans to forget the "helter-skelter" state of their beloved sport and to enjoy the excitement of a major matchup. Even the usually calm ND vice president, Father Cavanaugh, wrote a colleague, "This week at Notre Dame is extremely tense because everyone is thinking about the Notre Dame–Michigan game on Saturday. It will attract nearly 90,000 people [mainly Detroiters], the largest crowd ever to assemble at Ann Arbor. Michigan is rated Number 1 by most of the experts."

The Fighting Irish beat the Wolverines and claimed the top spot. Then the ND season, after successive wins over various opponents, built to the annual match with Army at Yankee Stadium. For the media and fans, this became the "test of Notre Dame's championship mettle," another opportunity to suspend their disbelief about the state of wartime college sports. Suddenly, a week before the event, star QB Angelo Bertelli, a Marine Corps enlistee who had been allowed to finish his ND degree work, received a notice to report immediately to the Marine base at Parris Island, South Carolina. Frank Leahy saw the hand of West Point coach Earl Blaik as well as those of Army higher-ups in the surprising and perfectly timed—from an Army point of view—call-up of his quarterback, but the ND coach kept his opinion private.

The departure of Bertelli on the eve of this important game set up one of the classic stories of this down period in college football history. Leahy had to turn to a young reserve QB, Johnny Lujack, to pilot the Fighting Irish. Sure enough, the talented Lujack threw for two touchdowns, ran for another, and led ND to a 26-0 victory. To describe Lujack's emergence, some New York and national sportswriters employed the storyline from the popular musical *42nd Street:* the star cannot perform on opening night of the Big Show, the director turns to the unknown understudy, exclaiming, "You're going out a nobody, but you're coming back a star." Lujack came off the field a hero, and the media and the fans loved the tale, repeating it often during the war years, and for the remainder of Lujack's playing career—eventually, in 1947, he won the Heisman Trophy. Meanwhile, Bertelli in 1943 won the same award for his brilliant but truncated campaign.

In 1943, however, even a glorious national championship campaign—the polls unanimously awarded the title to the Fighting Irish—was tarnished by the wartime conditions and the military super-teams. In ND's season finale, the Great Lakes Naval Station beat the Irish, 19-14. Adding confusion to the outcome was the key role played by Great Lakes's best running back, Emil Sitko, recently of Notre Dame.

In addition to awarding championship laurels to the team, a number of polls and newspapers proclaimed Frank Leahy "Coach of the Year," comparing him favorably to Rockne. Leahy's hero status was beginning to approach the master's. Then, in early 1944, when Leahy accepted a naval commission as a lieutenant, his hero image grew larger; he was handsome in uniform, and the wire services trumpeted his patriotism, featuring many photos of his induction. One observer summed up the media portrayal of the coach's enlistment: "He was 36 years old and had four children, a wife and a mother to support. But there was a war on . . . It was mid-April of 1944 and he could stand it no longer. Something larger than football was going on," and so he entered the military.

Behind the public narrative, however, a different scenario had unfolded. In November 1943, because of the War Department's decision to conscript every remotely able-bodied male, Leahy's draft board reclassified him 1-A, subject to definite call-up. In response to this, Notre Dame president O'Donnell wrote to the board, and argued that "the services now being rendered by this registrant" in his job at Notre Dame are "most essential to the war effort"; therefore the board should reconsider Leahy's 1-A status and allow him to remain in his current position. The school saw Leahy's work as analogous to that of former Missouri head man Don Faurot at Iowa Pre-Flight, as well as other colleagues directing teams at military installations. This analogy was false: the other coaches did not continue to run their own college squads, but enlisted and went to military base teams. However, the ND coach's service career turned out even better than theirs.

When the appeal failed, but before the Selective Service placed him in the Army, Leahy jumped onboard the Navy. Wells Twombley, the coach's biographer, described his war work: "He was one of America's great celebrity-officers, people of national importance who traded their civilian occupations for a comfortable tour of duty. Leahy was in charge of athletic programs" for the submarine fleet in the Pacific. "The country did not want to lose a single important name. Mostly Leahy talked football with submarine sailors, put on softball games and posed with other celebrity-officers in propaganda photos that pointed out to America that everybody was 'doing his or her share for the war effort.'"

During World War II, Americans wanted their sports heroes to live up to the classic ideals, and they accepted press photos and movie newsreel clips as proof of compliance. The newspaper shots of and articles on Frank Leahy's enlistment and tour of duty fulfilled public expectations, as did similar depictions of Joe DiMaggio, Joe Louis, and others. No sportswriter probed the pre-enlistment or wartime conduct of sports heroes; thus Leahy's appeal of his 1-A status departed to the filing cabinets. But the coach's actual story—similar to those of many other famous sports, political, and entertainment figures—reveals the distance between the classic images in the media and the reality of wartime life.

By the end of 1943 in intercollegiate athletics, the classical genre was breaking down, the changes in the basic elements—scheduling, player rosters, game rules, etc.—interfering with the fans' enjoyment of the sports. Wartime life had started to overwhelm the fun and games, causing their curtailment and, in some cases, threatening their existence.

To the rescue of college sports came Hollywood's war/sports movies, arriving wrapped in classical ideals and permanently changing the nature of big-time intercollegiate athletics.

12

Hollywood Reconstructs College Sports

When George Gipp died, he became a legend. Thousands marched, heart-broken and mourning, as they carried his body to the railroad station. His teammate, Hunk Anderson, now a famous coach, took what remained of George Gipp home, and they buried him in a little graveyard in the mining town of Laurium, Michigan. The years have passed and many snows have fallen on that grave. But George Gipp is a living memory to Notre Dame. And every fall, the memory glows with new life as the Fighting Irish go on to win "One for the Gipper."

> —Final words in the shooting script and short film, "The Gipper," *Bill Stern's Sports Shorts*, Columbia Pictures, 1943.

In his autobiography, Bill Stern mentioned that during the World War II period, he "did two MGM newsreels a week . . . [and] one filmed sport short a month for Columbia Pictures." His MGM newsreels appeared after the *Movietone News* and before the feature pictures in a majority of movie theaters, serving as the Hollywood equivalent of TV sports highlight films. The Columbia "Sport Shorts," usually fifteen minutes in length, were also popular with audiences and for them Stern took a famous sports story and put it through his myth machine. During World War II, the Gipper saga, with the athlete dying young and heroically, was a natural for Stern, and he intoned his conclusion, quoted above, over a scene of snow falling gently on a tombstone, George Gipp's name engraved upon it.

Stern's films and similar products indicate the overt connection between Hollywood and college sports during World War II, but a deeper symbiosis existed in the themes, characterization, and dialogue of Hollywood war movies. In establishing this new genre, screenwriters constantly used sports metaphors, and, increasingly, the sports media adopted military tropes. Underpinning this linkage was the United States military's emphasis on teamwork and suppression of individualism, and the cultural fact that for most American males, team sports, particularly football, provided a positive model of cooperation.

To understand this phenomenon and its significance for war films as well as the future of intercollegiate athletics, it is necessary to briefly examine wartime Hollywood and its products.

■   ■   ■

You'd open the doors [of movie theaters] and have to fall back. People were lined up because there was no [other] place to go. You had rationing and restrictions on travel, so we ran [movies] around the clock in some towns.

—1940s movie theater manager John Krier, 1996.

When the United States entered World War II, the Hollywood studios wanted to play a major role in the war effort. Early on, they worked with the War Department to produce instructional films for Armed Forces training; they also cranked out their regular flicks to entertain the troops and the home front. During the war, when almost every movie made money, the motion picture industry had no financial incentive to deviate from its standard forms.

Hollywood, however, required government assistance to obtain raw materials for film production, and as a less than essential industry, it needed ongoing permission to operate full tilt. Therefore the studio bosses, attempting to prove the absolute importance of their business to the war effort, ordered the production of patriotic war dramas. But in a genre age filmmakers could not instantly create a new cinematic form.

When the United States entered the conflict, the main experience of war for the film industry was World War I, but that human meat grinder had mostly spawned pacifist epics like *All Quiet on the Western Front* (1930). When, in the early 1940s, distributors rereleased *All Quiet,* it baffled and upset audiences, and was quickly withdrawn. Hollywood needed to remythologize the First World War, and *Sergeant York* (1941), a biopic about its most decorated U.S. soldier, proved a perfect vehicle for turning "the Great War" into a worthy patriotic cause—pleasing audiences and winning Academy Awards in the process.

The reworking of World War I was important in the development of the war movie genre, but recycling sports stories and metaphors proved as useful. In 1942, in typical Hollywood fashion, some RKO executives decided to combine a First World War story with a college football tale. One of them, Robert Fellows, had worked at Warners on *Knute Rockne—All-American* and wanted the new movie to imitate the successful Rockne biopic as much as possible, even to the point of casting Pat O'Brien in the hero's role. The film, *The Iron Major,* helped shape the war movie genre and, as importantly for college sports, it provided an important media solution to its wartime problems.

■   ■   ■

I just couldn't keep out of it [World War I]. Impossible [to do] after teaching so many hundreds of youngsters how to play and fight on the football fields . . . I'd want my sons to do exactly as I have, without hesitation and without whimpering. And without heroics, because, after all, we're doing now just what we ought to do—and what they would be doing [in a future war].

—From the film *The Iron Major,* 1943.

Frank Cavanaugh, a famous college football coach nicknamed "the Iron Major," used these arguments midway through the film to explain to his wife why, at the age of forty-one and with her and six young children to support, he intended to enlist in the American Expeditionary Force in the Great War. (When Frank Leahy signed up, some sportswriters pointed out the Cavanaugh analogy—not only their shared first names but also that both men had coached at Fordham and Boston College.) In keeping with Hollywood's classical cinema, Florence Cavanaugh accepted her husband's decision; in addition, the audience already knew how correct and prescient his words were.

The Iron Major had opened with a montage of young handsome males and one female—all named Cavanaugh and smartly dressed in Second World War uniforms—repeating the Oath of Allegiance at their inductions into various branches of the military. Then Florence Cavanaugh, a widow, told a friendly priest how "proud Cav would have been to see his kids" serving their country in this new struggle. The priest informed her that he was writing a biography, *The Story of Frank Cavanaugh—American,* because "not enough people remember Cav's story, and now, especially," with a war on, "his story needs to be told." Then the opening dissolved into Cavanaugh's life story, climaxing with his decision to fight in World War I, his triumphs on the battlefield and postwar gridirons, his death, and a final clip of his children's participation in the current conflict.

As with *The Iron Major,* Hollywood in this period frequently framed a tale with connected opening and final scenes, putting an almost literal frame on a picture. Usually the material in the frame was didactic, the filmmakers telling the audience how to view and think about the coming events in the movie and, at the end, summarizing and repeating the message one last time. The authoritarian frames mirrored the social and family structures portrayed in the films; they also reflected the controlling attitude of the studio bosses toward their products and audiences, as well as the wartime U.S. government toward its citizens.

Classical films, however, did not win over audiences with didacticism; Americans disliked "preachy" movies, condemning, for example, many British war pictures as "propaganda." Hollywood usually confined the overt political bulletins to the frames and some speeches in between. Yet American movies, particularly during World War II, were highly political. The genius of the Hollywood system was its ability to submerge messages into the plot and characters, rendering ideology inseparable from film artistry; in *The Iron Major* the depictions of the Cavanaughs' ideal family life reinforced Cav's decision to enlist and fight for the American way of life.

At the end of the movie's linear story and as a transition to the didactic frame, the film mounted a deathbed scene reminiscent of George Gipp's, with Cavanaugh's last words: "Fight for what you believe in, and believe in three things—love of God, love of country, love of family." In the classical cinema, these were not rhetorical abstractions. Viewers of *The Iron Major* could see God within the character of the priest as well as in the many religious episodes and artifacts in the film; the audience also witnessed constant scenes of a perfect country, and a flawless family. Considering the far above average box office response to the movie, and such critical praise as "he [Cavanaugh] believed in fighting for what you [readers] believe in," the film's message resonated with moviegoers.

■　■　■

Cavanaugh . . . relentless master of mighty teams, looked upon football as war. At the beginning of every season he'd assemble his players in the locker room and growl at them, "If any of you boys aren't willing and ready to sacrifice everything to win, then I don't want you on my squad."

—Sports broadcaster Bill Stern, 1943.

After the release of *The Iron Major*, Bill Stern did a radio portrait of Cavanaugh on his *Colgate Sports Newsreel*, emphasizing the coach's toughness and the appropriateness of his nickname. According to reliable historical accounts, Cavanaugh suffered terrible head wounds on a battlefield in France, while directing a gun battery exposed by staff error to German artillery; his survival as well as his promotion in rank earned him the nickname "the Iron Major." The film depicted the war scenes differently—he receives his almost fatal wound while leading a squad behind German lines—and it focused mainly on the war-and-sports metaphors. Cavanaugh has "to coach" his troops, and he gives them a prebattle pep talk in the rain: "We're going to the front lines to blast those Heinees out of their game position." When he returns to his first coaching job in civilian life, at an early practice he addresses his "troops" in the rain, telling them, "If you don't play as hard as you can, it's a mockery to even play."

Cavanaugh stresses the importance of winning to a much greater degree than did previous cinematic coaches, including Warners's Knute Rockne, and this aspect of the Iron Major's movie personality approached the historical facts of his life. By all accounts, he was a ruthless coach who frequently instructed his players to take the opposition's key men out of the game by any means necessary, including intentional injury. Many schools, after their initial encounters with his Holy Cross, Boston College, or Fordham teams, refused to schedule rematches; Rockne always declined games against Cavanaugh's squads, not simply because he disliked playing fellow Catholic schools, but also because he scorned "deliberately dirty play."

The film glossed over the nasty details of the historical Cavanaugh's coaching techniques, but it did convey his obsession with winning. Significantly, the script tied this to his war experiences. When a friend tells him that he pushes his players too hard, the coach replies, "I'm going to drive, drive, drive [them]. I'm going to make them learn what I learned in France." And Bill Stern, in his *Colgate Sports Newsreel* on Cavanaugh, highlighted this aspect of his coaching.

This marked an important shift in the classical treatment of college sports: previously in the media, sportsmanship had prevailed over obsessive winning, but the new bond between war and sports began to link the "unconditional surrender" sought by the United States in World War II with total victory on the playing field. Columbia coach Lou Little had proposed this connection when he attacked Grantland Rice's "It's how you play the game," but the cold print of the coach's words was far less persuasive than the cinematic depiction of the argument in *The Iron Major.* As Hollywood had long known, when cinematic images coat ideology, audiences swallow it more easily. Moreover, this movie, like Lon Keller's illustrations, portrayed the violence necessary for victory in war and football in stylized terms: in France, shells explode but no one bleeds openly; on the football field, players pile on but no one is carried off the field on a stretcher.

In the film, Cavanaugh answers his friend's criticism of his coaching with "A man's character is determined by how hard he fights for what he believes in." The film indicated that Cavanaugh's character and fighting spirit were shaped in large part by his Irish-Catholic background. In addition to his loving Irish-American parents and siblings, traditional Irish songs inspire him, as do discussions with a friendly priest. The climax of the Irish theme occurs in the locker room before a crucial Boston College game against powerful Yale. Cavanaugh calls aside the Irish-American players on his team and gives them a special pep talk, playing upon their sense of social inferiority and the importance of their beating haughty Yale. Then they lead BC to victory.

In addition to its Fighting Irish subtext, the film overtly used many of the *Knute Rockne—All-American* themes, particularly the importance of spirit, and the willingness to fight to the end. *The Iron Major* also echoed the earlier film in many specific scenes. An opening family dinner with the father's heavy Irish accent and the mother's insistence upon academics over sports evoked the Rockne immigrant saga, then the combining of athletic achievements with scholarly ones—Cavanaugh earns a law degree—paralleled the cinematic Rockne's success as a chemist. In addition, when Boston College offers Cavanaugh its head coaching job, it also asks him to teach an academic course (law), and, like Knute, he must choose between a promising scholarly career and coaching. In fact, Cavanaugh briefly practiced as a criminal lawyer, his temper gaining him frequent contempt-of-court citations; like the historical Rockne, by all accounts Frank Cavanaugh much preferred athletics to academics.

Pat O'Brien played both coaches, bringing his Rockne pep talk staccato to many of the Iron Major's speeches and his ND coach's loving-husband-and-father mannerisms to the family scenes. Most critics complimented his performance, but one found it "too reminiscent of his work as Knute Rockne." In addition, for many critics, not only did O'Brien-as-Rockne overshadow O'Brien-as-Cavanaugh, but *Knute Rockne—All-American* eclipsed *The Iron Major.*

Nevertheless, the later picture is an important transitional film to the war movie genre, continuing the sanctification of warfare as well as the equation between sports and combat. In addition, *The Iron Major* used many of the classic college sports tropes initiated by the Rockne film: the role of athletics in the melting-pot saga, the scholar-athlete, and the coach-hero. Most significantly, the Cavanaugh film began the Hollywood approval of total victory in sports; slowly but inevitably the demand for "unconditional surrender" in World War II migrated to the athletic fields and affected the approach to intercollegiate athletics. *The Iron Major* helped mark the historical boundary between such classical gestures as the 1940 Cornell renunciation of its fifth-down victory, and the post–World War II attitude, "Winning is the only thing."

■　　■　　■

ROCKNE:
Listen, boys. We've got a great thing in this shift if we do it right. I selected you four because I know that you *can* do it right. It's made to order for you!

—From the shooting script and film, *Knute Rockne— All-American*, 1940 (emphasis in original).

Not only did *The Iron Major* suffer from comparison with *Knute Rockne— All-American,* but it also sparked renewed interest in the Rockne biopic. As a result, Warners rereleased the earlier film on the bottom of double bills and, more importantly, printed a large number of sixteen-millimeter copies, distributing them free to the military for multiple showings. Many of these prints survived the war, remaining in circulation in school auditoriums and church basements, helping to perpetuate the fame of Rockne, Gipp, and Notre Dame.

In the end, *Knute Rockne* not only overshadowed *The Iron Major*, but, ironically, it also proved a more important movie for America at war. The military considered *Knute Rockne—All-American* "an inspirational motion picture," and a comprehensive study of football films in this period maintained that "the movie inspired America in its time of need," with the Gipper scenes serving as "a rallying cry to the nation."

The film became a protean force, viewers seeing in it their hopes and desires. In wartime, audiences ignored the elements of isolationism in some of Rockne's speeches, and instead focused on his pep talks on teamwork and winning. The scene where the coach teaches his shift to the Four Horsemen often drew applause; Moose Krause remembered that at a screening at his Marine Corps training base, "When Rock tells the Horsemen why he chose them, and how they can win with it [the shift], I felt . . . and other guys there felt that Rock's hand of destiny was choosing us to fight on the winning Marine Corps team."

Krause's comment indicates another important aspect of both films for a nation at war: the emphasis on the coach, the guiding force directing his men to victory. The media had long equated coaches with military commanders, and during the war the linkage between such icons as Knute Rockne, Frank Cavanaugh, and famous military officers comforted the public and the troops. Because commanders so controlled the lives of their men, the media's emphasis on their coaching qualities—their strategic creativity, their passion to win, and their concern for their "boys" à la Rockne and the Iron Major— aided many soldiers and their families through difficult situations.

■   ■   ■

PEACE & WAR

"Modesty forbids," grinned Knute Rockne when asked to name football's greatest coach. "But if I can name the two best football coaches in America, one of them is going to be Clark Shaughnessy."

In the twelve years since Rockne's death, Clark Daniel Shaughnessy has indeed proved himself a top-flight coach. Last week he uncovered a second talent: military tactics. In *Football and War* (Jacobs Press; $1) he convincingly underscores the remarkable similarity of football strategy to tactics and warfare.

—*Time* magazine, October 1943.

Hollywood movies stressed the strategic abilities of the officer-coach and, not surprisingly, the press emphasized the affinity between battle strategy and football, first in interviews with coaches and then by asking coaches to write out and diagram the analogies. Clark Shaughnessy, the inventor of the T-formation and an acclaimed football mastermind, put his ideas in book form, finding a receptive audience; in addition to excellent sales, important media outlets reviewed *Football and War* favorably, commenting on such sections as the "amazing parallel between Montgomery's victory at El Alamein and a 'fullback counter' run from Shaughnessy's T formation. The tactics are almost identical." (The Rockne blessing of Shaughnessy seems apocryphal—*Time* offered no source and the anecdote appears nowhere else in college football history—but it indicated the importance that Rockne's words, real and fictitious, held for the 1940s media and public.)

During this period, the linkage of officer and coach, war and football strategy gained widespread public approval and shaped the future of intercollegiate athletics. Even more than the press, Hollywood war films promoted it constantly. To understand this phenomenon, and the reasons the public accepted historical illusion for reality, we must examine the war movie genre.

13

War/Football Movies

One hundred and thirty-one days after December 7, 1941, a handful of young men, who had never dreamed of glory, struck the first blow at the heart of Japan.

This is their *true story* we tell here.

—On-screen printed message at the beginning
of *Thirty Seconds over Tokyo,* 1944.

Just as *Knute Rockne—All-American* and its imitators manipulated history, classical war movies, including those that claimed to depict actual wartime events, twisted reality. Hollywood never acknowledged the manipulation; instead filmmakers worked hard to convince audiences that their movies were "true stories."

Often both football and war films began with frames containing so much authoritative historical paraphernalia, including actors assigned the names of real participants, that audiences did not question the filmmakers' veracity. Another device to promote verisimilitude was the use of voice-over narrators reciting factual information, not only anonymous announcers but often well-known persons, like Ernie Pyle in *The Story of G.I. Joe* (1945). Also on the sound track, often from the opening frame to the final one, authentic anthems blared; in *Harmon of Michigan,* for instance, it was "Hail to the Victors," in *Thirty Seconds over Tokyo,* the Army Air Force's "Wild Blue Yonder."

The early 1940s football films preceded the war movies, the former pioneering and/or polishing the authenticity gimmicks and the war films quickly adopting the techniques. Facilitating the process were the Hollywood technical people who moved from sports to war films; one was Bryan Foy, the original producer of *Knute Rockne—All-American,* who produced *Guadalcanal Diary* (1943). In the 1930s, biopics had employed some of these devices, but only sports and war films made full use of them.

And the two genres often merged. Just as every 1940s college football movie contained long newsreel sequences of game action, the war films incorporated documentary clips of actual beach landings, air combat, and other military maneuvers; thus, in *Appointment in Tokyo* (1944), surrounded by documentary footage, Marines sing the "Notre Dame Victory March" as they approach combat zones. To media-savvy 1990s viewers, the authentic material in many war movies—too disparate from the Hollywood soundstage footage—seems intrusive; however, to visually unsophisticated 1940s moviegoers, the newsreels added to their sense of being there with Colonel Doolittle and his boys over Tokyo—just as the 1940s newsreels of Notre Dame game action enhanced viewer identification with Knute Rockne and his Fighting Irish.

Hollywood had long turned history into myth, and war films continued this practice. Moreover, like college football movies, the myths in combat pictures moved along well-charted lines. *Guadalcanal Diary,* based on the best-selling memoir by Richard Tregaskis, opens with a copy of the book cover and a voice-over narrator, supposedly the author, setting the scene. The frame then fades into a view of hundreds of soldiers sitting on the deck of a large troop carrier, a priest officiating at Sunday Mass. The narrator informs us that the priest graduated from "Notre Dame in 1917, [was an] All-America fullback for two years, now simply Father Donnelly." In historical fact, no one named Donnelly ever played on the Notre Dame football varsity, never mind attained All-America status.

Father Donnelly also does not appear in Tregaskis's book. The screenwriters created him—call it the "Fighting Irish trope"—as well as many of the other characters in the film. Indeed, the opening scene of *Guadalcanal Diary* so predictably set up a mixed ethnic crew and their conflicts that viewers immediately recognized a classic war movie, very far from Tregaskis's gritty journal of the Guadalcanal landing, and even further from the grisly footage shot by military photographers during the event (and not released until years after the war). Nevertheless, wartime moviegoers considered the Hollywood picture entirely genuine, the *New York Times* noting that it played "at the Roxy [Theatre, in New York] before an audience which was visibly stirred" from beginning to end, "and which, no doubt, had the impression that it was witnessing the Battle of Guadalcanal as it was fought."

■ ■ ■

In the [classical] war film, the most popular plot involves a group of men, individuals thrown together from disparate backgrounds, who must be welded together to become a well-oiled fighting machine. During the course of the film, the rough edges of the ornery and the cantakerous, the nonjoiners, the loners . . . must be smoothed down to make them fit. They must all hang together or all hang separately. The emphasis is on the team.

—Film historian Thomas Sobchack, 1975.

In addition to appropriating many of the cinematic devices used in early 1940s college football films, the screenwriters of war movies borrowed plots and themes from these pictures as well as from sports journalism. Before World War II, sportswriters had employed the well-oiled-machine metaphor for teams like Notre Dame and Army that had heterogeneous rosters and winning records. Then the scriptwriters at Warners used some of the tropes in *Knute Rockne—All-American,* particularly in the assimilation of Gipp into the team and in the emphasis on the Four Horsemen's names and backgrounds—Layden (Dutch), Miller (British), Crowley (Irish), and Stuhldreher (German)—and their coordinated mastery of the "Notre Dame Shift." Subsequently, war movie scriptwriters employed these themes, then the success of that film form fed back into sports narratives, adding new potency to the parables on cooperation and unity. College sports and war movies created a synergy, each using and enhancing the other.

The basic plot of classic war movies concerned two interconnected struggles: the fight against the external enemy, and the conflicts within the group-hero, the military team. The outside adversary symbolized "the Other," usually evil, always dangerous and threatening, whereas the group-hero was a microcosm of America, trying to integrate disparate elements into a unity to represent and uphold the nation's values. Much of the plot involved the internal conflicts, which the group-hero had to resolve successfully before it could defeat the enemy. The viewer derived pleasure from watching the crew work out its problems and then, as a cohesive fighting force, conquer the enemy. Moreover, for movie audiences, both the internal and external triumphs validated "the American way."

The popularity of war movies prompted many college sports coaches and fans to borrow some elements of the external conflict theme—hate your opponents—but they and the sports media mainly focused on the importance of overcoming internal strife to attain victory. The settings of the standard plot reinforced the war/sports tropes. For the stadium or arena, the war film provided a specific battle area to fight the enemy; for the locker room or athletic dormitory, a small, often tight place to contest internal quarrels, like a plane or ship or barracks. In addition, the military team became known by a collective name—the crew of the *Mary Ann* (the B-17 in *Air Force*), the crew of the *Copperfin* (the submarine in *Destination Tokyo*)—like the athletes of the Crimson Tide, the Big Red, or the Fighting Irish.

The players of the [1943] Notre Dame team . . . [are] a collection that offers satisfaction to many shades of ancestral pride. The left ends, Paul Limont and James Flanagan, are of Irish extraction. Captain Paul Filley, left guard, is Irish, and Bob Kelly, back, is not a Chinaman either.

Herb Coleman, the center, is of German extraction. Jack Zilley, at right end, is Irish-German. John Yonakor is Lithuanian. Connellsville's Johnny Lujack, at quarterback, is Polish. Creighton Miller, at left-halfback, is Irish-German. Jim Mello, at fullback, is Portuguese. Julius Rykovich, right halfback, is a Croatian.

More important they are all Americans . . . And [they possess] a common purpose to win for the glory of alma mater. This year's team, in the Notre Dame tradition, is a smooth harmonious aggregation.

—*Pittsburgh (Pennsylvania) Press,* November 1943.

War movies as well as many narratives about football teams during this era stressed the ethnic origins of the crew/team members. The melting-pot allegory provided the underlying premise: Americans originated in many different lands, but once here they all pulled together to form the *United* States, a totality much larger and more powerful than its diverse parts. Similarly, the players on football teams, with their disparate backgrounds, must achieve "a common purpose" and become "a smooth harmonious aggregation" to win. (During World War II, however, Asians did not qualify for the melting pot, hence the remark about not being a "Chinaman.")

Classic war movies began by introducing the members of the crew, signaling ethnic origins by physical appearance, names, and stereotypical character traits. These differences sparked the internal squabbles that initiated the plot action. Moreover, not only did ethnic traits cause immediate friction in the group, but regional and class differences also caused problems. Many WASPs came from small towns in the Midwest and West, and were portrayed as laconic, modest, and solidly middle class, occasionally wealthy; however, often one group of WASPs hailed from Texas, boasted constantly, and were farm boys, even cowboys. Some Irish characters from small New England towns were "lace curtain" bourgeois, but others were poor and urban, frequently coming from, like the working-class Jews and Italians, the quintessential Hollywood ethnic city of the period: Brooklyn, Noo Yawk. Brooklynites possessed street smarts, wisecracked constantly, and tended toward idiosyncratic individualism. In the first part of a war movie, the crew appeared so disparate, the class and cultural tensions so intense, that the viewer wondered if the group could ever unify, fight effectively, and win.

In this period and subsequent ones, many sportswriters began their pre-season surveys by asking similar questions about college football teams. Before the 1943 season, writers pointed out that Notre Dame had players from twenty-one different states, from cities as large as Chicago and towns as small as Chester, West Virginia, from places as diverse as Spokane, Washington; West Roxbury, Massachusetts; Fort Worth, Texas; and Ely, Minnesota. Moreover, as the *Pittsburgh Press* indicated, the Fighting Irish represented a wide variety of ethnic groups. In addition, the team not only reflected the class differences within the Notre Dame student body but also within the naval trainees on campus: Creighton Miller was from a wealthy, very old ND family; "Ziggy" Czarobski was the son of poor Polish immigrants; other players had equally diverse backgrounds. Yet, Notre Dame won the national championship, the press attributing the victory to the team's coalescing and "Fighting" as a unit.

Before World War II, sports media narratives about "melded units" were much less common than stories about individual athlete-heroes. Because most coaches recruited primarily in their schools' home regions, they produced homogenized rosters; the champion Minnesota Golden Gophers of the 1930s, for instance, were almost pure Minnesotan, as was their head man, Bernie Bierman, "the Hammer of the North." Even though some Southern coaches, armed with athletic scholarships, made raids into Northern states, usually they did not entice many players to venture below the Mason-Dixon line and they did not produce heterogeneous squads.

In the prewar period, only Notre Dame, Army, and Navy were truly national teams with athletes from many regions and backgrounds. However, World War II broke the traditional recruiting pattern in college sports, and after the war most coaches went far beyond their own territories to hunt for service-team veterans and other prime prospects. Many rosters began to resemble traditional Notre Dame and military academy lineups, and the narratives about college teams increasingly included the war movie metaphors on "melded units." (In the following decades, particularly with national TV coverage of college sports breaking down regionalism, the media polished the group-hero tropes. In the present era, when almost every major team recruits nationally, the media, coaches, and fans chant the metaphors of diverse-backgrounds-coming-together, fighting-as-a-unit, etc.; meanwhile, ironically, the military trumpets individual growth, "Be all that *you* can be in the Army.")

In an article on the 1943 college football season, Grantland Rice saluted the cohesion, in spite of war disruptions, of the Fighting Irish. In addition, Rice, although a Southerner, hailed an African American as one of the year's outstanding players, praising Michigan tackle Julius Franks for his ability "to fit like a cog" in the Wolverines' outstanding line. Similarly, Francis Wallace singled out various black players in his *Saturday Evening Post* football articles, including Penn State's Dave Alston, "Sophomore of the Year in Memoriam," for his personal, academic, and football abilities, as well as his untimely death from pneumonia.

Intercollegiate athletics was far ahead of other American institutions in integrating blacks into its activities. The Big Ten and the Pacific Coast Conference, particularly UCLA with Jackie Robinson, Kenny Washington, Woody Strode, and other outstanding African American athletes, led the way in the early 1940s. The Los Angeles sports media coverage of UCLA probably influenced some filmmakers to include black characters in the crews of war movies. In *Bataan* (1943), Private Epps, a former divinity student, is a demolition expert in the Engineers; in *Guadalcanal Diary* (1943), a black signalman identifies enemy and U.S. ships; and in *Crash Dive* (1943), Ensign Oliver volunteers for an extremely dangerous submarine mission. Not only did the African American characters fully integrate into the group-hero but, unlike many of the ethnics, they caused minimal friction along the way.

Significantly, these integrated Hollywood crews were historically inaccurate: during World War II, the armed services were totally segregated, African Americans could only fight in "Negro Units"; moreover, segregation in the American military continued until President Truman abolished it in 1948.

Yet Hollywood, like college sports, presented positive images of African Americans and of integration during World War II. The war movies were so persuasive that, a generation later, one of Ronald Reagan's favorite political stories concerned "a Negro sailor" at Pearl Harbor, and how his single-handed bravery in "blazing away [with a machine gun] at Japanese airplanes . . . coming down and strafing him" ended "segregation in the military forces" soon after. Reagan's critics pointed out the historical inaccuracy of his claim, as well as the lack of any photographic or documentary evidence of the specific incident. Nonetheless, Reagan persisted with his story. His biographers believe that the scenes from various war movies were so vivid for him that, in his memory, they became actual events; the lone machine gunner occurred in *Air Force,* and the black crew members in other films. No doubt other Americans, moved by war movies, made similar mental switches, and Hollywood, particularly with its synergy with college sports on this issue, contributed to the acceptance of integration in the postwar era.

■　■　■

WINOCKI (not having any [patience for his commanding officer]): Anything else, sir?

QUINCANNON:
Yes. Get this into your head—we all belong to this airplane. We're a single *team.* Each one of us has got to rely on every other man doing the right thing at the right time. *Teamwork* is all that counts. You used to play football, you ought to know. I happen to be running the team, that's all.

—From the shooting script and film of *Air Force,* 1943.

Winocki is the cynical outsider in the airplane crew, and his slow, painful assimilation into the team propels much of the plot of this classic war film.

When Weinberg, the Brooklyn Jew, asks him, "You played left tackle for Notre Dame? Chee, you must be smart—workin' your way t'rough college," Winocki replies, "I've seen guys with college degrees didn't know enough to come out of the rain." But eventually, by learning to respect and trust Quincannon, Winocki sheds his cynicism and, at the end, fights magnificently with the crew. This integration of an antisocial individual paralleled college football movies; for example, in *Knute Rockne—All-American,* George Gipp begins as a detached, hostile loner but then, through his love for Rockne, he becomes a team player, even inspiring an entire future team to glorious victory.

In addition, war movies placed commanding officers in coaches' roles, the scriptwriters often giving them football speeches. Not only does Quincannon make them in *Air Force,* but most commanders rattle them off in other war movies. Throughout the films, the commander-coach defines the acceptable parameters of the group's behavior, constantly stresses the importance of teamwork, teaches crew members their specific jobs, plots strategy, and directs the team in combat. Moreover, the officer-coach supplies stability in a fast-changing world, and continuity amidst the flux of crew members joining and leaving the team. The officer-coach usually becomes a hero to his crew, inspiring admiration comparable to what the players in *The Iron Major* feel for Cavanaugh and the Fighting Irish feel for Rockne.

And, like the cinematic Cavanaugh and Rockne, the officer-coach often dies in the last part of the film, and the military crew then wins its final and most important battle for its fallen hero. This trope or a version of it occurs in the 1943 movies that clarified the war genre: *Air Force, Destination Tokyo, Guadalcanal Diary,* and *Sahara.* In *The Iron Major,* in Cavanaugh's last season as a coach, he becomes increasingly blind, and for his team's final and most crucial game, he cannot see; nevertheless, the players, deeply molded by him, win it for "Cav." His blindness marks his death as a coach, and soon the audience sees his actual demise.

Like college athletes, the crew members in war movies divide according to age, experience, and specific duties. Every war movie has a "kid" character, a freshman who joins the group and has to learn "to play with the big boys," or fail and drop out. Usually a veteran crew member, a senior, befriends the "kid" and helps him fit into the group. The films, like college teams, situate other crew members, mainly sophomores and juniors, between the "kid" and the most experienced senior, the symbolic team captain.

The crew-team exhibits varying degrees of dissent and accommodation in all its early activities—eating, chatting, joking—as well as military duties. Eventually the men bond together and, in so doing, separate themselves from the outside world as well as other military units. In joining the military, they left their actual relatives, and when they finally unite, they achieve the closeness of a family. The synergy between war and sports films spun these tropes into the media's and the public's perception of actual teams and players, and soon they became the way that many sportswriters and broadcasters, as well as fans, discussed teams and, in an added twist, the way coaches and athletes began to perceive themselves. (In later decades, many teams proclaimed, "We are family," until, by the end of the century, the claim deteriorated into a cliché, applied by and to almost every sports unit, including highly dysfunctional ones.)

■　■　■

During the second world war, statistics were being put out about people who participated in sports being more successful in combat . . . [moreover] the men who were willing to be on a team and willing to give to a team and to their country were one and the same persons.

—Longtime USC coach John Robinson, 1993.

Throughout the war, the press and radio supported Hollywood's linkage of college sports and military service. Many contemporary magazine and newspaper articles, as well as radio programs, confirm John Robinson's comment. Attached to Grantland Rice's 1944 *Collier's* magazine "All-America" selections was the piece, "Postgrad All-Americas—Pacific Chapter," with the subhead, "Varsity Football Players Are Now Starring in a Bigger Game—the Pacific War." The author listed the names of former college football players on naval ships, particularly PT boats, in the Pacific. However, he did not give the names of the many non-athletes in similar roles.

Not surprisingly, writers often invoked Knute Rockne to prove the athlete-warrior connection. In the 1944 article, "Rock in These Days," syndicated to football programs around the country, Fred Digby, sports editor of the *New Orleans Item*, listed Rockne's attributes for a good football player—"brains, courage, self-restraint"—then advised, "Substitute 'a good aviator, soldier, or sailor,' and you have the description of the ideal American fighting man, of those warriors who today are at grips with the enemy on the far flung battlefields of the world." Digby also used Rockne to attack the wartime deemphasis of college sports: "How Rock would have tackled those softies who would kill football and competitive sports and substitute [for them] German *Turn Verein* physical education in the guise of intramurals"—thus equating the opponents of intercollegiate athletics with the German enemy!

The link between war and football tightened when the 1945 NCAA *Official Football Guide* featured an article, "Football Pays Off," by Commander William R. "Killer" Kane. A famous Navy air ace, Kane discussed the qualities necessary for success in football and aerial combat: in addition to "toughness" and physical "coordination," sheer "aggressiveness" brought "the yellow belly dead in the sights," and produced "the supreme thrill of splashing a Zeke." To readers, this pugnacity was appropriate to wartime combat, and also connected to the new aggressiveness in college sports. However, Kane refrained from describing the drowned pilots or other violent scenes.

Commander Kane's main point concerned "discipline": "We cannot all be ball carriers. Some of us must block. As it is in football, so it is in combat flying. Orders must be followed strictly. There is no room here for an individualist, a non-conformist, for he becomes a menace to his own mates. Teamwork in the air is as necessary (perhaps more so) as it is on the gridiron."

The mobilization of a huge, diverse society for war required tremendous discipline and coordination; by 1945, all institutions of American society marched together, thus Hollywood films, the NCAA, and the press connected to and reflected the wartime ideology. Even popular music, dominated by the totally harmonized "Big Band" sound, expressed the society's need and desire for conformity. Many of the wartime values were traditional, like discipline, but others were new and made a permanent impact upon the culture.

A distinctive element of classic combat films, different from all previous war movies, is that every crew-team member performs a special, often highly technical job. Some work with ordnance, i.e., linemen, and a smaller number of men pilot planes, ships, and tanks, i.e., offensive backfielders. Teamwork is essential, but only specialists can operate the individual parts of the new and complex military machines, particularly bombers and submarines.

Hollywood war films glorified this specialization and helped break down public hostility to it in many areas of American life, including college sports. Before the war, American popular culture still celebrated the all-around man—*Mr. Deeds Goes to Town* (1936), *Mr. Smith Goes to Washington* (1939)—and, in college football, the sixty-minute player. But the all-around man originated in the country's agrarian past and mythos, and during World War II, particularly because of the manufacture and operation of complicated war machines, the media extolled specialization.

With America's great military success in the war came public acceptance of technology and expertise on the home front, notably in the workplace but also in leisure activities. In college sports, football fans slowly began to accept the two-platoon system and players performing specific offensive or defensive tasks. After rooting for the tail gunner on the *Mary Ann* in *Air Force,* cheering for the offensive right end on the Washington Huskies started to make sense. Nevertheless, because of the deeply conservative nature of college sports organizations, change did not occur instantly in intercollegiate athletics; after the war, the NCAA returned to one-platoon football for a time. But reactionaries could not turn back the cultural clock; the media's increasing support of specialization doomed the sixty-minute men. Inevitably, expertise—every player with a narrow, specific job—triumphed.

■ ■ ■

QUINCANNON:
(To [his wife] Mary.)
I'll be back in a couple of weeks.

MARY:
Blarney! I can remember every honeymoon we didn't take—even the first one.

QUINCANNON:
(Slips his free arm around her. [He holds their baby in the other one].)
You oughta be glad the way things are—you never have time to get bored with me.

MARY:
I'll never get bored with you, Irish [her nickname for him]. It's been fun—every minute of it. Oh, such fun, I'm a lucky girl.   ·

QUINCANNON:
I'm a lucky guy.

(They look at each other deeply, seriously, saying things no words can say. Silently he hands her the baby and she takes it but keeps looking at him.)

So long, kid.

MARY:
(Whispers)
So long, Irish. Happy landings.

(He kisses her and abruptly she turns away toward the hangar, afraid he will see her crying, and Quincannon follows [his aide] White to the door of the airship.)

—From the shooting script and film of *Air Force,* 1943.

War movies, like college sports films, placed women in minor roles but never totally excluded them. During this era, because of the box office importance of female moviegoers, war and football movies always contained some scenes with mothers, wives, and girlfriends, as well as references to them in dialogue, letters from home, and so on. Often the scenes occurred near the beginning of the film: in *Air Force,* the Kid's mother accompanies him to the

plane before departure, handing him over to his symbolic father-coach, Quincannon; in addition, the commander has the above scene, the long, emotional
parting from his wife, Mary. These *Air Force* sequences were typical of classic war and football films.

Mary Quincannon, like the cinematic Bonnie Rockne, is loving, admiring,
dutiful, and perky. Because Mary's husband, like the famous coach and other
war and sports figures, is obsessed with his work, he has never taken her on a
honeymoon—paralleling the movie Rockne's failure to give Bonnie a vacation
for almost all of their marriage—but he does bring excitement and children
into her life. And, like Bonnie Rockne at the end of the biopic, the Quincan-
nons' parting and his air flight marks the last time she will see him.

The genius of Hollywood films in this period is that such scenes as Quincannon's departure conveyed a large amount of ideology without ever holding
up a single political sign. Mary behaves as a perfect wife and mother, fully
subordinating her needs to her husband's adventure. In the farewell scene,
she affirms the "little woman" role that Hollywood assigned her and most
other female characters in this period. Other war movies used similar
episodes and/or flashbacks or cameo shots of a female—the mother/wife/girl-
friend of one of the men—sitting at a writing desk or by a window at home,
visual emblems of women "keeping the home fires burning."

As in classic football films, women in war movies are cheerleaders, help-
mates, adornments, and prizes, but only rarely do they possess independent
personalities. Yet the males always claim that they are "fighting for the
women back home," that their mothers/wives/girlfriends personify America
for them. However, as in football movies, male conflict so drives the plot, and
male bonding so preoccupies the characters, that a viewer, particularly in a
later era, becomes skeptical of the claims. In these movies, war, like sports, is
clearly a male preserve, with hermetic customs and language, and the men
involved in war or football become wholly absorbed by their adventures,
which are often extraordinary struggles but always antithetical to the depicted
world of women. As a result, for all of the tributes to mom/wife/girl back
home, classic war movies, like their sports counterparts, keep females at a
great distance from the center of activity.

At many of the schools fielding the best football teams of this era, women
were not admitted. This had long been true of the University of Notre Dame,
and the ban was equally rigid at the Naval Academy and at West Point. Thus,
for the Army Black Knights, the team that came to dominate this era, like the
combat units that many of its graduates led, women had no role whatsoever.

14

Football Becomes the Black Knights and Colonel Blaik

[A smiling football player stands next to a beaming aviator, a Chesterfield cigarette in the latter's mouth. Beneath them in bold type:]

ON THE FIELDS OF FRIENDLY STRIFE
ARE SOWN THE SEEDS
WHICH ON OTHER FIELDS
IN OTHER YEARS
WILL BEAR THE FRUIT OF VICTORY

—Chesterfield cigarette ad, 1943.

In a national print campaign for magazines and football game programs, Chesterfield featured the American version of the Waterloo-Eton equation, penned by General Douglas MacArthur in 1919 when he was superintendent of West Point. Chesterfield ran this ad throughout the fall of 1943, placing it on facing magazine pages and in the midsections of programs. On the left page was the photo of the football player and the airman above the MacArthur quote; on the opposite page, in huge letters, "ON EVERY FIELD"—and in even larger letters and more vivid colors—"IT'S CHESTERFIELD." For the football programs, the names and numbers of the players were one-twentieth the size of the cigarette company's name.

Significantly, the ad never identified MacArthur as the author of the quote, probably because the advertising agency assumed that the passage and the author were so well known that attribution was unnecessary. Most likely, the agency was correct: General Douglas MacArthur was one of America's greatest heroes in World War II, and his West Point sports-war maxim was repeated constantly, not only by the sports media but also by the mainstream press as well as patriotic advertisers. In a sense, the public prominence of this U.S. Military Academy proverb symbolized the importance of MacArthur's alma mater for college sports in this era, underscored by the fact that one of the general's proteges, Colonel Earl "Red" Blaik, built the wartime Black Knights into the most powerful and attractive football team in the country and, in so doing, helped keep the sport alive. (Ironically, because of this success, when scandal engulfed Blaik's program a number of years later, immense harm resulted.) Every history of intercollegiate athletics in this era must consider the rise and fall of Colonel Blaik's Black Knights.

■   ■   ■

I want to emphasize that competitive athletics in our schools and colleges simply cannot be allowed to fall by the wayside if we are to go through to a win against the Axis.

Earl . . . how strongly I feel in this matter of development of the leader and how vital a part competitive athletics plays in it as a means at hand for its accomplishments . . .

So boy, keep driving ahead in your job [as West Point football coach], for it's a top-flight project in our war effort, and don't let anyone tell you anything else.

—General Robert Eichelberger, Commanding General, 1st Army Corps, to Colonel Earl "Red" Blaik, July 1942.

The Army football teams assembled and coached by Blaik during the war exemplified the total-victory mentality of World War II and also foreshadowed future attitudes in intercollegiate athletics, not only in the Black Knights' annihilation of opponents but also in their coach's and their school's ability to wrap an obsession with sports victory in idealistic and patriotic language.

Blaik began the 1940s as head coach at Dartmouth. In fact, on the day that his Indians played the "fifth down" game against Cornell, General Eichelberger, at the time West Point superintendent, watched the Army team lose to Penn, 48-0—the worst defeat in the academy's first half-century of football. Equally galling to Eichelberger and his Army bosses in 1940 were nine straight seasons of not beating Notre Dame as well as a mediocre record against Navy. The superintendent decided to end the years of second-rate teams and bring a hard-driving coach to the academy: West Point grad Earl Blaik. Eichelberger justified his move: "[Against Penn] the cadets cheered our team right to the end. It looks as if we are developing the finest bunch of losers in the world . . . I believe the cadets deserve a football team which will teach them how to be good winners."

Earl Blaik had been an outstanding West Point athlete in the period after the First World War when General Douglas MacArthur was superintendent.

As an article on Blaik noted, he is "an indoctrinated Army man whose idol of idols is" the famous general. MacArthur, who was sometimes compared with the Duke of Wellington and gave West Point its Waterloo-Eton axiom and various other mottoes, including one often quoted by Blaik: "Football, beyond any game invented by man, is closest to war."

MacArthur, however, was not simply a man of memorable phrases; he believed in plans and action, and as superintendent at West Point after World War I, he promoted athletics, particularly intercollegiate football. He augmented the Army tradition of bringing All-American grads from other schools to the academy to play three more years of college football; Blaik, for instance, had starred at and graduated from Miami University of Ohio before embarking on his Army playing career. West Point, using the excuse that it needed extra time to train officers, would not observe standard player eligibility rules; as a result, many schools—even Navy for a period—refused to play the Cadets. (Notre Dame, however, always took them on.) In the 1930s, President Roosevelt ordered Army to obey the eligibility regulations, and West Point's football fortunes declined—until in the 1940s the academy began to break the rules again.

When Eichelberger brought in Blaik, he also reinstituted open recruiting, not only of All-Americans at other schools but also of prime high school prospects, which spurred, among other things, the controversy with Notre Dame over Johnny Lujack. Army authorities convinced FDR and the War Department "to use the West Point football team . . . as an advertisement of the strength of the U.S. Army." But a losing team would prove a poor ad, hence Blaik got permission to win at any costs. Even with the severe shortage of trained officers during the early stages of American mobilization, the Army commissioned Blaik to coach football at the academy for the duration of the war, rather than assign him to a regular unit. And, unlike the 1920s and 1930s "Aw-Nuts" writers who had frequently reported on Army's "irregular proselytizing," the 1940s media enveloped Blaik with classical adjectives, never questioning his wartime coaching assignment or his recruiting methods.

Blaik began to construct powerhouse teams, and by 1944 sportswriters mainly used superlatives to describe them as well as the excellent Naval Academy squads, built in somewhat similar fashion.

> West Point and Annapolis . . . came into the [1944] football scene with stars from all over the country—veterans with three or four years experience at other colleges, and the pick of the high school stars. They were the two greatest teams in Army-Navy football history, packed with speed, power, experience, youth, spirit, and all-around class. Together they could send more than twenty first-rate backs into play.

> —Grantland Rice, December 1944.

Even though Rice spotlighted the amazing military academy teams, when he viewed the entire college football landscape, he indicated that the service academies held an unfair edge over their weakened opponents. Other schools and military base teams had unsettled lineups, with players inducted into the service or shipped overseas during the season, whereas, as Rice explained, because the War Department refused to disrupt West Point and Annapolis officer training, "Army and Navy had an advantage since neither of these teams lost a man." Indeed, for athletes, one of the attractions of attending the academies was prolonged shelter from active duty. As Francis Wallace later commented, some "athletes deliberately took refuge in the service schools to avoid the draft" and assignment to regular units. Indeed, a surprising number of service academy football players, including some All-Americans, sat out the entire war in these patriotic settings.

During World War II, however, the media never explained the West Point or Annapolis recruiting techniques or inducements. Only years later did the details of "Army's unofficial bureau in charge of steering players to West Point . . . operating at full wartime pitch" emerge, and then often in muted form. Moreover, compared to Army, the Naval Academy always had rust spots on its recruiting; it attracted some All-Americans, but it could not compete with the great Army squads—it lost 23-7 to them in 1944, and 35-13 in 1945—and Navy rarely overwhelmed opponents in the Black Knight manner.

One sports historian later termed Earl Blaik "the ogre of college football of the war years." In his approach to the sport, the Army coach more than fulfilled the description. His recruiting technique was simple and effective: he used West Point graduates around the country to scout for him; then, after selecting the best players from this pool, Blaik asked the appropriate members of Congress to appoint these athletes to the academy. During the war, most Congressmen and Senators as well as Selective Service officials considered it their patriotic duty to cooperate with Blaik and his Annapolis counterparts.

Typical of the coach's work was the recruiting of Army's most famous athletes, "The Touchdown Twins": Glenn Davis—"Mr. Outside"—and Felix "Doc" Blanchard—"Mr. Inside." Blaik first heard of Davis, a California high school "phenom," while he was coaching at Dartmouth. At Army, Blaik had scouts follow Davis's high school progress, and after the player's sensational senior year, Blaik offered him an Army appointment. However, Davis had a twin brother, Ralph, and, as he later revealed, "I told them [Army] I wouldn't go unless Ralph went too. The next thing we knew we both had Senatorial appointments." Unfortunately, neither twin "had high school grades accrediting them to West Point," but in building and maintaining his football machine, the Army coach often found ways to help his athletes over his school's strict entrance hurdles: special tutors—Blaik called them "academic coaches"—and a special preparatory school aided the academically challenged jocks.

In Blaik's recruiting scheme, Glenn Davis exemplified the best of the high school crop, whereas Doc Blanchard represented Army's transfer players. Blanchard started his college career at the University of North Carolina at Chapel Hill—his cousin, Jim Tatum, was the head coach—and Doc starred as a freshman Tarheel. After his first year, however, the Selective Service drafted and assigned him to a regular Army unit. Then Blaik, who had followed Blanchard's football career, intervened, found a senator to appoint Doc to the Military Academy, and arranged for the player to take the entrance exams at a special place and time.

Blaik's critics later charged that the Army coach frequently used this ploy, which they called "draft board recruiting." Blaik would allow a prime athlete to be drafted and placed in regular service, then he would intercede, organizing the West Point deal. A number of his players subsequently admitted that as high school seniors, they had no desire to attend the spartan, all-male academy, but after they tasted bleak regular Army life, the offer of escape to West Point and many years of big-time football suddenly held great appeal. Other players, with Blaik's aid, simply transferred to West Point before or when their draft boards called them up. In this category were All-Americans Tom "Shorty" McWilliams from Mississippi State, George "Barney" Poole from Ole Miss, and Dewitt "Tex" Coulter from Texas A&M—significantly, none ever saw active duty or graduated from the academy. Yet, the press always portrayed their choice of West Point in glowing terms, and the 1947 movie *Spirit of West Point* made the analogy between athletes selecting the Military Academy and young men choosing the priesthood.

After the 1945 season and the end of the war, McWilliams wanted to return to his original school, but Blaik refused to allow him to transfer out of the Military Academy—the coach invoked McWilliams's Army obligation! West Point superintendent Maxwell Taylor eventually permitted McWilliams to leave; he also admitted publicly for the first time that "the Army went looking for players: We do this deliberately . . . knowing from experience that the athlete makes the strong battle leader." Thus, even the confession dovetailed into the classic ideal.

Barney Poole and Tex Coulter hit upon a more efficient way to end their playing days at Army: they flunked out of the academy. Other All-Americans came and went during West Point's wartime glory years; some graduated and served, others did not. Some, like Bobby Dobbs from Tulsa, were All-Americans before they entered West Point; others, like Max Minor from the University of Texas, achieved All-American status while playing for Army. Blaik's players were so good that, according to one writer, " 'On Brave Old Army Team,' the popular gag went, 'On to the Pros!' " Indeed, after the war, many Army players entered the resurgent professional leagues. Sports journalist Jim Beach later noted, "Of all of them, it really surprised me that 'Doc' Blanchard did not go pro but instead made the military his career. I knew those players personally and 'Doc' always struck me as one of the most cynical, totally aware of Blaik's system and the West Point b.s." Apparently Blanchard stayed in the service because he loved flying—he became a first-generation Army Air Force jet pilot.

Following the war, particularly when Army and Notre Dame ended their annual series, a few details of Blaik's wartime recruiting methods leaked out. In a heated exchange in the letters to the editor column of *Sport* magazine, Army and Notre Dame fans pilloried each other, one ND fan charging that "our Military Academy is built on the idea of subsidizing players (with wartime deferments) and pouring it on other schools which have sent their men where the fighting is going on." Terry Brennan, at the time an undergraduate at Notre Dame and later its head football coach, wrote: "Perhaps you [the editors] can explain why the greatest football talent in the country was amassed at West Point in 1944-45-46. I suppose it was chance or some magnetic force." But the press was unwilling to print the particulars of Blaik's system, which only emerged in the wake of the 1951 West Point "Cribbing Scandal," and many years after that when the academy finally opened its files (see pages 351–52).

In the 1940s, Blaik responded to the recruiting issue in the manner of his hero, General MacArthur: he remained aloof, never acknowledging its existence. The coach, also like MacArthur, was rigid, cold, and intimidating in public and in private; he never discussed his recruiting with journalists, and, because of the media and public reverence for wartime heroes, no one pressed him on it. Sportswriter Jim Beach, covering Army for a wire service during this period, later explained that "back then, most press and radio people were cheerleaders for one team or another." Even Stanley Woodward, the sports editor of the *New York Herald-Tribune,* famous for his honesty, was "a notorious West Point and Blaik promoter." That important editors and journalists as well as readers would grant "a free pass" to a major sports figure like Blaik indicated the desire to keep the classical ideal intact, to believe that college football and its coaches, particularly prominent ones like Colonel Earl "Red" Blaik, played by the rules and upheld traditional values.

The popular 1947 Hollywood film *Spirit of West Point* further sanctified Blaik's wartime recruiting. The film focused much of its thin plot on Blanchard, portraying his Military Academy appointment as the fulfillment of his dying father's wishes. Blanchard senior had always loved football, had taught the game to his son, and the young man's acceptance by West Point marked the culmination of the father's life. The film also flashed back to Blanchard senior as a college football player in the South in the 1910s—however, it ignored the fact that he had been a "tramp athlete," playing for a number of schools under his own name as well as his "nom de football," Beaulieu.

Spirit of West Point depicted Felix "Doc" Blanchard—who awkwardly played himself—as a wide-eyed young man, very different from the "cynical" athlete whom Jim Beach and other insiders knew. Indeed, this movie provided an excellent example of a Hollywood transformation: because his actual father taught him the facts of football life, the real Doc Blanchard understood the system very well, but the movie reduced the father, son, college football, and West Point to warm Hollywood clichés. It even turned Red Blaik into an Army version of St. Knute Rockne.

The best parts of *Spirit of West Point* are the lengthy newsreel clips of Blanchard and Davis in action, illustrating in a much more convincing manner than the biopic scenes why Blanchard won the Heisman Trophy in 1945 and Davis a year later. The plot also presented the heroes with the dilemma of whether to go pro or to stay in the service and, in true classical fashion, resolved it in favor of patriotism (nevertheless, Davis subsequently went to the NFL). The movie, however, offered no insight into how Coach Red Blaik molded these players and his other All-Americans into national champions—teams so good that some football commentators consider them the best in the history of the sport.

∎　∎　∎

We [Army coaches] did not drive those cadets any harder than we drove ourselves. In my twenty-five years as a head coach, seven at Dartmouth, eighteen at West Point, I seldom took a vacation from the job, and then only when my doctor warned me some relaxation was necessary . . . During fall and spring practice, we worked [from early morning until] . . . far into the night . . . I always drove my assistants as hard as I drove myself, and I never found one who couldn't or wouldn't take it.

—Colonel Earl "Red" Blaik, 1960.

Of Blaik's many assistants who became head coaches in college and pro football, none was more famous than Vince Lombardi, who shared the work habits and the obsessive will to win of his Army boss. Like many workaholic coaches, including his great rival Frank Leahy, Blaik drove his players mercilessly, drilling them hour after hour on the West Point practice fields, frequently telling them, "You have to pay the price." The Army head man was not an innovative strategist; he used mainly standard formations, with at least thirty offensive plays and ten defensive "reactions," terming the set his "basic plays." Every week of spring and fall practice, according to his account, his teams "scrimmaged the basic plays more than a *hundred* times apiece" (his emphasis).

During the war years, because of his extraordinary recruiting and his football conservatism, Blaik did not use unlimited substitution. Instead he assigned his athletes to two-way units; the first and second elevens were almost equal in talent, with the third only a notch below. He told the press, bluntly and with no awareness of his arrogance, that the best college football he ever saw occurred when his Number One and Number Two squads battled each other in practice.

In his first seasons as head coach at Army, his teams grew increasingly powerful but still could not beat Frank Leahy's Fighting Irish, tieing 0-0 in 1941, losing 13-0 the following year, and 26-0 in the famous 1943 game when Lujack substituted for the departed Bertelli. However, after that season, Leahy entered the Navy—he was replaced by assistants Ed McKeever in 1944 and Hugh Devore the following year—and Blaik's recruiting and drilling attained maximum efficiency.

In 1944, against schools with rosters of mainly seventeen- and eighteen-year-olds as well as draft rejects, the Black Knights played relentlessly, beating North Carolina in the opener 46-0 and escalating from there: 69-7 against Pitt, 83-0 over Villanova. For the season, West Point scored 504 points to its opponents' 35. Moreover, in this period, because most offenses, including Blaik's, attempted fewer than fifteen passes a game, a team had to physically crush its adversaries to achieve a huge lopsided score with a running attack. Blaik practiced the football equivalent of "unconditional surrender."

The Big Game of 1944 was the match against Notre Dame. Blaik in his flat military prose acknowledged this: "Desire to snap the long series of losses to Notre Dame [Army last won in 1931] had established priority over the urgency to beat Navy, not only in the [student] Corps but among many graduates," i.e., the Army brass. Both schools as well as Yankee Stadium sold out their allotments of tickets months before the contest, and the New York press reported that "speculators have been getting top figures for tickets," often twenty-five times face value: $100 for $4 seats.

Army was a two-touchdown favorite to win, mainly because the Notre Dame "subway alumni" kept the odds down. Red Smith began his description of the 59-0 Army victory with "In the most horrendous Gaelic disaster since the Battle of the Boyne" and attributed this "travesty" of a football game to "the joint efforts of the best of all West Point's teams and one of South Bend's weakest."

Other accounts emphasized the ferocity of the Black Knights' attack, the AP noting that "Army showed no mercy" and, as the Fighting Irish tired, Blaik kept sending in fresh units, thus "Notre Dame felt the full blows of three great Cadet teams." However, ND partisan Arch Ward phrased his story line differently: "A courageous team from Notre Dame, made up substantially of 17- and 18-year-olds, today ran afoul of the powerhouse that masquerades as the Army football team." Ward hated the fact that this was the worst defeat in Notre Dame football history up to that time (and to this day); moreover, after the Army touchdown that established this record, the jubilant West Point player who scored it did a mocking dance from the end zone to his team's bench. Such in-your-face conduct was unusual for this period—

classical football forbade "rubbing it in"—but considering Blaik's take-no-prisoners approach to the sport, his player's actions seem predictable as well as a foreshadowing of a future football age.

Army fans also failed to show much sportsmanship. The United Press noted that "three of West Point's favorite sons"—Generals Jacob L. Devers, Carl Spaatz, and "Vinegar" Joe Stilwell—sat "proudly in the stands" and cheered loudly as "the Cadets poured it on." A female spectator later wrote *Sport* magazine that "I never in my life witnessed such poor spirit, [such] lack of sportsmanship as displayed by the Army Cadets [in the stands]. They screamed at the top of their voices, 'More! More! More!' . . . [Also, uniformed] officers by the hundreds were patting each other on the back and shouting, 'We did it! They'll never forget this one!' " Even Coach Blaik's public comments about the victory were less than gracious: "The magnitude of the victory, broadcast by short-wave radio all over the world, was [an] incredible [morale boost] to West Point men at war."

Notre Dame fans refused to bow their heads, and the cover of *The Notre Dame Alumnus* for Winter 1944 depicted their reaction: above a photo of a large crowd welcoming the team at Union Station in South Bend, a headline read, "The Tradition Lives On," and the caption explained that the "students had waited for two hours early Monday morning" for the arrival of the squad back from New York. "Emphatically this team was still their team."

At the center of the photo was, according to the caption, "The injured Bob Kelly, halfback, limping through the civilian student body." This aspect of the game troubled Notre Dame vice president Cavanaugh, and he wrote Arch Ward about "the terrific mauling our teen-age boys endured." The ND official also considered the Army rout a violation of the classical nature of college sports, telling Ward that "confidentially, I am greatly concerned about the one-sided competition" practiced by Army. In the long history of the Notre Dame–Army series, one or two touchdowns had been the usual winning margin, and even ND's 26-0 in 1943 was not a blowout. Nothing compared to the 59-0 game or the way that Blaik administered the thrashing—nothing, that is, until the 1945 game.

Before that season, West Point picked up more All-Americans from other college teams, including the great end Hank Foldberg from Texas A&M, and Army breezed through its games, smashing opponents like Penn, 61-0, and even military base squads by equally lopsided scores. The only team to give the Cadets a tough time was the young Michigan Wolverines. Coach Fritz Crisler realized that "we couldn't stay on the same field with Army, playing nose-to-nose," and so he made maximum use of unlimited substitution for the Yankee Stadium contest. For three quarters his team held Army's one-platoon units to a 7-7 tie; in the final quarter, West Point's offensive superiority finally wore down Michigan's defensive specialists for a 28-7 final score.

But the national sportswriters in the New York press box turned the game into a legendary David-and-Goliath event, equating Crisler's new kind of football with the biblical lethal stone. The fame of this game helped keep the demand for unlimited substitution football alive through the period when the NCAA tried to return to the prewar rules.

For the 1945 Army–Notre Dame game, no sportswriter predicted a Fighting Irish victory. Some ND fans hoped for a good game, but the young college boys only managed to lose by fewer points than the previous year: 48-0. West Point rooters were as jubilant and nasty as the previous season, and Fighting Irish supporters hoped that the conclusion of the war would end West Point's dominance. Arch Ward's biographer noted that the *Chicago Tribune* sports editor "took the defeats [59-0 and 48-0] as a personal affront. He could hardly wait for the revenge that" he expected "would be exacted upon the cadets after the war." Nevertheless, even in his disappointment and anger, Arch Ward, the consummate insider who knew all about Blaik's recruiting techniques, never wrote openly about them in his newspaper. Such were the rules of classical sports reporting.

15

The Wartime Irish
and Rockne's Other Heirs

My dear Joe:

From a newspaper account which I have seen this morning . . . a
Sergeant Gordon D. Marston is quoted: "I'm alive today because
there isn't a more courageous skipper in the South Pacific than Lieutenant John F. Kennedy." These words should be written in letters of
gold on parchment for the Kennedys of a generation to come.

The account goes on to say that . . . John helped [a man] to safety
by towing him to shore with a strap from a life jacket. Then, John
swam in darkness to islands in Japanese territory in search of rescue.
This is all wonderful.

—Notre Dame vice president John J. Cavanaugh
to Joseph P. Kennedy, October 1943.

During this period, Joe Kennedy was a member of the Notre Dame Lay
Board of Trustees, and he and his family always attended the Notre
Dame–Army games in New York, usually sitting near the ND president and
vice president. In his letter to Kennedy, Cavanaugh referred to JFK's heroism
in the PT-109 incident, emphasizing the classical ideals that such acts exemplified. In his reply, Joe Kennedy thanked the Notre Dame VP for his kind
words "about young Jack," adding "please steal me another box [at Yankee
Stadium] for the Army game" to give to some friends.

As the war progressed, Cavanaugh noted the bravery of many other members of the military, particularly former ND undergraduates, but unlike
administrators at many other schools, he never trumpeted the heroism of

varsity athletes over the actions of regular ND alumni. Even when the university listed in an October 1945 football program, "Notre Dame Men Who Have Made the Supreme Sacrifice," it did not single out the former athletes on the list. However, ND football programs in 1944 and 1945 did contain photos of Notre Dame athletic department staff now in the armed services. Among those featured was "Frank Leahy, Lieut. USNR," a reminder to fans that subbing for Leahy in 1944 was one of his assistants, Ed McKeever.

The transition from Leahy to McKeever went smoothly, with the press rolling out Rockne connections as a welcoming carpet for the new head man. A feature article in *Esquire* magazine began, "He [McKeever] wanted to play football for Knute Rockne, but the nearest he ever came was to be in the freshmen [Notre Dame] backfield" that scrimmaged against the varsity. McKeever left ND after one year to return to his native Texas, where he starred at Texas Tech and then became an assistant coach there, attracting the attention of Frank Leahy at a coaches' clinic. "From the outset," according to *Esquire,* the two men "went together like adjoining pieces of a jigsaw puzzle. It may have been because Rockne was McKeever's ideal and in Leahy he found 'a chip off the old Rock,' " the Texan transferring his love for the famous coach to his protégé, Frank Leahy.

Again, the press plugged a real person into a classic sports drama: the articles on McKeever resembled the products of a media assembly line, with his name penciled into the appropriate spaces. The *New York Times* titled Arthur Daley's column on McKeever's ascension "Successor to Rockne," and the columnist recited the McKeever-Rockne connections as well as some well-worn Leahy-Rockne ones before concluding, "Anyone who meets him [McKeever] will go away convinced that," as during the Rockne and Leahy years, "Notre Dame's destiny is in eminently proper and capable hands."

ND administrators also began to see their coaches in classical terms. Vice President Cavanaugh wrote to a fellow priest about "the value of Coaches Leahy and McKeever. Not only are they outstanding in their football ability, but they are exemplary Catholic gentlemen, of whom I am sincerely proud." And, to complete the loop, Leahy and McKeever regarded themselves in these terms and tried to act upon them, even repeating some of Rockne's most famous gestures.

In an article during the 1944 season, a syndicated columnist related how McKeever had received a letter from a GI "somewhere in Belgium, outside some flaming, nameless town," writing to the ND coach on behalf of his recently killed brother, a devoted Fighting Irish fan. The letter writer requested that McKeever "dedicate nothing so great as a game . . . but perhaps a touchdown or a kickoff to the memory of my brother." Before the Navy contest, the ND coach read the letter to the team, and dedicated the whole game to the departed fan. Unfortunately, Notre Dame lost 32-13. Afterward, McKeever remarked laconically, "Too bad we couldn't have won it for him."

Other media outlets retold this story with the traditional flourishes, e.g., the dead soldier had "suffered with the [ND] team in defeat, jubilated in victory." However, no reporter discussed McKeever's locker-room talk the following week—before the Army debacle—and that story only emerged later. According to Dave Condon, a Notre Dame student press assistant in 1944, before the Army game, McKeever told his players, "My father—the greatest Notre Dame fan I know—is critically ill and listening on radio. Doctors have given up hope, but if you beat Army, you'll save his life." After the Irish fell 59-0, one of the ND players remarked to some teammates, "Well, we sure took care of McKeever's old man."

Classical tropes turned upside down evoke laughter, but during the war the media avoided sports satires, always adhering to the straight versions. Indeed, for many writers, the classical form became so rigid that it nullified reality. Arthur Daley, *after* the 59-0 loss to Army and aware of the locker-room speech that preceded it, wrote in his column, "McKeever has the same instinctive knowledge of human nature and psychology which made Rock so great a coach." And the *Chicago Times*'s Warren Brown nominated McKeever for coach of the year, in part because "he was making discoveries about his material right up to the final play."

Because McKeever was the Notre Dame head football coach, the successor to Rockne and Leahy, apparently these journalists felt compelled to write about him in this way; they could not allow what they actually saw—the lopsided losses to Army and Navy—intrude upon their narratives. Thus Arthur Daley ended another column about the 1944 ND head coach with "Ed McKeever will some day be one of America's outstanding football coaches. He's much too hot for Notre Dame to hold as either assistant or pro-tem mentor."

McKeever believed this praise, and in February 1945 he resigned from his Notre Dame job to take the head coaching job at Cornell. The Big Red, in search of its prewar football prominence, guaranteed him *carte blanche*. Cornell kept its word, but McKeever did not fulfill either his part of the deal or the media predictions. As a reporter later explained, "He couldn't get along with the players . . . bawling them out at the slightest provocation, and gradually rebellion sprouted." Then, halfway through his first season, the players threatened to quit the team *en masse,* and the Cornell athletic authorities intervened, putting down the revolt by assuring the athletes that McKeever would not return the following year. Player strikes were rare in this authoritarian era, and Cornell hushed this one up.

McKeever's next head-coaching job, gained solely on the basis of his connections to Notre Dame, was equally disastrous, ending even more bizarrely than the Cornell fiasco. The University of San Francisco wanted to go big-time in college football, and it gave him a free hand to accomplish this. As Dave Condon later commented, "Ed built a powerhouse but wasn't discreet about eligibility rules"—many of his recruits had played semipro football or college ball under other names. When the president of the school began to investigate,

McKeever lined up a job with the professional Chicago Rockets of Arch Ward's All-America Conference. But before leaving San Francisco he wrote a detailed letter about his players' backgrounds—including the admission that twenty-two "were paid athletic bums"—and sent one copy to the school president and made sure that another would become public. After the press headlined the story, columnist Red Smith described the coach's motivation as "sheer malice" rather than any desire to repent or to reform college football: "McKeever held his tongue [about his ineligible athletes] when it profited him to do so. And loosed it when he could injure those he had left behind."

Ed McKeever, adrift from Notre Dame and the tight constraints of his coaching positions there, was a sad failure: Cornell, USF, 1-13 in his year as head coach of the Chicago Rockets, and then flopping again as recruiting coordinator at Louisiana State before finally slipping out of football.

McKeever's strange career raises important questions about college sports and the media, particularly the distance between the classic narratives and the reality of the individuals portrayed. McKeever's actual connection to Knute Rockne was marginal at best. In the late 1920s and early 1930s, Rockne attracted hundreds of young players to Notre Dame, assembling all of them for freshman football—team photos in the ND yearbooks of this period reveal the astounding size of the freshmen teams. The following spring, after grueling practice sessions, he moved a small number of freshmen to the varsity for the coming season; not surprisingly, many of the rejects soon dropped out of Notre Dame. Ed McKeever was one of these "Marching Hundreds." But the 1940s media ignored this reality, or never bothered to inquire about it; when McKeever became Notre Dame head coach, the press proclaimed his great bond with Rockne, who, in all probability, could not have attached McKeever's name to his face.

As for McKeever's work for Leahy, again the press avoided the facts: Leahy did not train his assistants to become head coaches—and few ever did. The head man demanded that his assistants carry out limited but time-consuming functions; McKeever's job was to train backfielders, which he did well. Sportswriters knew all about Leahy's coaching methods—they attended innumerable practice sessions—but again they refused to use their knowledge, instead substituting classical language and metaphors to describe McKeever's qualifications for the job of ND head coach. The writers plugged the name Ed McKeever into their ongoing Fighting Irish narrative but never bothered to inform readers about the real man or the nature of Leahy's system. Therefore, when McKeever disappeared into the black hole of failed sports figures, no writer explained why, or even waved good-bye. In a world that glorified heroes and victory, failure held no interest.

■　■　■

In Newark there is a big insurance man named Joe Burne [sic] who has been a great Notre Dame fan for years. It was Joe Burne [sic] who, one day back in 1929, took Hughie Devore, All-State end of the St. Benedict's eleven, over to New York to meet Knute Rockne at a hotel.

"How boutcha, boy?" greeted Rock in his famous pet phrase, "How boutcha, Hughie?"

"This boy," said Joe Burne [sic], "is going to be one of the greatest ends Notre Dame ever had. He's got it—everything: fight, smartness, hits hard, stays in there."

"Glad to have him. Glad to have him," snapped Rock in his characteristic staccato. "We've had some good ends. Can use some more."

Notre Dame is still using him. Tomorrow, Hughie Devore "embarks upon the great sea." Probably no other coach ever had so much at stake in so little time.

—*New York Mirror* sportswriter Ralph Cannon,
September 1945.

Hugh Devore replaced Ed McKeever as Notre Dame head football coach, and the "tomorrow" for Devore was the first game of the 1945 football season. Ralph Cannon neatly narrated the story of the first meeting between Devore and Rockne and, like a Hollywood film, recreated the scene as if he and the reader were present. However, the scene moves in too predictable a manner and contains too many internal errors to be totally accurate. The insurance man's name was *Joe Byrne Jr.*—he always used "Junior" because his father was his boss and extremely well known. Moreover, Joe Byrne Jr. was much more than "a fan": he had graduated from Notre Dame with Rockne and was the coach's closest friend. However, this reporter's final point—the extreme pressure under which the ND head football coach exists—was valid.

Other writers also plugged Devore into the Rockne narrative. A *Saturday Evening Post* feature on the new ND head coach stated, "Devore played under Rockne only as a freshman in 1930, but the Rockne stamp is upon him indelibly." This writer, too, ignored the hundreds of freshmen football players in 1930—none "played under Rockne"—but, unlike fellow freshman Ed McKeever, Devore did not leave ND, but starred on the teams of Rockne's successor, "Hunk" Anderson. Most likely that roller-coaster experience—Anderson won some key games but lost many others and was forced out—shaped Devore much more than did his brief and distant exposure to "Rock."

After graduating from ND in 1934, Devore worked his way up the college coaching ladder, first as a freshman coach at his alma mater, then as an assistant at Fordham along with Frank Leahy, next at Providence College, then Holy Cross, and finally returning to Notre Dame in 1943. Associates considered Devore a "serious man" and a realist—as opposed to McKeever who, by all accounts, contained a large quotient of "Texas b.s." In a July 1945 note to Vice President Cavanaugh about pre-season football practice, Devore wrote:

"We have the boys out there 'swinging' every day. However, I feel that I am not doing too much for them. They really don't seem to respond. It is either that I am a 4-F coach or they are 4-F players. I hope the former is true, because the boys have to play the games."

For the 1945 season, Devore's boys did "respond," and they beat their regular college opponents quite easily. They also managed to tie an excellent Naval Academy squad. However, they suffered against Army, 48-0, and also lost the finale to the Great Lakes Naval Station, 39-7.

At the end of the year, Frank Leahy returned from the Navy. Rather than revert to his ND assistant's job, Devore became head coach at St. Bonaventure and, according to the *New York Times* in 1950, "gave the Bonnies the best teams they ever had" until the school dropped out of big-time college football. He then coached at other colleges as well as in the pros—apparently, he advised the Green Bay Packers to hire Vince Lombardi—and, in 1958, Devore returned to his alma mater as freshman coach. He continued in that job until 1963, when he served another year as Notre Dame head man, between the Joe Kuharich and Ara Parseghian regimes. Subsequently, Devore worked at ND and then in the pros; in his final years, his alma mater honored him, including at a special halftime ceremony in 1990, as "The Oldest Living Irish Football Coach," and he held that distinction until his death in 1992.

The comparison of Devore's terms as Notre Dame head coach and McKeever's season is striking: the media plugged both men into the Fighting Irish football narratives, but only McKeever believed the press clippings; Devore had an accurate sense of his strengths and weaknesses as a football coach and used his judgments—not the media's—as his guide. McKeever quickly and bizarrely burned out of the coaching profession, whereas Devore quietly continued in football, ending as a revered figure.

■   ■   ■

Hugh Devore's separate terms as Notre Dame head football coach came at the conclusion of World War II and at the start of the Vietnam War. For Americans, from 1945 to 1963, the nature of warfare moved from the certainties of World War II to the Southeast Asia quagmire. In marked contrast to the classic war movies of the 1940s, during the Vietnam War Hollywood made very few combat films of any kind. Nevertheless, in the 1960s, many of the values and tropes of the earlier decade's movies migrated to the television commentary of college football, particularly as TV announcers moved from a 1950s "let the viewer watch the action" approach to a narrative style. The young Roone Arledge at ABC, with his emphasis on college football as pageant-and-fable, a panoply of camera shots and announcer storytelling, forever changed TV coverage of college sports.

Thus, even though most Americans placed the artifacts of World War II within a specific historical period, the core messages of that conflict continued to flourish for decades in parts of the culture, notably intercollegiate athletics. In the 1960s and afterward, as the American fascination with sports intensified, many of the war/sports metaphors and rituals as well as the moralism became so deeply ingrained within college sports that most participants, fans, and the media came to consider them inherent to the games—unaware that they were a set of ideas with definite origins and a documented history.

Yet, just as Hugh Devore's journey from head coach at Notre Dame in 1945 to that position in 1963 was circuitous, with many ups and downs, so too was the passage of the classic war/sports ideals. In fact, during the Second World War, omens of coming scandals in intercollegiate athletics, particularly in basketball, appeared, and after the war, the corruption in both that sport and in college football threatened at times to topple the entire college sports enterprise.

How intercollegiate athletics survived its scandals and overcame its critics provides the most fascinating chapter in its history.

Part 4

Postwar Years:
The Worsening
Crisis in
College Sports

16

The End of the
Notre Dame–Army Annuals

Forget Molotov [and the Cold War] and the price of butter [and post-war inflation] for a moment, and take a look at one post-war world which really lives up to your fondest hopes—the world of college football. Those circuses on wheels, the railroad football specials, will be running again . . . The college bands will be three-deep in material at every instrument. But, best of all, this year the young men in football suits will be the real McCoy—the greatest array of talent ever assembled for the great American roughhouse [sport].

—Francis Wallace in the *Saturday Evening Post,*
September 1946.

Victory in World War II did not instantly end America's problems: in fact, it created new international tensions with the start of the Cold War, as well as domestic inflation with too much disposable income and savings chasing too few goods and services. However, Americans could travel to and purchase seats in huge college football stadiums, and, with encouragement from such media giants as the *Saturday Evening Post,* as well as athletic department publicity campaigns, the sport experienced an attendance boom that equaled the explosion of the 1920s.

No teams were more popular in the first postwar year of 1946 than Notre Dame and Army, Numbers One and Two in the football polls throughout the season. West Point had many returning lettermen from the 1944–45 championship teams as well as some new All-American transfers, and Notre Dame possessed an excellent nucleus of players from 1945, plus a wave of ex-servicemen from earlier Fighting Irish units and such outstanding freshmen as future Heisman Trophy winner Leon Hart. In their opening games, Army beat nationally ranked Michigan and Oklahoma, and ND wiped out strong Illinois, Iowa, and Navy squads. The season moved relentlessly to the November Notre Dame–Army match at Yankee Stadium, with extra drama added because of Army's twenty-five-game winning streak and ND's desire to avenge the 1944 and '45 thrashings.

For the game, Yankee Stadium turned over ticket sales to the schools. Each received approximately 39,000, with the best seats going for $4.80 and general admission for $1. As early as the spring of 1946, the ND ticket manager warned prominent alumni that because of the huge initial demand, he had to reduce their allotment to a maximum of four seats each. Meanwhile, his West Point counterpart, facing even greater pressure, confined his sales to those who had graduated from the academy *before* 1932.

As soon as the box offices opened officially on August 1, sold-out signs appeared. Nevertheless, throughout the fall, the men in the Golden Dome received and had to refuse ticket requests from many important alumni and church officials, and the commanders of the Military Academy had to turn down appeals from armed services brass as well as prominent politicians. According to informed estimates, at least 750,000 people wanted seats, and a large percentage of them sent money to Notre Dame and West Point, resulting in more than $1 million in refunds. None of these ticket rebuffs made friends for the two schools. As one national columnist phrased it, "From a gridiron fixture, it [the annual game] appears to have grown into a Frankenstein monster" for ND and Army. Throughout the fall as the pre-game build-up intensified, other writers used the Frankenstein metaphor. However, the authoritarian Army officers and priests who ran the two schools wished to control the game, and they loathed its becoming a destructive monster lurching about unpredictably. These men wanted the annual match to be the epitome of the classical ideal in college sports, and the events of 1946 challenged, and eventually destroyed, that goal.

The official ticket situation was difficult enough, but in 1946 the black market in Army–Notre Dame game tickets—always a problem—spun out of control. Officials at both schools thought that they had sold seats only to authorized persons but, as the *New York Times* reported, the administrators became "considerably upset over the fact that speculators had got hold of tickets in large numbers." Moreover, scalpers "advertised openly that they had tickets," demanding—and obtaining—amazing amounts for them. This infuriated the regular fans, particularly those turned down at the box offices, and many aimed their wrath at Notre Dame and West Point, claiming that the institutions had profited from the ticket scalping. No document in the archives of either school provides any proof of this, and many indicate the contrary: the scalpers acquired many seats by tempting ND and Army alumni holding tickets with monetary offers they could not refuse; for school authorities, the fact that alumni—men claiming great affection for their alma maters and their schools' sports traditions—would sell their seats to the highest bidder was deeply disturbing.

For the media, the Army–Notre Dame game, long established as one of the country's two premier annual sporting events, surpassed its competitor—the World Series—that year. Because of the national media's concentration in New York, the Boston–St. Louis series became secondary to the football game in Yankee Stadium. The press proclaimed "the Football Battle of the Century"—the first time it used this term—and the demand for tickets drove the scalpers' price as high as $200 a seat (some new cars in 1946 cost $800). Even the snooty *New Yorker* magazine, usually only willing to cover Ivy League football, began a long article on the 1946 Army–Notre Dame event with "A sort of insanity seemed to seize the city last weekend . . ."

The school administrators, however, disliked the hype. They wanted to preserve the unique traditions of earlier encounters when Notre Dame and West Point alumni, as well as friends of the institutions like the Kennedy family, gathered for a full weekend of camaraderie in New York—but the frenzy surrounding the 1946 game completely disrupted the regular festivities. In addition, Notre Dame had designated the 1946 game as an "official student excursion," transporting its entire student body to New York for the weekend, but when the ND men arrived in Manhattan, scalpers swarmed over them, offering large sums of money for their tickets. Then, the entire Cadet Corps, as they had every year on the Saturday morning of the game, traveled down the Hudson by train to the railroad depot at 125th Street, marching from there to Yankee Stadium. However, during their 1946 march, scalpers besieged them and, ignored by the cadets, taunted them with shouts of "draft dodgers" and "slackers." Some rabid ND "subway alum" fans, smarting over the 1944 and '45 trouncings, joined in the jeering.

These student ceremonies had given the annual series its special place in the histories of both schools as well as of college sports, going back to the 1920s and the famous games played by Rockne's teams against superb Army squads, and beyond that to the first game on the "Heights above the Hudson," memorialized in *Knute Rockne—All-American.* The circumstances surrounding the 1946 contest threatened and ultimately severed that classical tradition.

The game itself was a defensive struggle, with coaches Earl Blaik and Frank Leahy, both desperate to win but apparently even more afraid of losing, ordering conservative attacks and fallback strategies. The contest ended in a 0–0 tie. The game's most vivid play was a defensive tackle made in the open field by Johnny Lujack against Doc Blanchard, preventing a touchdown. Few of the 78,000 fans at the game went home happy, nor were the partisans among the twenty-five million radio listeners satisfied. Only the bookies rejoiced: they had offered a half point on either team, and with a tie they kept all the money. Estimates of their take ranged from eight million to ten million dollars, an astounding amount in that era.

The conclusion of the November 9 game did not please the administrators of the two schools either, nor, to their amazement and dissatisfaction, did it end the problems that had begun long before that day. After the contest, the normally amenable press joined its grievances to the escalating alumni and fan complaints about lousy or no seats. In previous years, reporters had received complimentary tickets for friends as well as pressbox accommodations for themselves, but in 1946 the phenomenal demand for tickets and press passes not only ended the comps but shut many writers out of the midfield football press gallery, sending them to the baseball press box in a corner of the stadium, far behind one set of goalposts. Particularly upset with the move were many midwestern members of the Notre Dame sportswriters' network, as well as journalists from other out-of-town papers.

Some writers complained in their post-game stories, but others overlooked the problems and poured out the classical prose. Arthur Daley commented that the game exemplified "our American way of life," and even Red Smith enthused, "Never in living memory had two natural rivals, established early and beyond argument as the absolute best in existence, come together." However, in the weeks following the game, many sports journalists continued to whine. An AP columnist pointed out that "sports writers publicize" college football "and largely form public opinion, and when scores of reporters who couldn't get [complimentary] tickets to the game and were also shunted into obscure corners . . . go back home and write scathing accounts of their treatment, well, it just doesn't help the sport." Administrators at Notre Dame and Army understood the importance of these writers in promoting intercollegiate athletics and had attentively stroked them for many years, but circumstances in 1946 overwhelmed school officials and negated much of their previous work. They preferred traditional prose à la Arthur Daley to the carping of the new malcontents: they wanted the media to concentrate on the glories of the games, not the negative events surrounding them.

In the period after this fiasco, some writers friendly to the schools suggested other formats for the annual match, such as alternating Yankee Stadium with Soldier Field, a facility with more seats and pressbox space. Then another factor came into play: Yankee Stadium, under new ownership, demanded a total renegotiation of the rental agreement for the game as well as control of ticket sales. School authorities realized that the latter arrangement could lead to even more ticket scalping than in 1946. At this point, Arch Ward tried to use his clout with Notre Dame to move the game permanently to Soldier Field, with the schools continuing to distribute tickets. Army was willing to explore this option, but ND did not consider it a solution to the game's systemic problems, merely their relocation to ninety miles from its campus.

Then, in mid-December, an incident occurred at the 1946 NFL championship game in New York that persuaded the Notre Dame and West Point authorities to move toward ending the annual series. Hours before the kickoff between the New York Giants and the Chicago Bears, two key offensive players on the Giants—QB Frank Filchok and fullback Merle Hapes—confessed that gamblers had offered them money to "dump" the game. The Giants kept Hapes out of the contest, but Filchok played, throwing six interceptions. The Bears triumphed. Filchok claimed that he had played to win, but the league suspended him "indefinitely" (it allowed him to return a number of years later).

For Notre Dame and West Point authorities, this episode confirmed their fears about gamblers and sports, particularly because a key figure in the NFL incident had also played an important role in a 1945 Brooklyn College basketball fix (see page 288). Then FBI director J. Edgar Hoover, a patron of both ND and West Point, offered his opinion on the sports betting situation: "We are unalterably opposed to any attempts by doubtful characters to 'move in' on sports," particularly intercollegiate athletics. "We are opposed to any lessening of the standards that apply in sports . . . There's too much at stake" for America's youth and future.

School officials, however, knew that a large gambling subculture already surrounded college sports, increasingly legitimized by some national magazines with weekly columns of football and basketball predictions. For example, in 1946, *Newsweek* ran a "Fearless [College] Football Forecast" every week during the fall, picking winners for Saturday's games. Experts estimated "nationally now, gridiron betting [is] up in the hundred-million-dollar stratosphere" per year: the postwar gambling craze was fueled by inflation as well as many persons' sense of anomie in a swiftly changing world. A successful sports prediction provided the illusion of personal control, albeit temporarily.

After the 1946 season, Frank Leahy wrote to a top ND administrator, Father John H. Murphy, about the gambling situation in New York and other cities visited by the Fighting Irish. He received this reply: "The total effort that we [at Notre Dame] can put forth is to protect fellows on our teams from contact with these men [professional gamblers] . . . and that is being done quite satisfactorily" at present. Nevertheless, Leahy and Murphy knew that gamblers hung out in the lobbies of the city hotels where visiting college teams stayed, particularly in New York, constantly trying to approach the athletes. Possibly the best solution was to make fewer or no visits to New York.

Father Murphy then discussed an ancillary problem: "Also we can be careful in the information that goes out of our athletic offices. Even some of the priests around here last [football] year received long-distance calls from places as far off as Texas. These calls were placed by persons the priests did not know at all and inquired about the state of a player's health, etc." Similarly, at West Point in 1946, frequent telephone inquiries about player injuries burdened the officers on the Post.

The final factor that terminated the annual series was the change in administrative command at Notre Dame. Because of President O'Donnell's deteriorating health, Father John J. Cavanaugh assumed the top position in 1946. With a keener PR sense than his predecessor, he perceived that the events surrounding the 1946 game reflected badly on the entire University of Notre Dame, undercutting its attempts to promote its academic and religious missions to the general public. Similarly, the superintendent of the Military Academy, General Maxwell Taylor, also adept at public relations, felt that the 1946 New York City fiasco had hurt West Point's image.

Therefore, insiders at both schools were not surprised by the joint statement of ND president Cavanaugh and General Taylor on December 31, 1946, that the Army–Notre Dame series would end after the 1947 game. However, the sporting world did not expect the announcement, and newspaper headlines went to 152-point type to blare it out:

ARMY AND IRISH TO CUT GRID RELATIONS
Scalping, Gambling Reasons for Army-Irish Break

—*New York Telegram & Sun* above Associated Press story.

IRISH AND ARMY TO END ANNUAL GAME
Ticket Headaches and Gamblers' Activities Believed Factors in Break in Relations

—*San Francisco Call-Bulletin* above United Press story.

The Cavanaugh-Taylor statement noted: "Two reasons led to the decision. The first was the conviction of the authorities of both schools that the Army–Notre Dame game had grown to such proportions that it had come to be played under conditions escaping the control of the two colleges, some of which were not conducive to wholesome intercollegiate sport." Most newspapers running the story, from the *New York Times* to small weeklies, correctly interpreted the "not conducive conditions" as the gambling and ticket scalping surrounding the 1946 game. Arthur Daley added, "A Frankenstein monster had been unwittingly created and there was no recourse but to destroy it."

Daley also focused on the phrase "wholesome intercollegiate sport," comparing the 1946 event to "the classic Army–Notre Dame" games. He fondly recalled the "first one [Army-ND game] I ever saw, it was on the Plains [of

West Point] in 1922" and "I sat on the grass near the end zone and watched them [also] battle to a scoreless tie. Admission was free." Daley's love of classical sports mirrored the attitudes of the Notre Dame officials, and he interpreted their feelings with "The Army–Notre Dame clash had become too commercial just as all intercollegiate sport has become too commercial . . . It's sad to see the series end. But undoubtedly it's all for the best."

The West Point authorities had a somewhat different agenda, articulated in "the second reason" for the decision: "The desire of West Point as a national institution to [have] greater flexibility in the scheduling of intersectional opponents throughout the country." The context for this "second reason" was the autumn 1946 wooing and winning of Army by the Rose Bowl committee in Pasadena. During these negotiations, West Point had reversed its previous policy against bowl appearances and also had gained War Department approval for the January 1, 1947, contest. In late November, however, the Big Ten—after decades of rejecting bowl games—suddenly signed a long-term pact with the Pacific Coast Conference, the Rose Bowl host schools, for their champions to meet annually, commencing January 1, 1947. The agreement shut Army out of that game, but the foreplay had increased West Point's desire for a truly national schedule.

The "second reason" also clearly separated Army and the Big Ten from Notre Dame in their approaches to college sports. The Catholic school adhered to the "Fortress Notre Dame" strategy established by President John O'Hara in the 1930s. He had insisted that Notre Dame have stricter rules on intercollegiate athletics than all other schools; thus, because the Big Ten had shunned bowl games since the early 1920s, terming them "too commercial and harmful to the players," O'Hara and his successors enforced a similar anti-bowl policy. Late in the fall of 1946, when Army and the Big Ten committed to playing in bowl games, President Cavanaugh—refusing a top-dollar offer from the Sugar Bowl—continued the "Fortress Notre Dame" policy, convinced that it was the best course of action for his school.

A number of sportswriters commented on this aspect of the Army–Notre Dame break. In his column of January 1, 1947, the day after the Cavanaugh-Taylor statement, Arthur Daley noted that "perhaps there is something symbolic about the fact that the announcement . . . was made on the very eve of the most blatant display of football commercialism [in America], the bowl engagements." Daley was too polite to point out Army's double standard on this issue, but Shirley Povich in the *Washington Post* was not, mocking Army's recent "angling . . . for a trip to the Rose Bowl." Povich also saw hypocrisy in Army's condemnation of ticket scalping, calling the Rose Bowl, "a game which annually produces ticket scalping on a large scale." Therefore, as President O'Hara had originally envisioned, if the Catholic school maintained its "Fortress Notre Dame" strategy, ND would always hold the moral high ground, in this case over the almost sacrosanct United States Military Academy.

■   ■   ■

It [the Army–Notre Dame] is a game which has drawn close to $500,000 annually in Yankee Stadium, and has guaranteed $200,000 a season to Notre Dame.

—Sportswriter Dan Daniel, January 1947.

In the media coverage of the termination of the series, the amount of money at stake was rarely discussed. None of the wire service reports or major newspaper accounts mentioned it, and the only writer to touch upon it was Dan Daniel of Scripps-Howard, who buried the above sentence near the end of his story and did not elaborate. Sports journalists in this period rarely discussed the financial aspects of intercollegiate athletics but, as Daniel's figures indicate, the Army–Notre Dame game produced a huge amount of money for the participants: of the $500,000, approximately $200,000 went to each school, and Yankee Stadium received $100,000 for rent and services. Thus, shutting off this annual flow of cash deserves comment.

In 1946, the University of Notre Dame was not a wealthy institution. Its total endowment was only $4 million, and the $200,000 a year from the Army game (worth at least $2.5 million in 1990s dollars) helped fund most of ND's athletic programs, intercollegiate and intramural. Because the school planned to continue these programs at their current size, it had to make up the lost revenue by dipping into precious reserves. President Cavanaugh thoroughly understood Notre Dame's financial situation: a businessman by training, as vice president he had overseen the school's books for six years. Therefore he showed real courage in terminating the money flow from the annual Army game.

Some of Cavanaugh's motivations were practical—the loss of institutional control over an event involving Notre Dame—but others were idealistic. He truly believed in the classical sports ideals and wanted his school identified with them, not the sordid ticket scalping and gambling of 1946. In the break with Army, he acted according to his beliefs, even though it meant a huge money loss as well as many unhappy alumni and friends of the university. An astute administrator, Cavanaugh had long recognized the tension between the commercialism of large football revenues and the classic sports ideals. What distinguished him from the officials of most other schools in big-time intercollegiate athletics was the fact that he often made decisions on the basis of the ideals, not the dollars.

West Point administrators, particularly Superintendent Maxwell Taylor in late 1946, worked in different institutional circumstances. Money was not a problem for the academy. The United States military had won World War II and had embarked upon the Cold War: American taxpayers and the Congress were grateful and willing to generously fund the Army and its institutions, particularly beloved West Point. Indeed, academy officers spoke of the financial aspect of the Notre Dame series almost disdainfully. Sports editor Stanley Woodward, who had special access at West Point, wrote: "We derive the impression from residents of the post that the game produced almost nothing but money and unpleasantness." Since the officers did not worry about the former, ending the "unpleasantness" became their priority. (This also provides insight into Army's second reason for the break with Notre Dame: West Point sought a national schedule, not for commercial reasons, but because it considered itself "America's university," and wanted to reinforce this image with coast-to-coast games.)

Part of the "unpleasantness" for the West Point officers was the postwar ferocity of the fans of both teams, particularly the ND "subway alumni" and the civilian Army supporters. World War II had changed the nature not only of football, but also of the fans. Many now rooted against opposition teams with the same monomania that they had aimed at the Axis enemy. In addition, some rooters, now that they could no longer buy war bonds, tried to show their loyalty to and faith in their favorites by backing them with heavy bets.

When he became West Point superintendent in 1945, General Maxwell Taylor was shocked by the volume and tone of letters from Fighting Irish "zealots" complaining about Army's 1944 and 1945 routs of Notre Dame. In a private note to General Dwight Eisenhower, he described how "our coaches and players are now being flooded with threatening and often scurrilous letters and postcards." Another West Point insider stated that "officers of this post have received 5,000 vicious letters" from ND fans "in the past few years," many accusing the academy of anti-Catholicism.

ND president Cavanaugh abhorred this aspect of Subway Alumni behavior, and he sympathized with General Taylor: the Golden Dome received its full portion of hate mail from anti-ND fans, many of them Army supporters. Often these fanatics denounced Catholics in general, seeing Notre Dame football as an especially evil manifestation of the Papacy; others simply attacked Frank Leahy and his current Fighting Irish.

In his letter to Eisenhower, Taylor summed up the fan situation: "In the eyes of a large portion of the public, it [the Army–Notre Dame game] pits West Point against the Catholic Church." The academy had worked hard during the war to convince the public that "it belongs to everyone in the United States," but the rivalry with Notre Dame threatened to turn a portion of the population against West Point.

The University of Notre Dame was also unhappy with the "church versus state" attitudes of some of the fans. Although it recognized the special meaning of the Fighting Irish for American Catholics, President Cavanaugh was not a parochial priest. He had worked for General Motors as a young man, and he wanted his school and its graduates to enter the American mainstream; thus the narrow bigotry of the anti–Notre Dame letters as well as the anti-Army ones upset him. Arthur Daley, close to the ND hierarchy, noted that the situation "has made Notre Dame authorities more uneasy than they've ever admitted [publicly]. But now Notre Dame doesn't need that Army fray . . . It's become an educational institution that ranks at the very top scholastically."

In case the West Point and Notre Dame officials had any doubts about the fanaticism of both schools' "subway supporters" and their hunger for tickets, the fine print of the Cavanaugh-Taylor statement sparked a reminder. The end of the text mentioned that the two football teams might play in the future "from time to time," and announced that the final game in the annual series would take place at Notre Dame Stadium in 1947. The AP noted, "Ironically, within a few minutes after the" announcement of the "series finale . . . the Notre Dame ticket office was deluged with telephone calls for tickets" from both ND and Army rooters.

Contrary to Cavanaugh and Taylor's wishes, the fans did not put down their poison pens. As Earl Blaik described in his memoirs, because many ND backers blamed him for ending the series—they claimed he feared playing Leahy's teams—a "barrage was aimed at me. 'Blaik-haters' among the Subway Alumni and their press and radio spokesmen were numerous, thunderous, and vicious." Leahy, of course, received similar mail from Army fans, but the press treated him more kindly: the ND coach emphatically opposed the break and frequently said so in public. (Recently opened West Point files reveal that "Blaik did not particularly like the idea" of concluding the series, but kept silent, going "along with the decision.")

In fact, contrary to all sports histories on the subject, neither coach played a significant role in the decision to terminate the series. President John J. Cavanaugh and Superintendent Maxwell Taylor were men who consulted their subordinates but, in the end, exercised power as they saw fit. For institutional and personal reasons, they decided to halt the most popular annual series in the history of American intercollegiate athletics. Considering the morass of ethical, financial, and other college sports problems confronting American university presidents in the postwar era, the two men acted prudently, trying to steer their institutions away from the swamps threatening other schools.

Father Cavanaugh, however, saw the college sports world more clearly than did his West Point colleague; his university also possessed an athletics policy—"Fortress Notre Dame"—that charted a definite course of action and response. On the other hand, during the previous decade, West Point's approach to intercollegiate athletics had veered from somnolence to win-at-any-cost, and neither the academy administrators nor their Army bosses had ever decided upon a clear policy. Without a mandate or even general guidelines, Taylor acted mainly in an *ad hoc* manner.

The record shows that during the half decade after the ND-Army break, Father Cavanaugh steered Notre Dame safely through the most turbulent period in college sports history. West Point under General Taylor merely avoided one crisis to drift toward another. Without a coherent athletics policy, and by permitting Blaik *carte blanche* concerning the recruiting and retention of his players, Taylor and his immediate successors allowed the academy to crash into the "cribbing scandal" of 1951, horribly scarring both the school and big-time college sports.

In terms of American universities, West Point and Notre Dame are unique. Proudly independent, each has evolved in its own way, very separate from other institutions of higher education. However, as the 1946 termination of the Army–Notre Dame annual series proved, neither school was isolated from the prevailing conditions in college sports. To understand the enormity of the postwar problems and their importance to the future of intercollegiate athletics, particularly in terms of the rise of the NCAA, it is necessary to take a step back from specific events like the Army–Notre Dame series and to examine the general state of higher education and college sports in postwar America.

17

The Black Market and
the Birth of the Modern NCAA

When it comes to chicanery, double-dealing, and undercover work
behind the scenes, bigtime college football is in a class by itself . . .

Should the Carnegie Foundation launch an investigation of college football right now, the mild breaches of etiquette uncovered [in
the 1920s] . . . would assume a remote innocence which would only
cause snickers among the post-war pirates of 1946.

—*New York Herald-Tribune* sports editor Stanley Woodward,
November 1946.

World War II changed American society in profound ways, transforming most institutions, but few more so than higher education and
intercollegiate athletics. Many private colleges, sleepy and small domains of
privilege before 1941, became large, bustling, and democratic facilities after
the war; public universities grew exponentially, expanding their clientele
from the children of the middle class to multiclass and multiage students
after 1945. The main engine of change was the GI Bill of Rights, government
funding for all former service personnel wishing to attend university, permitting an entry into higher education and subsequent economic advancement
for many men and women who had previously considered college beyond
their means.

College athletes returning from the war were eligible for the GI Bill for
the remainder of their schooling, and this created an "athletic scholarship"
system funded by Uncle Sam. Stanley Woodward noted that many minor
"football factories" began combining their standard "small benefits" with the
government's generous ones, and schools "set up players in breath-taking

style." Many big-time sports programs could assemble even larger financial packages, and intercollegiate athletics entered, as Francis Wallace wrote, "a bizarre, unsavory period . . . The Black Market."

Complicating the situation was the chaos in college sports regulations during World War II and the lack of any national governing agency—the NCAA existed, but only as an advisory group. In the aftermath of the wartime situation, players could still transfer without losing a year of eligibility, freshmen could suit up immediately, and some conferences and schools openly permitted "athletic scholarships." As a result, many programs tried to lure star athletes to their campuses with "top dollar offers" and, in turn, as Wallace stated, many players "frankly peddled their services to the highest bidder." Numerous college team payrolls reached the $100,000-a-year range. According to the coach at Oklahoma State, rival Oklahoma assembled a winning squad by paying players $200,000 per year.

After the 1945 season, the attempt by All-American halfback "Shorty" McWilliams to move from West Point to Mississippi State, his previous school, broke into print—mainly because of Earl Blaik's loud and belligerent opposition to the transfer. The Southern university made McWilliams a "particularly lucrative offer . . . of $15,000 in cash, a $300 a month vacation job, the use of a car, and employment after graduation starting at $300 a month" (a package worth at least ten times as much in 1990s dollars). Eventually, an embarrassed West Point—pounded by "Aw-Nuts" writers' accusations that it was holding McWilliams "a football captive"—allowed the player to accept the Mississippi State deal.

The case of the great runner Buddy Young also attracted press attention. An early 1940s Chicago high school star and a University of Illinois standout, Young interrupted his college career to enter the Navy; while in the service, according to a national magazine, he "got more than 25 offers" from college and NFL teams to play for them after the war. UCLA led the bidding, but Illinois topped its offer and Young eventually rejoined the Illini. The unusual aspect of his story was not the price tag on his services—almost all returning college stars received big money propositions—but his race. Young was one of the first highly recruited African American athletes. In a sense, the illegal offers to him showed that segregation was ending in intercollegiate athletics and in American society. When schools started extending the same under-the-table deals to blacks as well as whites, they indicated that the pursuit of winning tolerated no creed, class, or color lines. (However, it took another generation for Southern colleges to join the bidding wars for black athletes.)

Breaking their normal silence on illegal recruiting, classical sportswriters featured Young's case, in part because he was an African American and thus beyond the regular boundaries. Nevertheless, as the postwar corruption increased and was exposed by the "Aw-Nuts" writers, joined by traditionalists like Stanley Woodward, many classicists retreated to defensive positions, trying to cling to the old ideals and avoid the rising and fetid waters of big-time college sports.

The returning servicemen created many instant college teams. In 1945, approximately 220 schools had fielded football squads; a year later almost 650 had full rosters, with many new powerhouses emerging. In this fluid boom time, as during the Roaring Twenties, various buccaneers strode onto the college sports stage, none more flamboyant or shrewd than Paul "Bear" Bryant. His first college head-coaching job illustrated the evolution of wartime football into its wild postwar phase.

Before World War II, Bryant had played at Alabama, then worked as an assistant coach at Vanderbilt. While in the service, he became head coach at North Carolina Pre-Flight Training School, where his abilities attracted the attention of University of Maryland officials. Maryland's president, H. C. "Curly" Byrd, had started his administrative career at the school as its football coach, and he wanted to build his institution into a postwar athletic power. During the summer of 1945, Byrd hired Bryant, but a week before the September opening game, Bear still had not shown up. A phone call to North Carolina revealed that Bryant had just received his military discharge and that he would leave in a day or so for Maryland. The school official remarked, "You can't hope to assemble a team by next Saturday" for the opener. Bear replied, "We won't have to assemble a team. I'm bringing one with me."

Bryant then piled a large contingent from his Navy Pre-Flight squad onto a bus, arriving the next day at College Park, Maryland, where, according to a 1950s article, "the young men double-timed to the registrar's office, enrolled as GI scholars, ate an early lunch, and reported" for practice. Five days later, they won the opener, 60-6, and began a successful season for the school. Bryant later boasted that each of his Navy veterans received "a double scholarship," the school's regular athletic grant plus the GI bill, "and that meant" a bundle of "extra money for them."

In 1946, in nearby Washington, D.C., the president of American University, Paul F. Douglas (later a U.S. senator) noted the events at Maryland and throughout postwar college football, and declined to enter his school in the big-time sports derby: "Post war college football has no relation to higher education . . . [Currently] a football player is nothing more than a human slave in the biggest black market operation in the history of higher education." Like many college sports critics, Douglas ignored the fact that most of the so-called slaves greatly enjoyed their status as well as their unprecedented high wages; however, he did indicate the growing unease of the higher education mandarins with the postwar situation in intercollegiate athletics.

■　■　■

In the years after the war, a marked increase [occurs] in transcontinental recruiting and intersectional scheduling . . . [and] a proliferation of postseason bowl games, with college teams competing intensively to gain invitations to one of these lucrative events . . . [Also] the G.I. Bill of Rights makes available millions of dollars [for college athletes] . . . The temptations [for recruiters] to "sweeten the pot" are obvious.

The NCAA, reacting to these fast-developing postwar changes, calls a special Conference of Conferences to meet in Chicago, July 22–23, 1946.

—NCAA official historian Jack Falla, 1981.

The first group to respond to the postwar crisis in college sports was not university presidents but athletic officials, particularly Kenneth "Tug" Wilson, the new commissioner of the Big Ten, and a number of his fellow conference heads from the West Coast and New England. Wilson invited them as well as selected university administrators and faculty representatives to a meeting in Chicago in July 1946 to discuss the deteriorating situation in intercollegiate athletics. As secretary of the NCAA, Wilson saw a role for that long docile group to play in the reform process; the NCAA at this time, according to one observer, was "a singularly toothless organization that contented itself with vague resolutions commending amateurism."

The official history of the NCAA places the association at the center of the July 1946 events; in fact, the conference commissioners, particularly Wilson, were the prime movers, and, for various ulterior motives, they proposed the NCAA as an umbrella agency for the regulation of college sports. In his opening speech, Wilson asked the conference officials, all of whose schools also belonged to the NCAA, to decide whether the association's "role was that of a 'recommending agency' or 'a policeman.' " Wilson considered the former—the NCAA's historic position—outdated because of the "tremendous increase" of shady practices in college sports, and the danger of intercollegiate athletics becoming a "semi-pro business." He suggested that the NCAA embark upon "an enforced policy of amateurism."

Most of the forty-two delegates approved the general concept—Wilson offered few specifics—and, on July 23, 1946, the modern NCAA was born. The association's official history contains no hint of the mixed and self-interested motives of the prime movers at that meeting. Because Tug Wilson owed his loyalty to and received his main paycheck from the Big Ten, his condemnation of the postwar "mess" reflected that league's discontent with the activities of competing conferences, particularly their poaching of recruits from the fertile midwestern football and basketball region. According to Wilson, often "plane loads of fine prospects . . . would be flown from the Big Ten area to other parts of the country and given most unusual entertainment," meaning nonstop party weekends as well as large cash offers and, in the South and Southwest, generous athletic scholarships. This further complicated Wilson's job as commissioner of the Big Ten because "naturally, the result of these raids was a step-up in our recruiting," as well as illegal activity "by alumni and coaches to keep our boys home." An arms race was beginning not only in the Cold War but also among competing athletic powers. The results included both escalating payments to athletes and better on-campus facilities than the competition could provide.

Money, often in the form of the illusory pot o' gold, had long driven college sports, and the postwar era exhibited the full range of financial problems. For most schools, no matter how many dollars came in from the increasing gate receipts and radio revenue, expenses spiraled even higher, usually propelled by recruiting costs. Tug Wilson termed the postwar period the "Era of Field Houses and Indoor Facilities." Many of his Big Ten members as well as competitors across the country erected new arenas for their booming basketball programs, modern training rooms for their football teams, and special living quarters for athletes, which were soon nicknamed "jock dorms."

In addition, many Big Ten and other schools greatly increased the capacity of their stadiums, and some of the latecomers to big-time football erected new ones. In spite of the postwar popularity of intercollegiate athletics, almost every participating school was losing money, leading one economist to conclude that the main motivation for the July 1946 meeting was "to cut costs" by reducing "competition for student-athletes among schools," i.e., to establish a set of rules on college sports, notably on recruiting expenses and remuneration to athletes; empower a national organization—the NCAA—to enforce the rules; and, by means of this "economic cartel," manage to "control costs" and achieve profitability.

Another area of concern to the organizers of the 1946 meeting was the proliferating bowl games and the problems they presented for the college sports establishment. The Big Ten, long claiming the greatest purity in intercollegiate athletics, had shunned the bowls since the early 1920s, regarding them as overly commercial and anathema to student athletics because they took too much time away from classroom studies. By 1946, college sports officials, including Tug Wilson, had observed the rise of such renegade but successful programs as the University of Tulsa Hurricanes, helped considerably by their participation in the Sugar Bowl in 1943 and 1944 and the Orange Bowl in 1945. However, Wilson's solution was not to ban bowl games, as most reformers suggested, but for the Big Ten to participate in them and for the NCAA to regulate the bowls, excluding the "outlaw" schools whenever possible, and making the New Year's Day events more profitable for the establishment. That fall, he led the Big Ten into negotiations for a long-term Rose Bowl contract using the argument that "the proposed agreement would prevent Southern schools from cutting into the Rose Bowl melon"—many had appeared in the game during the previous two decades—"and perhaps cajole them into altering their views on collegiate amateurism." Like his successors in the NCAA leadership, Wilson was a master at weaving self-interest into supposed reform measures, knotting the two so tight that the observer could not begin to tell where self-interest ended—if it ever did—and reform began.

The University of Tulsa and similar programs represented the worst nightmare of the college sports establishment, not only because of their bowl successes and athletic scholarships but, even more threatening, on account of their public flouting of the traditional ideals. Funded by oil men boosters who openly bragged about their cash payments to Hurricane players, Tulsa quickly earned the reputation, according to Stanley Woodward, of "a fine semi-pro club," stocked mainly with tramp athletes "whose eligibility wouldn't pass muster" at most schools. As Bear Bryant's Navy Pre-Flight/Maryland squad also illustrated, the disdain for even the pretense of student-based college sports was increasing, and the situation was attracting "Aw-Nuts" press attention. In a national magazine article, Woodward recounted the academic career of a typical player at "dear old Indian Territory Tech," Tulsa: "He was told that he could go to classes, or not, as he wished, but that he must be at football practice every afternoon at 2:30. He played very well in one of the bowls, incidentally."

The Big Ten—officially "The Intercollegiate Athletic Conference of Faculty Representatives"—had long insisted that its athletes were authentic students, and that faculty members controlled the conference as well as the athletic departments of the member schools. With this premise, Tug Wilson maneuvered Professor Karl Leib, Iowa's faculty representative, into the chair of the July 1946 NCAA meeting and also placed the academic issue on the agenda. (In fact, early in Big Ten history, the coaches and athletic directors had gained, and forever after retained, actual power in the conference, not only on their individual campuses but also in the commissioner's office. John Griffith, the first commissioner, had been a coach and athletic director, as had Wilson, for over twenty years at Northwestern.)

■   ■   ■

Delegates to this midsummer [1946] Conference of Conferences draw up the first draft of a statement entitled "Principles for the Conduct of Intercollegiate Athletics," which will prove to be one of the most influential documents ever written by the Association . . .

The principles concern adherence to the definition of amateurism, the holding of *student-athletes* to the same "sound academic standards" as those of the student body, the awarding of financial aid "on the basis of qualifications of which athletic ability is not one," and a policy of recruiting that basically prohibits a coach or anyone representing a member institution from soliciting attendance "of any prospective student with the offer of financial aid or equivalent inducement."

—NCAA official historian Jack Falla, 1981.

The organizers of the NCAA's first move toward national control of college sports, particularly Tug Wilson, always claimed that idealism motivated them. Whether the idealism was real or feigned, Wilson's strategy in 1946 was to link the NCAA and all of its members to the classic ideal of the amateur sportsman—hence "The Principles for the Conduct of Intercollegiate Athletics," with their conscious connection to the nineteenth-century "Gentleman's Code" on sports participation as well as to twentieth-century representations of amateur athletics.

Significantly, even though the NCAA official history uses the term "student-athletes" in its narrative of the 1946 events, at the time the phrase was unknown. (NCAA executive director Walter Byers invented it in 1953 to help member schools fight workmen's compensation claims by injured football players; see page 445.) The 1946 articulation of the amateur ideal subsequently evolved into the primary articles in the NCAA's constitution, which incorporated the student-athlete rhetoric and served as the premise of the association's rule book.

Tug Wilson strikes the modern observer as a quintessential college sports administrator, presenting a public persona very distant from his behind-the-scenes operations. As the main mover of the 1946 meeting, Wilson possessed detailed knowledge of the dark side of college sports, but his statements to the press were high-minded and optimistic: "We must set up a policy whereby a boy will choose a school for its educational value rather than the school choosing a boy for his athletic ability." As his memoir later made clear, his previous two decades in intercollegiate athletics had taught him the futility of this goal, but, in 1946, his desire to envelop the NCAA in the amateur ideal allowed him to issue such statements with a straight face.

In July 1946, however, Wilson overreached by encouraging the press to call the "Principles" "The Purity Code," implying that it would transform the cesspool of postwar college sports into a "pure" place. The term "Purity Code" prompted scorn from "Aw-Nuts" journalists, which escalated along with the corruption in college sports. Eventually, Wilson switched to the more appropriate "Sanity Code," suggesting that the authorities would bring sanity to an out-of-control situation.

Beyond the propaganda, Tug Wilson had major tactical problems: he had to move a large, diverse constituency—all the schools in big-time college sports, many stubbornly independent, others belonging to regional fiefdoms—to a common purpose and some basic agreement. Significantly, at the end of his opening speech, rather than appeal to the delegates' idealism, he used fear, advocating an "enforced policy of amateurism" because "it's either that or something will come up like another Carnegie report or a conflict with academic accrediting agencies."

Wilson's warning referred to the attempt by the Carnegie Foundation and its allies to reform college sports in the late 1920s and early 1930s. Most delegates would have remembered those events as well as the lucky break for intercollegiate athletics: the Great Depression had removed the college sports issue from the national agenda, forcing Americans to focus on much more important matters. However, as Wilson warned, in prosperous postwar America, big-time intercollegiate athletics would not escape so easily.

Wilson's solution to the current crisis—a strategy that became the *modus operandi* of the NCAA—was damage control: acknowledge the seriousness of the situation, try to curb the most visible abuses, punish the worst miscreants, but do not address the fundamental contradictions in the system. In other words, should and can institutions of higher education run huge sports entertainment businesses? If the NCAA and member conferences and schools endorsed the classic ideal, embodied in the "Principles," the basic contradictions would slip from view, papered over by the rhetoric on student-based college sports. To move his plan along, Wilson proposed that the "Principles" be sent to all NCAA members for their input, and that the schools and conferences vote on them at the next annual meeting of the association, in January 1947. Most delegates enthusiastically accepted this proposal and left Chicago to proselytize for the "Principles."

The press reaction to the conclusion of the meeting must have pleased Wilson. The AP offered a typical lead: "Twenty of the nation's college conferences today threw a haymaker at campus athletic commercialism, recommending sharp restrictions on financial aid and recruiting of athletes." However, a few writers dissented. Arch Ward in his *Chicago Tribune* column noted, "It is one thing to preach high standards. It is something else to practice them. College sport, especially football, is shot thru with hypocrisy. In many cases it is an out and out professional enterprise under an amateur cloak." This important friend of big-time college sports was moving away from his staunchly classical public stance—prompted in large part by Notre Dame criticism of the Big Ten–NCAA proposals (see Chapter 19). Ward had covered Big Ten athletics for many years, and he had also participated in the conference's squabbles with Notre Dame. Almost all of the disputes began with a Big Ten accusation that ND was cheating in recruiting or in its on-campus treatment of football players, whereupon Notre Dame would respond by providing the commissioner with lengthy documentary proofs that its athletes were closer to the classic ideal than those of any of its Big Ten accusers—and throughout, Ward would offer his private opinions on "Big Ten hypocrisy."

In July 1946, Ward went public with his comments: he viewed with skepticism the proclamations coming from the recent NCAA meeting in his city, but because of the dire postwar circumstances—"It [college football] unquestionably will die if the present trend continues"—he hoped that the NCAA "plan . . . will save a sport which has contributed more to the virility of the nation than any other contact game."

Ward also predicted that the NCAA's lofty "Principles" would encounter the reality of postwar college sports at the association's January 1947 national convention. At that meeting, the leadership would ask the entire membership to embrace the 1946 proposals, and Arch Ward, as well as other observers, suspended further judgment until the results were in.

18

The NCAA's "Principle of Amateurism"

1. *Principle of Amateurism*—An amateur sportsman is one who engages in sports for the physical, mental or social benefits he derives therefrom, and to whom the sport is an avocation. Any college athlete who takes pay for participation in athletics does not meet this definition of amateurism.

—From the NCAA's *"Principles for the Conduct of Intercollegiate Athletics,"* 1947.

The press covered the January 1947 annual meeting of the NCAA much more extensively than it had any previous gathering of the association. The *New York Times* ran a banner headline on its first sports page: "Firm Stand Urged to Stop Recruiting and Subsidization in College Sports." The paper's longtime football writer, Allison Danzig, called the NCAA's effort "the most significant step toward a general purging of the evils of recruiting and subsidization in the recent history of amateur athletics," and he termed the "Principles" much "more than a mere reaffirmation of glittering generalities."

The first principle, as well as subsequent ones on financial aid and illegal recruiting, created controversy at the convention for what they did not state but implied: in defining college athletes as pure amateurs, they banned the open athletic scholarships popular in the South and Southwest. One economic historian saw this subtext as the association's real agenda in the "Purity Code," terming it "the NCAA's strongest effort to date to eliminate the cut-throat [money] competition among its members for student-athletes" and a crucial step toward establishing the NCAA as "an economic cartel."

Indeed, the convention debate mainly concerned strategy on how best to create the cartel. Delegates supporting the "Purity Code" advocated a total ban on athletic scholarships as the best tactic, whereas their opponents considered this approach impractical and wrongheaded. Spokesmen from schools offering athletic grants argued that prohibiting them would not turn athletes into amateurs; instead, the ban would remove all control of payments from university authorities, resulting in alumni and boosters becoming the paymasters and escalating the practice of cash-for-jocks. Some of the opponents were remarkably outspoken: Dr. W. D. Funkhouser, the University of Kentucky faculty representative and the secretary of the Southeastern Conference, told the convention and the press that bans on paying money to athletes and recruiting "never had been adhered to and never would be, and could not be enforced." (Considering the involvement of his school's boosters, coaches, and players in the late-1940s scandals in basketball and football, his comments seem to presage coming events.)

At the 1947 meeting, the controversial prohibitions on athletic scholarships and recruiting passed by a 76-33 vote; the size of the opposition foreshadowed future discord on these issues. In addition, as the Kentucky delegate indicated, key questions on how to enforce the "Principles" remained unanswered. The AP quoted an NCAA insider as wondering whether "the code should be enforced by gentleman's agreement or a commissioner of college athletics. The official said he believed that there was little likelihood of the latter." Tug Wilson advocated a third way: "ostracization" of schools violating the code, i.e., members in good standing would drop offenders from their athletic schedules, and if the violators persisted in breaking the rules, the NCAA would ban them from the organization and big-time college sports.

Nevertheless, some sports commentators called for a commissioner, a "Judge Landis" to administer intercollegiate athletics. The autocratic Landis had cleaned up major league baseball after the Black Sox scandal, and *Sport* magazine—an immediate success after its launch in 1946—headlined an editorial on college sports with WANTED: THE LANDIS SPIRIT, sermonizing, "When your own house is in a mess, you don't call in the neighbors"—schools also cheating in college sports—"and ask them to clean it up for you." For many observers, the enforcement issue provided a test of the NCAA's true willingness to reform college sports. When the association did not even debate the question at this meeting, a number of "Aw-Nuts" journalists, joined by traditionalists like Arch Ward, charged it with "massive hypocrisy."

NCAA DEFERS ACTIONS ON BOWL CONTESTS

—*Chicago Tribune* headline, January 1947.

After agreeing to the "Principles for the Conduct of Intercollegiate Athletics," the NCAA members "deferred action on a surprise proposal to outlaw all bowl and post-season football games." The head of the Virginia Military Institute proposed the ban, and the delegates, rather than drain one of the worst swamps in postwar college sports, sent the VMI proposal to committee oblivion. In many ways, this maneuver said more about the NCAA's real desire to clean up college sports than did the "Principles."

The argument against bowl games, outlined by the VMI head and detailed by other reformers, was clear: bowl events occurred far from the natural campus settings for college sports; they were highly commercial and run by professional promoters; they required a great amount of extra training and travel for the college athletes involved; and they caused many ancillary problems, including gambling and ticket scalping. A few universities, notably Notre Dame, refused all bowl invitations for these reasons, but because of the rising expenses of big-time college sports, most schools pursued bowl bids and the supposedly large payouts that came with them. In the postwar era, almost sixty bowl games existed, among them the Glass Bowl in Toledo, Ohio, the Vulcan Bowl in Birmingham, Alabama, the Yam Bowl in Dallas, Texas, and the Papoose Bowl in Oklahoma City. Some only lasted for a holiday season or two, but every year in this period at least forty bowls operated.

In reality, the bowls ran a huge financial shell game. The top tier—Rose, Sugar, Orange, and Cotton—paid well, but almost all of the others kept most of the revenue or never made any. Furthermore, according to a *Collier's* investigation, even though all of the bowls claimed that they "are conducted for the benefit of local charities . . . the [bowl] contributions to charities are inconsequential. Figures revealed that only $5,000, or .003 per cent of the gross receipts had been donated to charity by 16 bowls in 1947." The other bowl games that year "refused to submit financial statements for audit," apparently because they gave nothing to charity.

Yet athletic directors fell for the con, often sending their team to more than one bowl game in the same year. After the 1948 season, Hardin-Simmons in Texas, attempting to jump from obscurity to big-time football, went to the Grape Bowl in Lodi, California, then the Camellia Bowl in Orlando, Florida, and finally the Arkansas Shrine Bowl in Little Rock, denying the players any semblance of final exam week or a Christmas holiday. In addition, the public believed that colleges made huge amounts of money from bowl appearances. In a typical expression of this myth, one fan wrote *Sport,* "Where else can they [universities] get that much money to aid them in building a new school or adding to the old one?" But the actual payouts from most bowls were negligible or nonexistent.

One group profited from bowl games: the promoters, meaning the members of the bowl committees. Not only did lots of cash, particularly from advertising and radio revenue, stick to their fingers but ancillary benefits flowed their way as well. When the Rose Bowl signed up the Big Ten for a long-term pact, shutting out southern and southwestern schools, one sportswriter noted that the deal assisted the California land developers on and behind the bowl committee because "more real estate can be sold, and at higher prices, to people from the Middle West [moving to California] than to the yokels from Dixie."

Bowl committee members also kept huge blocks of tickets for their own use, giving some to clients and friends but also selling many to scalpers. As a result, according to one authority, "Most of the [major] bowl games have, as their chief by-product, juicy ticket scandals." The 1947 Rose Bowl game was typical of the postwar ticket outrages. According to a Los Angeles sportswriter, the committee printed "89,000 plus tickets," but hoarded so many that it announced a sale of only 7,000 to the public. A large crowd lined up at the stadium, but when the box office opened, "only 746 [fans] received the coveted pasteboards," a maximum of two per customer. A riot ensued, during which, among other incidents, "a ten-year-old boy had his clothes partially torn off and his ticket taken away." The committee later acknowledged that it had kept 17,200 seats for its own use, but a press investigation doubled that number.

The Rose Bowl ticket scandal occurred a month before the 1947 NCAA "Purity Code" meeting; nevertheless, when the head of VMI argued that banning all bowl games would, in a simple and effective way, greatly aid the cleanup of college sports, NCAA leaders and delegates swatted aside his proposal. A further analysis of the 1947 Rose Bowl ticket allocation suggests why: more than 12,500 tickets went to Big Ten universities, with the best seats for their administrators and important alumni; another 36,000 went to Pacific Conference school administrators, alumni, faculty, and students, again with the best seats going to the VIPs; and 5,000 seats went to newspaper and radio personnel, to sell or to give to family and friends (the media also received free passes to report the game). Therefore, many university and media people—architects of intercollegiate athletics policy and of public opinion—received highly coveted tickets to the Rose Bowl game. Multiply the Pasadena system by forty other bowls across the country and it is not hard to understand why the VMI proposal to ban postseason games was a NCAA nonstarter.

Among those who attended the 1947 Rose Bowl and then went on to the NCAA meeting were Big Ten commissioner Tug Wilson and the new NCAA president, Karl Leib. Although fully aware of the ticket scalping and commercialism of bowl games, they had no sympathy for the VMI proposal either. Wilson had just completed years of lobbying his conference schools to end the Big Ten ban on bowl games and to sign a long-term Rose Bowl contract. His main motivation and arguments concerned money: because of the Rose Bowl's prominence, a large payout existed in Pasadena, ironically, mainly for the conference schools *not* making the trip.

To help persuade Big Ten members to end their bowl ban, Wilson had conceived of a way for all to share the spoils: a twelve-way split of the visiting team's payout, each member and the commissioner's office receiving one share, the participating team getting an extra one. In November 1946, with Karl Leib also lobbying the presidents and faculty representatives, Wilson gained a majority for the pact (West Point's agreement to play in the 1947 game pushed the issue to a final Big Ten vote). As Wilson suspected but did not mention before the ballot, the twelve-way split meant that the university appearing in the Rose Bowl, thanks to the major expenses from its huge traveling party, including school administrators, would *lose* money on the event. As examples, for the 1947 game, Illinois received $15,000 and spent $21,000, and a year later, Michigan's share was $18,000 while its costs were $32,000! (A half century later, this phenomenon continues, except that schools going to bowl games now lose hundreds of thousands of dollars; moreover, the administrators are still on the gravy trains—now charter jets—happily supporting their local athletic programs, complicit in the waste.)

At the NCAA convention in 1947, Wilson and Leib, with their Rose Bowl bias and experiences, also reacted negatively when the president of the University of Minnesota, Dr. J. L. Morrill, endorsed the VMI proposal. According to press reports, "Dr. Morrill entered rather emphatic objections to post-season bowl games" and "expressed disappointment that the [Big Ten] conference had seen fit to succumb to the bowl craze." Minnesota had opposed the Rose Bowl pact throughout the negotiations: Morrill had clashed with Wilson and Leib, always taking the moral high ground. At the final vote in November 1946, Minnesota was one of two nays. When the other dissenter, Illinois, received the bid to the 1947 Rose Bowl, Minnesota remained the lone opponent, and its president retained his public role as a leading spokesman for the reform of big-time college sports.

■ ■ ■

We have no [athletic] scholarships; we have no subsidies; and we are proud of it. The only thing that we do for any athlete is to procure him a part-time job at a recognized business in Minneapolis or St. Paul.

—University of Minnesota official Chester R. Roan,
December 1947.

Mr. Roan admits his university gets jobs for athletes . . . *If this isn't aid, then I'd like to know what is.* Does the university get jobs [like these] for other students?

—*Sport* magazine writer Dan Parker, December 1947.

The Morrill-Wilson-Leib nexus, each man representing a pivotal role in intercollegiate athletics, illustrates the difficulty of truly reforming college sports. In 1947, each called publicly for total "purification" of intercollegiate athletics, but, each had a separate agenda that conflicted with and undermined his reformist line.

Dr. J. L. Morrill, the university president, took the most high-minded position of the three, yet his own athletic department openly operated a jobs-for-jocks program as well as a semipublic network of alumni recruiters—clear violations of the NCAA's "Principles for the Conduct of Intercollegiate Athletics." Moreover, the Big Ten considered jobs-for-jocks legal—even though most positions involved minimal or no work and were funded by boosters. Possibly Morrill did not regard the "Job Plan," his conference's official term for the practice, as duplicitous, but because writers like Dan Parker discussed it in national magazines, and anti–Big Ten schools, particularly those giving open athletic scholarships, screamed about "Big Ten hypocrisy," Morrill could not have remained oblivious. Nevertheless, in his speeches, he never focused on such sordid details as the jobs-for-jocks policy in Minneapolis and St. Paul: instead, he offered lofty rhetoric. Possibly, like many university presidents, he wanted to reform other schools first and then have changes occur, somehow by osmosis, at his institution. In any event, Morrill's speeches remained words in the air, never bringing about real changes at his university or any other.

Tug Wilson, the conference commissioner, also supported the Big Ten Job Plan, particularly because it provided his schools with a crucial recruiting weapon. Wilson wanted to make his athletic programs as strong and rich as possible, and he never acknowledged the basic conflict between the Big Ten's increasingly commercialized college sports programs—money-seeking machines that he helped construct—and the classic "Principles" of amateur athletics in the NCAA charter that he helped write. His actions during this period defined his goals: Wilson never opposed the open athletic scholarships and under-the-table payments offered by competing conferences and schools for ethical reasons, but because they formed roadblocks to Big Ten dominance of, and greater revenue from, big-time college sports. However, to view Wilson as narrowly cynical is to underestimate his ability to wrap his political goals in the language of classic college sports, and to sell that line to the public.

Professor Karl Leib, the faculty representative, wrote much of the "Purity Code." As an academic, he should have insisted on actual reform—particularly as a means to prevent athletic departments from embroiling their host universities in scandals—but, like Wilson, he embraced the language of reform, not the substance. Leib, unlike Wilson, could have played a disinterested role in the governance of college sports: as a tenured faculty member, his job and salary were secure, totally separate from the promotion of intercollegiate athletics. Yet, like most faculty representatives, he was a "jock sniffer," infatuated by coaches and athletes, and willing to do his athletic department's bidding. (University presidents have long appointed "jock-sniffing" academics to faculty rep positions to ensure their compliance with—not their oversight of—the local athletic department.) Leib represented his species well and, as a result, became titular head of the NCAA during this crucial period in its history.

One item connected these men: their rhetoric about the classic ideal in college sports. The minutes of the 1947 NCAA convention contain lengthy samples of their high-principled speeches, but their utterances exist at such an immense distance from the actual conditions of postwar college sports nationally and within their own conferences and schools that the reader wonders whether these men were naive, self-deluded, or cynical. Considering their speeches within the context of their inaction on reform in their home bailiwicks, cynicism is the likeliest answer.

■　■　■

In one of his speeches at the 1947 NCAA convention, Dr. Morrill warned about the threat of a gambling scandal involving college sports, and offered concrete proposals to combat it. Again, his comments appear reformist and high-minded, and yet the largest bookmaking operation in the United States was situated near his university, employing many local people, including some of his own students, and he never attempted to have it closed down. The "Minneapolis Syndicate" established and published the point spreads on all college sports contests in the country, selling its services to almost every bookie joint in America. By 1947, it totally dominated the field. But at the 1947 NCAA convention, Dr. Morrill spoke with passion against the threat posed to college sports by gambling.

> The possibility of a devastating betting scandal hovers like a black harpy over the bigtime intercollegiate athletic scene. College basketball has been brushed by its dirty black wing [Brooklyn College in 1945]; professional football has smelled its foul breath [before the 1946 NFL championship game]. Intercollegiate football is ripe for the kill. If it comes, it will shake the big stadiums to their foundations.

Accompanying his warning, Dr. Morrill offered a number of specific suggestions: colleges should withhold all information that could aid bettors, for instance on player injuries; schools should send sports publicity only to "legitimate publications"—mainstream newspapers and magazines, not betting sheets; and coaches should cease their print and radio "prediction features." However, like the proposal to ban bowl games, Morrill's recommendations on combating the postwar gambling craze never made the "Purity Code" list, nor did he enforce them at his own university.

Nevertheless, aid on the gambling problem began to come from a number of major newspapers, including the *Los Angeles Times,* when they stopped publishing the point spreads on college games. But many other papers continued to run the betting lists—usually receiving them by wire from the "Minneapolis Syndicate"—and schools still sent their athletic teams to major urban stadiums and arenas, including Madison Square Garden with its wide open gambling and substantiated reports of fixed games (see Chapter 30). In addition, the NCAA refused to move its men's basketball tournament finals from the Garden and, at its next meeting, a large majority of members endorsed this venue. NCAA president Karl Leib explained that "the need for revenue was paramount at the present time," and the men's basketball championship, notably the games at Madison Square Garden, "were the NCAA's chief source of income last year, contributing a total of $57,635 to the coffers."

The discrepancy between the NCAA's espousal of pure amateurism and its actions concerned a number of observers. The *Washington Post*'s Shirley Povich noted that that "there's hardly a college that has subscribed [in practice] to the lofty procedures they have outlined" in the NCAA, moreover, "as long as the colleges hire high-powered publicity staffs to drum up public interest in their football and basketball games, they are setting them up as a betting medium." The contradiction was obvious: the NCAA and member schools talked classic amateurism but they acted in the most mercantile manner. Schools wanted to attract more fans, increasing gate and radio revenue, and yet they would not admit that many of the new as well as longtime fans attended or listened to the games primarily because they had bet on them. The NCAA and the schools constantly chased the fans' dollars, even into the gamblers' palace, Madison Square Garden. But officially they deplored gambling.

Finally, though the NCAA leadership, particularly Wilson and Leib, claimed to be reformers, they never confronted the contradictions in big-time college sports. And many of their critics within the NCAA, like President Morrill of Minnesota, talked even greater change, but never walked toward it on their own campuses. Still, these were the acknowledged reformers. In opposition to them stood many men like Curly Byrd, the president of the University of Maryland, pouring money into their openly corrupt athletic programs and unwilling to alter them in any way. With this cast of characters in charge of intercollegiate athletics in the late 1940s, not surprisingly it slid toward its worst crisis.

A few schools acted independently, trying to protect themselves. Though located in New York and lacking a viable arena on campus, Fordham refused to play at Madison Square Garden. Notre Dame curtailed its visits to the

Garden and turned down an invitation to the 1947 NCAA men's basketball tournament there. In retrospect, the presidents of these institutions showed a wisdom and a courage that most of their colleagues lacked. In actually putting principles ahead of payouts, they moved their schools far from the impending scandals in college sports, events that no amount of "Purity Code" rhetoric would cover up.

19

Notre Dame Reacts to
the NCAA's "Purity Code"

The type of reformers I refer to are those who play with the question
for public consumption, who seem to say that an indefinable something has to be done in a way nobody knows how, at a time nobody
knows when, in places nobody knows where, to accomplish nobody
knows what. I wonder if there are not grounds to suspect that the
reformers . . . protest too much, that their zeal may be an excuse for
their own negligence in reforming themselves . . . true reform in athletics will not be accomplished by the mere publishing of noble, high-
sounding codes which are often hypocritically evaded in actual
practice.

—Notre Dame president John J. Cavanaugh, January 1947.

Father Cavanaugh commented on the NCAA "Purity Code" in a speech at
a banquet honoring the 1946 Notre Dame national championship football team: the wire services carried the text of his talk, and many newspapers
across the country printed long excerpts from it. As a practical man who daily
confronted and attempted to solve real-world problems, he was offended by
the never-never-land of the NCAA "Purity Code." As a cleric and a university
administrator who sought consistency in words and actions, he disliked the
distance between the reformers' rhetoric and the actual situations within
their conferences and schools. Cavanaugh had long endorsed the classic
ideals in college sports, and annually he turned down large sums of money
offered by the major bowls. (The Sugar Bowl had made an $80,000 bid to ND
to play in its 1947 game.) Two weeks before his speech, he had helped terminate the largest guaranteed annual payday in American college sports history

up to that time: the ND-Army series at Yankee Stadium. He believed that no one could accuse him and his school of a disparity between word and deed.

The ND president also saw a hidden agenda in the work of Tug Wilson and his colleagues. A South Bend sportswriter sympathetic to Notre Dame interpreted this part of the speech: "Father Cavanaugh used polite language in referring to the pious hypocrites—some of them in the finger pointing Big Ten—who have recently adopted, or reaffirmed, a code of ethics which they have no intention of adhering to, and which has never been adhered to by any of them, among whom are many who are always 'wondering' about Notre Dame."

"Wondering" usually took the form of letters to the Golden Dome from the commissioner passing on accusations of ND cheating in college sports. Because this Big Ten dance with the Catholic school had gone on for a half century, why did Cavanaugh speed up the music immediately after the NCAA vote on the "Purity Code"? In the past, Notre Dame presidents usually responded to "wondering" by sending documentary rebuttals to the commissioner; then, if they were angry enough, they asked Arch Ward and/or other journalists on the ND network to step onto the dance floor and print some "blind items" in their papers about Big Ten cheating.

However, in January 1947, Father Cavanaugh was annoyed not only at the hypocrisy embedded in the "Purity Code," but also by the recent refusals by some of the most important Big Ten schools to schedule football games with the Fighting Irish. Illinois and Wisconsin, who had played ND during the previous seasons, declined future matches; Ohio State and Minnesota rejected all proposed games; and powerful Michigan had returned to its traditional anti-ND hostility. To Father Cavanaugh, these rebuffs suggested Tug Wilson's strategy of "ostracization" in action and, within that context, they implied that the Catholic school was violating the "Purity Code." Conference officials had already planted this idea in the press; one Chicago columnist quoted an unidentified Big Ten insider as stating that "unless they [ND] do some tall de-emphasizing at South Bend [immediately] . . . by 1949 the Irish will have a schedule made up for the most part of elevens [from] inferior" universities. The Notre Dame president suspected that the Big Ten campaign would escalate, so he fired back before public attitudes hardened.

Part of Notre Dame's problem in 1947, and for the next few years, was its overwhelming success on the football field. Winning, particularly in Frank Leahy's relentless manner, made enemies. It also caused many potential opponents to avoid scheduling ND, but without admitting that fear of losing was their main motivation—better to say that the "Purity Code" made them do it. (To their credit, a few Big Ten members continued to play Notre Dame through the Leahy years, but these schools, particularly Purdue and Iowa, had historically excellent relations with ND, and their games with the Fighting Irish greatly pleased their alumni, fans, and the local media.)

For Father Cavanaugh, part of the Big Ten's hypocrisy was the accusation that Notre Dame exhibited a win-at-any-costs attitude juxtaposed to the accusers' obsession with winning and willingness to commit major "Purity Code" violations to do so. When Illinois, with Buddy Young and other "semi-pro" athletes in their lineup, played Notre Dame in 1946, the Illini certainly sought victory. That the Big Ten team lost 26-6 did not indicate to Cavanaugh that ND was more obsessed with winning and/or cheating, only that Frank Leahy benefited from the unique and legal Fighting Irish recruiting system and also outcoached Illinois's Ray Eliot.

In his address honoring the football team, the ND president confronted the "winning" problem directly: "We at Notre Dame make no apologies about wanting winners. We want our students to go out and win in debates," and in sports, "and in the much more important battles in life. We shall always want Notre Dame men to win so long as there is a Notre Dame. But with even more emphasis, we want Notre Dame men to win cleanly and according to the rules."

After the war, the Notre Dame official began to preach this credo, and his protégé and successor, Father Theodore Hesburgh, reaffirmed it during his long tenure as ND president. Cavanaugh linked the dictum to the classic ideal, stating: "The American people worship a winner so long as he wins honestly and according to the rules . . . It must be remembered that the American way tolerates no penalty on success or winning provided success is achieved according to the principles of fair play."

With this formulation, however, Father Cavanaugh articulated a major shift in the concept of winning in college sports. In the proclamations of the classic ideal before World War II, sportsmanship—Grantland Rice's "how you played the game"—prevailed over "whether you won or lost." By 1947, the total-victory ethos of the war effort had so permeated American life and sports that a heavy emphasis on winning was now acceptable—as long as one achieved it "cleanly and according to the rules."

In his speech, the ND president also praised his football coach "for his extraordinary success in holding a team up to a high standard of perfection week after week, Leahy deserves to be ranked with the peerless Rockne." Adding the concept of perfectionism to winning was also new—traditionally, amateurs approached sports in a casual, fun-loving manner—but Cavanaugh cleverly tied this to the past with the reference to Rockne. Having been a student at the school in the 1920s, he referred both to the historical Knute Rockne, a true perfectionist, and to the cinematic coach in *Knute Rockne—All-American* who drilled his players in the intricacies of his shift formation. Like many protean heroes, the various forms of Rockne could serve multiple purposes and eras.

Father Cavanaugh's articulation of a perfectionist approach to winning marked a definite break with the past, but one that expressed the feelings of many people in the late 1940s. Moreover, his Fighting Irish football team came to embody his words: they did not lose a single game for almost five years, from December 1945 until October 1950, and became a symbol of this new ethos to millions of Americans.

Within the college sports pantheon, Knute Rockne—in his prewar and now postwar manifestations—represented the ideal. During the January 1947 controversy, some sportswriters also saw Frank Leahy and Father John J. Cavanaugh as classic figures. One Boston columnist drew parallels between their careers, emphasizing their hardscrabble childhoods (echoing the tropes in the Rockne biography and movie) and concluding: "Nobody knowing the background of these two men should be surprised, therefore, that they do not apologize for victories fairly won . . . They won their individual ways to the positions they now hold against the most burdensome of odds. Theirs is a story that is as old as our native land, and it would be strange indeed if these two did not wish to indoctrinate the students and athletes at Notre Dame with the same will to win in the battle of life."

In the postwar period, the classical depictions of Notre Dame athletics contrasted with the increasing amount of "Aw-Nuts" journalism about college sports. ND administrators observed this phenomenon and knew that it resulted, in large part, from their ability to keep their athletic programs scandal free.

■   ■   ■

I have the feeling—as Father Cavanaugh has—that everyone [in the NCAA leadership] suspects that Notre Dame must be the greatest sinner because it comes up with the most successful teams. And that hurts. It fails to take into account a great many other factors . . . [for example] the number of fine boys that are recommended to N.D. by our former players now coaching elsewhere, by priests and nuns, etc.

—Notre Dame vice president John H. Murphy,
February 1947.

Many of the accusations against Notre Dame concerned recruiting—the school's ability to assemble great football teams. Father Murphy explained to a correspondent that, as the favorite team of millions of American Catholics, the Fighting Irish harvested many outstanding players from the large parochial school system. Frank Leahy, a daily communicant, later admitted that when a Catholic recruit visited the campus, the coach showed him "Our Lady up on that Golden Dome and I didn't really have to say all that much";

the experience would convince "the lad" that "it was a blessing to play for Notre Dame and . . . [he would] find himself in a state of grace just by" agreeing to apply to the school. In that more innocent era, this appeal to religion worked wonderfully well, and sportswriters began to joke, "Notre Dame does not recruit, it gathers."

In his football banquet speech, Father Cavanaugh mentioned the religious recruiting phenomenon; he also noted that "in every town of any size in every state of the union, boys who hear of the Notre Dame spirit and the educational advantages here" from the media and especially the film *Knute Rockne—All-American,* "plan to come when they are old enough." And every season, the enormous press coverage of Notre Dame football, including the national radio broadcasts of Fighting Irish games, prompted many "athletes and non-athletes [to] want to enroll at this institution." These factors also helped Notre Dame gain a substantial share of public high school football talent. Therefore, contrary to the critics and their innuendoes, "there is no mystery about why good boys are here at Notre Dame and why still more will come."

An objective analysis of the situation reveals that the ND administrators were correct. From the 1920s through the 1940s, Notre Dame football had become a unique national phenomenon, able to enlist a larger number of the very best high school football players from all parts of the country than could any other college team. Only the military academies could compete in national recruiting, and when the World War II "draft board" aid ended, they began to trail the Irish badly. Many commentators acknowledged the school's recruiting superiority; Illinois's Red Grange, in the late 1940s a Big Ten football broadcaster, declared, "It's the natural ambition of almost every outstanding high school player in Catholic schools as well as many [athletes] from non-Catholic schools to want to play for Notre Dame."

Therefore, because ND recruited so well through legal means, the school did not have to offer prospects much more than a chance to play for the legendary Fighting Irish. With these advantages, other inducements made no sense. In addition, because of the school's adherence to the classic ideals, as well as the constant Big Ten scrutiny of its athletic program, cheating was out of the question for the men in the Golden Dome.

Reinforcing the will to abide by the rules was the structure of the university: the president and vice president, always priests, controlled all sports revenue and expenses, and closely supervised the ND athletic department. (At many schools in big-time college sports, athletic departments existed as separate entities, ADs and coaches running them in an almost autonomous manner.) Father Cavanaugh mentioned the ND system in his speech and also noted that at many other universities, "alumni aid to athletes tends to take [even more] control away from an institution and that is becoming the chief evil in athletics" (at the 1947 NCAA meeting, Southern college officials had warned that passage of the "Purity Code" would speed up this process). Notre Dame had never permitted its graduates or its legions of Subway Alumni any influence over its athletic department; it had also not allowed them to form Fighting Irish booster clubs, even though such groups would have willingly contributed huge amounts of money to ND athletic programs. The C.S.C. priests owned and operated the University of Notre Dame, including its football team, and they had no intention of yielding any power to the school's alumni or anyone else. Thus, longtime policy, institutional self-interest, personal beliefs, and unique circumstances helped Notre Dame live up to the classic ideal in college sports.

Outsiders, particularly some Big Ten and NCAA sports officials, "wondered" about Notre Dame's "cleanliness," and Father Murphy referred to their skepticism when he asked his correspondent, "Do you think that Father Cavanaugh would have dared make that speech if we were as bad as the other schools? Why, college presidents, athletic directors, and coaches would have had a field day against him. Can you point out one college president, athletic director, or coach who has attacked the speech? They know their athletic set-ups and they know ours. And they have remained silent." Murphy made an excellent point: considering the wide dissemination of Cavanaugh's talk, and its assault on the "Purity Code" and the many college sports officials behind it, the absence of counterattack was noteworthy.

In fact, at this time, one Big Ten insider admitted to the press: "No one questions Notre Dame's standard of athletic control. It is the finest. They always have observed our rules to the letter, as to eligibility, amateur ethics, and in every other respect." For many years, ND had used the Big Ten rulebook as its baseline. This official, however, complained about the relentless Fighting Irish victories: "They draw too great a football personnel for any other university to match, at least at this time. Boys with talent flock to South Bend."

How Notre Dame treated its athletes on campus was another source of Big Ten suspicions. In his letter, Vice President Murphy explained the rigid academic requirements: "students who participate in intercollegiate athletics [must] maintain a 77% average—70% is passing" for regular students. And often throughout this period, Notre Dame opened the transcripts of athletes to outside investigators; no examiner ever reported any fudging of the 77 percent rule.

Vice President Murphy also noted that the "discipline here" helped athletes academically, referring to the authoritarian nature of ND dormitory and student life. He added: "We still are old-fashioned enough to kick a boy out for intoxication or for immoralities that are winked at in every public institution." Indeed, Murphy's words were soon tested when star quarterback and varsity basketball player George Ratterman violated the dormitory curfew rule. True to its code, the school expelled him permanently.

■ ■ ■

> We never had a problem with Notre Dame officials, but after the war, some of their fans began driving us crazy. They began writing letters saying that other schools should imitate Notre Dame, not just in winning, but by winning absolutely cleanly and honestly. Sure, who doesn't want to do that? But no one could get players like Frank Leahy could . . .
>
> Also the fans said that Notre Dame sets an example that other schools *could* follow if those schools didn't like cheating so much. I really got angry when they started applying that to Purdue, as if we [Purdue] cheated.

—*Lafayette (Indiana) Journal & Courier* sports editor
Gordon Graham, 1961.

In this period, some Fighting Irish fans developed an aggressive "holier than thou" attitude about ND football. As Graham indicated and the letters to the editor columns of national magazines substantiate, these fans argued that because Notre Dame operated honestly, every other school should and could abide by the "Purity Code." Fathers Cavanaugh and Murphy never took this position—they understood the unusual nature of the Notre Dame system too well. They hoped that other schools would abide by the "Purity Code," but as realists they doubted it. Their statements on the issue always emphasized one point: the University of Notre Dame conducted its athletic programs in the way that it saw fit, in other words, according to Father O'Hara's "Fortress Notre Dame" policy. Because ND procedures were consistent with the NCAA's "Purity Code," so much the better; however, if the NCAA and the "Principles for the Conduct of Intercollegiate Athletics" vanished tomorrow, Notre Dame would still adhere to its own rules.

The term that best describes Notre Dame football in this period is "unique." Because of its exceptional demographic situation, Notre Dame could enroll more blue-chip prospects—athletes with definite pro football potential—than any other school. Moreover, ND could also find enough blue-chippers willing and able to endure its strict academic and student discipline to fill its team rosters. In contrast, such Big Ten schools as Purdue considered themselves lucky to obtain five blue-chippers a year.

To illustrate Notre Dame's success: after George Ratterman departed, Leahy returned the quarterbacking job to Johnny Lujack and his backup, Frank Tripucka; Lujack won the Heisman in 1947, and he and Tripucka went on to successful pro careers. In fact, in this era when rosters were still relatively small, forty-three members of the 1946–47 ND squads subsequently played professional football. Some of the All-Americans like Leon Hart and Jim Martin became All-Pros but, even more significantly, many third- and fourth-stringers went on to outstanding pro careers, like Vince Scott, who never played a down in 1947 but then starred for the Buffalo Bills, and afterward became a perennial all-pro in Canada as well as a CFL Hall of Famer. In addition, some members of the 1946–47 team, like starting halfback Terry Brennan, passed up pro football to immediately enter coaching. In contrast, five Purdue Boilermakers on the 1946–47 teams had pro careers.

In the end, the demographics of football recruiting indicate that Notre Dame was the exception that proved the rule on corruption in college sports. The fact that the Fighting Irish could win cleanly mainly confirmed that "Notre Dame was Notre Dame," a unique American institution, singularly capable of following the "Purity Code" and also gaining national championships.

Other universities, notably the Ivies, eventually enforced a version of the "Purity Code" within their league, but in so doing, they dropped out of big-time football. The schools that remained in the national championship derby faced the inexorable demography of recruiting. Universities like Ohio State and Michigan, with famous football traditions, had some advantages parallel to Notre Dame's, but no institution had the full Fighting Irish package, particularly the national media attention and the religious dimension. As a result, too many schools chasing too few blue-chippers created the "black market" in football players. To win in this climate, the traditional football programs had to cut corners, and the aspiring ones, like Bear Bryant's Maryland, had to ignore the rulebook.

At the conclusion of his football banquet speech, Father Cavanaugh told his audience: "Notre Dame has nothing to fear from any [NCAA] program that permits institutions to compete on a fair and even basis. I think that anyone who examines the history and nature of this university" will agree with that statement. His subtext was clear, albeit ironic: if, by some miracle, the "Purity Code" actually ruled college sports, no school would benefit more than Notre Dame; if the Fighting Irish could win in a corrupt world, imagine what they could do in an honest one! Until heaven arrived on earth, he would conduct Notre Dame athletics according to the school's historic policy.

■   ■   ■

A key part of Notre Dame's history was the media coverage of its football program. During this period in intercollegiate athletics, as the corruption spread, many sportswriters and broadcasters found it increasingly difficult to portray crooked college football and basketball programs in classical terms; however, they could not easily abandon their journalistic training and inclination. One solution was to crank out more classical portraits of the Fighting Irish. Thanks in part to this media need as well as to Leahy's victorious teams, the press and radio reports on Notre Dame football multiplied exponentially in the late 1940s. For some publications, another solution was to give more space to "Aw-Nuts" writers and their exposés, and this also occurred at this time, alerting the public to the growing crisis but, unlike the stories about the Fighting Irish, not providing any relief from it.

20

Sports Media Confusion

When the first issue of *Sport* hit the newsstands way back in August of 1946, almost everyone said that we couldn't possibly succeed, that nobody would read a general sports magazine. We defended our baby by saying that nobody had ever tried publishing stories about the *people* in sport—about the personalities who lure those huge crowds to the ball parks and arenas and stadiums all over America. We were sure our idea would click.

—The editors of *Sport* magazine, July 1949.

The men at *Sport* had many reasons for self-congratulation during the summer of 1949: their circulation had reached 700,000, an extraordinary figure for a new specialty magazine in this period, and, considering how fans passed the magazine around, readership was at least five times the print run. The editors also noted that "about a year ago, an expected rash of imitators began to flood the stands," but *Sport* withstood the competition by continuing to sign up the best sportswriters of the day.

A half century and a transformed sports world later, it is difficult to appreciate how *Sport* magazine—now a gaunt shadow—led media coverage of American athletics in the postwar period. Contrary to the editors' self-promotion, for decades many publications had run "stories about the *people* in sport." Newspaper sports sections had long adored "the personalities who lure those huge crowds"; general magazines like the *Saturday Evening Post* and *Collier's* had displayed portraits of athletes since the 1920s; and specialized journals on baseball, football, boxing, and horse racing had existed for many years, often carrying features on the personages of their sports. In 1946, the publishers and editors of *Sport* magazine plugged into this old tradition of athlete-hero writing, but they wrapped their "baby" in a new blanket.

Using the latest color and print technology and a "general magazine" format, they put out an attractive monthly totally devoted to athletics, with extensive coverage of baseball and football but also paying attention to most other sports. Moreover, *Sport*, with its striking color photographs of athletes, looked very new. Hollywood sports films and newsreels were still in black and white, as were newspaper and magazine photos, but in *Sport*, for the first time, fans could see their heroes "in living color."

In their 1949 birthday card to themselves, the editors also listed their "nationally famous" authors. They began with Grantland Rice, Frank Graham, and Tom Meany—all exemplars of classic sports prose—but then they included Dan Parker and Shirley Povich, writers who had inherited or adopted the "Aw-Nuts" style. In addition, the editors hailed Bill Stern, signaling their tie to national sports radio. Of the twenty names on their list, most were classical, and this approach dominated the first years of the magazine.

Grantland Rice anchored some early issues with long pieces on past heroes, like "I Remember Rockne," whose subhead explained: "A Great Sportswriter Sets Down His Personal Memoirs of Notre Dame's Immortal Grid Coach." Rice mainly retailed the old Rockne stories, particularly the chestnuts from the Warners's biopic, then concluded, "There are at least 50 high-class coaches on gridirons today . . . But Knute Rockne is the fellow you miss—the fellow you wish were still around. His ability, his color, his personality, his stories, and the stories about him, are still worth remembering. They'll be part of American football as long as the game is played."

In the turbulent postwar era, undoubtedly such portraits comforted the fans of college sports, as did Rice's emphasis on Rockne as a scholar-athlete and a scientist-coach. At a time when editorial writers, particularly in the national press, had started to attack the corruption in intercollegiate athletics, "Granny" Rice focused on the "old truths" as exemplified by Rockne and the Fighting Irish. For the patriarch of sports journalism, Notre Dame and St. Knute were the "Rock" upon which the classic ideal rested.

Rice always wrote for the fan who loved the athletes, coaches, and games as much as he did. However, from the 1920s to the postwar period, the average age of Rice's reader had decreased from adult to adolescent, the result of increasing national literacy and diminishing naïveté. Rice's work was perfect for *Sport* magazine's younger readers, who were still somewhat innocent and wanted to learn about the heroes of the so-called Golden Age of Sports, the 1920s.

Other *Sport* writers, aiming for both a teen and adult audience, tried to update the classical mode. In one of the first issues of the magazine, Bill Brandt contributed a feature with this subhead: "The Noted *Inside of Sports* Radio Reporter on [the] Mutual [Radio Network] Recreates a Fall Day in 1917 When the Whole Army Team Was Fooled, and Beaten, by a Notre

Dame Grid Immortal." The player was George Gipp, but instead of another retelling of his All-American year (1920) or the "Win One for the Gipper" speech and game (1928), the author related the events of the obscure 1917 Army-ND match, and Gipp's clever and effective play that day. The story concluded: "From November 1917 to November 1920, George Gipp paraded the gridirons of America, a football legend who came along just Once-in-a-Lifetime."

In this article and throughout its first years, as part of its appeal to adult readers, *Sport* claimed that its articles provided inside information, the "real lowdown." In the Gipp piece and elsewhere, however, the magazine mainly defined "inside sports" as a new angle within the classical spectrum, certainly not the whole truth about the subject: in 1917, his sophomore year, George Gipp did not show up at Notre Dame until the third game of the season, then dropped out of school in mid-November, a week after the Army contest.

■ ■ ■

> Last November [1946], in the gray light of an early morning, a heavily loaded New York Central train moved eastward through Indiana. It carried among its passengers a football team from the University of Notre Dame. As the train slowed down, moving through a small town, one of the players suddenly sat up straight in his seat and said, "Hey, look!"
>
> "Well, look at that," another added softly.
>
> Clustered at the station platform and strung out along the track were groups of school kids. Here and there among them were nuns. The kids ranged in age from seven to 16. It was not yet seven in the morning. It was cold.
>
> The kids held up two paper banners. One of them read BEAT ARMY; the other, in irregular letters, spelled out VICTORY FOR NOTRE DAME. One of the smaller kids was crying, whether from discomfort, or a rebuke, or emotion, the players would never know. The others were waving and shouting, but their sounds could not be heard over the powerful noise of the train. And then they were gone from sight.
>
> In dozens of small towns all the way from South Bend, through Indiana, Ohio, Pennsylvania, and New York, similar scenes were repeated.
>
> —*Sport* magazine writer Jack Sher, October 1947.

The opening paragraphs of a 1947 *Sport* feature on Johnny Lujack came directly from the classical Hollywood cinema—the train crossing the American heartland, the enthralled children, and so on—and the author maintained a consistent POV (point of view) from within the railroad car, hence the players cannot hear the shouts over the engine's roar. The diction is also from

Hollywood and network radio drama, e.g., " 'Well, look at that,' another added softly." How could the *Sport* writer possibly know the unnamed speaker's tone of voice? Jack Sher was not an eyewitness; he learned about the train incidents almost a year later. What Sher did know and understand were the tropes of classical Hollywood films and radio dramas: when someone spoke softly, it usually denoted awe, an important event unfolding.

Sher used other literary devices beloved by classical sportswriters. He indicated the ages of the children—"seven to 16," the specificity of detail here and throughout giving a glow of authenticity to the story—but, because the train did not stop, how did anyone determine the exact age range of the kids? He also described one child crying and, in a neat double-reverse, admitted that no one learned why—the withholding of a minor, never a major, bit of information made an account appear more credible, implying that in the story, as in life, some events were mysterious. Sher also echoed Ernest Hemingway—considered the paragon of truth-telling authors at this time—in the lines, "It was not yet seven in the morning. It was cold."

In its initial and most influential years, *Sport* magazine employed the masters of classical sportswriting, not only Grantland Rice but, even more effectively, his progeny, who incorporated the tropes of the Hollywood cinema and radio drama into their prose. They had seen so many Hollywood movies and heard so many radio plays that they had internalized this worldview. No doubt, they could distinguish these fictions from daily reality: however, they believed that *classical prose was the way to portray reality*. In a sense, authors like Jack Sher wrote their stories *before* they went on assignment; in the field, they mainly collected names, quotes, and events to plug into their preconceived narratives. They were well rewarded for their writing with the approval of their editors and readers, as well as monetarily. However, they were not cynics—if they had been, they could not have produced the same fable so enthusiastically and endlessly.

In historical fact, nuns and schoolchildren did gather on railroad platforms and alongside tracks to cheer the Fighting Irish as they journeyed to New York for the 1946 Army game. Sher fit this information into his classical tale. But other authors working in other modes and eras might have shaped this information into very different narratives; for example, a 1990s satirist might have portrayed the nuns as manipulative and the children as deluded. Like the classical sportswriters, the satirist would have written the story long before researching the event.

Fortunately for sportswriters in the turbulent postwar period in college sports, the University of Notre Dame and its athletes and coaches existed and neatly fit their stories. For that reason as well as the huge number of Fighting Irish fans—all of whom were potential subscribers—ND personalities received *Sport* magazine's constant attention, not only in regular articles but in the monthly "Book Special" section, 15,000- to 20,000-word profiles on a specific star.

For a 1947 "Book Special" on Johnny Lujack, Sher portrayed him in Hollywood terms: "Lujack is an unusually handsome young man . . . He has dark wavy, brown hair, a strong sensitive face, light-brown eyes, a mild, friendly smile. He is extremely well-poised, talks easily and intelligently, and has, as his teammates, teachers, and student friends will tell you, a quick sense of humor." Prewar and some wartime writers described star athletes in more "macho" terms; the word "sensitive" never entered their vocabulary. Sher's portrait was directly related to Hollywood films and fan magazines: postwar classical sportswriting, heavily influenced by the screen, tried to draw women into its discourse, and although most *Sport* subscribers were male, the magazine consciously attempted to attract female readers with movie magazine touches as well as some coverage of women's sports—hence the ND quarterback's "sensitivity."

The portrait of Lujack mainly consisted of retellings of standard stories, particularly the young Johnny subbing for Bertelli in the 1943 Army game, his military service, and his play in 1946 against Army. Unfortunately, the author used the classical formula so rigidly that the modern reader gains almost no sense of a breathing person inside the Notre Dame uniform. Most subscribers to *Sport,* however, probably did not want flesh and blood, and preferred an idealized hero.

The following year, the magazine profiled Lujack's replacement, Frank Tripucka, in similar terms. The theme was patience-pays-off: Tripucka had long "waited" behind Lujack to start at QB; indeed, he had "waited" to play for Notre Dame "ever since his sister bought the book *Knute Rockne—Man Builder* for him on his [eighth] birthday a dozen years ago. He waited while he read about Rockne, the Four Horsemen, and George Gipp. 'I'm going to Notre Dame,' he told his mother when he got his first football."

The author also employed an artificial nickname—"the Bloomfield Bullet" (Tripucka was from Bloomfield, New Jersey)—to render the player more memorable. In addition, like the formulaic "Hit Parade" songs of the period, classical sports stories usually contained catchy phrases. For Tripucka one went: "From Kansas to Killarney, from Dublin to Dubuque, the thousands of Irish alumni—real and subway—have their fingers crossed. They're wondering if it will be the story of the Bloomfield Bullet or the Bloomfield Bust." (Tripucka helped lead the Fighting Irish to an undefeated season, satisfying ND fan expectations.)

Readers frequently wrote letters to the editor of *Sport* praising the writers and the articles; however, the pieces on Notre Dame players and coaches sparked not only compliments but also occasional complaints. One Army fan griped, "I know that your magazine just has to include articles about Notre

Dame every Fall to build up its circulation but please tell your writers . . . not to lay it on so thick." The latter comment showed some awareness of the writing process, but no letter writer ever complained about the "thickness" of an article on his or her favorite team.

■ ■ ■

> The story of Doak Walker is more than the story of a boy who happened to be blessed with remarkable athletic abilities. It is the story of his parents, who reared him carefully and tenderly into a young man of character and poise. It is the story of his father, who blueprinted Doak's football career as meticulously as an architect plans every detail of a building. It is the story of Doak himself, who absorbed with rare understanding the wise words of his mother and father.
>
> In the Southwest, Walker is looked upon as a symbol of the ideal young man. He doesn't drink or smoke; he keeps in training the year around, and his phenomenal success hasn't turned his head. He is the most popular student in Southern Methodist University in Dallas.

> —*Sport* magazine writer Bill Rives, November 1948.

Sport featured athletes from schools other than Notre Dame, particularly when they achieved the classic ideal. Doak Walker, the 1948 Heisman Trophy winner, certainly qualified for a full "Sport Profile," and he received one in the magazine's "Big College Football Round-up" of that year. On the cover, in his flaming red SMU helmet and uniform, Walker gazed skyward, a football cocked behind his ear. An inside page—*Sport* innovated with full-page color photos (perfect for removal and attaching to a boy's bedroom wall)—featured a helmetless Walker, wavy brown hair, deep tan, and Texas "aw-shucks" grin. The text emphasized family—the perfect son shaped by the ambitious but concerned parents; complementing the text was a photo of Walker and his family examining a scrapbook of his football triumphs, and also one of a very young Walker in football uniform, the caption informing us, "As a small boy, Doak learned football from his father and was an ardent rooter for SMU's team."

Nowhere in the story was there a discussion of the Southwest Conference's controversial athletic scholarship plan, or the prominent role of alumni in SMU's recruiting and retention of athletes. A similar omission occurred in the photo and text on Walker's high school teammate, close friend, and service buddy Bobby Layne—a legendary hell-raiser and a well-paid college quarterback at the University of Texas in the late 1940s. *Sport* termed Walker "a symbol of the ideal young man," and everyone around him also had to fit the classic mold—hence the picture of him and Layne in naval uniforms, as well as a photograph of Walker with his girlfriend, the caption noting, "Doak's best (and only) girl is Norma Peterson, SMU's reigning beauty, [also] Queen of the Drake Relays this year. The other Walkers think Norma's wonderful too."

By all accounts, Doak Walker was an outstanding college running back and a decent person, but, as with profiles of Lujack and the other players, no flesh and blood spatters this story. This Doak Walker so conformed to the traditional motifs that he seems invented. Occasionally, between the lines, his father appears as an obsessive "sports parent," trying to fulfill his own athletic dreams through his son. However, the magazine refused to explore this possibility, instead reassuring readers that "Doak's general development was not sacrificed on the altar of athletics. In fact, the wholesome habits his parents inculcated in him, the sound and practical manner in which they reared him, share as much responsibility for his success as any coaching he has received." At the end of the narrative, we find Doak Walker traveling around Texas, fulfilling the Heisman ideal: "He particularly likes to talk to children. He tells them the story of how his Dad made him an All-American."

Equally adept at classical prose was Bill Stern—or his well-paid ghostwriters. In the late 1940s, his byline appeared frequently in *Sport* on articles and even on fiction—work recycled from his popular radio broadcasts. The magazine subheaded a Stern piece on coaches' halftime talks with "What Really Happens Between Halves? Are Football Fight-Talks Fact or Fancy? Here's the Lowdown from One Expert Who's Been There for the Spell-Binding." Any reader expecting the real lowdown—coaches throwing chairs, physically and psychologically battering players, spewing expletives, offering incoherent prayers—would have to wait another generation. The locker-room speeches quoted by Bill Stern, even from contemporary coaches well known as "screamers," were pure and inspirational; however, he quickly moved from the current scene to "the greatest coach of all for reviving 'dying' teams [at halftime] . . . of course, the immortal Knute Rockne."

Stern retailed the halftime chestnuts from *Knute Rockne—All-American* and the various hagiographies—the Gipper speech, the wheelchair talk, and so on—indicating that the ND coach continualy used locker-room oratory: "Football history will testify that dramatic speech usually got results. It was Rockne's fight-talk" that made his teams great. In reality, the ND coach rarely made locker-room speeches, preferring to carefully prepare his players for games and then allow them to do their work. A psychology professor once asked him about "keying up" athletes in the locker room, and the coach replied, "I do not make any effort to key them up, except on rare, exceptional occasions." But this aspect of Rockne's coaching would not have interested classical sportswriters or readers, and it would have flattened Bill Stern's article.

One of the best Stern contributions to *Sport* in this period was a short fiction piece entitled "Incident Over Kansas." It owed its theme and style to radio drama, including Stern's own Theater of the Coincidental, as well as such Hollywood movies as *Here Comes Mr. Jordan* (1941) and *A Guy Named Joe* (1943). The central character, Paul Hartley, is a former All-American who interrupted his playing career to enter the service; after the war, he returns to campus but football and its rah-rah atmosphere now turns him off. Paul quits the team, leaves school, and impulsively boards a plane for the West Coast. Over the plains, he strikes up a conversation with "a medium-sized man, with a shiny bald head, twinkling eyes, a large rugged nose, and a strong jaw . . . There was something about him that looked very familiar."

Paul trusts the man and explains his situation. The "bald-headed man leaned back," offering his analysis: "You think . . . football, and organized cheering, and school spirit [is] a lot of bunk just because you've been through the war. You think it isn't dignified for a combat veteran." The older man then tells Paul about the importance of "spirit" to past football players and teams, notably the Notre Dame Fighting Irish. Paul relaxes, and eventually falls asleep; when he wakes his companion is no longer on the plane, but the flight attendant points out that "right now we're over a place where they had a bad [plane] wreck . . . Bazaar, Kansas, down there back in 1931 an eight-passenger plane crashed and killed Knute Rockne." The story concludes: "A week later he [Paul] was back at school, playing football. Nobody could understand his sudden change of heart—and neither could he."

Readers would recognize the ghost-intervention motif and identify the bald-headed man as Rockne; they would also "understand" that the ND coach had inspired Paul's "sudden change of heart." Nevertheless, would readers believe that such an "Incident" could actually occur? In practical commonsense terms, probably not, but at a deeper, less rational level, many readers, especially younger ones, undoubtedly wanted such events to happen, wanted great men to intervene in their lives, tell them what to do, particularly to advise them to play more sports. Consumers of classical sports prose, films, and radio programs so loved these tropes that they suspended their disbelief and accepted the possibility of St. Knute appearing over Kansas.

The subtext of Stern's story is appropriately conservative and idealized: intercollegiate athletics must return to its prewar state, supposedly a time when players loved rah-rah, obeyed their coaches, and never demanded money to suit up for Old Siwash. But no matter how intensely Stern's readers wanted Rockne's ghost to return and correct the postwar problems, he never came. The volume of dirty linen in college sports increased, anxious NCAA officials tried the "Purity Code," and *Sport* magazine felt compelled to include some "Aw-Nuts" articles about the situation.

．　　．　　．

Pure as Pittsburgh snow [blackened by the steel mills] and as free from commercial taint as a roulette wheel with a gimmick, college football is with us again after its annual winter purification ceremony. This ritual is performed with whitewash, crossed fingers, and generous slices of bologna, by some of the nation's most accomplished liars and most colossal hypocrites.

—*Sport* magazine contributor Dan Parker, October 1947.

Parker began his piece with this diatribe, mocking the "purification ceremony . . . performed" by the NCAA in January 1947 with its adoption of the "Purity Code." Ten months after its passage, he assessed the code's effect. The title of the article left no doubt about his "Aw-Nuts" conclusion: "College Football Cleanup? PHOOEY!"

Parker also took the long view on college sports, seeing the NCAA's actions as this year's "ceremony" in an "annual" ritual to hoodwink the public. The article's subhead termed college football "Now as Clean as a Dirty Shirt" and proclaimed Parker "A Writer Who Can Spot a Fake a Mile Away." Accompanying the story was a two-page cartoon by Willard Mullin, creator of the Brooklyn Dodgers "Bum" character, depicting a mud-spattered football player entering a shower labeled "PURITY PROGRAM," then emerging covered with more mud than before.

Dan Parker was an heir to such 1920s sports journalists as W. O. McGeehan and Ring Lardner; although lacking their wit, he excelled at sarcasm and vituperation. His style clashed with *Sport*'s classical approach, but in the fall of 1947 the editors decided that the corruption in intercollegiate athletics had become so newsworthy that it merited space in their magazine. Therefore, because of their policy of engaging the best writers in every area of sports, they hired Parker, renowned for his "Aw-Nuts" columns and "inside information" articles in the *New York Mirror* and other papers.

This decision soon led to the magazine's most important contribution to American sports journalism: it became the first sports publication to devote space regularly to beyond-the-game concerns. From the inception of American sportswriting in the nineteenth century through World War II, every sporting paper and magazine had focused almost exclusively on the games and the performances and personalities of the athletes and coaches. Even during the Carnegie Foundation investigations and reports in the 1920s and early 1930s, only major newspapers like the *New York Times* and journals like *Harper's* carried articles on the off-field controversies. The sporting press ignored this aspect of athletics. One of the best chapters in the 1929 Carnegie report analyzed this phenomenon, attributing it to the symbiotic relationship between college athletic officials and sportswriters, and the refusal of the latter to criticize the former.

Sport's breakthrough, however, had limits: the editors only ran short articles on beyond-the-game questions, almost always in a pro-and-con format. The month after Parker's "Aw-Nuts" diatribe, Bill Stern answered with "Football Can Be Clean," whose subhead explained, "Attacked from All Directions as an Evil Swamp of Hypocrisy, the College Game Is Making Serious Efforts to Rid Itself of Its Unsavory Reputation." Furthermore, in its initial years, the magazine never ran critical profiles of sports personalities—even though many of them deserved debunking. Some "Aw-Nuts" writers slipped in exposé material on famous athletes, but always as examples for points in their argument, never as the main focus. For instance, in discussing the hypocrisy of the leading reform conference, the Big Ten, Dan Parker noted, "Nor did Buddy Young's resignation from Illinois right after the Rose Bowl embarrass that institution, although it was obvious that Buddy was under contract to the New York Yankees professional football team while starring for the Illini . . . The conference took no action."

Nevertheless, *Sport*'s policy of granting space to beyond-the-game controversies paid important dividends: the writers of their pro-and-con pieces took the analysis of sports, particularly intercollegiate athletics, to a higher level than previous journalists had done, preparing the way for the serious revisionist work during the scandal years. In discussing Big Ten hypocrisy, Parker examined the University of Michigan, pointing out that no conference member had expressed "more fervent devotion to the cause" of student-based intercollegiate athletics but that nevertheless in 1947, "Michigan was to demonstrate its own peculiar brand of de-emphasis with a $3,000,000 building program that called for enlarging its football stadium [to almost 100,000 seats] and constructing a fieldhouse that would seat a measly 18,000." Parker was also one of the first sportswriters to analyze how schools paid for this construction: they hired top athletes to stock winning teams to fill all the new seats. As he disclosed, Michigan had long done this. Their 1940 Heisman Trophy winner, Tom Harmon, had "owned two cars while at Ann Arbor," and received many other perks from generous alumni.

In yet another innovation, *Sport* also allowed its pro-and-con writers to use the discoveries of investigative reporters. In spite of the long history of American journalistic "muckraking," the sporting press had always shunned it, considering the discoveries embarrassing to their allies, notably the coaches, and of no interest to their readers. However, in his October 1947 article, Dan Parker used the work of a Pacific Coast Conference investigator who had turned up various scams involving PCC schools, including one where incoming students received extra money because of administrative "errors in computing [academic] grants-in-aid." Parker noted, "Strangely enough, all the students in whose behalf the 'errors' were committed were prospective athletes."

A half century later, one wonders what the average *Sport* reader thought of the "Aw-Nuts" pieces amidst all the classical prose. Possibly the response was cognitive dissonance: the reader saw the contradiction between the two views of intercollegiate athletics but could not act upon this knowledge. The editors of *Sport* encouraged this attitude when, in November 1948, they distanced themselves from the "Aw-Nuts" perspective. In an editorial, "Why Point the Finger at [College] Football?" they condemned the "savage attacks" by those writers who "put the slug on collegiate football." In spite of the evidence in some *Sport* articles, the editors felt that the "Aw-Nuts" journalists had gone too far, announcing: "Well, we're old-fashioned. We think [college] football is a wonderful sport. Not just because it's exciting and colorful to watch, but because it does a lot for the boys who play it."

What prompted this editorial recoil is impossible to ascertain. Possibly college sports officials, particularly coaches, complained about the "Aw-Nuts" pieces, even threatening to ban *Sport*'s regular writers and photographers from campuses. Or *Sport*'s editors, as advocates of the classic ideals, truly wanted the critics of college sports to shut up. In any event, they could not will away the rising tide of corruption and scandal in intercollegiate athletics. A year later, as savvy media men, they waded into the tumult further than before.

21

More Media Confusion—
but Not About Frank Leahy

THE TRUTH ABOUT CHARLIE JUSTICE—A *SPORT* PROFILE

Branded as All-America before He Entered College, the Phenomenal [University of] North Carolina Grid Star Has Been the Center of
the Sport World's Wildest Rumors. What's the Real Lowdown?

—*Sport* headline and subhead for a feature on Charlie
"Choo-Choo" Justice, November 1949.

One of the most celebrated college sports stars of the postwar era was
Tarheel halfback Charlie "Choo-Choo" Justice, not only an elusive runner but also the owner of a wonderful nickname that resonated with determination and power. *Sport* first profiled him in a 1947 classical piece, "Justice
Triumphs," placing him in the regular athlete-hero lineup: "Charlie, who
doesn't smoke or drink, is modest and unassuming. He hesitates to talk about
himself, but will always tell you what a great block the Carolina tackle made
on that touchdown play."

Choo-Choo, however, was from a part of America where universities gave
athletic scholarships, and encouraged their alumni to aid athletes, particularly
those with All-American potential. As a high school phenom in Asheville,
North Carolina, in the early 1940s, he was recruited by many universities, but
he entered the military instead of college. After he starred on naval base
teams during the war, the bidding for Choo-Choo's services escalated to the
top level of the postwar "black market." As a sensible veteran with a wife to
support, he considered more than fifty offers and signed with the highest bidder, the University of North Carolina at Chapel Hill in his home state. Some

of the losing schools did not leave his doorstep quietly, however; they leaked details of his UNC deal to the press. The 1947 *Sport* profile did not report this information, noting only that he chose the Tarheels because "he wanted to go to North Carolina all along."

Throughout the late 1940s, "Aw-Nuts" writers frequently pointed to Justice as an example of a pro player in a collegiate uniform. *Sport* revisited him in late 1949, this time stating that "Charlie's income at [North] Carolina is slightly under that of a top player in the National [Football] League or the All-America Conference. He has a car and plenty of spending money, all because some Carolina alumni think he's worth it to alma mater." Justice himself was quite forthcoming, acknowledging that UNC " 'gave us, my wife and me, full scholarships' " and, in spite of an acute postwar housing shortage in Chapel Hill, the school " 'agreed to find us an [off-campus] apartment.' " He also received GI bill benefits and "picked up commissions of varying amounts for helping sell [local] ads in the football program. For personal appearances, he received liberal 'expenses.' " In addition, in spite of the postwar shortage of automobiles, he had a new sedan from "the local GM dealer, a close friend." In this era, few UNC students, particularly married vets with children (he became a father in 1948), went through school as comfortably as Choo-Choo Justice—but none could shake off opposing linemen and break loose for long runs the way he could.

Nevertheless, this *Sport* profile, for all of its details about Justice's financial arrangements, contained dollops of classical sportswriting, including a defense of the player's motives: according to the author, Justice's critics "discount the altogether mundane possibility that Charlie might actually crave a college education, or have an overpowering urge to obtain a degree . . . Nevertheless, the motivating factor in Charlie's life so far has not been academics. It has been plain unvarnished gridironing, and the more the better." Huh?

The *Sport* magazine writer tried to plug Choo-Choo into the scholar-athlete formula but then backed away with weasel conditionals and double negatives: Charlie *"might"* want a college education, *"Nevertheless . . .* his life so far has *not* been academics." The writer seemed perplexed about how to portray his subject and, as a result, produced confusing, garbled prose. In another passage, after another assertion of Charlie's seriousness as a student, *Sport* mentioned that this autumn (1949), Choo-Choo's course load consists of "only three Phys. Ed courses—all laboratory," i.e., he was getting credit for playing sports. Such incongruities occur throughout the piece and mainly confuse the reader, as mixed-form works usually do. The writer sends some classical signals, but then undercuts them with "Aw-Nuts" comments and details, sometimes within the same paragraph.

Because of the constant contradictions, the profile fails. Undoubtedly, it did not satisfy fans anticipating a standard portrait à la Lujack and Walker, and it probably displeased readers looking for "Aw-Nuts" denunciations.

However, the failure mirrored *Sport*'s dilemma in the late 1940s. The magazine wanted to report the major story in college sports—the increasing corruption—and yet its initial and ongoing success was based on its classical viewpoint. Like many publications and writers in this situation, it tried to have it all ways, to give the readers items from both Column A and Column B, and in the Justice profile and similar pieces, it served up an indigestible mélange.

In this era, *Sport* could not explain Charlie Justice or great athletes like him. Neither the classical writers or the debunkers could clarify Choo-Choo's biography or his role as a hero in the South. *Sport* even tried again with a 1954 article that outlined Justice's college football record, then focused on his ordinary NFL career with the Washington Redskins. However, this piece mainly indicated that, at the end of Choo-Choo's pro days, he would probably vanish from the national sports scene.

This prediction proved accurate for more than two decades, until Justice's story attracted Frank Deford, one of the premier sportswriters of a later generation, who explored the UNC football hero in a novel, *Everybody's All-American* (1981), and a filmscript and movie (1988) based upon the book. Deford's nickname for his main character was "the Grey Ghost"—*Sport* had used "the Great Asheville Ghost," one of Justice's nicknames, in its subhead for the first profile—and even though Deford called his hero Gavin Grey, he sent him to the University of North Carolina, assigned him Choo-Choo's halfback position, made him a multiyear All-American, and then dispatched him to an average NFL career with the Washington Redskins. But beyond the biographical connections, Deford's approach allowed him access to a great athlete's life as well as his importance to his region, not simply as a football star but also as a culture hero. The contrast between *Sport*'s "Great Asheville Ghost" and Deford's "Grey Ghost" is startling and indicates the distance between America after World War II and America after the Vietnam War. (However, an analysis of those differences and what they reveal about American sportswriting belongs to the final chapter of this study.)

■　　■　　■

> In two seasons [as their coach], he ["Pappy" Waldorf] has pulled his usual rabbit out of the hat. The once-blowsy [University of California] Bears are a first-class power once more, ranking with the country's best. On the West Coast, the fans are asking: "Is it a flash in the pan—or has the Cal jinx met its master?"
>
> —*Sport* magazine writer Al Stump, 1949.

This piece on Lynn "Pappy" Waldorf stayed safely within classical boundaries, as did all of the magazine's profiles of college coaches. *Sport* could attempt mixed-form depictions of athletes, but coaches had real power over journalists, and this magazine was not about to explore the consequences of negative portraits of them. Nevertheless, it allowed some strong comments about football programs in "Aw-Nuts" articles, and from the information in one a few months before the Waldorf profile, observant *Sport* readers could have answered the question about the Bears' recent prosperity. In the Pacific Coast Conference, alumni and student associations participated fully in the football programs, often screwing them up; however, Waldorf controlled his school's groups, and generous Cal alumni and student fraternities helped him assemble first-rate teams at Berkeley. But in the portrait of Pappy, *Sport's* Al Stump ignored this crucial aspect of Waldorf's success, instead portraying him as an amiable fat man and, as the son of a Methodist bishop, an inspirational mentor.

Interestingly, Stump later confessed his classical sportswriting sins. At this time, he also whitewashed the life of baseball's Ty Cobb; subsequently, he revisited Cobb's biography and produced a harrowing account of one of America's most maniacal athlete-heroes. Stump's experience, with his own literary transformation as a central theme, became the basis of the 1994 revisionist film, *Cobb.*

■　■　■

His [Frank Leahy's] square-jawed Irish face would look fine in a [Hathaway shirt] collar ad. He is 38, married, the father of four children . . . If someone offers him a cigarette, he says, "I'll have one later." (He doesn't smoke.) If someone offers him a shot of whiskey, he may even hold the glass up to his lips. (He doesn't like the taste of the stuff.) But under the genteel velveteen is the real ironbound Leahy.

—From a *Time* magazine cover story on Frank Leahy,
October 1946.

Coaches like Cal's Pappy Waldorf remained regional phenomenons in the 1940s, but a few head men, notably Notre Dame's Frank Leahy and Army's Earl Blaik, broke through to national fame and fortune. Leahy also became the first postwar football coach on the prestigious cover of *Time.* In the pre-TV age, that weekly was the major source of national and international news for millions of middle-class Americans.

Because *Time* publisher Henry Luce and his wife Clare, a passionate convert to Catholicism, promoted traditional values, the portrait of Frank Leahy emphasized his straight-arrow qualities as well as Notre Dame's "simon-pure" athletics program in the midst of college football's "dark brown scheme." In addition, *Time* contrasted Leahy and ND to "the pigskin dollar derby" by citing examples of cheating across the country, from "the West Coast, where earnest [and phony] protestations of purity bloom all year round," through the plains, Midwest, and South, to "Yale, [which] landed the most sought-after halfback in the East, 190-lb. Negro Levi Jackson, a comfortably relaxed student." "Comfortably relaxed" was "Timese" for not qualified academically, but in fact, Jackson was a good student and became both captain of the team and an outstanding Yale graduate.

Another Luce publication, *Fortune,* the first magazine to examine American business in depth, also shaped *Time's* perspective: the cover story on Leahy depicted him as a corporate executive coach attuned to postwar America, very different from the good ol' boys like Pappy Waldorf. The text beneath a photo of Leahy in his thirty-foot tower above the ND practice field informed the reader: "From the tower he looks down on an operation that is as carefully calculated, as extremely complicated as the Studebaker assembly line in nearby South Bend."

Throughout the profile, *Time* emphasized Leahy's managerial characteristics: he "is meeting production quotas, [and] then some—nine touchdowns in the first two games—but the Man in the Tower is the kind of guy who always aims to do better." As *Time* glorified the new business executives of postwar America in their rising glass towers, it lavished similar praise on Leahy for his organizational skills and use of chain of command (the postwar phase of corporate America came directly out of the war's military methods). The magazine both described a real phenomenon—American life, including college sports, was becoming more corporate than ever before—and also helped to shape it—*Time's* constant paeans to company executives made them respected, even glamorous, figures in the postwar era.

For *Time,* Frank Leahy epitomized the corporate trend in American sports, and the Notre Dame coach very much accepted and enjoyed the role. And because life often imitates art, the ND coach became more corporate in his football methods after this cover article appeared.

Leahy's CEO manner and tower above the practice field fascinated other national periodicals, and soon after the *Time* article appeared *Collier's* sent a professional artist to Notre Dame to sketch the coach's operations. In suffused-color drawings, John Groth pictured "Practice Isn't Play": Leahy, high above the field, commanding the activities below; the backfielders and their coach in one area, the offensive line and coach in another; and so on. To add a classic Notre Dame touch, at the corner of one page, *Collier's* placed a small drawing of a priest in full cassock catching a football, with the caption: "Some of the priests are former players, and when a ball comes close to one, he is apt to grab it and throw it around."

In the late 1940s, many national publications carried portraits of Frank Leahy. One of the more interesting appeared in *Redbook,* at the time a "general format" periodical evolving toward the "woman's magazine" that it became. Under the title "Mr. Leahy's Winning Ways," author Francis Wallace used *Time's* executive motif: "Football is a business as well as a sport; the head coach is the general manager, and Leahy is a marvel of efficiency at this phase of his job . . . [And] his boys work efficiently in the businesslike atmosphere of the field."

After this article, Wallace began writing a book about his alma mater (*The Notre Dame Story,* 1949), and in it as well as subsequent magazine pieces, he discarded the metaphor of ND football as "a business" and Leahy as a CEO. The school's administrators vetted his book and suggested that he do a classic portrait of Notre Dame football. Privately, the ND administrators acknowledged that Fighting Irish football had its big business aspects; however, they did not like it depicted in those terms. President Cavanaugh believed that the emphasis on business prompted questions about commercialization and led to such phrases as the "Notre Dame football factory." ND officials had long bristled at that term, much preferring the classical metaphors, particularly those from *Knute Rockne—All-American.* They wanted these applied to their football program as well as to its head coach, Frank Leahy.

During this period, Notre Dame officials tried to take as active a stance as possible with the media. Not only did they work closely with the men in the ND sportswriters' network, like Francis Wallace, but they also directed the activities of their sports publicity director, Charlie Callahan. Through him they helped perpetuate the classic image of Fighting Irish football, so vital to their institution and to intercollegiate athletics in this period.

An examination of Callahan's work, as well as that of his fellow publicists at other big-time sports schools, provides important information on the relationship of the media to university athletic departments, and how this symbiosis shaped public attitudes to college sports, countering the increasing "Aw-Nuts" criticism during the crisis and scandal years.

22

Reporters Cover College Sports, and Notre Dame's Charlie Callahan Covers Them

On any Sunday from mid-September to December, 100 or more pub-licity purveyors are shuttling around the country by plane, spreading puffs on their football teams for games scheduled the following Sat-urday. Most of the advance men travel from 15,000 to 20,000 miles a season. Many more dollars go into "dope books" or fancy press brochures . . .

Treasuries are tapped heavily for such standard equipment as radio spots, free food and drink in press boxes, expensive glossy pho-tographs by the bale, postage, office supplies, hotel room rental for press and alumni parties, cases of bonded liquor.

—Sportswriter Al Stump in the *Saturday Evening Post,*
November 1949.

Athletic departments began employing on-campus sports publicists in the 1920s, and as with so many aspects of intercollegiate athletics, what began as part-time jobs for students soon evolved into permanent occupations for graduates. During World War II at many schools, the job reverted back to students, but after the war most athletic departments hired full-time flacks and poured many more dollars than before into their sports publicity machines. Nevertheless, a certain honesty about the position remained: the job title was still "sports publicist," and the job description included various promotional chores, including "hyping" future games. (A few years later, the NCAA urged schools to change the name to "sports information director," and to proceed as if the SID's handouts were no longer publicity releases but objective information. The media, hooked on the publicists' services, accepted the title and the "hard news" pretense without protest.)

In the late 1940s, the *Saturday Evening Post* began moving away from strictly classical articles on college sports and, in 1949, had Al Stump look at the "The Ballyhoo Boys of Football." Stump usually cranked out the traditional tropes, but now that the *Post* wanted a skeptical piece, he provided it. Stump began by discussing SMU "publicity man" Lester Jordan and his handling of Doak Walker in 1948: Jordan "batted out approximately 100,000 words about Walker," supplied countless photos, set up over 350 interviews for the athlete, and played a key role in turning the running back into a Heisman Trophy winner. The SMU handouts emphasized Walker's classical characteristics, which no doubt aided him; conversely, the University of North Carolina athletic department lagged in the promotional arts, and Choo-Choo Justice also fell short as a classic hero, never winning a Heisman in spite of his multiple-year All-American honors.

By 1948, the work of athletic department publicists had become so ubiquitous that an "Editors' Note" before *Sport* magazine's profiles of All-American candidates stated: "Here you'll read no mimeographed handouts from college publicity men, but keen analytical stories by great writers." Al Stump in the *Post* indicated that "sportswriters need only slit open the morning mail to write their pre-game stories. Big Ten press agents [create an] average [of] 150 news releases a year, sent to 200 of the country's leading papers, plus 500 . . . mailed to smaller sheets," for a total of more than 100,000 handouts per year. Stump never connected this activity to the Big Ten's hypocrisy concerning de-emphasis, but he noted that "proof that most schools are neck-deep in peddling sport entertainment lies in their promotional budgets and methods."

Big Ten and NCAA authorities made no attempt to curtail the publicity machines; indeed, they tried to use them for their own ends. The *Post* article discussed a meeting in which NCAA president Karl Leib informed a group of athletic department publicists "that they now face one of the most important selling jobs in college history" to persuade the public to support the association and its new rules. Leib urged the publicists to get behind "the new Sanity Code of the NCAA"—the new name of the "Purity Code"—and sell the package "to America."

The publicists attempted to implement this suggestion, and they persuaded many members of the sporting press to view the NCAA sympathetically. Nevertheless, sportswriters were less interested in the NCAA than in the college teams they covered, often reprinting the promotional material from the sports publicity directors verbatim in their articles and columns—but under their own bylines. The *Washington Post*'s Shirley Povich so scorned this practice that he endorsed the publication of betting lines as an antidote: "Sports fans have been victimized . . . by glowing pre-game accounts" written from the publicity handouts; "however, the reader is quickly informed of the reality of the situation when good old Wonderful U, despite its great single-wing attack, is a 21-point underdog in the betting. That one line can be very illuminating," and can combat all the puffery produced by athletic department publicists.

■   ■   ■

> Of all press galleries, Notre Dame's, seating 264 and always packed for games, is rated the finest. Arriving authors are handed a program, line-ups running three deep . . . Press Chief Charley Callahan, aware that the first sentence of a game report is the most difficult to write, also adds a special "if story" which covers all possible contingencies and practically puts a lead statement on paper. Callahan has one man on the sideline who does nothing but check injuries as they occur and report by phone; a corps of radio and newsreel spotters picked for their coolness and ability to memorize numbers; three men who turn out typed summaries within sixty seconds of the final gun; three experts on statistics who shoot for six minute post-game delivery; a travel agent to arrange accommodations on the spot; a staff of chauf- feurs to drive writers to their trains. There is even a doctor, who would come in handy if anybody suffered a cramp while reaching for a roast beef sandwich.

> —Sportswriter Al Stump in the *Saturday Evening Post,*
> November 1949.

   This description of the Notre Dame press box in the late 1940s provides an indication of the school's press relations at this time, and the pivotal role played by sports publicist Charlie Callahan (he spelled it "Charlie" but never corrected a writer's "Charley"). Stump marveled at the amenities in the ND press box, and although most became standard in big-time college sports within the next decade, Notre Dame, in large part thanks to Callahan, was well ahead of the curve in the 1940s, particularly in helping journalists write their stories. Stump called Callahan one of the "stars . . . in the [publicity] field, enjoying [professional] prestige comparable to that" of his school's head coach, and a large photo on the first page of the article featured the Notre Dame SPD—a thin man in a sports jacket, bow tie, horn-rimmed glasses, and a large fedora—standing next to Frank Leahy.

   Callahan had deep Notre Dame connections as well as an Irish Catholic background. An undergraduate at the school in the 1930s, and a student press assistant to the athletic department publicist of the time, after graduation he went to New York and did promotional work for a variety of employers, including Christy Walsh's "Sports Saloon" at the New York World's Fair (Walsh had been Rockne's agent), the New York Yankees football franchise, and the Boy's Club of New York City. In 1945, when ND sports publicist Walter Kennedy resigned, Callahan applied for the job. (Kennedy went into pro sports, eventually becoming commissioner of the National Basketball Association.) Bill Stern wrote a letter of recommendation for Callahan to President O'Donnell, as did radio newsman Bob Considine, who commented that in New York, Charlie had "observed" and learned from "the conduct of many another talented drum-beater."

Notre Dame hired Callahan, and he remained in the job for over two decades, mastering the thousands of tiny and large details that made up the sports publicist's duties. As his files indicate, he wrote daily press releases, corresponded with a legion of reporters as well as the growing number of fellow sports publicists, answered constant questions from Notre Dame fans and other members of the public, and tried to comply with the endless ticket requests from newspaper people as well as friends and acquaintances. In addition, like all sports publicity people, he spent many hours tracking down and compiling statistics on games and players, arranging for team and player photos, labeling them correctly, and attending to the mailing requests of the increasing number of Notre Dame coaches and assistant coaches, who wanted sports publicity releases and photos sent to their athletes' hometown papers. He had student assistants, but training and supervising them was an additional and time-consuming part of his job.

Callahan also had to respond to the letters that ND administrators and athletic department personnel carbon-copied to him. In 1947, for example, when Frank Leahy wrote Vice President John Murphy that "we have ever so many [ticket] requests from newspapermen, radiomen, and coaches who have befriended Notre Dame in the past, and I don't believe that because we are now in the number one position, we should forget those who were our friends on the way up," the ND coach sent a copy to Callahan, and the publicist tried to translate it into action during the fall season.

The SPD's single most important task, however, was to preserve the Notre Dame image, to make sure that his sports publicity machine presented the school's athletic program the way the ND administrators wanted. In October 1947, in a typical instance, he sent a note to Vice President Murphy concerning a request from the CBS radio program "We the People" to air a feature on Fighting Irish football from the ND stadium, and to involve former and current players in the broadcast. Murphy, after discussing the proposal with President Cavanaugh, replied: "Since the thing is definitely and exclusively more football propaganda," not even using the Rockne scholar-athlete themes, "neither one of us is particularly interested in accommodating these people . . . However, we might be interested if the people behind this broadcast will do . . . more than just advance Notre Dame's [on-field] football cause," and feature the school's academic and religious activities as well as its intramural sports programs. Murphy added that if CBS would do this, "We should insist on knowing definitely what is going into the program and perhaps providing them with some of the material. Let me know what comes of this."

It was this last part of the directive that was most complicated for Callahan. Almost all of Callahan's fellow sports publicists simply promoted their school's intercollegiate athletic programs, and if CBS wanted the varsity football players to sing the fight song on their heads in the shower, the SPD would arrange it, with no administrator overruling him. But Charlie Callahan's job was much more complex—in one sense easier than all of his colleagues because the fame and popularity of the Fighting Irish kept the media knocking on his door, not he on theirs, but also much more difficult because his school and its teams lived in the sports spotlight, with every event and incident magnified and measured against the media's and the public's concept of the classical ideal. And Callahan had to keep one eye on the men in the Golden Dome, and align his work with their concept of the University of Notre Dame's total image.

To accomplish this, the ND sports publicist had to enforce his bosses' policy on vetting stories and photos about their school. He had no problem imposing this censorship upon papers in northern Indiana: they were completely dependent upon ND's goodwill; in addition, the sports departments of many Chicago and midwestern city papers practiced self-censorship to accommodate Notre Dame. However, Callahan's dealings with the national magazines and newspapers sometimes became delicate. He could never impose conditions on *Time* magazine (hence its portrait of Leahy as CEO), and, in 1948, he wrote Vice President Murphy about his negotiations with *Life,* and their representative's balking at "our usual policy on magazine stories of okaying the script, captions," and photos. Specifically, the SPD worried about "a candid camera man going around [our stadium] taking pictures of drunks or any scenes that we might decide were not pleasing." *Life,* the largest circulation weekly in this golden era of magazines, eventually compromised, agreeing to do only shots of Notre Dame students, players, and coaches. Callahan agreed, then requested and received approval for the *Life* visit from his bosses.

■ ■ ■

LOUISVILLE, KY, JAN. 29 [1949]

Completely outplaying Notre Dame from start to finish, Kentucky's powerful basketball team, rated No. 2 nationally, tonight gained revenge for the 64-55 surprise thumping handed them last year by the Irish by trouncing the visitors from South Bend, 62-38. A capacity crowd of 8,000 saw the game.

—*South Bend Tribune* special correspondent
Charlie Callahan, 1949.

In addition to his many other chores, in the 1940s Callahan also wrote frequent articles and game stories for various newspapers and wire services, often under his own name. Callahan's reports were both factual and subtly favorable to Notre Dame; in the Kentucky story, he set up a "revenge" lead, working in ND's previous triumph before he got to the lopsided score of this game. He did not mention—because he did not know and would have been shocked to learn—that this great Wildcat team led by Alex Groza and Ralph Beard probably had "dumped" the previous year's contest (see page 336). In his game reports, Callahan also emphasized Notre Dame injuries and minimized poor performances. Against Kentucky, he noted, "Notre Dame was forced to play without the services of Captain Paul Gordon," and so on.

For 1990s readers, the concept of a sports publicist writing an impartial game report is ludicrous, but in the 1940s, when many newspapers could not afford to send a writer on the road with a college team, the publicity men often filled in for reporters, and few people complained. Undoubtedly, fans were more innocent and did not perceive the impossibility of a sports publicist producing an unbiased story. Indeed, in college towns where newspapers wanted sportswriters to promote intercollegiate athletics, particularly the local school's teams, bylined pieces by the athletic department's publicist seemed totally appropriate, and indistinguishable from the work of the journal's regular writers.

Charlie Callahan, like the SPDs at other schools, did away-game reports for the hometown paper, covering many Notre Dame basketball and baseball road contests as well as track, golf, and tennis meets. He also served as the United Press and International News Service stringer on the Notre Dame campus, supplying both wire services with copy about daily football practice and other ND sports activities. He and his colleagues at other universities continued this practice into the 1950s, when it began to die out. Practical concerns, not journalistic ethics, were what killed it: the wire services hired more stringers in small cities and college towns, and also lowered their rates to local newspapers. In addition, because a wire service ticker was much more reliable than an SPD dictating a story over the telephone, papers switched to "pulled copy" for away-game reports.

■　■　■

This is the day that an important football game takes place in San Francisco's Kezar Stadium. St. Mary's College versus the University of San Francisco. Naturally, folks in the Bay region and alumni of the two schools will be concerned about the result. On the novel side though is the fact that a good many people 2,000 miles away in South Bend, Ind., will be anxiously awaiting the outcome. So will scattered hundreds who were members of the Notre Dame Class of 1938.

—Charlie Callahan, *Our Sunday Visitor* columnist,
October 1950.

Much more influential than his signed *South Bend Tribune* pieces was Charlie Callahan's weekly column in *Our Sunday Visitor*, whose masthead proclaimed it "the Most Widely Circulated Catholic Weekly in the World." Printed in Indiana but with no direct ties to Notre Dame, *OSV* went to every Catholic church and parochial school in America, where it was available for a tiny donation from a table at the back of churches and given free to schoolchildren. In the late 1940s, *OSV* had a circulation of more than 800,000 and a readership much larger than that. For almost two decades, Charlie Callahan wrote the paper's only sports column, as well as most of its sports news.

The Notre Dame SPD focused on Catholic college and high school athletic programs, but, as with the column on USF playing St. Mary's, he found a Fighting Irish angle for most topics and quickly moved to it: the opposing coaches in the Kezar game, Joe Reitz and Joe Kuharich, were South Bend natives as well as teammates at ND; they had graduated in 1938 along with Charlie Callahan. (In the late 1950s, Kuharich became head football coach at his alma mater.)

From his platform in *Our Sunday Visitor*, Callahan promoted Notre Dame's classical ideals. He devoted most of the article quoted above to the current situations of other members of the 1937 ND football varsity; many had become coaches, teachers, and businessmen, but some had earned law and medical degrees, and one had entered the priesthood. In addition, Harvey Foster had joined the FBI and was moving up in the bureau, eventually becoming a deputy chief, and Mario "Motts" Tonelli, an accountant, had been an authentic World War II hero, surviving the Bataan Death March. In the same column, Callahan also described at length three "heady" and "inspirational" plays made by All-American Chuck Sweeney to save games for Notre Dame in 1937, adding that Sweeney was now a top executive for an oil company and "I've gone into all this detail on Sweeney to show you how All-Americans are made." As a sports publicist, he conveniently overlooked his profession's role in the making of All-Americans; Sweeney, an end, was a particularly hard sell because he did not catch a single pass all season!

Callahan's subtext here and throughout his *OSV* writings was that college football in general, and the Fighting Irish version in particular, turned out America's finest citizens. The cinematic coach in *Knute Rockne—All-American* had articulated this point in addressing the Congressional-like hearing, and Notre Dame sports publicists had repeated it ever since, none more enthusiastically than Charlie Callahan.

In their letters to the editor of *Our Sunday Visitor* as well as to Callahan personally, his readers praised his columns, enjoying and even expecting the Notre Dame viewpoint. No one saw a conflict of interest between his being both ND sports publicist and *OSV* columnist. More than a dozen Catholic universities played big-time football in this era—some of the St. Mary's and USF teams attained "Top Twenty" national rankings—but no alumnus or fan of another

Catholic school ever wrote to complain about Callahan's ND bias. Indeed, his readers saw him as an authoritative spokesman for a revered point of view. Readers also accepted Callahan's premise that all Catholics should support the Fighting Irish; aiding this proposition was ND's refusal to schedule football games against fellow Catholic schools, thus avoiding rivalries with them.

Probably Charlie Callahan's greatest impact upon college sports fans came from his *OSV* columns. He influenced many people with his ND press releases and other publicity work, as well as his articles in the *South Bend Tribune* and elsewhere, but judging from the reactions of his *OSV* readers, his Sunday sports sermons affected a greater number of people and in a more profound way than all of his other efforts. In a sense, his columns were the prose equivalent of *Knute Rockne—All-American,* and he tapped into his readers' emotional attachment to that film, to the classic ideals in college sports, and to Fighting Irish football. A generation of Catholic Americans had their loyalty to Notre Dame and its values reinforced by Charlie Callahan's weekly words in *Our Sunday Visitor.*

■   ■   ■

June 28, 1948.

Miss Lillian Genn [Nonfiction Editor],
Argosy Magazine,
205 E. 42nd St.,
New York 17, New York.

Dear Miss Genn,

Even though I wired you a week back that Frank Leahy was due on the campus by now, he still has not returned to his desk . . .
    My proposed solution will be to send you another [article under Leahy's byline], and, I think, [a] better story, one which I had intended doing under my own by-line. This I will now sacrifice because I know that you are getting close to your deadline. This article will deal with the importance of quarterbacking to a coach and to a team. I have not discussed it with the Coach but I'm sure it will be okay . . .

Sincerely,

Charlie Callahan.

In his article on "The Ballyhoo Boys of Football," Al Stump mentioned that for SPDs "it has become routine," among many other duties, to "ghost-write a few columns" for the coaches, athletic directors, and athletes at their school. In the late 1940s, national magazines and newspapers constantly sought Frank Leahy's byline, offering top dollar for it, and Charlie Callahan not only provided the main conduit to the ND coach but also served as his literary phantom.

The 1948 dealings with *Argosy* magazine were both typical and more complicated: Callahan had *carte blanche* from Leahy to use his byline, however, *Argosy* did not like the sports publicist's idea on "the importance of quarterbacking" and, because of the impending deadline, ordered an in-house writer to do another piece—still under Leahy's name. The magazine soon sent this article to Callahan, who replied: "We [Leahy and I] had dinner and discussed the story thoroughly. It is very good . . . Particularly good was the term 'combat intelligence.' It is an unused phrase in football stories which is unusual in itself . . . [Also] We both trust that your source was authoritative on the Rockne story on . . . Nebraska, for it is not a known story locally. Sounds good though."

The *Argosy* piece—under the byline of "Frank Leahy, Athletic Director and Head Football Coach, University of Notre Dame"—began, " 'Combat intelligence' is a polite phrase for knowing what's going on in the opposition camp" and, using war metaphors, discussed football scouting procedures. The second half of the article concerned a trip that Rockne, as a young assistant coach, supposedly took to Nebraska in 1915 to scout the Cornhuskers before ND played them. The story, however, was a fabrication. During the 1915 season, Notre Dame and South Bend newspapers placed Rockne with the ND team and/or semipro outfits for every autumn weekend. Thus, not only did he lack the opportunity to scout Nebraska but the ND administrators' very tight-fisted money policy during this era made it almost unthinkable that they would approve his round-trip train fare to Lincoln, Nebraska, as well as other expenses. But, in the 1940s, a few major details never derailed a good sports anecdote.

In late September 1948, Ms. Genn of *Argosy* wrote Callahan that "the Frank Leahy article . . . [went] to press and a check for $200 will be sent you shortly . . . I do hope that in view of the fact that the article gives Notre Dame excellent publicity, the price we are paying is satisfactory to both you and Mr. Leahy." Considering how little work they put into it, the $200 ($2,500 in 1990s dollars) was almost found money, and the coach and the publicist did their usual fifty-fifty split of the check.

Even *Sport* commissioned Leahy pieces from Callahan. In 1948, the magazine published "My Football Secrets by Frank Leahy," and a year later, "The Truth About My Future by Frank Leahy." Charlie Callahan had the ability to turn the coach's unusual speech patterns into readable prose. The 1948 piece began, "I have fond hopes that some day my three sons will play college football. When that time comes, I sincerely trust they will come under the tutelage of a strict coach." According to Father Charles Carey, one of Leahy's undergraduate classmates and later an English teacher at ND, "Leahy was not much of a student . . . he didn't come from a very literate background." The extant samples of the coach's handwritten prose, as opposed to the letters and reports edited by his secretary, also reveal Leahy's problems with written English. Callahan, however, could summarize the coach's thoughts and also give the reader the illusion that Leahy had actually composed them, as in the use of the word "tutelage" in the *Sport* lead. The coach always chose an elaborate term over a simple one, probably as an attempt to compensate for his background.

Ghostwriting for Leahy provided Callahan with a nice income supplement; however, the coach's successor, Terry Brennan, was less amenable to ghost-written articles appearing under his byline, and the ghost-dollars slowed for the SPD for a few years in the 1950s. However, because Callahan was the most prominent sports publicist in America, his own byline also generated good money, and he churned out pieces under it for many years, not only for local and parochial outlets, but also for national newspapers and magazines.

■ ■ ■

Mr. Arthur Daley, Sports Editor,
The New York Times
New York, New York

Dear Mr. Daley:

Just this morning one of the priests here on campus brought me your column from the January 31st [1949] paper. May I thank you most sincerely for a very excellent article . . . it always does my heart good (and thousands and thousands of our friends react in the same manner) to read an article that is as outspoken and kindly as yours. And I consider it a pleasure to sit down and type out this word of thanks— again in the name of our many friends, as well as in my own name.

—Notre Dame vice president John H. Murphy,
February 1949.

Arthur Daley had written about the recently announced Fighting Irish schedule for the coming season, as well as the history of the school's football program, "founded on the Plains at West Point in 1913 when Rockne and Gus Dorais revolutionized the game with their forward passing artistry." Daley had so internalized the film *Knute Rockne—All-American* that its version of the past had become real for him, as had St. Knute: "Never did he humiliate a foe" and run up the score, and because he coached in an era of low-scoring games, "Rock always sliced it pretty thin." If Daley had looked in the Notre

Dame *Dope Book* (later called the *Football Guide*), supplied to him by Charlie Callahan, he would have discovered that in Rockne's very first games as ND head man, his squad had won 26-6, and 67-7, and throughout his career, his teams regularly clobbered opponents, including in a famous game in the East during his final season—60-20 over Penn. But for this sportswriter, Knute Rockne and Notre Dame had become classic ideals, long ago separated from their actual histories.

Similarly, the administrators at Notre Dame, whether they knew the facts or not, much preferred the idealized version—hence Vice President Murphy's note to Daley. Frank Leahy remembered the Rockne years well, but he also understood the power of positive publicity. After receiving a carbon of Murphy's letter to Daley, the ND coach sent a note to the vice president: "Am very glad over [sic] your nice letter . . . Such gestures mean much more to sports writers than we realize."

The ND administrators not only reacted positively to articles about their school and its football program, but when they felt aggrieved, they expressed their displeasure through their media allies. If they did not spot the negative pieces, often a newspaperman in the Notre Dame network sent them a copy. Arch Ward supplied the Golden Dome with a stream of clippings about his alma mater, mainly his promotional pieces and his opponents' critical ones. In the summer of 1948, for example, he took exception to a sentence in the rival *Chicago Sun-Times* about a Chicago high school football player matriculating at Notre Dame. In the article, written by the young Jerome Holtzman, Ward underlined one sentence—"He [the athlete] was awarded a scholarship at Notre Dame because of his football ability"—and sent it to President Cavanaugh. The *Chicago Tribune* editor complained, "This type [of] publicity . . . injures the prestige of Notre Dame athletics. The implication is that any outstanding football player will get priority at the University." The ND president discussed Ward's letter with Vice President Murphy, and the latter wrote back to Ward: "I wonder if there is any way of combating it," meaning the implication that Notre Dame gave athletic scholarships—it did not—and that athletes do not have to "meet the necessary scholastic requirements."

The reactions of the ND administrators reflected the fact that because they controlled their campus so tightly, they often wanted to extend their command to all things concerning Notre Dame, particularly media portrayals. Not only did they try to censor photos and articles about their school but they actively supported pieces favorable to their point of view, not simply with postpublication congratulatory notes but often with prepublication assistance.

Alert to this situation, journalists in the Notre Dame network often sent article proposals to the Golden Dome; in 1947, alumnus Bill Fay, also with the *Chicago Tribune,* wrote President Cavanaugh about "an idea" for "a Lujack article with a different slant . . . saleable to a national magazine, perhaps [the *Saturday Evening*] *Post* or *Collier's*." Fay wanted to stress Lujack's academic career, noting that "the article could be newsworthy and interesting now with the re-echoing of over-emphasis charges" from the reformers about big-time college sports. He added: "Of course, I would ask you to approve the completed manuscript before submitting it to a publisher. If you believe that such an article would be helpful at this time, I'll make plans for it, and ask John Hinkle," the head of publicity for the entire university, "to obtain some of the material thru regular university channels."

Fay's article on Lujack never appeared. Apparently it was unable to go through the required ND filters and still interest the *Post* and *Collier's* in their newly skeptical phases.

■   ■   ■

March 27, 1946.

Mr. Bernie Masterson, Head Coach [& Athletic Director]
University of Nebraska,
Lincoln, Nebr.

Dear Coach:

In a recent column in this paper, in commenting on the resumption of Nebraska–Notre Dame football relations, I reviewed the history of the former football series between the two schools in such a manner as to arouse grave resentment on the part of Notre Dame academic and athletic authorities.

In that column I called attention to the then Ku Klux Klan attitude on the part of so many of the Nebraska players [and fans] of the 1915–25 era, when the Notre Dame games were played, and of the bitterness that attitude engendered on the field; a bitterness which resulted in relations being severed for 21 years.

The Very Rev. J. Hugh O'Donnell, C.S.C., president of Notre Dame; the Rev. John J. Cavanaugh, C.S.C., vice president and . . . Frank Leahy, head coach and director of athletics, all expressed both their personal and official resentment at the appearance of such a column . . . The column was quite thoughtlessly written and should not have been printed, and I hereby express my regrets and apologies to you as Nebraska's head coach . . .

Yours sincerely,

Jim Costin
Sports Editor.

Jim Costin, of the *South Bend Tribune*, had written honestly and accurately about the anti-Catholic and anti-Irish insults of the Cornhusker players, students, and fans during ND visits to Lincoln in the 1910s and 1920s. During this era, many Nebraskans joined the Ku Klux Klan, which had helped organize anti-Catholic crowd taunts. In 1925, KKK members had prompted and plastered the local newspaper headline, HORRIBLE HIBERNIANS INVADE TODAY, in store windows. Indeed, the events surrounding and during the 1925 game, particularly at halftime, persuaded ND officials to end the series. The halftime show had mocked the Four Horsemen, portraying them as hired, ignorant laborers, not real college students, and Irish Catholics as only fit for menial tasks. When, two decades later, Jim Costin described some of these events, ND administrators insisted that he recant and apologize directly to the Nebraska coach and athletic director.

Costin, totally beholden to Notre Dame, sent a servile apology, promising that "when the time comes for the resumption of the series in 1947"—the schools had contracted for a home-and-home beginning that year—"I hope to be able to write about it in a manner which will cause no embarrassment to anyone." He carbon-copied President O'Donnell and Vice President Cavanaugh of Notre Dame, also groveling to them: "I hope these letters will assure you again of my sincerity in attempting to make amends to you and the university for any trouble or embarrassment I might have caused you by my recent thoughtless and very careless writing." In addition, he apologized for a remark he had written about the postwar Notre Dame games against Army and Navy, and also apologized to their coaches, also sending copies of these letters to the Dome.

Why did the ND administrators want to rewrite history, particularly an episode that in no way reflected badly on their institution? The rupture with Nebraska illustrated how ND officials of the time put religious and ethnic convictions ahead of football profits, ending one of Notre Dame's most lucrative 1920s series. (Rockne, placing money over principle, opposed the break.) Moreover, O'Donnell had been a young faculty member in the 1920s, Cavanaugh an undergraduate, and both knew the history firsthand.

Possibly, in the 1940s, as Catholics increasingly entered the American mainstream, ND officials wanted to downplay the anti-Catholicism of the past and start anew in their relations with a large public university like Nebraska. Whatever their motives, because they controlled many of the journalists who wrote the histories, they used that power. After reading Costin's original article, President O'Donnell sent a memo to Vice President Cavanaugh: "Re: Costin spews—This Peru reporter [Costin was from Peru, Indiana] must be brought to time"—to dance in the correct time.

Ironically, Jim Costin was one of the tamest writers covering ND in this period, not a Notre Dame graduate but a religious Catholic who loved the Fighting Irish. Probably Costin's problem with the Nebraska column occurred because he knew that the historical events reflected positively on Notre Dame and badly on Nebraska, and he told the story fully expecting ND applause. He had not grasped the shift in institutional policy. (The history of

Notre Dame reactions to offensive halftime displays would add a chapter in the 1990s when Stanford's marching band mocked Catholicism and Fighting Irish traditions; this time, Notre Dame officials protested vigorously.)

In some ways, in the 1940s, the ND attempt to control journalists was old-fashioned, reflecting the imperial period of American journalism when publishers and their allies dictated the content of newspapers. In other ways, the ND administrators' premise about the impossibility of objective reporting, as well as the corruptibility of editors, writers, and the public, was almost postmodern.

Ironically, in one of its few nonclassical moments, *Knute Rockne—All-American* reflected the ND officials' attitude: when Rockne and his fellow coaches privately discuss the college sports reform movement, Rockne says, "The public isn't misled. They don't believe this stuff"—about the need for reform. Father Callahan, the cinematic president of Notre Dame, counsels, "The public believes whatever it reads in the papers, Knute. Unless it is denied in type just as large—and preferably larger," then people swallow the bolder headlines.

This comment reflected a long-standing position of the men in the Golden Dome. In early 1947, Vice President Murphy quoted the current ND president as saying that "old Father John Cavanaugh, a former President of ours," and upon whom the cinematic Father Callahan was based, "had the right slant on newspaper attacks. He said it never pays to answer a newspaperman [in public] unless you own a newspaper yourself" and, in lieu of that, to work behind the scenes and reply through friendly publishers and reporters. In this period, most American university administrators shared these sentiments, and acted upon them in their relations with local and regional media.

At Notre Dame, President Hugh O'Donnell was more authoritarian and less worldly than his successor, Father John J. Cavanaugh. Cavanaugh had a better sense of public relations than O'Donnell, and when he became president, he avoided confrontations with the media as well as direct reprimands of writers and editors. As one insider later noted, "Cavanaugh censored with a golden glove, rather than a mailed fist like 'Pepper' O'Donnell." In addition, in 1948, Cavanaugh reorganized the university's hierarchy, creating the office of executive vice president as well as various vice presidential positions, including one in charge of public relations. The ND president appointed Father Theodore Hesburgh to the former office and Father John Murphy to the latter.

Cavanaugh's administrative moves came at a fortuitous time for his institution. Not only did Notre Dame face a college sports world in flux, but its old nemesis, the Big Ten, wanted to change the basic rules of intercollegiate athletics and, through the NCAA, impose its will upon all other schools, including ND. As the university's executive vice president, Father Hesburgh represented Notre Dame in its dealings with the Big Ten and the NCAA, and when the inevitable conflicts occurred, he proved more than capable of dealing with all situations. Hesburgh's initial strategy, however, was to sit on the sidelines while the Big Ten and its opponents from the South and Southwest fought the opening rounds in the NCAA arena.

23

The NCAA's "Sanity Code"
Crashes into the Power Blocs

A major showdown is due at the National Collegiate Athletic Association conclave in January [1948], between the Job Plan, as exemplified by the Big Ten . . . and the legal athletic scholarship plan, chiefly identified with Southern institutions. "Semipros!" the job planners have been saying to the scholarship schools. "Hypocrites!" the scholarship boosters have shouted back.

—Francis Wallace's "Pigskin Preview,"
the *Saturday Evening Post*, September 1947.

Some sports historians see the NCAA's 1948 continuing ban on athletic scholarships as evidence of the association's sincerity in promoting truly amateur, student-based athletics. Not surprisingly, the NCAA's official history also espouses this line. However, an examination of the records of the time reveals a very different situation, one closer to Francis Wallace's description in the *Post*: a clash between power blocs and their different approaches to paying athletes—above or below the table—as well as the general cynicism of the founding fathers of the modern NCAA.

The main purpose of the 1948 NCAA annual meeting was to place the 1947 "Purity Code" at the center of the association's constitution (that process required the extra year's wait). However, the code's ban on overt financial aid to athletes sparked opposition from schools in the South and Southwest that granted athletic scholarships. As in previous years, critics questioned the motives behind the NCAA's plan to clean up college sports, seeing the lofty language of the code as a camouflage for Big Ten self-interest. Fueling their argument was the fact that Tug Wilson, Big Ten commissioner and secretary-treasurer of the NCAA, along with Iowa professor Karl Leib, president of the NCAA, led the association's move against athletic scholarships.

Wilson and Leib claimed that this prohibition would ensure the amateur status of college sports and preserve its classic ideals; their opponents pointed out that the "job plan" used by all Big Ten schools—paying athletes for minimal work or phantom jobs—was far worse than open athletic scholarships; moreover, because most schools in other conferences did not have "job plans" in place, an NCAA ban on athletic scholarships would give the Big Ten and its allies a major recruiting advantage. Thus, during this crucial early period of the modern NCAA, a huge gap existed between the association's idealistic rhetoric and the political motives of its main movers. Rather than close this space and opt for absolute amateurism—abolishing athletic scholarships *and* job plans—the Big Ten agenda prevailed, enshrining a basic contradiction in key clauses of the NCAA constitution.

Before the 1948 meeting, media and fans debated the pros and cons of job plans and athletic scholarships. *Sport* magazine headlined an article "Should College Athletes Be Paid?" and asked radio broadcaster Bill Stern to tell "why he stands firmly in favor of strict amateurism in U.S. colleges." Increasingly distressed by the postwar corruption in college sports, Stern emphasized the term "strict," condemning not only athletic scholarships but also the "phony job situation . . . the kind of job where the star halfback accepts a monthly pay check for ringing the dinner bell" in a dormitory once a month. He, as well as the millions of fans who listened to his radio broadcasts and read his articles, had internalized the scholar-athlete ideals: "Getting a higher education should be the primary reason for any youngster going to college. Athletic achievements, however sensational, should be secondary and should serve as a means to an end, namely a *legitimate* college diploma. Let's keep the record straight, when a college athlete plays for pay," receiving money through athletic scholarships or phony employment, "he's a professional no matter what uniform he wears."

In the postwar era, a large majority of sports reporters and fans believed in the classic ideals. Like Bill Stern, these college sports enthusiasts wanted the corruption to end, and probably they would have supported "absolute amateurism" as a reform measure. Nevertheless, almost all intercollegiate athletic officials considered true amateurism untenable; NCAA administrators only stated this opinion privately, but their opponents spoke openly.

In its next issue, *Sport* magazine had radio broadcaster Harry Wismer present the arguments for athletic scholarships—significantly, because the editors endorsed the traditional ideal, they had Stern do the "con" *before* giving space to the "pro" position. Wismer appealed to logic and pragmatism: "It's easy to say piously that college athletics should be snow-white pure, that they should be amateur with a capital A," but that ignores the reality of intercollegiate athletics as well as the importance of sports and winning in American society. Therefore, because no one can stop coaches and alumni from recruiting the best players for their teams, and paying them if necessary, instead of talking about "simon-pure" amateurism, "it's time someone proposed a practical plan for the operation of sports in American colleges and universities." For Wismer, the athletic scholarship program was the best proposal so far, and he enthusiastically endorsed it.

But, realizing that unadorned pragmatism would not convert the American public, he wrapped his argument in an updated version of traditional sports ideology: the "bootstraps" parable, the athlete-hero lifting himself from poor circumstances to great achievements. "This country won't lose anything by encouraging sports-minded young men to go to college. The boy who is a trained athlete goes into life with a deep-rooted desire to win. He's a credit to his family, to his schools, and to his country. If such men were prevented, by lack of money, from educating themselves, the United States would lose out on something big." When Wismer read this during a radio broadcast, "America the Beautiful" welled up behind his words, and he added: "We [Americans] would lose out on the kind of men who have made this country great in the past, and the kind of men we count on to make it great in the future."

The appeal to patriotism and altruism short-circuited the accusation that athletic scholarships were a cynical cover for paying college athletes. Wismer's position evolved into the line that athletic scholarships provide a wonderful means for poor boys to get out of the coal fields of Pennsylvania, et cetera, and, in later eras, the ghettos of America's cities. (Of course, this argument omits a key question about the societal purposes of higher education: why do colleges and universities intensively recruit poor kids with sports talent, and mainly ignore their classmates with greater academic but less athletic potential?)

In the *Saturday Evening Post,* Francis Wallace took a step back from the debate and described the dispute in real-world terms: the code's ban on money to athletes is "too easily broken—by the alumni, if not by the schools. And the urge to break the law will always be there, as long as colleges talk in terms of classic amateurism, yet operate football as a big-revenue proposition." Wallace underlined the fundamental flaw in the modern NCAA: its rhetoric and its rules based on "classic amateurism" mainly masked commercial greed.

COLLEGES ADOPT THE "SANITY CODE" TO GOVERN SPORTS

NCAA Bans Scholarships in Which Athletic
Ability Is the Major Factor . . .

Violators of Rules Can Be Suspended or Expelled

—*New York Times* headlines and subheads on the NCAA
convention, January 1948.

Not only the *Times* accepted the NCAA's reforms at face value; other major newspapers and the wire services added their applause. The Associated Press called the "Sanity Code"—the updated version of the "Purity Code"—"one of the most important documents in NCAA history." The *Times* trumpeted: "The revised constitution," incorporating the code, "has the effect of transforming the NCAA from an advisory body to a national [organization] with regulatory power over the 400 colleges in its sphere of influence."

Mainly because of Tug Wilson's parliamentary maneuvering, the expected fight at the 1948 NCAA convention did not occur. Before the meeting, he and Karl Leib appeased the opposition by appointing a number of its leaders to key committee posts, most notably Georgia Tech's Bill Alexander to the chair of the constitutional revision committee, which was in charge of putting the code in the NCAA's constitution. The respected football coach persuaded his southern colleagues to go along with the "Sanity Code," in part because it, unlike the "Purity Code," allowed off-campus recruiting. In addition, Leib promised, "We are putting the chief emphasis on compliance, rather than punishment." Therefore, wink and nod, schools could interpret and comply with the rules as they saw fit. Nonetheless, open athletic scholarships were forbidden, but job plans could continue—a situation that caused the compromise to begin to unravel later that year.

The "Sanity Code" also incorporated Tug Wilson's ostracism idea—the association could now suspend or expel rules violators—and, with these laws in its constitution, the NCAA moved from a purely advisory organization to one with regulatory powers. But many delegates, particularly the Southerners, regarded the NCAA regulations as paper tigers, lacking claws and teeth. The NCAA seemed to confirm this view when it announced the appointments to the new three-man Compliance Committee, the main instrument for judging cases and enforcing rules: the head of the Southwest Conference, a proponent of open athletic scholarships; the AD of Tufts University, an advocate of athletic department growth; and the longtime faculty representative of the University of Michigan, an apologist for the corrupt Big Ten job plans. Thus, as soon as the NCAA built its first constitutional "henhouse," it assigned foxes to guard it.

In its article on the 1948 NCAA meeting, the *New York Times* also reported that Iowa professor Karl Leib was "re-elected president of the NCAA for a second term," and he "expressed keen satisfaction at the adoption of the 'Sanity Code' with which he has been closely identified." Indeed, as Walter Byers, at the time Tug Wilson's assistant in the Big Ten and NCAA office, subsequently remarked, "In the late 1940s, I was one of a small group that patched together . . . the modern National Collegiate Athletic Association." Leib, Wilson, and Byers constituted the inner circle of the "small group," and through planning and maneuvering in this period, they molded the future form of the

NCAA as well as that of big-time college sports—a shape that reflects their political goals, not their classical rhetoric.

■   ■   ■

There is not a professional [sports] club which does not have written evidence and, in quantity, that the colleges have "professionally" induced boys to enter [to play sports for them]—boys, too, who are kept in college on such terms that we . . . define as professionalism.

Such men are just as much professional . . . as if they were on our [pro team] payrolls, but frequently with the added feature that neither the boys nor the college admit it. Surely, it is not part of the educational process to create or permit hypocrisy.

—Brooklyn Dodgers president Branch Rickey, January 1948.

The NCAA and the college coaches associations invited Branch Rickey to a joint session of their 1948 conventions, intending to rebuke him about the increasing number of signings by major league baseball clubs of undergraduate players. Nicknamed "the Mahatma" (a high-minded leader), Rickey was the most influential professional sports executive of this era; the college men assumed that a chastened Rickey would arrange an end to the baseball raids, setting a precedent against the signings of underclassmen by teams in all pro sports. The NCAA leadership backed the coaches because they too disliked college stars, particularly football players, leaving early, disrupting athletic programs and hurting gate receipts.

Branch Rickey, one of the shrewdest men in American sports history, completely outwitted his university opponents. He spoke with great moral authority—he had helped Jackie Robinson break the major league color barrier the previous year—and he bluntly told the college officials, "Your position would be stronger if your own house were in order." He then outlined the "written evidence" against the colleges, and stated his main point: "If you don't make your men professionals, we won't either."

Rickey, a former college athlete and coach, and a man proud of his university education, believed in the classic ideals, but he saw through the NCAA's invocation of them. He attacked the college sports officials at the point of their greatest weakness, their hypocrisy: "According to your own rules," if a college player "is not an amateur, then you are not entitled to play him, and particularly so since you made him a *de facto* professional . . . Baseball, I am sure, will conform fully" to your wishes and end the signing raids "if we are dealing only with *bona fide* college players," authentic students playing sports. The issue is simple: "If you will stay out of the professional field, we will stay out of" a truly amateur "college field."

The chairman of the baseball coaches association admitted that "he put us right back on the defensive." Rickey, however, was also a practical man; along with his criticisms, he offered a specific proposal: if intercollegiate athletic officials instituted real amateurism, pro baseball would only sign college players after their class had graduated and they had used up their playing eligibility. Within a decade, after further NCAA claims of reform as well as Rickey's departure from the Dodgers, his proposal became the *modus vivendi* for American professional and college sports for the next generation. Elements of it are still in place at the end of the twentieth century.

After Branch Rickey addressed the 1948 meeting, most coaches and ADs left the hall. If they had remained, they would have heard a short speech by the president of the American Council on Education. His words were unremarkable, but his presence foreshadowed a major event in the history of college sports reform: the early 1950s attempt—after the basketball "fix" exposés and many more football scandals—by the ACE and its special panel of college presidents (prompted by and including Father Cavanaugh of Notre Dame) to bypass the NCAA and to bring authentic reform to intercollegiate athletics (see Chapters 36 and 37).

■　■　■

> The football Black Market seems to be operating about as usual. If the brethren of the NCAA doubt this, they should read my mail [from coaches and ADs]. The working people in football obviously don't think what one called "The *Insanity* Program" will work. Here are some typical quotes:
>
> East: "It is being evaded, or the athletes I've talked to are liars . . ."
>
> Midwest: "We are through as a major power unless we go into the market and match them [other big-time programs] dollar for dollar . . ."
>
> South: "We thought we had a workable system [with athletic scholarships] but went along with the Purity Boys because we had to . . ."
>
> Rocky Mountain: "Gate receipts do most of the talking in football . . ."
>
> Pacific Coast: "So much hogwash."
>
> —Francis Wallace's "Pigskin Preview,"
> the *Saturday Evening Post,* September 1948.

According to Wallace, one of the best informed sportswriters of the time, from the January 1948 passage of the "Sanity Code" to the publication of his September article, the NCAA had reformed nothing—indeed, the association had not closed a single stall in the notorious college sports "black market." The three-man Compliance Committee had met in Tug Wilson's office in Chicago in April and drawn up a questionnaire on how athletes paid their college bills; the committee then sent the form to administrators of every NCAA school—not to the athletes—hoping for honest responses, though most observers expected the opposite. Then, in early August, the University of Virginia shocked the committee and the NCAA by holding a press conference to announce its multifaceted aid to athletes—most of it in violation of the "Sanity Code."

In the next eighteen months, UVA helped lead the fight against the code, and the school's position, as articulated by its president, never changed: "We want to be honest above everything else"—not pretend to be in compliance with the code while resorting to subterfuges as other schools do. More, because "we think it's too much to ask a boy to play football, keep up high academic standards and work also," UVA will continue to give athletic scholarships and advocate their open use. Significantly, Virginia also condemned the Big Ten's "job plan" and its enshrinement in the NCAA code: "We feel it is hypocrisy to give the boys clock-winding jobs to help pay their way. This is allowed under the Sanity Code," and benefits Big Ten schools and their allies with similar setups.

The NCAA mandarins responded angrily to Virginia's challenge, claiming that to keep reform alive, they had to punish UVA, possibly expelling it from the association. In 1948 and 1949, the Compliance Committee gathered the evidence—mainly UVA's public statements—for their case against the school, issuing high-minded bulletins as they worked. However, NCAA president Karl Leib revealed the association's Big Ten bias and actual agenda when he told the *Washington Post* that "the University of Virginia should step down a notch and play smaller schools if it cannot have a first-class football team and still comply with the NCAA code." In other words, if the upstart schools of the South and Southwest cannot finance their football players through a "job plan" as Iowa and its Big Ten colleagues did, "let them go down a notch and play within a smaller class," and allow the Big Ten and its friends to continue to rule big-time college football.

Leib, like other NCAA officials of the time and later, always tried to wrap *realpolitik* within moralistic language: "The NCAA is not conducting a witch hunt [against Virginia]. We are trying to draw up a workable set of rules to prevent professionalism in college football." Then, to poke UVA's wound, he claimed that Big Ten schools, "Pacific Conference, and [some] other big conferences are complying" with the code. "There will never be [athletic] equality among all schools. This is technically impossible . . . [some] schools are bound to have more jobs available." Finally, with amazing arrogance, he added, "For a school to assume it has a right to have a topnotch football team regardless of its circumstances" in providing jobs "is foolish."

The UVA football coach exploded at Leib's statement, pointing out that "circumstances" for "Leib's own school, the University of Iowa, located at

Iowa City . . . [were] not one whit larger than [UVA's] in Charlottesville." The only difference was Iowa's elaborate "job plan" for its football players versus UVA's refusal to establish one; as a result, Iowa played a full big-time schedule, whereas UVA faced NCAA expulsion. Moreover, to tell UVA to drop down in class and to invoke NCAA rules—written by Iowa and colleagues to ensure their exclusive big-time club—moved beyond hypocrisy and into a new realm of totalitarian thought.

Indeed, soon after the exchange with the UVA coach, Karl Leib's speech to the 1949 NCAA convention illustrated the "doublethink" and "newspeak" of George Orwell's *1984*, one of the most popular books of this period.

■　■　■

PROSELYTING, OTHER COLLEGE ATHLETIC EVILS DIMINISHING,
NCAA HEAD SAYS.

Improvement Seen Under Sanity Code

Prof. Leib Declares Definite Progress Has Been Made in Nation's Colleges

—*New York Times* headlines and subheads
on the NCAA convention, January 1949.

The *Times* did not record the membership's reaction to Leib's 1949 speech, but probably many NCAA delegates laughed privately at his Panglossian view of college sports. Within a few years, police investigations into the basketball fixes revealed massive and country-wide violations of the "Sanity Code" in 1948 and 1949, not just in basketball but also in football and other collegiate sports.

In the first years of its modern form, the NCAA had not yet mastered the art of public relations; the association's leaders, particularly Karl Leib and Tug Wilson, frequently confused their ambitions with reality, making public pronouncements as if their desires had already come true. If they had heeded the advice of their young assistant, Walter Byers, they would have toned down their rhetoric, avoiding listener skepticism as well as later ridicule when their claims crashed into actual events. (When Byers ran the association, he always preferred silence to inflated declarations; in addition, he concentrated NCAA PR campaigns on a few well-crafted themes.)

Two other issues that came before the 1949 NCAA convention seemed minor at the time but subsequently proved enormously important. For the first time in NCAA history, delegates discussed television. The AD of a school in an urban area where consumers had started to buy TV sets claimed that telecasting home games had hurt his gate receipts; Vice President Murphy of Notre Dame disagreed, noting that two years of televising home games in South Bend had not dented the demand for ND tickets. Michigan's Fritz Crisler, however, argued, "If colleges want to get out of television, it should be done this year"—as if schools could make that choice, could hold back what the AD at Berkeley called a "revolution to which all of us must adjust ourselves." Walter Byers attended this meeting but did not comment. No doubt he listened attentively, trying to work out a role for the NCAA in the dawning television age. His eventual plan enabled the association to monopolize the televising of college sports for many decades (see Chapters 39 and 40).

The other issue, one upon which almost all NCAA delegates agreed, was the need to regulate the post-season bowl games. At this time, fifty-nine bowl games existed, with most of the local promoters and committees keeping a huge slice of the revenue for themselves. In addition, the unsavory atmosphere surrounding many bowl events had attracted "Aw-Nuts" press attention, damaging the already shaky image of college sports. A magazine article, "The Case Against the Bowls," listed the problems, with Walter Winchell ellipses for emphasis: "Four-flushing promoters . . . ticket gouges . . . bigoted bids based on creed and color . . . wage payments to college 'amateurs' . . . shameless commercial advertising tie-ins . . . assorted minor 'fixes' . . . loss of precious vacation and pre-exam study time by the [athlete] students . . . plus other hazards and heartbreaks." The list read like an anticlassical parody, the bowls violating everything positive that college sports supposedly represented.

Shirley Povich in the *Washington Post* noted that the position of the real reformers was to abolish the bowls: "The Ivy League turned their faces against bowl games as an improper extension of the football season," and Notre Dame "has gained greater respectability by consistently declining" them. Nevertheless, NCAA leaders—Povich termed them the "self-styled righteous element"—ruled out abolition because they were not concerned with the unethical aspects of the bowls, only with the money questions.

At the 1949 convention, NCAA officials reported that very few bowl promoters would allow the association to inspect their financial books; in addition, schools participating in bowls were receiving diminishing payouts—in some cases, none at all. A group of conference commissioners, prompted by Tug Wilson, then proposed the creation of a "Bowl Game Committee" to establish rules on bowl game payouts and on bowl participation by NCAA members. The 1949 convention accepted this proposal, empowering the committee to meet, draw up regulations, and present them for approval at the 1950 meeting.

A year later, the committee submitted a plan to the delegates whereby the NCAA would certify all bowls and participants, ban uncooperative promoters, and require 80 percent of gross game revenue as well as a large percentage of tickets to go to the participating schools or to their conferences if they had shared-payout arrangements. In spite of bitter divisions at the 1950 convention on the "Sanity Code" issue, the membership overwhelmingly voted for these controls. The delegates also installed a permanent Committee on Extra Events to refine and enforce the bowl rules, ensuring that in the future NCAA members would only participate in "certified" bowls. An economist later commented that "in contrast to other NCAA regulatory efforts" like the "Sanity Code," "which were couched in public service terms, this move to control post-season football represented the most open [NCAA] maneuver to transfer [college sports] income to its members. Despite some brief discussion about protecting 'athletes from injury,' " and other bits of standard rhetoric, only one "interpretation of this plan" made sense: the association wanted *"to divert income from bowl game sponsors to NCAA members."*

Soon the Committee on Extra Events succeeded in weeding the chaotic landscape of post-season events into a controlled and profitable garden. The association's cartel behavior in regard to the bowls greatly pleased the membership and established the actual foundation of the modern NCAA: from the bowl precedent came the NCAA's monopoly on television contracts and on many other aspects of college sports.

Despite massive disputes over the "Sanity Code," at no time was the association in danger of disintegration. With the leadership's deft actions on the bowl issue, it demonstrated the true usefulness of the organization, specifically how it could funnel increasing amounts of money into members' pockets (and also into its own bureaucratic growth). No individual school or conference possessed the clout or could act in so monolithic and powerful a way as the NCAA if it moved with the solid support of its membership.

Most schools quickly grasped this truth. Despite angry internal disputes in future years, the association's success as a cartel on the bowl issue and other financial matters bred a loyalty as well as a dependence on NCAA-generated money that proved crucial for the organization's expansion.

Nevertheless, the NCAA's passage from 1949 to its future behemoth stature was not a straight line, and events in 1950 reveal much about that journey as well as about the association's true position on the reform of intercollegiate athletics. No single person and college sports program illustrated the latter issue better than Curly Byrd, the president of the University of Maryland, and his football Terrapins, contenders for the national championship in the late 1940s and early 1950s and the winner of the crown in 1953.

24

Curly Byrd Exposes NCAA Hypocrisy

[H. C.] "Curly" Byrd is a . . . college president who both played on and coached his school's football team. He coached from 1913 through '34 . . . From the time he became president in 1936, he pried funds out of the legislature to expand the school . . . and, of course, he did not overlook sports. He built an attractive [athletics] plant centered on Byrd Stadium, which seats 35,000 today and will some day hold 75,000.

—Sportswriter Tim Cohane in *Look* magazine,
November 1954.

In 1949, the University of Maryland, like Virginia a member of the Southern conference (a forerunner of the Atlantic Coast Conference), joined UVA in protesting the "Sanity Code." Maryland president Curly Byrd not only publicly denounced the NCAA's new rules but soon became the main organizer of the opposition to them. Byrd, like many college presidents of the time and forever after, believed that the way to build the fame and fortune of a university was through athletic triumphs, and he resented anything that impeded him, particularly the Big Ten and its manipulation of NCAA rules. In the postwar period, Byrd's University of Maryland Terrapins were typical of the rising powers in college sports, exemplifying the new model for success in intercollegiate athletics and operating in a manner antithetical to reform.

Like his opponents, Curly Byrd was also a master of classic rhetoric, wrapping his ambitions for sports conquest in traditional athlete-hero terms: "Men play football and engage in other athletics because they have within them that competitive spirit which differentiates between the aggressive fighter and one who is content to take things as they come." Byrd also liked to invoke the

American God of Progress: "And in the development of this aggressive fighting spirit is found the essence of human progress. Men who have objectives, who have ideals . . ." And so on.

Byrd's own aggressive spirit led to a ruthlessness that even surprised such cutthroat characters as Paul "Bear" Bryant, head football coach at Maryland in 1945. The Bear left College Park after a successful first season because the president "fired my [main] assistant . . . Straight out fired him without telling me a thing. And [then] I saw this big tackle *I had fired* going up the dormitory stairs. I asked why he was still there. 'Well, the boss [Byrd] just took him back,' " Bryant was told. Bryant did not pretend that his players were students: the fired "big tackle" was supposed to clean out his dorm room and leave school—and Byrd did not save him to continue his academic career, but to play football. The coach got the message: the school president "thought he knew as much football as the coaches he hired." Bryant "knew . . . that I couldn't coach for him," and so he immediately jumped to the University of Kentucky.

To replace the Bear and to continue to build the Terrapins into a football power, Byrd hired "Big Jim" Tatum, recently fired by Oklahoma for openly paying his players after a bowl game. A sportswriter described Tatum as wearing "flashy ten-gallon hats which add to his swashbuckling appearance," and replying to the question, "Is winning over-emphasized in the bigtime [college] game?" with, "I don't think winning is the most important thing. I think it is the only thing"—years before Vince Lombardi supposedly uttered this maxim.

In 1949, Byrd and Maryland clashed with the NCAA's Compliance Committee over the question of athletic scholarships. Byrd encouraged Tatum to recruit in football-rich western Pennsylvania, and to attract players to Maryland with offers of athletic scholarships. Tatum's assistant in charge of this recruiting area remarked, "If I saw a boy I liked, I could offer him a scholarship on the spot without checking back with Jim" or the school's admissions office; "we got a lot of good boys that way, because we could offer them something definite while other people were checking back with their head coaches" and university officials. The Terrapin traveling football admissions office violated all standard academic procedures but garnered All-Americans, including the Modzelewski brothers ("Big Mo" and "Little Mo") as well as other excellent players. It also became a model that continues at some schools to this day.

Throughout this period, the mainstream media, including the nearby *Washington Post*, treated Curly Byrd and his Terrapins kindly, never discussing the details of his behind-the-scenes football maneuvers and consistently reprinting his line about building his entire institution as well as its intercollegiate athletics program. The reality of Byrd's university only appeared in the press years later, with the belated publication of the Middle States Accreditation Committee's report on the school, done during the Terrapins' rise to the top of the national football polls. Among other criticisms, the investigators compared the expenditure of millions of dollars on a new stadium and a new field-house to the school's "grossly inadequate library" and minuscule budget for books and library services; moreover, "while football players constitute only 1.5 percent of the student body, they receive . . . 54 percent of the [university's entire] scholarship money."

■   ■   ■

[On the eve of the 1950 NCAA convention], Dr. H. C. (Curly) Byrd, president of the University of Maryland, had this to say about the possible expulsion of several schools [including his own] from the NCAA for code violations:

"A school like Ohio State claims to comply with the code, yet it comes up with a Rose Bowl team. What practices did they employ to build this team? . . . VPI [one of the schools facing expulsion] has won only one game in the last two years. Ohio State and Michigan [won 28 and] say they are complying. We want to know how they turn out those [powerhouse] teams."

Byrd, a former Maryland coach, will be the spokesman for the three protesting conferences—Southern, Southeastern, and Southwestern—at tomorrow's [NCAA] meeting.

—Associated Press report, January 1950.

Curly Byrd saw NCAA politics as he did football: as a rough, mean struggle where underdogs should use any tactic, including biting and gouging, to win. Because a month before the 1950 convention, the Compliance Committee had charged his school and six others with "Sanity Code" violations, recommending their expulsion from the NCAA, he fought back by attacking the Big Ten universities behind the NCAA maneuver.

When Byrd spoke at the convention, he stated bluntly, "I understand that Ohio State University has what we'll call unusual jobs for its athletes. The Compliance Committee looked into the situation and found that it conformed with the code . . . Does Ohio State want to vote for the expulsion of Virginia," and other schools, including Maryland, "when Ohio State has facilities to take care of" its athletes like this? Byrd and his allies were less concerned with the details of OSU's job plan than with Big Ten/NCAA hypocrisy in punishing schools that granted athletic scholarships. However, his comments caught the interest of the *New York Times,* which subsequently revealed that the Ohio State "athletic office has lined up . . . 150 jobs" for OSU athletes, the most questionable ones being for the "football players as [Ohio] State House pages or [carried] on the payrolls of the Highway Department and other state agencies." The *Times* also interviewed Professor Ralph Aigler of Michigan, a member of the three-man NCAA Compliance

Committee, who acknowledged that in Ann Arbor "not a few employers prefer athletes" to regular students; however, when a reporter ranged beyond the job issue, confronting Aigler with proof that two Wolverine hockey players had previously played for a professional team, "Aigler brushed him off with the statement that Big Ten investigators had given Michigan a clean bill" on that matter, and all other questions about U of M athletics.

The Compliance Committee's accusations against the "Seven Sinners," the press nickname for the schools facing expulsion, and the countercharges from Curly Byrd and his allies caused an important event midway through the 1950 NCAA convention in New York—an event significant because it did not occur. General Dwight Eisenhower was supposed to give the convention's "Principal Address," extolling the traditional virtues of intercollegiate athletics. In 1950, Ike was president of Columbia University in New York, but at the last minute, rather than make the short trip downtown and speak before the increasingly rancorous NCAA—a group moving far from the ideals he espoused for college sports—he canceled his appearance, sending a perfunctory excuse. The disjuncture between the language of the "Sanity Code" and the reality of the NCAA's activities obviously bothered observers like General Eisenhower. Nevertheless, the NCAA leaders as well as their opponents seemed oblivious to this situation.

At the same time as Ike's snub, the *New York Times*'s Arthur Daley, a longtime supporter of college sports, indicated his diminishing opinion. "The sheer hypocrisy which exists in intercollegiate athletics [today] is monumental and almost beyond belief," particularly the constant denials of "countless instances of subsidizing and proselyting. But no writer in his sane mind would dare print a word of it" for fear of being maligned by the perpetrators. The disgust of this influential sportswriter reflected a much wider media discontent about big-time college sports, indicating how profound were the problems faced by the NCAA and its members at this time.

The day after Ike's canceled speech, the delegates were ready to vote on the expulsion of the "Seven Sinners." The NCAA leadership called it "one of the most important [events] in the history of college athletics," whereas their opponents termed the vote "an instrument of hypocrisy." Byrd and his allies had lined up a large number of supporters, not only all the Southern and Southwestern schools but, as the AD at Louisiana State noted, "a lot of independents are coming over to our side, they have started thinking for themselves instead of following the [Big Ten] leader."

After tallying the ballots, NCAA president Karl Leib tried a dubious trick: because a small majority favored expulsion, he declared, "The motion is carried." But the opposition leaders knew that the NCAA constitution required a two-thirds majority to expel members and, from the floor, immediately and loudly pointed this out to Leib. The AP reported that the NCAA president finally announced, " 'The action failed,' but declined to concede [that] the result was a victory for opponents of the Sanity Code."

At this point, Curly Byrd moved to the podium. Showing that his exposure of NCAA hypocrisy did not prevent him from engaging in similar double-dealing, he pledged his own and his group's allegiance to the association: "We want to back the NCAA to the end, so that athletics in this country shall be on a higher plane than ever before. We are in complete sympathy [with] moves to raise the standards of the NCAA." In reality, Byrd and his allies wanted a code without teeth but, for public relations purposes, with classical trimmings.

The 1950 vote pointed toward the former, but only a strong PR machine in full damage control mode could effectively use traditional rhetoric for cover. The problem in 1950, later acknowledged by the NCAA's official history, was "that the only penalty provided under the [Sanity] Code was expulsion . . . a severe penalty," provoking the revolt led by Byrd and exposing the association to the scorn of many observers. Expulsion was too blunt an instrument. Damage control requires subtlety and gradations of response; the NCAA needed minimal penalties to minimize crimes. The association's leaders learned from these events. In subsequent years, they installed flexible and light penalties— for violations much more serious than those committed by the so-called "Seven Sinners"—and perfected the NCAA's damage control strategy.

In 1950, despite the success of the revolt, an indication of the viability of the new NCAA order occurred when the members passed, almost unanimously, the resolutions granting control of bowl games to the association and the establishment of the Committee on Extra Events. Curly Byrd's Terrapins had already participated in a number of bowls, receiving disappointingly small payouts; the school president understood the wisdom of having an NCAA with enough power to extract the maximum number of dollars and tickets from the bowl promoters. For that reason, as well as his desire to establish a toothless association, he and his allies wanted to work within the system. They realized that beneath the NCAA's elevated rhetoric was a flawed and malleable organization. So, before the convention ended, Byrd steered himself and a number of his allies into high positions within the association.

In addition, the rebels demanded the head of Karl Leib, which they quickly gained when he chose not to run for another term. Replacing Leib was Hugh Willett, faculty representative of the University of Southern California, a school famous for its corrupt athletic practices, but with the cover of membership in the Pacific Coast Conference.

In his autobiography, Walter Byers discussed his train ride home from New York to Chicago after the 1950 convention. Seated in the club car with Tug Wilson, who had managed to retain his NCAA secretary-treasurership, and

Hugh Willett, the association's new president, the young assistant remarked that all three members of the NCAA's inner circle "were depressed over the loss of the Sanity Code" vote on the "Seven Sinners." Byers claimed that the gloom resulted from the convention's rejection of true reform; an outside observer might have connected the mood to the censure of the Big Ten/NCAA leadership, and the realignment among the power blocs controlling the association.

Despite all the classical language emanating from the NCAA in the postwar period, the arguments within the organization were not about the fundamental reform of college sports. They mainly concerned power and money, how to share the former in order to divide the latter more equitably. The Big Ten and its allies greedily wanted to resume their prewar domination of big-time college sports and its revenues; the upstart Southern, Southeastern, and Southwest conferences wanted to expand their athletic programs, acquiring a larger piece of the economic pie—but Big Ten/NCAA barriers impeded them. Curly Byrd and his colleagues corrected this situation at the 1950 convention.

25

Notre Dame Responds
to the New NCAA

Football is not out of hand at Notre Dame and we won't let it get out of hand. If the time ever comes when it threatens to get out of control, we'll handle it here, and we won't have to be reminded by someone else.

—Notre Dame vice president Murphy, November 1947.

Throughout the late 1940s, Notre Dame remained remote from the controversies within the NCAA. In 1947, President Cavanaugh's hostility toward the "Purity Code" evolved into nonconfrontational skepticism. Late that year, with the vote to ratify the "Sanity Code" approaching, Father Murphy reiterated his school's independent position in the statement above. Then, after the 1948 convention, Murphy privately advised Cavanaugh: "I think you should write . . . to Tug Wilson, stating our intention to comply" with the code. "No doubt most others," particularly in the Big Ten, "have already done so, and they may very well be waiting to see what Notre Dame will have to say . . . [and] how we shall meet the new requirements. As I say, I think we shall be meeting them more honestly than any other school." Cavanaugh did as his vice president suggested.

In late 1949, with another NCAA convention approaching, the ND Faculty Board in Control of Athletics noted in its minutes, "In light of the subsidization practices and abuses now in vogue in many universities, Notre Dame's position was reviewed, and there was emphatic agreement that we would meticulously continue to observe the NCAA recommendations applying in this area," and articulated in the "Sanity Code."

During this period, Notre Dame was less interested in being an NCAA "goody-goody" than in traveling an autonomous and loftier course than the association. Adding credibility to the Catholic university's position was its open invitation to college sports officials and reporters to inspect its academic and financial books. Notre Dame, a private institution, had no obligation to allow anyone to examine its internal affairs; however, it repeatedly issued the invitation because, as ND officials maintained, "We have nothing to hide." Visitors saw student files and transcripts, and confirmed the school's claim that its athletes needed a 77 percent GPA to be eligible for intercollegiate sports. In addition, ND permitted the publication of its financial statements. At this time, most state universities, including those in the Big Ten, refused to open their academic and financial books.

In addition to cooperating with investigators, Notre Dame officials implemented their athletics policy in other ways. Because of the fluid "black market" in college players, various people contacted the ND athletic department about excellent athletes willing to transfer to Notre Dame from other schools. ND coaches forwarded these inquiries to their bosses in the Golden Dome, and the vice president would then inform the inquirers that, even though "transferring" was within NCAA rules, Notre Dame had long rejected the practice, a few wartime exceptions notwithstanding. On occasion, when the original letter came from an ND alumnus, the administrator added that the antitransfer rule helped Notre Dame maintain good relations with other schools and squashed all rumors of ND "poaching" other teams' stars—a constant charge against football programs that accepted transfers during this period.

Similarly, on recruiting, even though the "Sanity Code" allowed coaches to hunt for prospects, Notre Dame maintained its conservative policy. In 1949, the chair of the Faculty Board in Control of Athletics told a man who had found an outstanding high school player that "the young man himself [must] write to our athletic director, Mr. Frank Leahy, or his assistant, Mr. Edward Krause, informing them of his desire to enter Notre Dame. We do not . . . contact boys until they have signified their desire to enter Notre Dame." And, once the Catholic school admitted a player, it invoked the 77 percent GPA regulation, with Father Murphy often proclaiming that this was "7 percent over the requirements of the Big Ten Conference," and "7 percent more than any other college or university that I know of."

The most public aspect of the "Fortress Notre Dame" strategy, however, was the school's ongoing refusal to participate in bowl games. With each successive championship season in the late 1940s, the bowl game offers escalated, reaching $120,000 for the 1950 Sugar Bowl; the chair of the bowl committee also informed ND that his group had adopted the "proposed NCAA postseason bowl football plan," thus guaranteeing Notre Dame the promised minimum or a higher amount if revenue warranted ($120,000 was the largest guarantee to one school for a single game at this time). Executive Vice President Hesburgh politely refused: "I know that you perhaps will think us old-fashioned in this, but we feel very strongly about our obligation of seeing that these boys [on the football team] receive a good college education," thus, when the regular football season ends, "they need every moment of extra study to prepare for [final] exams," and cannot continue in daily practice for a bowl game.

Notre Dame's invocations of scholar-athlete values differed from those made by the NCAA and other big-time college sports schools in one major respect: after invoking the ideal, ND did not turn around and pocket the dollars. As Hesburgh explained to a correspondent in late 1949: "We were offered large sums of money for . . . post season games this year [again], and while the University is having a very difficult time making ends meet, we feel that the education of our athletes is something that we cannot sell or barter. If we are not true to this primary interest of the University, we should not play football at all." In 1949, Notre Dame had permitted publication of its most recent annual financial statement, revealing a net operating loss and an endowment of less than $7.5 million; therefore, $120,000 in 1940s dollars would have helped the school's finances. The books also revealed that the priests running Notre Dame kept football expenses as well as coaches' salaries to a minimum.

■   ■   ■

We at Notre Dame have ever tried to steer a middle course between the two extremes which either condemn football out of hand or make football an end in itself . . .

Notre Dame will continue to play football as she has in the past . . . *within the rules and regulations we set ourselves to follow.*

—The Rev. Theodore M. Hesburgh, December 1949.

Father Hesburgh became executive vice president of Notre Dame in 1948, but a year later he was still so little known that in its report on his speech at the annual ND football banquet, the *Chicago American* called him "Fred A. Hesburgh." The dinner occurred two weeks before the 1950 NCAA convention. This impending event, and NCAA president Karl Leib's attendance at the banquet, provided part of the context for Hesburgh's remarks, as did the recent demands for total football de-emphasis by a number of prominent educators. Hesburgh rejected the condemnations of college football, and he also scorned those who made the game "an end in itself," Curly Byrd's Maryland being a prime example. Most of all, here and in other speeches, Father Hesburgh emphasized Notre Dame's independence in intercollegiate athletics, the fact that ND did not belong to an athletic conference, and would not join a political bloc within the NCAA. Undoubtedly Karl Leib left disappointed because of ND's refusal to enlist in the Big Ten campaign against the "Seven Sinners" slated for expulsion at the NCAA convention.

Reinforcing Notre Dame's position was the historic separation of Catholic higher education from state universities and most private institutions. In addition, in 1950, two of the schools facing NCAA ejection were Boston College and Villanova University, Catholic schools belonging to different religious orders from Notre Dame but equally skeptical about secular American higher education. At the 1950 meeting in New York, the head of Boston College articulated the Catholic viewpoint when he explained his school's refusal to cooperate with the NCAA and its Compliance Committee: BC "simply cannot admit that a body set up for the handling of intercollegiate athletics can conceivably be more competent to judge a college's education standards than the college itself." Unlike Maryland and Virginia, BC and Villanova did not grant athletic scholarships: they simply refused to surrender any authority over their internal affairs to a secular organization like the NCAA.

Because Notre Dame's late-1940s situation diverged from that of its Catholic colleagues—the Fighting Irish won three of four national football championships, whereas other Catholic schools had lower profile athletic programs—ND chose to cooperate with the NCAA, but always indicating that its regulations were its own, and stricter than the association's. This plan not only fit the school's traditional "Fortress Notre Dame" policy, but also allowed it to remain the classic ideal for the media and millions of fans during this dark time in American college sports.

In 1950, after the tumultuous NCAA convention, the Associated Press asked Father Cavanaugh whether his school continued "to subscribe to the Sanity Code." The ND president answered affirmatively, adding that even though the code was not "the perfect answer" to the problems in college sports, "at least it is a move in the right direction." This remained Notre Dame's position throughout 1950 and for the remainder of the short existence of the "Sanity Code."

■　■　■

> The abuses and evils [in college sports] have grown to a point where it has become a public scandal. Whether intercollegiate football is a racket is beside the point, but the public has come to think it is a racket, and some kind of curbs must be put on it.
>
> —Tufts College AD Clarence Houston, January 1951.

During his service on the NCAA's Compliance Committee, Houston saw the underside of intercollegiate athletics up close. At the January 1951 NCAA convention, he spoke in defense of the "Sanity Code" and its attempt to regulate college sports. Other NCAA officials also pleaded for keeping the code on the books. The association's president warned that if the member schools totally destroyed it, "we face . . . a crisis in American collegiate athletics."

Nonetheless, Curly Byrd and his allies, after a frustrating year of working on NCAA committees and trying to remove all possible teeth from the code—and facing annoying opposition—decided to dispose of it once and for all, driving a stake through its heart. They came to the 1951 convention well armed, having lined up the two-thirds majority necessary for the execution.

The Big Ten and the Pacific Coast Conference stood against them; in addition, some small colleges, seeing that Byrd's world of wide open recruiting and subsidization meant enormously increased costs for everyone, lined up with the NCAA establishment. During the meeting, supporters of the code spoke at length, but opponents rarely responded, not even to direct attacks. According to reporters, the opposition only came alive when the "president of the NCAA announced the result of the vote"—the death of the code—then "there were cheers and much back-slapping."

But in removing the "Sanity Code," the delegates had also blown away the NCAA's fig leaf of traditional rhetoric, leaving big-time college sports in a more exposed position than ever before. Nonetheless, throughout the code's history, sports commentators and fans, rather than fully examine its appearance and reality, focused on such seemingly peripheral questions as "two-platoon football," complaining loudly about it.

In this unsettled era, however, even the platoon dispute began to transcend simple sports chatter. It connected directly to the major issues in big-time college sports, the split with the one-platoon past evoking both the classic ideals and the uncertain future.

26

Fan Confusion—
"Block That Two-Platoon System"

SATURDAY AFTERNOON MEAT GRINDERS

Fans in the Stands Are Yelling like Mad—Block That Two-Platoon System. Some Football Experts Believe the Only Way to Save the Game Is to Throw Out the Unlimited Substitution Rule.

. . . the two-platoon hipper-dipper [deception] wraps up all the abuses of college football in one untidy package. Since more players are needed to make the thing work, more intense proselyting is required. Keener competition for talent boosts the 'inducements' given to some very odd, road-show scholars.

—*Collier's* magazine title, subhead, and quote from an article,
October 1949.

Two-platoon football started in 1942 as a temporary measure to help the college game survive the wartime emergency. So many all-around players had entered the military that coaches began using large numbers of pre-draft freshmen and "4F-ers" in limited one-way roles. After the war, with plenty of good athletes returning to college or entering from high school, coaches continued to train players as offensive or defensive specialists, markedly increasing the level of play. In this period, coaches also prevailed upon their conferences and the NCAA to maintain unlimited substitution, but they agreed to end freshman eligibility.

Many fans and sports reporters disliked two-platoon football, as did a number of older coaches who were unwilling and/or unable to switch to the new

248

system. One of them, Knute Rockne's pal Jimmy Phelan, told his colleagues, "The fans are confused by the terrific numbers of men you're using. It detracts from the game" because coaches are taking the sport away from the players. "It's time to stop such methods—they're making a farce of the game."

By 1949, with the end of military demobilization, other problems began to occur. With only the pool of high school grads to stock two-platoon rosters, well-funded programs competed ferociously to assemble scores of good recruits, leaving fewer prospects for the middling and poor teams. As the *Collier's* article indicated, two-platoon football escalated the cost of and the cheating in college sports as well as the academic frauds involving athletes. As a result, some schools started to de-emphasize the sport. Ratcheting down his program, the president of Fordham announced that football at the big-time level "doesn't do us any good financially, scholastically, socially, or [even] athletically." Other colleges, to keep their programs afloat, began to sell games to the powerhouse schools; for a decent guarantee, they agreed to play in the big-time team's stadium, even though they had almost no chance of winning. Gene Rossides, an Ivy League standout in this period, said of this practice, "I wouldn't respect my school if it put me on the field to have my brains knocked out" in an intentional mismatch for money. (The selling of games and players by small and medium-sized programs continues to this day; particularly during the early part of the season, undermanned squads lose to Top Ten teams like Nebraska by lopsided scores, but the visiting school receives a nice paycheck.)

The October 1949 article in *Collier's,* a major mainstream journal, indicated the growing media hostility to various aspects of big-time intercollegiate athletics. It also cited one exception on the bleak college football landscape: "Football has not conferred enduring benefits on any school except Notre Dame," mainly because ND does not cheat, and the Irish do not schedule games against "patsies." In addition, Frank Leahy had not fully embraced the two-platoon system, preferring such sixty-minute players as Leon Hart, outstanding at offensive and defensive end and the 1949 Heisman Trophy winner.

Nevertheless, many of Leahy's coaching colleagues favored unlimited substitution, most notably Fritz Crisler of Michigan with his young teams during World War II, and then with his massive squads in the postwar period. In the 1948 Rose Bowl, the Wolverines humiliated USC, 49-0. According to one sportswriter, Crisler amazed and dismayed the huge crowd and the national radio audience by sending "in a complete new eleven every time the ball changed hands."

Crisler's success persuaded other big-time coaches to install the two-platoon system, and, in the late 1940s, Colonel Earl Blaik of Army, remembering a close call against Michigan in 1945, followed suit. In the postwar period, the supply of great players to the military academies diminished significantly, and Blaik saw the advantages of unlimited substitution. His defection from one-platoon football helped sanction the new method, and during these years, the American Football Coaches Association reacted to the increasing criticism of two-platoon by voting endorsements of it at its annual meetings.

In addition, Frank Leahy started experimenting with "group substitution"; in 1948, when ND went on defense, he replaced his offensive backfield with a set of defenders. Leahy remained conservative compared to Crisler and Blaik; nevertheless, his methods were radically different from those of his mentor, Knute Rockne. After the war, Leahy hired Marty Brill, one of Rockne's best halfbacks, to coach the offensive backfielders. However, a reporter noted, "There are no longer a simple shift and a few major plays" in the ND offense. "Now he [Brill] faces a complicated system of innumerable plays." Brill admitted that "I'll have to stay up nights to learn the details of" Leahy's system. Apparently he could not adapt to the new game, departing after one season.

In the postwar period, many fans also had trouble adjusting to the new game; conservative by nature, they wanted football to return to its simpler prewar state. *Sport* magazine explored their discontent in a 1948 pro-and-con debate: "Is Free Substitution Bad for Football?" Radio announcer Harry Wismer argued, "Football was always tough to follow . . . But now, only the coach knows who's in the scramble of defensive lines, offensive backs, and 'messenger boys.' " College football in this era, with its somber uniforms and smallish numbers, was not spectator-friendly, and, according to Wismer, two-platoon "made football even more confusing to watch—and incidentally, to report over the radio—than it ever was before . . . you have to be a certified public accountant to give an accurate radio description of a football game." Moreover, for many fans and media people, coaches calling every play by sending in "messenger" substitutes violated the classic ideal: university athletes were supposed to think for themselves, on the field and off.

The complaints against two-platoon strike a 1990s reader as quaint; however, in the pretelevision age, fans only experienced a football game from the stadium seats or a radio description. One-platoon football placed the same twenty-two players on the field for much of the contest, but "free substitution" not only doubled that number but added "messengers" and other subs from lower on the depth charts. Many fans—as well as an announcer like Harry Wismer, famous for spending more time in the hotel bar than in game preparation—were reluctant to learn the new offensive and defensive alignments and to master the expanding rosters.

Some media people, however, loved two-platoon for its razzle-dazzle, and also saw its potential for enhancing their careers. Answering Wismer in *Sport* magazine was Bill Stern, NBC sports director. He claimed that "free substitution" created "much faster football" and more interesting games. "What's so wrong with [player] specialization," he asked, when it delivers such a superior product? Stern's attitude reflected an important cultural trend in postwar America: specialization had helped win the war, Hollywood war movies celebrated it, and postwar industry glorified it in the shift to the consumer economy. Eventually, when a majority of Americans endorsed specialization, most football fans accepted unlimited substitution.

In the radio booth, Bill Stern, with many more assistants and spotters than announcers like Harry Wismer, understood his advantage over his competitors and quickly adapted to two-platoon football. Nevertheless, in his *Sport* article, he situated his main argument for "free substitution" within the traditional ideology of intercollegiate athletics; the subhead stated his main point that unlimited substitution "Gives More Boys a Chance to Win Their [Varsity] Letters." Stern maintained that now every player "has a definite chance to see some action, no matter what his [athletic] shortcomings are. Thus more boys can get into the games and realize a lifetime dream, the chance to earn a coveted college letter. This promotes better spirit on a big squad."

Just as Harry Wismer, in another *Sport* pro-and-con, tried to convince readers of the wisdom of athletic scholarships by invoking American patriotism and altruism, Stern appealed to equality and fair play as well as an idealized view of college football as amateur fun-and-games. In reality, many coaches considered two-platoon the most efficient way to crush opponents and win. Stern's arguments, like Wismer's, indicate the malleability of the ideology of college sports. To persuade fans to embrace a particular position, proponents construed the core beliefs in extraordinary ways, always linking their self-interest—like Wismer's inertia and Stern's ambition—to idealistic rationales. This era put this rhetorical strategy in play; in subsequent decades, college sports changed in many ways, but each move was enveloped by invocations of the traditional ideals, and even today, every new proposal is packaged in classic language.

In a *Saturday Evening Post* article, sportswriter Fred Russell saw the implications of unlimited substitution, and he did not like them. Mocking the main promoters of two-platoon, the big-time coaches, Russell wrote: "Many builders of character [also] plan separate kickoff and receiving units. Some will go so far as to insert a special place-kick crew for the point-after-touchdown attempt." He then quoted the lament of a coach at a small college: " 'Soon there will be no such thing as an all-around football player. And the bigger colleges will employ sets of offensive and defensive coaches.' "

Russell understood that the big-time coaches drove the two-platoon system, that its existence enlarged their programs and budgets, expanded their empires, and, most important of all, enhanced their personal prestige and earning power—as long as they won. However, the new football system was more Darwinian than its predecessor. Every head man with a "Top Twenty" team created many losing coaches; two-platoon not only enabled the best-funded and most ruthless coaches to thrive but speeded up the demise of the less "fit." The end of Harry Stuhldreher's coaching career illustrated the post-war realities, including the new breed of college football fans.

■   ■   ■

FOOTBALL'S DIRTY LINEN SOMETIMES SHOWS

Taken by itself, the Stuhldreher story might be passed off as an amusing account of the tribulations of a football coach. But it cannot be so interpreted. Rather, it is still another manifestation of the moral paralysis which has made college football at most institutions a frankly professional enterprise . . .

For more than ten years, every literate American has known that college football stars, despite Purity Codes and pious protestations to the contrary, are paid for their services either by the college itself or by alumni groups. Almost without exception, institutions that deny the charge are either woefully ignorant, painfully sanctimonious, or nonparticipants in big-time football.

—The editors of the *Saturday Evening Post*, October 1948.

This editorial underlined the *Post*'s shift from classic treatments of college sports to a more critical approach. If "every literate American" had "known" all about the underside of college football for more than a decade, they had not acquired much of their knowledge from the *Saturday Evening Post*. Until the postwar era, despite a few skeptical articles and some scattered comments in Francis Wallace's "Pigskin Previews," the *Post* had mainly featured traditional portraits of coaches, players, and college sports programs. But by the fall of 1948, with the obvious failure of NCAA codes and other reform attempts, the *Post* not only criticized the schools in big-time football, but, in the same issue as the editorial, it printed Mary Stuhldreher's attack upon the fans—the people who kept the enterprise afloat with their ticket purchases and radio listenership. After this, the magazine ran many more critical and/or behind-the-scenes articles, culminating in a series of exposés of college sports in the 1950s. The *Post*'s shift both reflected and shaped the growing skepticism of "literate Americans" about intercollegiate athletics.

In the 1940s, Mary Stuhldreher's husband, Harry (the QB of Rockne's Four Horsemen), coached the University of Wisconsin Badgers. After limited success during the war and immediately after, his team sank to the bottom tier of the Big Ten in 1948, mainly because he did not adapt to the postwar football system. The *Post* titled Mary Stuhldreher's article "Football Fans Aren't Human," and subtitled it "[She] Tells What Happened to Her Family Because

Her Husband Happened to Produce a Losing Team. A Shocking but True Picture of Big-Time Football." Not only did the Wisconsin students mock the coach with insulting signs, particularly when the Badgers lost to teams like Yale, but townspeople made nasty phone calls to the Stuhldreher home as well as crude remarks to Mary and the Stuhldreher children in stores and school. Mary wrote, "I minded for the children, because other children taunted them about their father," and the jibes "were getting under their skins."

Mary also indicated that the Wisconsin situation was not unique; she listed the experiences of other coaches' families during losing streaks—all had tried to ignore the insults but most failed; one wife couldn't eat and her "children refused to go to school." Neither the author nor the editors, in their work on this piece and in their editorial, offered much historical perspective on the situation, other than insisting that the volume of abuse was much louder and meaner than prewar student protests about losing teams. Those had been campus "hi-jinks"; these were cruel and unrelenting.

World War II had permanently changed college sports fans: the concept of "total victory" had migrated from warfare to other areas of American life, particularly to college sports, eroding the traditional "sportsmanship" approach. In the prewar era, most fans of "down programs" maintained a grin-and-bear-it attitude, whereas postwar partisans showed much less patience with teams and coaches who failed to deliver victory. Despite Mary Stuhldreher's denunciation of all fans, many remained traditional, but the number of "rabid rooters" was growing quickly, and they stood out from their polite brethren. By 1948, probably many fans would still have applauded such classic gestures as Cornell's renunciation of its 1940 fifth-down win, but a large number would not. The wartime and postwar ethos had spawned the modern fan—a branch of this species eventually devolved into the body-painted maniacs of the late twentieth century.

The Stuhldreher case revealed other aspects of postwar college sports. The University of Wisconsin student newspaper offered a very accurate analysis of the reasons for Stuhldreher's coaching failures, not only his unproductive on-field tactics—his offense remained similar to Rockne's Notre Dame Shift—but also his inadequate recruiting. The student editorial board asked a number of pointed questions: "Are race and color considered in choosing players?" and "Do other universities in the [Big Ten] conference offer greater inducements to attract players than . . . Wisconsin?" The writers obviously knew the answers but wanted readers to think about these issues. Stuhldreher, like his fellow Notre Dame alumnus, Frank Leahy, had made no attempt to recruit African Americans, even though many Big Ten schools had improved their teams with black players, in the process passing Wisconsin in the standings, and as for the Badgers' meager "job plan," Mary Stuhldreher offered the excuse that the school was not "located near large cities where it is possible to find better jobs for athletes," ignoring Madison's status as the state capital—Ohio State in Columbus had long used a similar situation to great "job plan" advantage. With a few deft strokes, the student analysis revealed Harry Stuhldreher's failures as a Big Ten program head, and, after the Badgers' 2-7 1948 season, he resigned, departing intercollegiate athletics for private business and never coaching again.

A decade earlier, the Wisconsin student editors would not have asked such questions in print, if at all. In the heyday of classical sportswriting, sharp analysis of college sports—particularly of off-field matters—rarely appeared, never in heavily censored student newspapers. But just as the war had sparked specialization in many American occupations, including college football coach and player, it prompted more expert journalists and even fans.

The week after Mary Stuhldreher's article appeared, the *Saturday Evening Post* ran a feature about a college sports enthusiast in New York who, "By Steeping Himself in Gridiron Data 70 Hours a Week . . . Has Become the No. 1 Authority of Football Lore." The fan—a true forerunner of today's sports collectors and trivia nuts as well as serious researchers—"crammed" his apartment with "150,000 clippings, 200,000 photographs, [and] some 30,000 books and guides, costing $25,000." The *Post* writer explained: "Originally a Saturday diversion, football has become the compensating substitute for the disappointments and frustrations of . . . [his] social and professional life."

Reading today about this fan and his piles of paper prompts the standard quip "Get a life"—until one learns that the man, Dr. Louis Henry Levy, began in 1945 to write football guides and trivia books, which became very popular, evolving into best-sellers when taken over by mainstream publishers. Moreover, Levy served as a research source for various people, including, in 1948, "George Allen, assistant coach of Michigan's 150-pound team, [seeking] data on the origin of football scouting, the subject of his master's thesis" (the same George Allen who became a successful NFL head man).

In the postwar era, few fans were as obsessed as Dr. Levy; most took a more casual approach to college football. Immediately after the war, rooters were so delighted to have their favorite sport and teams return that they attended games in record numbers. Later in the 1940s, however, as two-platoon took firm hold and the off-field scandals escalated, they began to grumble and stay away. But for the supporters of one school, Notre Dame, 1946 through 1949 was a golden era, a period when "Leahy's Lads," as the press called them, lived up to the classic ideal—and never lost a football game.

27

Leahy's Lads Capture
the Spotlight

A record crowd of 70,000 will jam [the University of Illinois] Memorial Stadium Saturday in hopes of seeing a modern counterpart of Illinois' famed Galloping Ghost in super-speedy Buddy Young; and invading Notre Dame is not scoffing at the possibility.

—Associated Press pre-game report on the Illinois–Notre Dame game,
September 1946.

No schools benefited more from the immediate postwar college football boom than Notre Dame and the Big Ten powers. A matchup like Illinois versus the Fighting Irish attracted local, regional, and national attention, and also served important social and cultural functions. As indicated by the AP report, which was based on an Illini publicity handout, some Big Ten universities had started to promote their best black players as stars; Illinois was even comparing Buddy Young to the school's and the conference's greatest football hero, Red Grange, the "Galloping Ghost."

The halftime show of the 1946 game marked another social and cultural breakthrough, one that could not have occurred at a Big Ten school in the prewar era. According to a newspaper account, "the 175-piece Illini band formed a human Golden Dome and accompanied a voice teacher in an 'Ave Maria.' The largest crowd ever to watch a game at Champaign stood reverently until the song ended." Popular Hollywood films like *Song of Bernadette* (1943) had made "Ave Maria" and other Catholic hymns known to millions of Americans, but the Illini band's gesture indicated the increasing goodwill felt by average Americans, even in the Protestant heartland, toward Catholics and toward their most famous university, Notre Dame. This meshed with the

Catholic school's attempt to move into the cultural mainstream; as one pro-ND sportswriter enthused, "Notre Dame, with its French name, Irish nickname, and other foreign names [is] a truly American university."

Unfortunately, this was the only game between Notre Dame and Illinois in this period. That year, the minutes of the ND faculty athletic board recorded a letter received "From Mr. [Doug] Mills, Director of Athletics, University of Illinois, telling us that the Notre Dame–Illinois football relationship would not be renewed after 1946." Mainly because of Tug Wilson's "ostracization" strategy, Illinois joined other important Big Ten universities in banning ND from its schedules. In fact, this proved to be a supremely short-sighted tactic, hurting the schools that adopted it, not the Fighting Irish.

■　■　■

> So what if after the war some Big Ten teams avoided us [Notre Dame]? We never had trouble getting good games. We still played Southern Cal, they were regular opponents like Navy and others . . . we also added some of the best teams in the country like Southern Methodist when they had Doak Walker and Kyle Rote . . .
>
> The press couldn't get enough of us. Even for regular football practices during the week, you'd see lots of reporters from the big city papers and national magazines along the sidelines. Then on football weekends when the radio boys showed up . . . and soon TV started, it was like the circus coming to town.
>
> —Edward "Moose" Krause, 1991.

In the late 1940s, sports media covered most big-time college football contests adequately, but they blanketed Fighting Irish games as if they were as important as World War II battles. In part, the lengthy undefeated streak created intense media interest but, just as important, the multitude of longtime ND rooters provided a huge base audience for print articles and radio programs about the Fighting Irish. When they were joined by millions of regular sports fans, the readership and radio ratings soared.

In addition, in this period Notre Dame began to attract increasing numbers of supporters for nonreligious and nonethnic reasons. Francis Wallace attempted to explain "why the American public, and not just the Irish and Catholics, like it [ND] and root for it." Using Hollywood war movies and their "Notre Dame characters" as his reference, he discussed one of the school's greatest heroes, Jack Chevigny. As a player, Chevigny had starred in the "Win One for the Gipper" game; the film *Knute Rockne—All-American* highlighted his deeds. Then, although overage, he joined the Marine Corps during the war and died on Iwo Jima. Wallace maintained that Chevigny's

"Notre Dame credo"—"My *team,* my *school,* my *family,* my *friends,* my *faith,* my *country*"—was simply the basic "American credo," and that the public had started to see Notre Dame as a quintessentially American phenomenon, not merely a Catholic and Irish one.

That Wallace could plug Fighting Irish football so effortlessly into the metaphors of World War II movies attests to Notre Dame's distinctive place in the popular culture of the 1940s. In addition, because he had been a Rockne press assistant, he could readily draw on the ideology of *Knute Rockne—All-American.* Wallace concluded his discussion of Jack Chevigny by invoking basic American icons—Notre Dame "will continue to build upon its two great sources of strength, God and the Melting Pot, upon which our country was also built"—leaving readers unable to separate his articulation of Notre Dame beliefs and values from his desire to wrap his alma mater in the most sacred American totems. Nevertheless, most readers in the late 1940s seemed to like his work, if the letters to the editor of the *Saturday Evening Post* and Wallace's book sales are accurate indications.

No matter how Notre Dame fans and alumni felt, if the late 1940s media had not seen a story in the Fighting Irish—one that sold newspapers and magazines and boosted radio ratings—they would not have continued to lavish so much attention upon ND football. In 1947, a South Bend sportswriter began a feature on a Notre Dame home game with "Telegraph lines leading out of South Bend [tomorrow] will hum with approximately 138,000 words describing the football battle for a little patch of green earth Saturday in Notre Dame Stadium." Most of the wires connected to the ND pressbox and the almost three hundred sportswriters who filled its seats—not only local and regional journalists but often the luminaries of the profession, including Grantland Rice, Stanley Woodward, Red Smith, and other New York columnists. The *Notre Dame Alumnus* termed the pressbox "The Headline Helicopter," because it seemed "to hover over the game."

Because ND continued its radio policy of accommodating all broadcasters, often as the South Bend reporter noted, "At the microphones [for the game] will be 'Red' Barber for CBS; Ted Husing for Mutual; Bill Stern for NBC," and such leading regional and local announcers as "John Harrington, WBBM, Chicago; Jimmy Dudley, WJW, Cleveland; and Joe Boland, WSBT, South Bend." This blanket radio coverage ensured that almost every football fan in the continental United States could find a station carrying the ND game, whereas supporters of other college teams—even of the top-rated powers—had to be near the contest and/or the home area of the school to hear their favorites play.

In 1947, telecasting of Notre Dame games also began, not only in the South Bend region but by coaxial cable to stations in Chicago and other midwestern localities. In a quaint headline, the *South Bend Tribune* announced:

"230,000 Fans to See Irish" play tomorrow, "175,000 of Them Will View Game by Television," while the others would be in the stadium. The article explained, "In the Chicago area alone nearly 10,000 television receivers will be available for the televised broadcast. Many of the receivers will be set up in" public places so that large numbers of people can watch. Again, other schools began televising games in this period, but none could match the instant size of the ND viewing audience.

Similarly, other college football teams in the postwar period had strong fan bases in their states or regions, but none remotely challenged the national supremacy of the Fighting Irish. Crucial to ND's dominance was the fact that from December 2, 1945, to October 7, 1950, "Leahy's Lads" did not lose a game. Notre Dame came to symbolize the best in college football in the same way that the New York Yankees epitomized it in baseball, and Citation in horse racing. This greatly pleased the millions of ND supporters; the aura of excellence enveloped them. And for ND rooters as well as most other college sports fans, Notre Dame not only meant Number One on the field but, because it was a scandal-free program, the Fighting Irish also represented the traditional ideals.

Some fans who climbed onto the Notre Dame bandwagon in this period had different motives. Many people simply loved winners. Others, particularly wealthy Americans, came to regard the national champions as a "must-see"; they wanted to witness Fighting Irish games as well as the World Series, the Kentucky Derby, and heavyweight championship fights. One ND alumnus commented that because of the team's popularity at this time, the school's alumni increasingly "spread" their seats "among close friends and business contacts, and you almost had to 'be somebody' to get a ticket to the game," with the favored few becoming "a blue-chip audience." But upscale spectators tend to sit on their hands, rarely cheering enthusiastically for or against any team. The number of such fans, along with the ND alumni ticket holders, helps explain the quiet crowds at many Notre Dame contests during this time. (A similar phenomenon occurred at many ND home games in the final decade of the century.)

Grantland Rice remarked in a 1949 article on ND's football schedule that "all one has to do is book Notre Dame and then be sure of a complete sellout . . . I'm afraid the same thing couldn't happen to Michigan, Army, California, North Carolina, or Georgia Tech. Not on foreign soil, away from partisan rooters." Thus, even at the height of their postwar popularity, the other great teams of the era could not fill stadiums away from home. Only the Fighting Irish could, in part with their national supporters but also with those "blue-chip" fans who wanted to see and associate with the best team in the sport. Moreover, by 1949, with the increasing scandals and the public cooling toward college sports, when the market began to sag for the major football powers and crash for the minor ones, Notre Dame sailed along, filling stadiums, beloved by fans. In part, ND achieved this by winning and upholding the classic ideal, but, in addition to its new supporters, it maintained its huge fan base including the Notre Dame Family, the Fighting Irish Fanatics, and the Subway Alumni.

■ ■ ■

When any of us [in the Big Ten] meets Notre Dame, [even in a Big Ten stadium], 70 percent of the spectators are for Notre Dame. Why? It's a matter of religion, not of football. We simply didn't care to mix athletics and religion, so we dropped Notre Dame.

—An unnamed Big Ten president to Grantland Rice,
January 1949.

This statement ignored the conference's "ostracization" strategy as well as the high percentage of ND fans, particularly in Big Ten stadiums, who rooted for Notre Dame for nonreligious and nonethnic reasons. Nevertheless, many Fighting Irish supporters did "mix athletics and religion," but not in the simple way suggested by the university president; moreover, because Notre Dame rooters divided into distinct groups, their conduct was far from uniform.

The Notre Dame Family—the C.S.C. priests, the faculty, students, staff, and alumni—cheered for their football team but never turned the games into a religious crusade. These fans, however, constituted a small fraction of all ND rooters; because of the university's modest size, by 1949, there were about 30,000 Family members, including all living alumni.

Fighting Irish Fanatics—people with no tie to the school other than similarity of religion and ethnic origin—made up a larger percentage of fans, numbering probably about 250,000—although their numbers kept increasing because they, like their counterparts elsewhere in college sports, represented the new breed of fan. The Fanatics regarded Notre Dame football as part of a "holy war" against Protestant America, and they demanded "total victory" every time the Fighting Irish took the field. Some Fanatics obtained tickets to games, but most of their activities occurred in other public places, like the streets of New York before and after Army-ND contests, and in urban bars when TV broadcasts of ND games began in the late 1940s. In addition, during the final years of the Army-ND series, they sent nasty letters to West Point officials and, later, to the coaches and administrators of other schools on Notre Dame's schedule. In a sense, these fans demanded "unconditional surrender" from ND's opponents.

The Fighting Irish Fanatics had no power over the operation of Notre Dame football—the Golden Dome always kept tight control—but their behavior often annoyed and/or embarrassed school authorities. For the Fanatics, the University of Notre Dame existed primarily to win football games, and they even sent hostile letters to ND after the two tie games that kept the 1946–49 undefeated streak alive. Then, in the 1950s, when some losing seasons occurred and the press wondered whether Notre Dame was "de-emphasizing" football, the Fanatics' outrage at this prospect approached dementia.

Nevertheless, the Fanatics were a minority of all ND supporters. By far the largest group of ND enthusiasts in this era, estimated by the press at about nine million, were the Subway Alumni, who were similar to the Fighting Irish Fanatics in their religious and ethnic identification with Notre Dame, but much more polite and less aggressive than the Fanatics. To become a Subway Alum, one did not need to live in New York City, merely to cheer for ND and not belong to the Notre Dame Family.

In this period, a letter writer to *Sport* magazine from Cleveland, Ohio, calling herself "a member in good standing of the Subway Alumni Ladies Auxiliary," tried to explain the appeal of Notre Dame football to her, her family, and friends: ND, because of its national recruiting, usually connected to "your own parish" through players from your area and/or ethnic group; when you combined this personal link "with the fact that you love football, you want a team to root for, you want a team that has color and tradition, [then] Notre Dame fills the bill." She added, "Yes, religion has something to do with it, but in a roundabout sort of way."

For such rooters, the Fighting Irish had not embarked on a Holy Crusade against Protestant and public schools, but represented an extension of religious and ethnic identity. That the team won continually in this period boosted the self-esteem and group pride of the Subway Alum; however, as with the Notre Dame Family and unlike the Fanatics, tie games and eventual losses never inspired rage in them.

For the men in the Golden Dome who ran Notre Dame football, the various groups of fans created multiple problems, not simply because of negative behavior but also because those fans wanted to see their beloved Fighting Irish in action. This caused a huge, ongoing ticket demand for too few seats, and raised questions about the football program's "commercialization." The ND administrators usually solved these difficulties by adhering to the school's "Fortress Notre Dame" policy.

■ ■ ■

Dear Father Murphy,

Recently Messrs. Perini, Quinn, and Sullivan, the Owner, General Manager, and Publicity Director of the Boston Braves Baseball Club, visited us in South Bend. During our conversation they offered Notre Dame a guarantee of One Hundred Thousand Dollars ($100,000) if Notre Dame would play Boston College in Boston, at Braves Field on September 27, 1947.

> In view of existing conditions it would seem prudent on our part to accept their generous offer . . . [because] our net profit has been, and will be considerably lower this coming season . . .

> —Notre Dame AD Frank Leahy
> to Vice President John H. Murphy, May 1947.

The cancellation of the annual game with Army at Yankee Stadium had created an expected shortfall in ND athletic department revenue, and also removed the team's only appearance in the eastern United States from the Fighting Irish schedule for that year. As AD, Frank Leahy wanted to generate as many dollars as possible, and an extra $100,000 (worth over $1 million today) seemed too good to pass up; the game in Boston would also please ND alumni and fans in the East. Nevertheless, Father Murphy quickly replied that "the answer must be 'No,'" adding that he did not "even submit this matter to the Faculty Board in Control of Athletics." The vice president's response reveals how ND administrators carefully shaped the school's football schedules and sports image, always aware of the massive public interest in, as well as media scrutiny of, the Fighting Irish.

Vice President Murphy reminded Leahy "that a similar request was submitted [by you] earlier" this year, and because it meant "a tenth game on your schedule this year, [it] was ruled out." Part of the school's "Fortress Notre Dame" policy involved adhering to the length of the Big Ten season. Because no team in that conference would play more than nine games in 1947, neither would Notre Dame. Even though this meant missing some major paydays, it avoided charges of overemphasizing football.

The exchange also indicated the ongoing tension between the ND administrators and their increasingly powerful AD/head football coach. Leahy had previously proposed tenth games against state schools, but possibly he thought that an end run involving another Catholic institution would succeed. However, the coach had overlooked one of the basic tenets in Notre Dame's scheduling strategy, one initiated by his coach, Knute Rockne: *do not schedule fellow Catholic schools.* In the 1920s, Rockne had worked hard to make Notre Dame "Catholic America's Team," and after he achieved that goal, he refused to share football fame, fortune, and fans with other Catholic institutions, pleased that his program far surpassed theirs. From his point of view, scheduling another Catholic school could only hurt ND's dominance. Mainly because of his dictum, only once between 1928 and 1975 did Notre Dame play a fellow Catholic institution. (In 1951, the Irish visited the University of Detroit as a special favor to the latter's longtime coach and AD, Gus Dorais, Rockne's college roommate, the QB on the 1913 Notre Dame squad, and crucial to the "invention" of the forward pass.)

Memo to Father Cavanaugh:

This man, an ND grad of five or six years back, proposes establishing a weekly ND football mag, to appear each week during the football season . . . [He] thinks there are thousands of ND fans . . . who would eat up such a magazine. More literary indigestion!

—Vice President Murphy to President Cavanaugh,
August 1946.

Across the bottom of this memo, the Notre Dame president replied to his VP by writing, "Frankly, I don't think much of this. I think that we already get plenty of [narrow] football publicity," and Murphy conveyed this rejection to the alum. During the next few years, as public interest in Fighting Irish football increased, other ND alumni explored the possibility of starting fan magazines. Because the copyright laws of the time gave Notre Dame exclusive rights to the Fighting Irish name, and also because the magazine promoters knew that they needed Golden Dome cooperation as well as Charlie Callahan's aid to succeed, they framed their requests in the most polite terms—but they always failed to receive an official approval.

The ND authorities, continually facing accusations of football overemphasis from Big Ten schools, did not want an even brighter spotlight on Fighting Irish football, so weekly fan magazines made no sense to them. But as the team kept winning national championships and attracting media attention, they encountered the old conundrum: how do you dismount from a tiger? They tried by vetoing publications like the fan magazines, and they also discouraged sports publicity in other areas, even ones with religious tie-ins. Father Murphy sent a memo to Father Hesburgh in late 1949 concerning the "All-Catholic All-American Football Team": "I am in agreement with you that the idea of an All-Catholic team is not too happy a suggestion," and although ND should not oppose it publicly, the school should only cooperate in minimal ways.

During this period, the Fighting Irish came from many different ethnic groups and religions, as well as diverse geographic locations—in 1948, one even hailed from the orphanage at Boys Town, Nebraska (a perfect theme for a classical article). Notre Dame administrators wanted the media to feature the ecumenical nature of the team and school and tone down the Irish-Catholic emphasis. In 1949, Father Hesburgh wrote to a sports columnist about the latter's comments on a Jewish football recruit: "I trust that you did not mean any slur when you speak of Julius Epstein as a 'synthetic Gael' because he is Jewish. We would not like to be snobbish about this Irish business, because as a matter of fact we have a good many Jewish boys in our student body, several Jews on our faculty, and even one among the priests of our Community who run this University."

In the late 1940s, as the University of Notre Dame attempted to move toward the cultural mainstream, its "mix of athletics and religion" became increasingly complicated and vexing to its administrators. In 1949, Vice President Murphy wrote to an acquaintance about the problem: he disapproved of the "Irish partisans" (his term for the Fighting Irish Fanatics), as well as the rabid fans of opposing schools, both groups making "the unpardonable mistake of confusing football prowess with" religion. "If Notre Dame wins, the Catholic Church somehow triumphs; if we lose it is a blow to Catholicism in the United States!"

Murphy noted that "most persons I know" in the Notre Dame Family and the Catholic Church "resent this attitude very much." He sympathized with Subway Alumni who cherished the Fighting Irish for religious and ethnic reasons, but he disdained the "Irish partisans" and their mirror images among ND's opponents. For Murphy, the partisan mentality was either a "thoroughly un-American attitude of bigotry" or an "entirely vincible [surmountable] ignorance." The ND vice president hoped for the latter, believing that a lack of information about the real University of Notre Dame had caused the confusion about "football prowess" and religion, and that possibly "a public relations campaign" could alter attitudes. As a realist, however, he acknowledged that media and public misconceptions about his school would not change quickly.

In a letter to Notre Dame president Cavanaugh in this period, Francis Wallace suggested a PR effort built around the theme of his forthcoming book, *The Notre Dame Story* (1949), and the ND official seemed receptive to the idea. Cavanaugh realized that for his university to succeed on the national scene, it had to stand for more than winning football teams. And the ND president represented the Notre Dame Family, acting on its behalf, certainly not that of the "Irish partisans" or the Subway Alumni. (Unfortunately, at this time, many other college presidents did not construct this wall between their university constituency and their rabid fans, particularly when the latter included "fat-cat" boosters seeking control of the school's athletic program.)

According to Wallace's outline: Notre Dame "football will be subordinated to its proper place . . . football is the store window [of the university] which can be effectively used to bring people into the store where they can see the more important [educational and religious] things we have to offer. There *is* a University located there, and the excellence of our football is a reflection of the true excellence of the University" (emphasis in original).

At the time, Wallace's words contained a large element of wishful thinking; as Father Hesburgh later commented in his memoirs, in the late 1940s, academically Notre Dame was far from Wallace's claim in his book that "our athletic excellence merely reflects the excellence of the school as a whole . . . [including] every department." However, in a 1949 letter to a correspondent, Father Hesburgh noted Wallace's general formulation, and "Notre Dame excellence"—first articulated in 1947 by Cavanaugh—later became Hesburgh's credo during his long tenure as ND president. He also worked hard to turn it into reality.

> Father Hesburgh tells the story that as a young Executive Vice-President in 1949, he went with the football team to the University of Washington to represent the university. In those days, he always wore his cassock. In Seattle, the press photographers kept asking him to lean forward, raise his cassock, and pretend to hike a football that they had brought along as a prop.
>
> He refused, but he says that then and there, he decided he would try to change all this; he wouldn't de-emphasize football but he would make Notre Dame so famous an educational institution that, in future, the press would ask representatives of the University about academics first and foremost.

> —Notre Dame vice president Richard Conklin, 1991.

In a photograph of Father Hesburgh at a banquet in Seattle during this trip, the ND administrator is scowling, appearing ill at ease and unhappy. Conklin suggested one reason for his dissatisfaction; in his memoirs, Hesburgh also mentioned an unpleasant dispute with Frank Leahy. The argument concerned the number of players going to Seattle: the ND administrator believed that thirty-eight was sufficient—it conformed to the standard ND traveling squad number—whereas the football coach, increasingly experimenting with two-platoon football, wanted forty-four. When Hesburgh imposed his number upon Leahy, an athletic department employee told the priest, "Frank is very angry. He's ready to explode." However, the coach avoided Hesburgh during the long train ride to the West Coast, and the two met only at a dinner given by the president of the railroad line. Hesburgh noted that Leahy "was cold and uncommunicative, which made everybody uncomfortable, especially me."

This was the first of a series of disagreements between two of the strongest personalities in Notre Dame history. Inevitably, because they represented differing views concerning intercollegiate athletics and, as significantly, the power of the football coach within the University of Notre Dame, they would clash again in the coming years.

■　■　■

In the late 1940s, Notre Dame had minor questions of institutional control of its athletics program, while other universities contended with major problems, some even encountering well-documented press charges about their fraudulent recruitment, admission, and retention of players. Nevertheless, in some areas of the media, the traditional images of athlete-heroes continued; Hollywood studios and Madison Avenue advertising agencies treated college sports with particular kindness, trying to preserve its classic appeal for the American public.

Because the films, magazine advertisements, and football game programs of these years occurred on the cusp of the worst scandals in college sports history, a late-twentieth-century observer might view them as exercises in futility. However, because intercollegiate athletics survived the scandals and went on to greater popularity than ever before, a more accurate interpretation of these film and print images is that they helped construct a bridge from the idealized past—over the troubled present—to the prosperous future.

28

Images of College Sports
from Hollywood and Elsewhere

Something for everybody is the order of the Christmas show at the
Radio City Music Hall . . . From the frosty and tinkling snow maidens
of a sparkling and spectacular stage revue to the lively and Charleston
stepping [college] juniors of a bright movie version of *Good News*,
there are splendors for every age . . . Tinsel and turtle-doves and
touchdowns—they're all in the Hall's big Christmas show.

—*New York Times* film reviewer Bosley Crowther,
December 1947.

For its main Christmas movie of 1947, MGM released a lavish version of
an old musical comedy, *Good News*. Originally a 1920s stage show and
then a film, MGM recycled it for postwar audiences, bordering its ads with
Christmas wreaths, associating the movie with the festive season. Through all
of its forms, the simple tale of college football players and their girlfriends
endured, so much so that the *Times* critic remarked: "Curiously, Metro
[MGM] hasn't troubled to change matters very much, permitting the old plot
to work out in a rigidly old-fashioned style." But that was MGM's main purpose with the movie: to resurrect 1920s images of college life and sports—a
time when, supposedly, real students played intercollegiate football and worried mainly about whom to take to the Big Dance, and whether the star quarterback would pass his French exam and be eligible for the Big Game. The
movie's "old-fashioned style" was not due to studio error or lethargy but to
clever planning.

MGM's musical comedies were always highly artificial. In one locker-room
scene in *Good News*, the football players burst into an elaborate song and

dance number, and the studio's fully saturated Technicolor added to the otherworldliness of its films. Moreover, by paying top dollar to production people, like the talented Betty Comden and Adolph Green, who wrote the screenplay of *Good News,* and for the production elements—the film's music included the hit song, "The Best Things in Life Are Free"—MGM produced the most entertaining and successful musicals in Hollywood.

During its ninety-two-minute running time, *Good News* attempted to transport viewers from their postwar problems to a stylized and idealized college world. A later generation of moviegoers might regard MGM's strategy as ambiguous—for a rich corporation to tell Americans struggling with rampant inflation that "The Best Things in Life Are Free" seems rather cynical. However, probably because of the underlying optimism generated by victory in a great war, audiences embraced this film and its messages, turning it into a huge box office hit and very "good news" as well as a "best thing" for MGM's owners (who did not give away tickets to it for free).

Good News also urged the public to ignore the "black market" scandals darkening intercollegiate athletics and to return to an earlier era when a pretty co-ed could persuade a football hero, a bright but inattentive student, to hit the books. The player then passes the crucial exam, rushes to the stadium, and leads his team to victory in the Big Game. The resurrection of these classic images was good news for college football fans, as was the message to forget the current unpleasantness in their favorite sport and count on a better future.

Hollywood made other football films in this period, most of them classical and far from the "Aw-Nuts" view of college sports beginning to appear in the national magazines. The uplifting but inaccurate biopic on Army's "Touchdown Twins," *The Spirit of West Point* (1947), was typical (see page 142). Nevertheless, by 1949, as the increasing popularity of television eroded box office receipts, a few studios decided to incorporate the postwar sports controversies into their classic films—to piggyback on the headlines and to bring back the TV viewers.

Twentieth Century Fox's *Father Was a Fullback,* released for the 1949 fall season, portrayed a losing college coach beset by the new, ferocious fans, as well as excitable members of his own household, particularly his teenage daughter. With its comic viewpoint and constant family interaction, it resembles the emerging TV sitcom genre, especially shows like *Ozzie and Harriet* that migrated from radio to television, where Mom and the kids help Dad out of various professional predicaments.

Moviegoers enjoyed *Father Was a Fullback.* One reviewer attributed its success to its "chucklesome approach" to college football, a "game being taken so seriously" by fans as well as editorial writers "these days." The film mocked the controversies, even dismissing the gambling issue by having the loudmouthed family maid bet openly and comically against Father's team. As for the obnoxious fans and the temperamental daughter, the scriptwriters resolve their complaints by giving her a wonderful new boyfriend—a prized high school football recruit. The athlete then turns down a chance to go to Notre Dame, instead joining Father's squad and becoming the cornerstone of his rebuilding program. This conclusion terminates all domestic and football difficulties, leaving even the demanding fans believing in a better future: Father's winning team.

An adequate script and first-rate acting, particularly by Fred MacMurray as the coach, kept *Father Was a Fullback* afloat. However, *Yes Sir, That's My Baby*, another college football comedy released for the fall 1949 season, sank. Like its competitor, *Yes Sir* tried to use and mock some of the controversies in postwar college sports, in this case, returning GIs who have to balance football and family demands. The film alludes to the "black market" in recruiting—the hard-nosed coach orders his star prospects to play well or pay back their signing bonuses—but then the movie veers off into the "Baby" part of its title. The players have young children and their wives insist that the athletes do some of the baby-sitting—the wives also attend the local university and, indeed, are much more serious about academics than their husbands. But rather than explore this assertion of feminism, the film focuses on football players changing diapers, including during song and dance numbers.

Out of this mishmash came neither a coherent statement on postwar college football nor a successful musical comedy about it. One reviewer commented that *Yes Sir, That's My Baby* "represents a sorry attempt to make something bright and funny" out of its material, and "the script indulges in banalities" throughout. Indeed, the script is simultaneously obvious and obtuse: it ignores the very problems, notably the football "black market," that provides its premise. In fact, as Universal Pictures, the studio behind *Yes Sir*, discovered the following year—and as *Good News* had proven previously—despite press attention to the growing scandals in college sports, movie audiences still preferred purely classical films on this subject.

For the 1950 football season, Universal released *Peggy*, a movie with no references to contemporary controversy. The woman of the title secretly marries the star of the Ohio State football team, then moves to Pasadena, California, and enters the Rose Bowl Queen competition, which is only open to unmarried women. In addition, her father, a former OSU professor, dislikes the athlete and does not know about the marriage. The plot climaxes when Ohio State goes to the 1950 Rose Bowl, and the festival crowns her queen. The scriptwriters sort everything out for a happy ending: OSU beats Cal in actual game footage, the Queen resigns in favor of her runner-up sister, and the professor accepts his son-in-law.

The *New York Times* reviewer remarked that the scriptwriters "concocted" the picture from extensive newsreel footage—for the first time movie audiences saw Rose Bowl game and parade highlights in color—and "from the most familiar ingredients" of Hollywood comedy, all "designed for the sole purpose of making the customers chuckle folksily for an hour or so. The crowd at the Palace yesterday . . . ate it up." And, unlike the poor box office receipts for the incoherent *Yes Sir, That's My Baby,* Universal did remarkably well with the classical *Peggy.*

The main disjuncture between the reality of college sports and *Peggy's* frothy representation of it concerned the Ohio State football star. The film depicted him as a traditional athlete-hero, clean-cut and upright. In fact, OSU's star of the time and 1950 Heisman Trophy winner was Vic Janowicz, an athlete far from the traditional ideal. "Aw-Nuts" journalists had detailed the sordid story of his college recruitment: various schools openly bid for his services, which Ohio State won when a millionaire booster offered the player a lucrative "college job" on his horse farm outside of Columbus. Janowicz helped lead the Buckeyes to the Rose Bowl and victory, but in many of his statements to the press, he mocked the standard pieties; during his Heisman season, he stopped attending classes and subsequently flunked out of school.

Even though *Peggy* contained newsreel shots of Janowicz in action, not a hint of his reality—other than his triple-threat football talent—appeared in the OSU hero character. The scriptwriters knew about Janowicz but disregarded the information, instead portraying him in the most orthodox athlete-hero manner. However, because the movie uses actual team names and game footage—as opposed to the fictional "State U" squads and staged contests in other college football films of the period—*Peggy* seems calculated to convince moviegoers that it represents both current news about and the enduring values of college sports. If the NCAA had made the film, it could not have turned out better propaganda for big-time college sports.

Ironically, the Rose Bowl parade and game in *Peggy* occurred within a week of the calamitous 1950 NCAA convention in New York. Yet the two events were more than a continent and several days apart; the distance between the Hollywood film images and the meeting in Manhattan helps explain why, despite the coming scandals and increasing press invective, intercollegiate athletics survived its most troubled period. Millions of Americans loved the Hollywood depictions of big-time college sports and its athlete-heroes, and they held on to those through both good times and bad.

■　■　■

IRISH STAR MAY FOLLOW GRANGE,
HARMON, AND DAVIS INTO FILMS

You don't have to be an actor to crash the movies anymore. Just the nation's No. 1 football star of the season and you're in. Hollywood's hepped on turning gridiron aces into actors, and the latest is Johnny Lujack.

—United Press headline and report, January 1948.

The UP writer detailed Hollywood's pursuit of the ND quarterback and 1947 Heisman Trophy winner; because of the success of earlier films starring Red Grange and Tom Harmon as well as the recent *Spirit of West Point* with Blanchard and Davis, various studios offered contracts to Johnny Lujack. Even though Glenn Davis had publicly bad-mouthed his own film—"Save your dough, it isn't worth [the] 85 cents" admission charge—nonetheless, according to the UP, "every football fan in the country bought a ticket to see it."

Unfortunately for Lujack's movie career, apparently the studios never offered him the amount of money he wanted, and in the end he opted for pro football with the Chicago Bears. Possibly the difficulty of dealing with real football heroes—Lujack did not sign, and Glenn Davis embarked on various messy romances, including an engagement to Elizabeth Taylor—soured the studios on Heisman winners. Thus, in the late 1940s, Hollywood began to use more fictional heroes in its football movies than actual athletes; with this ploy, the studios not only bypassed contract disputes but gained the ability to shape a character like the Ohio State star of *Peggy* to film specifications, avoiding negative histories like Vic Janowicz's. In addition, Johnny Higgins, the fictional OSU player in *Peggy*, could never criticize the product.

Yet, for many people in the movie industry, the infatuation with real college football heroes and the sport continued, well illustrated by the excitement generated by the Notre Dame visits to Los Angeles for the annual USC game. From 1947 through 1951, ND played four of the five matches in the Los Angeles Coliseum, mainly to make up for the missed wartime games, but doing so placed the Fighting Irish at the center of Hollywood consciousness.

The West Coast press covered the ND visits in week-long multipage spreads, including lengthy columns of quotes and game predictions by movie celebrities. Bing Crosby, a serious ND fan, always favored the Irish; LA-based actors like Robert Taylor usually liked the Trojans; comedians pushed their trademarks, e.g., Jimmy Durante backed "Notre Dame by a nose"; and actresses stayed within well-defined personas, with Lana Turner merely suggesting sexuality, "I like the Trojans because they're so cute," while Mae West indicated something more direct: "Never mind the game, what are you doing afterwards, big boy?"

Newspaper accounts of ND-USC Saturdays in the Coliseum described the box seats full of Hollywood luminaries, with many California politicians, including Governor Earl Warren, behind the USC bench, and national leaders, usually a Cabinet secretary, and men like Joseph P. Kennedy, near the Notre Dame team. In addition, on the ND side sat most of the movie people responsible for *Knute Rockne—All-American,* not only the actors— Pat O'Brien attended every ND-USC game in this period, and Ronald Reagan only missed when on location for a film—but also members of the Warners production staff. In addition, many of the celebrities went to the private functions generated by the ND visits, particularly the annual banquets hosted by the local Notre Dame alumni club.

Pat O'Brien often served as toastmaster of this event, always providing the evening's most dramatic and memorable moment with his full-throated rendition of the famous "Win One for the Gipper" talk. On occasion, Ronald Reagan gave Gipp's deathbed plea. What the audience loved most of all, though, was O'Brien's reprise of the locker-room speech. O'Brien also took his cinematic Rockne on the road, attending many banquets throughout the year, Notre Dame functions as well as those given by other groups.

Pat O'Brien helped keep the legend of Knute Rockne alive, but he was not alone in this endeavor. Because of the military's use of *Knute Rockne—All-American* during the war and the resulting abundance of 16-millimeter copies, the movie lived on in public and parochial schools, church basements, and youth assembly halls. In addition, Bill Stern and other radio broadcasters frequently lifted stories from the film for their evening programs, and even comic-book companies reproduced versions of it for their readers. Of all Hollywood products about college sports, the Rockne film lived longest and multiplied most fruitfully. By the late 1940s, it not only embodied the traditional sports ideal for millions of Americans, but its version of the coach's life had become the "real story" of Knute Rockne for most people interested in athletics. Crucial to that process was a series of newspaper articles by a Notre Dame faculty member, Father John A. O'Brien, first syndicated in 1947 and frequently reprinted in following years.

> [In] *A Yank at Eton* [1942], Mickey Rooney expresses the thought of high school youths throughout the nation when he says: "I don't want to go to Eton. I want to play football at Notre Dame." The courage and the daring which Notre Dame teams traditionally display have won for her millions of [fans like this young man] . . .
>
> The tradition of an invincible will to win and of gameness under fire cluster around the immortal Knute Rockne who brought such magic, wizardry, and even dramatic appeal to the gridirons of the nation.
>
> —Father John A. O'Brien, Ph.D., 1947.

In his articles about Notre Dame football, Father O'Brien tried to update Rockne's life, but because he quoted mainly *Knute Rockne—All-American,* he set the film version in concrete. Father O'Brien was not an unsophisticated Notre Dame fan: he had earned a Ph.D. from the University of Illinois, taught the first courses in religious studies at an American public university, and written many well-received books. He brought scholarly credentials to his series on the Fighting Irish, and he proudly listed his Ph.D. on his byline.

" 'If I have learned any one fact,' he is saying again to the educators," O'Brien quotes Rockne as telling the Congressional-like committee, " 'in my twenty years of work with boys, it's this—the most dangerous thing in American life today is that we're getting soft, inside and out.' " O'Brien, active in academic politics at Illinois during the 1920s, must have known that this committee never existed and that therefore Rockne never made this speech to it. Yet, the power of the cinematic words, and O'Brien's approval of them—" 'We're losing a forceful heritage of mind and body that was once our most precious possession' "—led him to ignore the boundary between fact and fiction, conveying filmscript lines to his readers as if the coach had actually spoken them.

Similarly, O'Brien repeats Gipp's deathbed speech as truth, lovingly reproducing in print all of the film's pauses and dramatic breathing. Again, he placed his scholarly training on hold: he mentions that the coach kept silent about the player's dying words for eight years, but he never explores the reasons why or the possibility that Rockne fabricated the story. In addition, at Notre Dame, where Father O'Brien started teaching in 1940, the older priests clearly remembered the real George Gipp and his far-from-pristine character, yet in an article on this athlete in the series—"George Gipp Wrote Epic of Courage as Notre Dame Star"—O'Brien portrays him as a paragon, devoid of defects.

O'Brien's work perfectly captures the willful innocence of many 1940s fans toward college sports, the desire of readers and film and radio audiences to believe the classic narratives, and the alacrity with which many members of the media gave it to them. Just as the viewers of *Peggy* enjoyed its idealized portrait of intercollegiate football, its icons of athlete-heroes and parade queens, readers of O'Brien's series on Notre Dame football received similar, albeit more austere, pleasures. In addition, because of such treatments of *Knute Rockne—All-American,* most younger sports fans, including students at Notre Dame, accepted the cinematic biographies of Rockne and Gipp as accurate.

■   ■   ■

IRISH OUT TO WHIP ARMY AS MEMENTO FOR "ROCK"

The little man always wanted this one above all others, so the Fighting Irish of Notre Dame will go out tomorrow to win it for him.

This was Rock's prize, this Army game . . .

—United Press headline and lead
before Notre Dame–Army game, November 1946.

Forties sportswriters often wove Fighting Irish myths into their Notre Dame pre-game and game stories, invariably invoking *Knute Rockne—All-American*; the above UP account also included the entire Gipp deathbed scene. In fact, because the 1946 contest followed the Army routs of '44 and '45, it was mainly revenge that motivated the Fighting Irish players—but this did not comply with the Rockne legend or the "memento" theme. (The sports media's love of traditional motifs still exists in TV announcers' claims such as "Joey Jock wants this one for his mom.")

For the 1947 ND-Army game, the finale of the annual series, the mammoth press coverage included carloads of Rockne reminiscences, usually beginning with the first contest in the series, 1913, and the "invention" of the forward pass, and moving through "the fabled twenties." But Notre Dame games against other opponents also received the gloss of legend. In 1947, when Nebraska played ND for the first time in more than twenty years, sportswriters returned to the past, coating it with a golden hue; for example, "What a parade . . . on the bright stage of memory. There will be Knute Rockne . . . the immortal George Gipp, and the dancing Four Horsemen."

Despite increasing postwar press interest in the dark side of college sports, Notre Dame football, past and present, received only classical coverage. No journalist discussed the cause of the break in the ND-Nebraska series: the rabid anti-Catholicism that the Notre Dame traveling party encountered in Lincoln. In part, this resulted from the Golden Dome's position on the issue and writers in the ND network learning about this (see page 223), but the blackout included national and regional journalists far from Notre Dame's influence. The younger men may not have known the story, but undoubtedly some veterans remembered it; yet, in the many pieces on the history of Fighting Irish–Cornhusker football, no writer discussed the KKK-inspired incidents, and only a few alluded to them, typically in such sanitized remarks as "a Notre Dame–Nebraska game was one of the spectacular, unpredictable fixtures of the gridiron calendar, with surprises on and off the field." Probably the older writers ignored the episode because it so contradicted the classical view of college football, particularly during the Rockne era.

Despite the evidence to the contrary, the sporting press—from beat reporters covering college teams to scholarly authors like Father O'Brien—claimed to be objective. On the other hand, Bill Stern and most of his colleagues in sports radio considered themselves not news reporters but entertainers, for their game announcing and especially for their evening shows.

In this period, partly in reaction to the current rot in college sports, broadcasters like Stern also turned to the past, particularly the 1920s (disregarding the rampant corruption during that era). Stern began many evening programs with "It was in the fabulous twenties, the Golden Age of Sports, when Knute Rockne was the most famous football coach in America," and he would then retell the St. Knute stories based on the biopic, or segue into fables about Pop Warner, Red Grange, Babe Ruth, and other bygone sports heroes. In addition, Grantland Rice began to earn a nice supplementary income from his radio reminiscences of the 1920s, and many other sportswriters and broadcasters joined in, all of them fleeing to the idealized past to escape the increasingly troubled present. Moreover, media symbiosis linked the radio and print nostalgia to Hollywood, and to the popularity of such late-1940s films as *Good News, Take Me Out to the Ball Game* (an MGM musical about old-time baseball), and *The Babe Ruth Story* (a sanitized and hokey biopic), and aided those movies' successful runs.

Bill Stern also tried to fuse the past with the best of the present, often connecting the Rockne tales to the current head coach at Notre Dame. Sometimes he named Leahy in the opening line and moved through his playing career, injuries, and the trip with "Rock" to the Mayo Clinic; in other broadcasts, Stern only identified Leahy as "a player," then, at the end, dramatically announced that "the player became a famous football coach and, curiously enough, some years after Knute Rockne's death, he stepped into the shoes of the 'old man' to become the football coach of Notre Dame. His name is Frank Leahy!"

In the postwar era, the actual Frank Leahy lived far from Bill Stern's Sports World, working very long days in his office and on the practice fields at Notre Dame. As head football coach and AD, Leahy focused on the mechanics of producing a winning team and running an athletic department, but he also spent time on a crucial and less routine part of his job: keeping Fighting Irish football within the classic ideal. His various responsibilities converged each year when he approved the program packages submitted to him for the games at Notre Dame Stadium.

29

Postwar Programs as Propaganda

Dear Father Murphy . . .

We are genuinely delighted in . . . our 1947 souvenir programs . . . It is our strong conviction that Notre Dame fans deserve an exceptionally fine program—the best that we can arrange for. It is our aim now, as it shall be in the future, to stress quality and the best workmanship we can procure.

> —Notre Dame AD Frank Leahy to Vice President Murphy,
> September 1947.

In this era, football game programs provided athletic departments with a highly effective and dependable means of positive publicity. Because on every autumn Saturday, millions of Americans read the programs, usually for many hours, the traditional images and articles in these publications formed a massive counterattack against the criticisms of college sports. Indeed, as Leahy suggested with the word "souvenir," and as contemporary accounts confirm, most fans took them home, showed them to family and friends, and saved them for years, extending their influence far beyond game day.

In his 1947 report to Father Murphy, the ND athletic director also complained about the mounting printing costs due to postwar inflation, but he applauded the healthy advertising revenue, explaining: "Some of our national advertising is procured for Notre Dame by the Don Spencer Agency in New York, and some by the Ed Daly Agency in Chicago. Both of these firms are in the football program business on a nationwide scale, and they procure advertising for us" at top rates.

The Spencer Agency mainly obtained color ads from cigarette companies for the important middle sections and back covers of the programs, and Daly delivered such sponsors as appliance manufacturers for black-and-white inside pages. In addition, since the 1930s, Spencer had sold generic packages of front covers and inside feature articles. The agency offered about ten standard drawings and twenty articles per season, and ADs selected what they needed for their four or five home games, placing host's and visitor's names in the blank spaces on the generic covers. In the late 1940s, approximately 80 percent of the schools in big-time college football used Spencer's services; the remainder, mostly West Coast universities, worked with regional or local agencies.

Every autumn, millions of people saw the same Spencer illustrations and a smaller number read the articles; thus, this single media source had a profound influence on American attitudes toward college sports. Athletic directors like Frank Leahy, having experienced the successful propaganda campaigns of World War II, understood the importance of promotion and advertising, particularly with visual messages, and their input helped form the Spencer Agency's postwar product.

> This season we are planning on having a special cover for the Army program, which will feature a picture of the Army captain and the Notre Dame captain, in addition there will be some art work which will have campus scenes and the team mascots featured. Judging from the early sketches this cover will be unusually outstanding and attractive in a very dignified way.
>
> —Notre Dame AD Frank Leahy to Vice President Murphy,
> September 1947.

At the end of the war, some of the Spencer artists tried to resume their prewar cover themes, particularly the depictions of "smash-mouth" football popular in the 1930s. However, ADs like Leahy did not want to return to images of the raucous past and insisted that the agency provide more "dignified" work. Because universities like Notre Dame shaped opinion in college sports, and also ordered some special covers from Spencer—even though the generic ones were cheaper and most schools took them—the agency illustrators, led by senior artist Lon Keller, willingly moved in a new direction.

Keller, a devotee of Norman Rockwell, started to portray a kinder, more Rockwellian version of college football. One of Keller's most popular postwar covers, first done on special order and then recycled into generic form, pictured the helmeted head of a lineman in pre-snap position; the handsome athlete leans forward, smiling as if advertising toothpaste, revealing lovely white teeth—he is definitely not a "smash-mouth" victim. That Frank Leahy, an advocate of intensely physical football, endorsed this gentler image indicates his awareness of the power of publicity as well as his desire to counter criticism about his team's fierce play.

Though the Spencer artists toned down the violence, they continued some of their wartime imagery, particularly the quarterback as pilot, eyes intently scanning the horizon. But instead of placing fighter planes in these drawings as they had during the war, they now sketched dancing cheerleaders or other upbeat symbols of intercollegiate athletics. As postwar football evolved from running to aerial offenses, this theme proliferated on the program covers. In addition, *Life* magazine imitated sports art and, on a fall 1947 cover, displayed a photo of Johnny Lujack staring up at a shining blue sky; a year later it was Doak Walker, football cocked behind his ear, searching the Texas heavens.

In the late 1940s, Spencer artists also promoted college sports by linking football to U.S. political power. The agency's Number Two illustrator, Larry Tisdale, tied the sport to America's new superpower status by placing a football helmet upon a globe floating through space, trailing red, white, and blue streamers. In another of his geopolitical designs, a cheerleader's megaphone extends from a map of America—the country decorated in red, white, and blue bunting—to the heavens. Many universities chose these two covers, placing their names on the patriotic symbols, fusing themselves and their football teams to American nationalism and mainstream values.

Tisdale also created a series of "King Football" drawings. One of his 1948 designs, a pigskin with a gold crown on its top third, appeared at the home games of more than fifty schools. He followed this in 1949 with an equally popular sketch of a football wearing a laurel wreath, spotlights illuminating it from various angles. These covers implied that the strength and power of "King Football" would triumph over all nay-saying critics.

Most colleges and universities took the standard Spencer covers, but a few schools, like Notre Dame and the military academies, commissioned individual illustrations. For the Army-Stanford game in 1948, Lon Keller did the profile of the Stanford Indian in the background, West Point cadets carrying American flags beneath it. Not only did the Army and Navy programs have all of the national advertisers but they also included many pages bought by military-industrial companies, proclaiming jingoistic slogans and trying to please the service brass who attended these games—the men who ordered the military hardware. In the late 1940s, the average college football program was sixteen pages; some Big Ten and Pacific Coast Conference schools went to thirty-two, and the major powers in those groups as well as Notre Dame had sixty-four for their most important games. As the Cold War intensified, though, because of the military-industrial ads, the football publications of the military academies never contained fewer than one hundred pages, and they often topped two hundred.

In 1947, Notre Dame ordered one special cover for the Army contest and another for the Nebraska game. For the former, the football captains dominated, Army's mule and ND's Irish terrier appearing as tiny peripheral figures. However, for the Cornhuskers' visit, Spencer hired a landscape painter to render the Notre Dame Church and the Main Building, the many crosses on the church visually dominating the left side of the canvas and the Golden Dome with the statue of Mary commanding the right side. In between, backed by a burst of sunlight, the Stars and Stripes flew atop a high flagpole. Undoubtedly, the ND administrators who approved the painting appreciated the coupling of American Catholicism and patriotism, but, considering the history of the ND-Nebraska series, one wonders if the artist and the officials wanted to subtly remind the visitors that the University of Notre Dame triumphed on its own terms. As significant, this was one of the very first Spencer covers without a football theme, emphasizing instead a nonathletic aspect of a university; subsequently, Notre Dame commissioned many more non-football covers and also non-football articles, beginning a trend that other schools followed.

Another special cover in this period, one that also evolved into a generic mainstay, was done by a West Coast artist for the 1948 Notre Dame visit to Southern California. Using visual designs popularized by such 1940s Hollywood nostalgia hits as *Meet Me in St. Louis*, the artist foregrounded a snoozing middle-aged businessman in an easy chair, dreaming about his youthful football triumphs—above his head was a sketch of him in an old-time uniform, carrying a pigskin. On each side of the player, handsome young women in period dress eye him and begin to swoon. This image connected to Hollywood's use of the past as well as West Coast fans' discontent with the difficult present: a reformist commissioner, an ex-FBI agent, was investigating Pacific Coast Conference schools, including USC, and discussing his findings in the press. Old-time football imagery soon became a staple for the cover artists. The West Coast agency and Spencer people often employed it to evoke traditional sports values and, for many years, used it as the motif for homecoming game programs.

However, the 1948 USC–Notre Dame cover, like Hollywood films and other nostalgia products, rewrote history. Not surprisingly, no hint of the sad fate of ballcarriers in the "flying wedge/smashed body" era appeared in the sketch. The drawing also revised the role of women during football's early period: rather than swooning for athlete-heroes, women rarely attended games or followed the sport. Indeed, photos of crowds during the early eras of college football indicate mainly male spectators in their standard hats and suits.

Immediately after World War II, however, because athletic departments wanted to fill their long-empty stadiums, they and the cover artists intensively promoted college football as entertainment for everyone—hence the appearance of large numbers of women, children, even pets on the front of football programs for the first time in college sports history. Often female characters wore mums—as did the increasing number of women attending college games—and Larry Tisdale promoted this phenomenon in a 1946 drawing of a confident young woman in a tailored suit, orange mum in her lapel, sitting happily on a huge pigskin. This promotional campaign never abated; in fact, it came to dominate the program covers in the late 1940s and the 1950s.

In the single most popular cover of the postwar period, bought by almost every school and repeated for many years, Keller presented the profile of a golden blonde and blue-eyed female, wearing a kerchief dotted with small footballs, basketballs, and other sports equipment, her upraised right arm revealing a bracelet of sporting charms—football, basketball, etc. She is a postwar creation: for the first time in American sports history, promoters wanted females to attend events, and this young woman is obviously cheering for her favorite college team and athletes. The subtext is clear: women are now permitted to love sports—but as spectators, not participants.

The marketing of college football to women and children reached a new and remarkable level in 1948 when Lon Keller did a Rockwellian illustration of a gentle, brown-eyed cocker spaniel trying to grip a pigskin. Many schools bought this cover, including Baylor for its home game against the Texas Long-horns; one wonders what good ol' boy Bobby Layne and his cohorts thought of this football program when they visited the Baylor Bears that day.

But the cover artists did not ignore the masculine fan base, often depicting college football as part of the natural progression of American males to adult-hood. Lon Keller did Rockwellian panels of a baby holding a pigskin aloft in 1930, then as a child tackling a sandlot opponent in 1935, as a junior high ball-carrier in 1940, a high school kicker in 1945, and finally a college senior QB in 1949. For the athletic department officials selecting this drawing, the images probably articulated their personal and professional worldview. More important, considering the popularity of this cover, fans agreed with the message, treating it as another link between college sports and the natural order of American life—and not as propaganda for an embattled enterprise.

In this era, not only playing football but attending the games defined the masculine experience. In a cover as popular as the cradle-to-manhood one, Keller drew a father and three sons watching a game. All the sons are blond and blue-eyed, and all have animated faces, as if viewing a particularly excit-ing play. Every school that purchased this cover placed its initials or insignia in the rooters' buttons worn by the father and sons: "BU" for the Baylor home game against Tulane in 1948, "ND" for the Notre Dame home game against Michigan State in 1948, and so on.

Advertisements in the programs also reinforced the equation between football and male development; 7UP ran a national ad featuring a sandlot player taking a break to "Fresh up with 7UP," while his mother and sister look on approvingly. Again, females aided male athletes as supporters and cheerleaders. One especially vivid cover captured this phenomenon: a sandlot player, about ten years old and in full football uniform, signs autographs for two young girls gazing at him adoringly. This image merged with the multitude of similar ones defining male-female relations in the culture at this time, all of them influencing viewers at an almost subliminal level. Probably few purchasers of the "autograph party" cover criticized the illustration; more likely, they glanced at it and said, "How cute," thus endorsing contemporary male-female roles and the linkage of sports to these comforting mainstream stereotypes.

Other images in the football game programs reinforced elements of American postwar culture in equally subtle and effective ways. Nowhere in these publications are subliminal messages more in play than in the ubiquitous ads for cigarettes—part of the tobacco industry's campaign to portray, according to a later critic, "the cheerful association of cigarettes with youth, energy, and athletic excellence."

■ ■ ■

A   B   C
Always Buy Chesterfield
Voted Tops in Colleges from Coast to Coast

—Text of 1946 Chesterfield cigarette ad in midsection of
college football programs, below a photo of singers
Perry Como and Jo Stafford.

I'd Walk a Mile for a Camel

—Text of 1949 Camel cigarette ad on back cover of college
football programs, below a photo of a smiling, healthy
female college student on her way to the game,
holding a cigarette in her upraised hand.

The middle sections of the programs included the team lineups and uniform numbers, thus during games fans viewed these pages more often and intently than any other part of the publication. Cleverly, in this still predominantly black-and-white media era, the tobacco companies placed in this section multicolored ads so large and eye-catching that they dominated the pages, dwarfing the small type used for the players' names and numbers. Usually one company bought the space for an entire season, like Chesterfield in 1946, Camel in 1949. These ads began the modern commercialization of college sports. A direct line exists from the cigarette brands' sponsorship of the football game lineups to the "official sponsorship" by various companies of the NCAA tournament and other events, and, in our own time, the transformation of almost every college sports program into an advertising vehicle.

After World War II, Chesterfield featured famous and healthy looking entertainers, including the Gipper, Ronald Reagan, who informed fans, "My cigarette is the *MILD* cigarette—that's why Chesterfield is my favorite." By the late 1940s, however, Camel, a much stronger and more addictive brand, began to dominate the program advertising. Camel had long bought the back covers, which were well viewed at halftime and on the way home. Then the company started to purchase the midsections. Instead of famous entertainers, Camel featured college-age models, mainly female, in university settings; Camel, traditionally a "male" brand, wanted to enlarge its customer base by persuading women to smoke it. Camel did not neglect male smokers, however, soon launching a campaign of famous athletes endorsing the brand in sports and men's magazines.

In this period, most universities would not accept advertising from beer or liquor companies for their game programs; school officials understood the dangers of alcohol consumption and refused to promote it, particularly because drinking during and after football games caused problems for many schools and worked against the postwar "family entertainment" theme. But, despite mounting evidence on the hazards of smoking, university administrators ignored these studies, most done in their own laboratories, and they approved the close association between intercollegiate athletics—one of the most visible sports activities in America—and smoking, thus helping to promote cigarette consumption. In addition, some of the loudest critics of college sports "commercialization" headed schools that took the Spencer Agency packages along with the money from the tobacco companies, allowing the cigarette ads to dominate their football game programs.

■   ■   ■

> The suggestion you make about including a page or two on Notre Dame's scholastic and intellectual achievements in our football program is an admirable one, and I shall see what can be done in this regard for the coming fall. I know that Mr. Leahy and everyone else concerned will be most happy to cooperate on this point.
>
> —Father Murphy to Notre Dame alumnus Frank E. Cane,
> April 1949.

In the postwar era, the Spencer Agency supplied text articles to schools buying its season packages. Usually prominent sports journalists wrote the pieces and focused on football, often rendering traditional portraits of athletes and coaches. In the postwar era, with player substitution rules changing annually, a piece was included on each year's version, like "Number Please!—'47 Rule Changes Liberalize Substitution."

The host universities always produced some program text, mainly articles about their players and coaches and usually a note from the director of the alumni association. In this period, Notre Dame programs carried columns on the starting players, indicating their ethnic and geographic origins—"Espenan, Charles Raymond (Ray), French-German senior from New Orleans"—and their academic work: "[Leon Hart] is an excellent student in mechanical engineering and possesses an 83.5 average." However, no school, even those in the Ivy League, published stand-alone articles on the university's academic programs.

Prompted by an ND alumnus, Father Murphy began to implement changes in the fall 1949 program. An article entitled "Notre Dame . . . 'Upon the Moveless Rock,'" discussed the school's religious and academic traditions, but alluded through the play on "rock" to Rockne's nickname and Notre Dame's football fame. Throughout the following year, in a major breakthrough, the ND souvenir program carried feature articles that never mentioned athletics, only academics. One began, "Every three minutes someone in the United States dies of cancer," and then outlined the oncology research being done on the Notre Dame campus.

Because of its unique history as a school originally famous for its football team and much less well known for its academic achievements, the University of Notre Dame did not need to boost its college sports programs. Indeed, as their vetoes of the proposed Fighting Irish fan magazines demonstrated, its administrators preferred to downplay the purely athletic aspects of its intercollegiate teams. In the late 1940s, ND expanded this policy to include publicizing the university's religious and educational activities in athletic publications.

For many officials of other universities, the non-football covers and non-sports articles in the game programs seemed odd, even artificial. However, in the aftermath of the scandals, the NCAA ordered the Spencer Agency to use this approach in their season packages, and to try to persuade the public that the student-athlete ideal still existed (see page 446).

Notre Dame, in a variety of ways, including its innovations in football game programs, distanced itself from other schools in big-time college sports. As a result, ND remained far from the coming basketball fixes, the worst scandals in the history of higher education. The university kept its classic ideals intact and was able to present them to Americans both in its publications and in its actions. Ironically, the Notre Dame basketball team had helped popularize the sport, particularly in urban arenas like Madison Square Garden. But before the postwar basketball popularity turned into the fixing scandals, the Fighting Irish had returned home to "Fortress Notre Dame."

Part 5

Scandal Years

30

The Rise and Odor of College Basketball

Notre Dame has come to town and once again the cry is heard, "Where can I buy a ticket?" Other teams with good records have been here this year to play on the Garden basketball court and the demand for seats for those games has forced Ned Irish to go into hiding. But the hysteria for tickets for the NYU–Notre Dame contest has been unprecedented in Garden history.

—*New York Post* sports columnist Leonard Cohen,
February 1946.

During the first decades of the twentieth century, at Notre Dame and most other schools, intercollegiate basketball was a poor cousin to football. In the 1930s, however, in midwestern states like Indiana and Illinois as well as in the New York City area, college basketball emerged as a major spectator sport, filling many campus gymnasiums and city arenas. Crucial to its urban growth was Ned Irish, a New York sportswriter turned promoter. In 1934, he persuaded the owners of Madison Square Garden to allow him to stage college basketball games on nights when the facility was empty; for his first major promotion—counting on the fame of the University of Notre Dame and its many New York "subway alumni"—he brought the ND basketball squad to the Garden to play the best local college team, the New York University Violets. The game almost sold out the arena, greatly boosted Irish's promotional career, and inaugurated an annual series between the schools that continued to fill the Garden for a number of years.

After this initial success, Ned Irish scheduled other local universities against well-known visitors, usually as part of college double-headers. These games helped popularize the teams of St. John's, Seton Hall, CCNY (City College of New York), Manhattan College, LIU (Long Island University), and Brooklyn College, as well as many visiting schools.

The success of college basketball in Madison Square Garden prompted the owners of Chicago Stadium to invite local and regional teams to their facility; Northwestern games did well but, in the 1940s, the Notre Dame–DePaul matches quickly became fan favorites. Other urban promoters, particularly in Philadelphia, Washington, D.C., Milwaukee, and Kansas City, invited major college basketball teams to their arenas, and the fans turned out for games. By the early 1940s, the city arenas began to surpass the smaller campus gyms as the main venues for college basketball, increasing the sport's popularity and media coverage. Ironically, wartime government restrictions accelerated this process.

Because college basketball traveling squads during the war consisted of about ten players, a coach, and a trainer, the government permitted much more train travel for basketball teams than for football squads. The small size of basketball rosters also helped coaches avoid the severe manpower shortages afflicting their football colleagues; in addition, because the armed forces did not induct men over six feet, six inches (standard uniforms, beds, etc., did not fit them), many of the best players never entered the military. This situation began the permanent evolution of the game away from small, quick athletes to extremely tall front lines and bigger guards, with the sport's first "giant" stars— Bob Kurland of Oklahoma A&M, and George Mikan of DePaul—emerging during the war period.

College basketball's two major tournaments, the National Invitational Tournament and the NCAA playoff, also experienced significant growth during the war. The NIT, set up by Ned Irish for Madison Square Garden and featuring the best teams in the country, consistently filled its venue. The NCAA tourney, at first a poor relative of the NIT, moved from campus gymnasium, where it lost money, during the late 1930s, to various city arenas for the finals in the early 1940s and small profits, and then, in 1943, to Madison Square Garden and the big time—full houses and substantial revenue. For college basketball, urban arenas seemed like valhalla, and coaches and athletic directors scrambled to schedule as many games as possible in them. They ignored the fact that a growing number of city fans regarded college basketball less as a sporting event than as a gambling opportunity, particularly with the advent of point-spread betting.

> In the early 1940s Charles K. McNeil, a former math teacher in a Connecticut prep school, opened a bookmaking operation in Chicago. Looking for a way to attract customers and make gambling more interesting, he introduced a revolutionary form of betting which he called "wholesaling odds" . . . McNeil rated each team and then estimated how many points the favored team would win by. Gamblers bet . . . not

on the odds but on the point spread . . . As one ex-bookie noted, "The point spread was the greatest discovery since the zipper."

—Sports historians Randy Roberts and James S. Olson, 1989.

Before McNeil's invention, betting on basketball was no more attractive than wagering on any other sports event. Even with favorable odds, for instance, 5 to 2 on Purdue over Indiana, a gambler had to bet on one team winning or losing. The point spread changed everything. Suddenly games between mismatched squads became interesting: if the bookie made the superior team a ten-point favorite, the bettor could wager that the underdog would play well enough to come close, at least not to lose by ten points or more. The point spread transformed basketball betting into the favorite wintertime action of many sports fans, greatly increasing interest in and attendance at college basketball games.

But the point spread, as the college sports establishment would soon discover, had a definite downside: the infusion of millions of dollars in bets attracted professional gamblers who wanted to fix the contests and create lucrative "betting coups." The point spread also allowed fixers to persuade players to "shave points" but still win games. Every competitive athlete hates to lose, and this fundamental tenet of sports psychology had prevented many previous fixes; the 1919 Black Sox achieved infamy because they had actually thrown the World Series, intentionally losing games to obtain the gamblers' payments. However, shaving points seemed much less serious; with a ten-point spread in their favor, athletes could miss or allow some baskets and win by less than ten. They could accept the bribes and still triumph, including in championship games. Even the language of basketball fixing made "shaving" sound much more innocent and palatable to players than "dumping," losing on purpose.

In 1944, the night before the NCAA men's basketball championship final in Madison Square Garden between Utah and Dartmouth, an incident occurred that foreshadowed the coming scandals in college sports. A gambler went to the hotel room of Utah coach Vidal Peterson and proposed that the coach fix the final game by keeping key players on the bench at crucial times. Peterson, in a move out of a Hollywood Western, responded by decking the gambler with one punch and throwing him into the corridor.

The punch-out in the New York hotel room attracted almost no press attention. It so violated the classical sports ideals promulgated by the media that even New York's tabloid newspapers, then as now fascinated by underworld activities, did not mention it—even though sports reporters quickly learned about it. And seven months later, when Kansas coach Phog Allen discussed the incident in a speech, the media gave his comment and the fix attempt minimal space.

Forrest "Phog" Allen was an important coach and the heir at the University of Kansas to Dr. James Naismith, the inventor of the sport. In 1945, he began a campaign to warn the public about a coming gambling scandal that would "stink to high heaven"—but the media dismissed his statements. Allen had observed and become alarmed at the amount of betting in Madison Square Garden and some other city arenas. Gamblers would congregate in the entranceways and corridors before games, taking bets, and then they would distribute payoffs immediately after the contests. Fans would scream for their team "to cover the spread" and boo winning teams that failed to do so. Allen not only attacked the gamblers but also the NCAA, charging that it "teams up with professional promoters to hold tournaments in arenas where everyone knows big-time gamblers operate." NCAA officials, aware that basketball tourneys were the association's main revenue source, ignored his complaints.

Phog Allen's voice cried in the prairie wilderness, but his predictions started to come true a few months later. By chance, during a New York police stakeout of an underworld "fence," two members of the Brooklyn College basketball team appeared at the suspect's house. The police wondered why the players were there and, under questioning, the athletes confessed that they were involved in fixing games and that the suspected fence was the gamblers' go-between. The New York press treated the story as a one-day-wonder, and the school expelled the five players involved—except one of them, a starting guard, who was not even a registered student!

Harold Olson, the head basketball coach at Ohio State, articulated the general reaction of the college sports authorities: "Just because a couple of kids are stupid enough to accept bribes doesn't mean there's anything wrong with [college] basketball." Indeed, the collegiate sport was enjoying unprecedented popularity and expansion, while the professional version was still barnstorming in its pre-NBA phase.

■　■　■

In view of the importance which all major institutions of higher learning are attaching to basketball, I believe we should allow ten incoming players per year in the sport. With air travel being so popular, plus the fact that some colleges have stadia which can accommodate crowds in excess of ten thousand spectators, we should take advantage of Notre Dame's popularity. It is my sincere hope that we can soon have a suitable stadium for our home basketball contests. Should the latter recommendation become reality, our income from basketball would be a pleasant surprise. Just as soon as the material can be procured, I think we should break ground for a basketball stadium.

—Notre Dame AD Frank Leahy to Vice President
John J. Cavanaugh, July 1946.

A number of schools, including Notre Dame, took notice of the unsavory conditions in college basketball and tried to protect themselves. Even though its powerful athletic director wanted to expand the basketball program, the ND administrators refused his request. Leahy, unlike many football men who devalued all sports except their own, saw the postwar possibilities in college basketball as a way to build his school into a powerhouse. The record shows that none of Leahy's wishes were answered: ND continued to admit only a few basketball recruits a year, and the school kept its old 4,500-seat field-house for another generation. The priests in charge of Notre Dame were not antibasketball—they respected the school's tradition of success on the hard-wood—but they worried about the postwar problems in the sport.

The annual series with NYU in Madison Square Garden presented imme-diate difficulties, and in the summer of 1945 the Notre Dame Faculty Board in Control of Athletics, chaired and guided by Vice President Cavanaugh, voted "to discontinue this series because of its professional-promotional" aspects—coded language for their unhappiness with an arena full of gamblers. However, New York University officials as well as Notre Dame alumni in the East energetically protested the decision, and one NYU faculty member, a for-mer president of the NCAA, urged Notre Dame to reconsider its cancellation. Because the association and other college authorities dismissed the possibility of widespread fixes, ND disliked acting in a unilateral manner and eventually agreed to the 1946 game. Because of its excellent team that season and the magic of the Fighting Irish name, on February 9, 1946, in New York, when the few remaining tickets for the NYU game went on sale, "a riot" occurred with "8,000 fans stampeding the Garden wickets," prompting police intervention, according to a *Newsweek* report.

After this contest, Notre Dame again wanted to pull out of the series, but later that year, because the football annuals with Army had been terminated following the 1946 game, the New York alumni increased their pressure on the Golden Dome to continue the annual NYU contest; many ND alumni functions centered around athletic team visits. The Notre Dame administra-tors had ended the most popular college football series in America because, in large part, the gambling and ticket scalping surrounding the event had grown unmanageable. They wanted to terminate the Madison Square Gar-den game for similar, albeit smaller-scale reasons, but after the trauma of the break with West Point, ND officials decided to postpone the end of the NYU series for at least another year.

Notre Dame played and beat NYU in New York in 1947, subsequently fin-ishing the season with a 20-4 record and receiving a bid to the NCAA men's basketball tournament. During this era, the NCAA only invited eight teams and the participating schools split the large payments from the sold-out are-nas. However, with increasing rumors of fixes, and the NCAA tourney sched-uled for Madison Square Garden, Notre Dame turned down the invitation to "the Big Dance." The ND administrators wanted to keep their entire inter-collegiate athletics program within the classic ideal, and they realized that the "professional-promotional" events at the Garden existed far outside its boundaries. Ironically, as ND was pulling away from New York, the national magazines based in that city increasingly used Notre Dame's pristine image as a way of promoting college basketball.

■ ■ ■

> When you see him [Kevin O'Shea] in a Notre Dame [basketball] uni-form, you can't help thinking he was born to wear it. Not only is his name a natural for the roster of the Fighting Irish, but his whole appearance is just what the average sports fan expects a typical Notre Dame athlete to look like . . . He's definitely a good-looking young man. Not pretty, in the matinee hero sense. But wholesome and appealing . . . He's a driving, never-give-up competitor, but in a crisis he's as calm as they come.

> —*Sport* magazine writer John Carmichael, February 1948.

In 1948, *Sport* did a traditional portrait of ND All-American basketball player Kevin O'Shea. The magazine also featured photos of O'Shea playing the game, studying in his dorm room, and kneeling in prayer at a campus shrine. The latter picture was captioned, "Kevin and his pals often stop at the Grotto on the campus to say a prayer. It's a copy of the famous Lourdes Grotto." By using these familiar Fighting Irish narrative and visual tropes for a portrait of a college basketball player, the magazine gave readers a well-trod path into a newly popular sport, furthering its growth and contributing to the creation of its modern form. (Pro basketball, lacking a stable league and long-term franchises, had yet to appear on media radar screens.)

In the postwar era, the editors at *Sport* sought new trends and helped to shape them. Because of their Manhattan base and their personal affection for basketball, they wanted to promote the sport to equality with college football. Other national media outlets headquartered in New York, particularly the wire services and press syndicates, had a similar goal; the growth of college basketball would increase the size of their sports departments. Notre Dame cooperated by producing Top Twenty teams, and the national media ran fre-quent articles on ND stars like O'Shea and on Moose Krause, head basketball coach from 1946 through 1951, often exaggerating their actual abilities. Gor-don Graham, longtime sports editor of the *Lafayette (Indiana) Journal & Courier,* later commented:

> It didn't make sense that Kevin O'Shea was on everybody's All-America team for four years [1946–47 through 1949–50]. Sure he was

talented, but he had bum knees and they'd pop out of place, so you'd never know how he'd play on a given night. The AP, UP, Helms, *True* [Magazine] . . . all those national guys with their All-America awards must have only seen him on his good nights, and the rest of us, on his lousy ones . . .

[Also] "Moose" is a great guy, I've shared many a bottle with him, but he's mainly a football man . . . So it was ridiculous when the New York writers glorified him as some sort of "basketball genius."

In the postwar period, also for the first time, the major general-interest magazines spotlighted college basketball. For the 1946–47 season, *Collier's* inaugurated a "Basketball Forecast." Written by Hank Iba, a prominent coach, the article promoted the game, and so did the photos; one sequence of fan reactions was captioned, "Basketball has become the Number One spectator sport of the country. These frenzied enthusiasts were snapped at Madison Square Garden, New York." (The total attendance for all high school, college, club, semipro, and pro basketball games surpassed that of all other team sports but trailed, by many lengths, horse racing.)

The *Collier's* pictures also indicated the major problem in the sport: the betting on college basketball that was increasing geometrically in the postwar era, and MSG as the gathering place of many professional gamblers, including some intent on fixing games. Hank Iba ignored this phenomenon, no doubt hoping that it would disappear, but he did mention the "dozens of returned servicemen" on college rosters, their years of experience in "service basketball," and the colleges' eagerness to enroll them.

A small but active "black market" in college basketball began after the war, but it did not compare in national scope or size to college football's recruiting bazaar. The rosters of the "40 Strongest Teams of 1946–47 and Their Stars" in the *Collier's* preview indicated the transitional nature of the sport. Kentucky, rated Number One, possessed such highly recruited basketballers as Dale Barnstable and Jim Jordan as well as football scholarship winners Ralph Beard and "Wah-Wah" Jones; the New York area schools in the top ranks— NYU, St. John's, CCNY, LIU—mainly featured sought-after basketball recruits, but Notre Dame at Number Three listed football players Johnny Lujack and George Ratterman along with basketball prospects Kevin O'Shea and Leo Barnhorst. Many other teams had rosters with multisport athletes, and Yale at 20, Dartmouth at 30, and Harvard at 33 had some unrecruited regular students on their starting fives.

Collier's main rival, the *Saturday Evening Post*, also began to pay attention to college basketball, using the late 1940s rise of St. Louis University as a case study for a major article whose subhead was "Tired of Sinking Money in Hopeless Football Teams, Colleges Have Found a Cheaper, Quicker Path to Big Time. At St. Louis U. They Traded a Gridiron for a Court—and a National Reputation." Terming the Billikens "one of the big success stories of postwar sports," the *Post* tracked the basketball team's home attendance from a few hundred before 1945 to more than 10,000 a game in the late 1940s.

St. Louis University was typical of many Catholic schools, particularly urban ones, in this period. With the wild inflation in football costs, and scant fan support for their mediocre gridiron squads, these schools started to focus their small athletic department budgets on basketball. In an article on this phenomenon, *Sport* magazine pointed out, "From the time [in 1946] that Notre Dame and its magic name invaded" St. Louis's largest arena to play the Billikens and produced "a packed house . . . the St. Louis U. athletic director felt a bonanza was within reach." Then, in 1948, when St. Louis ended a long Notre Dame winning streak, the local papers put the news in banner headlines on their front pages—the first time basketball had attracted maximum attention in the city. The Billikens' AD continued to build his program, and as his team moved up in the national polls, it became the winter sports rage of the area.

The media also aided the ascent of other Catholic college teams by devoting increasing amounts of space to them and their best players, often with full classical portraits of and catchy nicknames for the athletes. *Sport* featured a profile of "Easy Ed [Macauley] of the Billikens," and other publications focused on Holy Cross's Bob Cousy—"The Couz." In 1947, Holy Cross became the first Catholic institution to win the NCAA title, but the Massachusetts school was so new to the big time that during its championship year "the Cross" did not possess a campus arena, playing all of its home games in downtown Worcester or Boston.

Non-Catholic urban colleges also started to spend more athletic department dollars on their basketball programs, and local newspapers reacted accordingly, augmenting coverage and often creating the position of basketball beat reporter. In addition, many radio stations began to broadcast home games and then, because of the excellent ratings, to send announcers on the road. In the postwar era, New York, with its 1930s head start, produced the best group of college teams, the largest amount of local press coverage, and such famous play-by-play broadcasters as Marty Glickman. But in other cities, many colleges also promoted their basketball programs, and the media and fans responded. Philadelphia, with its mix of secular and parochial schools, was typical. There the press, radio, and fans embraced the "Big Five" games and tourneys of Temple, Penn, Lasalle, St. Joseph's, and Villanova, and Temple also produced a national scoring champion with the best sports nickname of the era: Bill Mlkvy, "The Owl Without a Vowel."

In addition, many traditional basketball powers improved, with some of the best teams and players coming out of the Big Ten as well as schools farther west. However, some conferences and universities, particularly in the

Southwest and the South, remained committed solely to football, limiting college basketball's growth.

Media attention started with the new basketball teams and their star players, then expanded to the coaches, previously not well known personages who quickly moved toward the celebrity status accorded their football colleagues. The *Post* piece on St. Louis U. featured a photo of coach Ed Hickey, nicknamed "Little Napoleon" because of his diminutive size, and described his innovative coaching techniques: "Hickey goes over movies of St. Louis games a frame at a time, searching for player mistakes. Student assistants keep voluminous statistics on every Billiken scrimmage . . ." and so on. Also during this period, magazines began to run classic portraits of basketball coaches. In 1948, *Collier's* profiled North Carolina State's Everett Case, detailing his rise from Hoosier schoolboy to successful Indiana high school coach, and eventually big-time college mentor. However, the three college coaches spotlighted most often in the national press were Nat Holman of CCNY (City College of New York), Clair Bee of LIU (Long Island University), and Adolph Rupp of Kentucky. During these years, they won more games and titles than any other trio, and they achieved a prominence equal to most football coaches of the time. But the fame of their great teams turned to infamy when the fixing scandal broke, because their players were among the worst offenders in the sordid story.

Finally, the postwar media recognition of college basketball also included the universities involved. The *Saturday Evening Post* article on the St. Louis U. program ended with "Looking back on the changes basketball has wrought, [school president] Father Holloran sums up the university's attitude . . . Says he, happily, 'You could not purchase what basketball has done for this school.'" Basketball attracted free media attention and even some money to universities with a winning big-time program. However, as other school presidents—including those at CCNY, LIU, and Kentucky—would discover, publicity is a two-edged sword, capable of swinging back upon an institution when its athletic program generates negative news, creating ugly headlines about player and/or coach misconduct, seriously injuring a school's reputation as well as its investment in intercollegiate athletics. The sharpest blade to ever slash college sports—the basketball fixes of the late 1940s and early 1950s—began its trajectory, oddly enough, not on college campuses but in the vacation resorts of New York State's Catskill Mountains.

31

College Basketball Starts to Implode

In the summer of 1946, Bob Cousy was playing for the Tamarack Lodge in the Borscht Belt in a league including [such great players as] George Mikan, Ed Macauley, Dolph Schayes, and Don Forman. Heavy betting among resort guests was common and common knowledge. When the story of a dumped game was exposed, the players involved were fired from their summer sinecures, and the fixer guest was kicked out of the resort.

—Sports historian Neil Isaacs, 1975.

In an era before air conditioning and easy air travel, the pleasant weather and summer resorts of the Catskills attracted many vacationing New York City residents. (Borscht, cold beet soup, was a popular dish served by the hotels, and the origin of the area's nickname, the Borscht Belt.) Not only did middle-class families travel to the mountains to escape the city heat, but Manhattan show business and sports people, including professional gamblers, also made the trip. To entertain guests, hotels hired young musicians and comedians—some of the most famous stars of TV's "Fabulous Fifties" began on the "Borscht Circuit" after the war—and, for added diversion, management staged basketball games.

Beginning in the 1930s, resorts sponsored teams, and after World War II, they also employed college coaches to recruit players and to run the squads efficiently. As a result, every summer in the late 1940s, more than five hundred college players from across the country suited up for Catskills basketball, making it the single best showcase for basketball talent in America, far better than the ramshackle pro leagues of the time and, because of the all-star lineups, superior to regular college games and tournaments.

To maintain the athletes' amateur status under the various NCAA and conference codes, the coaches arranged for the hotels to hire and pay the players as waiters, bellhops, etc., but, in fact, to demand little if any work beyond basketball. The official employment met the regulations for NCAA "summer job plans," thus university authorities ignored the reality of the situation. Moreover, because the under-the-table deals paralleled the inducements that coaches offered athletes to play regular college ball, summer rule-breaking seemed business-as-usual to all involved. Combine this corrupt system with the other "black market" scams of the time—some summer league participants had played for schools when not registered as students, others had benefited from forged transcripts, etc.—and the context for fixing games becomes clear.

Because of the postwar popularity of sports betting, bookmakers worked the Catskills resorts, setting point spreads and taking bets, and many guests, not just the Broadway crowd, wagered. It made the games more interesting, and was all part of the entertainment package. Professional gamblers ventured big bucks on the summer contests. They were also among the most prominent guests at the hotels, giving betting advice to ordinary folk, generously tipping the staff for their real work and the athletes for their nominal jobs. Many gamblers also slipped the athletes money for playing well; then they would "put some money down" on behalf of the players, and if the outcome was favorable, the gamblers would give the players "their share of the winnings." Therefore, the next step—a gambler's suggestion to a player to shave a few points in a summer game for extra money—was not gigantic. Indeed, it seemed logical to many athletes, all part of "doing business," of being a college basketball star in this place at this time.

Dumping a game, however, was usually over the line. As Neil Isaacs suggested in his account of the 1946 incident, the hotels wanted their teams to win, and, although they accepted the gambling because it pleased the guests and even tolerated some point shaving, they objected to intentional losses. Most hotel owners wanted a winning team and bragging rights over their peers. A recent social history of the Borscht Belt summed up the situation: "It was here on the Mountain courts that athletes learned to shave points and rig games," and it all "ended as one of the greatest scandals in the history of American amateur sports."

Neil Isaacs also said that the "heavy betting" was "common knowledge" in the Catskills and beyond. When asked about this many years later, Notre Dame's Moose Krause responded:

> My friends at Toots Shor's [Manhattan bar] certainly knew about it and told me . . . I told our boys not to go there for summer ball. I can't recall a single one ever going. But I know that other basketball coaches thought it was okay, they said it exposed a boy to great competition . . .

> I remember some of the crowd at Toots Shor's saying that it [the Catskills' betting and point shaving] was only the tip of the iceberg . . . sooner or later, lots would come out, players on regular college teams were working with gamblers. I was sick about that. Of course, it all came out . . . But I was really glad that we [Notre Dame] kept as far away from all that as possible.

At the time, a few coaches did comment publicly about the summer leagues and the gambling surrounding them, as well as in the city arenas. Forrest "Phog" Allen of Kansas had spoken out after the 1945 Brooklyn College scandal; two years later, he told journalist Dan Parker that "things have not improved insofar as the gambling angle in college basketball is concerned. In fact, the gamblers have grown a little wiser and are playing their angles a little more shrewdly" by getting to know the coaches and players through summer basketball. Allen also saw the problem within a larger context, one that included football: "Today is the Golden Age of [intercollegiate] athletics. There isn't enough silver in the country to meet the demands of [college] athletes. A few years ago there were college men, so-called amateurs, drawing $7,500 a year for participating in amateur sports. Today the ante has been raised considerably." If Allen's original number is merely doubled, and then adjusted to 1990s dollars, it becomes the equivalent of $150,000—an astounding amount for college athletes to receive under the table, and a figure that contradicts those sports nostalgists who look back at the postwar era as a true "Golden Age" in intercollegiate athletics.

In the late 1940s, the highest "salaries" still went to football players, but basketball stars were closing the money gap. Thus began the modern era in college basketball, a sport marked by dazzling play and equally spectacular corruption.

■   ■   ■

BASKETBALL'S BIG WHEEL

Ned Irish—Who Made College Basketball a Box-Office Success and $150,000 a Year for Himself—Is Today Both the Most Frequently Praised and Most Often Damned Man in Sports. Do His Double-Headers Encourage Gambling . . . ?

—*Saturday Evening Post* title and subtitle, January 1949.

From 1946 through 1948, few media stories stated or even hinted that college basketball players were rigging games in the summer leagues and during the regular season. The 1950s investigations, however, revealed a multitude of fixes and extensive knowledge of them during the postwar period, notably in university and press circles. Occasional "Aw-Nuts" items by Dan Parker and like-minded colleagues surfaced, but, on the whole, a conspiracy of silence smothered the subject. It was as if all those in charge of college sports—the NCAA, university administrators, athletic directors, coaches, event promoters—believed that the problem would miraculously vanish. Moreover, the sports media, energetically promoting college basketball, wanted to fatten, not flatten, the golden goose.

Many sportswriters, especially New York basketball beat reporters, went to the Catskills during the summers, partly to vacation but also to report on the important games. As members of the Broadway sporting crowd, they knew the professional gamblers and bookmakers working in the mountains, and they talked basketball betting with them in the Catskills and in the city. Ike Gellis, sports editor of the *New York Post* in this period, later stated that the New York basketball reporters were fully "aware of the monkey business . . . Any sportswriter worth his salt had to know what was going on," and yet none tried to expose it.

Finally, in 1949, the *Saturday Evening Post* lifted one veil but, as the subtitle of its article on Ned Irish indicated, it presented the gambling problem mainly with question marks, not assertions. Irish ran Madison Square Garden and other arenas in the East, dictating college basketball scheduling to an extraordinary degree. Not only were the final rounds of the two championship tournaments, the NIT and the NCAA—of equal importance in this era—played at the Garden, but Irish's double-headers throughout the season helped build or destroy a team's ranking in the polls and its chances for the major prizes at the end. The *Post* suggested that Irish rewarded his friends and bulldozed all opponents; one athletic director remarked that "you play it his way because you need the money and he's the only one who can give it to you."

Irish did generate unprecedented paydays for college basketball programs—and for himself—but the *Post* wondered about the "gambling flourishing in and around the Garden. Naive spectators constantly are mystified in the closing moments of games by the furious commotions accompanying [plays] . . . that can't possibly affect the results. The yammering comes from people who have bet on the point margin between the teams." The *Post* noted that "Irish strenuously tries to soft-pedal references to gambling because he knows it can wreck his empire," and he also knew that betting greatly contributed to the popularity of college basketball, attracting many spectators who came to see and cheer the team carrying their money. Thus the head of Madison Square Garden winked at the rampant gambling activity at his New York facility, and at his arenas in Philadelphia, Buffalo, and elsewhere.

Just as the gambling was an open secret, so were the fixed games. Stanley Cohen, a young fan at the time and later the author of a history of the scandals, wrote: "All through the postwar years of the forties, every kid in the streets of New York knew that the scores of college basketball games were being manipulated. Not all of the games, of course, [because] . . . a team would have to establish a pattern of excellence before the point spread would go high enough to warrant a fix" by point shaving. But the cognoscenti could spot the fixes—beforehand if possible, to piggyback onto the "betting coup," but often, as a game unfolded, if they were on the losing side of a setup.

The great 1949–50 CCNY team, which won both the NIT and the NCAA championships, shaved many points and, during a game that season against a badly outmatched SMU squad, made the fix so obvious and the game so unnecessarily close that, according to an eyewitness, "an irate bettor" who had taken CCNY and the large point spread "couldn't take it any more and he single-handedly stormed the City bench, 'You guys are dumping!' he screamed," in the faces of the players and the coaches. CCNY won, below the spread and avoiding the "dump," yet for this game and all of the other rigged ones, the officials on hand—the referees, the coaches, and Ned Irish—denied the possibility of a fix.

Sports bettors frequently feed upon unsubstantiated rumors, but a more authoritative indication of the fixes came from the bookmakers. These tough-minded businessmen wanted college basketball to thrive. They made their money by taking a percentage of total volume; therefore the more the fans bet, the greater the profits. Bookies never backed one side; indeed, they worked hard to even up the amount wagered on each team. A fix, if it generated a lopsided amount on one club and a huge payoff, could destroy them. Thus, in a final irony, the bookmakers, more than any other group connected to college basketball in the postwar period, wanted honest games and hated the fixes.

At this time, almost all bookies subscribed to a service in Minneapolis that set the point spreads for every college contest in the country. As early as 1945, the "Minneapolis Syndicate," suspecting point shaving by Brooklyn College, had taken that team off their board. During the following years, the service declined to give betting lines on increasing numbers of college teams. Then, in 1948, according to the *Saturday Evening Post*, they "refused to quote figures for all New York [college] games. The inference was plain: the boys suspected the games were not strictly on the up-and-up. The [Minneapolis] syndicate has also been shying away from Philadelphia games for several years." (Nevertheless, because of the volume of money bet in these cities, some local bookies ignored the Minneapolis warning and set their own lines; as a result, some lost their shirts.) The *Post*'s comments on the syndicate's suspicions were as close any mainstream publication came to exposing the basketball scandal before the House of Shaved Points collapsed.

In the late 1940s, "all of the New York basketball writers had contacts with bookies," an insider recalled. "A lot of them played the ponies" with the "books." Eventually some writers grew tired of the "smart bookies' " taunts about "covering up the fixes," and they started planting clues in their game stories. Never an exposé or a direct accusation, only veiled sarcasm and double entendre. Ironically, the comments did not prod the authorities to action, but they did begin to affect the players "doing business." CCNY star Floyd Layne later remarked that the years of his team's "shaving" made him increasingly nervous, and "the newspapers didn't help keep you at ease." Previously, sportswriters had idolized the players, but by 1949, according to Layne, because the journalists knew "what was going on," they changed their tone and "you could see it in the sarcastic stories they'd write about certain games. There were broad hints of fixes."

Nevertheless that year, when a player on the George Washington University team informed New York authorities that gamblers had tried to bribe him to fix a game against Manhattan College at Madison Square Garden, the press as well as college sports officials treated the incident as an aberration. District Attorney Frank Hogan investigated and arrested the gamblers, but much more important fixes, including those of championship tournament games, went unapprehended.

Like their basketball writers, most New York sports editors knew about the shenanigans at the Garden and other arenas, permitted the printed insinuations about them in game pieces, but kept the lid on the larger story. However, Max Kase, the sports editor of the *New York Journal-American,* was out of the basketball mainstream—he knew little about the sport and had never even seen a college game—but became increasingly curious about the fix innuendoes appearing in his beat reporters' articles. In late 1950, he visited his gambling world contacts and discovered the extent of the basketball rigging, but then, rather than assign sportswriters to the story, he turned it over to his newspaper's investigative crime reporters.

Kase's actions underline the complicity of the sporting press, particularly the beat writers, in the fixes, as well as their inability to write accurately or even honestly about intercollegiate athletics. Most of these writers were so close to and dependent upon athletic department personnel, particularly the coaches and the publicists, that they feared upsetting them as well as jeopardizing their own careers by exposing the fixes. Then, in early 1951, when events overtook the press, including the *Journal-American's* crime crew, and the scandal came tumbling out through player confessions, most sportswriters still hesitated to investigate fully and/or tried to cover up for their athletic department friends, particularly the coaches.

The conduct of the sporting press during the fixes and even after their exposure—not only in New York but in the other cities and towns with teams involved—was, with a few exceptions, shameful. Gordon Graham, the Indiana newspaperman, summed it up well: "Most sportswriters at that time treated their readers like mushrooms—they kept them in the dark and covered them with manure."

Nevertheless, the events of 1951 prompted some changes in newspaper and magazine sports departments. More significantly, it cracked the classical lens through which most Americans viewed intercollegiate athletics.

32

Scandal/Scoundrel Time:
Players Confess, Coaches Escape

The ball game begins and the fans turn into shrieking aborigines. At least two-thirds of them have money riding on the contest. The fans greet each shot with horseplayers enthusiasm. Junius [Kellogg, Manhattan center] is so unnerved that his game falls apart. He fumbles easy passes and is a step behind everyone else. "Fix!" the fans start yelling. "Dumper!" they scream . . . The Manhattan bettors are shouting obscenities and racial epithets [at Kellogg, an African American].

—Basketball historian Charles Rosen, 1978.

The January 1951 contest described above, between Manhattan College and DePaul, seemed to fans a typical Madison Square Garden outing, but it was, in fact, an extraordinary event. The previous week, two of Junius Kellogg's former teammates had offered him $1,000 to rig the DePaul game, promising even bigger payoffs from their gambler patrons if Kellogg fixed future games. The Manhattan College player, a young Southerner who was totally out of the NYC-Catskills loop, went to the authorities; then the police enlisted his help in trapping the fixers. Kellogg's extreme nervousness about the latter situation caused his inept play. After the game, the police arrested the two former Manhattan players, co-captains on the 1949–50 squad. They quickly confessed to attempting to bribe Kellogg, and continued talking, admitting to shaving points in games the previous year and naming their gambler contacts.

Many newspapers led their stories on this incident by praising Junius Kellogg, but none acknowledged the implications of the Manhattan College confessions. The *New York Times* treated them as a regrettable episode, "the third of its kind in New York in the last five years," but not an indication of a huge system. Actually, it was more like the three-hundredth "of its kind" in New York and elsewhere since 1946. Another journal ended its article on the Manhattan revelation with "What the effect will be on Garden college basketball remains to be seen."

New York Times columnist Arthur Daley, a Catholic, found the Manhattan College fix, because it involved a parochial school, "far more stunning, far harder to believe than any of the others" in recent years. Probably Daley had heard scuttlebutt about the situation, but, at the Olympian height of his "Sports of the Times" column, he lived far from the Broadway sporting crowd and the Garden. In his commentary on the Manhattan College scandal, he focused on Junius Kellogg, "the elongated Negro center [who] had the inherent decency, the high moral fiber, and the deep religious scruples to report the bribe offer." As for the player-fixers, Daley displayed uncharacteristic rage. Because they had landed "the lowest and most contemptible punch below the belt" possible in sports, violating all traditional standards, he wrote, "The personal preference here would be boiling [them] in oil."

In the two previous New York fix cases, the district attorneys had prosecuted the felons but not initiated wider investigations. This time, DA Frank Hogan sent out detectives; within a month, they scooped up enough evidence to arrest three players on CCNY's national championship team as well as their gambler contacts. This news generated newspaper headlines and large photos of the fallen CCNY players with heads bowed before a booking officer's high desk—a startling pose for athlete-heroes.

These photos and similar ones of other arrested players—always with heads lowered, avoiding the camera's stare—became the dominant icon of the fix scandals. Reproduced repeatedly, they achieved a fame previously only attained by such sports images as Lou Gehrig at the microphone in Yankee Stadium, and Knute Rockne addressing the Fighting Irish at halftime—except the arrest photos signified the close of the classical sports age.

> There are two seemingly unrelated news items in yesterday's paper. The headline of one read: "Educators Plead for Moral Values." The headline of the other read: "Three City College Aces Held in Basketball Fix."
>
> —*New York Times* columnist Arthur Daley, February 1951.

Daley admitted his shock at "still another basketball fix," and he linked the immorality of the CCNY athletes to the plea by a panel of prominent university presidents "for a moral reconstruction" of American values. The *Times* columnist had hoped that the scandal would end with the Manhattan College revelations; now, ever the optimist, he saw the CCNY arrests as the "most stunning denouement" to the horror story, the final unfolding of the fix plot. But a month later, the headlines in his newspaper refuted him again: "3 MORE ATHLETES FROM CITY COLLEGE SEIZED FOR 'FIXES.' "

Arthur Daley responded to this news with silence. In his next column, he escaped into sports history. As if overwhelmed by the magnitude of the scandal—the police had also started to collar players from other schools, indicating a nationwide conspiracy—the most important sportswriter in America retreated into the world that he knew and loved best, the classic sports past with its mythic heroes. In a long, lyrical piece on Knute Rockne, the writer exhaled a literary sigh of relief, beginning, "He was an immigrant boy from Norway who became a football coach. But that is akin to saying that the Museum of Modern Art is a building on Fifth Avenue. It doesn't even hint at the treasures inside."

Daley obviously enjoyed writing this column, laying on his favorite tales—inevitably the Rockne-Dorais invention of the forward pass, and the "Win One' for the Gipper" speech—and, with each paragraph, he moved further from the current reality of college sports. His only reference to the awful present was the oblique comment that Rockne "made Notre Dame the No. 1 football power in the land and he didn't do it by proselyting or subsidizing," i.e., unlike most athletic programs today. That the ND coach had engaged in extensive recruiting and subsidization was probably known to Daley from his 1930s Fordham association with such beneficiaries of Rockne's system as Jim Crowley and Frank Leahy, coaches at Fordham during that decade and quite open about the methods of their Notre Dame mentor. However, in 1951, surrounded by the fix scandal, Arthur Daley had no interest in the historical Rockne. He wanted to use the mythic St. Knute as a "shining example" of all that was "good and true" in intercollegiate athletics. Thus: "Any schoolboy exposed for a single second to the magnetic charm of this dynamic man was forever lost [in it]. Every kid in the country dreamed of playing football for Rock."

Daley's use of the Rockne-as-inspiration-to-boys trope echoed the dedication and central theme of *Knute Rockne—All-American*, but for all of its golden hue, it contained an ironic and tragic subtext. A few days after the Manhattan College revelation, the *New York Times* ran the headline, "ROCKNE'S SON SHOT," and an article about the coach's eldest son Billy, age thirty-five, who, while drunk and in search of more liquor, had broken into the home of a bootlegger in Wichita, Kansas, and been shot by him. The *Times* and other papers also carried follow-up stories as Billy went from the "critical list" to limited recovery. Arthur Daley must have read these articles, some of which even appeared in the *Times* sports pages. But for this writer, the sad fate of the coach's boy (he had long drifted around the country), as well as the reported alcohol problems of Rockne's other sons, was incredibly far from the traditional world of St. Knute—yet uncomfortably close to the sordid netherworld of the current scandals. Finally, the disjuncture between Rockne-as-inspiration-to-boys and the lives of the coach's actual sons indicated the growing tension within classical sportswriting, as well as the revisionist reality threatening it.

■   ■   ■

When the gambling scandal broke, an official of one of the schools . . . involved said: "I can't believe our boys could do such a thing."

"Why not?" a reporter asked. "You paid them for campus jobs they didn't work at; you gave them passing grades for classes they didn't attend. You bribed them to play for you; the gamblers bribed them not to play too well. What's the difference?"

—*Collier's* author and Yale University basketball coach
Howard Hobson, December 1951.

That many of the best college basketball squads in the country, including CCNY, the winner of the 1950 NCAA and NIT championships, consistently rigged games seems as extraordinary to fans a half century later as it did to most basketball rooters at the time. The explanation for it resides less in the aberrant criminality of the players involved—"a few rotten apples," according to the college athletic establishment—than in the corrupt system within which many college sports programs existed. Indeed, the extent of the corruption was much greater than fans at the time believed. Ultimately, law enforcement officials claimed a total of seven crooked teams, thirty-two dishonest players, and eighty-six fixed games. However, basketball experts now maintain that the actual numbers were much higher in every category; the official statistics were kept artificially low because many DAs in college towns and in some cities were unwilling to investigate and/or prosecute local sports heroes and damage their schools' reputations.

The fixing system was both widespread and deep within individual programs. One of the CCNY fixer-players later revealed that "shaving points was a time-honored tradition at City. The choice was to go along with everybody else or to tell the authorities." But because everybody was "doing business," including players on other teams, it made sense "to go along." Indeed, according to Norm Mager, the sixth man on the CCNY championship team, "It could get messy out there [on the court] when the other team was shaving too," but for different gamblers. "We'd know [a double fix] when we purposely threw away a pass, and we'd get it right back."

As Yale's Howard Hobson indicated, the corruption at CCNY and other schools extended beyond the players to the coaches, and to the athletic recruiting, admission, and retention system. The revelations about CCNY exploded early and, because of the team's stature, attracted enormous attention, but, as subsequent events demonstrated, the basketball program at "City" was far from unique. Indeed, it was depressingly typical of many schools in big-time college ball.

The architect of CCNY basketball was the famous coach Nat Holman, and to him went the tributes when the team won championships. Strangely, he escaped all blame when the fixes were exposed. Nevertheless, examining Holman and his basketball system provides an excellent explanation of how and why the fixes occurred.

■   ■   ■

> If Babe Ruth had masterminded as many pennant-winning clubs as John J. McGraw, or if Jim Thorpe had been the football coach Knute Rockne was, they would have achieved in their sports the same sort of unique position Nat Holman holds in basketball. A host of highly regarded experts consider Holman the greatest player and coach that basketball has ever seen.
>
> —*Collier's* magazine writer Stanley Frank, February 1950.

In an age of classic embellishment, the praise for Nat Holman exceeded the usual inflated hyperbole. Because of his well-known vanity and his preference for sycophantic scribes, even the national magazines approached "the Master," as Holman called himself, bearing accolades. Yet, within his laudatory columns, Stanley Frank provided clues about the real man: "He always has recognized himself as the game's ultimate authority," and "he firmly believes his name and the words 'Mr. Basketball' are interchangeable." Modesty was a traditional virtue, but Nat Holman skipped his portion—in 1950 he even attempted to register and copyright his self-appointed title of "Mister Basketball"! And beneath the hype was the reality of a corrupt basketball system.

Holman, an outstanding player on the famed "Original Celtics," the first great basketball team, started coaching CCNY part-time in the 1920s. He and his program went full-time in the 1930s, and by the 1940s he employed two street-smart assistants, Bobby Sand and Sam Winograd, to do the messy business of locating prospects, getting them into CCNY, and keeping them happy while there, including making deals for them in the Catskills. Holman's aides even spent their summers in the mountains, Winograd at a hotel where, in addition to his basketball duties, he ran the betting pool. Both men knew basketball thoroughly. Sand was so astute that many magazines, including *Sport*, asked him to contribute technical articles on the game, but Nat Holman always vetoed such proposals, telling his assistant, "I'm the big shot here."

Holman wanted Sand to concentrate on assembling prime basketball talent, and although the recruiter found many excellent prospects, particularly when the service teams broke up at the end of the war, he had difficulty getting players admitted to CCNY. As a tuition-free institution, the college attracted a multitude of poor but very bright New York area high school graduates; as a result, City had very high admission and academic standards. *Collier's* depicted Holman's players "as the few school-boy phenoms" in the nation who legitimately "qualify" for CCNY entrance; furthermore, they are such ideal scholar-athletes that they attend the school even though "they can find easier ways of getting a free education at other colleges."

The reality was different. After the scandal broke and the New York Board of Education, in charge of CCNY, investigated the basketball program, it reported that "between 1945 and 1951, the high school transcripts of fourteen [players] were changed" by the basketball office "to establish their eligibility for admission." One of the players later commented that "forging transcripts was a widely accepted practice at City," and it went much further than the board claimed—indeed, so far that the board stopped investigating. Holman's assistants did the heavy lifting on player admissions and retention, and later carried the full censure of the board—it condemned their "cynicism and disregard of academic and ethical standards"—but many observers considered their boss equally guilty. "All Nat wanted was ballplayers," a former recruit charged. "He didn't care how he got them."

Just as they knew about the transcript fraud, as well as the schemes to keep the athletes in school and to slip them money, Sand and Winograd came to realize that the players were involved in other deceptions, particularly with gamblers. From their contacts in the Catskills and in the city, the aides heard the rumors about CCNY fixes, and they watched the uneven play in games. In 1949, after one particularly error-filled and infuriating performance by a key player, Sand informed Holman of his suspicions. The head man told him to "quiet down," and forget the matter. The assistant persisted, subsequently pointing out to Holman instances of questionable play in other games, but he could never persuade his boss to move on this issue.

Sand became more frustrated as the fixes continued. When his team actually dumped to underdog Missouri in 1950, and he learned that many bookies had refused to take bets on the game, he spoke to an administrator at CCNY about the situation. The official approached Holman, who responded by swearing that there was "no chance in the world that a City College ball player would ever do such a thing" as fix a game. The administrator then informed colleagues in the CCNY hierarchy and was rebuffed by them. Explaining this bureaucratic malfeasance, an observer later remarked: "Administrators were warned but they were so enamored of the glamour of seeing their school in a bigtime [college sports] environment, they looked away. Though the young men were forced out of school, no administrator lost his job or was censured." As at other universities involved in the fixes, the CCNY authorities—the persons with ultimate responsibility for their school's athletic program—formed a crucial link in the corrupt basketball system.

The moment of greatest enchantment for CCNY officials came at the campus celebration after the team's victory in the 1950 NCAA championship game. The school president announced, "This is one of the proudest days of my life," and then with words indicating his total obliviousness to the facts—or his willful ignorance of them—he intoned: "This team came here to study, not to play basketball. I am proud of the team and what it has done for the college. I want to emphasize that the players have been given no scholarships to play ball. They are not imported mercenaries." (CCNY did not need to give athletic scholarships: the school was free for all students.)

This invocation of the classic sports ideals matched the press portrayals of the team, capturing what the public as well as university officials loved about intercollegiate athletics. With its rigorous academic tradition and its working-class commuter students, CCNY seemed an unlikely candidate for collegiate sports supremacy, but, in winning college basketball's double championship—a feat never managed before or since—Holman's program illustrated, according to the press, "all that is great about collegiate athletics and America." That the reality was so far from the ideal turned the team's descent, less than a year later, into a free fall, accompanied by bitter press and public denunciations, almost all of them aimed at the players.

■ ■ ■

> The American people have a romanticized view of athletics. They want to identify with the entire fantasy that the world of sports has come to represent. Whenever you break a moral code that people are supposed to believe in, you are confronted with a stronger wrath than any burglar or common thief ever faces.
>
> —CCNY starting center and fixer Ed Roman, 1978.

Because in the postwar era the traditional ideal of athlete-heroes held the public imagination, fed in large part by the media's promotion of it, the public and the press denounced the player-fixers as "Judases," "betrayers of America's youth," and various kinds of monsters. The City players and the arrested athletes on other teams admitted their guilt, paid their official debts to society—some even with prison time—and became social pariahs, enduring years of internal exile. Most of them came to terms with their sad fates, but many also carried a major grievance: "All of the [head] coaches yelled their innocence from the rooftops," Ed Roman explained. "We [athletes] took the rap." Floyd Layne, another of the City fixers, later realized, "If you told the truth," as the players did in their confessions, you were crucified, but if you "lied and maintained an air of respectability," as the head coaches did, then "you could ride right through and everything would be okay."

Roman concluded, "Above all else, I've learned that the entire universe of sports is based on illusion." Although his comment is too general, it definitely applied to his coach, Nat Holman—a master of illusion before the scandals broke and, even more amazingly, during the revelations and after.

MAN OF THE YEAR IN SPORT

Nat Holman Didn't Score a Point for the City College of New York Basketball Team Last Winter, but His Imprint Was on Every Play . . .

—The editors of *Sport* magazine, December 1950.

The highest praise for Holman rolled in after CCNY won the NCAA and NIT championships in 1950. Many magazines and newspapers gave him full profiles and some, their annual awards. *Sport* magazine changed its most important prize from "Athlete of the Year" to "Man of the Year in Sport" so that it could honor him. The *Sport* accolade appeared a few months before the web of CCNY fixes unraveled; the irony of the award to Holman embarrassed *Sport* into taking a more balanced line on college sports—but not on Holman or the other coaches involved in the scandals.

Sport began the award article by detailing Holman's rise from the "melting pot that is New York's Lower East Side" in the first decades of the century to his seasons as a star player for the "Original Celtics," then his years as a winning basketball coach at CCNY, culminating in the 1950 championships. Using the tropes of the immigrant myth made popular by such films as *Knute Rockne—All-American,* the editors trumpeted: Holman "has lived the ancient American dream . . . [His] selection as Man of the Year . . . serves to re-state in a troubled time the vast area of opportunity that beckons in this free country."

When the scandal exploded, this identification of Holman with the deepest American myths made it much easier for him and colleagues in similarly tight spots to defend their innocence. Could any fan possibly believe that the heirs of St. Knute would look the other way while their players rigged games? And just as the media had promulgated the myths about coaches, it now proclaimed their innocence. What's more, to expose their guilt would not have helped the promotion of college sports or the careers of individual sportswriters and broadcasters.

When Ed Roman condemned the total-denial strategy of the coaches, he also denounced the "free ride" provided to them by the press. In the case of his coach, Nat Holman, it was as if reporters refused to connect the dots discovered during years of covering the CCNY program and reach the most commonsense conclusions. Not only did the facts of Holman's life supply indicators—the "Original Celtics" rigged many games, he owned a profitable camp in the Catskills and watched many hotel games, his confrontations with Sand and others leaked out, and so on—but his coaching techniques provided important clues concerning his ongoing knowledge of the fixes.

Yet the media treated Holman's denials as scripture, and later generations of sports journalists, including Ira Berkow, a current writer of "Sports of the Times," continued to support the coach's line up to his death in 1995 and afterward. Even scholarly studies of the fixes treat Holman and other coaches of crooked teams gently, accepting their explanations. Fortunately, the historical record on these men is voluminous, and readers can connect the dots for themselves.

■   ■   ■

Holman is a purist. He teaches the basketball he himself played—short, incisive passes in a game that features ball handling and maneuvering for position, and which culminates in a deft lay-up shot.

—*Collier's* writer Stanley Frank, February 1950.

The profiles of the CCNY head man usually described his coaching techniques. *Collier's* also termed him a "harsh perfectionist [who] invariably turns out beautifully drilled teams" and quoted his philosophy of coaching: " 'I have no patience with mediocrity . . . You correct mistakes by pounding at them. Easygoing guys who don't demand the best don't win many games.' " Reports of Holman at work confirmed his words, one observer noting, "Nat's practice sessions were models of efficiency and seriousness. They began at 4 [P.M.] sharp, and for the next three hours, every minute was accounted for." Furthermore, when the coach spotted an error and "blew his whistle during a scrimmage, the terrified players would freeze while they waited for the wrath to descend on whoever was out of sync."

Like most successful coaches, Holman taught a specific system. He had refined the "Original Celtics" method into a "total team" concept: careful ball control, short passes, precise movement on offense, and the highest percentage shot possible, preferably a layup. In a period before the shooting clock, Holman's clubs could maneuver the ball and wait patiently for the best shot; similarly, on defense, he preached teamwork—assume defensive positions, help out teammates, and force the opposition into turnovers. For players trying to rig games with bad passes and blown shots as well as defensive lapses, Holman's system presented major problems, not only in executing the fix but in remaining undetected, particularly by the man who devised the system.

In contrast to Holman's deliberate style was "Racehorse Basketball." Originating in Indiana high school basketball in the 1930s, and introduced into the colleges in the early 1940s by men like Everett Case, "Racehorse" gained popularity throughout the decade. Emphasizing the fast break and the running game, this approach allowed spontaneity and innovation, in the process creating high scores and many player errors and turnovers. This system was perfect for athletes shaving points, and when the full scandal unfolded, some "racing" teams were implicated. However, Nat Holman abhorred the uncertainty of "Racehorse Basketball"; it violated his basic concept of the sport and his perfectionist, controlling personality. His teams always played careful, positional ball.

Nevertheless, Holman made some concessions to the modern basketball age. He had assistants film every game and many practices, and he spent hours examining his players' moves, careful to spot their mistakes and to upbraid the offenders during team meetings. He also wrote books about his coaching methods—his *Winning Basketball* went through many editions—and he gave clinics on his techniques, bringing along film clips to illustrate his points and to demonstrate the value of filming one's players.

> In many respects Holman is like Notre Dame's brilliant football coach Frank Leahy. Both take themselves and the game they teach seriously, both work themselves unsparingly. Both expect their athletes to do the same . . . Both like to win and being sticklers for fundamentals . . . their teams, win again and again and again.
>
> —From *Sport* magazine's "Man of the Year Award" profile, December 1950.

The parallels between Holman and Leahy seem accurate but still raise a crucial question: if ND players had rigged football games, won but made deliberate errors to stay under the point spread, would their coach have detected a pattern and, most significantly, suspected a fix? One does not have to be a Fighting Irish fan to believe that Frank Leahy, with his perfectionism, his constant use of films, his attention to the movement of every player on every play, would have discovered the "rigging."

Football, with its frequent stoppages, is a more static sport than basketball; nevertheless, considering CCNY's deliberate style and Holman's insistence that his team always remain within his system, one has to conclude that when "the Master" studied his players in game action and on film, he noticed their intentional errors—*he spotted the fixing*. Assistant coach Bobby Sand certainly saw it. Yet, when the CCNY arrests came, Nat Holman constantly denied any knowledge of, or even suspicions about, his players' shaving and rigging, and the press and public believed him.

> When my players were making bad moves, I saw them as technical errors, basketball mistakes. When I chastised them for their mistakes, to them it must have sounded like an expression of suspicion on my

part. But it wasn't, I was seeing basketball errors . . . I had seven of them against me. My first seven men [the starters and first two reserves] were all in on the fix. I was strapped.

—Nat Holman in *Sport* magazine, December 1951.

The CCNY coach reacted to the confessions of his seven players with a full-court offense. Not only did he accuse his "boys" of terrible wrongdoing behind his back, but he preempted their potential counteraccusation that he knew about the rigging: his locker-room criticisms might have "sounded like . . . suspicion" but they were innocent. Holman even managed to appear aggrieved: all of his key players were "against me . . . I was strapped." But between the lines, this suggests that, because exposing the seven fixers would have wiped out his greatest team, being "strapped" might have become a major incentive for silence.

Nat Holman extended his innocence to all other coaches, all equally inno-cent—indeed, like him, also oppressed by their bosses, *and* the players, *and* American life. In his *Sport* article, he condemned the "general relaxation of morals in the country . . . boys at loose ends have brought this on. And in this climate, the responsible authorities of bigtime basketball have failed in their duty. *They have allowed the game to fall into the hands of the boys.*" Even a half century later, the brazen hypocrisy of this statement is astonishing.

Nat Holman, however, realized that a pose of virginal innocence strained credibility. In the *Sport* article, he acknowledged, "The rumors about dumps had been prevalent for some time . . . Oh, I was slightly suspicious of some players on other teams who would make glaring mistakes out on the court. But I couldn't be suspicious of my boys. No coach could and still do a job. I'm sure Clair Bee, Forddy Anderson, Ken Norton, and Gerry Bush [coaches of other crooked teams] will know what I mean." Holman indicated the coaches' paralyzing predicament: if they confronted their players with well-founded suspicions and the athletes confessed, the coach would have to go to school administrators, then the district attorney, the media, and the public; in the alternate scenario, if the coach accused his players and they lied, the coach would still have to go to school officials, the DA, and the rest.

Either way, how could the head man's reputation remain at its current high level, never mind his earning power from his clinics, speeches, books, and other ancillary activities? He had allowed his "boys" to become involved with gamblers, and to commit the most heinous sports crime possible; even if he exposed their fixing, he was still the head man, responsible for his "boys." The law courts would convict the crooked players, but, in a sports age still bound by traditional rules, coaches feared that the court of public opinion would condemn them to very harsh punishments. In this no-win situation, the coaches apparently felt that the best course of action was no action. The initial response of Kentucky coach Adolph Rupp to the CCNY arrests probably summed up the coaches' attitude: "The Chicago Black Sox threw ball games, but these kids only shaved points." In other words, they did not hurt the win-loss record.

■ ■ ■

> Basketball is a great sport. A youngster itself, it has come to serve youth throughout the world. City playgrounds are built around a basketball court. Bushel-barrel rims have become standard equipment on garage doors all along the American countryside. Today more youngsters play basketball than any other sport.
>
> It has developed a phenomenal following of millions. Giant arenas—on college campuses and in metropolitan main streets—have been built to house it. Schools have made money from it. Coaches have received better salaries because of it. Newspapers, radio, now television have recognized its growth into a major sport and have benefited from it.
>
> —Nat Holman in *Sport* magazine, December 1951.

The magazine titled this article "How We Can Save Basketball," but, considering the platform it provided for the coach's rationalizations, *Sport* should have called it "How We Can Save Nat Holman." The subhead revealed the magazine's position: "Himself a Principal Sufferer from the Vicious Plague That Struck the Sport This Year, City College's Great Coach Analyzes the Sickening Scandal and Courageously Charts a Course for the Future. Punish the Guilty, He Says, but Not the Game."

The public reaction to the scandals provided the context for Holman's self-serving piece. Along with fan bewilderment and outrage, as the scandal spread and the arrest tally rose, various authorities, including the editorial writers at the *Saturday Evening Post* urged Americans "Not to Duck the Real Issues in the Sports Mess," the systemic corruption in college sports. To avoid gamblers and their city arena hangouts, some universities considered moving all college basketball games back to their campuses. More radically, to short-circuit future scandals in a sport with the inherent lure of the point spread and point shaving, some editorialists called for the complete de-emphasis of college basketball, returning it to "a par with college wrestling." The seriousness of these proposals and the weight of their proponents, including the *New York Times*, led *Sport* to enlist "Mr. Basketball" to reply, and also to give his excuses.

The CCNY coach began his article with a clever invocation of traditional basketball scenes: "youngsters" on "city playgrounds," and country boys shooting at "bushel-barrel rims." Having invoked a scene as far from the scandals as he could get, in his second paragraph he addressed his real audience: university officials and the media. He placed his main point in the subtext here and in subsequent paragraphs: if the attacks on college basketball continue, Holman argued, the goose will die, and its golden eggs to schools will disappear; moreover, media assaults on the sport harm the media itself and jeopardize the jobs of many writers and broadcasters. Therefore, "punish the guilty"—the players—"but not the game"—the coaches, the schools, and the media.

By featuring Holman's article and a variety of follow-ups, *Sport* magazine championed this argument. In addition, by including his total denials, it sanctioned them, encouraging other media outlets to do the same. Finally, *Sport's* portrayal of the coach as a "Principal Sufferer from the Vicious Plague That Struck the Sport" helped Holman remain on his pedestal. One New Yorker noted that "Nat was still 'Mr. Basketball,' but now people addressed him with the majesty due to a genius who suffers unjustly."

Nevertheless, the New York Board of Education, the coach's employer, showed less immediate forgiveness toward him, and began a series of investigations and hearings on his basketball program. Holman fought back with total denials and, because of the political nature of the proceedings and his political clout, eventually triumphed, leading to the long-standing tag line, included in his *New York Times* obituary, that he "was cleared of any wrongdoing." Yet, the record of the hearings reveals that he insisted upon being either confronted by a smoking gun, such as evidence of his accepting a bribe from a gambler, or "exonerated." By cleverly forcing board members to consider only acts of commission, not omission, he maneuvered them into an acquittal, as well as assent to his improbable argument that "nobody could possibly detect deliberate bad play." Holman returned to coaching, retaining his master status, and became an early inductee in the Basketball Hall of Fame.

In protecting Nat Holman during and after the scandals, the authorities and the media acted mainly out of self-interest and self-deception, but why did the public accept the claims of total innocence from this coach and his colleagues in similar situations? To understand that response, the reader has to re-enter the world of midcentury America.

■   ■   ■

A Marine captain named Richard McCutcheon became the first contestant to go all the way [on the quiz shows] . . . For $64,000 he was asked to name the five dishes and two wines served by King George VI of England for French president Albert Lebrun [at an obscure state dinner] in 1939. He did: *consommé quenelles, filet de truit saumonée, petits pois à la francaises, sauce maltaise,* and *corbeille.* The wines were *Château d'Y'quem* and *Madera Sercial.* The nation was ecstatic—it had a winner.

—Author David Halberstam, 1993.

Most consumers of 1950s sports and other entertainment were remarkably naive and uncritical. The great television scandal of the decade, the fixed quiz shows, demonstrated this: huge TV audiences believed completely in the honesty of the programs, even though the parade of contestants rattling off perfect answers to amazingly arcane questions defied all common sense. Moreover, the press never inquired about the utter improbability of the situation. Like the basketball scandals, the truth eventually came out, and Americans learned that the TV producers had rigged the quiz shows in a variety of ways; during practice sessions, for instance, they asked McCutcheon the exact questions that appeared on the show that night.

Similarly the public, even sports fans, knew very little about the complexities of various games, particularly basketball. The sport had only entered the big time in the 1940s. Most people did not understand its playing styles and tactics and could barely recognize a hook shot from a jump shot. In addition, fans could not easily learn the nuances of the sport: although television had started to carry important college games, cameras were far from the floor, and could not capture intricate action under the basket or elsewhere. Slow-motion, stop-action, and video replays were years away; 1950s announcers mainly identified the players' names and statistics but did not discuss strategy or, even if they did, they lacked on-screen devices to illustrate their points. In the early TV period, basketball consisted of ten players, wearing uniforms that appeared similar because of the black-and-white telecasting, moving up and down a distant court, with closeups mainly occurring when the camera froze on a player taking a foul shot.

As for film, even though its clarity surpassed early TV images, only in occasional movie theater newsreels could fans see clips of college basketball. In addition, basketball aficionados could obtain some of the "training movies" that coaches screened at clinics, but these were not in wide distribution. Even more difficult for fans to locate were the film strips used by coaches like Holman to analyze their teams and their opponents, and to instruct players in team meetings.

Of course, fans could buy tickets to games, which many did, but in most city arenas, spectators sat away from the floor and lacked the means of analyzing the game's subtleties, or even becoming aware of them (video replays on the Jumbotron were not even a science fiction dream). The average fan in an arena did not see the rigging—mainly because he or she did not have a clue what to look for. As in postwar football, with fans bewildered by the complexities of two-platoon play, most college basketball spectators did not understand the technical aspects of the sport. They mainly cheered for their favorites, or the side they bet on, but they did not know the reasons why their team won or lost. Even the fans booing a club not covering the point spread could not explain what was actually occurring—they could merely count the difference between the score and the spread. Only the cognoscenti in places like Madison Square Garden understood the rigging and could spot it, but they were a tiny minority of all basketball fans.

Thus, in this period of sports ignorance, the public, predisposed toward the coaches as the heirs of St. Knute, had no trouble believing that Nat Holman and his colleagues could watch from the bench during games, and later view films of their teams' play, and never suspect a fix. The public did not understand Holman's system or how it made point shaving difficult to execute, as well as simple for "the Master" to spot. A half century later, with many fans as knowledgeable about basketball as some of the 1940s coaches, total denial would never fly as high or as well. Moreover, the press understands the sport better than ever before, and has also moved to a more skeptical stance on coaches.

A direct connection exists between the coaches' denial strategy during the scandals and the fact that it would not work as successfully today. More than any other event in American sports history, including the 1919 Black Sox disgrace, the postwar college basketball fixes and the Army football scandal changed media and public attitudes toward sports, starting the erosion of faith that ended the Age of Innocence and purely classic portraits of athlete-heroes. The events of 1951 shaped all subsequent fan and media perceptions of American sports, particularly intercollegiate athletics, and helped create the sports age in which we still live.

33

Coach Bee vs. Author Bee:
The Death of the
Frank Merriwell Hero

No athletes were viewed as more virtuous than the college All-Americans. They formed a natural aristocracy based not on birth, wealth, race, or religion, but on ability. Visions of . . . Frank Merriwell, [and other] fictional All-Americans, continued to dominate American thinking about college athletics. They were heroes who were modest in victory, gracious in defeat . . . and at all times fair and honest. Before 1950, the periodic college recruiting scandal failed to erase this myth. Then came 1951.

—Sports historians Randy Roberts and James S. Olson, 1989.

Sports novels about Frank Merriwell and his compatriots remained in print during the first decades of the century, but by the late 1940s readers wanted similar heroes in more contemporary settings and situations. To meet this demand and to expound the traditional virtues, author Clair Bee created Chip Hilton, "a clean-cut, All-American scholar-athlete," excelling in basketball, football, and baseball, and also "a perfect son, great friend, and an A-plus student." Bee's novels were immensely popular; Chip Hilton outperformed all rivals and his books outsold all competitors.

For Clair Bee, the Chip Hilton series was only part of a production line that included many volumes on basketball coaching and tactics. His main job, however, was as athletic director and head basketball coach at LIU (Long Island University), one of the major postwar basketball powers and a team deeply involved in the fixes. Thus, Clair Bee's story contains fascinating biographical questions—like Nat Holman, he denied any knowledge of the rigging—and also provides insight into the demise of classic sports heroes.

■ ■ ■

Coach Henry Rockwell, Valley Falls' veteran football mentor . . . was biting off his words as he moved back and forth in front of the weary players, "I thought you fellows were going to report in shape . . . Football's a fast man's game—not a fat man's game. You fellows who don't want to play badly enough to get in shape, just remember to bring some nice, soft cushions to the games. Then you and I can . . . watch kids who love this game—love it enough to get in condition."

—From the opening chapter of Clair Bee's first Chip Hilton novel, *Touchdown Pass,* 1948.

KNUTE ROCKNE'S VOICE. A rapid, clipped and staccato manner of speech, especially when addressing groups.

ROCKNE [TO THE CROWD OF PLAYERS AT THE OPENING OF FALL FOOT-BALL PRACTICE]:
If there are any of you spoiled high school stars here who don't want to get in shape and learn to block and tackle—turn in your suits tonight. You can't make the team here. The Notre Dame System is based on teamwork which means a combination of self-sacrifice, brains—and sweat!

—From the shooting script and film *Knute Rockne—All-American,* 1940.

When readers encounter Chip Hilton's beloved mentor, Henry Rockwell, they hear echoes of the Rockne film speeches. They also learn that the man's nickname is "Rock," and although he tends to wear "a plain, gray, warm-up track suit, it couldn't conceal his muscular build . . . compact and well proportioned"—as in the photos of the Notre Dame coach, and of Pat O'Brien in the movie role. In addition, "the Rock . . . was pressing sixty [years old] but he didn't look it"—Clair Bee introduced his "Rock" to the public in 1948, the year that Knute Rockne would have reached sixty.

The analogies continue as the Hilton novels unfold. Rock mentors Chip through many high school football, basketball, and baseball seasons; Rockne coached more than one sport, for many years heading the ND track program but also dabbling in boxing and basketball. Then, when Chip moves to college ball, Rock goes with him, coaching for State U, and continuing to impart such aphorisms as "Courage is an important thing in life and in athletics." During sports seasons, Rock also emphasizes that "it takes courage to study when you're tired just as much as it does to fight out there on the court [or field] when the going gets tough. Often a game gets more important to a player than school—that's bad. School's first. Basketball's second," as are all other sports.

In the Rockne film, immediately after the coach discussed "self-sacrifice, brains—and sweat," he proclaimed, "And the brains come first . . . I'll expect you to keep a high average in your classes. We want to win if we can—but you didn't come to Notre Dame to play football," but to get an education. "Five years from now the public will have forgotten even the *best* of you. Remember that!" The scriptwriters at Warners were both correct and wrong. The public quickly forgets most college athletes, but it long remembers and treasures the scholar-athlete ideal espoused by the Rockne movie and other classic representations of college sports.

In addition, like the players in *Knute Rockne—All-American,* Rock's advice propels Chip to athletic, academic, and social triumphs. As a result, Chip considers himself "one of the luckiest fellows in the world," having achieved sports and school success, and with "so many friends he could scarcely count them." At the top of the list was "Henry Rockwell," and then Chip's teammates, "Soapy Smith, Biggie Cohen, Speed Morris, Red Schwartz, Fats Ohlson, Jimmy Lu Chung," and so on. Like the combat crews of World War II movies and the Fighting Irish football squads, Chip's pals— and Rockwell's teams—represent diverse races and ethnic groups, and they usually overcome internal strife and external prejudice on their way to athletic victory, with teamwork solving all character and plot problems.

In his freshman year in college, Chip excels in many intercollegiate sports, leads his dormitory as its president and the freshman class as vice president, coaches an intramural basketball team, works at a soda shop, and, most important of all, "as a top-flight student . . . he had a lot of studying to do." In succeeding years, he continues to work his way through school, star in many college sports, earn top grades, lead various campus groups, solve crimes, but never party or waste time. As Clair Bee often stated, "Chip Hilton wasn't a loafer."

Neither was his creator. *Sport* magazine did a full profile of Clair Bee in the early 1950s entitled "Basketball's Busiest Bee." It listed his activities: assistant to the president of Long Island University, also the LIU athletic director and head basketball coach; in addition, he "occupies himself with . . . farming, writing, radio and television broadcasting, book and game publishing, speaking at basketball clinics . . . [operating] a summer basketball school," and "a daily newspaper column which he insists on writing himself." By all accounts, Bee was one of the great entrepreneurial coaches of his era, not unlike his idol Knute Rockne during the 1920s. And like Rockne and other people from hardscrabble backgrounds, Clair Bee, who was from the coal fields of West Virginia, drove himself and those around him as if only nonstop work could keep his success afloat.

Like all winning and money-hungry coaches, Bee increased his annual earnings to the point where, according to one study, "Bee's salary had risen by 300 percent from 1941 and 1950," whereas his athletic department continuously showed a deficit: the profits were siphoned to coaches and players, not to the school. And during the 1940s, Bee's outside income grew at a much greater rate than his salary. *Sport* noted that Author Bee churned out four books a year for large advances and royalties, and he also earned money from subsidiary rights—national magazines like *Senior Scholastic* for high school students frequently printed excerpts, as did other journals. In addition, the coach realized significant amounts from his summer camp in the Catskills, as well as his association with the sports program at nearby Kutscher's Hotel. By 1951 when the scandals broke, Bee topped $75,000 a year—$750,000 in 1990s dollars—but to maintain and enhance his annual income, he had to continue to win games as Coach Bee, and to expand his writing and speaking business as Author Bee.

The situation in the Catskills indicated the deep contradictions within the two worlds of Clair Bee. Like Nat Holman, the LIU coach was totally plugged into Catskill summer basketball, and in the postwar period all of his fixer-athletes worked the mountain circuit. In addition, from 1949 to 1951 one of Bee's favorite players, Eddie Gard, operated as the gamblers' main go-between, recruiting athletes from LIU and other colleges during the summers for the wintertime fixes. Gard inherited this job from an LIU teammate who had graduated into the big-time rackets. According to one historian, the primary gambler-fixer, Salvatore Sollazzo, "and Gard traversed the Mountain roads scouting [hotel] teams for corruptible talent."

Catskill basketball existed on another planet than Chip Hilton's, that wonderfully idealized place where Rock tells his "boys" how he feels "about *outside ball playing*," including summer basketball: " 'Sooner or later you'll meet a thirty-cent promoter [e.g., hotel manager] who will want to cash in on your publicity. Fly-by-night leeches like to capitalize on players whose names are on the sports pages.' " Rock absolutely prohibits outside ball, telling his players to obey his dictum or otherwise " 'turn in your [school] uniform! Is that clear?' " Unfortunately, the other planet from Chip's was Earth, and not only did Clair Bee condone his boys playing outside ball but he often set them up with Catskill teams. Yet, he later denied any awareness of the gambling and fixing going on in the mountains.

In Chip Hilton's world, excellent athletes show up for the club, and Rock molds them into winners, on the court and off. Historically in college sports, very few superior athletes have wandered into major programs; Coach Bee at Long Island University—a school with limited athletic facilities and even less sports tradition—had to hustle for talent, often cutting corners to obtain it. In the 1930s, when he coached LIU's football team, according to one of his former players, "Bee would head for a coal mining town . . . and recruit a team to represent LIU"; "Bee [also] brought some shady baseball players" into that LIU program, the player said, including athletes registered at other schools, and his first basketball star, Julie Bender, "was a nonmatriculated student in LIU's night school and . . . ineligible to play varsity sports."

But Coach Bee built up his school's athletic program, particularly in basketball, and his Blackbirds became favorites at Madison Square Garden, climbing to the top level of the national rankings. By the mid-1940s, Bee and his assistants continued to recruit aggressively and with little regard for academic niceties. Bee found Eddie Gard in the Merchant Marine, but because the player could not gain admission to LIU, the coach placed him in a prep school, paying his way there, and then brought him to LIU, paving and paying his way at the university. Similar schemes later became standard-operating-procedure in many college programs; however, during the 1940s they represented unusual and innovative cheating.

By the end of the decade, recruiting became easier for Bee, his Blackbirds having achieved such prominence that he attracted legions of prospects to his mass tryout camps—except the athletes had no academic affiliation with LIU. With these assemblies, Bee violated NCAA and all other college rules on recruiting, and outbrazened most other coaches of the era, who tended to hold discreet workouts for individual recruits. Sherman White, subsequently one of LIU's best players and deeply involved in the fixes, explained: "Those [LIU] tryouts are really something"; Bee and his assistants "get about 200 boys in from all over and put a number on each one's back." The tryout "goes on for a couple of days and each day they cut the group down. For what they call the finals, they play a regular game. I played in that game and made out fine. So Clair Bee set up a scholarship for me, effective that September."

Sherman White gained admission to LIU—he had been turned down at other schools and had flunked out of Villanova—as well as an all-expenses-paid deal. Bee called these grants "athletic scholarships." The "Sanity Code" specifically banned them, but he justified them, as well as the admission of academically questionable athletes, with what later became a standard coaches' argument: "Just because a kid is big and strong and is able to play basketball, is that any reason for him to be offered any less help than another kid who is good at music or math?" (Subsequently, many coaches, including Nebraska's Tom Osborne, have even rationalized the presence of convicted felons in their programs with this academic-institution-as-help-agency line.)

In contrast to the sordidness of the LIU program, Author Bee offered readers a college sports nirvana. Chip Hilton disdained "athletic scholarships" as "wrong because they are compensating players to represent" universities. Moreover, because coaches "hire three or four outstanding players for every position on a team . . . the fellows on athletic scholarships are hand-picked specialists," not "true representatives of the normal student body."

Thus, they take "the enjoyment [out of sports] that comes from playing for fun." Finally, "making sacrifices"—Chip always worked his way through college—"because a fellow loves a sport is a lot like patriotism." But giving athletic scholarships is "the same as hiring mercenary soldiers to fight a war." Chip always wore the Stars and Stripes; LIU's "Blackbeards" flew the Skull and Crossbones.

A half century later, the differences between the worlds of Author Bee and Coach Bee appear so huge that one wonders if the man suffered from multiple-personality disorder. He wrote the Chip Hilton books with such passion and sincerity that he persuaded millions of readers to love and believe in his heroes and their traditional values. He also ran his basketball program so cynically that the New York judge who sentenced the LIU player-fixers excoriated Bee, wishing that he could send him to prison along with the athletes because "all of the players entrusted to the care of LIU were openly exploited in behalf of Mr. Bee and the university . . . The acts of these defendants are merely the symptoms of the disease" spread by the LIU coach and like-minded colleagues.

The best critical article on Clair Bee's fiction termed "the Hilton series as the last of its kind, the final representative of what might be called the Frank Merriwell genre." Critic Jack McCallum suggested that because media styles change, Chip became old-fashioned by the early 1960s when the publisher stopped printing the books. However, more complicated factors were involved: Chip and his pals did not die of time, they imploded. Because their form of the classic athlete-hero was pure fantasy, when the reality of postwar college sports kept bursting into the daily news, including shrill headlines about Bee's LIU player-fixers, it became increasingly difficult and finally impossible for readers to believe in Chip and his teammates.

Nonetheless, even if these fictional athlete-heroes expired, traditional sports ideals continued in other forms, sometimes fragmented but often with amazing tenacity. Because the St. Knute legend was connected to an actual person, it persisted, aided greatly by Notre Dame's immense distance from the scandals. According to McCallum, when readers of Clair Bee's fiction remember the series, they recall "the Rock," and such typical passages as "Chip turned away from the trophy case to speak to Coach Rockwell but he had disappeared [into his office]. A wave of gratitude swept over the boy as he stood there alone in the gym foyer, and a mist came over his eyes and a painful lump in his throat," full of thanks for his coach. Not surprisingly, a similar public warmth toward college coaches helped Clair Bee survive the fixing scandal, and allowed his total-denial strategy to fly.

·　·　·

In the first half of the century, Bee was basketball. There wasn't a thing he did that didn't affect the game, and there wasn't a thing that affected the game that he didn't do. He was one of the most singularly brilliant minds ever involved with athletics, and one of the greatest analytical basketball minds we've ever had.

—Indiana University men's basketball coach
Bob Knight, 1995.

Knight came to know Bee in the 1960s and always claimed that the older man taught him more about basketball than any other person. Without dispute, Bee changed the sport significantly, inventing the 1-3-1 zone defense, the three-second lane violation rule, and many other basic elements. In addition, in specific coaching situations, according to another basketball authority, "Bee was the game's greatest strategist . . . He had a knack for spotting the opposition's weakness and exploiting it. Bee plotted the strategy that 'locked in'" and nullified all of the great offensive players faced by his LIU teams. Most experts who saw him work hailed Bee as "a basketball genius," recognizing that "when it came to scouting, analyzing, and defense, he was the best."

Unlike Nat Holman, who proclaimed himself "Mr. Basketball" and "the Master," Bee was modest about his accomplishments, content to win games, write basketball strategy books, hold clinics, make training films, and increase his annual income. In fact, Bee's output exceeded Holman's; not only did he achieve a higher winning percentage, but he produced many more technical books, everything from *Drills and Fundamentals* to *Zone Defense and Attack* to *The Science of Coaching*, for a total of twenty-three non–Chip Hilton volumes. Furthermore, multiple and reissued editions of his works, as well as translations into many languages, augmented his production to the point where he became the single most published authority on basketball in the world.

By the mid-1940s, the media had recognized Bee's abilities and were producing increasing numbers of articles about him. In 1947, *Collier's* spotlighted him in a feature on basketball scouting—a relatively new phenomenon in the sport and unknown to the general public. The LIU coach not only sent scouts to chart future opponents but announced, "I'm using movies this season . . . to scout the weaknesses of my own team." He also discussed how "colleges send scouts secretly armed with 16-mm cameras and telescopic lenses to film future football foes in action," and how this will become "a widely accepted practice" in basketball. Bee also liked to scout in person; Frank McGuire, who played against Bee's LIU teams and later became a great college coach himself, claimed that Clair Bee "had the best basketball brain anybody ever had. He saw things on a basketball court which I doubt anybody else could see."

Author Bee gave his fictional "Rock" a similar talent. Chip's coach analyzes opponents with astounding precision, and he understands his own athletes equally well, not only their playing strengths and limitations but also their behavior; for example, "He was perfectly aware," even though the players believed otherwise, "of the rupture between Bollinger and Hunter and

Knute Rockne smiles down benignly on college sports.

Grantland Rice in a sportswriter's snazzy hat, carrying his home paper, the *New York Herald-Tribune*.

"Smashed-face football" of the 1930s—note the knee to the face, lower left.

College football literally wraps itself in the flag during World War II.

The 1944 Madison Square Garden basketball program marking the tenth year of Notre Dame–NYU games; the bomb inscription reads, "TO ADOLPH AND TOJO WITH LOVE ON OUR 10TH ANNIVERSARY—IRISH AND VIOLET."

The men who ran Notre Dame athletics in the postwar period. From left to right: Father John J. Cavanaugh, Frank Leahy, Edward "Moose" Krause, and Father John H. Murphy.

BELOW LEFT: Arch Ward inscribed his photo, "To Frank Leahy, America's No. 1 College Football Coach."

ABOVE: Sportswriter Francis Wallace beaming at his success.

ABOVE LEFT: Radio broadcaster Bill Stern at a mike—his mouth is uncharacteristically closed.

ABOVE RIGHT: Army coach Earl "Red" Blaik in his "Peerless Leader" stance.

Notre Dame quarterback Johnny Lujack in the jump-pass pose beloved by 1940s photographers.

Cigarette companies and college sports tried to woo women supporters with this typical postwar football program ad.

College football program covers reinforced 1950s gender roles.

ABOVE LEFT:
The scandal caused by
his team's fixing games
removed the smile from
the face of basketball
coach Clair Bee.

ABOVE RIGHT:
Big Ten commissioner
Kenneth "Tug" Wilson
often seemed worried.

LEFT:
Nothing bothered
Adolph Rupp, the
"Baron of Bluegrass."

Michigan State president John Hannah (left) eyes Notre Dame president Theodore Hesburgh warily.

BELOW LEFT: Football coaches Frank Leahy and Bud Wilkinson, in gray flannel suits, scan the sky as 1950s "Men of Vision."

BELOW RIGHT: A popular 1950s program cover: submerged by books, an NCAA "student-athlete" tries to change the image of college sports.

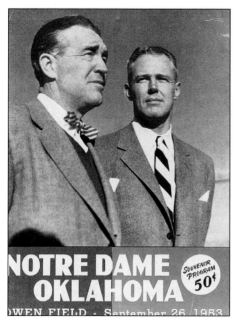

RIGHT:
Johnny Lattner, the
1953 Heisman Trophy
winner, poses in front
of the Golden Dome.

BELOW:
Notre Dame sports
publicist Charlie
Callahan holds a 1966
National Football
Championship prize;
Father Edmund Joyce
smiles at lower right.

Farley on one side and Morris and Bitsy Reardon on the other." A *Sport* magazine profile of Bee, published just before the arrests of the LIU fixers, enumerated the coach's skills, concluding, "Best of all is Bee's ability to spot [player] strength and weakness . . . as the game is being played." This portrait ignored his off-court activities—no mention of his Catskill camp and hotel connections, among other things—but if we connect Bee's superb analytic skills to his full operation, his ongoing knowledge of the fixes emerges.

> It was simply taken as fact that LIU was shaving points . . . It was the bookmakers who were putting the finger on LIU, and there is no more reliable source in the world of sports. To a bookmaker, a fixed game is a greased chute to oblivion.
>
> —Basketball historian Stanley Cohen, 1977.

The bookies caught on to LIU when they spotted a clear and consistent pattern of on-court behavior: the team whomped strong opponents when the point spread narrowly favored the Blackbirds, but won by smaller margins against weak teams when the spread was wide. Bee's players wanted to win and, taking no chances with thin spreads, played up to their potential in those games; however, with sufficiently large spreads, they shaved. Because New York papers carried the betting lines, and because Clair Bee not only read the dailies but published a column in a number of them, one has to assume that he also noted his team's pattern.

A bookie later remarked, "It was a crazy time. There were players dumping, coaches dumping, and referees dumping." In fact, in one LIU loss at the Garden, Bee spotted the refs' conduct and openly stated, "We lost to Arizona simply because the referees wanted us to lose. They took the game away from us. There's no doubt in my mind that their actions were deliberate." If the LIU coach could see referee fixing, why could he not detect rigging by his own players, whose abilities he knew intimately?

The *Sport* magazine profile of Bee contained a large photo of the coach instructing his prize pupil, Sherman White—*The Sporting News*'s 1950–51 college basketball player of the year. Bee had made White a special project, transforming him from an awkward goliath into one of the premier big men of the era. In the process, Bee came to know and understand White's every on-court move. But just as this player had problems acquiring positive basketball skills, White later described his difficulties in learning to fix: "You'd think it would be easy to hold back but it isn't. Basketball is a fast game and it's hard to hold back. Some things you do instinctively, you don't think"; however, a player has to shave consciously and often looks bad in the process. Again, it defies belief that Clair Bee, the greatest basketball scout and analyst of his generation, never noticed that the man he had molded into his star player was rigging games.

. . .

Ignoring the fixing probably became more difficult for Bee than spotting it. During games when opponent ineptitude or double-fixes made it tough for the Blackbirds to stay under the spread, and they had to commit frequent and obvious errors, the cognoscenti near the LIU bench, according to witnesses, would "jeer and shout insults . . . 'What's the points tonight? Huh, ya bums.'" At such moments, Clair Bee sat like the monkey trio See No Evil, Hear No Evil, and Speak No Evil. And when the coach examined the films of his players in action, the monkeys remained on his back.

Like Nat Holman, Bee could not easily blow the whistle on his fixers. Not only would he damage his reputation as Coach Bee, but, because of the Chip Hilton novels and their advocacy of traditional values, going public about his players' fixing would jeopardize Author Bee's career. And his high annual income would melt away. Such situations often create paralysis of action, along with the hope and prayer that the secret will remain hidden. Clair Bee also understood better than any other person of the era how little the press and public knew about basketball tactics and on-court play, and how actual evidence of fixing could stay buried, conceivably forever.

By all accounts, the coach never expected the player confessions. However, in February 1951, when the police arrested the first wave of CCNY athletes, they also picked up LIU's Eddie Gard, who had functioned as the contact man between the City athletes and the gamblers. Gard confessed, implicating the current stars of Bee's team, Sherman White, LeRoy Smith, and Dolph Bigos (the LIU captain), and this led to their arrests and confessions. Clair Bee needed the best offense ever devised to survive this crisis.

> Come the questions that put me and every coach whose team was corrupted squarely on the spot. I'm supposed to be a smart basketball man. Why didn't I suspect that games were fixed? Didn't I see things on the court that led me to believe something funny was going on?
>
> Those are fair questions, and I only can answer them now as I did when they were first asked. I never dreamed that a boy who played for me could be crooked. Had I thought it was necessary to police his conduct off the court, I would have given up coaching . . . Sure I was a naive chump—but I was so sure of my boys because I was so close to them.
>
> —Clair Bee in the *Saturday Evening Post*, February 1952.

Like Nat Holman, Bee always denied any knowledge of the fixes, and he cleverly attempted to turn his supposed faith in his players—Henry Rockwell's classic virtue—into the source of his undoing: his total belief in his "boys" caused him to suspend his famed analytical powers. The major problem with this explanation is that it contradicts Clair Bee's clear division between Coach and Author. Cynically, the Coach obtained his athletes in "cattle-call" tryouts, paid them, greased their way through college, and was close to them professionally, not personally; as a workaholic, he did not have time for social events. Yet Author Bee wholly condemned such practices, banishing them from his books, always trumpeting Rockwell's unlimited fatherliness toward "his boys." Coach Bee produced winning teams because he grasped the cutthroat realities of college basketball; the Author succeeded because he understood the fantasies of traditional athlete-hero fiction. Up to the arrests of his players, a high wall separated Coach from Author, thus, the convenient *ex post facto* demolition of the barrier appears false.

Yet the media and the public believed his explanation. Reporters accepted Bee's total denial, and the public approved. After the arrests and convictions of the player-fixers, LIU de-emphasized its athletic program, and Clair Bee moved on to the NBA for a few years, before retiring from coaching in the mid-1950s. He then spent many years in athletic management, also operating successful basketball camps and clinics. In 1967, the Basketball Hall of Fame inducted him with full honors, his past sins falling away. Not only did a new generation of coaches, men like Bob Knight and Frank McGuire, treat him as a beloved father figure, but important sports journalists extended similar kindnesses. Ira Berkow of the *New York Times* even put a new spin on Bee's total denials: "Because of his intensity [as a coach], he never suspected that something fishy was going on with his team." (Wouldn't Bee's "intensity," combined with his analytic powers, make his awareness of his players' fixing more, not less, likely?) And sports historians also accepted his denials, endorsing his golden mantra, "A coach has to believe in his players or he might as well quit."

Less kind toward Bee were his arrested players and their families. Like the CCNY fixers, those at LIU resented the media's portrayal of their coach as "a victim of the scandal," monstrously oppressed by his players. They watched as Bee's total denials worked, rescuing his career as well as his ancillary businesses; meanwhile Sherman White aptly described the players' fates with his title for a magazine article: "The Basketball Fix Wrecked My Life." White's father remarked bitterly: "It would have been different if Sherman was raised on the streets," and had become a criminal there. "But Sherman" was from a good family and "had to go to college" in Bee's LIU program "to learn something he was never taught at home."

Least kind to the coach was Judge Saul Streit, the New York General Sessions Court judge who presided over the fix trials. He scorned the disclaimers from Bee as well as Holman, underlining his disgust in his judgment: "*The equivocation and the denials of the coaches . . . concerning their knowledge of gambling . . . would be comical were they not so despicable.*" Unlike Coach Bee, the jurist truly believed in the classic sports ideals, invoking them while sentencing the key fixers: "I find that suspended sentences will not suffice for these defendants," but prison terms "will serve as a warning to other college athletes . . . that they cannot break the ideals of American sport and then escape with a mere reprimand." Streit also analyzed the systematic corruption in Clair Bee's athletic department, contrasting it to "the Temple of Amateur Sport," where athletes serve as role models for America's youth. Finally, in a comment that could have come from Henry Rockwell, the judge condemned all those like Clair Bee who defile the Temple, "undermining the faith of young Americans and shattering their ideals and belief in integrity and character."

Unlike Nat Holman, who responded to Streit's and other condemnations with arrogant counterattacks, Clair Bee continued his denials but also offered limited contrition. In his 1952 article in the *Saturday Evening Post*, "I Know Why They Sold Out to Gamblers," Bee condemned his athletes but acknowledged that "public confidence in college basketball is shattered, and the fault is partly mine . . . I was a 'win-em-all' coach, who, *by resorting to established practices*, helped to create the emotional climate that led to the worst scandal in the history of sports."

Bee offered here what later became a standard coaches' excuse, "I only did what my competitors were doing"—ignoring his much larger scale and innovative cheating. Nevertheless, he assumed partial responsibility—"I, every coach under the pressures of bigtime sport, was so absorbed in the victory grail that I lost sight of the educational purposes of athletics"—and he assessed the damage caused by the scandal. The *Post* telegraphed his assessment in its subhead, "The Basketball Scandals . . . Have Shocked America." This went beyond headline hyperbole into accurate commentary.

At the end of the twentieth century, sports commentator Heywood Hale Broun summed up the scandals: "Corruption in college sports wasn't new [in 1951]. But we [the media] had covered it over with Knute Rockne piety and Frank Merriwell sugar." As a result, the basketball scandals truly shocked most Americans, ending the college sports Age of Innocence and consigning the Chip Hilton athlete-heroes to oblivion.

34

The Fixes Play in Peoria
and Find an Old Kentucky Home

Everyone seems to be talking about bringing the game back to the campus. But the way things are, you could play in the attic or the cellar, and the gamblers would still be operating. I guess that from now on coaches will have to start sacrificing talent for character.

—New York University men's basketball coach
Howard Cann, April 1951.

The fix scandal touched NYU—the police nabbed one of its stars with the first wave of CCNY players—but then it moved on, sparing the school and the coach, a longtime New York area favorite. Howard Cann denied any knowledge of the fixes, arguing that a single player, even a high scorer, could not sufficiently affect the final result of a game to merit a coach's special notice. The NYC press and public liked Cann, who operated without Holman's arrogance or Bee's intimidating expertise, and they accepted his denials, enabling him to continue his NYU career for many more years. Also, in the spring of 1951, Cann offered a clever New York response, quoted above, to the growing national criticism of the city and the Madison Square Garden basketball scandals, as well as the calls to move the game back to the campuses.

Provincial newspapers had started to portray the scandal as a peculiarly "Noo Yawk" phenomenon, involving only NYC colleges and players, and an unjust reflection upon the All-American sport of basketball, as well as the wholesome hoopsters and fans in the rest of the nation. In fact, as events proved, the most New York element about the fixes was District Attorney Frank Hogan's willingness to expose them, in contrast to his colleagues in the provinces. By the summer of 1951, Hogan had connected the fixes to players at midwestern schools, who were not only rigging games while visiting Madison Square Garden but also on their home courts.

Hogan's first target was the University of Toledo in Ohio. An unscrupulous coach, Gerry Bush, recruiting athletes with money on all sides of the table, had launched the Rockets to the top of the national rankings in the late 1940s. Basketball success had attracted betting on the team as well as gamblers trying to fix games. The fixers easily convinced Toledo's best players, many of whom had Catskills experience, to shave points. According to one sports historian, "the gamblers became so bold as to sit near the Rockets' bench and shout instructions to the players. It became necessary to have uniformed police stationed at the field house to keep known gamblers" away from the bench. Yet, when DA Hogan revealed the Toledo fixes, the Rockets coach claimed, "There never was a question in my mind that my boys were absolutely clean. *If great coaches like Clair Bee and Nat Holman could be fooled by their players, then so could I.*"

Obviously, the Toledo head man recognized a great excuse when handed one, and he clung to this career preserver throughout the messy scandal that involved his best players and many fixed games. Aiding him was the local district attorney's refusal to prosecute the fixers, and the Toledo media's and public's support for this nonaction. Many locals agreed with a fan's comment in the *Toledo Blade:* "Who cares how many points they [the Rockets] win by, as long as they win." These rooters reflected the new postwar breed of college sports fans who placed winning above all else. As the scandal spread through the Midwest, their counterparts in Illinois and Kentucky offered similar opinions.

In addition, unlike the aftermath of the revelations at LIU, the University of Toledo administration did not de-emphasize the school's basketball program, although its officials pledged to shun invitations to Madison Square Garden and play mainly in the campus fieldhouse—where the majority of fixes had occurred!

GENE MELCHIORRE—LITTLE MAN, BIG STAR

Basketball May Be Surrounded by the Big Fellows, but It Hasn't Been Captured Completely by Them Yet. Proof Positive Is Offered by Bradley University's Agile Captain. "Squeaky" Not Only Holds His Own Against the Step-ladder Brigade; He Even Muscles In on Their Pet Racket with His Show-Stopping Pivot Stunt.

—*Sport* magazine headline and subhead, March 1951.

The *Sport* editors chose unfortunate metaphors for their classic profile of Gene Melchiorre, particularly "Big Fellows," i.e., gangsters, and "Their Pet Racket," fixing games. The first New York arrests had occurred by the time

Sport published this article, and although the Bradley athlete was not indicted until the following summer, Melchiorre was well known as one of the worst player-fixers *and* as a contact and "bag man" for the gamblers. By all accounts, he was also an exceptional basketball player, a talented small guard who could move the ball quickly and score easily. For 1950–51, he earned consensus All-America honors, and, in previous seasons, he led the Braves to high NIT and NCAA finishes; in 1950, Bradley lost the final games in both tourneys to CCNY. Melchiorre always claimed that he had not rigged those games.

The Peoria school became a basketball power after World War II because of an excellent coach, Forddy Anderson, and total support from the university's president, David Blair Owen, a former public relations executive. Dr. Owen organized a booster club to fund a lavish athletic scholarship program, traveled with the squad, and promoted it constantly, preaching that the publicity from basketball success would "put the school on the map." Bradley recruited many veterans of service teams, players who had polished their games and cynicism in the military; Melchiorre later admitted that his main duty during twenty-two months in the Army was playing basketball. Upon discharge from the service, these athletes usually went to the college offering the best money deal.

Once at Bradley, players became aware, as Melchiorre recalled, "that fixes were going on for years," and they joined in, suspecting that "sooner or later, somebody was going to get caught," but not believing that "we were the ones." And even after the CCNY arrests in New York, President Owen mounted his high horse, proclaiming that Bradley would no longer visit the Garden because of "its unsavory atmosphere." Soon enough, Frank Hogan knocked him to the ground with the announcement that eight Bradley players had rigged games over a number of seasons. Hogan wanted the athletes extradited to New York to answer charges about their fixes at Madison Square Garden; the Peoria authorities showed minimal interest in helping him or investigating possible fixes in their jurisdiction, in part because Frank Hogan identified Melchiorre, a local hero, as the key offender. Not only had he fixed games as a player but, according to the DA, "he met with gamblers in both Chicago and New York, he arranged the deals, settled on the price, collected and distributed the payoff money."

Governor Adlai Stevenson of Illinois intervened, threatening to extradite the athletes to New York if they did not go voluntarily. They went and confessed, mainly to their Garden activity and some fixes in Peoria. Illinois officials refused to follow the leads, never examining the fixers' activities at home. Bradley's president announced that rather than de-emphasize the school's big-time basketball program, he would continue full speed ahead "with the natural hope that our teams will win." The president's actions and attitude caused Judge Saul Streit, while sentencing the Bradley players, to note that Dr. Owen, with his "subsidization and his extensive traveling with members of the team while their studies were being ignored, gave official sanction to their moral debasement." (The NYC trial did force the NCAA—a number of years later, when it finally reacted to the scandals and tried to restore the image of college sports—to penalize Bradley in one of its first infractions cases.)

Again, Judge Streit showed that he believed more sincerely in the scholar-athlete ideal than did the university officials he encountered. At institutions like Bradley, Toledo, and then Kentucky, the passion to win in big-time college sports transcended any desire to balance academics and intercollegiate athletics. This lust for victory began with the school trustees and presidents, caught up the fans and students, and came to rest in absolute support for the coaches of the crooked teams. Bradley's Forddy Anderson, in spite of his players' rigging many games over many seasons, perfunctorily denied any knowledge of the fixes, and continued in his post for three more years before jumping to a better job as head man at Michigan State, where he remained for more than a decade.

Even more successful at living happily ever after the scandals was Adolph Rupp of Kentucky, coach of the most corrupt team in the fixing scandals and one of the most revered figures in the history of his sport, nicknamed "the Baron of the Bluegrass." More than any other, the Kentucky story indicates the differences between the classic past of intercollegiate athletics and the cynical future, where, although schools and coaches pay lip service to the old ideals, winning becomes "the only thing," justifying every means to achieve it.

■ ■ ■

> [At the University of Kentucky] it is impossible to put football and basketball in its proper place in university education because some of the alumni, fans, and sports writers demand winning teams with such force that their demands cannot be resisted . . .
>
> Athletics in the University of Kentucky, as in many other universities, has become professionalized, though it is still considered to be amateur. As such, athletics has no worthy place in a university. The University of Kentucky and many other state universities, as soon as possible, should return intercollegiate athletics to its amateur standing.
>
> —Griffenhagan Associates Consulting Report for the
> Governor of Kentucky, 1947.

In 1946, to help the Commonwealth of Kentucky move from a poor agrarian economy to an industrial one, and to define the role of the state's primary university in this economic development, the governor hired a prestigious Chicago consulting firm to examine the University of Kentucky. The consultants found a woebegone academic institution but a school where everyone, except a few faculty members, loved the intercollegiate athletics program, particularly Adolph Rupp's basketball squad, and the emerging football team of coach Paul "Bear" Bryant, who had recently come from Maryland. Reinforcing the power of the fans within the university was the support of influential outsiders, including state legislators and the media. The consultants concluded that unless university administrators gained control of their athletic department, UK would never become a major academic institution, able to help the state's economy in a meaningful way.

The Chicago experts also criticized UK president H. L. Donovan for promoting college sports in a senselessly enthusiastic manner. When Donovan became president in 1941, a decade after Adolph Rupp arrived at the school, he institutionalized support for UK teams: he set up a booster foundation to extract maximum dollars from supporters, he taxed the students in the form of fees channeled to the athletic department, and he allowed his coaches virtual autonomy in the recruiting and retention of players. Not surprisingly, in this coaching paradise, buccaneers like Adolph Rupp and Bear Bryant prospered with, according to one commentator, "no restrictions on the number of players on a squad, or on scholarships."

Kentucky belonged to the Southeastern Conference, and officially gave fifteen full rides in basketball and sixty in football until the "Sanity Code" outlawed them in 1948. Nevertheless, Rupp and Bryant carried many more men on their rosters before and after 1948, and also paid starting players well above the athletic scholarship limit. When the fix investigation exposed the UK operation in 1951, Judge Streit discovered 113 football and basketball players on athletic scholarships for that year, and dozens of "walk-ons" on special deals. The jurist termed the Wildcat athletic department, *"The acme of commercialism and over-emphasis,"* commenting: "I found undeniable evidence of covert subsidization of players, ruthless exploitation of athletes, cribbing on examinations, illegal recruiting, a reckless disregard for the players' physical welfare, matriculation of unqualified students, demoralization [corruption] of the athletes by the coaches, the alumni, and the townspeople." In the postwar "black market" in college sports, the UK program was hardly unique, but, as Judge Streit noted, the Wildcats violated the rules in a particularly outrageous manner.

The New York judge, however, did not discuss what citizens of the Commonwealth of Kentucky found at UK in the late 1940s and early 1950s: winning teams, with national championships in basketball and major bowl victories and high rankings in football. As one observer stated: "Kentucky showed how a newcomer could ascend to the top ranks of college sports, also its primary vehicle was basketball, not football," but even in the latter sport, Bear Bryant's "impact from 1946 to 1953 marked the greatest transformation of any football program in the nation."

This writer also remarked that "if football had its Knute Rockne, then college basketball's own legendary figure was Adolph Rupp" and, after Bear Bryant completed his career, he did not trail far behind the Notre Dame coach. The three men possessed some similar characteristics; nevertheless, as legendary figures, Rockne resided at the opposite pole from Rupp and Bryant. For Americans, St. Knute embodied the traditional virtues, but the Baron and the Bear mainly represented one thing: ruthless winning. Rupp and Bryant offered scant lip service to the classic ideals, instead stating, "I am not engaged in a popularity contest, I want to win" (Rupp), and "I don't want to be the greatest coach in the world, I just want to walk off the field a winner" (Bryant). And sports history has judged them accordingly: "The man [Rupp] was dedicated to winning as the only reason for playing basketball," and "The Bear had only one object in life—to win, and he'd walk over his mother to do it."

Rupp and Bryant personified a new breed of college coaches. In the past, men had wanted to win—Rockne certainly did—but they paid real or feigned obeisance to the classic pieties; Cornell's Carl Snavely, a notoriously hard-driving coach, even gave back a national championship because a key victory violated the sportsmanship ideal. In the postwar years, the old-fashioned coaches began to retire, and such successors as Frank Leahy evolved into CEOs, but both types still endorsed—at least publicly—the academic side of their universities. Privately, they avoided conflicts with professors at their schools.

Not Adolph Rupp and Bear Bryant. At Kentucky, they had adjoining offices in the athletic department, and in his memoirs Bryant commented: "Like him [Rupp] or not, you had to be impressed by the way he took the bull by the horns. One year they had a faculty group investigating the Kentucky athletic department . . . when they got to Rupp he was ready for them. I could hear it plain as day . . . He just ate their fannies, and they haven't sat down yet. They haven't even opened their mouths. They're in there trying to investigate athletics and he's attacking academics." To underline his contempt for the educational side of the university and to help his players with an easy class, for many years Rupp taught a course in "Advanced Basketball." Moreover, he openly "proclaimed himself the best professor in the university because all his students got A's."

In many ways, Rupp and Bryant descended from the outlaw tradition in American life, mocking and attacking the proper citizens. Some coaches at other universities, particularly schools with academic inferiority complexes, had built renegade programs; Gerry Bush at Toledo and Forddy Anderson at Bradley had used their schools' and fans' resentment of the Big Ten, chiefly Ohio State, Michigan, and Illinois, to their advantage. But Rupp and Bryant perfected the outlaw routine, thriving first on the geographic and social frontier in Kentucky, and then, for Bryant, in Texas and Alabama (he went to Texas A&M in 1954 and Alabama a few years later), areas where not only colleges existed outside the mainstream of American higher education, but many citizens felt left out and aggrieved by the industrial prosperity of other regions. Thus, when Rupp's and Bryant's teams could symbolically redress these grievances by beating the best varsities of the established universities, their supporters cheered them on, only caring about the victories, not how the coaches achieved them. These men did become culture heroes in their states, but they represented very different cultures than did St. Knute.

In the 1940s, the national press attempted to assimilate Rupp and Bryant into the traditional mainstream, but the coaches resisted, preferring to remain outsiders:

OLD RUPP AND READY

The Wildcat mastermind is a bulky, middle-aged gentleman, very frank. A perfect subject to interview. He talks quickly and spiritedly, punctuating his remarks with funny phrases.

—*Senior Scholastic* headline and text on Adolph Rupp,
February 1948.

In the late 1940s, this classic periodical for adolescents tried hard to portray the Kentucky coach in standard terms, but those who knew Rupp could translate "very frank" into "scathing diatribes, and "funny phrases" into "frequent obscenities." In spite of *Scholastic*'s efforts, some of the real Rupp came through, especially when the coach told a long anecdote about his successful recruiting forays into Big Ten states, and how he turned the ensuing insults into the proud title, "Carpet-Bagger in the Holy Land." Similarly, in 1947, *Saturday Evening Post* attempted a traditional profile—"The Crafty Wizard of Lexington"—but Rupp's arrogance shone through: even if they "fire him tomorrow," the coach brags, he "still will have a 200-acre farm twelve miles from Lexington, a thriving insurance business, and a substantial block of stock in . . . a tobacco warehousing corporation that bills itself as the largest in the world." Of course, the Kentucky authorities never considered firing him, even after the fix revelations concerning his team, and Rupp grew richer, becoming one of the wealthiest men in the commonwealth.

The postwar press also attempted traditional treatments of Bear Bryant but, like Rupp's, his personality and behavior resisted. The *Saturday Evening Post* titled one portrait, "Football's Jittery Genius," offering standard tropes, including one from the life of Abraham Lincoln: "Bryant's urge to excel stems from a childhood of privation. One of twelve children, Bear worked on the family cotton farm in Arkansas and walked three miles each way to Stonewall Grammar School." But the adult Bryant bothered the *Post* enough for the magazine to note that "Bear liked a sympathetic and pliable press. He asked writers to submit practice-session stories for approval" before publishing them, and he hauled "one writer who wrote with irksome objectivity" in front of "the whole football squad one day," taunting and humiliating him. "Jittery" applied more to the media's attitude toward Bryant than to the straight-ahead, authoritarian coach.

The *Post* also noted that within Kentucky, "The Bear" had started to challenge "The Baron's" supremacy. Bryant later discussed how, at UK, he "had a social position coaches seldom have—good friends" among the most important political and business leaders in the state. Moreover, in practical coaching terms, "whatever I wanted, I could go to" the head of the boosters' association and, "if I asked for money," I could get "a sackful." However, because Bryant played second fiddle to Rupp, reflecting the relative status of football and basketball at UK—a major source of tension between these supreme egotists—the Baron's social standing and ability to tap boosters always surpassed the Bear's.

Bryant had applied for the UK job in 1946, and immediately won over the head of the booster association: "We were talking contract and I said, 'Just pay me so much for a win and so much for a bowl game and I'll be satisfied.' They [Kentucky boosters] hadn't had any coaches who talked that way, and the idea must have appealed to them because" the eventual contract had plenty of "incentive clauses." Bear was a new kind of college coach, one who made few pretenses about "scholar-athletes" and "character building" and who requested pay based on his won-lost record. His "performance clauses and incentives," as he called them, so violated college sports traditions that they prompted censure at the time from outside Kentucky, but, a half century later, they have become routine in intercollegiate athletics—as has the friendship between "power coaches" and the "power elite" of a state.

Bear pioneered in other ways, particularly in recruiting. Not only did he regard prime high school prospects as "princes," but he treated their coaches as "kings," realizing that for the long-term success of his teams, the goodwill of the high school mentors was more important than any individual recruit. According to a 1951 report, high school "coaches were entertained royally at Lexington time and again . . . [and] many of them have attended bowl games as guests of the Kentucky athletic department, all expenses paid." Bryant's system yielded dividends for him throughout his coaching career; his ability to harvest fertile football areas like western Pennsylvania produced such great players for his programs as Vito "Babe" Parilli and Joe Namath.

Other college coaches denounced Bryant's tactics. According to one report, during one recruiting season "the NCAA received 17 complaints from rival schools on Kentucky's eager-beaver bushbeating, a sure sign that Bryant's agents were most persuasive." In his autobiography, Walter Byers, longtime director of the NCAA, conceded, "There was evidence of" Bryant committing "NCAA violations simultaneously with those of Coach Rupp . . . [One] report said the Kentucky [football] recruiters left $1,000 in $20 bills at the prospect's home." Yet according to Byers, Bear went "unscathed because of the public's and our own [NCAA] preoccupation with the basketball problems" at Kentucky.

■   ■   ■

The "Baron of the Bluegrass" drove his athletes the same way he raised Hereford cattle and grew choice burlap tobacco; with an uncompromised devotion and discipline.

—Sports historian Gregory Sojka, 1989.

By all accounts, Rupp matched Bryant in recruiting. He cast a large net in assembling his teams, and after a player worked his way to the varsity, Rupp paid him well, with bonuses for outstanding games. Crucial to his system was his use of Clair Bee's concept of "cattle-call" tryout camps; in 1948, for instance, Bill Spivey, a seven-foot center from Georgia, showed up for "a 100 player tryout." According to a witness, in sorting out the prospects, the coach threw Spivey a ball, ordering him to "take it the length of the floor, and put it in." Spivey moved to the basket and dunked the ball—an unusual maneuver in this era. Rupp shouted, "By God . . . I'll keep that one."

Rupp favored a more up-tempo playing style than did Nat Holman and Clair Bee, allowing the Wildcats to fast-break at times. His teams achieved victory and fame, according to observers, with "a bruising man-to-man defense," and a totally planned and well-drilled offense where "even the fast breaks were models of precision." Rupp's squads won three NCAA titles in four seasons—1948, 1949, and 1951—and his first group of championship players acquired the nickname "the Fabulous Five." They were selected as half of the United States Olympic basketball team for the 1948 games, where they helped the United States win the gold medal. Then, in the fall of 1949, for the inaugural season of what *Sport* hailed as "the newly-formed . . . National Basketball Association, the finest array of players and teams ever assembled in one league," the Wildcat stars became the nucleus and principal owners of the Indianapolis Olympians franchise. (The NBA's fiftieth anniversary celebration in 1997 was two years too early, and based on marketing, not historical, concerns.)

The "Fabulous Five" consisted of center Alex Groza, forwards "Wah Wah" Jones and Cliff Barker, and guards Ralph Beard and Kenneth Rollins. Even after the revelations of their fixing, Rupp always maintained that the "Fabulous Five was the greatest basketball team of all time," and he had their uniform numbers retired by the University of Kentucky.

■   ■   ■

Lou and Alex Groza of Martins Ferry, Ohio, are two wonderful examples of smalltown boys whose love for sports made them national heroes. From their modest inconspicuous beginnings, they have catapulted to fame on the twin springboards of talent and hard work . . . But corny and Hollywoodish though it may sound, they'd both rather chew the rag in their Dad's unpretentious tavern back home than be guests of honor at the most plush banquet in the biggest hotel in America's largest city.

—*Sport* magazine writer Bob Richelson, December 1948.

Alex Groza's older brother, Lou, was an outstanding lineman at Ohio State and then as a pro with the Cleveland Browns; he also became the first great NFL field-goal kicker. By all accounts, he was a very tough and cynical player, but *Sport* portrayed him and his brother in the classic manner, even using a reference to sports movies to bolster the portrait: readers might be skeptical about cinematic heroes, the writer conceded, but "corny and Hollywoodish though it may sound," the Groza boys really did qualify for the laurel wreaths. Moreover, *Sport* continued, "All this may sound like a combination Paul Bunyan–Frank Merriwell tale, especially in these days of fixed fights and betting coups, but that's how the Grozas are regarded by those who know them."

The tension in these lines is palpable, the writer and editors struggling with the decline of the classical sports age but not knowing how to describe athletes in any other way except with classic metaphors. A half century later, one wonders how they reacted to the disclosure of Alex Groza's years of fixing. Were they ashamed of their profile of him, or did they lamely explain, "If the Baron never knew"—Rupp, even less convincingly than his fellow coaches, denied any knowledge of his players' fixing—"how were reporters supposed to figure it out?"

By investigating the rumors, which were widespread after the Wildcats actually dumped an NIT game to Loyola of Chicago, with Groza in a key and conspicuous role. Rather than play Rupp's tight man-to-man defense on Loyola's weak pivot man, Groza first committed obvious fouls and then backed off, allowing his opponent to score easily; he also left his own offense in the locker room. Groza and his fixing teammates somewhat redeemed themselves to Rupp, who was furious, by then breezing through the NCAA tournament and winning the championship.

If the media did not know the details of the UK fixing while it occurred, many reporters, including the writer of the *Sport* profile, must have learned while doing interviews in Lexington about the open subsidization of the Kentucky players. In a small town, with all eyes on the Cats and taking tender loving care of them a source of civic pride, only a young Jimmy Breslin, after visiting UK, was willing to say in print that "promising athletes like 'Wah Wah' Jones, Alex Groza, and Ralph Beard were sponsored by people who saw to it the boys never wanted for much of anything." Breslin did not name the sugar daddies, but many UK fans knew that Groza received regular payments from Owen Campbell's liquor-distributing company, with instructions "to come down to the warehouse during the off-season, one or two days a week, if you have some spare time." Boosters never offered these sinecures to Frank Merriwell or Chip Hilton; if they had, the hero would have flatly refused, then reported the scams to his coach. In Groza's case, Adolph Rupp knew all about the deal, and the other ones involving his "boys."

After the *Sport* portrait of Groza, and months closer to the exposure of the fixes, the magazine profiled UK guard Ralph Beard, under the subhead "There's No Distraction Powerful Enough to Break Through His Devotion" to basketball. (A modern reader wants to add, "Except Gamblers and Boosters Offering Him Money and Other Gratuities.") But for *Sport*, Beard's "big weakness is ice cream. He doesn't drink and he doesn't smoke, but he's a sucker for ice cream." Like all disintegrating literary styles, classical sportswriting had entered its baroque and absurd phase with such inanities as Beard's obsession for ice cream: "A plateful of ice cream is only a teaser for Beard. He likes to eat it out of a good-sized cereal bowl," and so on. Thus, the magazine depicted the sports-hero-on-the-take as Andy Hardy at the soda shop (ironically, by the late 1940s, Andy Hardy, a.k.a. Mickey Rooney, had embarked upon a life of booze and sex).

Many years later, with more honest forms of journalism in play at most sports departments, Dave Kindred of the *Washington Post* wrote: "I like Ralph Beard. We have played golf" many times. "But he took money" from gamblers and boosters. "He took it because it didn't seem that bad a thing to do. Shop owners in Lexington gave him discounts on clothes, some saying he didn't have to pay at all. Men who shook his hand after games left $20 bills in his palm . . . If a man won some money betting on Ralph's [basketball] talent, it seemed almost right for the kid to get part of it," and so it became a small step to taking money to fix games.

Kindred explained the context of the fixes: in a totally crooked environment, drawing a border to exclude one form of corruption—fixing—from all other kinds became difficult. Yet, in the history of college basketball, many clubs have existed in corrupt situations and have not rigged games. Preventing fixes is the job of the team's border guard: the head coach. At UK during the postwar years, the Baron always looked the other way.

■   ■   ■

It was a gambler's catechism in the late forties. The smart money knew never to bet against the Yankees in baseball, Notre Dame in football . . . [or] the University of Kentucky's basketball team.

—Basketball historian Stanley Cohen, 1977

Not wagering against the Yankees and Notre Dame was a no-brainer. Speculating that the Bronx Bombers or the Fighting Irish would fail to cover the spread was a sucker's move; it happened occasionally but no one could predict when. Different reasons, found in the daily papers, prompted savvy bettors to avoid Kentucky basketball: the Cats won most of their games—130 out of 140 in the postwar era—but frequently under the spread.

When police arrested the first group of CCNY fixers, Baron Rupp offered the disinformation that New York "gamblers couldn't get at my boys with a ten-foot pole." In fact, the New York underworld had used a better implement: one of Bear Bryant's athletic scholarship holders, Nick Englisis from Brooklyn. Nick never fulfilled his football potential but became an All-American go-between for the gamblers and the Wildcats. Judge Streit later noted that Englisis "ranked 219th in a [high school] class of 230," and did not begin to meet UK's low "admission standards for out-of-state students."

When apprehended by Frank Hogan's office in 1951, Englisis and the UK players confessed to rigging games in various big city arenas, including Madison Square Garden, and they acknowledged fixes in Lexington and other college fieldhouses. DA Hogan had no jurisdiction beyond New York and could not pursue the leads outside the city. Not surprisingly, the Kentucky authorities showed zero interest in them or in the Wildcats' connections to local gamblers with whom the players worked in addition to their New York contacts. Why not get paid twice, the athletes asked themselves, for the same fix?

Because of the state's horse race betting culture, Kentucky gamblers had long thrived, and inevitably some of them buzzed around UK basketball, striking deals with the fixer-players. Thus the team began to shave Southeastern Conference games for the locals and for the New Yorkers; in a conference devoted to football, the Cats easily controlled their weak basketball opponents and stayed under the spread. After the "Fabulous Five" fixers departed, their subs moved into starting positions and continued to rig games. But the transition produced some problems. A Wildcat shave of a non-conference match against St. Louis University turned into a loss, after which one of the gamblers complained to a Cat "that the game was so obviously fixed it was hard [after that] to get bookies to accept substantial bets on Kentucky games."

And through it all, according to his subsequent testimony, the Baron of the Bluegrass never noticed anything unusual. Like Nat Holman and Clair Bee, Rupp taught a disciplined, calculated basketball system; in addition, he constantly drilled his players and thoroughly understood their strengths and weaknesses. Rupp was also one of the best basketball analysts of his time and, as he told *Collier's* in 1949, "Not many fans realize game movies are equally important in basketball" analysis as in football. "It isn't generally known that basketball coaches film all their big games for postgame study. But we do."

One assumes that the Baron had film of his team's famous dump to Loyola in the NIT and of other fixed games, and that he analyzed the play of Alex

Groza in the NIT debacle as well as Groza and his teammates in other contests. Yet Rupp later denied any knowledge of the rigging of approximately seventy-five games—the total of admitted and probable UK fixes from 1946 through 1951. Some basketball coaches saw events more clearly. In the aftermath of the fixes, Yale's Howard Hobson wrote that "coaches *can* spot" player mistakes; he and an assistant had "sat together at that Kentucky-Loyola game and commented several times on the defensive lapses" made by Groza, analyzing them in detail. Because Kentucky officials refused to follow DA Frank Hogan's leads as well as many others, no one will ever learn the exact number of UK fixes, but its enormity is indisputable, as is the hollowness of Rupp's denials.

Nonetheless, as with the other coaches involved, the media and even subsequent sports historians accepted the Baron's word, in part because of his intimidating reputation as the winningest coach in college basketball history (until Dean Smith broke his record in 1997) and also because no photos existed of Rupp holding a "smoking gun." Only proof comparable to that would have prompted the Kentucky authorities and the sporting press to indict the UK coach. However, the evidence against the Baron was stronger—and the distance between dots shorter—than in the case of any other coach. Particularly incriminating was Rupp's relationship with the most important gambler in Lexington, Kentucky, Ed Curd.

■   ■   ■

> Alex Groza contended that Rupp showed the team slips before every game carrying the point spread . . . Dale Barnstable said he was bawled out [by Rupp] after one game because his missing a crucial shot had cost one of Rupp's friends $500.

> —*Sport* magazine writer Furman Bisher, March 1959.

Adolph Rupp took his title, the Baron of the Bluegrass, literally, acting as if he owned the University of Kentucky and its environs, immune to reproach or criticism. (*Sport* only criticized him after the scandal and a change of editorial policy, but the journal's comments never bothered Rupp.) With his impervious attitude, he saw nothing wrong in his friendship with Lexington's leading gambler, Ed Curd, a man connected to the national Mafia. Rupp visited Curd's home and also saw him while traveling with the Cats, including in New York. The Baron never hid his ties to Curd, nor did he have any problem enjoying a very public dinner with him at Manhattan's Copacabana Club, which was famous for its Mob ownership and patronage, after a UK game at Madison Square Garden. Apparently on this occasion, Curd introduced Rupp to Mafia head Frank Costello.

Unlike the other coaches of fixing teams, the Baron acknowledged his interest in basketball betting, admitting his calls to Ed Curd about the point spread on UK games—the probable source of the slips mentioned by Groza.

However, if the Baron could not reach Curd, another way to obtain betting information, according to locals, was to walk "four blocks from the school [to] a large restaurant that had the point odds and the score by periods of major college games . . . plastered in big white chalk letters on a permanent, blue cardboard scoreboard which hangs over the bar . . . [In] there, people were [always] talking money, cash won and lost on the day's games."

In the gambling culture of Lexington, the Baron shared the citizens' regard for betting as well as their aversion to puritans who condemned it as evil. Most Kentuckians were open-minded, open-walleted, and open-mouthed on the subject, hence Dale Barnstable's story about Rupp's friend's loss of $500 (at least $5,000 in 1990s currency). Nonetheless, Kentucky book-makers, despite their support of open gambling, became upset at the Wild-cats' actions, as well as the Baron's apparently ho-hum attitude about point shaving, indicated by his often-quoted comment, "The Chicago Black Sox threw ball games, but these kids only shaved points."

After a very obvious Wildcat fix against Tennessee in early 1949, the Lex-ington bookies protested loudly. Far too much money had flowed to the Vol-unteers' side, and the UK stars looked inept in winning the game but staying under the spread. The Lexington revolt spread to Louisville, and, soon after, the *Courier Journal,* the main paper in that city and the entire state, ran the headline "Bookies Give Up Net Play." The accompanying article explained that all college basketball games were off the betting boards in Kentucky for the rest of the season.

To argue that Adolph Rupp was oblivious to these events and "a victim" of his player-fixers seems foolish, yet throughout the subsequent UK fix revela-tions, the coach's supporters maintained exactly that. This so infuriated one UK alumnus, a lawyer in Lexington, that he sued the Baron, charging that the coach and Ed Curd had engaged in a conspiracy and "debasing scheme" to benefit from the fixed games—that they had known about or even arranged the fixes, and wagered accordingly. No evidence of Rupp's personal gambling emerged, although he could have easily laundered it through Curd. However, even if the coach never bet, his ongoing concern about UK point spreads indicates an awareness of his players' activities.

If Rupp suspected point shaving, why did he tolerate it? Possibly he con-sidered it unimportant, as his Black Sox comment implied. Possibly, like Nat Holman and Clair Bee, his "living legend" reputation trapped him into inac-tion, along with his high annual income, which was less dependent on bas-ketball than that of the other coaches but might have been hard to sustain after a major hit to his culture hero status. In addition, blowing the whistle on Groza, Beard, Barnstable, and their teammates would have dismantled the Fabulous Five and their championship successors, and the UK coach loved to build teams, not tear them apart. In the end, Adolph Rupp confined his whistle blasts to the practice floor, probably hoping that the point shaving would go away. Autocratic rulers like the Baron often confuse their wishes with reality, and Rupp later admitted that the public hue-and-cry about the fixes surprised him, especially the animosity toward the players.

In his lawsuit against Rupp, the Lexington lawyer also asked, "Why does he stay on while the boys have to leave?" As at the other schools in the scandal, the UK athletes carried the can and the coach survived. The lawyer concluded that "Rupp cannot escape justice simply because he is a coach" loved by the fans. For this alum's trouble, a local judge—an elected official in the heart of the Baron's Bluegrass country—dismissed the suit and suspended the plaintiff from his law practice for a year!

More objective observers also questioned Rupp's innocence. Gordon Graham of the *Lafayette (Indiana) Journal & Courier* later remarked, "Lots of sportswriters, particularly the Kentucky boys, knew that Rupp knew about the fixing . . . The Baron just didn't give a damn about point-shaving as long as his teams won, and they sure did that except for a few times like the NIT game with Loyola. Then, I understand, he got real mad and tore their hides off. But no Kentucky reporter would put the truth in his paper, his by-line on the article would've been the signature on his death warrant."

However, New York judge Saul Streit did not fear the Wildcat wrath. In sentencing the player-fixers for their activities at the Garden, he stated: "In view of the evidence presented, Rupp's sanctimonious air . . . is ridiculous . . . *With his knowledge,* the charges in his care were openly exploited" by many people, including gamblers, and the coach did nothing about it.

In the previous fixing cases before Judge Streit, the chastised schools had slunk away or remained silent. Not the University of Kentucky and important Wildcat supporters, including the governor and the university trustees. In true frontier fashion, the Kentuckians shot back by denouncing the New York judge as a biased and uninformed city slicker—ignoring the fact that Streit had obtained most of his evidence about the school's athletic program from the sworn testimony of UK players and athletic department personnel. Kentucky officials also proclaimed that "our policies will not be dictated by Judge Streit," although the jurist had merely recommended that the school return to traditional athletic values.

The year after Streit's judgment and Kentucky's hostile reply, *Sport* sent Jimmy Breslin to Lexington. The magazine headlined the article, "Kentucky Apologizes for Nothing," highlighting the passage:

> Far from being chastened or stirred to a revision of its program by these events, Kentucky, from its president . . . right down to the 107th man now in school on an athletic scholarship, gives every indication that it only has one thing to say about the whole affair: "We'll be back stronger than ever in basketball [and other sports] . . ."

Sport's premise was that Kentucky *should* apologize. Most of the other schools involved in the fixes had offered some sort of apology, usually mumbling in the passive voice that "mistakes were made," the absent pronoun obscuring specific responsibility. But no one at the University of Kentucky—certainly not the Baron or his bosses—showed the slightest contrition. And UK fans totally supported this position; Breslin remarked that "in the Bluegrass country, [Rupp] remains as strongly entrenched as" ever, and "everywhere in the state of Kentucky, the Baron is sympathized with as a man who was betrayed."

A baron wronged need not apologize for anything, not his players' rigging or his corrupt recruiting and retention system. Moreover, the UK president, deaf and dumb through it all, told Breslin that the only "failure was in the boys who disgraced coach Rupp and the school. There would have been no trouble here if it were not for that fact." To his credit, the Baron never attacked his former players; instead, he planned his revenge on his critics. The latter, including officials at other SEC schools, called for Rupp's resignation or, if that were not forthcoming, his firing. The Baron waited patiently because, as he later revealed, "There never was a chance that UK would fire me. The Board of Trustees [had] told me, 'Adolph, as far as we're concerned, you didn't know a damn thing about the fixes.'"

From his frontier outpost, the Baron also observed the national calls for de-emphasis of big-time college basketball, and he reacted predictably, telling Breslin: "I must say I'm getting a little tired of this de-emphasis business. Do they want us to de-emphasize a player's athletic ability? Or de-emphasize the interest of the spectators? Or shall we de-emphasize the winning of a ball game? I think it's time we de-emphasized the de-emphasis. And I am perfectly willing for the good people of Kentucky to be my judges."

For all of his bluster and bravado, Adolph Rupp understood college basketball and its fans, particularly the new breed for whom winning was "the only thing." He also knew that for these partisans, bigger is better; the higher a player can jump and dunk, the more the fans want to see him, and the faster a team can move the ball and score, the louder its supporters will cheer it on. In the aftermath of the fix scandals, various academics had proposed the de-emphasis of big-time intercollegiate basketball, returning it to a student game played only on campus. Adolph Rupp, with his far-outside-the-academy viewpoint, wanted to mobilize college basketball fans and the media against this. The Baron lacked the academic critics' formal education, but he saw the future of college sports more clearly.

■　■　■

At the University of Kentucky, Bear Bryant also saw his future at the school and decided to leave: "The trouble was we [Rupp and I] were too much alike, and he wanted basketball Number 1, and I wanted football Number 1. In an environment like that, one or the other has to go." The football coach, acknowledging that he would always hold UK's short straw, opted for Texas A&M and, after that, Alabama.

Also prompting Bryant's move was the slow but inexorable outside pressure upon the UK athletic program. First the New York court and national media judgments, then an SEC investigation, and finally the NCAA began an inquiry: UK's systematic violations had gone too far, and the college sports establishment needed to punish the school as part of its damage control propaganda (see pages 493–94). During the New York trials of the UK fixers, Bryant realized that, outside the state of Kentucky, "the bad publicity was hurting my program. I was trying to recruit at the time and I thought, 'Why the hell do I have to go through this, as tough as it is to recruit for Kentucky [football].' " After the SEC penalties, and then NCAA Case Report No. 1, as well as "the fact that Kentucky's athletic department," including Bryant's football program, "was likely to be watched closely by the NCAA," the Bear moved to the quiet plains of Texas. There, according to the NCAA's Walter Byers, Bryant continued to cheat and produce winning teams but avoided NCAA attention for a number of years. (When he received it, he went to Alabama and built an impenetrable castle.)

Nothing budged Adolph Rupp, not even the cancellation of the Wildcats' 1952–53 season. The following year, Jimmy Breslin returned to Lexington and wrote, "The Baron Is Out to Get Even." The UK coach had never enjoyed the traditional sports virtues; now he felt justified in demolishing an important one.

> There's not going to be any of this point-shaving by Kentucky this year. When we run up one of those 95- or 97-point totals . . . and there's still a couple of minutes to play. I'm not going to pull my boys up and have them stand around at midcourt and try to hold the score down so we don't humiliate somebody. We'll just keep playing our game and let those 100-point scores fall where they may. We used to try to be nice about things like that, but those days are gone.

Rupp's 1953–54 Wildcats went undefeated, covered their point spreads, and finished Number One in the polls. The Baron's subsequent teams won many honors, including an NCAA championship, and also lost a famous title game: in 1966, the all–African American Texas Western (UTEP) starters humiliated his lily-white squad, marking the last stand of segregated college basketball. After that, even Adolph Rupp began to recruit African Americans, as did Bear Bryant in his final coaching years.

In the end, after the Baron and the Bear became the winningest coaches in big-time college basketball and football, the halls of fame in their sports inducted them with laudatory ceremonies, proving that in modern college sports, winning washes away all sins.

35

Football Becomes
the Postwar Scandal
and Colonel Blaik

The [1951 West Point football] scandal touched off a nationwide discussion on honesty in American life. The profiteering of the Korean
War, bribery in college basketball, the fur coats and deep-freezes
[given for political favors] to the Truman administration had shaken
the nation, but they all paled beside the cheating at the Military
Academy. Nothing ever illustrated quite so clearly how high was the
pedestal on which the public had placed West Point as the reaction to
the scandal.

—Historian Stephen Ambrose, 1966.

When the Army football scandal broke in August 1951, the *New York
Times* used 216-point type for its front-page headlines, and filled
many front-page columns, full inside pages, and numerous follow-up articles
with the story. Every other major American newspaper covered the West
Point scandal in similar fashion and, like the *Times,* with even greater editorial outrage than had been aimed at the basketball fixes. The media immediately focused on the large number of athletes involved—thirty-seven
members of the current Army football team, and twenty-three participants in
other intercollegiate sports—and the press highlighted the statement by the
U.S. Army Chief of Staff that "the serious infractions of Academy regulations
and [the Honor] Code had started with the football team and had spread to
other [sports] groups."

For most Americans, the Army team was not a typical collegiate squad.
Colonel Earl "Red" Blaik, head coach since late 1940, had always presented
his Black Knights as "the Nation's Team," and his wartime champions and

postwar powerhouses sold this concept to millions of Americans. Furthermore, Blaik and his media supporters always proclaimed that his superb athletes were regular West Point cadets, hence future leaders of the United States Army. Even before the events of 1951, many Americans regarded successful basketball clubs like CCNY's and LIU's with suspicion, and outlaw athletic programs like Kentucky's with hostility, but they considered West Point football sacred. Its conquests under Blaik were woven into the country's recent military triumphs.

Out of historical context, the crimes of the Army athletes seem minor compared to those of the basketball fixers; however, in August 1951, the announcement that so many football players had systematically violated the West Point Honor Code over many years upset the public far more than had the news of basketball rigging. Not only was college football at the center of American popular culture, and the Black Knights among the elite of the sport, but their school—the United States Military Academy—had produced the country's most celebrated living warriors, including Generals Eisenhower, MacArthur, and Patton. "My heart sank that summer day when I heard about it," recalled Notre Dame's Moose Krause. "Although Army was our toughest rival for decades, I respected them so much . . . And their officer corps meant so much to me as an American. My gosh, their graduates had just led us to victory in the war. I hated the basketball fixes but the Army scandal was a lot worse."

At the core of the United States Military Academy was its Honor Code. Compiled in 1818 by the "Father of West Point," Colonel Sylvanus Thayer, the Code stated that "no cadet will lie, cheat, or steal, and every cadet is honor bound to report any breach of the Code." West Pointers considered the Code holy writ, a guide to life and to war. On the battlefield, it allowed officers to accept the word of a colleague instantly, never questioning the speaker's veracity or motives. Through the nineteenth and twentieth centuries, as Academy men fought America's wars, the Code became encrusted with a sacred patina. General Eisenhower responded to the news of the scandal by explaining that for a West Point alumnus the Code, along with "the honor system" based on it, "occupies a position in his mind akin to the virtue of his mother or sister."

Because of the Honor Code, West Point had unproctored exams. During World War II the school depended on the Code when it started giving the same tests to half the students in a course on one day, and the other half on the following day. (The demand for officers during the war and afterward greatly enlarged the student body, necessitating the split class and exam schedule.) Unfortunately, because of the rigors of football—Blaik's training was ferocious—and the fact that many players were less academically qualified than regular West Point students but had to take the same courses, the temptation for some athletes in the first-day sections to provide exam questions to their second-day teammates became irresistible. Thus the "cribbing system" began, becoming widespread through the late 1940s and into the 1950s; what's more, athletic department tutors organized and facilitated the dishonesty. Eventually, two young cadets—non-athletes—discovered the cheating, and felt "honor bound to report the breach" of the Code to the authorities. This prompted a major investigation, elicited many confessions, and resulted in the August 1951 announcement, headlines, and public outrage.

The Military Academy quickly expelled ninety cadets (most of the thirty non-athletes were tutors), but it refused to bring charges against any offenders who had already graduated, a group that included many former athletes and tutors. In addition, West Point would not name the disgraced cadets, but the media quickly fingered many of the thirty-seven football players because other schools began recruiting them. The NCAA and most of its members exhibited neither surprise nor distress at the Army scandal, and many coaches regarded it as an opportunity to grab some prime beef from Blaik's storehouse.

The most heartfelt reaction came from classical sportswriters like Arthur Daley, still shell-shocked from the revelations of basketball fixing. The *New York Times* columnist wrote that, at first, the Army scandal "seemed like a bad dream. But it is stark, sickening reality . . . Caesar's wife, regarded as beyond reproach, is no better than the rest of" the cheaters in college sports. Previously, Daley had criticized some big-time programs, particularly outlaws like Kentucky, but for him Army was different, at the center of the American establishment, like his own *New York Times,* residing far above the grubby crowd. Now, with "the terrifying impact of the latest scandal" came the realization that "intercollegiate athletics is rotten to the core and the Army episode proves it." Meanwhile, college sports officials offered only the hollow "Sanity Code, pious platitudes and hypocritical mouthings . . . The entire system was careening downhill and out of control, heading for a crash. It has come."

Then, anticipating the attempt to minimize the Army players' conduct as compared to the basketball fixers, Daley stated: "The West Point scandal might not seem even vaguely related to the basketball scandals. But they are blood brothers, spawned by over-emphasis, commercialism and bigness. Educators have lost sight of their primary goal, which is education. They have let themselves be lured into seemingly attractive detours that are marked by tinsel road signs offering athletic prestige, victory, and gate receipts." Then Daley uncharacteristically revealed some inside information: Army footballers "had been [specially] recruited for the Point and assured that they'd get all possible help in graduating . . . they were there on a double standard—the Honor Code and a special athletic code."

The *Times* columnist never wrote another word on the Army scandal, but many newspapers and magazines reprinted this column. The largest religious weekly in the country, *The Christian Century,* carried it, pronouncing Daley's "lesson . . . the most important" one offered by the press so far. As the scandal unfolded, as the details of Blaik's recruiting and academic tutoring system became public, as the famous coach engaged in damage control, denying any personal knowledge of Honor Code violations, Arthur Daley's lesson about West Point and college sports corruption proved instructive.

▪   ▪   ▪

> The first mistake was made years ago when [Military Academy officials and] alumni, probably with the full approval of the War Department, started to try to recoup West Point's football fortunes and to "recruit" or "attract" athletes extensively. There followed a period of intense intercollegiate rivalry [with competing schools]. West Point [also] had phenomenal winning streaks and the pressure was on to keep them going.

> —Military analyst Hanson Baldwin, January 1952.

For Baldwin, "the first mistake" leading to the football scandal occurred in late 1940 when the West Point superintendent and top administrators, after many mediocre football seasons, decided to resurrect Army gridiron glory and hired Earl "Red" Blaik to accomplish this task. With a win-or-else mandate and mentality, the coach enlisted West Point alumni to help him scout and recruit, and then capitalized on the Military Academy's attractions and advantages during wartime. Within a few years, Blaik constructed the most powerful team in college football. (See Chapter 14.)

After the war, in the vicious football "black market," the Army coach had to recruit more intensively, and also to work out new ways for his athletes to gain admission to and remain at West Point, which was improving academically. Blaik asked his alumni allies to perform tasks similar to those done by the boosters of most big-time athletic programs, for instance, to fund all-expenses-paid visits to West Point for prospective players—a perk never offered to regular candidates to the Military Academy. In addition, for the first time, the head coach and his assistants made extensive recruiting trips; Blaik amazed a California blue-chip prospect, Gene Filipski, when he "popped up unexpectedly one afternoon on [his] high school campus in North Sacramento. 'I was really awed,' " the athlete remembered.

Filipski, however, had academic problems, and Blaik worried about the player's ability to pass the stiff West Point entrance exams. To ease this situation and similar ones involving other promising athletes, Blaik "arranged for him . . . to attend the West Point Prep." As *Time* magazine later revealed, the Prep, despite its fancy title, was a "cram school" in operation for the sole purpose of preparing football recruits for the Academy's entrance exams. Blaik and his alumni allies established it, with the latter picking up the tab. The Prep constituted a crucial part of the West Point recruiting package in the late 1940s and early 1950s. One prospect described the complete deal as an "easy appointment to the Academy, promises of help passing the entrance examinations, and draft-free status while playing football at West Point"— with the commencement of the Korean War, the military had started drafting regular college students again.

In addition to success on the entrance exams, every West Point candidate needed the sponsorship of a member of Congress to enter the Academy. Usually members appointed the most qualified high school graduates in their districts or states. However, one unofficial exception had long existed: for football players. Blaik always worked this loophole, according to *Time* often using high-ranking Army officers stationed in Washington, D.C., "to wangle appointments for boys [he] selected as good football material." One recruit recalled that the coach had tried to arrange the "deal" with a U.S. Senator from his state, West Virginia, but the legislator only rated the young man as a "third alternate" and gave the appointment to a more academically qualified student. The athlete related that "as far as I was concerned that was the end of it. Then one day I got a telegram from West Point informing me that my appointment had been granted. How it was and where it came from, I don't know to this day."

In the wake of the scandal, when the details of the typical West Point package emerged, many Americans, including those in the military, protested. General Carl Spaatz, wartime head of the U.S. Air Force and a West Point grad, wrote in *Newsweek:* "It is unthinkable that the American people could accept any relaxation of the Code of Honor or any fundamental change in the Academy itself," particularly its egalitarian admissions and retention policy. Most Americans viewed the Academy as a bastion of democracy, not only defending it but upholding its principles in all ways; frequently, people cited the career of Dwight Eisenhower, his beginnings in ordinary circumstances in Kansas, his admission in open and fair competition to West Point, and his rise in the Army and the nation on the basis of hard work, intelligence, and merit. Coach Red Blaik's special deals for football players totally violated this ideal, and deeply offended many of his fellow citizens.

In his comments on the scandal, Blaik appeared oblivious to his offense. He always defended his recruiting and appointment maneuvers, as well as the special "on Post" treatment for his players. At heart, despite his military rank, Earl "Red" Blaik was a big-time football coach, in love with winning and willing to accomplish it by almost any means. And he surrounded himself with similarly committed men. His offensive line coach from 1949 to 1953 was Vince Lombardi, who eventually became more famous than his mentor for his desire to win and his supposed axiom, "Winning isn't everything—it's the only thing." (Lombardi was less original than obsessive—he took his football ideas and sayings from others, and he pushed them to their limits.)

Blaik's Black Knights showed opponents no mercy, often running up lopsided scores. The coach reveled in the wartime routs of Notre Dame, but after the termination of the series with the Fighting Irish—Blaik opposed the break—he most enjoyed the annuals with Navy, particularly when his team controlled the outcome. From 1943 through 1950, except for an occasional Navy upset and one tie, his Black Knights thumped the Middies.

The Naval Academy, with a succession of head coaches who lacked Blaik's dynamism and ruthlessness, could not keep up with the Army football program during World War II, and it slipped even further behind in the postwar era. By 1951, according to an informed reporter, "There was a wide disparity in football talent between . . . the two service schools. It was just as obvious that Army's unofficial bureau in charge of steering football players to West Point was operating at its old wartime efficiency," whereas Navy did not recruit aggressively, or establish "cram schools" for admission or offer special tutors to aid academic retention. Some Navy alumni and fans grumbled about the string of losing seasons after 1945, but when the Army program hit the rocks in 1951, they bragged about the Naval Academy's "total freedom from scandal."

John Lardner, one of the most astute sports journalists of the period, wrote: "The naked point of the Army scandal is that high-pressure football and high-pressure education will not mix. Army wanted championship football" and could only achieve it by cutting corners like most other big-time football schools. Therefore, "when Army's stern code of ethics collided with her football ambitions . . . the code of ethics temporarily broke down."

The scandal prompted a public debate on the appropriate role of college sports at the Military Academy. General Spaatz argued for de-emphasis: his alma mater's problems began, he believed, when "an athletic clique," with its "overemphasis on [intercollegiate] athletics, especially on a winning football team," gained undue power within the West Point administration and the cadet corps. The general blamed Blaik's athletic system and its "distorted values" more than the "offending cadets" for the scandal—the latter merely entered the system and "assumed that football and the maintenance of a winning team was the ultimate objective of their service at the Academy."

Spaatz's statement and similar criticisms, particularly from West Point officials, infuriated Blaik and his supporters. The coach fought back, never conceding a millimeter of wrongdoing, or any ongoing knowledge of the "cribbing system," or any problems resulting from his big-time football team. Even though the military, the media, and the public accepted his denials of personal complicity in the Honor Code violations, Blaik remained dissatisfied. The criticisms of his football program permanently enraged him, and he sought total vindication on his own terms. Almost fifty years later, with much more evidence in the public domain than there was at the time, Blaik's quest mainly illustrates the concept of hubris.

■   ■   ■

"They are passing [out] examination information," he [my football teammate] told me, and that's how I became aware of the cribbing system . . . My buddy said this practice was accepted throughout the Corps and even *condoned by the authorities.*

—Expelled Army football player Gene Filipski, October 1952.

Filipski, who gained admission to the Military Academy through Blaik's "cram school" and an arranged appointment, participated fully in the cribbing and, when apprehended, confessed. Nevertheless, he took his expulsion hard, later discussing it at length in an article, "Railroaded Out of West Point." He accused Military Academy officials of ignoring the cheating when it suited their purposes but, when the scandal erupted, acting hypocritically and penalizing the offenders far too harshly. Many of Filipski's expelled teammates voiced similar complaints.

As with the basketball fixers who also blamed "the system," the question becomes whether these Army athletes were resorting to a standard excuse or whether in fact West Point officials, including the football staff and Blaik, possessed an ongoing knowledge of the Honor Code violations and were as guilty—if not more so—than the condemned cadets. Once again, the search for the answer begins in the nature of the Army athletic program and the way the coaches ran it.

The year before the West Point scandal, *Sport* magazine presented a classic profile of Red Blaik, portraying him as a paragon of American virtues. Along with the glowing adjectives, the reality of the coach's workaholic life appeared: "He devotes almost every minute of his time in and out of season to his job. *He personally attends to every detail.* He shepherds each football player through the Academy, sees that he stays up in his classroom work." Blaik later acknowledged his workaholism: "How many of the thousands, yes millions, who have thrilled to Army . . . in a packed stadium on a bright, windswept autumn Saturday, ever stopped to contemplate the years of sweat and worry that went into the production of the inimitable drama unfolding down there below them?"

The author of the *Sport* profile, Stanley Woodward, had unusual access to the reserved and often hostile Blaik: he was the only journalist allowed behind all the scenes at West Point, and was even invited on the coach's private camping trips. In a 1950 article for *Collier's*, Woodward again emphasized Blaik's total control approach and his high degree of organization, how his office contained many file cabinets with "hundreds of movie reels and scouting reports" on his Black Knights, and "on every team and every player Army is scheduled to or conceivably may play against."

Woodward also described the football program's "academic coaching staff": Blaik called the tutors "coaches," and, as an example of their concern for the athletes, the head academic "coach makes all [football road] trips along with one or two of his assistant coaches, and works over the potential academic delinquents ceaselessly." Years later, when the Military Academy opened its files to public scrutiny, researchers discovered less laudatory details about the football tutoring system and could better ascertain what Blaik knew about the cribbing system and when he knew it.

> [By 1950] the football "poop" was much more than [tutoring] help; it was providing answers to tests so that the recipient could pass even without understanding the material . . . With more than twenty tutors specially assigned to help football players, and with [the tutors'] organized collection, and selected clandestine distribution of test questions and answers to selected players, it was now a full-fledged cheating ring.

> —Military historian James A. Blackwell, 1993.

When the Freedom of Information Act became law, the United States Military Academy had to open its files to researchers. While examining them as well as Pentagon and other Army archival material, James A. Blackwell discovered the genesis and growth of what he termed the football cheating "conspiracy." It began after World War II when recruiting pressures forced Blaik to take less academically qualified players than before, and also when Superintendent Maxwell Taylor upgraded the course content at the Academy. This created a situation where Blaik's academic "coaches" had to focus intensively on those athletes, often key parts of the Army football machine, in danger of flunking out of the Academy.

With the split class and exam procedure, the tutors worked with players in the first-day and second-day cohorts and, as part of ordinary tutoring, debriefed the first group about that day's exams. As the pressure to keep athletes in school increased, the academic "coaches" started to go beyond regular exam preparation and feed second-day men the upcoming questions. Blackwell noted that the cheating was "designed initially to provide only a few selected football players [with] help once or twice at strategic times in the course of an academic year." However, like the gamblers and the player-fixers who began with a few shaved points of occasional games and moved to regular rigging, the "cribbing system" escalated, and "by 1948, many football players" received many exam questions ahead of time, in addition, they "were getting *answers* to exams just prior to taking them."

The cheaters developed their own jargon: "It became known as 'the poop,' a term derived from the military slang of the day . . . getting 'the poop' meant to obtain the answers to an upcoming graded event," not simply major exams but, by 1950, minor ones, and even the daily quizzes in courses. The coach-tutors believed that their actions were "preserving the winning [football] tradition so painstakingly built by Red Blaik." Reinforcing their beliefs were "such benefits" as permission "to eat at the training table," enjoying its excellent and abundant fare as opposed to the spartan West Point regular "chow," as well as trips to away games with the team.

Did Red Blaik, who *"personally attends to every detail"* in his program, including his players' classroom progress and their work with his academic "coaches," know about the huge and long-term cheating conspiracy? Soon after the scandal broke, Blaik called a press conference to discuss the Honor Code violations. "I wish I had heard of it [the cheating] at the very beginning," he stated. "I'm sure I would have been able to stop all this business in short order." Moreover, according to a reporter at the conference, "He counted himself guilty to the extent that, as a coach of a squad that had been 'a close family,' he had not known what they were doing." He also revealed that his son Robert, slated to be the starting QB, was one of the expelled cadets.

Possibly Blaik had noticed that Clair Bee's guarded apology played better with the media and the public than did Nat Holman's arrogant denials, and the Army coach took the former approach. Nonetheless, in this two-hour press conference, he never mentioned the role of his academic "coaches" in the cheating, nor did he ever discuss this topic afterward. It only emerged publicly with the opening of the archives. Of course, in 1951, West Point investigators knew about it immediately—hence the expulsion of the tutors.

In all of Blaik's later statements on the scandal, including long chapters in two memoirs, he never deviated from his initial declaration of innocence. He also never denounced his players the way Holman had, agreeing with Filipski and others that they were unjustly "railroaded out of West Point." He entitled one of his memoir chapters "The Ninety Scapegoats."

Despite Blaik's denials, the question remains: what did he know about the Honor Code violations and when did he know it? Because of the small number of original cheaters, possibly the coach had not "heard of it at the very beginning" but, by the late 1940s and early 1950s, because the cheating involved so many players and tutors, and occurred constantly, it seems incredible that Blaik—a total control head man—did not learn about it. Moreover, during this period, stories circulated at West Point about a math instructor going to Blaik with evidence of a star player's cheating, being kicked out of the coach's office, and not pursuing the matter because Blaik "was the most powerful man on the Post." However, neither before 1951 nor subsequently did Army officials aim their investigation at Blaik—after all, he was a fellow officer—and eventually they closed the "cribbing case" without commenting on his possible complicity in it.

Between the lines of Gene Filipski's article resides the most plausible explanation of Blaik's behavior. When the player discovered "the cribbing system," he asked himself whether he could "risk ruining the football team by reporting these men, some of them big names, who were also my schoolmates and teammates and friends? Could I jeopardize their careers?" If we see the situation from Blaik's viewpoint—*my* football team, *my* big-name recruits, *my* beloved players, including *my* son—we can understand why, upon discovering widespread cheating, he might hesitate to act and ruin all that he had built, including his current varsity as well as its members' present and future careers.

In his article, Filipski concluded: "I decided, right or wrong, that friendship and the football team came before the Honor Code." Within the closed system of Blaik's Army football club, with its elitism and contempt for ordinary rules—from the recruiting process on—Filipski demonstrated how the decision by players and tutors to cheat seemed logical to them. Because Earl Blaik had constructed this system, he too could have believed that his players and academic "coaches" could ignore regular West Point regulations, and that he could look the other way on the cribbing. A postmortem Army report on the scandal, though it didn't accuse him of complicity, noted that "Blaik's loyalties to the football program transcended his loyalties to the Corps and its traditions," even the Honor Code.

Blaik had other reasons for inaction. Like the basketball coaches, he had much to lose by revealing the huge conspiracy. He was not money-hungry like them and fearful of a decline in income, but his vanity equaled theirs, and he was obsessed with his reputation. By the late 1940s, the sports media, with many classic profiles, had elevated Colonel Blaik to the top rank of American coaches, much higher than any contemporary basketball or football head man other than Frank Leahy, and challenging "the Immortals," Pop Warner and even Knute Rockne.

When the Army scandal exploded, like his basketball colleagues Blaik denied any prior knowledge of the cribbing—how else could he explain its occurrence on his watch and still retain his "Living Legend" status? Moreover Colonel Blaik, like Holman, Bee, and Rupp, possessed the self-confidence to launch and sustain a total-denial strategy, and survive an immense crisis.

Most sportswriters at the time and afterward accepted the Army coach's word on the scandal. One belated dissenter was Jim Beach, an AP reporter who covered Army football during Blaik's years and was the coauthor of an excellent study of the Army–Notre Dame series. In a 1996 interview, Beach stated:

> Blaik knew all about the cribbing—it was total bullshit then, and it still is, that he knew nothing about it. He called his tutors "coaches," and he worked with them like he worked with his football coaches. Blaik introduced me to some of them, and it was obvious that he was totally on top of their work . . . Earl Blaik was on top of every single

thing at the Point that had to do with his football players, including the cribbing . . . Of course, the AP would never let me work on this story.

At the time, a few other sportswriters privately questioned Blaik's denials, but none dared investigate it. According to Moose Krause, "Frank Wallace believed that Blaik knew about the cribbing when it was going on, and Frank knew lots of inside stuff but, believe me, he would never put it in the *Saturday Evening Post* or anywhere else . . . Anyway, we weren't playing Army those years, and I had no reason to doubt what he [Blaik] said."

Like the AP's Jim Beach, Francis Wallace never wrote about the Army coach's awareness of the Honor Code violations. Indeed, no writer has. Even James Blackwell, after assembling the archival evidence on the "conspiracy," did not assess Blaik's role in it. Possibly Blackwell's many pleasant interviews with the players involved, including Blaik's son Robert, inhibited him, but a book reviewer commented that Blackwell "doesn't condemn Blaik . . . though much evidence" in his text "seems to point to his [Blaik's] knowing about the cheating." In the end, however, examining the evidence now on the public record leads to the inescapable conclusion that *Colonel Earl "Red" Blaik learned about the cribbing conspiracy while it occurred and did nothing to expose it.*

As with the basketball coaches involved in the fixes, the media has always avoided connecting all of the dots in the Blaik portrait. At the time of the scandal, the reluctance of the sporting press to criticize the Army coach was so ubiquitous that it prompts basic questions about traditional sports journalism as well as big-time college sports during its worst crisis.

■   ■   ■

Last week's repercussions to the scandal centered around a New York appearance by Army's athletic director and football coach Earl Blaik . . . Colonel Blaik called his sportswriter friends together . . . at Leone's Restaurant in Manhattan—which brought out more cameramen and curious sidewalk neck-craners than usually attend a motion picture premiere.

—*Time* magazine, August 1951.

After the initial Army announcement about the Honor Code violations, Blaik called a press conference in Manhattan to give his version of events. According to his memoirs, he invited "a group of some forty metropolitan and national-wire-service newspapermen to meet with me for lunch" at Mama Leone's famous restaurant. In this period, orchestrated news conferences had not yet become standard. For an athletic coach to call a formal one was unusual; for a West Point coach, a ranking Army officer, to hold a special one in New York City was a first. But Colonel Blaik operated his own way, correctly expecting that the sporting press would treat him gently and that he could put his spin on the scandal and see it printed without critical comment in the next day's papers.

A conference highlight occurred when Blaik, responding to the rumor that he would resign from the Military Academy, stated his determination to "remain at West Point," and "this statement was greeted by cheers" from the assembled journalists. This revealing reaction did not occur because sportswriters loved Blaik—most disliked him and his previously high-handed treatment of them. They cheered because they interpreted his statement as a signal that Army football would remain big-time, and they could continue covering it in the same manner as they had during its recent glory years. They cheered for their own jobs and their importance as prominent sports journalists; de-emphasis at Army could mean de-emphasis for big-time football in their region, and a scaling down of their coverage.

Moreover, with the Army scandal coming immediately after months of basketball fix revelations, and the blows to that sport as well as to its leading coaches, sports reporters did not want to investigate and topple the great Colonel Blaik. His descent might jeopardize the existence of college sports itself, certainly its big-time form. Cleverly the Army coach signaled this danger during his press conference; as Nat Holman in his article had cautioned journalists not to bring down the sport of basketball, its coaches, and its reporters, Blaik posted a warning: "Let's not put this country on an intramural [college sports] basis . . . true vitality and the urge to do great things stem [solely] from varsity competition." Every journalist at Leone's knew that the public demand for coverage of intramural college sports hovered around zero. Therefore, sportswriters had to help save major intercollegiate athletics—and their own jobs.

Throughout the meeting, the Army coach repeatedly called the assembled press "my friends"—which *Time* mocked with its double-edged comment about the coach's "sportswriter friends." After years of the colonel's frostiness, the surprised scribes appeared to enjoy the flattering salutation from their newfound pal; most importantly, they agreed with his attack on de-emphasis. And, in 1951, who represented big-time college sports more than the famous figure standing at the microphone at Mama Leone's? Every season, the media and the public watched the parade of players pass by, but coaches remained on the scene for much longer periods. Hollywood, with films like *Knute Rockne—All-American,* portrayed the coaches as the essence of college sports, and the media had long depicted Colonel Blaik as a true heir of St. Knute. Thus, to preserve big-time intercollegiate athletics, to preserve their own positions, the media had to keep Blaik on his pedestal.

If any sportswriter at Leone's wanted to inquire about Blaik's "academic coaches"—the beat reporters knew all about the omnipresent tutors in the West Point program—they kept silent. Indeed, so awesome was Blaik's aura that most journalists probably repressed such queries, not permitting them into their consciousness. After all, for their cooperation during the present crisis, Colonel Blaik was calling them "my friends" and feeding them some of the best Italian food in New York.

> He [Blaik] went on to defend Big Football, the very influence which—by his own words—had done most to cause the cribbers to violate the Honor System. Army football players, he said earlier, were "unbelievably fatigued" after hours of practice on the gridiron, and [still] had to face the iron scholastic schedules of the Academy . . .
>
> He seemed involved in a contradiction. If the [expelled] cadets were to be defended on the ground that the pressure of Big Football was too strong for the honor system, then something needed to be done either about football *or* the honor system!
>
> —*Time* magazine, August 1951

The day after the meeting at Leone's, newspaper stories were as positive as the Army coach hoped. The following week, however, some criticism appeared, typified by the *Time* piece about the press conference. The magazine had sent a non-sports journalist, placing the article in its "Manners & Morals" section, not in "Sports," and the reporter not only shunned the sports media lovefest with Blaik, but jumped on the coach's failure to see the basic "contradiction" in his position: the incompatibility of Big Football and the Honor Code at the United States Military Academy.

This journal's coverage of the press conference and the scandal—its focus on the larger social questions rather than the coach's narrow sports concerns—paralleled the increasing editorial criticism of big-time football at West Point, and of commercialized intercollegiate athletics in America. (Observers often described the distance between the editorial board and the sports department as the same as that between "the Ivory Tower" and "the sandbox.") In fact, even though Colonel Blaik easily survived his personal 1951 crisis, big-time intercollegiate athletics was entering its most difficult period, one where, at times, its future actually seemed in doubt (see Chapter 37).

At the Military Academy, Blaik was allowed to stay on; the coach had shrewdly boxed in his bosses by publicly stating that he would not resign. Nevertheless, after the investigations into and reports about the Honor Code violations, West Point officials curtailed Blaik's recruiting and appointment abuses, monitored his players' classroom work closely, and abolished his academic "coach" positions, which forced athletes to seek help from the regular West Point tutors available to all cadets. Historian Stephen Ambrose summarized: "Football, and especially the Navy game, were still important at West

Point, but the scandal and the reaction to it made it clear that other things counted more," particularly the Honor Code and academic integrity.

Not surprisingly, the 1951 season was Blaik's most difficult. In a "Pigskin Preview" article, Francis Wallace commented that before the expulsions, "Army looked to have the third-ranking team in the nation . . . and a solid chance at an unbeaten year." Now, having lost thirty-seven players, including his stars, disaster descended; at the end of the year, Blaik's hastily rebuilt team had a 2–7 record, beating only Columbia and The Citadel, losing to Navy, 42–7.

In subsequent seasons, Blaik constructed a working version of an Army team, nothing to compare with his previous powerhouses but a squad that could operate successfully in 1950s postscandal football. Aided by the general de-emphasis in the eastern college game, particularly the Ivy League's total de-emphasis, and the NCAA's return to one-platoon football, he had a series of winning seasons until he retired in 1957. Friendly sportswriters also awarded him various year-end honors.

The College Football Hall of Fame inducted him in 1965, and subsequently, he accumulated many more honors and awards, including the Presidential Medal of Freedom in 1986. President Ronald Reagan always loved the great Black Knight teams of the 1940s, and he saw them in purely classical terms, hailing Blaik: "One of America's great coaches, he brought a winning spirit to his team, honor to his branch of service and pride to his nation." The only holdout among the award donors was the United States Military Academy, which in spite of pressure from Blaik's supporters refused to name a building or anything else after him. Probably the West Point authorities had read the archival material closely.

When Blaik died in 1989, most of the obituaries briefly mentioned the 1951 Army scandal, typically commenting that "he was in no way involved, other than to defend players he thought were the victims of circumstance." Thus, the love of classic college sports triumphed over the facts of history— even over indications of who had created the scandal "circumstances." Invariably, the good-bye to the coach underlined his "record . . . 166–48–14, a winning percentage of .728."

In August 1951, no one questioned that Blaik produced winning teams, but many Americans doubted that the Army coach had bestowed "honor to his branch of service and pride to his nation." The fallout from the West Point scandal was profound, and despite a later generation's amnesia on the subject, the event had a permanent and lasting impact upon the future of American college sports.

36

ND President Cavanaugh and the ACE Try to Reform College Sports

FOOTBALL IS A FARCE

Many of the colleges still seem to consider football their No. 1 contribution to the U.S. One might have thought, after the basketball fix scandals of last winter and the West Point cribbing scandal of this summer, that the colleges would have learned their lesson—and that athletics would be coming in for a healthy de-emphasis.

—*Life* magazine editorial title and text, September 1951.

In a full-page editorial, the country's most popular magazine—the great glorifier of American life—denounced big-time college sports and listed its condition as "more critical" than the public realized; the basketball fixing, for example, "involved many other teams and players whose names have never been published because prosecuting attorneys preferred to ignore the facts rather than wound local pride." This attack and those in other mass circulation weeklies—the *Saturday Evening Post* headlined an editorial during this period, "Maybe It Takes a Cribbing Scandal to Deflate [College] Sports"—reflected the truly low standing of intercollegiate athletics during the fall of 1951. Readers responded positively to these editorials, one telling *Life:* "I couldn't believe it. College football is such a sacred cow that I have never seen such an outright denunciation in a national magazine. Congratulations." Not only had the scandals cost big-time college sports a huge amount of public support and official approval but, to many observers, the enterprise seemed incapable of regaining health.

Even the sporting press began to waver in its backing of intercollegiate athletics. *Sport* editorialized: "Our first reaction to the announcement of The Case

358

of the Cribbing Cadets last August was, 'Oh, for crying out loud, this is the last straw.' We were still dizzy from the impact of the non-stop basketball scandal." The magazine complained, "It's the system we're sore about," and after surveying the many abuses and frauds in college sports, its editors concluded that unless "responsible educators . . . grasp the need for a re-examination" of the entire system, "the alternative—and this is no laughing matter—is very likely the abolition of intercollegiate sport."

The most prominent sportswriters in the country also joined the critics. Unlike their colleagues who cheered for Colonel Blaik at Mama Leone's, many national columnists overcame narrow self-interest. Red Smith, commenting on Judge Streit's jail sentences for some of the player-fixers, urged that the culprits, "when they go behind the [prison] wall . . . be accompanied by their accomplices—the college presidents, the coaches, the registrars, the alumni who compounded the felony." Smith also mentioned a recent radio broadcast during which Grantland Rice, one of "the best friends [college] football ever had . . . said that unless the colleges scrubbed up fast, there were sure to be [more] scandals that would invite the reformers to abolish intercollegiate sports altogether."

Grantland Rice, however, did not share Red Smith's disdain for university presidents. The previous year he had written an "Open Letter to a College President," imploring the generic executive to gain control of his athletic department and restore the classic ideals to college sports. For Rice, the problems had become systemic—not just a few rotten apples but a quickly spoiling barrel—and so entrenched that they "make you wonder whether [big-time college] football . . . should be allowed to survive in its present form." Rice then exhorted, "Mr. College President . . . bring the great game of football back to its true place in college life—on a par with baseball, crew, track, etc."—in other words, de-emphasize it. That the writer who created the Four Horsemen, the Galloping Ghost, and other national heroes, who promoted big-time college football constantly for more than forty years, now called for its de-emphasis must have astounded readers. Nevertheless, his position was linked to his traditional viewpoint; at this time he also campaigned for the abolition of two-platoon football and a return to all-around athletes, deploring the fact that "we don't talk of the great player any more, we talk about the specialist."

Additional pressure upon "Mr. College President" came from a massive six-part series in the *New York Times* in early 1951. Beginning with front-page headlines—"College Emphasis on Sports Found to Victimize Students/ Study Shows 'Subsidizing' of Athletes by Some Schools Establishes False Values and Lowers Academic Standards"—the paper relentlessly explored the underside of intercollegiate athletics and published a long list of offending universities and their crimes. Among many violations, the *Times* discovered widespread transcript tampering, dubious admissions procedures, and curriculum fraud.

The *Times* also found some university presidents willing to criticize the current system. A. Whitney Griswold, head of Yale—one of the pioneering schools in big-time college football—condemned "the confusion of values represented by semi-professional bigtime athletics [as] . . . a betrayal of the traditions of higher learning." A few years earlier, Griswold had helped organize the Ivy League and start its move toward athletic de-emphasis.

The newspaper also gave high marks to Notre Dame president Cavanaugh for his opposition to athletic scholarships. However, unlike Griswold and most Ivy League administrators, the Notre Dame official did not want to abolish big-time college sports. Football not only enabled his school to reach millions of Americans, but it generated almost a million dollars a year, an important source of revenue for an institution with a total endowment of only $9 million.

For the *Times*, the answer was de-emphasis, and Notre Dame was an exception that did not contradict the "case for deflation." Father Cavanaugh disagreed with this solution; nonetheless, as he watched intercollegiate athletics become increasingly corrupt and disreputable, he realized that despite Notre Dame's historic independence, the Fighting Irish still sailed on the ship of big-time college sports, and that craft was sinking. To help save it—both because he believed in intercollegiate athletics and because the task was in his school's self-interest—he launched a campaign in early 1951 that, in the end, not only preserved big-time college sports but shaped its modern form. That the eventual outcome differed greatly from his original plan does not negate his crucial role in initiating it.

■　■　■

> We are flatly and irreconcilably against paying football players directly [with athletic scholarships] or indirectly [with phony jobs]. We think that the chicanery by which this is done is the major injury from which intercollegiate athletics is suffering, and that this injury threatens the influence and good name of the game.

—Notre Dame president John J. Cavanaugh, December 1950.

The ND president first articulated his reform proposals in a speech at the annual Notre Dame football banquet. For Cavanaugh, "paying" a college athlete was "manifestly unfair to the boy" because it made him an employee, not a student, of the university. He insisted that real scholar-athletes must receive "a genuine college education." Therefore, "entrance requirements for them will not be lowered by the university," and "there will be no soft courses" for them; also they will have to make "satisfactory progress toward a degree." His institution already followed these procedures, additionally, all of its "athletes have to attain a 77 percent average rather than merely get by" in their courses—all part of the school's historic "Fortress Notre Dame" policy.

In this speech, Cavanaugh not only stated his traditional premise—"We want Notre Dame to play to win cleanly and according to the rules"—but, between the lines, he revealed his pragmatic purpose: if the Fighting Irish could compete on a level playing field against opponents enforcing similar academic regulations, the Catholic institution, with its exceptional recruiting advantages, would triumph. However, in the deteriorating college sports climate, because Notre Dame would not lower its standards, the more that other schools cheated, the more difficult it would become for ND to win. The banquet speech came after Frank Leahy's worst season, a 4-4-1 record, and some of the losses had been to universities with questionable athletic programs. Thus, for Cavanaugh, the practical and the idealistic coalesced in late 1950 and early 1951. The need to pull college sports out of its current morass coincided with the desire to ensure the future success of Fighting Irish football. For the ND president, the bottom line was clear: no one would benefit more from the results of effective national reform than "Fortress Notre Dame."

Father Cavanaugh began his campaign in late January 1951 by writing to a number of important colleagues, including the head of the University of California system, Robert G. Sproul:

> Dear President Sproul,
>
> You have, no doubt, shared with me the concern that has in recent years attended the direction of intercollegiate athletics . . . It appears to me that the time is ripe for leadership from those who head up our leading institutions.
> Faced with the actual situation, and wishing to do something concrete about it, we at Notre Dame have determined to contact the various schools that we play and hope to play in future. We think that the presidents of these schools provide a fine cross-section of the various leagues and conferences throughout the country, and if something could be accomplished by our group, it would have a good effect on a nation-wide basis.

The ND president then offered a list of the major maladies in big-time college sports, and also his long-standing belief "that neither the NCAA through its [recent] Sanity Code nor the conferences through their regulations have solved" or can solve these problems—indeed, the NCAA compounded them when it abolished the "Sanity Code" at its recent 1951 convention (see page 247). Cavanaugh contended, however, that if a group of important university presidents could agree on such controversial issues as prohibiting athletic scholarships and then enforce their pact, this would aid big-time college sports and represent a partial counterweight to the current decay. It would also have allowed the universities involved, Notre Dame, Cal, and others, to escape to a lifeboat and continue playing at a major level.

Father Cavanaugh received mixed responses to his letter. Some university presidents were enthusiastic, but Sproul, head of both the Berkeley and UCLA campuses—schools with increasingly corrupt athletic programs—was noncommittal. On the other hand, the head of the University of Pittsburgh noted, "The dissolution of the NCAA as a regulatory body throws the door open for even more cutthroat competition than previously existed . . . [Thus] it is time for these matters to be settled at the top level and I will heartily join a meeting" at "Notre Dame or any other place."

Cavanaugh also received replies from a number of Big Ten universities. He had not written to conference members antagonistic to ND in this period, but he did send letters to Iowa, Purdue, and Indiana, schools that still played the Fighting Irish. Indiana president Herman B. Wells jocularly dismissed Cavanaugh's campaign by indicating that "the problems of which you speak . . . seem a little less urgent" and "dangerous to us" because "we have not been 'afflicted' with any continuing success in football." (Ironically, a few years later, Wells hired and failed to control a football coach whose constant cheating brought down the full wrath of the Big Ten and the NCAA upon his school.) The responses of the other Big Ten executives contained less wit but no greater enthusiasm for the ND plan.

Many presidents also fell back on academic procedures, some replying that they had to take the ND proposal to various internal committees and/or they could act only through their conferences. The chief executive at Iowa used the latter excuse, also remarking, "There are some diseases, of which 'footballitis' is one, that must run a course before anything constructive can be done, and I feel that the course has not yet been run." This president then hired a buccaneer coach, Forest Evashevski, and presided over a virulent multiyear outbreak of Hawkeye "footballitis." In light of subsequent events during the reform attempt of 1951–52, these executive sidesteps and evasions clearly foreshadowed the attitude of many university presidents toward systemic change in big-time college sports. Nonetheless, at this point in the process, Father Cavanaugh suspended his usual skepticism and pressed ahead.

The ND president correctly anticipated the public demand for reform. The *New York Times,* joined by other major newspapers and national magazines, continued to campaign for a "total collegiate sports cleanup." In addition, the *Times* and others prominently featured Judge Saul Streit's sentencing of the basketball fixers, including his declaration "that the evils could be uprooted if the [college] presidents assumed direct control of athletic activities."

Cavanaugh also argued for tight presidential supervision of college sports programs. At his school, with its authoritarian traditions and top-down management, the Golden Dome had long governed the athletic department.

In late summer 1951, after the revelations of the basketball fixing and West Point outrages, as well as football scandals at such schools as William and Mary, the American Council on Education (ACE) adopted the concept of presidential reform. With his one-man campaign, Father Cavanaugh had encountered opposition and recalcitrance, but with the backing of the most important organization in higher education, the prospects for change improved. In confidence, Cavanaugh told a colleague that the ACE was "establishing a committee to study intercollegiate athletics" and to propose reforms, but had not yet gone public with its plan. The ACE had asked Cavanaugh to serve on its panel—the appointment of the chair was still undecided—and he had accepted, looking forward to the assignment.

On November 9, 1951, in Washington, D.C., the ACE announced its committee of ten prominent college presidents, including Cavanaugh and Yale's Griswold, chaired by Michigan State's John Hannah. Apparently the ACE felt that Notre Dame's long independence from and aloofness toward the main associations in college sports and higher education ruled out its president as chair. The *New York Times* remarked that the "members of the committee represent colleges that, with one exception [Notre Dame], are affiliated with athletic conferences," and active in academic affairs. In addition, in an era when overt anti-Catholicism still existed, few Catholics and even fewer priests became heads of high-profile national boards. Nevertheless, the ACE's choice of MSU's Hannah prompted criticism: rather than place a proven reformer in the chair, one with a mix of idealism and pragmatism, the organization had selected a president in charge of an athletic program well known for its rule violations.

Many of the ACE's other appointments also raised questions about its commitment to reform. Except for the heads of Wesleyan and Western Reserve, the other presidents ran institutions with reputations for dubious practices in college sports, particularly Southern Methodist University and the University of Washington. Earlier that year, the *New York Times* had revealed that SMU permitted "134 athletes to continue on free tuition with an average" below or at passing, and the school operated a plush dormitory specially for football players, one of the first "jock dorms" in the nation. In the same article, the *Times* mentioned academic deals for athletes at the University of Washington, and that school's rampaging boosters had also attracted the attention of the commissioner of the Pacific Coast Conference, resulting in various sanctions. The panel members from the universities of Nebraska, Utah, and Mississippi also presided over athletic programs with suspicious pasts and presents, and even the head of Furman had attracted NCAA attention for condoning violations of the "Sanity Code." As important, most of these institutions belonged to conferences that wanted to expand their college sports programs and achieve big-time status.

Apparently the ACE's strategy was to bring the miscreants and their allies into the reform movement and, by including them in the deliberations, ensure that they would support the eventual proposals. But because many of these presidents were weak and/or hypocritical, the tactic was perilous. Possibly if Whitney Griswold or John Cavanaugh—strong personalities with clear agendas and formidable persuasive powers—had chaired the committee, they would have brought the other members into line behind them. Instead of Griswold or Cavanaugh, the ACE appointed John Hannah, one of the slyest foxes in higher education, to guard the henhouse of reform.

Late 1951 marked an exceptional moment in the history of American college sports—the only time in the twentieth century when meaningful change was possible. The political and academic establishments, the public, and even the media were demanding systemic reform. As the president of Purdue University told Cavanaugh, strict national "rules and regulations" would give every "president an external force to back him in trying to make his own [athletic] constituency live within such regulations." But many of the ACE's appointments to its committee, particularly John Hannah as chair, rendered this moment of great opportunity uncertain.

Because of Hannah's crucial impact on the ACE reform attempt—he played the key role in its outcome—his character and career deserve special attention.

■   ■   ■

THE MICHIGAN STATE CONSTRUCTION JOB

> The ingredients of Michigan State's rise from an "also-ran" in the football picture to a top ranking power include an athletic-minded college president; an aggressive, free-spending football-conscious alumni group; a head coach who is a sound fundamentalist; a staff of assistants who are talented and persuasive "salesmen"; a liberal academic admissions policy . . .
>
> —*Sport* magazine title and text, December 1953.

John Hannah represented an important species in American higher education: the Booster President, the executive who believes that he can promote his school regionally and nationally through success in big-time college sports—only victory, in his view, attracts attention and an aura of accomplishment—and who averts his eyes when his coaches, alumni, and admission officers break the rules to build winning teams. The NCAA's Walter Byers termed Hannah's strategy "athletic bootstrapping," and he considered the MSU president its greatest proponent, as well as the forerunner of many future university heads.

In this period, the presidents of schools like Maryland, Bradley, and Kentucky also believed in boosterism—and openly participated in the cheating. Hannah refined athletic bootstrapping to its modern form, the supportive chief executive who keeps his distance from the grime, carefully cultivating "deniability." As a result, Hannah considered himself "a reformer" while his work at Michigan State offered an Orwellian definition of that term.

In 1941, Michigan State College, not yet a university, appointed Hannah to its top position. Shortly after, he used a major bequest to the school to permanently fund a large number of athletic scholarships. He announced that "football is a college's show window," and that he intended to build a winning team to help his institution to, according to Byers, "climb from the status of an instructional school for tradesmen and farmers to a nationally respected university." After the war, when the Big Ten sought a replacement for the University of Chicago, Hannah campaigned successfully for MSC's admission to the conference. He also enlarged his football stadium from 14,000 capacity to 51,000 and cheered as coach "Biggie" Munn's winning teams filled it; Hannah attended every Spartan game at home and on the road.

Football success, however, brought both desired and unwanted attention. The state legislature elevated his school to university status, but the Big Ten office, according to commissioner Tug Wilson, "began to get many complaints and charges that unearned aid" to MSU athletes, including substantial amounts of cash, "was being made through" the off-campus Spartan Foundation. Most Big Ten athletic programs cut corners, but the MSU cheating was on a larger and more organized scale than the others; also the established powers, particularly in-state rival Michigan, wanted the commissioner to show the "new kid" that the MSU felonies went far beyond regular Big Ten larceny. Tug Wilson investigated and subsequently accused Michigan State officials, including the president, of making no attempt to control the boosters: "The notoriety of the Foundation fund was such that . . . it could not have been ignored and . . . should have been the subject of searching inquiry by the college authorities, but was not."

The Spartan Foundation's "notoriety" was well known before the ACE appointed John Hannah to chair its panel, but many of the boosters' specific activities became public only during and after his work with the committee. Throughout the Big Ten investigation, the MSU president took the unusual line that "a university could not be held responsible for the operations of an outside slush fund" funneling money to its athletes. As Wilson stated, if higher education accepted this argument, "This would repeatedly become the pattern of illegal aid" to athletes. That Hannah claimed no responsibility for the boosters indicated his problems as a reformer of college sports and exposed him to constant accusations of hypocrisy.

■   ■   ■

COLLEGES' INQUIRY ON ATHLETICS OPENS

Committee of Presidents Begins Two-Day Hearing, Pledges No Whitewash.

[According to John Hannah] "the chief executive officer of the university is responsible for the conduct and integrity of the institution, including athletics, and . . . there is real concern for the protection of the integrity of higher education."

—*New York Times* headline, subhead, and quote from text,
November 1951.

Soon after the ACE formed its panel, the members met in Washington, D.C., to discuss their priorities and a plan of action. Their major deliberations occurred on the same day that Judge Streit sentenced a group of player-fixers, and many newspapers juxtaposed the two stories, featuring the comments of Streit and Hannah on the importance of university presidents initiating a college sports cleanup.

Most papers, however, placed an equally important item well below the Streit and ACE stories. An AP dispatch from Chicago announced: "The NCAA's policy making Council today proposed a program of rigid athletic controls. It hit especially at lax academic standards, professionalism trends," and so on. In other words, the NCAA Council, in damage-control mode, proposed revisiting the "Sanity Code." The association's timing and announcement signaled its objection to the ACE as a regulatory agency in intercollegiate athletics, as well as its own refusal to depart quietly from the college sports stage. Thus, on the day when the long-awaited reform revolution began to choose a specific route, the forces of counterrevolution also started to march.

Examining the NCAA Council's proposal is instructive. The NCAA termed it a "12-Point Code," its official history later proclaiming that this code "will evolve in the years to come as a fundamental part of the Association's position regarding the conduct of intercollegiate athletics." Yet, the actual twelve points reveal the NCAA's longtime strategy of cooling out all serious reform initiatives. The list offered conditional and improbable propositions, with zero assurance that any one of them would produce results. The call to "reexamine post-season games," for instance, was a sham. The NCAA leaders assumed that ACE presidents like Griswold and Cavanaugh wanted to *ban* all bowl games, but the NCAA also knew that most schools liked the bowls. Even the apparently positive points, like "limit the number and amount of financial grants to athletes," contained tricks; the association could, and eventually did, set a *high limit:* more than a hundred grants per school in football. To consider the NCAA's approach as real reform is to confuse propaganda with reality.

Nevertheless, the NCAA's Walter Byers worked hard to sell the association's plan. According to an official of the Football Writers Association, Byers asked that group's "help . . . to save the endangered college sports which are so important to us [sportswriters] as well as to the NCAA." Then, at the ACE's next public hearing, Byers presented the association's twelve-point code; however, unlike the football writers who responded positively to the NCAA appeal, "some of the ACE presidents," according to their spokesman, "felt that this was 'more [NCAA] double-talk.' "

The latter comment underlined the crucial question of the ACE panel's relationship to the NCAA. At this time and later, arguments about this issue occurred within as well as outside the ACE committee. One commentator noted that many college presidents not on the panel "thought that the ACE committee was to act independently" of the NCAA, "even to react to the NCAA's . . . failures to reform college sports," and to pursue a totally separate course. Some inside members, including Griswold and Cavanaugh, also advocated the independent route. On the other hand, John Hannah talked autonomy but walked in another direction. His moves eventually influenced the ACE proceedings as well as the fate of the reform initiative.

The same day that Byers appeared before the ACE presidents, the president of the National Football Coaches Association gave the panel his group's position on reform: "When asked if college sports needed 'cleaning up,' [Lloyd] Jordan said, 'Not necessarily. There are some corrections needed [but] I don't think it [the current situation] is as bad as it's made out to be.' " Even though he coached at de-emphasized Harvard and could have embraced reform, Jordan represented his personal and his association's point of view. His intransigence also indicated the depth of coaches' opposition to any significant changes in college sports, and Jordan almost taunted the committee when he added, "We must recognize that colleges" with intercollegiate athletic teams "are in the entertainment business. The only question is . . . if we do it at all, shouldn't we do it well?" The president of Western Reserve objected, remarking that he had "yet to find a college charter that includes" a sports entertainment mission "as a legitimate objective."

Jordan's cynical realism contrasted with a certain amount of presidential naïveté, which appeared when some members of the panel argued that "de-emphasis . . . will not affect the quality of athletic competition . . . [college sports] will be just as interesting under [reform] proposals as it is now." Most coaches worried that if they could not recruit the best possible athletes— regardless of their academic abilities—they would put an inferior product on the field. Who would pay, they asked, to see Phi Beta Kappas play football? The coaches believed that de-emphasis would result in lower attendance and, inevitably, diminish their importance as well as the size of their annual incomes.

The argument between the ACE presidents and the coaches was as old as big-time college sports, and underscored its core contradiction. Most Americans wanted college football players to be superb athletes *and* authentic students, thus fulfilling the classic ideal. That model required boys from early ages to spend enormous amounts of time perfecting their sports skills and, at university, to perform at a very high athletic level. That model also demanded that these young men succeed at a totally different endeavor: intellectual analysis, which also required a huge amount of prior training, as well as successful performance in college classrooms, America's highest educational level.

Some exceptional scholar-athletes could handle these conflicting demands, and a few athletic programs could gather a fair number of them, but tens of thousands of participants in big-time college sports fell short, particularly academically. The system could not support the traditional scholar-athlete ideal; indeed, it had long ago spawned its evil twin, the "dumb jock" stereotype. Therefore, for reform to please all the constituencies in intercollegiate athletics—education-minded presidents and faculties, career-minded coaches and athletic directors, sports-obsessed alumni and fans, as well as the media—reformers had to square the circle of academic and athletic excellence, by definition an impossibility.

On the other hand, if each group followed the logic of its position, the presidents would de-emphasize and accept a lower quality athletic product, and the coaches would overemphasize and live with their professionalized programs. Thus, when the ACE panel considered its first specific proposals in November 1951, it had to choose a definite direction. To its credit, it did. (In the history of intercollegiate athletics, only the NCAA has more or less tried to appease all constituencies, but it does so by pretending that the disparity between academic and athletic excellence does not exist.)

The basic contradictions of college sports confronted the ACE panel in late 1951, but many observers remained optimistic about its ability to achieve viable reform. The important Catholic weekly *Commonweal,* long scornful of big-time college sports, noted that "the protracted over-emphasis of American intercollegiate athletics is happily under fire," with the ACE presidents making a "concerted effort to cut intercollegiate athletics down to size."

37

The NCAA Finds an ACE Traitor
and Subverts Reform

COLLEGE PRESIDENTS ASK BAN ON BOWL GAMES

The abolition of all post-season football bowl games was recommended today by [ACE] college presidents studying intercollegiate sports. The recommendation was part of a proposed program which would supervise the athlete from high school until he finished college.

—*Washington Post* headline and lead, December 1951.

In mid-December 1951, the ACE panel floated a short list of proposals to keep the media spotlight on their reform effort, and to preempt attention from the NCAA's promised enactment of the "12-Point Code" at its January 1952 convention. The ACE presidents, pushed by ND's Cavanaugh and Yale's Griswold, called the bowls "the height of college sports commercialism and exploitation of student football players," and because of the bowls' prominence and symbolism, the panel made their abolition its first item of business.

The "Bowl Game Ban" headlines sparked instant protest, particularly from sportswriters. One important Southern columnist also included John Hannah in his attack, pointing out that the MSU president's current criticism of bowl games "was more double-talk. One year ago, December 1950, he approved the appearance of his team in a bowl but couldn't get the Big Ten's O.K." on it—because of the conference's exclusive deal with the Rose Bowl.

In addition to the sportswriters, coaches immediately denounced the ACE proposal. Tennessee's famed General Robert Neyland argued that post-season games were wonderful events and "a reward to kids for a job well done" throughout the year. He did not mention that many bowls also rewarded participating coaches with fat bonus checks and, because bowl appearances capped winning seasons, they also helped coaches gain enhanced annual contracts.

The AP polled "over 100 of the nation's sportswriters and sportscasters," many of whom enjoyed the free trips and other gratuities provided by the bowls, and they voted "4-to-1 . . . that bowl games are harmless and should be retained." At this time, however, the AP also ran the story that "Stanford's McColl, AP Lineman of the Year, Is Opposed to Bowls," quoting the player's contention that "the commercialism connected with the larger bowls out-weighed the honor" of playing in them. Bill McColl was interviewed after a practice session for his team's appearance in the coming Rose Bowl, but he still "agreed with the anti-bowl stand taken by the ACE college presidents." A straight A pre-med student, he represented the scholar-athlete ideal, and he offered his "endorsement of football de-emphasis." However, such critical comments on these questions from All-Americans appeared infrequently on the sports pages, which were usually swamped by jock endorsements of big-time college sports.

Meanwhile, behind the scenes, NCAA officials worked to torpedo the ACE's antibowl proposal. They reminded university presidents that in recent years the NCAA had gained control of the previously chaotic bowl scene, making them profitable for participating schools and conferences, and asked the chief executives to oppose the ACE panel on this issue and others. When the NCAA argument combined with pressure from coaches and athletic directors, anti-ACE incidents began to occur. At a late December meeting of Southeastern Conference presidents, the head of Vanderbilt University intro-duced a motion to support the ACE bowl ban, but according to the AP, "the failure of the measure to get even a seconder follows right in line with a warn-ing from [SEC] head coaches and athletic directors yesterday that college presidents should keep hands off the SEC's liberal bowl policy."

As the antireform forces gathered strength, the ACE panel became con-cerned that some of their fellow college presidents, even those inclined to fol-low ACE directives, would never overrule their powerful coaches and ADs, and gain control of their athletic programs. This problem had sunk some previous reform efforts, and according to many observers, it defied solution. However, in late 1951, pushed again by Cavanaugh and Griswold, the ACE presidents devised a way to cut this Gordian knot that had long entangled the reform of college sports, and to bring about meaningful change with one swift blow.

■ ■ ■

Enforcement [of the ACE proposals] would be left to the nation's five accrediting organizations [that] . . . set standards not only for the col-leges and universities but also for the high schools.

They are the North Central, the Middle States, the New England, the Northwest, and the Southern Association. All belong to the American Council on Education and representatives of each will be at the [ACE] committee's next meeting.

—United Press report, December 1951.

When the ACE panel announced its enforcement strategy, some reporters failed to understand its implications. One asked, "What if a school doesn't want to go along with" an accrediting agency's decision "and ignores it?" An ACE spokesman replied, "A knowing violation of an accrediting ruling is a very serious breach" and could lead to the institution's losing its degree-granting powers. The spokesman added, "I think that any faculty and president would think many times before they would jeopardize their [accreditation] standing" over a college sports dispute.

The accrediting agencies of America separated legitimate colleges and universities from the "diploma mills" and fly-by-night operations, certifying that students of approved institutions earned valid course credits and that graduates had amassed sufficient credits to receive valuable degrees. Schools worked hard to obtain and keep accreditation for their academic programs because without this seal of approval their legitimacy vanished, and their students could not transfer credits to other institutions or gain admission to professional or graduate schools.

The simplicity and directness of the ACE enforcement plan appealed to panel members: the accrediting agencies, trained to investigate and evaluate university programs, would examine athletic department procedures, holding them to specific ACE rules. If investigators found violations, according to the head of the American Council on Education, "They will appraise the institution of them, and recommend that changes be made . . . if the changes aren't made, the [school's] accreditation will be withdrawn." As importantly, the independence of the accrediting agencies gave them immunity from the pressure that college sports interest groups, particularly boosters and the media, always imposed upon university presidents—demands that had scuttled previous reform attempts.

In early January 1951, newspaper headlines announced, "Accrediting Groups Offer Help in De-emphasis of College Sports," and the articles described the cordial meeting in Washington between leaders of the five organizations and the ACE panel. The accrediting officials saw the ACE concept as a solution to a major problem in American education—they had long complained about the corrosive effect of big-time college sports upon universities—and also they liked the fact that the plan would increase their own power and importance.

With the accrediting groups on board, the ACE presidents decided to work out a detailed list of reform proposals to announce on the eve of the 1952 NCAA convention. They wanted to present the association members with a *fait accompli*—the ACE vision of the impending future of college sports. The *Chicago Tribune* declared: "In the past, the NCAA has been the enforcement body for the colleges. The [ACE] presidents' plan would take it [enforcement] away from the NCAA entirely."

COLLEGE HEADS CRACK DOWN
ON BOWLS, SCHOLARSHIPS

College presidents who have been studying intercollegiate athletics yesterday proposed a sweeping new code that radically would alter the American sports scene.

NCAA HEAD CALLS
PROPOSALS "PREMATURE"

Dr. Hugh Willett, president of the NCAA, tonight described as "premature" proposals by a committee of college presidents.

—*Washington Post* headlines and leads on adjoining stories,
January 1952.

Added to its previously proposed ban on bowl games, the ACE reform list now included the abolition of out-of-season athletic practices, including football spring sessions, and the end of all athletic scholarships and job plans—henceforth, schools would treat athletes like all other students, only providing grants on the basis of academic merit and/or financial need. The NCAA objected to these proposals, and president Hugh Willett, USC faculty representative, led the counterattack. However, just as John Hannah was compromised by his school's questionable athletic program, Dr. Willett had a similar problem: his Trojans had long flauted Pacific Coast Conference rules, not only in football but in other collegiate sports.

In 1950, the Boston Braves had complained about the $22,000 bonus "we had to pay" a player, Joe Andrews, "to sign with us. We had to pay this figure not to beat [professional] baseball competition . . . but rather to beat the figure offered by Southern Cal." Considering that the value of this bonus in 1990s dollars is about $220,000, and that baseball trailed Trojan football as the school's most important sport and the object of its boosters' money, the offer to the baseball player indicates the scale of USC cheating in the postwar period.

Nevertheless, Hugh Willett was a master at holier-than-thou attitudes and pronouncements—one observer mocked his attempts at "regulating the morals of honest persons"—and he became the front man for the NCAA's assault on the ACE reform initiative. One of Willett's tactics was to proclaim NCAA reforms, and only acknowledge their actual provisions if questioned directly. Before the 1952 NCAA convention, headline writers repeated his assertion, "NCAA Plans New Sanity Code with Potent Enforcement Means," but one reporter got him to admit that "we will have a Sanity Code but implementation and enforcement will be left to the member institutions." In other words, if they do not want to clean up their athletic programs, we cannot make them do so.

Moreover, many groups within the NCAA not only rejected minimal reform, but loudly attacked the ACE's proposals. Maryland football coach Jim Tatum condemned the ACE "presidents who are embarked on a campaign to de-emphasize [college sports] . . . There is nothing wrong with football," opined the coach of one of the most corrupt and successful programs in the nation (third in the 1951 polls). "There is definitely something wrong with some of these [ACE] people trying to run it." Maryland president Curly Byrd attempted an end-run around the ACE by announcing that "most of their recommendations already are in force [at this university] . . . For one thing, we always have insisted that the school control any aid to athletes," with the president totally in charge of the grant money. Beyond the blatant lie—the ACE wanted to ban athletic scholarships, and Maryland gave more than most schools—Byrd put an ironic twist on the issue of presidential control: indeed, he personally supervised all aid to athletes, even handing out pay envelopes to some!

As NCAA members gathered in Cincinnati, the denunciations of the ACE panel escalated. According to the United Press, the Louisiana State University athletic director "charged today that college presidents advocating drastic athletic changes are 'publicity hounds and opportunists who are out of their field.' " Other ADs also condemned the presidents, one adding that if the ACE men were successful, you "might as well discard the NCAA." The commissioner of the SEC echoed this opinion, remarking that the ACE presidents "should work through the NCAA, otherwise this organization is dead."

The demise of the NCAA was precisely the goal of such ACE presidents as Whitney Griswold and John Cavanaugh, and also the reason why NCAA officials fought the ACE initiative so tenaciously and ruthlessly. At this juncture in the controversy a key event occurred: John Hannah went to Cincinnati, ostensibly to answer any questions that delegates might have about his panel's proposals. In fact, Hannah had another purpose, one that became crucial for the future of the ACE plan.

The first press reports of the ACE chair's visit stressed, "Presidents Predict No Compromise with NCAA," as well as Hannah's declaration that the ACE "report is final," and the NCAA will have to live with it. Behind the scenes, however, Hannah presented a different scenario, one that offered the NCAA maximum room to maneuver. In a private note to Hugh Willett, he assured the association president that "we are all trying to accomplish the same general objective in spite of the newspaper efforts to make it look as though we are engaged in a civil war with the athletic directors and coaches and the NCAA on the one side, and the [ACE] college presidents on the other."

Because of Hannah's habitually unclear use of "we"—sometimes he employed it as the royal "We" referring to himself, sometimes he included others—the reader cannot determine whether the Michigan State president acted alone, or whether others on the panel supported his conciliatory position. Certainly Cavanaugh, Griswold, and some other presidents on the committee, as well as many outside it, did not want a rapprochement with the NCAA at this time. Moreover, the newspapers, even though siding with the NCAA, had accurately described the gulf between the ACE's activist plan and the NCAA hesitancy on reform. But Hannah approached the NCAA with white flag raised, and his tactic changed the future of college sports. Instead of pressing the ACE demands upon the NCAA, he helped the association move into its damage-control mode and appear reformist, painting new labels on its old system.

In Cincinnati, John Hannah switched sides. The day before the convention opened, according to an insider's report, he met in "closed session" with the NCAA Council and Executive Committee, resulting in "a harmonious get-together." After this meeting, Hugh Willett stated that Hannah "showed clearly that the objectives and athletic philosophy of the presidents' committee are the objectives and philosophy of the NCAA."

The results of Hannah's sellout soon became apparent in the headlines and stories about the 1952 NCAA convention: "NCAA Maps Athletic Reforms Less Drastic Than Proposed by Presidents/Association Asks No Bowl Game Ban," and, at the convention's conclusion, "Bowl Game Study Voted/ Spring Practice Is Retained on Limited Basis." The headlines implied what the stories revealed: the NCAA's damage-control strategy had inched the association toward change but had stopped miles from the ACE proposals—although, typically, the association agreed "to study" the presidents' ideas. In addition, the NCAA opened the door to athletic scholarships, and made its compliance procedures less complex. However, as the AP noted, the new enforcement committee "is not expected to initiate investigations but to act only when there is 'critical need.' "

The NCAA also spun a perfunctory PR resolution "endorsing the philosophy and general objectives of the ACE." This allowed such longtime press allies as Allison Danzig, the main football writer of the *New York Times,* to conclude that, although "the NCAA did not see eye to eye with the ACE," the association gave an "unmistakably clear" sign that its members "mean strictly business in correcting the malpractices that marked 1951 as the blackest of all years for intercollegiate athletics."

At the convention's conclusion, reelected NCAA president Hugh Willett indicated his pleasure with Hannah's actions and the association's cooptation of the ACE initiative, stating that he "felt certain that [the ACE] college presidents would now look to the NCAA for enforcement of their athletic code." Then, in a statement emphasizing Hannah's surrender on the most crucial point of the ACE plan—enforcement by the accreditation groups—Willett announced, "I am convinced that the accrediting agencies will be called upon only as a last resort," not as part of any regular enforcement process. In other words, most big-time athletic programs, including Willett's Trojans, had dodged the most deadly bullet ever aimed at them.

Willett concluded, quite correctly, that "the NCAA would continue to be the chief instrument for guiding and enforcing intercollegiate athletic policies." He did not thank John Hannah personally, but he remarked, probably from inside knowledge, "It is quite possible that the ACE will modify the recommendations of its presidents' committee." In fact, whether the ACE did so or not had become moot; Hannah's sellout to the NCAA had made it impossible for the presidents' panel to regain the reform momentum and to impose its will upon the reluctant college sports establishment. Unless a true reformer led a coup on Hannah's chairmanship—an unlikely scenario because the MSU president could probably summon a majority of committee votes—John Hannah would carry the corpse of ACE reform through the rest of the year, then quietly bury it in an unmarked grave.

Why did John Hannah betray the ACE reform initiative? At the time, some observers accused him of hypocrisy, but none grasped his full deception or probed the reasons for it. (Only the availability of internal ACE documents now makes this inquiry possible.) Hannah usually explained that he went to Cincinnati to obtain NCAA acceptance of the ACE plan and facilitate its translation to reality; however, his actual agenda concerned his position as president of Michigan State.

Because Hannah had dealt with the NCAA for many years, and had observed its unwillingness and inability to change college sports, he understood the futility of working with the association on reform. Nevertheless, his knowledge of the NCAA led him to the realization that his beloved Spartan athletic program would exist much more happily under loose NCAA regulations than in the harsh new world of ACE reforms, policed by the North Central Accrediting Agency, in charge of the Midwest. Just before the NCAA convention, that agency had become the first to sign on officially to the ACE college sports assignment. For MSU athletics and its Spartan Foundation, this action was akin to a noose fitting. Probably this incident, more than any other, prompted Hannah's behavior in Cincinnati. In confronting this crisis, his longtime loyalty to Michigan State transcended his temporary allegiance to an outside organization.

. . .

The NCAA's official history later pronounced the 1952 convention, with its introduction of "new regulatory legislation," a pivotal event in the chronicles of intercollegiate athletics. At the time, not only did self-interested sportswriters endorse the NCAA proclamations, but many other journalists went along with the official line. Even *New York Times* columnist Arthur Daley termed the convention a "step in the right direction." Describing previous NCAA meetings as burdened by "too many hypocrites for genuine reform to have a ghost of a chance," he declared that "this time, though, it is different."

Daley's emotions often outran his critical abilities, and, in this important column, his desire to see big-time college sports leave the intensive care unit overcame his analysis of the events in Cincinnati. "In effect," he argued, "the NCAA took the lofty, utopian proposals of the [ACE] presidents and watered them down slightly," beginning the real reform of college sports. His key adjectives were "utopian" and "slightly." But the ACE plan, as the Ivy League soon proved, was not utopian but highly achievable, and even a cursory comparison of the NCAA and ACE proposals indicated an ocean between them. For example, before the Cincinnati meeting ended, the NCAA approved athletic scholarships for the first time, a form of aid anathema to the ACE panel and, according to his previous writings, to Arthur Daley.

Nevertheless, Daley's love of big-time college sports prompted his applause for the NCAA's moves. With this column, he placed the weighty "Sports of the Times" imprimatur upon the NCAA's 1952 convention, and many other journalists and even some editorialists followed with similarly favorable pieces. Soon these media endorsements calmed the public storm, lowering the pressure on college sports authorities to make substantive changes. In his column, Daley also offered a metaphor that became a mantra for many sportswriters and their readers: "The recent scandals acted as a hotfoot on the collegians. They jumped. Perhaps they weren't too willing about it but it was impossible [for them] to stand still any longer." The implication was that the black clouds of 1951 had started to clear, and a bright new college sports era, presided over by the NCAA, was dawning.

38

ND President Cavanaugh
Reacts to the ACE Failure

It was only a year ago that the NCAA threw out the Sanity Code and went its merry way in corrupting the youth of the country by permitting illegal recruiting and subsidizing. The situation deteriorated so rapidly that college presidents led by Father John J. Cavanaugh saw the necessity of taking command if college football [and basketball] were to continue. The American Council on Education appointed a committee to study the problem and recommend a solution. The group did such a thorough job that the NCAA . . . [including the] hypocrites who comprise the majority, fell back in dismay. The NCAA is on its knees, pleading for a chance to prove its sincerity.

—*Chicago Tribune* sports editor Arch Ward, January 1952.

Not every sportswriter embraced the NCAA PR line at this time. Just as his ultraconservative *Chicago Tribune* marched to a different political beat than most other American papers, Arch Ward viewed the 1952 convention differently than most sports journalists. In addition, because of his links to the Notre Dame hierarchy, Ward's opinion transcended the personal, providing a good indication of the ND viewpoint on the events in Cincinnati.

This writer would have never vilified an organization as prominent as the NCAA if Notre Dame officials disapproved. After depicting the NCAA "on its knees," Ward wrote, "Maybe it will get it" and honestly reform college sports, "but we doubt it. The [ACE] presidents' committee has ruled out bowl games . . . It has abolished spring practice in football," these being the first litmus tests of authentic change. But "despite pious proclamations from Cincinnati, there is no intention on the part of many coaches and athletic directors to change their *modus operandi,*" and because of their power within the NCAA, the association can never bring meaningful reform to college sports.

Unlike Arch Ward, Father John Cavanaugh did not make a public statement on the NCAA convention, or on John Hannah's deal with the association. In part, the ND president chose silence because he hoped to revive the ACE initiative, but also because, in Cincinnati, Notre Dame had fought the NCAA over the latter's emerging TV monopoly, and future battles on this issue loomed. (This is discussed in the following chapters.) Therefore, Cavanaugh decided not to criticize the NCAA publicly for edging toward reform, no matter how gingerly or insincerely it moved. Nevertheless, as often occurred during Arch Ward's long career as sports editor of the *Chicago Tribune*, the men in the Golden Dome allowed him to serve as their amanuensis.

Joe Doyle, the main columnist for the *South Bend Tribune* and, like Ward, close to ND administrators, outlined the school's athletic policy after the 1952 NCAA convention: Notre Dame already followed all but one of the ACE proposals, thus it had no need for the NCAA's watered-down or nonexistent versions of them. About the only ND exception to the ACE rules concerned spring football practice. Moose Krause informed Doyle that "with clarifications" on that one "it won't be too much trouble for us" to follow it as well.

Cavanaugh had been skeptical about the NCAA's proposal "to study" the ACE's resolutions, particularly the bans on bowl games and spring practice. After the convention, he watched as the Big Ten hemmed and hawed about ending its multiyear pact with the Rose Bowl; similarly, the Big Ten and the NCAA refused to prohibit spring football practice, they merely shortened it to "twenty days within a thirty-day period." In Cincinnati, NCAA leaders had made noises about "phasing it out," but the coaches had dug in their cleats, joined by the legion of sportswriters who depended upon spring football sessions for weeks of articles and columns on "Old Siwash's Prospects for the Fall Campaign."

In early February 1952, ND head coach Frank Leahy wrote to Vice President Hesburgh: "Am extremely anxious to learn as to whether or not we will have spring practice this year . . . With the usual spring practice, I firmly believe [that] our 1952 club would lose at least five games. If spring football is completely eliminated here, we will do worse than that." Leahy was famous for his unjustified fears about losing, and Father Hesburgh replied coolly that he could not give him "definite word on spring practice at this time . . . Father Cavanaugh told me before leaving [for the ACE meeting in mid-February] that it would depend a great deal on the action of the American Council on Education" panel. Hesburgh referred to the coming attempt by Cavanaugh and Griswold to persuade their ACE colleagues to go it alone on reform, to follow through on the accrediting agencies' enforcement plan, and to ignore the NCAA's 1952 convention moves. Hesburgh then made a statement that to Frank Leahy must have sounded like one of the worst heresies ever uttered: "The feeling at present seems to be that if everyone would do it [abolish spring practice], all of the schools would be *lower in quality,* but of similar quality" during the fall season.

The vice president did provide the coach with one straw to grasp: "I do not think that there is any intention to put our team in a disadvantageous position by making them do what others won't do" in terms of physical conditioning and preparation, therefore, "I believe that we shall do whatever is done by the people we play." The 1952 schedule featured such Top Ten opponents as Oklahoma and Texas. For ND administrators, to assemble and maintain Fighting Irish squads according to the school's "Fortress Notre Dame" rules made sense, but to play high-powered teams without proper conditioning seemed unfair to the athletes. Thus, Cavanaugh and Hesburgh postponed the decision on canceling spring practice.

Throughout its February 1952 meetings, the ACE panel dithered, discussing various strategies and not pressing ahead on definite agreements with the four accrediting agencies. Chairman Hannah, a master of obfuscation and delay, blocked Cavanaugh, Griswold, and their allies on the panel. One observer described Hannah's technique: "Deliberate in speech, he would deflect or simply not acknowledge arguments that ran counter to his mission."

Then Yale's Griswold departed, joining his Ivy League colleagues in announcing that group's official intention to de-emphasize, to play almost exclusively within conference and according to its own rules, most stricter than even the ACE's. For a number of years, the Ivy League had moved away from the mainstream of big-time college sports, but the February 1952 announcement made the separation permanent. This action helped the Ivies ascend to the pinnacle of American higher education, but it removed them from the college sports reform movement.

In the *New York Times* article, "Ivy League De-emphasizes," NCAA president Hugh Willett gave the association's response to the Ivy announcement: the latter's code, as well as the ACE one, "would not bring about any changes in college sports until after" future NCAA conventions studied them; thus despite the Ivy League bans on bowls and spring practice, "There will be a full schedule of New Year's Day bowl games next season, and spring football practice would be eliminated only in certain sections this year," meaning the Ivy League.

Throughout the rest of the winter and into the spring, chairman John Hannah did not budge from his pro-NCAA position, so, reluctantly, Father Cavanaugh allowed Frank Leahy to call spring practice—much later than in previous years. (Leahy still managed a 7-2-1 record in 1952.) Cavanaugh felt that because Notre Dame was committed to a very non-Ivy schedule for the foreseeable future, he had to compromise on this issue. In a letter to a long-time journalist friend, he showed his anger and exhaustion with the ACE committee: "I am writing this to you personally, without any intention that it be published. You asked me for my own frank views, and I want to give them to you . . . [The ACE rules were] a very good minimum guide for any institution to follow. If all institutions would be able honestly to say that, in practice, they observe these regulations, I think intercollegiate athletics would be good, would be highly interesting, and would be beneficial to the boys themselves." However, in the current college sports world, hypocrisy dominated.

When Cavanaugh joined the ACE panel, he had written to a colleague, "An institution says one thing and does another, whereas it sends boys on the field committed to good sportsmanship," off the field it demonstrates "abuses of this sportsmanship through deceit or otherwise." Now, near the end of the ACE process, events had validated his original insight.

Later in 1952, Frank Wallace offered his summary, and probably the Golden Dome's, of the actions of John Hannah and his allies on the ACE panel: those college presidents, "whose laxity was most responsible for the explosion" of public outrage, "holler loudest" for change "and then run wild in a righteous scramble to lead the way to reform. In this case, the officials were certain college presidents who knew all along that the stork did not bring winning teams and large gate receipts," and, not surprisingly, these men proved insincere about reform. Between the lines Wallace implied a sarcastic "Go Spartans! Go Ponies! Go Huskies! Go Huskers! Go Utes! Go Rebs! Go y'all!"

As John Hannah wound down the ACE panel's activity, and dealt with the Big Ten investigation of his own athletic program, various university presidents not on the panel wrote to the ACE expressing their disappointment at "the seeming reversal of attitude . . . in turning back the policing of [intercollegiate] athletics to the NCAA. It has been the failure of that body to adequately police athletics that has caused, in large part, the present abuses."

In appointing the Michigan State president to chair its panel, the ACE had not only given him too much power—including the ability to demolish the wall between the ACE and the NCAA—but had tied the committee's fate to his. As the Spartan Foundation scandal grew, the reputation of John Hannah and the ACE panel sank. Then the Big Ten placed Michigan State on probation, giving it a year "to put its house in order or face" serious consequences. And, ironically, in one of its first infraction cases, the NCAA handed MSU a similar sentence. Apparently the Big Ten and the NCAA not only wanted to embarrass Hannah, but also to drive a stake through the heart of ACE reform. John Hannah should have heeded the axiom, "If you swim with sharks, don't bleed."

Nonetheless, as the MSU president well knew, Big Ten and NCAA probations were mild compared to what could have occurred if the North Central Accrediting Agency had investigated his athletic program. Hannah did curtail the Spartan Foundation's most overt abuses, but, according to Walter Byers, MSU never really cleaned up its athletic act, and subsequently it came "back for major encores" of investigations and penalties. In addition, it spun off coaches from its 1950s football program who cheated at other schools.

In late 1952, *Sport* magazine wrote an epitaph to the whole sorry ACE-Hannah episode: "The [ACE] recommendations never gained wide acceptance and Dr. Hannah's vigorous role in the movement was a source of embarrassment" to the reformers. Many college officials "who couldn't reconcile the Spartans' brilliant [football] record with the aims of the council said, 'Why doesn't Dr. Hannah start practicing what he preaches?' " In a sense, he did: he preached athletic bootstrapping, and he practiced it to an almost infinite degree, even to sabotaging a major attempt to curtail its potency and the power of big-time college sports.

■　■　■

> The reformers have punted on third down and gone on the defense. The Big Ten is liberalizing its scholarship program to give more assistance to athletes. The bomb to de-emphasize bowl games proved to be a dud. A good financial time is being had by all participants in the New Year's Day spectacles, not to mention the conference brethren who share the spoils . . . Only in the East have new stringencies been imposed with the organization of the Ivy group.
>
> —*Saturday Evening Post* writer Fred Russell,
> September 1953.

While still in Cincinnati in 1952, NCAA leaders had started to defuse the bowl-game "bomb" by stating that, even if the membership wanted a ban, no prohibition on bowls could begin before "existing commitments with the bowl committees have been fulfilled." Then, in late 1952, the association's Extra Events Committee extended the certification of nine New Year's events through 1954, including the Salad Bowl and the Refrigerator Bowl. Therefore, the NCAA could "study" a possible ban in perpetuity, while always having to honor the "existing commitments."

The standard bowl contract now gave 75 percent of the admission and media revenue to the participating schools and/or conferences; this greatly pleased most association members, as did NCAA approval of spring football practice. In addition, a majority of conferences now endorsed athletic scholarships, and even the Big Ten, long preferring its "job plan" payments to athletes, began to reconsider the issue of direct grants to jocks.

Most significant of all for many NCAA schools, the accrediting agencies turned away from intercollegiate athletics. The inaction of John Hannah and his ACE panel on this enforcement plan caused four of the agencies to depart the field in 1952. Then, according to the *Saturday Evening Post*, the aggressive North Central, confronting maximum hostility from Big Ten presidents, "back-pedaled" away from college sports. All of "which suits the NCAA just fine. It wants to retain . . . this [enforcement] function" for itself. And, that year, the outrageous Kentucky and Bradley basketball fixes finally caught the NCAA's attention, and it decided to investigate and penalize the schools.

■   ■   ■

During the crisis of the early 1950s, the worst in the history of intercollegiate athletics, NCAA leaders discovered an important device for their damage-control strategy: the appearance of reform—loud proclamations accompanied by minor alterations to the rules, as well as enforcement of those regulations—convinced much of the media and the public that the NCAA was the agent of reform in college sports. This ploy also helped the NCAA destroy the ACE's authentically reformist initiative, the most serious campaign to transform big-time college sports ever mounted.

An economist later remarked that in this formative period of the modern NCAA, the association's new rules always "purported to preserve amateurism," but, in fact, they mainly increased the NCAA's cartel domination of intercollegiate athletics. This was most evident in the association's move into the televising of college football, and its closing down of all competition, notably the first Fighting Irish TV network—a power play that was accompanied by maximum NCAA rhetoric on the preservation of traditional college sports ideals.

On the television issue, Notre Dame battled the NCAA tenaciously for a number of years. In retrospect, it is clear that even though the Irish lost this war, their arguments further exposed the true nature of the NCAA and foreshadowed the association's dominant but dubious role in modern college sports.

39

The NCAA Battles
Notre Dame on TV Rights:
Opening Round

Notre Dame started live television of home football games in 1947 . . .
Our home football games during each of the years that the games were
televised [1947 through 1949] . . . have been sell-outs with the exception of two games [that almost sold out] . . .

We think it would be unwise [for the NCAA] to move too quickly
or prematurely against television, before it has been given an adequate test. According to the television people, it is still in its infancy.
After all, the appeal of football and sport generally is to the public,
and [NCAA] legislation if taken against commonly accepted public
opinion, might hurt the whole game and the general sports' attendance more than it would benefit it.

—Notre Dame executive vice president Theodore Hesburgh,
December 1949.

Father Hesburgh offered his analysis of the TV situation in response to
questions from a news reporter. As he noted, his university started televising its home games very early in the medium's history, and had no problems with home attendance. However, some other schools claimed a drop in
their football gate receipts, their main source of athletic program revenue,
when they invited in the TV cameras and/or when fans in their areas could
watch more attractive college matchups on TV, particularly Fighting Irish
games. At the January 1950 NCAA convention, the delegates formally asked
the association to examine these issues and possibly draft legislation to control the current laissez-faire market.

In his statement on TV, Hesburgh added an analogy with radio. Colleges
had faced the football attendance question during the early years of that

medium and, in 1934, "the Eastern Conference decided to prohibit live radio broadcasts of [its] football games." This ban had no effect on game attendance, but it provoked complaints from angry radio listeners, thus the schools involved "hurt themselves by such action." Moose Krause described the episode more pungently: "We can look back now with amazement" at this radio ban. "It obviously served no point at all."

During the 1950s debate on the televising of college sports, Notre Dame officials frequently invoked the radio precedent, not only the failed prohibition but also the fact that their school had benefited greatly from its open-door radio policy. In the 1930s, ND permitted all stations and networks to broadcast its games for free, and in the 1940s it still kept the door wide open but began to charge minimal rates. Schools and conferences with restrictive radio policies and/or high rates did not gain the national fame of the Fighting Irish or satisfy their alumni and fans as ND did. For Notre Dame administrators, the university's radio policy led naturally into its television strategy. In 1950, Father John Murphy stated that "our decision to televise our football games over as wide a network as possible" was prompted "by our wish to please as many of our followers throughout the country as possible," as well as to alleviate the huge demand for tickets to Notre Dame Stadium games: many people who cannot buy them for "our home games" can now watch the contests on TV.

In this period, Notre Dame also allowed the TV newsreel companies to film its games for minimal fees, and movie companies, like Paramount News and Movietone, to shoot for free. In its contracts with the latter group, however, it stipulated that they could only use the game film in their movie theater newsreels, and they could not resell it to TV. Very early in their dealings with the television industry, ND officials had sensed the new medium's potential, and they treated it warily.

From 1947 through 1949, for entire seasons of home game telecasts, the school received low, then high, five-figure sums from various TV companies. For 1950, the television revenue jumped to $160,000, yet, in the contract negotiations for that season, Notre Dame rejected the highest bids, from NBC and ABC, and instead selected the Dumont Network, mainly because of its willingness to air ND educational programs along with the football broadcasts.

> In allowing our games to be televised, we have been able to present sidelight stories on the educational, cultural, and religious aspects of the University of Notre Dame. And, in itself, this latter [procedure] has become a point of far greater importance to those guiding the destinies of Notre Dame than the mere televising of an athletic contest.
>
> —Charlie Callahan for Edward "Moose" Krause,
> September 1950.

Notre Dame officials realized in the late 1940s that television not only had the Midas touch, but the new technology possessed persuasive powers far greater than those of all other communication media. Father Hesburgh believed that TV gave his school a unique opportunity to counter the "football factory" charges sometimes hurled against it, and to stress its academic and religious missions. Moose Krause did not agree with his bosses about selecting the Dumont package over higher money offers, but he put the best face on this situation in a press handout. Subsequently, however, Krause not only bragged that ND had the first television football network—in fact, it shared that distinction with the University of Pennsylvania—but, more accurately, that his school pioneered the educational spots aired during college athletic events. In a 1990s interview, he remarked, "The next time you watch a college game on TV, and a school promo comes on at halftime . . . and you're on your way to the refrigerator or the toilet, remember that we started it all."

During the halftime of a number of Notre Dame games in 1949, at the insistence of the Golden Dome, the TV broadcasters aired live interviews featuring Father Cavanaugh and various ND faculty members. In early 1950, a Dumont executive, in making his company's pitch for the contract with ND, noted, "The very favorable response to the short half-time interviews" last year "indicates that the viewing public may now be ready to accept this [educational] program" on a regular basis, "at least we are willing to try."

Father Hesburgh, in charge of negotiations with Dumont, wanted more than brief interludes of talking heads at halftime, and he requested a twenty-minute pre-game program, consisting mainly of films on "the non-athletic features of the University" of Notre Dame, as well as shorter films of similar material "on the visiting school"—ND's opponent that day. The network not only complied but added ten minutes to the program, announcing its plans in a press release entitled "Dumont Fashions New Type Program as Notre Dame Pre-game Feature." With a text calculated to please the men in the Golden Dome, the network exclaimed, "This program will demonstrate that Notre Dame is more than a college outstanding in football . . . We intend to show the study, worship, and play that add up to the development of a Notre Dame man."

Dumont, however, was the passive partner in the enterprise, merely shooting and airing what the school wanted. First, the ND publicity office generated a number of film synopses, each of them emphasizing different faculty and student aspects of the university, and then the Notre Dame PR people created the shooting scripts.

In one example a "cut to interior [of Science Building], student with test tube" leads to a lab scene with the student and a professor, then the script directs a "dissolve to" a dorm room, where the "exhausted student is joined by three of his buddies. They hold a small bull session." The voice-over narrator intones:

But student life at Notre Dame was never designed to be all study. Equally important are the friendships of the residence halls, and the give-and-take of bull sessions, where every man is an expert.

"There's a strong connection between studying hard and playing hard." Those words of Knute Rockne's explain why sports are the fourth quarter in Notre Dame's concept of the whole man.

The scene ends with a "slow dissolve to [the] bust of Knute Rockne" on the Notre Dame campus.

Significantly, Dumont and Notre Dame did not try to portray the school as something it was not, for instance, a high-powered academic institution like the University of Chicago. Instead the Dumont films invoked the traditional college sports ideals, and their great exemplar, Knute Rockne, chemist and athletic figure. This approach reaffirmed the school's self-image and its public image as portrayed in *Knute Rockne—All-American*.

But before Fighting Irish football had even aired in 1950, Notre Dame encountered hostility from a more powerful opponent. When Dumont assembled its Notre Dame network of forty-three stations based mainly in eastern and midwestern cities—Frank Leahy boasted that "83 percent of all the television sets in the country will be tuned in on us"—a number of Big Ten universities became alarmed at the huge potential TV audiences for ND football in their regions. They wanted the conference to address this issue immediately.

■ ■ ■

Mr. Inside (the Mid-Western member of that know-it-all family) sends word that Notre Dame is in the wrong with the other football-playing colleges for . . . [the Dumont] television contract. At a recent Chicago meeting, he says, [Big Ten] schools read the riot act [to ND] and insisted the contract be canceled . . . Incidentally, the chief spokesman against TV was Fritz Crisler [Michigan AD], who can pack 97,000 into Michigan Stadium anyway.

—Associated Press writer Hugh Fullerton Jr., May 1950.

The conference leaders, especially Crisler, claimed that the Notre Dame telecasts would hurt their game attendance as well as that of small colleges in their areas—Big Ten schools had never expressed concern for the latter when expanding their stadiums in the late 1940s and petitioning state governments for better highway access to them. In the *Saturday Evening Post,* Fred Russell commented that the "idea, of course," of ADs like Crisler "is to get" all the college football "dough" for themselves, and their motto is a "cynically paraphrased" version of Grantland Rice's famous stanza: "And when the One

Great Scorer comes/ To write beside your name/ It's not whether you won or lost/ But how many paid to see the game."

In 1950, a large part of the Big Ten frustration with Notre Dame was due to the conference's inability to do anything about the Fighting Irish TV deal. At the NCAA convention that January, the delegates had postponed all actions on the television question until they could study it further; therefore, schools could still act unilaterally in the laissez-faire TV market.

In the spring of 1950, Big Ten commissioner Tug Wilson informed Vice President Hesburgh that the Big Ten wanted "to ban live television for [its own] 1950 football games but realized that the matter should be discussed with . . . other institutions," particularly Notre Dame, in the hope of persuading every school to institute a similar blackout. Wilson also mentioned that recently "my assistant, Mr. Byers, discussed the subject with Mr. Krause" and "requested that Notre Dame attend a meeting" with all the Big Ten athletic directors. A month later when the meeting occurred, the Big Ten "read the riot act" because Notre Dame would not cancel its Dumont deal.

Using the TV-ruins-attendance argument, the conference leaders demanded that Notre Dame forgo its independent course and cooperate with them—the Big Ten had decided to proceed with its TV blackout for the 1950 season. ND officials smelled hypocrisy: at the NCAA convention, the Northwestern AD had stated publicly that his school had "televised for four years," had competed with Fighting Irish telecasts pumped into Chicago, and "I would say definitely it [TV] does not have an effect on our season tickets" or attendance; moreover, "Wisconsin figures it did not affect their season ticket sales," and Ohio State says that "It has not affected them whatsoever." Nor was attendance down at Michigan or the other universities attacking Notre Dame.

Moose Krause saw the Big Ten assault on his school as an obvious power play, and more neutral observers shared this viewpoint. NFL commissioner Bert Bell claimed that "Crisler, Big Ten commissioner Tug Wilson, and others were afraid that Notre Dame would monopolize TV . . . [and] get the receipts, and deprive some of those selfish men (Crisler et al.) of trying to control the situation." After Notre Dame's rejection of the 1950 TV ban, the Big Ten men decided to work directly through the NCAA—Wilson and Byers were key leaders in the association—to nullify the Fighting Irish TV network.

■   ■   ■

When we [the NCAA] finally left the [Madison Square] Garden in the early 1950s, *it had nothing to do with the gambling scandals there.* The main reason was the rental charge [for the NCAA basketball championship tournament]. It was very high. We figured we could make more money on campuses. Schools would usually give us the gym for cost. It was more profitable to go to campuses at that time.

—NCAA official Arthur C. "Dutch" Lonborg, 1979.

Through the postwar years, dollars, not ethics, shaped almost all NCAA decisions; the association's obsession with profit and growth rendered other considerations secondary, even the Garden fix scandals that almost ruined college basketball. Thus, in constructing their first television plan, the NCAA leaders never raised their eyes from the ledger sheet. Moreover, they defined their revenue stream very narrowly—mainly gate receipts—and refused to envision different financial strategies for the new TV era.

In the discussions about TV at NCAA conventions during these years, Michigan AD Fritz Crisler always acknowledged the leadership's preoccupation with money. He knew all the pro-TV arguments, including Father Hesburgh's "public service" one—that the more that Americans watch college sports on TV, "the wider support we [universities] should get" for all "our programs," academic as well as athletic. But Crisler's standard response won delegates' applause: "I appreciate the public service aspect. However," after television has destroyed football attendance, "I don't believe that our stadiums full of [mainly] good will and public service on five or six afternoons in the fall will help us a bit on our [athletic department] budget."

The first direct NCAA attack on ND's television contract came at the association's 1951 convention. Crisler announced that the Big Ten would continue its TV blackout for the coming season, and he urged all NCAA member schools and conferences to do the same. To support this position, association leaders cited the results of a survey commissioned by the NCAA the previous year.

The National Opinion Research Center (NORC) claimed that, from peak years in 1947 and 1948 to 1950, football attendance had declined by 4.2 percent in areas with competing games on television, and this decrease translated into almost 500,000 fewer fans for the 1950 season. NORC then offered a highly questionable conclusion: "If there had been no televised games in 1950 . . . attendance at college games would have been 40 percent higher," which translated into 1.4 million more fans, "than it actually was." (NORC calculated its projection from the 1947–48 high, ignoring all other factors.) One commentator remarked that, after hearing the NORC report, "the stunned delegates voted overwhelmingly for a moratorium on the wholesale telecasts of football games in the 1951 season," and also gave the association the power to enforce the suspension. Previous NCAA success at bowl game regulation had prepared the way for the 1951 resolution on TV, but the leadership's arguments and its strategic use of the NORC survey ensured the 161 to 7 vote, with Notre Dame in the lonely minority.

An economic historian noted that "this resolution gave the NCAA more power to limit competition between the producers [the schools] in the intercollegiate athletic industry than it had ever before enjoyed in its 45-year history," instantly augmenting the association's cartel status. Furthermore, the NCAA television monopoly helped the leadership extend cartel rules into all other aspects of college sports, leading to the association's dominant role in intercollegiate athletics.

If carefully analyzed, however, the NCAA's anti-TV position and the NORC reports appear bogus. The open television market was, at most, a minor cause of the decline in football attendance; much more important factors, including some exacerbated by the NCAA itself, created the slide. An examination of the situation reveals how the NCAA leaders manipulated the NORC numbers for their own ends and, in the process, annihilated their opponents' legitimate arguments and rights.

College football crowds did decline at the end of the 1940s and into the 1950s, but so did attendance at major league baseball games and most other sporting events. One writer termed it "the Great Sports Slump," attributing it to "a revolution in the ways that Americans had begun to spend their spare time . . . a shift from public forms of recreation to private, home-centered forms . . . [an] increased privatization of leisure." Prompting this shift was the movement of millions of middle-class Americans to suburbia and their involvement in such new forms of weekend activity as boating, golfing, and barbecuing, as well as their decreasing interest in traveling to stadiums and sitting through long sporting events. In its TV policy, the NCAA never considered this crucial social change, which was occurring all around it.

In addition, the NCAA/NORC baseline for football attendance, 1947–48, marked the postwar period's economic high point: consumer demand, pent up during the war, peaked during these years. In 1949, an economic dip began, and by 1950 many businesses were suffering, especially those dependent on discretionary spending, like spectator sports.

Finally, by 1950, with the last of the World War II veterans having passed through the university system—in 1947–48 more than one million attended college—student enrollment dropped significantly. This caused a major slide in football attendance, primarily because most students received free tickets to all home games, as did their families. (NORC only measured attendance, not gate receipts.) Furthermore, in 1950, with the Korean War intensifying and the Selective Service drafting many male students, the campus population sank to an artificial low. The NCAA always ignored these demographic factors; therefore, a few years later, when football attendance increased with the end of the Korean War and a new influx of vets on campuses as well as a return to regular male enrollment, the association attributed the growth solely to its restrictive TV policy!

One other major factor contributed to the decrease in football attendance: corruption in college sports. Most NCAA members refused to recognize that the scandals provoked public anger and a decline in popular support, including at the box office. In addition, they would never acknowledge that Notre

Dame's excellent gate receipts *and* TV ratings resulted, in part, from the school's distance from the scandals.

■   ■   ■

> In this situation, the chief comment to be heard from college and university officials is "hush-hush." Trustees, presidents and faculties are so busy looking innocent or embarrassed that they are fumbling the ball in a championship game [including on the TV front].

—Amherst professor Albert E. Lumley, spring 1952.

In the early 1950s, in the lengthy NCAA discussions on TV policy, very rarely did a speaker mention the effect of the basketball and football scandals upon game attendance. Averting their eyes from this obvious reality and its implications for the future of college sports allowed NCAA officials and most member schools to hug their TV-ruins-attendance security blanket. This separation of corruption and attendance was obviously false: fans did not erect a similar barrier when they discussed the current state of college sports, when they expressed their feelings about their favorite teams, particularly if tainted by scandal, and when they considered whether or not to attend games.

Because so many Americans cherished intercollegiate athletics for its traditional ideals, which were so violated by the scandals, apparently many people temporarily turned away from college sports in this period. Neither NORC nor any other research group ever surveyed public opinion on this question. However, by tracking the media condemnations of intercollegiate athletics, and assuming that they created a negative climate for college sports products, including game tickets, the commonsense conclusion is that the scandals hurt attendance (how much and/or for how long is impossible to quantify). Ironically, the NCAA, by severely limiting television coverage and its positive portrayals of college sports, diminished a powerful source of counterpropaganda, one that could have tempered public disapproval and probably lessened the attendance slide. (At this time, however, Walter Byers did craft a "positive" PR print campaign for the NCAA, stressing the classic ideals of college sports; see Chapters 45 and 46.)

The NCAA's separation of scandals and attendance resulted from its leadership's realization that to acknowledge any connection between the two would hurt its case for TV restrictions, and also aid the advocates of systemic reform. If the association openly admitted that the corruption threatened attendance, the lifeblood of college sports, then the NCAA's main reaction to the scandals—damage control and cosmetic surgery—would appear insufficient. However, neither the leaders nor most members wanted meaningful reform, so they found it easier to ignore the scandals-hurt-attendance factor and blame the drop solely on television.

The NCAA also disregarded all evidence contrary to its position, even when directly confronted by it. Up to the 1951 convention, the TV-and-attendance experiences of a number of universities contradicted the association's case. Not only had Notre Dame sold out almost all home games from 1946 on, but crowds increased at the University of Pennsylvania, another school that televised every home contest during these years. Moreover, in the late 1940s, more television sets existed in the Philadelphia area than in almost any other part of the country, and viewers could watch as many as five games on some Saturdays. The articulate Penn AD, Francis Murray, frequently attacked the association's TV arguments and the NORC findings, but he could only persuade a handful of schools to side with Penn and Notre Dame against the leadership's television policy. The 1951 NCAA resolution on TV and the resulting 161–7 vote illustrated his isolation.

> Whereas, there is positive evidence that live television broadcasts have an adverse effect on attendance at college football games and,
>
> Whereas, the future growth and further expansion of the television industry indicate that this adverse effect on attendance will become increasingly great, and . . .
>
> Whereas loss of football gate receipts from [the] drop in attendance threatens the economic structure of college athletics . . .
>
> It is resolved that the members of the NCAA agree to declare a moratorium on live telecasting of college football games for 1951.
>
> —NCAA television committee chair Thomas Hamilton,
> January 1951.

In arguing against this resolution, Father Hesburgh criticized the delegates for their old "habits" of financial thinking, their concept of "full stadiums . . . [as] the only way we can support our [athletic] programs." Because "we are living . . . in a new world, [with] new communication problems, new cultural problems," the old formulas no longer applied. He urged every school to explore this new reality, including the ways that television could help them gain greater public support for all of their activities, and not to step backward into a TV blackout. But the delegates voted overwhelmingly for the draconian television resolution, agreeing with the NCAA's "old mode" argument: if fans could not see games on TV for free, they would flock to the stadiums and buy tickets. Attendance, however, continued to decline in 1951, non-TV factors prevailing.

The press and most of the universities voting on the resolution did not see it as a historic event, one that would subsequently empower the NCAA beyond its leaders' fondest wishes. The *Chicago Tribune* remarked that the "television vote merely is a recommendation. Individual universities cannot be bound by this decision," subheading this item "No Penalty Possible." Its reporter also asked Moose Krause for his reaction to the resolution; the ND athletic director replied that officials of his university will decide "whether Notre Dame will continue television" for its home games.

In the past, Notre Dame had cooperated with all NCAA resolutions; in fact, its own athletic policies were far more stringent than the association's, and it had never experienced a problem with the NCAA's control of bowl games because it refused to play in them. However, the moratorium on television for 1951 seemed specifically aimed at Notre Dame and Penn, and before agreeing to it, ND officials decided to explore their options. Father Hesburgh had warned the 1951 convention, "We realize that . . . we can't merely think of ourselves. We don't want to, but we also do not want to commit ourselves . . . to an [NCAA] action that is taken hastily or perhaps not advisedly."

Soon after the 1951 meeting, Notre Dame president Cavanaugh went to New York to discuss the moratorium with television executives. One advised him "that Notre Dame should endeavor to get a three-year contract for televising as many of its games as possible on a network. Such a contract should establish a good price for the 1951 season, with 1952 and 1953 to be negotiated based on [new] sets installed and new markets opened," no doubt resulting in higher payments for ND football. Other network executives liked this idea, and, informally, they began the bidding process for the Fighting Irish television package. Moose Krause later told the International News Service that the high bid was "$600,000" for 1951; in addition, for 1952, "I would estimate" that ND would receive "$1,000,000," and "probably an even greater" amount for 1953.

As with the previous contract, Father Cavanaugh stressed the inclusion of non-football material "illustrative of the educational nature of the schools" participating in the televised games—moreover, from now on, the educational programs "should be continued on a year-long basis. I would make this so definite that any commitments to televise our football games, which are a great attraction, would be conditioned upon the willingness of the network to carry [the] educational projects . . . throughout the year."

At this time in early 1951, Cavanaugh also launched his college sports reform campaign, and he mentioned his ideas on educational programming in his letters to university presidents. The confluence of these two major ventures—the ND television contract and the reform initiative—persuaded the Notre Dame president to place formal TV negotiations on hold and to abide by the NCAA moratorium for the present. Moose Krause later commented, "Father told me that the NCAA might even go out of business if the scandals got worse, so he didn't see any point in fighting them head-on about their television blackout . . . But when their committee came out with its Game of the Week plan, he had more than second thoughts."

■   ■   ■

The constitution of the NCAA in no way provides, as far as we see, that the NCAA should act as an agent for any individual school either in the scheduling of games or in the coverage of these games by radio, television, or any other means of communication.

—Notre Dame president John J. Cavanaugh, May 1951.

As part of the NCAA's 1951 TV resolution, the association had empowered its Television Committee to shape and supervise a plan for the coming season; most delegates expected the committee's members to endorse a total blackout. In the spring of 1951, the committee surprised Notre Dame and other schools by approving "a program of limited telecasting" of one game for most fall Saturdays, with the committee to negotiate and administer the contract. According to an NCAA spokesman, the committee realized that "a complete ban on television likely would encounter great public displeasure, while a return to totally unrestricted television would continue and probably accelerate the decline in attendance." Therefore, it decided upon a middle course of "limited telecasting."

Behind this propaganda facade stood the 1951 reality of increasing public anger at the proposed blackout and the possibility of state and even federal action to nullify it, as well as the desire of NCAA leaders to establish the association's control of TV revenue from college sports. To meet these demands, according to football historian Beano Cook, the committee allowed the Game of the Week but was determined "to keep Notre Dame off the tube every Saturday. They limited the number of exposures" of the Fighting Irish to as few as possible.

An economist equated this action to a rigged "division of the marketplace, and a limit on competition that is part of cartel" behavior. Hence, the flattening of those schools with previous success in the open marketplace, especially Notre Dame and Penn, so that others could succeed: the cartel helped the large number of weak members at the expense of the strong few. Additionally, to ensure that *all* members followed the cartel rules, the NCAA Council—controlled by the leadership, like the TV Committee—recommended that any institution violating the new television policy be branded "a member not in good standing" and, if the violations continued, be expelled from the association. In a mail vote, a large majority—with NCAA bowl game regulation as a precedent, and hoping for similar benefits from the "limited TV" plan—approved the penalties.

. . .

Father Cavanaugh, in his comment on the NCAA constitution and in other statements, protested this sudden turn in the association's TV policy. The president of the University of Pennsylvania, Harold Stassen, condemned the NCAA's plan in much stronger terms, and also began accepting bids from the networks on a TV contract for all of Penn's 1951 home games. The television industry sided with Notre Dame and Penn. Most companies wanted an open market, believing that laissez-faire would benefit them more than would NCAA cartel control of limited telecasting. In May 1951, *Billboard* magazine reported that legal "counsel for the webs [networks] have completed an exhaustive study" of the situation, concluding that "any network and schools joining in such a scheme" as the NCAA's, "would violate the Sherman and Clayton anti-trust laws."

Penn then signed a TV contract for 1951. Pressure on Notre Dame to sign and countervailing pressure to adhere to the NCAA TV policy increased. In mid-June, Fred Steers, an ND alumnus close to the school's administrators, wrote Vice President Hesburgh about a recent phone call from Tug Wilson during which the Big Ten/NCAA official remarked that "it would be difficult for schools which did not abide by the [NCAA] television edict to schedule games [against other NCAA members]. Whether all of this was in the form of a veiled threat to be carried back to you" at Notre Dame, "I do not know," but Steers passed on "this information for what it is worth."

For Notre Dame officials at this time, threats from Tug Wilson, covert or real, counted for less than did other matters. The American Council on Education had become interested in Father Cavanaugh's reform proposal. The ND president considered this endeavor more important than the TV question, therefore he postponed the decision on whether to defy the NCAA's television policy until the ACE's plans became clearer. In addition, as the scandals continued to unfold in 1951, many observers, including Father Cavanaugh to some extent, believed that the NCAA had entered a terminal stage, rendering all of its actions moot.

This judgment proved incorrect: even though the association could not control—indeed, contributed to—the corruption in college sports, it could move effectively, and with the consent of most members, when in a cartel mode. Soon after the University of Pennsylvania began implementing its 1951 TV contract, the NCAA Council declared it "a member not in good standing" and threatened to act similarly against any institution that allowed its football team to play on TV against the Quakers in 1951. Four Ivy League schools then told Harold Stassen that they would cancel their fall games in Philadelphia if Penn insisted on violating the NCAA TV policy. Reluctantly, Pennsylvania backed down, voiding its television contract.

For the first time in NCAA history, the association had forced a recalcitrant university to do its bidding. From this important incident, as well as the death of the "Sanity Code" a half year previously, NCAA leaders learned a crucial lesson, one that they and future association directors would obey: when dealing with cartel money matters, most members would support strong actions, but on questions of meaningful reform, the majority wanted damage control, not change—thus the failed expulsion of the so-called "Seven Sinners" in 1950.

∎   ∎   ∎

> This year [1951], we had nothing whatsoever to say about the televising of the [Notre Dame] football games. Under the experimental television plan of the NCAA, we are permitted to televise only one home game and one away-from-home game . . . the matter is completely out of our control.
>
> —ND president John J. Cavanaugh, September 1951.

In the summer of 1951, after his appointment to the ACE panel, Notre Dame president Cavanaugh decided to avoid a Penn-like public dispute with the NCAA and go along with what he regarded as the association's "one-year TV experiment." Also during that summer, the NCAA Television Committee refined its fall plan, arriving at a hodgepodge system of three national games for the entire season and regional contests on other Saturdays. Not only did the narrow schedule spark fan protests but the blackouts of many important games prompted reactions more dangerous for the NCAA, including the threat of government intervention.

Notre Dame rooters, after years of watching many Fighting Irish contests, were furious at the meager NCAA TV ration: an October national telecast and a November regional game. As the 1951 season continued, many non-ND fans joined in the demand for more national telecasts featuring the Fighting Irish, particularly for their November visit to Number One–ranked Michigan State. The NCAA TV Committee had scheduled a regional broadcast of this game for some parts of the East; midwestern fans yelled loudly to see it, and yelled even louder after MSU sold out Spartan Stadium, invalidating the NCAA's TV-ruins-attendance premise for the blackout.

Politicians responded to the public outcry, including GOP congressional leader and future president Gerald Ford of Michigan, who criticized the NCAA blackout as "extremely arbitrary . . . an inflexible program" that "inevitably will lead to state or federal legislation." A few days before the ND-MSU contest, *Washington Post* columnist Shirley Povich advised readers that on Saturday, even though no D.C. college team played at home that day, government officials and all other local residents "can spin their video dials until their knuckles moan," and they still will not find the ND-MSU game because the NCAA had blacked out the District of Columbia. In addition, to "expose" their own "dunderhead thinking," the NCAA would allow the ND-MSU tele-cast in Baltimore even though two local teams, Navy and Maryland, played in the city or nearby that afternoon! Finally, Povich called for the U.S. Department of Justice to investigate the NCAA and its probable violation of the antitrust laws.

Lo and behold, the very next day the NCAA lifted the blackouts in Michigan and the District of Columbia, and those viewers and many others saw Michigan State crush Notre Dame, 35-0, the work of the Spartan Foundation paying off on the playing field. The NCAA's "naked reverse" indicated how much the association wanted to avoid government scrutiny of and possible legislation against its cartel behavior. Fortunately for the NCAA at this time, its television policy did not interest the Justice Department, and during the next few years association leaders learned how to cool congressional hostility with the judicious removal of blackouts as well as the placement of bowl games and basketball tournaments in the home districts of key legislators.

For the MSU-ND game, possibly to anger Fighting Irish rooters, the NCAA blacked out the South Bend area. Father Hesburgh mentioned this to a friend, adding that the ban is "for no good reason as we have no other games" at local colleges "to compete with" the match on television.

Other elements of the NCAA's 1951 TV policy annoyed Notre Dame officials. Not only had the Big Ten rescinded its planned conference blackout for that season, but its members appeared on television more often than did the schools of any other group. ND administrators sensed a large amount of Big Ten hypocrisy and manipulation in the 1951 TV plan: Notre Dame, instead of a probable $600,000 in television revenue for that year from its own TV network, ended up with less than a tenth of that amount from the NCAA's deal, whereas Big Ten universities jumped from an expected $0 to more than $200,000 in TV money while their attendance remained high.

Also displeasing to Notre Dame officials but apparently of no concern to the NCAA hierarchy was the failure of the network (NBC) to include educational programming in the football telecasts. Only advertisements for the sole sponsor of the TV package, Westinghouse Corporation, appeared. Considering the NCAA's cartel leverage on the contract, it could have ordered the educational promos; however, "instead of the films on the academic parts of the universities," as Moose Krause later remarked, "all you got was some woman named Betty [Furness] waving at the shelves of a refrigerator . . . and lots of cartoons of dancing light bulbs."

■ ■ ■

In his letter about the South Bend blackout for the ND-MSU game, Father Hesburgh also remarked, "The real fight in this [TV] problem will come in January at the annual [NCAA] meeting. Our immediate problem is to get a good lawyer to draw up a brief on the case, and I am currently engaged in seeking one out. We want the top man in the country." Notre Dame planned to present this brief at the 1952 convention to convince the membership of the illegality of the TV plan and the necessity of terminating it. But if the delegates refused to act, ND did not rule out a court challenge.

During the fall of 1951, the University of Pennsylvania embarked upon a similar course of action. Its athletic director informed the press that it would present its own legal brief to the NCAA convention, including its contention that "NCAA and the ECAC [Eastern College Athletic Conference] face possible anti-trust suits" if they continue their unfair and restrictive television practices. In addition, the Penn AD asserted that "centralized national control" by an association such as the NCAA "is contrary to the basic principles of free institutions" and, in the case of the TV policy, it clearly violates the rights of its members.

In the long run, the allegations by Penn and Notre Dame against the NCAA proved correct, and years later a number of federal courts, including the United States Supreme Court in a 7-1 vote, supported them. However, in the charged atmosphere of the 1952 NCAA convention—when the association, with the help of John Hannah, hijacked the ACE reform proposal—rational legal arguments counted for little. More important to the NCAA leaders and most delegates was the codification of the TV plan and steamrolling over Penn's and Notre Dame's objections to it.

40

The NCAA Battles Notre Dame
on TV Rights: TKO

Whenever a group of producers colludes to form decisions collectively, one of the first problems to emerge centers on income distribution . . .

Without the NCAA's limitations, Pennsylvania and Notre Dame attracted generous television contracts. With the NCAA limitations, the Pennsylvania and Notre Dame revenues were, in effect, redistributed to those other schools that appeared on the NCAA's weekly telecast. Furthermore, under the NCAA's decision-making rule, the two schools could do little about it. Because a majority of NCAA schools stood to gain from the television policy, Penn and Notre Dame found themselves constantly outvoted on questions of television policy.

—Economic historian Paul Lawrence, 1987.

After losing yet another NCAA convention vote on TV policy in the early 1950s, Moose Krause described the NCAA actions more succinctly than could any economist: "The NCAA started as an advisory body, then became a regulatory body, and now has become a confiscatory one." The association attained its financial dominance of college sports at the 1952 and 1953 conventions, mainly by appealing to the delegates' fear and greed.

As members gathered in Cincinnati in January 1952, NCAA leaders issued the latest NORC report, weaving its conclusions into the opening clauses of their new resolution on television policy: because "the NCAA plan of restricted television in 1951 substantially reduced the adverse effects upon attendance at college football games," be it resolved that the association continue and strengthen the policy. In reality, 1951 attendance had dropped 6 percent from the 1947–48 high—as opposed to a decline the previous year, with laissez-faire TV, of 4.5 percent—and the NCAA TV plan had in no way stopped the slide. However, the association's leaders refused to admit this, and, by juggling NORC numbers, they claimed that a statistically projected drop from 1947–48 would have been *worse* than 6 percent, thus the policy had "reduced the adverse effects."

George Orwell's popular book of this period, *1984,* described similar rewritings of history, and suggested that mental laziness and misguided self-interest caused a majority of people to believe the altered versions of reality concocted by the authorities. The NCAA world of the early 1950s possessed an Orwellian quality, not only in the way the members swallowed the ever malleable NORC numbers but also in their acceptance of the leaders' arguments on the legality of the TV monopoly.

According to the *New York Times,* at the 1952 convention session on television policy, Penn AD Francis Murray quoted an assistant United States attorney as recently declaring, "Any agreement that restricts the sale of television or broadcast rights by group action and takes away the individual right of choice" of a group member "is illegal," and this antitrust regulation "would apply to non-profit organizations such as colleges." However, when asked to respond to this statement, Joseph Rauh, "legal counsel of the NCAA Television Committee, refused to be concerned by this opinion" and dismissed it, to the approval of the delegates.

Murray persisted in listing the Sherman and Clayton antitrust violations in the NCAA's TV policy, but Rauh and Professor Ralph Aigler of the University of Michigan Law School continued to swat the Penn arguments aside. Aigler, a longtime Big Ten and NCAA leader, added that he had "no hesitancy in saying to the NCAA, as my client, 'You are not running any great risk in going ahead' " with the TV plan.

With these assurances as background, Murray thought that he saw an opening. When the NCAA resolution on the 1952 TV plan reached the floor of the convention, he introduced a simple amendment "aimed at ending all questions as to the legality" of the NCAA's TV policy. He proposed that the Television Committee "petition the Justice Department for a decision at once as to the legality" of the policy. American businesses did this frequently, not only for short-term answers but for long-term protection against potential lawsuits, and the Penn AD appealed to the delegates' common sense in this matter: if the NCAA went ahead with its television monopoly and subsequently lost a court challenge, particularly to a TV network plaintiff, a devastating settlement could cost the members a fortune.

Murray's amendment made perfect sense and should have won unanimous approval. If the opinions of the NCAA's legal counselors were correct, delegates had nothing to fear from petitioning the Justice Department; if, on the other hand, the TV plan were deemed illegal, members would have learned a most valuable fact. Nevertheless, when put to a vote, as the *New York Times* reported, "The amendment was beaten overwhelmingly, and Murray knew then and there that his cause was too." Fairness and even common sense had no place in the NCAA at this time. A herd mentality then carried the delegates to a vote of 163–8 on the main resolution, with Penn and Notre Dame in the minority.

■ ■ ■

First honest bit of work I've been asked to do all week was check the NCAA Television Committee meeting. Took a long, warm walk to the Biltmore [Hotel] and couldn't even find the bastards. Not in the room where they were supposed to meet and no sign of them anywhere else. When they do come out with a statement, I think I'll refuse to mention their names.

—Associated Press writer Hugh Fullerton Jr.
to Charlie Callahan, April 1952.

The NCAA 1952 convention directed the Television Committee to design and administer a TV plan for the coming football season. Key members of the committee were the association's newly promoted executive director, Walter Byers, and Eastern Conference commissioner Asa Bushnell—a duo that retained an almost absolute control over NCAA TV policy for the next two decades. Byers was renowned for his secretiveness—which possibly explains why Hugh Fullerton could not find the committee meeting in April 1952—and for his cunning. His ally, Bushnell, headed a group composed mainly of small schools, and he relentlessly championed their concerns.

The final 1952 television plan called for a national game every week, as well as weekly "games of regional interest" featuring small colleges—a step that included these schools in the TV money. Most importantly, the TV Committee ruled that a school "may appear on television only once per season," and, after it released the 1952 schedule, many observers interpreted this restriction as anti–Notre Dame and pro–Big Ten: the committee gave the Irish one appearance, and granted six Big Ten schools national TV exposure (the conference still endorsed the line that TV ruins attendance). Byers and Bushnell justified the "one appearance" rule as a means to spread the wealth—NBC and the sole sponsor, General Motors, paid $1,144,000 for the package—and the NCAA did funnel a substantial amount to the small colleges appearing on TV, but the largest percentage went to Big Ten coffers.

When Notre Dame saw the plan, President Cavanaugh protested to Byers. Rather than attack the "one appearance rule" head-on, the ND official indicated that the TV package "seems to put a premium on mediocrity and cast suspicions on success." In other words, in the committee's attempt to please a large number of schools by scheduling them for TV—whether they had good football teams or not—it restricted successful and well-run football programs like Notre Dame's to one appearance. Moreover, this plan, like its predecessor, would prompt a "very negative . . . public reaction. We see no point in unnecessarily antagonizing the public, especially when the case for restricted television . . . in the opinion of many, is illegal."

This last point related to the most important paragraph in the letter: "On the advice of legal counsel, our conviction is that the plan is illegal and unfairly restricts an institution's right to televise." The ND president did not explicitly state that his university would sue the NCAA, but he implied that it retained that option. More, what was moving Notre Dame toward the courts, in Cavanaugh's words, was the Television Committee's "startling proposal for the future that all proceeds from television should be shared by [all] member colleges." Up to and including the 1952 plan, the schools with games on television split the total revenue according to the number of their appearances, with the NCAA also taking a share. The Television Committee now proposed that, after the coming season, all members of the association share the TV revenue equally, regardless of whether their teams appeared on television or not.

Father Cavanaugh told Byers, "Such a proposal is socialistic in nature and hardly to be expected of an official committee of the NCAA." Not surprisingly, some Big Ten universities, even though pleased with the 1952 schedule, also disliked this sweeping share-the-wealth concept and complained. Byers, however, pushed the proposal more for personal than altruistic reasons. With this plan, he saw a way to depart from his Big Ten patrons Tug Wilson and Fritz Crisler (knowing that if he stayed with them, he would always remain under their thumbs), and to build his own power base upon the bloc of small colleges. That group, numerically large and very important under the NCAA's one-school-one-vote constitution, would benefit most from NCAA "socialism," and Byers, with the endorsement of Bushnell and his ECAC, courted the small colleges with visions of TV sugarplums for all.

■   ■   ■

In a press report last week, Bushnell and Hall [another TV committee member] said that I was too "excited" [about the TV-revenue-sharing proposal]. My reply to them is, yes, I am excited.

Wouldn't you be excited if someone tried to come into your home and steal your furniture? I'll remain excited as long as they try to infringe on the private rights of our institution. I say the plan is illegal, immoral, un-American, and socialistic.

—Notre Dame AD Edward "Moose" Krause, October 1952.

During the fall of 1952, when the NCAA Television Committee began serious campaigning for its share-the-wealth plan, Notre Dame officials became alarmed. Moose Krause led the counterattack, sometimes escalating his rhetoric to "Our stand is that it is Communistic," as if hoping that the Cold War language would persuade other schools to help Notre Dame kill the plan before the 1953 convention.

Krause also criticized the fall TV schedule, which confined the Fighting Irish to a single appearance and a small payout ($50,000), and he mocked the NCAA's disregard of the academic promo spots: "We spent that much money showing the public the advantages of higher education during our TV program two years ago. All this year's program did was sell automobiles and try to sell the NCAA's policy to the public." (Walter Byers used his keen PR sense to promote his group's policies, not higher education, and he would only include the latter in NCAA halftime spots a few years later, after his association had gained secure command of college sports.)

Beyond Moose Krause's jibes was a serious complaint, which stemmed from his many years at Notre Dame as well as that school's unique history. For Krause, the share-the-TV-wealth "program invades our private right by encroaching on our traditions and the prestige we have spent 100 years building up." As a Catholic institution in a hostile Protestant region, the University of Notre Dame had long adhered to an independent course, totally supporting itself, never requesting or expecting aid from any outside force, even the Catholic Church. (Notre Dame's C.S.C. founders and their successors belonged to a tiny order far from the Vatican.) Until well into the twentieth century, ND even operated farms next to the campus, providing the school's food supply; similarly, in intercollegiate athletics, Notre Dame had gone its own way, independent of conferences, carefully building its own fan base and support. From this history of autonomy came the deep belief that not only could and should Notre Dame take care of itself but, when it earned money from football, it had a right to keep every penny. Conversely, when the school lost money, unlike many universities, it had to cover its deficits; it could not turn to state legislatures or other sources to mop up its red ink.

At this juncture in Notre Dame history, in the fall of 1952, Father Cavanaugh left the presidency to head the Notre Dame Foundation; he wanted to turn it into a modern fund-raising operation and build a large endowment. Father Theodore Hesburgh moved into the top position, and Father Edmund Joyce became the executive vice president. In one of his first public statements on the NCAA share-the-TV-wealth plan, Joyce remarked, "I really don't know what we'll do if they keep this up" and push it through the convention. The reporter added that "Father Joyce . . . hinted that the university might go against the NCAA wishes," but that decision had not been made. With this as background, a large Notre Dame contingent, including

Hesburgh, Joyce, and Krause, prepared for the 1953 NCAA convention in Washington, D.C., intent on presenting their university's position and persuading the delegates of the Television Committee's "socialistic" folly.

■   ■   ■

IRISH WON'T DEFY NCAA STAND ON TV.

Notre Dame's battle for unrestricted television of football games will be carried to the floor of the NCAA convention in Washington, but Ed Krause, the Irish athletic director, today denied rumors that his school is thinking about defying the NCAA and televising its home schedule in 1953.

"We've been against the NCAA controlled TV plan for two years," said Krause . . . "But the NCAA serves a definite purpose in college athletics. There's absolutely no foundation to the story [that ND will resurrect its TV network], even though we strongly oppose controlled TV."

—*South Bend (Indiana) Tribune* report, December 1952.

In fact, in the maneuvering before the convention, various pro–Notre Dame reporters floated rumors that the school might defy the NCAA TV plan. The association responded through its press allies that if Notre Dame resurrected its TV network, it invited a boycott by all potential opponents and expulsion from the NCAA. Yet the association worried that a huge Fighting Irish television contract would prompt enough defections to cause, according to Francis Wallace, "the formation of a TV League among the 'haves' "—ND and some other big-time football schools. This threat persuaded the Television Committee to shelve its share-the-TV-wealth proposal, and Notre Dame officials decided to fight the NCAA's television policy from within the association rather than from outside with a revived TV network. They hoped that rational argument, as well as some new evidence, would convince a majority of delegates to rescind the policy.

The NORC figures for the 1952 season were even worse than in previous years: football game attendance had dropped 16 percent from the 1947–48 baseline, and the NCAA's statistical sleight-of-hand concerning real loss versus projected loss approached the ludicrous, particularly the party line that the TV plan "does, in fact, accomplish its primary objective—it reverses not the loss, but the rate of loss."

A more informative survey, introduced into the convention record by Penn AD Francis Murray, was done by the *Chicago Herald-American* in late 1952. It revealed that "only four percent of 18,056 persons answering a printed questionnaire approved the present college football TV arrangements"; on the other hand, "35 percent favored unrestricted TV, 33 percent expressed a willingness to pay a small fee to witness college football on their home television sets, and 28 percent supported a regional television plan whereby each section of the country would have its own special game of the week" and individual teams could appear frequently. Even factoring in the many Notre Dame rooters in the Chicago area, a mere 4 percent support for the NCAA's TV policy represented massive public disapproval, and this statistic persuaded some schools to press for a more flexible NCAA TV plan, especially in the area of pay-TV and other non-network options.

The Notre Dame administrators at the convention hoped to capitalize on this sentiment for change, and, on the eve of the official opening, they gave every delegate and media representative a lengthy handout written by President Hesburgh. After reiterating his school's objections to the NCAA's television policy and his "public service" arguments for unrestricted TV, he added his personal view of the situation: he considered the current plan, because it so limited individual schools, "a removal of the incentive to excellence." This emphasis on "excellence" became a catchword of his long ND presidency, and his career in American public life.

Hesburgh then aimed a very telling comment at the NCAA leaders and the many athletic department officials who supported them: "It is a strange commentary on those who direct athletics, one of whose main values is to teach honest competition, that they alone in the field of television have been afraid to meet competition and have attempted to restrain it through athletic boycott." He added, "Nor do we think that there is [any] valid argument for monopoly and boycott," and abrogating the rights of individual members of the association.

Father Hesburgh made his first appearance as Notre Dame president at this convention, which also marked the debut of his longtime assistant, Father Joyce, as the school's executive vice president. In his initial speech, Joyce invoked Notre Dame's traditions and its greatest hero, Knute Rockne, reminding the delegates that when "different conferences were planning to ban radio, Rockne then had the vision to see that radio would help rather than hurt football in popularity as an American sport." Similar foresight, he said, should apply to the televising of college football.

In the formal debate on TV policy, Father Joyce also offered some new perspectives: "The Television Committee frequently has referred to television as [schools] giving a person a free ticket to a game. I question this sincerely. I do not think there is that connection between the two." The NCAA loved the "free ticket" analogy, basing it on the old-fashioned model of gate receipts, but in the new reality, television *paid* schools for the right to deliver viewers to advertisers. Thus schools gave nothing away for free; indeed, selling their broadcasting rights soon proved a wonderful financial boon for them. Later in the 1950s, as the annual amount of the NCAA's television contract escalated, the association came to understand this concept.

Father Joyce also questioned the entire TV experience and its actual impact on game attendance: "A game watched on television is not anywhere near the same as being in the stadium itself. There are too many factors you receive in being present at the game which you will never get over the television set." Indeed, a telecast of a 1950s college football game consisted of one or two anchored cameras of the single lens variety, showing the action from a great distance, with an occasional panorama shot. Additionally, not only was telecasting confined to black-and-white—often, because of inadequate transmission and antennas, with fuzzy images—but frequently the announcers made mistakes and could not explain the action. Not surprisingly, Father Joyce and millions of other fans considered a televised game far inferior to a stadium seat. Nevertheless, game attendance at many schools continued to drop—as Notre Dame and University of Pennsylvania officials kept insisting, for reasons other than television.

For the delegates at the 1953 convention, the most important part of Father Joyce's speech concerned his school's reaction to the current TV policy. In his opening, he said that "it is not particularly pleasant being in the minority position opposing a rather large majority," but he signaled that Notre Dame would not defy the association, either by departing or by mounting a court challenge. However, his explanation for his school's acquiescence probably did not comfort the delegates: "We think this [TV] policy is a reactionary one, an artificial one, and one which is doomed to failure within a few years." The only surprise in the ensuing vote on the policy—172 to 13—was that the opposition broke into double digits.

Notre Dame did not leave the convention empty-handed. Because the Television Committee also had control of nonstandard telecasting—i.e., pay-TV and theater television—for 1953, it gave all schools permission to act individually in this area. (ND had already experimented with theater TV in the late 1940s.) The NCAA leadership not only saw this as a wise concession to Notre Dame, which probably would benefit most from theater TV, but it rationalized the move as the equivalent of selling game tickets. Thus, in midsummer 1953, Notre Dame signed a contract with Box Office Television, Inc., for theater TV of all of its home contests. BOT had 110 screens and predicted an audience of 250,000 for each fall game.

At this time, another TV technology promised much greater monetary rewards than theater television; because it also sold "tickets" for individual games, the NCAA Television Committee approved it: pay-TV. Three systems competed for college sports contracts: Phonevision, which used the telephone line as a cable; Telemeter, which used a coin deposit meter attached to the set; and Skiatron, which used a plastic ticket insertion method. At first, fans liked pay-TV, so much so that one commentator predicted that "the days of free TV football are numbered. Within a few years, subscription or pay-as-you-see TV will replace free television." In fact, public acceptance soon cooled. Americans were growing used to the apparent bargain of standard TV, without grasping the concept that broadcasters delivered them to advertisers, with financial consequences for viewers that were far from free.

The writer who predicted the end of "free TV football" based his guess, in part, on his observation of "the TV discussions" at the 1953 NCAA convention concerning nonstandard television. Notre Dame officials also came away from that session with an optimistic sense of the future of alternative TV systems; this accounted to some extent for their decision not to continue to butt heads with the NCAA on its network television policy. Later that year, Francis Wallace explained that "the opponents of NCAA control are presently passive—with Notre Dame sitting it out with a theater-TV experiment"; however, "the situation is unique, complex and much too big to be permanently controlled. One of these days—and it could happen suddenly, most likely with the advent of subscription TV. . . it will jump up and control itself."

With his pipeline to the Golden Dome, Wallace most likely reflected ND administrative thinking on the TV issue at this time. Except for failing to substitute "glacially" for "suddenly," his prediction came true—three decades later. In the early 1980s, subscription TV finally took hold in the form of cable, forever altering the college sports TV landscape. As importantly, in 1984, a number of schools challenging the NCAA's control of their television rights won a landmark Supreme Court decision, ending the association's monopoly on college football telecasts. In the early 1950s, if Notre Dame and/or Penn had taken the NCAA to court, they most likely would have gained their TV freedom; however, because they adopted a passive attitude, mainly hoping for outside intervention by pay-TV or some other force, they did not instigate legal action.

In addition, in the early 1950s, critics of NCAA policy, both within and outside the association, made the crucial mistake of underestimating the tenacity and shrewdness of Executive Director Walter Byers, as well as his ability to strengthen and promote his association. Opponents watched as Byers persuaded the media and the public to accept the NCAA as the agent of reform in college sports, deserving of control of all aspects of intercollegiate athletics, including television. This public relations campaign proved to be the most important in NCAA history, consolidating its power and launching its phenomenal growth.

Aiding the NCAA's PR drive was the shift in Hollywood movies in this period. Even though the motion picture industry had lost some of its cultural dominance to television, it still influenced public attitudes on many issues, including college sports. During the scandals, Hollywood—attempting to profit from the widespread concern about them—produced a number of exposés of big-time college football and basketball that, according to one commentator, "touched America's collective conscience, asking questions that needed to be asked." When the NCAA, after coopting the ACE reform attempt, appeared to provide answers, Hollywood then marketed less critical views of intercollegiate athletics as well as a number of classical college sports films, including one that helped rehabilitate West Point football. Significantly, from this mélange of early 1950s films evolved the college sports movie form that continues to this day, and also the basic TV treatments of intercollegiate athletics. The media had always aided college sports, never more so than in helping them recover from their worst scandals.

Part 6

Recovering
from the Scandals:
Media-Made
College Sports

41

Hollywood and College Sports
in the Early 1950s

By the early fifties Hollywood's problems were very evident, particularly at the box office. From a record weekly attendance of 82 million in 1946, film audiences alarmingly plummeted to about 36 million by 1950. Labor troubles, higher production costs, adverse court rulings, highly publicized anti-communist hearings all hurt the movie industry. Added to this was the challenge of television.

—Historians Douglas T. Miller and Marion Nowak, 1975.

Like many ultrasuccessful businesses, Hollywood's command of American entertainment during the 1930s and the Second World War bred industry-wide complacency and an adherence to old formulas. The aging men who ran the studios were ill prepared for the postwar situation, not only its unexpected economic, legal, and political problems, but also its greatest danger to them: a new and immensely popular competing entertainment medium, one that broke America's weekly movie-going habit, TV.

By 1950, movie executives realized that they lived in a changed world, but rather than adapt efficiently to it, they spent the rest of the decade seeking ways to return to the glorious past. To fill theaters again, they poured fortunes into superficial products not available on television: a deluge of Technicolor pictures, Cinemascope epics, 3-D thrillers, and so on. And because television entered the family living room and practiced intensive self-censorship, churning out shows like *Father Knows Best* that resembled Hollywood's classical films, the studios began to differentiate their products from TV's, creating some pictures with "adult" themes and more overt depictions of sexuality than they had previously.

Critics termed the best of the new movies "revisionist," noting that they used the traditional formulas as points of departure to explore more realistic areas of character and theme. The 1952 Western, *High Noon,* presented one of the premier heroes of the classic cinema, Gary Cooper, as a less than noble sheriff, a man questioning the values espoused in standard Westerns. *High Noon* attracted attention and did satisfactorily at the box office, indicating to Hollywood that some ticket buyers enjoyed the revisionist form. Yet other moviegoers still loved the classic Westerns, especially those on TV like *Gunsmoke.* Thus, the deeper cultural message was that the massive American movie audience of the 1930s and World War II years had fragmented, with many members of it departing to Television Land, taking with them the worldview that had dominated previous Hollywood films but would appear less and less in 1950s movies.

Even some war pictures, including a few about the ongoing Korean War, received revisionist treatment. Samuel Fuller's 1951 films, *Steel Helmet* and *Fixed Bayonets,* contained elements from the World War II cinema but, as one critic noted, "the tone is cynical and tough." Fuller sought a greater realism in his war films than had previous directors, and rather than glorify combat with patriotic slogans, he focused mainly on its gritty, brutal elements. Moreover, his treatment seemed appropriate for the ambiguous and unresolved Korean War, and although he represented a minority view in the early 1950s, his revisionism influenced many subsequent directors and permeated film culture.

Critics characterized the worldview of revisionist films as pessimistic. "Instead of the optimism . . . [and] the typical celebratory or complacent view of American life in the classic text, such as *Bells of St. Mary's* (1945), the overall atmosphere of these films is bleak, cynical . . . and/or highly ironic." Like other Hollywood genres in the early 1950s, college sports movies began to move from the sunny and self-satisfied mode of *Knute Rockne—All-American* and its heirs toward cynical worldviews. In previous periods, particularly the 1930s, some filmmakers had produced "Aw-Nuts" college sports films, but these lacked the thorough pessimism and the complete critique of intercollegiate athletics found in such 1950s revisionist pictures as *Saturday's Hero* (1951). Aiding filmmakers in their exploration of this new territory were the scandals and corruption in intercollegiate athletics in this period, and the public's increasing skepticism about the old college sports pieties.

■   ■   ■

> I'm through. I can't play anymore. I'm glad. The game I loved as a kid is all gone. It [college sports] is a business, and you don't get paid nearly enough. Then they kick you out like a dog.

> —Steve Novak, the main character in *Saturday's Hero,* 1951.

Novak delivers these lines after a career-ending injury—caused when his coach insists that he play while seriously hurt. Reviewers characterized the "script's dialogue as cynical," noting that the entire film "treated college football with distinct cynicism rather than the time-tested rah-rah spirit." *Variety,* the entertainment industry's main trade publication, lauded this approach, heading its review: "Topflight drama probing college football with exploitable b.o. [box office] chances," explaining that "the forthright baring of" college sports corruption "furnishes a sizable exploitation peg on which to push *Saturday's Hero* into promising box office possibilities."

Variety also praised the Sidney Buchman and Millard Lampell film script, which was based on the latter's ironic novel, *The Hero.* Significantly, anti-Communist groups had long condemned Lampell for his leftist politics, but Columbia Pictures still employed him for *Saturday's Hero,* and then ignored the anti-Communist pickets outside theaters exhibiting the picture. Undoubtedly, Columbia acted less out of civil libertarian convictions than its belief in the film's commercial potential. The studio's bet paid off. One commentator later remarked that "*Saturday's Hero,* nurtured by a variety of sports scandals, became a highly successful movie," one of Columbia's most profitable in 1951. Thus, just as the traditional movie audience was fragmenting, so were the college sports fans among it, with many willing to see serious criticisms of intercollegiate athletics.

Not only did the main character in *Saturday's Hero,* with his cynicism and weariness, differ from previous college football heroes, but many of his teammates shared his point of view as well as the illegal payments from boosters, and their personalities differed radically from the usual supporting players. When the team first gathers, a prep school walk-on announces, "I'm the fourth one in my family to wear this uniform." The hero's closest friend, a spokesman for the ex-GIs and working-class men on the squad, replies, "I'm the fourth one in my family to wear shoes." Steve Novak, from a poor Polish American background in urban New Jersey, smiles.

As the team's afternoon practices, run by a drillmaster coach, become tougher, the professional athletes survive and the amateurs depart. The head man is far from the coaching ideal of *Knute Rockne—All-American,* not only because of his brutal methods but also in his blunt locker-room talks. Before a crucial game, he tells his players, "Just do your job and they will go down. Nothing more or less. Just do your job." One critic commented, "It was all so different from the old days when [college] football . . . was considered a great character builder," not simply a mean business, "when Pat O'Brien, the ultimate in moral uprighteousness, always played the coach" and made riproaring speeches.

The movie revises other college sports stereotypes in both obvious and surprising ways. An English professor exhibits standard faculty contempt for jocks, but when the hero—who wants an education despite the athletic department's discouraging him from getting one—recites an assigned poem perfectly and with feeling, the professor responds, "You don't understand, Novak, you're supposed to stand there like a dumb ox while I make a fool out of you."

This overturning of expectations and exploring of new ground characterizes revisionist film, and makes *Saturday's Hero* one of the most distinctive movies of this period. The scriptwriters also take the standard sportswriter character, often the hero's mentor and/or confidant in traditional sports movies, and they not only portray him as corrupt and undependable but, in the end, they assign him to the job of sports publicity director at the football school!

The themes and values of revisionist films consistently oppose those of the classic cinema, often attacking them directly. The negative reviews of *Saturday's Hero* noted the film's "hooting with fiendish derision at all the good old rah-rah-college attitudes so often expressly ennobled in certain items from Hollywood," like *Knute Rockne—All-American*. But even this reviewer admitted that the movie's relentless exposure of college sports corruption led him to wonder if " 'over-emphasis' is a euphemism that deserves some sort of journalistic prize" for understatement.

The film shows such obvious forms of "overemphasis" as boosters slipping cash to athletes, but it also reveals more subtle and rarely discussed kinds. In Steve Novak's final season, because he has to help promote his school's football program as well as his own All-America candidacy, he must attend frequent booster meetings and dinners throughout the region. As a result, his grades—even those fixed by compliant professors—fall, but as the ticket-selling and All-America campaigns escalate, the athletic department increases the speed on Novak's travel treadmill. (For many college athletes, this problem persists to the present day but never attracts much attention; the media are too busy covering the banquets and interviewing the players.)

Revisionist filmmakers also experimented technically, breaking with the standard photography, music, editing, and other components of the classic cinema. Instead of the well-lit, comfortable scenes of traditional college sports movies, much of *Saturday's Hero* occurs at night, featuring visual devices from the most revisionist area of Hollywood cinema, film noir. In addition, the sound track does not blare the usual football fight songs; rather it contains the brooding, unsettling score of Elmer Bernstein.

The film made another significant technical departure from classic college sports movies. Instead of incorporating large dollops of newsreel footage of actual football games, a standard method from *Knute Rockne—All-American* on, the filmmakers of *Saturday's Hero* created their own action shots, emphasizing the brutality of the linemen's "war in the trenches," the ferocity of open field blocking and tackling, and the regular attempts to intentionally injure opponents. All the reviews commented on these scenes, and most subsequent sports movies, even some trying to continue the traditional form, did their own game footage, aided by the lighter cameras that were becoming available.

Finally, revisionist films end very differently than classical movies. The latter emphasize the famous Hollywood "happy ending," with the hero and heroine going off into the proverbial sunset. This closure, the tieing together of all plot strings, indicated to audiences that, like the movie characters, they too lived in a tidy world, one where good always triumphed over evil.

On the other hand, revisionist films disdained closure, usually ending ambiguously, stressing the complexity of life, and the improbability of neat conclusions. One critic wrote of *Saturday's Hero:* "In an atypically bleak ending for" a college sports movie, the hero leaves the university, and "returns home to an ordinary job and night school." Moreover, his college girlfriend, the rebellious niece of the team's main booster, might join him, but then again, she might not; her wealthy Virginia background is a large impediment to life with Steve Novak in his poor Polish neighborhood in New Jersey.

College sports movies, even revisionist ones in later eras, rarely end this somberly; audiences tend to dislike unresolved and pessimistic conclusions, and Hollywood knows that when people leave a theater after a "down ending," usually they do not recommend the film to friends, thus negating the crucial word-of-mouth factor in ticket sales. That *Saturday's Hero* resisted closure but became a box office winner implied massive agreement with its conclusion: Steve was better off starting again in his poor neighborhood and at night school than continuing as a regular student at the rich but corrupt university (the English professor befriended Steve and offered to sponsor him). More than any other event in 1951, a turbulent, watershed year in intercollegiate athletics, the commercial success of *Saturday's Hero* underlined the shifting public attitudes on big-time college sports and related to their declining popularity, as well as to the calls for their reform.

■　■　■

In his *New York Times* review of *Saturday's Hero,* Bosley Crowther wondered how "the people who run the college football leagues—or for that matter, the ones who run the colleges" will react to this film. In a publicity release, Columbia Pictures supplied one answer:

> An effort to preview the disenchanted football motion picture, *Saturday's Hero,* on the campi of representative American football universities has met with serious resistance. It begins to be apparent that most college authorities do not wish to encourage the ideas that are put forth in this picture, i.e., that football in American colleges is a gigantic racket, that players are recruited, subsidized, given passing marks by courtesy, and discarded when they get hurt.

The Hollywood studio had offered to screen the movie free of charge at schools around the country, but only six had accepted. University administrators either ignored the offer or made feeble excuses, as at Berkeley, where "sudden repairs on Wheeler Auditorium made it necessary for university authorities to halt the project." In 1951, college officials preferred an ostrich position on the issues in the film; only when the public outcry reached a higher decibel level did they lift their heads and turn to the NCAA for damage control and a semblance of reform.

One of the schools that allowed screenings was Notre Dame, and moviegoers there had a variety of reactions. Sports publicist Charlie Callahan claimed that he "could not believe the episodes in *Saturday's Hero* can be typical of college football." Other Notre Dame viewers saw the film as fairly accurate about the corruption at many schools. Stanley Woodward, former sports editor of the *New York Herald Tribune* and no fan of the Fighting Irish, commented privately: "Notre Dame does not resort to low practices in football. However, Frank Leahy knows they go on and we can't believe that Charles [Callahan] is as naive as he says he is. Last spring, Leahy said to this writer, 'Before I would stoop to some of the practices that are carried on in [college] football, I would recommend to the authorities at Notre Dame that the game be dropped.'" Nonetheless, Woodward did not publicize his beliefs, preferring a classical approach in print.

Increasingly, during this dark time in intercollegiate athletics, various members of the media, including longtime ND antagonists like Stanley Woodward, saw the Fighting Irish as the exception to the rule in big-time college sports. They also suggested that the ND model could provide a way out of the current imbroglio. The Hollywood studios later picked up this theme, but first they turned out more films based on the scandals.

■   ■   ■

[In *The Basketball Fix*] a talented young athlete is led down a primrose path strewn with shaved points . . . [The movie indicates] that intercollegiate athletics . . . is an extremely lucrative business, a professional endeavor that is piously designated amateur . . .

While *The Basketball Fix* is on the timid side, it is worth the effort put into it, and points the way to better and more constructive social comments [on college sports].

—*New York Times* film reviewer Oscar Godbout,
September 1951.

Godbout did not find *The Basketball Fix* (1951) revisionist enough, and *Variety* made the same criticism, leading its review with "Some exploitation value but mild chances . . . Some ballyhoo situations may scare up a profitable booking by strong exploitation, but overall outlook is for lower-case, programmer release." The film's problem was not its revisionism, but its botching of that form.

Unlike *Saturday's Hero,* the basketball film did not present a thorough and dramatic critique of college sports, or even deliver its initial voice-over promise: "There's more to this fix story than meets the eye." The movie takes a very innocent collegian, sends him to work and summer basketball at a country club where a professional gambler hangs out, and depicts the latter's corruption of the athlete. *The Basketball Fix* focuses on an individual's mistake: the player, needing money to support his younger brother and to get married, accepts the gambler's bribes to shave points in college games. But the movie ignores the culture of corruption that surrounded college basketball at this time; instead of entire teams and legions of gamblers, we watch one player and one fixer. Thus, when the athlete blunders and the authorities discover his actions, they punish him with a prison sentence, the last line of the film intoning, "It's going to cost *him* much more than *he* figured." The movie never transcends this single story, and its narrow focus frustrated reviewers and audiences more than it pleased or enlightened them.

The Basketball Fix, an independent production, was released in September 1951. The public already knew many details of the CCNY and LIU fixes as well as the open gambling at Madison Square Garden; not surprisingly, the *New York Times* reviewer found the film "on the timid side." Yet *The Basketball Fix* contained authentic revisionist elements, including a film noir quality and the actor John Ireland, "a popular tough-cynical hero of the early 50s," as a hard-boiled newspaper reporter. In addition, the ending, with the athlete on his way to prison and a very uncertain future, resisted closure.

Finally, for all of its problems, *The Basketball Fix* indicated that *Saturday's Hero* was not an aberrant college sports picture but part of a larger trend, one that also affected big budget Hollywood products, including major studio releases like Warner Brothers's *Jim Thorpe—All-American* (1951), with the highly bankable Burt Lancaster; Universal's *The All-American* (1953), with the hot, young Tony Curtis; and Warners's *Trouble Along the Way* (1953), with superstar John Wayne. For these pictures, however, the filmmakers combined revisionist elements with classical ones, producing a new kind of college sports movie: a mixed-form hybrid. Some 1930s pictures, with their attempt to blend "Aw-Nuts" and "Gee-Whiz" elements, had confused audiences and failed. The 1950s mixed-form movies were much more effective and successful.

■ ■ ■

In England, in the very first game of football . . . really a soccer game, an enterprising young man picked up the ball and ran through his amazed opponents. That's how football was born—illegitimately.

It moved to America and someone took advantage of a loophole in the rules and invented a formation called "The Flying Wedge." So many young men were maimed and killed by this clever maneuver that President [Theodore] Roosevelt had to call the colleges together and ask them to make the game less brutal. He was, of course, defeated in the next election . . .

Football [today] is an industry, the price of a good running back surpasses that of a professor . . . Take my advice and stay out of [big-time college] sports.

—The John Wayne character in
Trouble Along the Way, 1953.

Early in this film, when the rector of a small Catholic college, St. Anthony's, asks Steve Williams (John Wayne) to head his football program, the cynical coach offers the above history of the sport. Not only does he stress its inherent corruption, but, in his comment about Roosevelt's election defeat, he suggests that the American public wants the sport to remain brutal and nasty.

Wayne plays the role with macho humor, effectively delivering the straight-from-the-shoulder punchlines. The *New York Times* reviewer commented: "John Wayne makes a thoroughly believable coach who is given an opportunity to expound on the reasons for 'buying' outstanding players, faking school records, and sundry off-the-norm practices" and, in the course of the movie, commits all of these college sports "sins" and many more.

John Wayne had achieved superstardom in some of Hollywood's most traditional Westerns and World War II combat pictures, but reviewers and moviegoers accepted him in the role of a crooked college coach because, from his opening scene, they realized that Steve Williams was *not* a purely revisionist character, an anti-Rockne, and that *Trouble Along the Way* contained many classic elements.

The rector must rescue his Catholic college from financial bankruptcy to keep it open—an often-used plot device in classic 1940s films involving parochial schools, orphanages, churches, and so on. However, the title *Trouble Along the Way* suggested a new twist, playing off the title of the most famous classical film about Catholic institutions, *Going My Way* (1944). The priest decides that a winning football team and full stadiums will produce the money to achieve his goal, and, because the college cannot afford a regular coach, he must hire a reprobate (Steve Williams/John Wayne) who will work for minimum wage. The hero tells him, "I've been kicked out of the Big Ten, Ivy League, and Southern Conference, they won't even let me coach at Alcatraz," but he accepts the St. Anthony's job because it will help him appear as a "good citizen" while he contests a child custody case with his ex-wife—he wants to keep his sweet young daughter. *Variety* summed up the film: "There's a lot of unobjectionable hokum mixed into the story, plus some sharp kidding of big-time gridiron talent and how it's found and subsidized, all blended with any number of socko laugh sequences."

This mix of revisionist and classical material allowed John Wayne to function in the role—the cynical coach is a wonderful father—and to utilize his screen persona as an American hero. One film scholar explained the mixed-form phenomenon: "What is so fascinating and confounding about Hollywood [mixed] genre films is their capacity to 'play it both ways,' to both criticize and reinforce the values, beliefs, and ideals of our culture within the same movie."

Mixed-form pictures allow the filmmakers to score points on a hot topic—in *Trouble Along the Way,* the corruption in college sports—while avoiding the risk of depressing the audience with an unrelieved revisionist vision. Mixed-form films also permit box-office stars like John Wayne to work in them—rarely do "hero actors" agree to play totally against type and assume anti-hero parts. In this movie, Wayne can deliver some very sardonic lines, like "The race is not always to the strong and to the swift, but that's the way to bet," and still be a loving father and, at heart, a good man. In assembling his football team, he can break all the rules, but because he is trying to save the school, he is not a true scoundrel. Viewers can also enjoy his early season victories over powerhouse clubs because they sense that his crooked schemes will unravel in the end.

Yet the film's revisionist criticism of big-time college sports is unrelenting. After Steve Williams bribes his former assistants to break their current contracts and join him, they agree, explaining, "For once we'd like to make as much as the [college] players." The head coach recruits athletes by making them "shareholders" in the team, giving them hefty percentages of the game program sales, parking, and other concessions. The filmmakers depict college sports corruption with humor, but they continue their attack throughout the movie. However, they exempt one big-time program from their critique: Notre Dame.

In the opening scene, when the rector explains his idea of assembling a winning football team to save the school, he invokes Notre Dame as his model: "We'll be like Notre Dame, outstanding in academics and athletics." The film visually reinforces the concept of ND football as the ideal when the rector puts his school's slim, threadbare yearbook on a table next to Notre Dame's thick, prosperous one. Later, the rector achieves a great triumph, with the aid of a cardinal, when he schedules a game against the Fighting Irish for the coming season. By establishing at least one school as an ideal in college sports, the movie suggests the possibility of reform, and an end to scandal and corruption.

But before St. Anthony's plays Notre Dame, the coach's dishonesty is exposed. The press does not uncover it—the film portrays sportswriters as compliant hacks—but Williams's ex-wife, to win the custody case, informs the rector of her husband's cheating with his current team, which her private investigators have discovered. The rector decides that his big-time football plan was a horrible mistake, and he cancels the remainder of the season and the program.

Trouble Along the Way concludes, like many mixed-form movies, with elements from both classical and revisionist endings. The school is saved, the cardinal promising to support it financially for many years. The coach apologizes for his actions and resigns, but the rector rehires him to run St. Anthony's now permanently small-time team. In addition, the ex-wife is exposed as a vengeful, uncaring mother. But the ending veers off the traditional track when the coach does *not* win the custody case or the hand of his new girlfriend, the social worker in charge of his daughter's case. In the final scene, this woman takes the child from the coach, placing her in foster care. Even though the filmmakers imply that if Steve Williams becomes an authentically "good citizen," he will regain his daughter and marry the social worker, they end the scene with the woman and the child walking away from the coach and the college.

One commentator saw this "novel twist to the usual ending of a football drama . . . as indicative of a change in the wind as movie audiences grew receptive to a more realistic approach to" college sports films. Moreover, "the conventional [college] football movie . . . was becoming a part of the Hollywood past."

Trouble Along the Way did well at the box office, its mixed form pleasing audiences. Its revisionist criticism of college sports seemed up-to-date and appropriate to the reality of the early 1950s, but its traditional elements and humorous tone rendered the movie cheerful and upbeat. Finally, even though the film resisted standard closure, it suggested a positive future.

Hollywood produced many sports movies in this period, from the thoroughly revisionist *Saturday's Hero* to John Ford's classical paean to West Point, *The Long Gray Line* (1955). But *Trouble Along the Way,* with its mix of forms, proved to be the true forerunner of future sports films, the one most similar to the mainstream cinema of later eras, including our own. The most successful contemporary sports films, particularly those of Ron Shelton—*Bull Durham, White Men Can't Jump,* and *Tin Cup*—are lineal descendants of *Trouble Along the Way.* Shelton's only box-office bomb was the thoroughly revisionist *Cobb.* In addition, on TV, the relentless combination of traditional sentimentality and revisionist sarcasm on programs like ESPN's *SportsCenter* comes directly out of Hollywood's mixed-form treatment of college sports.

42

Mixed-Form Films
Become the Norm

Why and how has the grand old game [of college football] changed so much—if, indeed the particular media image of the game . . . is a fair image? Why has the relation between the audience and the game changed . . . Why does almost everyone feel some vested interest in the structure of [college] football, experiencing a sense of historic occurrence and discontinuity if that structure seems to be undergoing change?

—Social critic Reuel Denney, 1953.

This observer wondered about the early 1950s media depictions of college football, particularly those containing a mix of traditional and revisionist elements. He saw them as central to a historic shift in public attitudes on college sports, but he did not explain the images, how they mirrored and shaped the public discontent with college sports in the early 1950s, how the scandals and corruption violated the media-made ideal, particularly such potent representations of it as *Knute Rockne—All-American* and its heirs. Thus, as Hollywood experimented with new depictions of college sports to fit the changed circumstances, people were "experiencing a sense of historic occurrence and discontinuity."

In a less media-savvy age, even sophisticated commentators like Reuel Denney failed to appreciate the effect of images upon audiences; they still believed that people perceived public events directly, making judgments based upon those perceptions and not upon their viewing of the highly mediated representations—increasingly the way that Americans saw such mass spectacles as college sports, and also politics. In 1952, for the first time, a media consultant crafted the campaign of a major presidential candidate.

A mixed-form movie that illustrated the motion picture industry's involvement with and shaping of college sports "reality" during this period was Universal's *The All-American* (1953). All of the key production people—producer Aaron Rosenberg, director Jesse Hibbs, editor Cotton Warburton, and screenwriter D. D. Beauchamp—had been All-American football players at the University of Southern California in the late 1920s and early 1930s. In addition, the cast included current and past All-Americans, most notably Frank Gifford and Tom Harmon. For this movie, the line between image and reality totally blurred.

Undoubtedly, the personal histories of the filmmakers drew them to the classic elements in the magazine story upon which the movie was based; however, their knowledge of big-time college football's present condition led them to a revisionist depiction of the game's underside. The reviewers recognized the mixed nature of *The All-American,* one noting that "in Merriwell fashion [Tony] Curtis plays the self-confident hero [Nick Bonelli], who is a whiz on the gridiron . . . [but] flashy off in his 'sharp' clothes and long haircut." Modest Frank Merriwell wore unostentatious clothes, and his 1950s imitators sported crewcuts, not DAs (duck's asses) like the movie's central character. But Tony Curtis was a hot young actor who looked good in flashy clothes, and the script called for him to learn life's lessons and to clean up his act—and eventually get a shorter haircut.

The film begins with the hero's parents, hard-working Italian immigrants, traveling to see their son play. Unfortunately, they die in a car crash, but when Bonelli's ruthless coach receives the news before the opening kickoff, he refuses to tell Nick and risk a mediocre performance from him. Outside the dressing room, the coach also fails to recognize a former player, crudely brushing him off. Bonelli almost single-handedly wins the game, but after discovering the coach's cynical maneuver, he quits the team, loses his athletic scholarship, and leaves school. Revisionist scenes and dialogue dominate the first part of the movie, many of them with a distinct film noir quality.

But *The All-American* soon takes a classic turn, and Nick, always a good but frustrated student at the "football factory," accepts an academic scholarship to an Ivy League–type college with a de-emphasized sports program. Moreover, he refuses to go out for football, and the coach does not pressure him to join the team. Thus, the filmmakers, by contrasting a corrupt big-time program with an academically oriented smaller one, set up their response to the current controversies in intercollegiate athletics. They also reflect their own desire, as well as that of college sports fans, for, according to the script, authentic "scholar-athletes" as opposed to the "hired mercenaries" at the "football factories."

Various scenes of college life follow, including a romantic triangle with Nick and a demure "good girl" and a sexy "bad girl." Then, on a beautiful autumn day, a sandlot football game with some young boys rekindles Nick's love of the sport, and he joins the varsity, quickly mastering its one-platoon system, which the film endorses (all the USC filmmakers played one-platoon during their college years), and Nick leads the team to inevitable victory.

Reviewers recognized *The All-American's* traditional elements, terming them "rah-rah," but they overlooked the filmmakers' message on the current corruption in college sports: bring back the honest, old-fashioned programs. Significantly, the film also exempts Notre Dame from its indictment of big-time college football; the script calls Nick Bonelli a "Notre Dame type guy"—ethnic Catholic, authentic student, and superlative athlete.

Finally, the film indicates that Nick is a true All-American, not only for his outstanding football talent but because, even more important, he fulfills the immigrant dream. By the end of the movie he embodies the All-American virtues of clean living—he rejects the blonde bombshell for the "marrying type girl"—and hard work, gaining an honors degree in architecture.

The All-American used the symbolism of its title in an obvious manner, but at this time a much more important mixed-form film was utilizing the same phrase and some of the themes: *Jim Thorpe—All-American*. This biopic from Warner Brothers, the studio behind *Knute Rockne—All-American*, resonated with traditional All-American allusions, but it also contained many revisionist elements, marking a definite departure from standard depictions of great athletic heroes. The differences between *Knute Rockne—All-American* (1940) and *Jim Thorpe—All-American* (1951) map the historical distance from the center of the classical college sports age to the beginnings of the new mixed-form period.

■　　■　　■

> *Jim Thorpe—All-American* follows the pattern set by previous sports sagas. It is a story recognizable from former film performances and not from the unique Thorpe's life.
>
> That, in itself, is unfortunate, for Michael Curtiz, the director, as well as the cast and scenarists have not glorified their subject beyond credibility. They have indicated that Thorpe's career was not one long series of triumphs but was studded with setbacks.
>
> —*New York Times* film critic A. H. Weiler, August 1951.

Reviewer A. H. Weiler recognized the mixed form of *Jim Thorpe—All-American* but did not like it, preferring a more revisionist treatment to the classical emphasis. The film contains a very traditional frame—it begins and ends at a 1950 banquet honoring Thorpe as the greatest athlete of the half century—and it uses his college football coach, Pop Warner, as the voice-over narrator of his life story. The frame surrounds a familiar narrative and plot line: the hero rises from poor Indian boy on a reservation to collegiate football and track star at Carlisle Institute, and then his ultimate triumph, his sweep of gold medals in the pentathlon and decathalon at the 1912 Olympics. The film includes many classical touches during the athlete's ascent: Thorpe never sees a football before being handed one in college, and he becomes an instant star; countless American flags, repeated playings of the national anthem, and huge parades surrounding his Olympic victory. In addition, as part of his trajectory, the filmmakers provide a classic romance with a pretty classmate. But then, at the apex—Olympic triumph and marriage to his beloved—the hero starts a long, painful descent, the plot departing radically from traditional narrative until, near its conclusion, it swerves back to a "happy ending."

The *Times* critic praised the revisionist detour and wanted it to dominate the film, but other reviewers enjoyed the mixed nature of the biopic, none more so than the critic for *Variety:* "The scripters haven't spared the whip in reciting the ups and downs of the famous Oklahoma Indian . . . It is not always the story of medals and trophies, this is also a recital of the downfall that can so easily envelop any athlete." *Variety* predicted "neat b.o. [box office]" for the film, and *Jim Thorpe—All-American* did even better than expected, becoming a hit for Warner Brothers.

In the film, Thorpe's fall begins when the Olympic authorities discover that he had played professional baseball one summer while in college and, because of their rules on absolute amateurism for all Olympic competitors, they strip him of his medals. This debacle propels him into a full-time professional sports career, beginning with the New York Giants baseball team, but it also prompts anticlassical behavior: he refuses to be a "team player." His negative attitude ends his baseball career, and he enters pro football. Soon he spirals down in that sport, becoming less effective as a player and increasingly alcoholic and boastful off the field. He also encounters anti-Indian prejudice—and makes some amazingly revisionist statements about it—but sadly drifts into a netherworld of cheap hotel rooms and booze straight out of film noir. Finally, his wife leaves him, and he becomes a pitiful creature, his athletic talent confined to arm-wrestling in skid-row bars.

The crucial late scene in the film, the turning point that pivots the plot toward its classical ending, occurs during the 1932 Olympics in Los Angeles. Pop Warner finds Thorpe working in that city as the emcee of a seedy dance marathon, forced to wear Indian headdress and costume. The coach tries to persuade Jim to accept personal responsibility for his decline, to refute the charge that "the great Jim Thorpe turned out to be a powder puff" and turn his life around.

Thorpe at first rejects his old coach but, in the end, accepts his advice, finding regular work as a truck driver. In the final scenes, Jim comes upon some kids playing sandlot football in a junkyard and offers to coach them. His work with the youngsters restores his love of football and his faith in the future. This trope appears in many sports films, including *The All-American*, and serves here as the bridge back to the 1950 banquet, and the movie ends with Pop Warner honoring his most famous player and unveiling a painting of the young Thorpe in his United States Olympic uniform.

Fifties moviegoers saw *Jim Thorpe—All-American* as Hollywood presented it: a mixed portrait of a great athlete. Even though the scriptwriters did not reveal the historical Thorpe—his descent was much more sordid and painful than portrayed, and he never came out of it, dying in 1953 in extremely sad circumstances—the filmmakers offered a somewhat revisionist outline of his post-Olympic life. They also broke with the saccharine biopics about other famous sports heroes, typified by *The Babe Ruth Story* (1948).

Nevertheless, they set one major character in the film in classical concrete, Pop Warner. Ironically, their treatment of him was wholly inappropriate. The discrepancy between the film version of the famous coach and the historical facts concerning his relations with Thorpe and other Native American athletes reveals a great deal about Hollywood in this period and also about media-made college sports history.

■ ■ ■

There was also testimony [at a public hearing] that Warner bet heavily on the 1913 game with Dartmouth and told the team at half time that if they won he would cut them in; they did and he did, to a modest percentage. Warner, in [Carlisle football captain] Welch's judgment, was a fine coach but a man with little principle . . .

Welch and other team members apparently did not mind being exploited as athletes, but they objected to [such Warner tricks as] the way he sold fifty to seventy-five tickets in hotel lobbies on Friday nights and then pocketed the money.

—Sports historian Jack Newcombe, 1975.

Glenn "Pop" Warner was one of the great buccaneer coaches. As Newcombe documented in his comprehensive study of Carlisle athletics, Warner scheduled long barnstorming tours for his college football team, personally pocketing the money from his ticket allotment as well as a sizable percentage of the gate receipts, and he often wagered large amounts on games, including the famous 1913 contest against Dartmouth. In addition, Warner liked to use other Native American schools as farm clubs and to suit up players for many years beyond their normal college eligibility. Pop accomplished this, according to his friend Knute Rockne, by "changing legal names to Indian names as they switched schools . . . The famous back, Emil Hauser of Haskell, became Chief Waseka at Carlisle, etc."

The film *Jim Thorpe—All-American* depicts Pop Warner as a model of integrity, who was personally aggrieved by the revelation of his greatest athlete's wrongdoing: Thorpe's summer pro baseball job in North Carolina, the offense that lead to the loss of his Olympic medals. In fact, Warner set up Thorpe and other Carlisle athletes with summer baseball-playing jobs; finally, the coach's misdeeds in this area and others became so well known that, in 1913, the Department of the Interior, in charge of Native American institutions, forced him to resign his Carlisle position. However, because of Warner's ability to produce winning clubs, he went on to further fame and fortune at Pittsburgh and Stanford, the latter university even changing its team nickname to "Indians" to lure him west.

The Hollywood whitewash of Pop Warner in 1951 has direct parallels to the media cleansing of other famous college coaches during this period. The press embraced the proclamations of innocence by Nat Holman, Clair Bee, and even Adolph Rupp; moreover, newspaper descriptions of Colonel Blaik's denials of any knowledge of his Cadets' cribbing echoed the film depiction of Pop Warner's ignorance of his athlete's summer pro baseball activity. (The movie appeared shortly before the Military Academy scandal broke.) However, even more than his counterparts, Warner held a special place in the pantheon of American sports heroes. Not only was he famous in his own right and considered almost the equal of Knute Rockne, but he is also the patron saint of the Little League version of his sport: Pop Warner Football.

A Philadelphia businessman had founded the junior football program in 1929, naming it after Pop in 1934 when Warner, on the downside of his career, arrived in the city to coach the Temple Owls. After the war, Pop Warner Football became a national phenomenon, attuned to the expansion of suburbia and promoted for its supposed character-building attributes. Thus, Hollywood had no interest in presenting a revisionist and accurate portrait of Warner to accompany its sketch of his greatest player, Jim Thorpe.

Throughout the film, Warner lives up to his nickname as he "fathers" his Indian "boys," always available for counsel and aid, and he also provides inspirational locker-room talks as well as lectures on life. His character is saintlike, and in the end he helps Thorpe see the true light, an action crucial to the picture's optimistic conclusion.

Despite the revisionist scenes of Thorpe's descent, the film's happy ending left moviegoers with a positive feeling, as did its sanctification of Pop Warner. The highlighting of classical material foreshadowed a temporary comeback of traditional college sports films.

Even though this revival proved short-lived—America could not return to the less sophisticated and more homogeneous society that first embraced *Knute Rockne—All-American* and its immediate heirs—the best of these retrograde pictures, *Crazylegs, All-American* (1953), and *The Long Gray Line* (1955), offer an important insight into mediated college sports in this period as well as in future ones.

43

The Temporary Return of Classical Football Films

It gives me great pleasure to present this award to a man [Elroy "Crazylegs" Hirsch] whose name is a byword to every boy in the Midwest, and throughout the nation . . . A man who is a true All-American in all the ways that honor indicates.

—Arch Ward in the film *Crazylegs, All-American*, 1953.

At the beginning of this biopic, Republic Pictures filled the screen with the printed message: "This is the true story of an American boy—one of the greatest athletes of our time. All football sequences are taken from games in which he played." In addition to the stress on "actuality," including the old-fashioned use of newsreel clips, the movie starred Elroy Hirsch himself. Most critics considered him "likable and credible," his handsome, chiseled "All-American looks" enhancing the movie's carefully constructed "reality." (Hirsch was more cooperative with his studio than other All-Americans like Glenn Davis had been with theirs; see page 270.)

The plot begins with Hirsch as a high school player in Wisconsin; his coach, "Win" Brockmeyer, watches as Elroy remains after football practice, trying to perfect different aspects of his game until, finally, darkness forces him to stop. The coach, played by an actor with a mellow and authoritative voice, also functions as the Voice-of-God narrator, informing the audience that "none of us realized then that a sports legend was being born, like Red Grange and Tom Harmon." The classic cinema often engaged in elbow-nudging, telling viewers how to think about the material on screen; *Crazylegs, All-American* had particularly sharp and active elbows. (A few 1950s TV sportscasters adopted elbow-nudging as their main technique, and the tradition continues to this day.)

Elroy Hirsch became a high school star and, in 1941, joined the University of Wisconsin football team, coached by Harry Stuhldreher, the quarterback of Knute Rockne's "Four Horsemen" backfield. The movie depicts Hirsch's first college game, Wisconsin against Notre Dame; Elroy leads the Badgers to a 7-7 tie, his play against the celebrated Fighting Irish "elevating him to the highest level of the sport." That season, because of his distinctive running style, a reporter calls him "Crazylegs," and the nickname sticks, adding to his popularity and, when he makes the 1941 All-America team, his "legendary fame." Then, in December of that year, with the U.S. declaration of war, he enlists in the Marine Corps and immediately finds himself among a group of ethnics, WASPs, urban and country boys straight out of a World War II combat film.

By setting so much of this movie in the heyday of classic college sports and war pictures, the filmmakers summon up that period and attempt to evoke the response that audiences made to such pictures as *The Iron Major. Crazylegs, All-American* also implies that intercollegiate athletics existed in an ideal state before the postwar corruption and scandals, and can recapture that mode again. Of course, Eden never existed in college sports history, and *Crazylegs* offers no suggestions on how to restore it.

The Marine Corps sends Hirsch to a training program at the University of Michigan, and soon he suits up for the Wolverines, leading them to victory in the Big Ten. The film contains little plot movement and mainly features Crazylegs's athletic triumphs—he wins All-America honors in football again—as well as examples of his conduct as an All-American male. For the latter, the movie includes a traditional romance with a lovely young woman named Ruthie, his eventual wife. When he joins the Marines, she tells him, "I'll wait for you, Roy," and wherever he journeys, he places a photo of her on his desk or bureau.

Ruthie, played by starlet Joan Vohs, resembles the blonde co-eds on the football game program covers in the 1940s and 1950s, and the movie posters for this film displayed Hirsch hugging Vohs, her head and eyes upraised, gazing adoringly at him, identical to the iconography of the game programs. The photo of Ruthie on the desk of his room at Michigan motivates him to join the Wolverine basketball team so that when they play at Wisconsin, he can travel along and see her (the film contains no hint that the Michigan basketball coach might have recruited Hirsch).

Crazylegs is so talented an athlete that he becomes an All-American in basketball, and later in the spring he wins Big Ten honors in baseball and track. Finally, the Marines ship him to Parris Island for further training, and, as a parting gift from Michigan, he is awarded a monogrammed "Wolverine blanket," reserved for graduating senior athletes. This climaxes his college career and is the main thrust of the movie. It also indicates the boring nature of the traditional sports plot, the predictable pageant of athletic triumphs and human virtues, a monotony that contrasted with the lively revisionist and mixed-form treatments of college sports.

The plot then outlines Hirsch's postwar professional career. First he plays in the *Chicago Tribune*'s College All-Star game, receiving the MVP Award from Arch Ward, then the movie includes lengthy footage from his games with the Los Angeles Rams, the sound track blaring the truly awful "Rams Fight Song." In these scenes, the filmmakers self-consciously compete with TV, showing game action and up-close-and-personal scenes with Hirsch and teammates Bob Waterfield, Norm Van Brocklin, "Deacon" Dan Towler (who leads the club in a prayer), and other stalwarts from Hirsch's years with the Rams.

The pro football sequences demonstrate the fragility of the purely classical college sports movie: increasing numbers of collegians were turning pro for the money—the movie makes a point of Hirsch's only doing it to pay his father's hospital bills—and the polished NFL play contrasts to the early 1940s college football scenes. Nevertheless, *Crazylegs, All-American* broke even at the box office, and did not end Hollywood's interest in such films.

■   ■   ■

At this time, because the studio bosses believed that Cinemascope movies sold the most tickets, Columbia Pictures, for one of its major movies, combined two traditional genres—the college sports picture and the military school film—into a big-budget John Ford epic, *The Long Gray Line,* which was eventually released in 1955. Columbia did not foresee that future film historians would label this picture "the last of the [school] 'spirit' movies" and "a fitting close to an era," but the studio's short-sightedness reflected Hollywood's frequent misreading of America in the 1950s, particularly the movie industry's reluctance to accept the fragmentation of its once monolithic audience.

Columbia made and marketed *The Long Gray Line* as if the weekly moviegoers of the early 1940s still existed; in fact, they had split into a number of factions, many still appreciative of the pure classicism of this film but others indifferent or hostile to it. One critic characterized "this kind of movie" as "contrived and fantasized," also "displaying a code of honor and standard of behavior that are no longer credible . . . as old-fashioned today as the patriotic mood that inspired it."

The attitude of many Americans toward the military started to shift, particularly after the frustrating Korean War, and so had their perspective on another institution featured in *The Long Gray Line:* big-time college sports. At times a direct homage to *Knute Rockne—All-American* in its re-creation of the first Notre Dame–Army game and its casting of Donald Crisp (Father Callahan in the first film) as Patriarch Maher here, this film tried to recapture the prewar college world, with only partial success. Many moviegoers still loved the college sports ideals portrayed in this picture, but others found them hollow and/or improbable after the early 1950s scandals.

In part, *The Long Gray Line* was Hollywood's final effort to revive the huge and homogeneous audience of *Knute Rockne—All-American* and *The Iron Major*. In failing to accomplish this, the picture underlined the fact that college football itself was losing market share, particularly as the popularity of the NFL increased. Nevertheless, *The Long Gray Line* did demonstrate that for the loyal fans of college sports, the classic ideals remained powerful, especially when enveloped in traditional iconography.

Just as Columbia had its goals for *The Long Gray Line,* the U.S. military authorities involved in the picture had theirs: they considered the movie a crucial part of their campaign to rehabilitate the image of West Point and Army football after the 1951 "Cribbing Scandal."

■   ■   ■

The Long Gray Line was Ford's first picture in Cinemascope . . . Though ostensibly based on Marty Maher's autobiography, *Bringing Up the Brass: My 55 Years at West Point* (1951), and proclaiming itself, "The True Story of an Enlisted Man Who Was There for 50 Years," virtually all of the movie is pure invention.

—Film scholar Tag Gallagher, 1986.

Columbia studio executive Jerry Wald later admitted that he "pitched" this film for many years before his bosses finally gave it the green light. In the mid-1940s, he read about longtime West Point athletic trainer Marty Maher in a newspaper article, and then he heard Maher discussing his "years at the Post" on a national radio program, but Wald's concept for a film on Maher's life stalled until the West Point scandal of 1951 occurred. Suddenly, a New York publisher brought out the Maher memoir—described by one critic as an "almost unreadable collection of locker-room stories and talk of old Ireland"—and the Columbia bosses approved Wald's project, hiring the great classical filmmaker John Ford to direct it.

Long before the invention of the phrase "spin control," the United States military had practiced it, primarily during World War II but also in the postwar era, and never more assiduously than when putting the best spin on their own affairs, particularly those concerning their cherished West Point. Neither Wald nor anyone else associated with *The Long Gray Line* ever acknowledged the film's propaganda content, but much of the movie appears as West Point's postscandal response to its critics as well as reassurances to the American public that all was well in this important institution. Some reviewers sensed the film's PR subtext, but they did not dislike it, one noting, "It is frankly sentimental, very human, proudly patriotic." (The filmmakers did admit that Army officials had the right of approval over the script and also controlled the shooting at West Point, where almost every scene occurs.)

The opening of *The Long Gray Line* immediately invokes familiar West Point icons, both visual—the heights above the Hudson, the rows of cannons, the fabled barracks—and aural, the Cadet chorus singing the "Alma Mater" and other Academy hymns. The opening fades into a contemporary scene, the gray-haired Maher at the White House asking one of his favorite former students, Dwight Eisenhower, president of the United States, for a special waiver from the Army's mandatory retirement policy. This episode sends a clear message to 1950s audiences: this is an important film.

While the president ponders Maher's request, the frame dissolves into a scene with Maher, played by Tyrone Power, the hero of many classic action pictures, arriving in America as a young Irish immigrant at the end of the nineteenth century. Much of the subsequent plot involves Maher's fulfilling the immigrant dream and becoming a true American. In addition, he must adjust to West Point's way of life: his first job in America is as a waiter on the Post, then he enlists in the Army, remaining at the Military Academy in various positions until a bluff but kindly officer (played by Ward Bond, a Ford regular and a former USC football hero) makes him an athletic trainer.

One of Maher's first direct encounters with the Cadets concerns the Honor Code, which was crucial to the 1951 West Point scandal. A group of his friends in the Corps violate the Code. Their offense goes undetected, yet they discuss turning themselves in and accepting the draconian punishment, expulsion. Maher tells them that they are "mad" to consider this course of action. Nevertheless, the Cadets confess to the authorities, also explaining to Marty that the Honor Code transcends "being caught or not." For them, it embodies a spiritual truth—the essence of the United States Military Academy.

Later in the film, Maher's godson Red Sundstrom, who had made Marty immensely proud with his admission to the Academy, tells his godfather about his violation of the Honor Code and his intention to remain silent about it. Maher has come to love the West Point ethos, and he refuses to approve Red's action—in fact, he demands that the young man abide by the Code and accept expulsion from the Academy, even though Red is about to graduate and receive his officer's commission. Red follows Marty's order, and, because this incident occurs during World War II and in a classic film, he enters the Army and becomes a combat hero. Again, the movie emphasizes the transcendent importance of the Honor Code, a crucial element in the expulsion of the ninety athletes and tutors in 1951.

Maher's actual memoirs do not contain any of these events or even a godson: the scriptwriters concocted the Honor Code incidents and the Cadet characters in them. Similarly, they created a scene where a brash politician on a VIP tour of West Point gets into an argument with Marty about the Code.

The visitor, the governor of a large state, contends that "West Point is overwhelmed by tradition, and has lost touch with reality." In 1951, many apologists for Blaik's powerhouse program used this line to attack the severity of the punishments to the athletes and their tutors for cribbing. But Marty Maher, clearly the hero of the film and a truthsayer, defends the Academy's traditions as necessary for the training of officers. He then names the great West Point graduates—Eisenhower, MacArthur, Patton, and others—who led the Allied forces to victory in the recent world war. The case for the Honor Code rests.

Throughout his years at the Military Academy, particularly in his role as football trainer, Maher dispenses personal advice and aid to the young Cadets. A running joke concerns his attempts to help Ike stave off baldness. Marty also deflates some of the football stars, always insisting that they study hard and reminding them that they came to the Academy to become military officers, not professional athletes. As with the film's treatment of the Honor Code, Marty's position here is a postscandal response to the criticism of Blaik's questionable football recruits, a reassurance that this phenomenon was an aberration, far from West Point tradition.

■　■　■

Midway through the movie, the voice-over of Marty Maher introduces the first Army–Notre Dame game: "I'll never forget that day in 1913 when we played that little school from the far, far west." Except for the Cinemascope process and the suffused color, John Ford's recreation of this event is remarkably similar to the one in *Knute Rockne—All-American.* Ford depicts the same small football field at West Point, the rickety wooden stands and sparse crowd, and the informal gathering of teams on the sideline. On the surface, each film attempts historical authenticity, but at a deeper level, because they strive for a "golden glow," they create an idealized old-time football game.

In 1913, the Notre Dame visit to Army was not a huge event, but both teams were nationally ranked and played before much larger crowds— including for this game—than these films imply. In addition, even though both movies include helmetless players and muddy uniforms, no athlete suffers an injury, not even a bloody nose—unlike the ferocious collegiate game of the era. (In 1913, the Notre Dame student newspaper mocked this brutality in its headlines for one game: "Darwin's Original Football Squad Met Barnum's Pets . . . Results—Six Dead, Seventeen Wounded.")

Technicolor also allowed John Ford to add a historical error not in the earlier film: he placed Notre Dame in green uniforms, though they only wore blue and gold in this early period. But Ford, born in Ireland, could not resist green for the Fighting Irish, nor the inclusion of various "stage Irish" characters familiar to Americans from vaudeville and Hollywood but far from authentic Irish culture. Maher's father, Old Martin—played by Donald Crisp—talks with the thickest of brogues, dances jigs, and fulfills the "Old Sod" stereotype, particularly during the 1913 Army–Notre Dame game, when he leads spontaneous cheers for the Fighting Irish and wagers heavily on them. Yet, in keeping with Crisp's Father Callahan character in the Rockne biopic, in times of family crisis, Old Martin exhibits great strength and wisdom.

During the first half of the Army–Notre Dame game, because the Cadets dominate, Old Martin is downcast (in the actual game, ND scored first and led 14-13 at the half). Then, the voice-over of Marty announces, "In the second half, something happened never before seen in football": the introduction of the forward pass. The film shows the Notre Dame coach substituting Rockne into the contest (he played the whole game), and soon the All-American end catches a touchdown pass. His teammates call him "Swede," as they do in *Knute Rockne—All-American* (he was Norwegian) and he snares other TD passes to lead his team to victory.

John Ford never shows Rockne full face and up close—probably because Americans knew his face so well and would dislike an actor other than Pat O'Brien playing him—but the effect is to render "Rock" ghostlike and omnipotent. Old Martin cheers him and his teammates on, and when Notre Dame coasts to victory, he tells his son never to bet "against Mother Church." Then, as the Fighting Irish leave the field victorious, a nun joyously leads a brass band of parochial school students in the "Notre Dame Victory March."

Finally, John Ford's account of the first Army–Notre Dame game is even less historically accurate than the one in *Knute Rockne—All-American* and, if possible, more sentimental. Both films also perpetuate the myth that Rockne invented the forward pass, and that Notre Dame won the 1913 contest with this brilliant tactic. (Authoritative studies credit Eddie Cochems, coach of St. Louis University from 1906 to 1908, as the probable inventor; moreover, in 1913 at West Point, ND used the pass to spread the Army defense and create space for its running backs, scoring more often on running plays than passes.)

Significantly, in his memoir, Maher gave the accurate scoring details of the game, and he also mentioned that Army had used the forward pass for a number of years, primarily when near its opponents' goal line. His clear statement of these facts indicates how the scriptwriters of *The Long Gray Line* willfully ignored them, choosing instead the idealized fable from *Knute Rockne—All-American*. Similarly, in his book Maher commented, "Nowadays I hear the name of Knute Rockne a lot, spoken almost in a whisper," but rather than genuflect, Maher discussed the actual "man who understood what [sports columnist] Red Smith calls 'the biological urge to bet' " on college games (Rockne ignored his players' large betting pools on Army games).

Mundane details, even though historically accurate, do not make a classical film—the form demands that events and characters be extraordinary in all respects. More than any other Hollywood director, John Ford knew how to create classic movies, so he ended the ND football sequence in the Army locker room with the West Point coach telling his downcast players that they had just learned one of life's most important lessons: be prepared to encounter the unexpected, particularly because warfare always contains surprises. He cheers them up with the prediction that, as officers, they will take the lesson of this defeat with them into coming battles and, as a result, achieve great victories for their nation. Since the audience knows that West Point men led the American armies in World War I, soon to begin, and then in World War II, *The Long Gray Line* fuses the first Army–Notre Dame game and college sports with America's most glorious military triumphs.

In all probability, Charlie Daly, the Army coach in 1913, did not make this post-game speech or any other one. In this era at West Point, at game's end usually the families and friends of the players came onto the field and talked with them at length, after which the Army athletes eventually drifted back to their locker room to change and resume their Cadet duties. But applying historical facts to *The Long Gray Line* misconstrues John Ford's intention, his lack of interest in documentary-like realism, and his fascination with an ideal world. Thus, at the end of the film, back in the 1950s, after Ike agrees to Marty's request, the West Point authorities honor Maher with a special full-dress parade. During it Marty gazes off, suddenly seeing the ghosts of his loved ones, all dead but all eternally "real" to him and the moviegoer.

John Ford's genius was his ability to evoke an ideal world that his audiences wanted to exist. Particularly in his 1950s films—now termed his "Age of Myth" period—Ford created a world in which moviegoers could witness heroic men accomplishing splendid deeds, supported by beautiful and passionate women (Maureen O'Hara plays Marty's soulmate and wife). In *The Long Gray Line*, viewers can attend the first Army–Notre Dame game, know their war heroes as young men, and walk the glorious heights above the Hudson. Intercollegiate athletics holds a similar appeal for its devoted fans, including the witnessing of great events, "knowing" outstanding athletes as college players, and visiting the hallowed stadiums and arenas.

In the end, John Ford's world is a better one than humans have experienced at West Point or anywhere else in the universe, and in the 1950s, even though some moviegoers, those inclined toward revisionism, dismissed the world of *The Long Gray Line* as a fantasy, and some regretted its passing (mixed-form enthusiasts), many others refused to believe that it no longer existed and that its heroes had vanished.

■　　■　　■

The Long Gray Line achieved the U.S. military's goal for the picture: it helped return the West Point image to its former lofty place in the American sports pantheon. In addition, almost miraculously and accompanied by great media and public hosannas, the Army football team returned to national prominence. Crucial to its ascendancy, and to Coach Blaik's ability to remain within the rules, was the NCAA's restoration of one-platoon football—an on-field equivalent of the idealized college sports scenes in *Crazylegs, All-American* and *The Long Gray Line.*

At the time, for the media and for football fans, this NCAA rule change seemed monumental; a half century later, because one-platoon disappeared forever within a decade, it appears marginal. Yet the 1950s media portrayal of one-platoon football and fan enthusiasm for it—in large part due to media representations—form an amazing and important chapter in the history of intercollegiate athletics. Moreover, because NCAA leaders played a crucial role, their handling of the one-platoon legislation reveals their understanding and manipulation of the traditional ideals, as well as their continuing drive for control of college sports.

Focusing on these events is similar to—after a long matinee of 1950s films and their engaging narratives—exiting into the harsh sunlight outside the movie theater.

44

Fan Pleasure: The Return of One-Platoon

DOWN WITH THE PLATOONS

All hope is not lost, folks. The great game of [college] football may yet be saved and its popularity restored . . .

This column prefers to remain impersonal, but I am so violently opposed to the two-platoon style of play that there is no other way to treat the subject . . . I was a football fan long before I was ever a football writer, and I'm still a fan even though I find my interest wavering and my zest for the college game disappearing fast.

—*New York Times* columnist Arthur Daley, January 1953.

Prompting Arthur Daley's joy and potential reconciliation with college football was the surprise announcement on the eve of the 1953 NCAA convention that the association's council had recommended an end to unlimited substitution in college football—a return to the old one-platoon system. The council, controlled by the leadership, saw the move as a response to the many problems bombarding the sport, and Walter Byers, with his superb PR sense, promoted it as a major reform. Significantly, the ACE presidents' panel had not considered the platoon issue important enough for their agenda; it was definitely peripheral to the substantive reform of college sports.

Throughout the late 1940s, as increasing numbers of coaches employed separate offensive and defensive units, the controversy on unlimited substitution had escalated (see Chapter 26). In the early 1950s, the Pacific Coast Conference petitioned the NCAA to abolish two-platoon football, mainly because this would, "at one stroke, reduce the inflated costs" of funding the new, massive squads. The association did not respond, even though the football schedule for 1951 contained almost thirty fewer schools than in 1947–48, the recent dropouts including such prominent programs as St. Mary's of California and Georgetown University. When Georgetown quit football in the spring of 1951, its president revealed that the deficit for the sport the previous year had totaled almost $240,000 ($2.4 million in 1990s dollars), and he announced that "the extravagances of football," including eighty-one athletic scholarships, "have forced us to re-examine our educational, institutional, and social objectives. On no account could we see any justification for big-time football."

By the time of the 1953 NCAA convention, another twenty schools had dropped out, and for most small colleges the combination of declining football attendance and increasing expenses seemed a fatal potion. Sympathizing with them, Walter Byers also saw a way to consolidate their support for his administration: he pushed for a return to one-platoon and lower costs, hence the NCAA Council's action in early 1953. But this proposal was not an automatic PAT: the American Football Coaches Association presented a major obstacle. Indeed, on the very day that the council made its recommendation, the association moved in the opposite direction, announcing the results of its vote on the issue: 207 for the status quo on two-platoon, 246 for completely unlimited substitution (the current rules had some restrictions on when a player could return to the game), and only 71—mainly small-college coaches—for modifications of the present regulations, but not total one-platoon.

Nevertheless, Byers and his allies had a clever strategy for passing the rule change: rather than bring the council's proposal to the convention floor and watch famous coaches stomp it to death, they sent it directly to the Football Rules Committee for approval and implementation. The NCAA constitution permitted this maneuver, and, with the coaches howling that such a monumental change required a full floor debate and vote, the leadership zipped around their end.

The rules committee, mainly ADs and older coaches, met not only after the convention ended but in Florida, a thousand miles from the main meeting. It endorsed the ban on unlimited substitution, offering two reasons for its action. One was economics; as one member explained, "The coaches like free substitution but they don't have to balance the books." The other was the return to traditional football: "Many fans complain that the modern game, with constant streams of players running on and off the field, is too confusing. This group would like to go back to the era of the all-around 'iron man' performer."

On this issue, NCAA leaders always invoked "the will of the fans" as an impetus for this "reform," although the association never commissioned any surveys on unlimited substitution. The new, faster game of specialists probably pleased some spectators and bewildered many others, possibly discouraging the latter group from attending, but the NCAA offered no numbers. Predictably, the NCAA avoided such surveys because the results might contradict the official line that only TV ruins attendance.

When the NCAA Football Rules Committee passed the council's proposal, the *New York Times* placed the news on its front page, alongside articles on President Eisenhower's first inauguration. To illustrate the football story, the *Times* printed a large photo of a change-of-possession situation, captioned "Platoon Traffic Jam: Four complete football teams are on the field in this typical game played under the two-platoon system as the ball changes hands . . . Under the new college rule that was adopted yesterday, mass movements of troops would be virtually eliminated."

The *Times* congratulated the NCAA: "The scuttling of the two-platoon system . . . is the best thing that has happened to the gridiron game since the scuttling of the flying wedge" almost a half century ago, but "it must be confessed that the action was totally unexpected." Thus, with a simple move—one that did not reform big-time college sports in a meaningful way—the NCAA defused its most powerful newspaper opponent.

Many other dailies and magazines as well as a who's who of prominent sportswriters also hailed the NCAA rule. Grantland Rice particularly liked the fact that now "coaches have to do more coaching . . . get down on the ground," as Rockne did, "and teach the one-way operators" how to play the whole game. And *Sport* magazine began an editorial, "We're among the large majority of college football fans who greeted the timely end of the free-substitution rule with a rousing cheer."

The sporting press always maintained that it understood the fans; as Arthur Daley stated, "I have yet to meet a fan who doesn't agree with me" on the platoon issue. Whether the public influenced the media or vice versa or whether, as is most likely, they interacted, the appeal to classic sports ideals probably persuaded many people of the wisdom of returning to one-platoon. And the bottom line for Walter Byers and his association was that the symbiosis on this issue between the NCAA and the media, and between both and the public, played a major role in restoring the popularity of intercollegiate athletics, as well as obliterating the memory of the scandals.

Some football coaches also endorsed the rule change, particularly mentors of de-emphasized and/or small-college programs. Columbia's Lou Little believed that his team and similar ones "can come back now, [live] within their means, and restore football without trying to overextend themselves." One-platoon did help the Ivies to improve their record against non-conference opponents, but it and the Cold War military draft aided the service academies even more, returning Colonel Blaik's Army squad to national glory, helping Navy make the Top Ten again, and assisting the new Air Force

Academy to break into big-time college football. Each military school could attract at least one platoon of outstanding players who could also survive academically. The football success of the military schools delighted the media and received full coverage in the most important national magazines; in the mid-1950s, according to *Life,* the Army-Navy annual became America's "Big Game" again, featured on its cover and those of other weeklies, with long photo essays inside.

■   ■   ■

> I think the new rule sets football back a generation. It definitely will make for an inferior game. On almost every team, for example, men will be playing defense who never played defense before. Inevitably, they'll make more mistakes than a defensive specialist working in the two-platoon system, and cheap touchdowns will result.
>
> —Michigan State coach Clarence "Biggie" Munn,
> August 1953.

Despite all of the media and fan endorsements of the new rule, big-time coaches like Munn articulated the main football problem with the return to yesteryear. Not only was one-platoon regressive—in fact, offenses became as error-prone as defenses, the game suffering more in that area than Munn had envisioned—but the rule change ran counter to the deeper cultural currents of the 1950s, particularly the era's love of bigger-and-better in everything from huge refrigerators to massive automobiles.

Ultimately, the tide of modernity submerged the reactionary one-platoon rule, but why did the fans, after viewing its negative effects during the 1953 season, continue to accept it for the remainder of the decade? Did the ideology of traditional college sports actually outweigh their desire to see the best possible football product on the field? Richard Miller, the author of a 1953 book on college sports, offered one important clue:

> The average fan, although he may believe himself to be an authority on football, doesn't know [for example] . . . when the line pinches, waits, loops, or even charges straight ahead. I do not say this to belittle the fan's knowledge of the game, but instead to emphasize the highly complex and scientific nature of modern football . . . [The fan] cannot expect to become an expert by having played for a few years some time ago, by watching a few games each year, and by discussing the games with friends.

This description of the early 1950s college football rooter seems accurate: how would this person acquire expertise when neither sportswriters nor radio and television broadcasters discussed technical matters? Football fans of this period were as uninformed about their favorite sport as most basketball root-ers were about theirs; the latter group did not understand basketball well enough to dispute the coaches when they denied any knowledge of the fixes. However, TV eventually taught the fans the complexities of college sports. As the announcers became more skillful—particularly when "color commenta-tors," often former coaches, joined the play-by-play men in the booth, and used illustrative devices—the fans started to learn when the linemen pinched, looped, and the rest. But those lessons were still a few years away.

In the early 1950s, a period of rapid change in most areas of American society, many college football fans seemed to welcome the ban on unlimited substitution as a time-out from the sport's rapid evolution. Just as many vot-ers hoped that the Eisenhower presidency would provide a respite from the profound social upheavals that had occurred during the FDR and Truman years, college football fans, conservative by nature, considered the restoration of one-platoon a suspension of the game's swift development. In addition, in hearkening back to a supposedly simpler and more honest period in college sports history, one-platoon transported fans from the aftermath of the scan-dals, and the absence of meaningful reforms, to a recognizable and comfort-ing gridiron world. Therefore, even though the impossibility of resurrecting the past doomed the rule, for a number of years it served its NCAA masters well and satisfied most of the media and the public.

■   ■   ■

Because big-time coaches always embrace bigger-and-better, one-platoon never pleased them, and led by Biggie Munn and other famous football men, they constantly criticized it, sometimes offering very accurate and prescient comments. As soon as the NCAA Football Rules Committee passed the reg-ulation, Woody Hayes of Ohio State condemned it, pointing out that coaches "simply cannot train a boy to play both offense and defense" in ordinary after-noon sessions, and therefore "the rule will mean longer practice sessions, something I thought the" NCAA's so-called "reformers were trying to avoid." Not only did Hayes indicate the hypocrisy inherent in the association's move, but NCAA leaders never questioned his premise: even with one-platoon play, they wanted college football to remain at the highest possible entertainment level and to fill stadiums, particularly since economic revival was one of the main goals of the rule change.

Other big-time coaches made similar arguments, and support for their beloved unlimited substitution came from a surprising source: Red Grange, the Galloping Ghost of the Illini, one of the greatest heroes of 1920s one-platoon football. Unlike many sportswriters who saw his 1920s playing career through a misty haze, Grange was clear-eyed, stating that his alma mater's recent "Rose Bowl champions would have whipped my own best Illini team by 50 points." Grange also liked the two-platoon game "because today's specialists are better football players" than their predecessors, and "thanks to frequent rest periods on the bench, they can go at top speed every second they're on the field. The ironmen of my era would have melted down in a hurry if they'd ever have attempted to play a full, 60-minute game at the tremendous pace demanded by modern football." Finally, for a knowledgeable football fan like Grange, the complex modern game was much more fascinating than the "stereotyped and unimaginative" 1920s version.

Nonetheless, the level of play in the revived one-platoon system did not decline to the 1920s level, mainly because the big-time coaches exploited the same loophole used by Knute Rockne: assemble a large number of players, form at least two complete units, and, according to one 1950s analyst, "employ Rock's 'shock-troops' idea . . . wherein a No. 2 team starts [each half] to wear down the opposition for the No. 1 team to enter and make the kill. [As a result] there won't be many sixty-minute players" in the new era. But this solution meant that the rich teams would stay wealthy and put fans in the stands, whereas the poor would still go to the hell of empty stadiums. Even Grantland Rice recognized this in a 1953 season preview: "In one-platoon football, as in two-platoon, the 'have' schools, those with more 'liberal' recruiting and subsidizing programs, or those with superior organization . . . will prevail." Rice placed Michigan State in the first category—"liberal" was his euphemism for cheating—and Notre Dame in the second—the Catholic school's recruiting advantages and Frank Leahy's coaching abilities ensuring success.

For many fans, however, the brand of football played by the "Have" schools seemed an excellent solution: it allowed the big-time teams to remain large, with their units going at a good speed when in the game, but it ended the massive and confusing substitutions with every change of possession. In addition, coaches had to install simpler offenses and defenses, and the fans could gradually learn the new formations.

■ ■ ■

Throughout the 1950s, most coaches with big-time programs continued to detest the one-platoon rules and to lobby against them. They demanded total abolition, but their leaders urged a more subtle approach: a widening of the loopholes that already existed in the regulations. After the 1953 season, the American Football Coaches Association requested that the NCAA Football Rules Committee allow players "to return once in each quarter." The Committee turned this down, but the close 10-7 vote encouraged the coaches. In the next few years, they not only obtained this change but began to stretch the loopholes until finally Woody Hayes could send his entire lumbering offense through them.

Hayes's "three yards and a cloud of dust" style of play characterized much of the game in this period, and most sports historians now scorn 1950s one-platoon ball as "dull" and "unimaginative." Because coaches could teach defensive play easier than offensive execution, defenses tended to dominate, but, other than the military academies, the one-platoon game did not help the smaller programs recoup their football fortunes—they could not play it as well as the big boys. Moreover, none of the schools that had dropped out for financial reasons came back, and others joined them on the sidelines; the big-time programs triumphed, and small-college football teams continued to limp along. Eventually, the NCAA regrouped them into lower divisions.

Yet, in terms of public relations, the NCAA's restoration of one-platoon was a great success. From the rule's inception in 1953, the media hailed it as a profound change, with pronouncements like, "Seldom has any sport" or sports system "undergone such a drastic revision from one season to the next" (the *Saturday Evening Post*), and because one-platoon was so connected to the traditional ideals, the public believed that it signified reform for other aspects of intercollegiate athletics. However, the rule was cosmetic surgery and never dented the corruption in college sports; indeed, it increased the abuses as coaches searched for authentic two-way players, offering ever larger amounts of money and perks to induce them to sign. One former coach joked that with two-platoon, he and his colleagues always needed "a third platoon to go to class" and satisfy the faculty; even though the 1953 rule eliminated one unit, coaches still required an extra one for classroom duty, more so now because of the lengthier football practice sessions.

In the end, for the NCAA, the return to one-platoon lasted about as long as the contents in the hip flask in a fan's pocket. The NCAA nursed its potion through the entire 1950s, regularly adding water and diluting it, but finally the association totally emptied the flask and set out for the next contest, the explosive 1960s version of the sport. Once the average fan's knowledge of football caught up with the current game—with NFL telecasts accelerating the process because the pros never deviated from unlimited substitution— the cultural demand for bigger-and-better college football brought back two platoons and much more: massive squads of new and improved specialists as well as special units.

■   ■   ■

> Quite possibly sports historians fifty years from now will mark the passing of free substitution as the end of an era [of corruption in intercollegiate athletics], and the beginning of a trend toward collegiate football and basketball in keeping with the purposes of a college education.

> —Author Richard Miller, 1953.

No sports historian at the end of the century would agree with this statement; indeed, its optimism and inability to see beyond the surface of the rule change is startling today. The restoration of one-platoon football now appears as an artificial attempt to return to the past—not even to actual history but to an idealized version of it—and analogous to Hollywood's brief attempt to revive classical college sports movies. Thus, 1950s one-platoon was doomed before it began, and for that reason it is mainly remembered as an aberration or a curiosity. All sports histories dismiss it quickly, ignoring even its important cultural dimension.

Nonetheless, this incident did "mark . . . the end of an era": the media's last hurrah for the classic college sports ideals in their pure *Knute Rockne—All-American* form. One-platoon not only prompted many columns and articles by Arthur Daley and like-minded sportswriters, but also radio and television shows. Most importantly, it was linked to the NCAA's counterattack on the critics of intercollegiate athletics and the association's attempt to represent post-1951 college football and basketball as scandal-free and reformed.

Led by Walter Byers, the NCAA not only altered the public image of intercollegiate athletics, but it started to change the vocabulary of college sports. The association began with its own publications as well as the official ones of member athletic departments, particularly their most visible products: football game programs, seen by millions of Americans every fall.

45

Programs as Propaganda—
When Needed Most

A 1953 case was filed by a player named Nemeth, who was injured during spring football practice at the University of Denver . . . The court ruled that the state Industrial Commission's award to Nemeth [for workmen's compensation] was correct, since "Nemeth was an employee of the university and sustained an accidental injury arising out of and in the course of his employment" [as a football player] . . .

[As a result of] the dreaded notion that NCAA athletes could be identified as *employees* by state industrial commissions and the courts, we crafted the term *student-athlete,* and soon it was embedded in all NCAA rules and interpretations as a mandated substitute for such words as players and athletes. We told college publicists to speak of "college teams," not football or basketball "clubs," a word common to the pros.

—NCAA executive director Walter Byers, 1995.

In an amazing confession, Byers admitted inventing the term "student-athlete" and ordering its use in all NCAA documents. (In addition, the term soon appeared on English professors' lists of oxymorons.) His motivation was practical, not idealistic, and his pronoun "we" was less modest than royal. With the costs of college sports continually rising in the 1950s—one-platoon football did not make a serious dent in expenses—Byers realized that if athletic programs also had to pay workmen's comp fees for their athletes, and also faced lawsuits and potentially huge settlements for employee/players suffering catastrophic injuries, many schools would drop football; some might even quit intercollegiate athletics. Also, the NCAA now permitted athletic scholarships, which, according to critics and even some IRS agents, constituted pay-for-play.

Therefore, because the NCAA could not make intercollegiate athletics even remotely amateur, it would use sleight of language and insist to the courts, the IRS, and the public that the verbal appearance was the reality, that the amateur ideal actually prevailed. This campaign succeeded, and since the 1950s the NCAA and its member schools have rarely lost a lawsuit on these issues, never an appeal.

A year or so after mandating the "student-athlete" and "team" terms, the NCAA also changed the title of the sports publicity directors to "sports information directors," as if these men and women now dispensed only factual information, not PR puffery. Some members of this cynical profession viewed their new title with amusement. In a letter to his fellow athletic department publicists, an editor of a SID publication joked, "The annual directory of Sports Information Directors (*that's you*) is in the works." Nevertheless, most changed their stationery and desk plaques.

In this period, NCAA newspeak reigned—the leadership's favorite reading seemed to be Orwell's *1984*—and other college sports items also received new names. The "dope sheet," because of its allusion to betting, became the "scouting report," and the venerable "dope book," published by athletic departments for the media, mutated into the "football preview guide" and the "basketball preview guide." Guidebooks also went public, first at Notre Dame under the aegis of Charlie Callahan, and then at other schools, pleasing devoted fans and earning some money for athletic departments.

The NCAA also pressed SIDs to work harder on the football and basketball game programs, not only by cooperating fully with the national advertising agencies that produced most of them but also by including items reflecting the association's policy on various issues. As in previous periods of widespread public and media discontent with college sports, in the early 1950s, the NCAA and member athletic departments counterattacked with a stream of visual and written propaganda, all of it linking their commercial enterprise to classic college sports ideals. Walter Byers and his colleagues believed that if their PR offensive succeeded, not only would it help big-time college sports survive its worst crisis and scandals, but it would set the student-athlete image in the public consciousness for years to come.

■   ■   ■

A huge graduation mortar board hovers above the head of a football quarterback at the center of the drawing. The QB, pigskin in his right hand, arm cocked, scans the sky. Textbooks frame the upper half of his body, and his torso and legs disappear behind the large front covers of other books, big block letter titles—BUSINESS ADMINIS-TRATION, ECONOMICS, LAW, ENGINEERING, MEDICINE— identifying them. The textbooks monopolize the picture.

This passage describes one of the most popular football game program covers of the 1950s. From the origins of collegiate football game programs in the late nineteenth century, this illustration marked one of the few occasions a cover depicted the educational aspect of the university, and the very first one in which academics overshadowed sports.

In the 1950s, the Don Spencer Agency on New York's Madison Avenue dominated game program production, and one of its artists produced this illustration as part of a series of covers on the student-athlete theme. More than 150 schools used it for home football games, superimposing the names of their institution and the visitor's onto the image and the date of the game at the bottom of the page. Thus, millions of Americans saw the ad agency's merger of academics and athletics, its insistence on the student-athlete, and its response to such criticisms as "dumb jocks" being sheltered in "Mickey Mouse courses." (See the photo section of this book for a copy of this cover.)

Another popular cover in this period by the same artist, Larry Tisdale, attempted to portray the balance between the two sides of a student-athlete: the left panel of the drawing displayed a tweed-jacketed shoulder and arm, the hand holding thick textbooks; in the right panel, a football-uniformed shoulder and arm, the hand grasping a pigskin; and in the middle panel, a gold football trophy in front of a graduation gown. (A contrary but private view of such images appeared at this time as the lead item in the newsletter of the Football Writers Association of America: "Profs and players/ Might be buddies/ Except for emphasis/ On studies." In public print, however, most FWAA members went along with the NCAA line.)

Larry Tisdale produced many variations on the student-athlete theme, as did other Spencer artists. The agency's premier illustrator, Lon Keller, also created an important version: football as a thinking man's game with high intelligence required to play it. In an often repeated and imitated drawing, Keller placed a ballcarrier in the center of the sketch, and foregrounded the Xs and Os of a diagrammed play, indicating the amount of information the athlete had to process for the play to succeed. Again the Football Writers Association of America dissented, preferring the dumb-jock model; the lead item in a 1950s newsletter joked, "Heck of a halfback from Hangover Tech/ Exploded through enemy wall/ Raced into the clear and ran like a deer/ But somebody else had the ball!"

Lon Keller also drew many covers featuring student-athletes of "bygone era football." Usually he situated the game in the 1920s or the late nineteenth century, but he always portrayed a nonviolent, good-natured version of the sport. In addition, he often depicted old-time players carrying books and football equipment to and/or from practice, balancing classroom and athletic responsibilities. Many schools used these covers, particularly for their annual homecoming games, presenting a sanitized and exemplary past to the fans.

At one of the annual meetings of the sports information directors during this period, a panel discussed the game programs and concluded that "a good cover does more than anything else to sell a program" to spectators. And the excellent sales of the student-athlete covers—the contemporary as well as the nostalgic ones—implied that the fans liked the images of football players as authentic students, wanting to believe in the traditional college sports ideals.

Throughout the 1950s, the Don Spencer artists produced many illustrations on the academic-athletic connection, millions of copies of their work appearing every autumn. In a period when advertising agencies began to see themselves as "hidden persuaders," creating subtle, even "subliminal messages," the football game programs provided excellent examples of Madison Avenue's wizardry. Thus, the Spencer Agency's nondidactic images also contained messages: its regular depictions of football heroes playing the game, with adoring fans cheering them on, invoked an idealized world, one far from the reality of 1950s intercollegiate athletics.

Lon Keller favored handsome, crewcut young men, with modest grins and gleaming white teeth; often, below their reassuring faces, he foregrounded stylized drawings of 1950s football action, with no hint of violence or even roughness in the tackling or blocking. Another Spencer artist, C. C. Breall, sketched the faces of smiling football players floating above colorful marching bands: college sports as American pageant. Breall also did Norman Rockwell–like drawings of young boys dressed in adult football uniforms, standing in front of bedroom mirrors, pretending to be All-American heroes. Keller frequently used a variation on this trope: a Pop Warner League QB, arm cocked, superimposed upon the larger image of a college QB, arm cocked.

Keller was also adept at other aspects of Rockwellian art. In one popular drawing, he depicted four football players in the locker room after the game, singing as a quartet, imitating the male groups of the period, like the Four Freshmen and the Four Lads, entertainers who often topped the Hit Parade and performed at college proms and other campus events. Thus Keller, like Rockwell, recycled the pop culture of the time—in this case, the puerile Tin Pan Alley music of the 1950s—and clearly linked college sports to this polished, artificial world.

Another favorite set of images in this period, used by every athletic department working with the Spencer Agency, featured young blonde co-eds admiring their football heroes. One cover in particular endured for many years, appearing at the home games of almost every big-time football school: a beautiful young co-ed with ruby lips, blue eyes, and long blonde hair snuggles her head against the shoulder of her boyfriend, a handsome football player in uniform, gazing up lovingly at him, her hands clasped as if in prayer to emphasize her adoration of her athlete-hero. (Frank Deford in *Everybody's All-American*, published in 1981, wrote about a similar 1950s couple; the young woman was the school's "Magnolia Queen" and the player a Heisman candidate. However, Deford also presented the reality behind this fantasy world.)

Variations of the "adoring co-ed" theme continued throughout the decade. Sometimes she gazed up from a book to daydream, the football hero's image floating at the top of the drawing; at other times, she was a cheerleader on the sideline; always she was a fervent supporter as well as a reward and prize for "her man." She was almost always blonde, and, as the decade continued, she often looked like Doris Day and wore pink-and-blue sweaters and poodle skirts.

These conservative depictions of young women apparently pleased all involved, reaffirming their sense of college sports as a bastion of traditional male-female relations. Similarly, many program covers in this era revived the motifs and icons of the World War II years—another crisis period in intercollegiate athletics—and appealed to patriotism. The goal of the NCAA's relentless PR campaign, brilliantly brought to life by the Spencer Agency, was to render college sports as American as mom and apple pie, to present the playing of "The Star-Spangled Banner" and the display of Old Glory at games as the unassailable reality of big-time college sports, and to imprint this all-American image upon the public. Not surprisingly, in the mid-1950s, when Chevrolet became the major sponsor of the NCAA's TV football package, it began to add its name to the cherished All-American list, also presenting a weekly award to the outstanding "student-athletes" of the televised game.

For the 1950s program covers, the Spencer artists also continued the theme of female-as-spectator, begun the previous decade. With football attendance in decline, the NCAA and member schools wanted to emphasize this role for women, and many covers illustrated and even glorified it. One popular illustration showed a thirty-something married woman (less sexual than the co-eds, hence dark-haired), carefully placing a mum in her lapel before leaving for the game; her husband sits at the wheel of the family car, fuming as he waits. But wait he did, her role as a fan fully sanctioned.

■　■　■

Mr. Edward W. Krause,
Director of Athletics,
University of Notre Dame.

Dear Moose:

Herein is a brief report of the Fourth Annual Mid-Winter meeting of the college and university sports publicists . . .

Program Problems . . . *Academic features,* it was thought, *should not run over two stories a program,* it being general opinion that feature stories on football are what are desired by the buying public . . .

—ND sports publicity director Charlie Callahan,
February 1951 (emphasis added).

The Notre Dame publicist, after attending the national meeting of his association, returned with the opinion of his colleagues bolstering his own in an ongoing dispute with his bosses about the contents of the Notre Dame football programs. In the late 1940s, the school had innovated with text articles on education and religion in its football programs, and by 1951 its administrators wanted many more "academic features" per issue, not only for home games but also in the programs of the schools that the Fighting Irish visited. Callahan balked, but his immediate boss, Moose Krause, agreed with the men in the Golden Dome, and, as the scandals of 1951 unfolded, the ND officials demonstrated that they were far ahead of the curve on the "academic features" question. In the next few years, the NCAA and some SIDs endorsed this position, swayed by the excellent sales of programs with student-athlete covers.

The early 1950s Notre Dame programs featured general articles on the university's educational and religious traditions, and specific pieces on academic departments, programs, and special events: "The Medieval Institute," "The Marriage Institute," "A Symposium on Soviet Russia," and so on. Then, the season after Father Cavanaugh left the school presidency, articles on his accomplishments in office appeared and, in the following years, Father Hesburgh contributed many columns on his administrative plans. In the mid-1950s, the ND football programs added more academic features, including a series on "Notre Dame's Great Teachers—Yesterday & Today."

Slowly, in the Big Ten and the East, various universities began to add academic features to their game publications. Nevertheless, in other parts of the country, particularly the South and Southwest, despite NCAA urging, the norm remained one short and perfunctory piece on the school's founding.

The ND programs, like those of all other schools, did contain photos of the football coaching staff and athletic department officials, as well as the main administrators of the university. However, the Notre Dame publications were unique when, in the mid-1950s, they began to carry photos of the academic deans and department heads. Another important breakthrough—one that eventually had a profound effect on every "student-athlete" in big-time college sports—occurred in an article published throughout the 1955 Fighting Irish home season.

Under the innocuous title, "What Becomes of Notre Dame Football Players," Executive Vice President Joyce discussed the findings of his recent survey on the graduation rates of ND players: "During the past quarter century . . . less than 3% of Notre Dame's football players have failed to graduate. Only two monogram [varsity letter] winners since 1945 left school without receiving their degrees." The inquiry also revealed that, after graduation, most of the ND players succeeded in business and/or professional careers. Father Joyce undertook the survey in 1954, in part, to examine a criticism often "levied against intercollegiate football . . . that the average foot-ball player is incapable of doing college work and therefore he either fails to graduate or is given snap courses." His school had long claimed that its ath-letes received genuine and full educations, and Joyce, trained in accounting, sought the actual numbers.

He announced his findings at the Notre Dame football banquet in Decem-ber 1954, publishing them in the game programs the following season. He wanted to help college sports during this dark period, and he certainly enhanced Notre Dame's reputation; however, the NCAA would not touch his survey or, more significantly, his idea of examining graduation rates. The NCAA leaders knew from personal experience and anecdotal evidence that a thorough study of the graduation rates of athletes at most big-time college sports schools would reveal much lower numbers than Notre Dame's 97.5 percent.

Ironically, even though the Fighting Irish grad rate more than fulfilled the student-athlete ideal, the NCAA never publicized it. The association much preferred the "crafted" game program images of athletes surrounded by text-books and mortarboards to the reality of national graduation rate statistics. The association definitely did not want the Don Spencer Agency to include pieces like Father Joyce's in its "features packages"—after reading them, spectators might wonder about the rates for the teams on the field that day.

Not surprisingly, Joyce's innovative use of graduation statistics languished for many years, though he continued his surveys of Fighting Irish athletes and released the results in ND publications. Finally, decades later, when investiga-tive journalists—not sportswriters—began to examine this question, they dis-covered grad rates that moved the NCAA into major damage-control mode.

■   ■   ■

ROCK STARTED SOMETHING
In Olden Days 11 Men Played an Entire Game—but Now . . .

In our undergraduate days we thought "Rock" was the greatest man that ever lived. We still do, which shows how a fellow matures over the years.

—Headline, subhead, and text from an article written by Red Smith for the Spencer Agency's "Features Package," 1953.

Red Smith reminisced about the Notre Dame of his student years in the twenties, and his favorite coach's use of "shock troops." With the 1953 restoration of one-platoon football, the national columnist managed to be both topical and nostalgic, also invoking Rock-as-classic-ideal throughout, both great football mind and magna cum laude graduate.

St. Knute was a perfect subject for the game programs of the 1950s, and sports information directors across the country ordered the articles on him, not only when the Fighting Irish came to town but on many other occasions. (During this period, many layers of hagiography covered the actual man.) Undoubtedly, the college sports establishment wanted to connect the postscandal period to the Golden Past and obliterate unpleasant events in between. Thus the Spencer Agency cranked out "Rockne Specials" for its national packages, using various anniversaries as pretexts: in 1953, the fortieth anniversary of the first Notre Dame–Army game and "the invention of the forward pass"; and in 1956, "the 25th anniversary of his tragic plane crash." In 1955, on the thirtieth anniversary of Notre Dame's first trip to Los Angeles, the Los Angeles Coliseum placed a plaque with Rockne's name and likeness in its "Coliseum Court of Honor . . . on the south side of the field," and USC ran a season-long article in its home-game publications, "Rock—The Headman." Then, two years later, when Army resumed football relations with Notre Dame, the Military Academy carried special photos of and articles on the famous coach in its programs.

In the mid-1950s, ND administrators and their West Point counterparts had decided on a two-year reappearance of the famed series, but not a return to annual games. (The teams did not meet again until the mid-1960s, and then only for another home-and-home.) In part, the school authorities wanted to bury the rumors about bad relations between the institutions that had circulated since the 1940s termination of the series, but, as important, they wished to help college football recapture past glories. Not only did Notre Dame and Army play a version of one-platoon football again, but real students wore the Fighting Irish and the Cadet uniforms.

The 1957 Army-ND game, played at Franklin Field in Philadelphia, generated massive football nostalgia, much of it centered on the Rockne legends. The game program, a Spencer special production, had "1913–1957" emblazoned in the upper right, and an old-time quarterback rising ghostlike upper left, about to launch a forward pass, while below him, 1950s players pass-blocked and pass-rushed. The supernatural motif resembled the conclusion of *The Long Gray Line.* Inside, the main article presented all of the previous game program covers in the ND-Army series, page after page revealing their traditional iconography and themes, from the early drawings and photographs to the World War II era with its entwining of college football and American patriotism. The 1957 program also included many full-page photos of the administrators of the two schools, as well as articles about the institutions' academic, military, and religious activities. And on game day, the teams provided 95,000 fans with an exciting contest that Notre Dame won, 23-21.

For the following year's meeting at Notre Dame Stadium, the hosts also ordered a special program cover from Spencer: old-fashioned picture frames occupied each quadrant of the page, photos of the 1913 Army coach and player-captain in two of them, and the 1913 ND coach and player-captain in the others—the viewer's eye moved quickly to the picture of the undergraduate Rockne. Inside, fans found a full complement of academic features on the two schools, and from the stands that day, they watched a dull 14-2 Army victory, similar to many of the actual old-time matches in the series.

Nevertheless, college sports enthusiasts and much of the national media so loved this restoration of traditional football that *Life* magazine featured the 1958 match with many pages of pictures and text. Supporting the classical representation was the Army hero of the game, Pete Dawkins, an excellent halfback and student, who was soon to win a Rhodes Scholarship as well as the Heisman Trophy. One of *Life*'s photo highlights was "Dawkins Gets Loose for 11 Yards," a major gain in this game, inadvertently indicating the blandness of the contest. Dawkins, very savvy with the press, frequently stated, "At West Point, a football player must be a Cadet first and a football player second," thus helping to remove the shadows of the 1951 "Cribbing Scandal."

■ ■ ■

Unlike Notre Dame and the military academies, most schools did not add many of their own articles to the Spencer features package. However, they took one or two of the agency's articles for each program. The typical Spencer piece extolled "student-athletes" in the most traditional terms; for example, Charles Loftus, SID at Yale University, wrote a long paean to them: "Nobody else can cram into one mind [the] assignments for an end run, an off-tackle slant, a jump pass, a quarterback sneak," and so on, except this "hard working, untiring, determined kid doing the very best he can for his school or college."

The Spencer Agency also provided the multicolor ads from the tobacco companies, the main sponsors of game programs as well as other college publications. The back covers usually presented a beautiful co-ed holding up a cigarette, and the middle pages—the ad dwarfing the team rosters—revealed healthy young people enjoying outdoor activities, including watching college football games, while puffing away. The ad agency further concealed the disjuncture between the glossy appearance and the toxic reality of smoking when it created a mid-1950s campaign specially for the game programs: a university scientist, peering through a microscope and gripping a cigarette, announces, "Science discovered it, you can prove it . . . More college men and women buy Chesterfield than any other cigarette." A half century later, these ads seem primitive and transparent, but according to sales figures of the time, they proved highly effective, helping persuade a majority of 1950s college students to adopt or continue the nicotine habit.

The football programs also contained pages of local advertising, sold by the athletic department to businesses in its area, on occasion with a message contradicting the Madison Avenue themes on amateur athletics. In the 1951

Baylor University publications, a local jeweler proclaimed "My offer to the 1951 Baylor Football Squad—If you win the S.W. [Southwest] Conference Race, you will each receive $100 Gruen 'Regal' Diamond Dial Wrist Watches." Baylor won and probably the jeweler happily paid off.

As the decade continued and Walter Byers assumed absolute control of the NCAA, the Spencer Agency sent out increasing numbers of pieces promoting the association. In 1955, many articles used "Intercollegiate Athletics Observes NCAA's 50th Anniversary" as their excuse for trumpeting the wisdom of the association's policies. However, every season after the 1953 passage of the one-platoon regulation, because the fans wanted to understand the rules of the game to which they had bought tickets, the programs also carried an NCAA article explaining that year's modifications of one-platoon. As early as 1955, the annual piece admitted, "It is possible for the coach to use the same player eight times during the course of the game . . . [but] this change, although liberalizing the Substitution Rule, is not intended as a step toward the old 'Two Platoon System' which was outlawed several seasons back." In subsequent years, as one-platoon ebbed away, the explanations became increasingly tortured, as if written in Orwellian newspeak where "War is Peace" and "Two-platoon is One-platoon."

■   ■   ■

A Noble Cause Is at Stake

We hold these things important:

Our purpose in honoring the heroes of the past in the Hall of Fame is to remind our youth and all of our people through great historical exhibits and through print and over the air that *there shall be no soft-ening of our fibre as we [Americans] face the task of world leadership.* There should be a clear recognition of the qualities developed through sport, of which amateur football is our finest example . . .

  Finally, *we hold that the game shall not be de-emphasized;* that the same standards of competitive excellence be held high on the field of sport as are held in the classroom . . . Football should continue to be a VITAL focus of general undergraduate and alumni interest.

—The Credo of the College Football Hall of Fame,
reprinted in most college football programs
in the 1950s (original emphasis).

In the late 1940s, various business and media groups in Brunswick, New Jersey, pushed for the creation and construction of a college football Hall of

Fame in their area (most sports historians recognize Rutgers University as the site of one of the first games of American football). A number of national figures, including Tug Wilson and Grantland Rice, liked the idea and helped promote it. However, it did not take hold until 1953 when the NCAA decided to use the Hall as part of its student-athlete PR campaign, asking member schools to "designate one home football contest [per season] as the Hall of Fame game, and to turn over a portion of the receipts to the project." In addition, the association requested that members print the Hall of Fame's credo in their programs throughout the season. This statement contained the traditional sports pieties as well as 1950s Cold War rhetoric—it italicized *"no softening of our fibre"* as the United States assumes *"the task of world leadership"*—and also included the political self-interest of the NCAA: *"we hold that the game shall not be de-emphasized."*

The authors consciously echoed the Preamble to America's noblest document, "We hold these truths to be self-evident," but the contrast with the Hall's version, "We hold these things important," as well as the one on de-emphasis, underlined the inadequacy of the promoters' language and ideas. Nevertheless, most NCAA member schools designated a "Hall of Fame game," placing a banner across their program cover for that contest and generating contributions to the project. Yet, throughout the 1950s, even after retired General Douglas MacArthur became honorary chairman and aided the Hall's fund-raising efforts, the organization never accumulated enough money to guarantee the venture's success.

The minutes of Hall of Fame's Executive Committee meetings reveal the difficulty: rather than parallel the NCAA's relentlessly classical portrayal of college sports, the Hall of Fame directors veered to the right politically, becoming involved in partisan disputes, often issuing extreme statements. Indeed, the organization came to see its role as "eventually . . . to build the Hall of Fame [but] of far greater concern is the Foundation's mission to serve as a spokesman for college football," superseding the NCAA because of the latter's "soft" attitude toward the critics of big-time college sports.

The president of the Hall of Fame Foundation, Chester J. LaRoche, often pressed its executive committee to attack "the negative influences which have inveighed against the game in the public print, such as the [famous] articles by James B. Conant, Henry Steele Commager, and others," and he issued frequent denunciations of the "enemies" of intercollegiate football. Conant, the president of Harvard, chaired an important U.S. commission on education in the 1950s, and had questioned the role of big-time college sports in American universities; Commager, an eminent historian, had posed similar queries in a *New York Times* magazine piece. To denounce these pillars of the American establishment, as LaRoche did, was folly. In contrast, the NCAA's Walter Byers, though undoubtedly disagreeing with Conant's and Commager's views, avoided public disputes with these men and other prominent critics.

But not LaRoche. Describing himself as "the best friend college football ever had," and speaking "on behalf of the Hall of Fame," he became obsessed with all real and imagined opponents. At one committee meeting also attended by General MacArthur and Colonel Earl Blaik, LaRoche worried about the many schools that had quit the sport, sounding off:

> In the matter of dropping football, the strongest case is the University of Chicago. To answer our critics, we should dig into the facts concerning Chicago. It is probable that the character of their student body has dropped off badly, and they are now overloaded with beatniks, leftists, and undesirables. It could be proved that dropping football was a disaster.

At the time and subsequently, University of Chicago officials replied to such charges by comparing the number of Nobel Prizes won by Chicago faculty to the number of Big Ten football championships captured by the Maroons before they left the conference (the current total is sixty-nine Nobel laureates to six Big Ten titles). Even General MacArthur, no lover of "beatniks, leftists, and undesirables," seemed annoyed by this LaRoche tirade, responding succinctly and accurately: "Our problems, public relations and otherwise, are of two parts, money and personnel." MacArthur realized that with incompetent ideologues like LaRoche in charge of the Hall of Fame Foundation, its prospects for raising sufficient funds were dim, and its future problematic. His analysis proved correct. The Hall of Fame never succeeded in New Jersey, stumbling along there before departing for King's Island, Ohio, in the late 1970s. Failing there, it then moved to South Bend, Indiana, in the mid-1990s, hoping that the proximity to and glow from Notre Dame football could provide a stable and permanent home.

The NCAA kept the designated Hall of Fame games until the 1960s, then quietly dropped them, shifting its efforts to a massive PR campaign for the 100th anniversary of college football in 1969, a century after the first contest at Rutgers. Walter Byers understood the value of college sports history, particularly when enveloped by traditional imagery, much better than did the Hall of Fame men supposedly in charge of preserving and exhibiting it. For Byers and the NCAA, intercollegiate athletics had to appeal to as many Americans as possible; it had to be as inclusive as the flag, the national anthem, and Mom-Apple-Pie-and-Chevrolet. Narrow sectarian attacks would never help big-time college sports overcome its critics, strengthen its fan base, boost game attendance, and, when the NCAA came to understand the power of television, increase TV ratings and payouts.

The Hall of Fame's 1950s dogmatism on intercollegiate athletics contrasted sharply to the NCAA's pragmatism, as did Chester LaRoche's rigidness to Walter Byers's opportunism. LaRoche told Americans what to think about college sports; Byers figured out what Americans wanted to think about college sports and tailored NCAA policy and publicity accordingly. For their efforts, LaRoche and his original Hall of Fame disappeared long ago, whereas Byers now enjoys a multimillion-dollar retirement while his association encompasses a multibillion dollar operation, the most powerful in American sports.

■　■　■

In overcoming the worst crisis and scandals in the history of intercollegiate athletics, the easiest part of Walter Byers's job was crafting the PR campaigns and dealing with the Spencer Agency: he could issue orders and, usually, have them obeyed. However, the relations between the NCAA, its member schools, and the press were more complicated, particularly at a time when "Aw-Nuts" carping was evolving into thoroughly revisionist views of college sports. Moreover, unlike the public, the sporting press—even the writers who loved the traditional pieties—knew the realities of 1950s intercollegiate athletics, discussing them in their newsletters, private correspondence, and stadium and arena pressboxes, as well as at their favorite "watering holes" around the country.

Yet Byers and the SIDs understood the symbiotic relationship between the press and athletic departments, and the sports officials played to this mutual dependence, not only in their relations with the beat reporters in college towns, but with sports journalists on the most important newspapers in the country. If the administrators of college sports could persuade most members of the sporting press—indeed, could merely prompt them to convince themselves—that they should help big-time intercollegiate athletics survive the 1950s scandals intact and basically unchanged, then both sides would benefit. In fact, that process developed more rapidly than expected, with most sportswriters never deviating from self-interest into such abstract ideals as a fair hearing for meaningful reform and/or de-emphasis.

46

College Sports Publicists and Sportswriters: Symbiosis Squared

1851 Hundredth Anniversary 1951

The New York Times
Times Square, New York, N.Y.
November 2, 1951.

Dear Charlie,

As you may remember, Allison Danzig and I were working on a sports book of stories for *The New York Times.* The book, which is called, *The Greatest Sports Stories from The New York Times,* is finished and it will be published [shortly] . . .

We thought that you might be able to place something [about it] . . . in one of your football programs, the school paper or the Alumni Magazine . . .

Sincerely,

Pete Brandwein

Notre Dame sports publicist Charlie Callahan replied to this letter from Pete Brandwein, a *New York Times* sportswriter, that he would do the *Times* writers an even bigger favor than they requested, "I will plug your book in *Our Sunday Visitor,* national Catholic weekly (circulation 815,000). Also will do what I can locally." In fact, Notre Dame administrators did not approve of gratuitous "plugging," except for works by important sportswriters on the Notre Dame network like Arch Ward, and Callahan did not plant anything about the *Times* book in the game programs or other ND publications, although the *South Bend Tribune* accepted an item. However, he did write a fulsome column about the anthology in *OSV*, focusing on the Notre Dame–related material, and undoubtedly he helped sell some copies.

That the *New York Times* sportswriters made this request in the fall of 1951, following the basketball fix and Army cribbing revelations, is significant. The editorials in their newspaper condemning the current college sports system, including the role of the media in it, as well as "Sports of the Times" columns by Arthur Daley with similar themes, never affected Allison Danzig, the *Times*'s main college football writer, and Pete Brandwein, his assistant. They maintained business as usual, and their request for a plug, sent to many athletic department publicists, signaled the continuation of you-scratch-our-backs, we'll-scratch-yours. Thus, after Callahan's puffery appeared in *OSV*, Brandwein sent him a "thank you from Allison Danzig and myself for the splendid send-off you gave [our book] in your column in *Our Sunday Visitor*. It was swell and greatly appreciated." He added, "Hope you will drop in as usual" at the *Times* when you are next in New York, "then I [and Danzig] can thank you personally."

Probably at this time, few American sportswriters, including those at the country's most important newspaper, and even fewer college sports publicists saw anything wrong with this mutual aid society. It benefited both sides professionally and monetarily, and the concept of conflict of interest never entered their thinking. Moreover, this symbiosis explains why criticisms of big-time college sports rarely appeared on the sports pages and, if they did, received scant attention. Indeed, the publicist-journalist alliance was so entrenched that when the scandals broke, most newspaper editors, including those at the *Times*, assigned news and crime reporters to the stories, knowing that these men and women would cover them more honestly and thoroughly than would the sportswriters. Nevertheless, newspapers gave the coverage of the NCAA annual meetings to their sports departments, which explains in large part the press's presentation of those crucial events from a pro-NCAA perspective and, when the ACE reform attempt occurred, an anti-ACE one. Leading sportswriters like Allison Danzig reinforced this bias by always accepting the NCAA spins and PR handouts without critical comment, setting the pace in a follow-the-leader profession.

As important, the public did not know about the sports publicist-journalist alliance. In a more innocent age, readers tended to swallow the sports pages, including the puff pieces, whole. As Richard Miller commented in *The Truth About College Sports* (1953): "A majority of sports fans depend upon the sportswriters and broadcasters for their thinking [about intercollegiate athletics]. If the sports communicators decide" to support one side on an issue, "chances are good that they will succeed" in moving the public to that position. This writer concluded with a line certain to displease the sporting press: "Big-time [college] sports are given considerably more news space than they deserve." Not surprisingly, even though a major New York publisher brought out Miller's book, the sporting press ignored it, no doubt contributing to its quick death. On the other hand, the thoroughly hyped Danzig and Brandwein anthology sold extremely well.

At the end of the century, the athletic department publicist-journalist system remains intact—indeed, in a much more polished and elaborate form than in earlier decades. Ironically, the symbiosis between sportswriters and publicists has spread from the sports department to the rest of the newspaper; one expert noted the constant late-century "blurring of distinctions among advertising, public relations, and journalism." However, the public is much less naive than in the 1950s and now treats all media pronouncements with a large amount of skepticism. In addition, in opinion polls, Americans consistently rate journalists, including sportswriters, among the least respected professionals, vying for the bottom rung with lawyers and used-car salespeople.

■　■　■

> You have to remember that most sportswriters work on tight deadlines, and when I started working for Charlie Callahan, first as a student, then his assistant, he always emphasized helping a writer meet a deadline, even if that meant feeding him material that we wrote . . .
>
> The most important thing, though, is that we never lied . . . I've taken pride in the fact that my credibility is high in this [sports] business and that's because I learned early to give reporters what they wanted to hear but to never lie. I would never lie to a newspaper guy or a [media] reporter. I wouldn't risk losing my reputation or Notre Dame's . . . Anyway, the SID job is tough enough without having to cover up, back track, all that sort of thing. It's a lot easier to go straight ahead.
>
> —Former ND sports information director
> Roger Valdiserri, 1991.

Callahan's successor, like most SIDs, considered himself in a "helping profession," forever on duty. As a result, Roger Valdiserri, like his mentor, valued efficiency, getting through long, intricate days, and lengthy, complicated football and basketball seasons with a minimum of mistakes and screwups. To accomplish this, these men set up smoothly running publicity machines within the Notre Dame athletic department, and they also worked with their colleagues at other schools.

In the 1950s, sports publicists began printing rosters of media people, constantly updating and distributing these guides among themselves. In addition, at their national meetings, they swapped ideas on how to "work the press and broadcasters." The topic of one 1950s panel discussion for publicists, "When You Take a Football Trip," offered such tips as this one: "Los Angeles Area: Radio and TV stations are all out to help college football publicity . . . [However] You must arrive by Sunday [before the following Saturday game]. Monday writers luncheon very important. If you work [it], you will hit well but be prepared to move fast" around the room.

In the 1950s, college sports publicists still resembled old-time "drummers" who needed to press the flesh of buyers and traveled on hectic schedules. But rather than compete with each other, the sports publicity directors cooperated fully, sharing their lists of prospects. In 1952, for example, before football teams visited Michigan State, their SPDs received a guide from the MSU publicist beginning, "The following [twenty] radio and press representatives are the key people [in the state of Michigan] interested in receiving information released by Spartan opponents, particularly for contests in East Lansing. *Please service them.*"

The final phrase prompts images of prostitutes "servicing" clients, but the term was standard SPD/SID jargon, used without irony. Sports publicists also told their colleagues to "feed" various reporters; for instance, the Michigan State SPD suggesting that, for Lyall Smith, sports editor of the *Detroit Free Press,* "feed him column materials [a] week or so before [the] game" with your team.

The SPD/SID "tip sheets" also rated the media in terms of pliability, and some were more thorough than others. The University of Pittsburgh's Bob Wycoff and his successor, Beano Cook, always provided very lengthy and detailed lists, including the correct pronunciation of the media person's name; for example, the *Pittsburgh Sun-Telegraph's* "George Kiseda (Ka-*seed*-a) . . . will cooperate with you on regular football stories and [he will] use whatever stuff you give him." Cook even added some humor to his missives: in apologizing for misspelling a name on a previous communication, he noted, "I went to an Ivy League school for one year and that is the reason I cannot spell." (Cook also avoided the phony SID title, calling himself an "athletic publicity director" into the 1960s.)

As the typical tip sheet indicated—"John Golightly is the man to see at INS [International News Service] . . . a *stout booster* and *will use everything he can*"—the publicists most valued those sportswriters who "boosted" college sports uncritically, and also consumed the publicity handouts whole, printing them without word changes, or only making alterations to conform to their publication's style sheets. Again, the public had no knowledge of this situation, believing that all published items originated with the writers under whose bylines they appeared.

■　■　■

Mr. Arch Ward,
Sports Editor,
Chicago Tribune,
Chicago, Illinois.

Dear Arch:

A couple of items for The Wake [of the News, Ward's column].

"And an Irishman led them all," could have been the caption of many of the pictures taken by the news photographers and newsreel men on the opening day of Notre Dame football practice . . . William James Patrick Flynn, senior left tackle from Gary [Indiana], was decked out in complete Irish regalia, Green frock, black topper, white lace vest, knickers and black button shoes . . .

—Notre Dame's Charlie Callahan, September 1950.

Through the years, the ND sports publicity department regularly supplied Arch Ward with items for his front-page column in the *Tribune's* sports section. Callahan surpassed his predecessors in knowing what pleased Ward most, and how to phrase items in the Chicago writer's style. As a result, most of Callahan's contributions appeared in "The Wake" complete and unedited, including the above item on one of the first Notre Dame sightings of what became the school mascot, The Leprechaun. (At this time, a scruffy Irish terrier named Clashmore Mike officially occupied the mascot role, mainly because its forebear had been a gift to Rockne.)

Throughout the 1950s, Charlie Callahan continued to send "Wake" items to the *Tribune,* the saga of Clashmore Mike and The Leprechaun slowly unfolding, as well as such typical bits as "Paul Reynolds, Notre Dame sophomore halfback candidate from Springfield, Illinois, has an interesting background in that he is of Irish-German-Scotch-English descent." No single item meant very much in itself, but taken together—at least two hundred pieces in the column per year—they reinforced Notre Dame's traditional image, emphasizing its connection to the American immigrant saga and the melting pot as well as its student-athlete ideals, such as "Jack Mayo, now an outfielder with the Philadelphia Phillies, was captain of the Notre Dame [baseball] club, and carried a 81% average in Engineering."

Not only did Charlie Callahan's items for "The Wake" please his friends at the *Chicago Tribune,* but every fall he spread more joy by sending them free season tickets for Notre Dame home games. In the 1950s, he had a lengthy comp list, with many Chicago media people on it, as well as their colleagues in other cities. In 1954, Harry Caray at KMOX in St. Louis received four season tickets. But Callahan distributed the largest number to writers on the Notre Dame network: twelve to Arch Ward and also twelve to Warren Brown, sports editor of the *Chicago American;* twelve to Joe Doyle at the *South Bend Tribune,* twelve to Bill Fox at the *Indianapolis News,* and so on. Considering the difficulty of obtaining ND tickets in the early and mid-1950s, and the top-dollar sums that scalpers gained from the resale of the few tickets appearing in their market, the comps for media people were authentic gifts.

Nevertheless, the demands of some sportswriters knew no limits. In 1951, Bill Fox asked Frank Leahy for permission to sit on the Notre Dame bench for Fighting Irish home games. Fox did not pitch his request in terms of wanting a fresh angle for a story, but he did mention that other schools had extended this privilege to other writers. The coach informed the newsman (an ND alumnus) "that it will be impossible for me to comply with your request to sit on our bench. Right off hand I can think of four of your colleagues who are fairly close friends of ours, who have asked permission to sit on our bench in the past. Because I have turned them down I honestly feel that it would be very imprudent to make an exception, even in the case of such a loyal Notre Dame man as yourself." Frank Leahy had an excellent PR sense and valued the promotional work of men like Bill Fox, but after staring into the apparently bottomless pit of sportswriter yearning, he wisely turned down the request.

That Fox and his colleagues would make such proposals—and have them accepted by some coaches—illustrates their own as well as their readers' obliviousness to the concept of objective sportswriting (another of the era's oxymorons). By publicly identifying themselves with one team, these writers did not pretend to report honestly about that team and its opponents. Often writers on the bench or in the pressbox rooted openly for their favorite club. Longtime *Columbus (Ohio) Dispatch* sports columnist Paul Hornung wore head-to-toe Ohio State scarlet and gray outfits to all OSU games, constantly cheering for his beloved Buckeyes. (At the end of the century, with university journalism schools, rather than old-time apprenticeships, training newspaper staffers, some sportswriters and editors attempt a balanced approach to intercollegiate athletics; ironically, the sports department of the *Chicago Tribune* exemplifies the new style.)

In the early 1950s, not everyone associated with intercollegiate athletics ignored the bias of the sporting press. Occasionally a dissident voice sounded. When announcing the demise of Fordham University's big-time football program after the 1952 season, the school president, Father Robert Gannon, included the press in his critique of college sports. Characteristically, one of the few outlets that quoted his remarks set them up with a negative lead: "Just to make sure that no segment of the population was left unoffended," by Fordham's move, "Father Gannon took a passing swipe at the sportswriters.

'They are the tyrants of tyrants. They think that the university's one purpose is to provide them with an income.' "

The demise of another Jesuit university's football program, Georgetown's, prompted an article in the *Saturday Evening Post* and subsequent letters to the editor. One correspondent, a dean at the University of South Dakota, wondered how these "cancellations" would affect "those sportswriters who make their living ballyhooing this pseudo-educational monstrosity [big-time college sports]. They love the groveling and salaaming [by university administrators] for tidbits of favorable publicity . . . and then they [the sportswriters] drool about character-building and educational values" in intercollegiate athletics.

But these 1950s critics were crying in the media wilderness, confined to the bottom inches of news articles and letters to the editor columns. Moreover, unlike the Fordham president and South Dakota dean, who had day jobs and could not devote much time to criticizing the sporting press, the media and their SPD/SID allies in full-time positions cranked out endless streams of publicity promoting their product. The outcome of this lopsided fight to persuade the public to support big-time college sports was obvious from the beginning. Of greater interest was the strategy of the victors, its origins, evolution, and role in the eventual triumph.

■　■　■

Dell Publishing Company, Inc.
261 Fifth Avenue,
New York, N.Y.

Dear Charlie,

First thing we'd like to get across about [Bob] Williams [Notre Dame QB] is that he has to do an awful lot of *brainwork*. Unlike most students at Notre Dame, he not only faces curricular problems but also has to spend a great deal of time brooding over football problems. In this connection we'd like two [photographic] shots.

    1. Williams poring over some ponderous problem—really concentrating—together with one of his instructors—preferably in clerical garb.

    2. Skull session with Leahy. Preferably no one in the picture but Williams, Leahy, and perhaps a blackboard.

—Stanley Woodward, editor of Dell Publishing's
Stanley Woodward's Football Guide, March 1950.

In the late 1940s, the respected sports editor, after a long career at the *New York Herald Tribune*, left the paper to edit a series of books and guides for Dell Publishing as well as to write articles for leading periodicals. Not only did this career move improve his financial situation, but Woodward stepped out of the editorial shadows to place his name in the title of various publications. His immediately successful annual football preview, the first pre-season guide in national distribution, dominated the preview market for a number of years. For the 1950 edition, Woodward decided to put Notre Dame starting quarterback Bob Williams on the cover, and to include a detailed photo essay on the player. As his requests to Charlie Callahan indicated, he wanted to present his featured athlete in classical terms.

Considering Stanley Woodward's long-standing affection for West Point and his dislike of the Fighting Irish, his choice of an ND player seems significant. The 1950 Army team had All-American candidates, but apparently none could serve as Woodward's "poster boy"; Army's best player that year, Al Pollard, was notoriously thickheaded. However, because of the increasing corruption in college football—highlighted by the NCAA convention fiasco over the "Sanity Code"—the New York editor seemed determined to present a traditional "scholar and athlete" (his term), and he turned to Notre Dame to find one.

Woodward's ideas for the Williams portrait referred to *Knute Rockne—All-American* and similar films at many points, the photo of the player with an ND instructor "in clerical garb" plugging into 1940s Hollywood depictions of strict but kindly teaching priests. The editor's concept for the ND player also looked forward to the NCAA/Spencer Agency's "student-athletes" and, because of the popularity of *Stanley Woodward's Football Guide,* served as a link between past and future icons of college sports. Moreover, as the scandals of the early 1950s unfolded and the editor refined his formula, his images helped provide a bridge over those events.

In his letter to Callahan, Woodward listed fifteen separate photo requests, many as specific as the ones above, but also some general ones, for which he requested input from the Notre Dame publicist. Woodward wanted "to get across that a football player's life is a pretty dedicated affair. Not much time for comedy. Here, of course, I'm quite at sea and shall rely heavily on you for suggestions." Callahan replied, "I think a religious shot taken at our Grotto would be good. This fits into the Notre Dame theory of 'A clean mind in a clean body,'" and "Another locale for pictures would be the Rockne Memorial. There is a good bust of Rockne in the lobby. And since this building is devoted to the non-varsity athlete, it is a good point to bring out," and Williams could pose in the exercise rooms.

Thus, Stanley Woodward and Charlie Callahan wrote the narrative of Bob Williams's life, and presented it to a large number of American sports fans. Whether the ND player actually engaged in the scripted activities or not was irrelevant to these authors. They wanted a perfect athlete-hero, and, after visiting the campus, the Dell photographers provided the shots of Williams to fit the narrative. Thus, in the published magazine, in the section of the story headlined "He Studies like a Scholar" Williams sits at a desk, contemplating the pages of a thick book. Another shot of Williams at his desk also shows a priest standing next to him, the photo captioned: "The Rev. Thomas Kelly,

CSC, head of the classics department, stops by to help Williams in his work. Except on fall Saturdays, Williams is just another college student to the faculty, encouraged and helped, but expected to hold to high grades."

In an adjoining photo, Williams stands at a blackboard with Frank Leahy discussing a diagrammed play; in another, the player sits at a desk with the coach, the caption noting, "Coach Frank Leahy spends many hours with Williams as they plot the moves that will confound the enemy this coming fall." Woodward emphasized the player in his narrative—Leahy only appears in these two photos out of a total of twenty-five. The editor knew all about Leahy's authoritarian coaching style and the fact that he and his players did not "plot" football strategy together: the head man *dictated* game plans, and his athletes, including the QBs, carried out his orders. But throughout Woodward's annual guides, he downplayed the role of college coaches and amplified the importance of the players, particularly intelligent ones like Williams, who had an 83 percent average as a liberal arts major.

Most likely Woodward did this because some of his readers were young men and he wanted them to identify with the athlete-heroes; he also hoped to please his adult readers with these traditional portraits. The following year, when the corruption in college basketball and football reached high tide, prompting not only revisionist films but also negative articles on college sports, Woodward and most other sports editors persisted with the traditional approach, particularly in their portraits of outstanding athlete-heroes. Indeed, in 1951, when the latter were in short supply, the press created some, even for the Heisman Trophy.

■　■　■

> Richard William Kazmaier is one of the nation's best football players. He is also a refreshing reminder, in the somewhat fetid atmosphere that has gathered around the pseudo-amateurs of U.S. [college] sports, that winning football is not the monopoly of huge hired hands taking snap courses at football foundries . . .
>
> He is a slender 5 ft., 11 inches, 171 lbs. He is a senior at a small university (3,000) that does not buy its football teams. At Princeton, he has a [academic] scholarship, just as 42% of his teammates have (and 40% of all Princeton undergraduates). He is an above average student majoring in psychology.
>
> —*Time* magazine cover article, November 1951.

In the long history of Heisman Trophy winners, Princeton's Dick Kazmaier seems the least qualified victor—an underweight back in the de-emphasizing Ivy League, with few prospects of starring in the NFL. Nevertheless, he beat out such future pro Hall of Fame running backs as Hugh McElhenny and Ollie Matson for the most prestigious award in college sports. But in the fall of 1951, Heisman Trophy voters—mainly sportswriters—were less concerned about actual on-field football talent than off-the-field image. After the horrendous college sports scandals earlier that year, they wanted to find someone who embodied the "scholar and athlete" ideals, and Princeton's Dick Kazmaier met those qualifications.

Various press sports departments supported his candidacy, *Time* pushing particularly hard. As the above paragraphs indicate, this magazine still criticized the college sports system, but it also treated favorite players and teams positively—most *Time* writers had attended Ivy League schools. The cover article on "Kaz" portrayed him in relentlessly classical terms: of the three photos accompanying the text, one placed him in his dorm room chatting with a roommate, captioned, "Friends and studies come first"; a second pictured his smiling father, with the caption line, "Mother sends the cookies"; and the third showed him in action against Harvard. The text confirmed the iconography: "A serious youth, he rates his serious interests in this order: 1) friends, 2) studies, 3) football. He plays the game because he likes it."

In December, the Downtown Athletic Club of New York announced Kazmaier as the winner with 1,777 votes, well in front of his nearest competitors, and far ahead of such great running backs as Washington's Hugh McElhenny, and University of San Francisco's Ollie Matson, who finished eighth (103 votes) and ninth (95), respectively. Yet the 1951 on-field performances of the West Coast backs outdistanced Kazmaier's, McElhenny running for almost 1,000 yards in the tough PCC, Matson gaining over 2,000 yards to lead the entire NCAA, whereas the Princeton tailback had 861 on the ground, plus passing yardage. Even in an age of East Coast bias against athletes in other regions, few informed sportswriters contended that the Princeton player was better than his West Coast rivals; however, his image far outshone theirs. Ollie Matson played for a corrupt USF program and was black (no African American, even the great Jim Brown, won a Heisman until the 1960s); and Hugh "The King" McElhenny, although white, was the college sports establishment's worst nightmare, a high-living jock who openly ridiculed the traditional pieties.

At the same time as the *Time* cover issue on Kazmaier appeared on newsstands, *Sport* featured a surprising article on McElhenny. *Sport's* editors, increasingly disillusioned with big-time college athletes, began exploring new ways of portraying them, moving from "Aw-Nuts" stories to full investigations. The subhead on the McElhenny piece charged that "This Touchdown Star Followed a Trail of $20 Bills . . . to the Washington Campus," and the story contained some startling quotes from the player: " 'As things now stand,' he says without batting an eye, 'I've got three cars, $30,000 in the bank [$300,000 in 1990s dollars], the promise of a lifetime job from four companies, and two professional teams are paying my way through school. Also a wealthy guy puts big bucks under my pillow every time I score a touchdown. Hell, I can't afford to graduate.' "

McElhenny benefited from the competition between two pro leagues, the NFL and AAC (Arch Ward's All-American Conference) for the best college players, but they merged before he left school, deflating the market, later prompting his famous boast that he was "the first college player to take a cut in salary to play pro football." Moreover, while at Washington, he refused to mouth the platitudes of "Jockspeak." As *Sport* reported, "Unlike most [college] football players, he makes little secret of his distaste for the goings-on between book covers, especially book covers which house intelligence on chemistry, English, and mathematics . . . 'Why should I kid people,' he says with refreshing candor, 'I'm not a top student, and I'm not crazy about school. Football is my life, and that's where I'm making my money.'"

But 1951 America was not ready to accept an outspoken athlete like Hugh "The King" McElhenny, no matter how great his running abilities; his poor finish in the Heisman balloting was proof of his unpopularity with the media and most football fans—except in Seattle. However, Princeton's Dick Kazmaier represented the classic ideal, and he continued through the year-end awards derby, picking up other trophies, then capping off 1951 by capturing the Associated Press "Male Athlete of the Year" prize, beating out golf great Ben Hogan, National League batting champ Stan Musial, and other exceptional athletes, including the NFL player of the year, Otto Graham, and the New York Yankees' Allie Reynolds, who had had two no-hitters that season.

Almost a half century later, the AP results astound the reader: Kazmaier, 70 first-place votes; "Bantam Ben," 27; Stan "The Man," 21; Graham and Reynolds, 7 each. That sportswriters could consider a 171-pound Ivy League back, playing against mediocre opponents, *a better athlete* than Hogan, Musial, Graham, and Reynolds in their prime and conquering the very best in their sports seems absurd. Yet, the dire times and the ideology of traditional college sports, as well as a huge amount of self-interest, prompted this vote.

Sportswriters knew that part of their livelihood—the coverage of big-time intercollegiate athletics—could soon diminish significantly, and if voting for a Princeton halfback as the "Athlete of the Year" would help restore public confidence in college sports, they would follow the Chicago dictum to "vote early and often." Sports journalists and their editors knew all about the seamy reality of big-time intercollegiate athletics, but rather than attempt to change it by massive investigative reporting, they preferred to paper it over by altering negative public perceptions of it. In late 1951, the elevation of a Princeton student to Heisman Trophy winner and then "Athlete of the Year" was an important step in the propaganda campaign.

■   ■   ■

Subsequent Heisman winners in this period also conformed to the classic image, although as the crisis passed, their football-playing credentials surpassed Kazmaier's. In 1952, Oklahoma running back Billy Vessels won mainly because his coach, Bud Wilkinson, possessed a talent for public relations and for assembling winning teams, and Sooner publicist Harold Keith conducted a clever Heisman campaign. Wilkinson, handsome and articulate, ran a reasonably clean program, and always courted the national press; meanwhile, Vessels attended classes and gained over 1,000 yards his senior year. Keith, using the invented nickname "Billy the Kid," emphasized the athlete's Oklahoma small-town background and hardscrabble childhood. The SPD also turned Vessels's initial academic problems into part of the Heisman narrative, the press often repeating the story, "A failing student as a freshman at Oklahoma, he hit the books as hard as he did the defenses" of opposing teams. In addition, Vessels had one of his best offensive days in 1952 on national television against Notre Dame, in a game that broke TV ratings records.

As important for Vessels's election, however, was the handicap of his main competitor, Maryland QB Jack Scarbath, an exceptional passer. Because of Maryland's years of cheating in football, approved and supervised by President Curly Byrd, by 1952 the Terrapin program had attained a foul odor that was impossible for the national press to ignore, particularly after *Sport* magazine ran a confession by a former Terrapin headlined, "I've Been Through the Football Mill," subheaded, "Big-time Football, Says This Ex-Maryland Star, Is an Octopus That Strangles College Life."

So Vessels easily defeated Scarbath and two other challengers, Minnesota's triple-threat junior, Paul Giel, and UCLA linebacker Donn Moomaw. (No junior had yet won the award, and the UCLA program had corruption problems.) Trailing the front-runners in 1952 was Notre Dame's Johnny Lattner, a versatile player on offense and defense but not a leader in any NCAA statistical category. ND publicist Charlie Callahan recognized that Lattner, the team's best all-around player, was a long shot for the Heisman for his senior year—until January 1953, when the NCAA restored one-platoon football.

■ ■ ■

Callahan had succeeded previously with Johnny Lujack in 1947 and Leon Hart in 1949, but both were exceptional players, clearly dominant at their positions. Yet both gave credit to Callahan for his help, particularly Hart, the only lineman to win a Heisman: "Notre Dame won it, I didn't . . . [The] publicity department [deserves] it most of all. Charlie Callahan deserves it." For Johnny Lattner, the ND publicist would have to craft a special campaign, one appealing to the same nostalgia that resurrected one-platoon football. To do this, Callahan had an advantage over most SPDs/SIDs: for the press and the public, the Fighting Irish continued to represent traditional college sports values. Thus, to promote Lattner, Callahan emphasized the player's "old-fashioned" qualities, both on the field—the first statistic listed on all Lattner promo sheets was "Minutes Played per Game" (even in two-platoon 1952, he topped forty minutes per contest)—and, equally important to his Heisman candidacy, the athlete's off-the-field character and experiences.

> As a freshman at Notre Dame, he [Lattner] was required to watch the film *Knute Rockne—All-American.* He was moved by the "Win One for the Gipper" speech. In the spring, his father was in the hospital dying of cancer. Lattner took varsity quarterback Johnny Mazur to visit his father, and Mazur assured Mr. Lattner that his son would score a touchdown in his first varsity game. Mr. Lattner died that spring. In John's first game of his sophomore year, he was sent into the game for one offensive play (he had played defense) . . . true to his promise, Mazur called Lattner's number, whispering, "This one is for your father." Lattner scored, dragging two tacklers over the goal line.

> —Author John T. Brady, 1984.

Throughout 1953, Charlie Callahan frequently told the Gipper/Lattner story to the press. However, when sportswriters asked the player about it, he confirmed it but declined to elaborate. One writer noted, "He is a shy, bashful introvert" who dislikes talking about himself, and "is embarrassed by praise and annoyed by adulation." Charlie Callahan never forced Lattner to open up, aware that the player's modesty would appeal to the media and the public, particularly when combined with his other athlete-hero attributes.

The Notre Dame publicist's best move during this Heisman campaign was to persuade a number of national magazines to profile his candidate. Since the scandals, some of these publications had run revisionist articles on college sports, and their editors were much less amenable to Notre Dame's customary censorship than they had been, but Callahan accepted these risks, hopeful that the school's and Lattner's classic appeal would triumph. His calculation paid off, first in the pre-season guides; not only did Stanley Woodward, as expected, praise Lattner, but Jimmy Breslin interrupted his attacks on college sports to laud the ND player in *True* magazine's entry into the preview field. Breslin termed Lattner "pretty good proof that they [Notre Dame] still pour youngsters from the old-time mold—and don't do a bad job of it either." Furthermore, "The only thing that Johnny regards as more important than a winning season for the Irish is a B [grade] in Accounting. He is a serious student."

The previews helped convince many sportswriters and fans of Lattner's credentials, but to put the campaign over the top Callahan needed, in addition to the candidate's excellent play on offense and defense during the season, "showcase features" in the leading national magazines. Lattner cooperated and played well, but his main competitor, Minnesota's Paul Giel, kept compiling amazing offensive statistics (he ended up with over 4,600 career yards). Nevertheless, Charlie Callahan pulled off his magazine coup. In November, the *Saturday Evening Post*, the foremost repository of revisionist articles on college sports in this period, ran a long, classical portrait of the Notre Dame athlete, extolling his "Iron-man virtues," particularly his two-way play, his punting, and his "truly all-around" athletic ability—Lattner had also played ND varsity basketball. The *Post* reporter emphasized that "to usually derisive old-timers, the development of Johnny Lattner has been a delight. Lattner is out of the old mold," and, more, "At twenty-one, John Lattner is still an unpretentious youngster. He is devout—he goes to mass every morning at Notre Dame."

Then, just before the Heisman voting, *Look* magazine published a huge photo spread on "Johnny Lattner of Notre Dame," subheaded "The Fighting Irish of 1953 Have No Glamour Boy. But the Fans See a Touch of George Gipp in the Halfback Heroics of Johnny Lattner." The *Look* editor apparently referred to the Gipper of *Knute Rockne—All-American*, not the actual person, who, except for his all-around athletic ability, in no way resembled the sedate Lattner. The *Look* photos, filling many of the magazine's 11-by-17-inch pages, reproduced some of Charlie Callahan's favorite campus shots: Lattner in class, captioned, "John maintains an over-80 average. He intends to become an accountant after [military] service"; Lattner in ROTC uniform with other cadets, preparing to serve his country "after graduation"; Lattner in front of the Golden Dome, chatting with Vice President Joyce; Lattner "at the Grotto, a Notre Dame replica of the one at Lourdes, France. Lattner kneels to pray that nobody will be hurt in next Saturday's game"; and Lattner at football practice on Cartier Field where "before Notre Dame Stadium was opened in 1930, early Fighting Irish teams under Knute Rockne . . . played their home games."

The *Look* photo album on this ND player captured and summed up a generation of classic college sports iconography. It invoked *Knute Rockne—All-American* and many of the movie's motifs, including the religious ones; it referred to the World War II years and the link between college football and military patriotism; and it used the old/new student-athlete tropes, prominent in the Rockne film and now proclaimed by the NCAA. The final photo showed the ND player in game action: "On the loose against Purdue: This is the Johnny Lattner the football crowds know for his *all-around* performances." The underlined phrase—keywords in Callahan's publicity for the player—helped clinch Lattner's Heisman Trophy in 1953.

In the 1953 Heisman ballot, almost all of the nine runners-up had better numbers in one or more offensive categories than Lattner, but the ND athlete's defensive talents exceeded theirs, particularly those of Paul Giel, who finished second. In addition, some of the best qualified candidates played for troubled programs—UCLA's Paul Cameron, Maryland's Bernie Faloney—or were black, like Illinois's J. C. Caroline. In 1953, Johnny Lattner represented what the media and the public wanted to think about college sports, and voters rewarded him with the trophy. (In this era, many sportswriters, particularly in the South, refused to believe that an African American could be an outstanding student or a truly great football player, hence Ollie Matson's ninth-place finish in 1951, Caroline's seventh in 1953, and Jim Brown's fifth in 1956. But America changed, and Ernie Davis broke the Heisman color barrier in 1961.)

■   ■   ■

Notre Dame, Charlie Callahan, and Johnny Lattner derived great benefits from the 1953 Heisman Trophy, but the individual and organization that profited most were Walter Byers and the NCAA. Lattner's triumph, like Dick Kazmaier's and Billy Vessels's, reinforced the image of student-athletes, adding momentum to the NCAA drive to win back the public after the scandals.

Yet, for big-time college sports, the road to victory still contained many bumps and potholes, none more annoying and potentially disrupting than the revisionist articles in the press and the events that provoked them, including the famous "Fainting Irish" incident of late 1953. Although it made the final vote extremely close, that episode did not derail Lattner's Heisman, but it did contribute to the resignation of Frank Leahy. It also ended an era in Fighting Irish football as well as the media's St. Knute portrayals of big-time college coaches.

47

Magazines Discover Revisionism

TOO MUCH FOOTBALL

Apart from the moral breakdown at West Point and the taint of professionalism in one college after another, what has big-time football
been doing to the player who has gone to college in honest search of
an education? ALLEN JACKSON was a first-string guard at the University of Michigan, from which he graduated this year. He won his
[varsity] letter on three consecutive [Big Ten] championship teams
and played in the Rose Bowl. Here is his account of his own experiences at a University where the slogan is: "When Michigan Loses,
Someone Has to Pay."

—Title and subhead on an *Atlantic Monthly* article,
October 1951.

In the wake of the 1951 scandals, many mainstream magazines ran editorials decrying big-time college sports; in addition, some featured revisionist
articles as well. Unlike the "Aw-Nuts" grumbling of the past, these new
pieces presented well-documented indictments of intercollegiate athletics,
in no way condoning its activities or proposing any solution other than total
de-emphasis. Moreover, some of the articles came from men within the
system—players, coaches, and university officials—who described the
abuses with an authenticity and detail that far transcended the "Aw-Nuts"
complaints.

The *Atlantic Monthly,* a leader in periodical literature, printed one of the
first revisionist pieces, Allen Jackson's "Too Much Football." The former

player demolished the "scholar and athlete" shibboleth: "The coaches are aware that, in theory, studies come first, but they are also aware that, in a big-time league, if studies actually come first, second-rate teams are likely to result." Jackson then detailed his attempts to achieve a meaningful education, and how the Michigan football program opposed that goal, forcing players "into the over-organization and over-perfection which the big-time game demands," so controlling their lives that the athlete "can no longer decide for himself what he should study" or when; everything was governed by the coaches' fixation on producing a winning team.

Jackson opposed the increasing emphasis on training and specialization in postwar two-platoon college football. The NCAA later tried to nullify this widespread complaint with the restoration of one-platoon, even though coaches accurately predicted that the rule would cause longer and more intensive practice sessions. Most importantly, Jackson's analysis of the split between the "student" and the "athlete" roles in the Michigan program indicated a systemic problem in big-time college sports, one that became enormous in subsequent decades and remains unresolved to this day.

As disturbing to 1950s readers because it directly violated traditional sportsmanship was Jackson's discussion of the intentional violence in the college game. Using his program's motto, "When Michigan Loses, Someone Has to Pay," as an ongoing metaphor, he described the coaches' pressure on players who made errors as well as the orders to destroy "scout squads" in practice and opposing teams on Saturday, including with "gang-tackling" reminiscent of the "flying wedge" era: "Michigan's maize-and-blue [uniformed] players . . . [were] ordered to cover the opposing ballcarrier with 'a blanket of blue.' "

In the fall of 1951, this on-field ferocity probably reminded some readers of the brutal football scenes in the recently released *Saturday's Hero*. Like that revisionist film, Jackson saw the intercollegiate game from a bleak and ironic viewpoint, one that not only challenged the myths of big-time college sports but also the premises of the entire enterprise. However, the former player resisted cynicism. He was weary, disillusioned, and pessimistic about reform, but he was not ready to abandon all hope.

A few years later, after the NCAA assumed full command of intercollegiate athletics, the *Atlantic Monthly* ran another revisionist article: "College Athletics / Education or Show Business?" Written by former college president Harold W. Stoke, this piece crossed the line from pessimism to cynicism. Stoke, after administrative tours at Louisiana State University and the University of Washington, asserted that "big-time college athletics is now a major part of the entertainment business," and university officials merely "pretend that the athlete must go through the motions of meeting, like other students, the usual academic requirements."

In a long, well-argued essay, with much supporting evidence, Stoke demolished the student-athlete myth as well as the NCAA's claims of reform: "No matter what the regulation, if it prevents [intercollegiate] athletics from supplying the public entertainment for which it exists, a way around [the rule] must be found" by university and athletic department personnel, "and even the NCAA itself." Not only had his experiences with big-time college sports made him cynical, but he cited the corrosive effect of the entire enterprise: intercollegiate "athletics requires an atmosphere of academic accommodation to its necessities, to the great cynicism of faculties and students" who know all about the special deals for jocks. As a result, it "has bred a kind of humiliating schizophrenia in educational administrators who are compelled to defend with platitudes what they do not believe or to keep an uneasy silence."

Almost a half century later, these arguments seem familiar and relevant, mainly because intercollegiate athletics has never solved its systemic problems and because, through the decades, many authors have made similar criticisms. In fact, the early 1950s scandals spawned a genre of revisionist works on big-time college sports that flourished during later periods of scandals and continues to this day. Nonetheless, the revisionists have always occupied a small section of the upper stands of the college sports arena, loud but unable to alter the system. Indeed, the main difference between the early 1950s critics and their successors is that a few of the former held positions of power, including college presidencies, and tried to make meaningful changes.

■   ■   ■

THE FOOTBALL HEADACHE

> In this article, a university president tells why his school has withdrawn from big-time football. In next week's issue, a big-time coach, Blair Cherry, formerly of the University of Texas, tells why he got out of the game. The *Post* is not opposed to intercollegiate football . . . We do feel, however, that the game is getting out of hand in many cases, and that the testimony of Father Guthrie [of Georgetown] and Mr. Cherry may help to reverse a regrettable trend.
>
> —Title and editor's comment in the *Saturday Evening Post*,
> October 1951.

During the late 1940s, this magazine had included a number of "Aw-Nuts" pieces in its coverage of college sports, along with traditional profiles of college athletes and coaches. The scandals of 1951 moved the editors to a revisionist approach, soliciting articles from well-informed but disillusioned participants in big-time intercollegiate athletics.

In "No More Football for Us," the president of Georgetown detailed his reasons for dropping the school's once-illustrious football team, which had employed such coaches as Lou Little, Jim Crowley, and Frank Leahy. Even more than the program's increasing expenses and deficits, Father Guthrie disliked its commercial entertainment aspects; he listed as his "first reason for stopping football at Georgetown" the fact that it "is a big business exploiting a small number of 'students' for the benefit of paying spectators. It forms no part of an honest educational system . . . It has as much reason to subsist on the campus of an educational institution as a night club or a macaroni factory."

Accompanying this criticism was the question whether "it is possible for the liberal arts college to assume, in addition to its traditional education, the training of the professional athlete?" Because of an anomaly of American sports history—the college version of football and basketball became popular before professional leagues in those sports took hold and developed minor leagues—the Jesuit priest found his school and others in the training business for the NFL and NBA. Adding this "absurdity" to the list of his other criticisms of big-time college sports, the Georgetown president concluded, "History, recent experience, and common sense seem to vote unanimously in the negative" for continuing the football program; therefore, he terminated it, also de-emphasizing the basketball team to the authentic student-athlete level.

The following week, also in the *Saturday Evening Post,* Blair Cherry revealed "Why I Quit Coaching." Accurately described as "a coach who resigned at the height of his success," Cherry, the mentor of the great Longhorn teams of the late 1940s, denounced the corruption and hypocrisy in big-time college football, much of it centered on the ferocious recruiting game: "It has become as much a problem to land a star athlete as to elect a congressman. You have to devote more time to recruiting than coaching." Once landed, however, the pampered recruit became a freshman under the coach's thumb; players like Michigan's Allen Jackson criticized the coaches' control of athletes, but Cherry analyzed the system's control of coaches, particularly the pressure from university administrators and trustees to win the recruiting and all other games. (Cherry hinted at his own cheating while recruiting players like Bobby Layne but never directly admitted it.)

Most of all, the Texas coach despised his bosses' "double-standard of morals," their claims to "stand for amateurism, for . . . conference rules, for this fine thing and that," and yet, when "cheating is going on" by coaches, alumni, and boosters, somehow "these people don't know about it—and *don't want to know about it.*" Nevertheless, Cherry believed that the hypocrisy transcended individual administrators, connecting to a system of university compliance with powerful football fanatics, often men in state legislatures and corporate seats of power. For these reasons and others, Blair Cherry resigned after the 1950 season, never to return to coaching. His pessimistic article in the *Saturday Evening Post* served as his farewell statement.

Unlike the pieces in the elitist *Atlantic Monthly,* which were calculated to influence university administrators but, as Cherry explained, were not likely to accomplish that task, the articles in the *Post* reached millions of readers, including many college sports fans. Letters to the editor applauded these pieces and hoped that they signaled major changes in intercollegiate athletics. In late 1951, various reformers, including some active in the ACE movement, cited these and other *Post* articles; however, a few months later, when the NCAA coopted the ACE plan, it did not address Guthrie's or Cherry's criticisms, opting instead for damage control and a public relations campaign.

■   ■   ■

The following year, as television made inroads into the popularity of the weekly magazines, the *Saturday Evening Post* decided to publish more revisionist articles on college sports as well as on other American institutions. Because TV offered only a classical view of intercollegiate athletics, the *Post* wanted to distinguish its product from the small screen's, providing readers with information and a viewpoint unavailable on the tube or even in newspapers. In a typical 1952 piece, the magazine focused on the booming football programs in Florida, explaining in the subtitle that "They May Be De-Emphasizing College Football in Some Sectors but the Battle Between the Universities of Florida and Miami, Who Meet This Saturday, Grows Fiercer Than Ever. In Florida, Even the Race Tracks Stage Athletic 'Scholarship Days' to Raise Money for Subsidizing Players."

Instead of the traditional before-the-Big-Game feature, *Post* sportswriter Fred Russell exposed the many corrupt practices in the Florida and Miami programs, including the state law sponsored by Gator boosters in the legislature mandating extra racing days to fund athletic scholarships at the University of Florida, and to a lesser extent at Florida State: "Receipts from . . . betting at thirteen dog tracks, three horse tracks, and one *jai lai fronton* netted $158,246" last year (more than $1.5 million in 1990s currency) for Gator football. The Miami Hurricanes, supported by the city's Chamber of Commerce and the Orange Bowl committee, raised large amounts privately and, according to the *Post,* then sheltered their well-paid recruits in such courses as "fishing, boat handling and elementary sailing, folk dancing, social dancing, and similar subjects."

Like the *Post*'s other revisionist articles, this account regarded substantive change as impossible. It depicted politicians and university authorities enthralled by the current system, and it treated college sports corruption as inevitable. A typically cynical passage ended the article, mocking the optimistic closure characteristic of classic sportswriting: "A neutral observer has but one suggestion. He thinks that all the horses and dogs in the state who helped to bring racing money to the assistance of football should be admitted free" to all college games.

Because *Post* readers apparently liked these revisionist works, *Collier's,* trailing the *Post* in circulation and even more vulnerable to TV competition, began running them too. And, like Hollywood movies that used their increasingly sexual images and themes to outpace television, *Collier's* sensationalized its revisionist articles on college sports. In 1953, 216-point headlines proclaimed THE HYPOCRISY OF COLLEGE FOOTBALL, with the subtitle, "An Ex-Coach Tells How the Present System Reduces Star Players to Perjurers, Scalpers, and Football Gigolos. 'I've Broken the Antiproselyting Rules with the Best of Them,' He Says—and Names Names in Revealing How. Who's to Blame for the Mess? What's the Remedy?"

For this feature, *Collier's* focused on Jeff Cravath, USC head coach from 1942 through 1950 (by 1953 he was out of football and a ranch owner in California's Imperial Valley). Cravath not only admitted to cheating while at USC but he placed it within the context of a totally corrupt college sports system, explaining the underpinnings by quoting a longtime coaches' axiom: " 'If you have to choose between breaking the rules and losing games, wouldn't it be better to break the rules? If you lose your games, you're certain to be fired. If you break the rules, *you have to be caught before you're fired.*' " No one caught Cravath during his years at Southern California—he supervised the extensive Trojan alumni/booster cheating system—but, in 1950, after his only losing season out of nine, USC axed him.

This article emphasized that cheating corrupted both the coaches involved and the players, the objects of the recruiters' largesse. According to Cravath, because the Pacific Coast Conference insisted that an intercollegiate athlete annually "sign an affidavit . . . that he has not accepted and will not accept any help whatever from persons outside his immediate family . . . the minute a boy accepts money or a gift from an alumnus" or booster, he violated that oath. Other conferences and then the NCAA adopted similar statements for athletes to sign, and the affidavit procedure still exists; thus, Cravath's comment on the dishonesty of this situation remains as true today as it was when he made it in 1953: "Educators say that football and other [intercollegiate] sports strengthen a boy's character, yet before a football player has appeared in a single game, he has been forced to become a perjurer" and commit other crimes.

Because *Collier's* published this article in the fall of 1953, after the NCAA proclamations of reform, Cravath also commented on that "charade": "The system controlling the game is pure hypocrisy. You may read that faculty leaders have agreed to curtail spring practice, limit athletic scholarships, or take other measures to de-emphasize college football. But" because of carefully placed loopholes, "the decrees actually have little effect . . . To keep up the pretense of purity and to still produce winning football teams is no small job. And the central figure in this intrigue is usually the college president." According to the former coach, university officials spout traditional jargon but ignore or evade the rules—the result is massive "hypocrisy."

After the *Collier's* article appeared, USC rooters, in their letters to the magazine and to Los Angeles newspapers, tried to "kill the messenger," dismissing Cravath as "a failure," bitter because he could not keep his job or stay in coaching. Other football fans as well as many sportswriters joined the *ad hominem* attack, adamantly refusing to consider the substance of the former coach's words. Cravath also drew criticism for his pessimistic conclusions: "Despite [current] resolutions of purity, college football still has most of the evils it accumulated in becoming a big business" and, as it grows larger, it will never purge those evils. *Collier's* had asked in its subhead, "What's the remedy?" but, true to the revisionist form, the article resisted resolution and closure, offering no cure for the systemic problems.

Considering the power of the college sports establishment and its symbiotic relationship with the sporting press, not surprisingly, the early 1950s revisionist criticisms did not dent big-time college sports. Nonetheless, they helped establish the foundation of the revisionist genre, visual as well as literary, and contributed to its viability. In the postscandal period, as important as the print features in the mainstream magazines and such films as *Saturday's Hero,* were a number of startling photo essays in America's most popular weekly, *Life* magazine. (Although *Life* began to portray college sports negatively in the 1950s, including Notre Dame at times, the magazine's love of the U.S. military dictated the classic coverage of service academy teams and the 1957–58 Army-ND games.)

■　■　■

ROUGH DAY IN BERKELEY

. . . The second time that Cal's great [runner] John Olszewski carried the ball, he was pounced on by USC's human gorilla, Pat Cannamela. He was the first of several California stars retired by injuries . . . the men of USC [were] impersonating Murder, Inc.

—*Life* magazine headline and text, October 1951.

Entering this game, the California Golden Bears held the Number One ranking in the polls, but USC upset them 21-14. Instead of its traditional portrayal of "Big Games," *Life* took a revisionist approach, featuring many photos of injured players being treated on and/or carried off the field, including Cal's "Johnny O." However, the most shocking photo revealed, as the caption explained, a USC "tackler taking a fist in the eye from California ballcarrier Bill Powell (who is studying to become a minister), as a big Trojan end" choked Powell from behind. *Life's* interpretation contrasted with the television and newspaper accounts of this game, and the magazine's photos of the violence offered readers a view not available elsewhere. (TV replays and freeze-frames began over a decade later, and shots of college football brutality occurred a number of years after that.)

The final picture in the photo essay, which took up a full page, showed "The Happy Destroyers, crippling Linebacker Pat Cannamela . . . and unstoppable Halfback Frank Gifford" hugging in the locker room, the caption adding, "Cannamela [who] helped USC incur roughness penalties, was congratulated by teammates when he disabled California star Johnny Olszewski." (In his *Collier's* article, Jeff Cravath revealed the illegal payments to induce Cannamela to sign with USC, and the bidding war for Olszewski, won by Cal.)

Years later, Frank Gifford discussed this game and the *Life* feature on it. Claiming that the magazine "taught me something about a certain type of journalism," Gifford contended that *Life* set out "to do a big cover story on the nation's top team," Cal, but when the USC victory "ruined their story, they got ticked off, and then they got even" by portraying the Trojans, particularly Cannamela, as animals. The vivid photo of the Cal ballcarrier punching the USC tackler in the eye contradicts Gifford's interpretation, as does the 1951 context of media interest in revisionism. Nevertheless, Gifford's account does point to the formulaic nature of sports reporting, and how the media can select items for a revisionist story as easily as for a classical one.

For all of *Life's* photo essays, including this one, the magazine's photographers took a huge number of shots; subsequently, the editors in New York chose the pictures for the story they wanted to tell. For Cal versus USC, they told a revisionist tale. Nevertheless, a vestige of classicism appeared with some opening shots of happy USC students in a railroad car on their way to the game. Obviously, the *Life* editors had enough photos to do the entire piece in traditional form, but decided that the revisionist version more accurately depicted the events of the game and would attract the most attention.

Because of the ongoing violence in college football during the postwar era, *Life* could have assembled similar features for many games from 1946 through 1950; however, only in 1951 did it begin to do so, in large part because of the sudden popularity of revisionist films and articles about college sports. Thus, the week after the USC-Cal game, the magazine presented a photo essay that shocked many more readers than had the events in Berkeley. Titled "Caught by the Camera," the text revealed how Oklahoma State players had disabled Drake University's outstanding halfback Johnny Bright, with photographers catching the Aggie brutality frame by frame. Exacerbating the situation was the racism of the Oklahoma State fans and their taunting of Bright, an African American.

On the first Drake offensive play of the game, the camera revealed Bright, who is not carrying the ball and who is, as the caption explained, "completely out of the action, flat-footed, concentrating on the play's outcome." In the next photo, on Bright's blind side, an Aggie lineman approaches, fist cocked. Then the Aggie "smashes a right cross to Bright's jaw that broke it." But the

Drake player stayed in the game. On a subsequent play, the camera showed the designated assassin charging Bright and "slugging him again." This time Bright "had to be helped off the field" and could not return. Oklahoma State won, but the photo essay upset most college football fans; the flagrant disregard of sportsmanship mocked all traditional ideals.

In the fall of 1951, various factors shaped *Life*'s revisionist approach. The editors considered college sports hypocrisy and corruption as the main story in big-time intercollegiate athletics and, after editorial denunciations of the "evils plaguing the game," decided to expose them in the most graphic way. They also wanted to sell magazines and maintain *Life*'s high circulation in the new television age. For these multiple goals, revisionism provided a perfect vehicle, supplying sensational, never-before-seen photos of college football's "actual sportsmanship." This mode proved effective because, ironically, after years of only classic photos of game action, it never occurred to players and coaches that the media would record violent behavior—so *Life* could capture such remarkable scenes as the blatant attacks on Johnny Bright.

Because the 1951 articles attracted so much attention, the magazine continued this approach into the 1952 season, even applying it to Notre Dame players. In a September piece, "The Fighting Irish Look Tough Again," the magazine featured large close-up photos of four different players, all of them open-mouthed, missing many teeth and, according to a newspaper commentator, looking "like a quartet out of a Boris Karloff–Bela Lugosi horror movie." *Life* accentuated the ferocity motif by captioning the photos, "Glowering guard Virgil Bardash . . . ," "Belligerent back Tom Carey . . . ," and so on.

However, unlike *Life*'s 1951 photo essays, the facts did not remotely support this treatment, and attacking the Fighting Irish sparked a firestorm of protest. One newspaper headlined its piece, "*Life* Observes National Newspaper Week with Shoddy Slur on Football," the writer arguing that these were atypical players because they resided far down the depths charts and saw limited game action; furthermore, as a Notre Dame press release indicated, they were among the few athletes on the team with missing teeth. Compounding *Life*'s slanted selection was its retouching of the photos to emphasize the "snaggle-toothed goon" motif. In one case, teeth were blackened out "to convey the impression that two of the player's teeth are bloody stumps."

Life's attempt to plug the Fighting Irish into its revisionist approach to college sports failed because of Notre Dame's classic image and its importance to intercollegiate athletics in the postscandal period. The magazine's blunder prompted a huge outcry and provided the college sports establishment and its newspaper allies with an excuse to attack all revisionist critics. Recognizing its mistake, *Life* not only apologized in print but ran large photos of the four players with their regular teeth and/or bridges, as well as the full text of a statement by Notre Dame vice president Edmund Joyce.

The ND official found no apparent "justification for the gross misrepresentations and the false impressions created by a publication which prides itself upon an accurate portrayal of American life and institutions . . . Nor is it in keeping with the basic fairness which perhaps, most of all, characterizes American life." Between the lines, Father Joyce suggested that *Life* abandon its new style and move on to more objective coverage of college sports.

But *Life* was the most important magazine in America, and one fiasco did not deflect it from its revisionist angle on college sports. In a subsequent 1952 article on the Fighting Irish, it portrayed Notre Dame in more neutral terms, allowing unstaged game photos and straightforward text convey the brutality of college football. "Forced Fumbles Beat the Irish" depicted the ND loss to Michigan State, the text informing readers, "Both teams were hitting opposing backs so hard that the football squirted from their hands," and at one point in the game, the "Michigan State bench began to chant, 'Make 'em fumble, make 'em fumble.' "

A featured photo revealed an MSU back plunging over the line, face contorted in pain, tacklers pummeling all parts of his body. Opposite this shot stood one of an ND ballcarrier also trying to penetrate the line, his face contorted, and the faces of the players beneath him in the pile exhibiting extreme agony. Another photo showed an ND player being carried from the field, the caption indicating that a "broken collarbone puts Notre Dame's David Flood on a stretcher late in the game."

A few Fighting Irish fans protested these grim pictures in letters to the editor, but the magazine's neutral tone apparently mollified most readers. The photos communicated *Life*'s stance on the violence in college football; moreover, Americans had never seen these images before and could only view them in *Life* and its magazine imitators, not on TV or in newspapers. In addition, like the explorations of new techniques in Hollywood's revisionist films, because *Life* considered itself on the cutting edge of photojournalism, it wanted its photographers to depict college sports in new ways, and the revisionist approach allowed them to do so. The traditional shots of the QB throwing a jump pass had become clichés, but the photos of players in agony were new. Thus, many motives drove *Life*'s coverage of intercollegiate athletics in this period, not the least of which was apparently, as Notre Dame discovered in 1953, getting even.

48

The Fainting Irish and
the End of Frank Leahy's
Notre Dame Career

Leahy was not prepared for the stormy reaction which followed [the ND-Iowa game in 1953] . . . he even expected commendation for the way the Irish fought back with so desperately little time, not once but twice, to pull even with a team that had looked a sure winner most of the afternoon.

"Why damn me?" he asked, "That's the way to play the game."

—*New York World Telegram & Sun* columnist Joe Williams,
February 1954.

he 1953 Notre Dame–Iowa contest provided the media with a Rorschach upon which to project their varying approaches to college sports. As Joe Williams noted, the Hawkeyes outplayed the Irish most of the game, but in the last minute of the first half, ND got a touchdown to even the score at 7-7, and in the final minute of the game, the Irish came back again with another TD, avoiding defeat and grabbing a 14-14 tie. In the Sunday newspaper accounts, some writers placed this game on the list of Fighting Irish "miraculous comebacks," portraying a never-say-die team in the Rockne tradition. Coach Frank Leahy certainly saw the game in those terms and expected that portrayal; moreover, *Life* and other publications had photographed the key Notre Dame scoring plays and could have done the story in the classic mode.

One observer later commented, "It was Monday before anybody realized that a grievous sin had been committed against the entire moral structure of the nation. Notre Dame had cheated!" What prompted this interpretation was the charge that ND, having used up its time-outs, had resorted to unsportsmanlike conduct by faking injuries to stop the clock, notching both TDs as a result. *Life* headlined the story, "The Clock-Stopping That Got Iowa's Irish Up," with photos capturing, according to the captions, ND players "claiming injuries to stop [the] clock and gain time in [an] attempt to tie the score." In one sequence taken during the final minute, "Notre Dame players, Hunter (photo left) and Penza (photo right) prostrate themselves simultane-ously . . . Seeing them down, [an] official calls 'time out' and stops [the] clock. Then they got up, ran off the field." A similarly faked injury by ND lineman Frank Varrichione had obtained a referee time-out in the final minute of the first half, allowing ND to run the play that tied the contest at that point.

In an age when the rules did not permit an abundance of time-outs and TV stoppages did not exist, every team resorted to feigned "injury time-outs" to halt the clock. Clubs had "designated fainters," but usually the tactic did not help the side doing it or affect the outcome. Notre Dame's initial sin was scor-ing with the aid of this maneuver and gaining a tie. Its more serious and over-riding one was its violation of the classic ideal, and Iowa coach Forest Evashevski, although he often used the same strategy, quickly fell upon this "grievous" transgression.

When the Hawkeyes returned to Iowa City, "Evy" addressed a student rally, and, according to *Life*, "He expressed his feelings in a parody" of Grantland Rice's most famous lines: "When the One Great Scorer comes to write against our name / He won't write whether we won or lost / But how we got gypped at Notre Dame." *Life* featured a picture of Evy making his speech, the parody lines highlighted above the photo. Evashevski also termed this ND team "The Fainting Irish." The combination of a catchy name and the photo images of "unsportsmanlike conduct" turned the incident into a national controversy, and also hastened the end of Frank Leahy's coaching career.

After Evashevski's opening salvo, Grantland Rice himself weighed in, inform-ing Americans that "I consider it a complete violation of the spirit and ethics of the game and was sorry to see Notre Dame, *of all teams,* using this method. Why in heaven's name was it allowed?" Rice also criticized Frank Leahy, pointedly disagreeing with the few press compliments to the coach for using the tactic so effectively: "Some people are calling it smart playing, I think it was disgraceful playing."

Rice's remarks and similar criticisms gave the public the impression that Leahy invented this trick, whereas he had merely employed a longtime strat-egy. In an amusing comment, Cal Hubbard, a former All-American and at the time a major league baseball umpire, told the *Chicago Daily News,* "Hell, where do they get off trying to give credit to Leahy. I thought I invented that play 30 years ago when I was at Geneva College. They've been stealing it ever since. Nothing's sacred anymore, not even the good old fainting play."

When other teams and coaches had triumphed in this manner, their stories had not lasted till Monday morning, never mind made it to national headlines; however, many of these incidents surfaced as a result of this controversy. If Iowa and Forest Evashevski had used the tactic to tie the game, the media would not have raised a hue and cry. Evy was famous for bending the rules. His great All-American Alex Karras had boasted that he became a Hawkeye solely because of the lucrative deal that an Iowa assistant coach offered his entire family. As New York columnist Joe Williams asked, "Why, then, all the brickbats at Notre Dame and Frank Leahy?"

Williams offered an astute answer: "Actually the criticism of Notre Dame is a unique tribute to the position it holds in the heart of the average football fan, and having earned this position, Notre Dame has a responsibility the like of which exists in no other college. The Irish must play it impeccably clean and straight at all times." Many fans, including Fighting Irish rooters, believed that Frank Leahy had violated this revered "position," and they demanded that he pay for it.

A majority of sportswriters agreed with the fans. Some acknowledged the historic use of the phony-injury tactic but then quoted Grantland Rice's "Notre Dame, *of all teams.*" The sports editor of the *St. Louis Globe-Democrat* asked, "Should Notre Dame, like Caesar's wife, be above suspicion?" and, answering affirmatively, argued, "Ever since Notre Dame, under Knute Rockne, became the nation's No. 1 football team—a place it has held in [Americans'] affections even in lean and losing years—its operation of football, of necessity, has been under scrutiny," but it has passed every test—until now.

Life kept the Fainting Irish incident in the national spotlight for a number of weeks, and the criticism of Frank Leahy and Notre Dame increased in volume. It came mainly from fans who saw intercollegiate athletics through a classical lens and who deeply believed that the Fighting Irish had violated the sacred ideals. They expressed themselves in letters to newspapers as well as to the University of Notre Dame.

■   ■   ■

> Notre Dame has always been regarded as the Number One football institution in the United States. As such it must be above reproach. Its reputation has definitely been damaged by the conduct of the Notre Dame team in this football game. I cannot help but feel that it is only fitting and proper for Notre Dame to forfeit the game to Iowa, and I am sure that many fans throughout the country . . . would regard Notre Dame in a better light for taking this action.

> —John A. Andresen to President Hesburgh, November 1953.

The letter writer, a resident of Flushing, New York, described himself as "a follower and admirer of Notre Dame football for a good many years." His suggestion "to forfeit the game" evoked the memory of Cornell's action in its famous "fifth-down" game against Dartmouth in 1940, but the college sports world had changed significantly since that event, and Cornell had not won with a tactic but through referee error. Nonetheless, in a flood of letters to the Golden Dome and to the ND athletic department, as well as to local and national newspapers, including Catholic ones, the fans invoked the traditional ideals and found Frank Leahy and his school guilty of violating them.

A man in Montana wrote directly to the coach, informing him, "I cannot believe that Knute Rockne would have, for one moment, tolerated the feigned sickness of a player for the purpose of stopping a time-clock in order to get his team coordinated [so] that a game might be won, or controlled, under any circumstances. I have always thought that you were a grounded disciple of Knute Rockne." Leahy was, and he had often witnessed his mentor using a "designated fainter"—a few months later, he publicly discussed this—but the fan's comments demonstrated the power of *Knute Rockne— All-American,* and how Notre Dame and its current football coach were now reaping the St. Knute whirlwind.

Leahy, a hard-driving coach who slept in his office during the football season, had long suffered physically from his exhausting perfectionism. In 1953, a few weeks before the Iowa incident, he had collapsed during the Georgia Tech game; his condition appeared so grave that Father Joyce administered the last rites of the Catholic church. The Fainting Irish storm also brought on a hospitalization. Then the press began to create and feast upon rumors that he would soon retire, and when he did not deny the speculation forcefully enough, the gossip increased. Throughout this period, however, Leahy mainly wanted to give his side of the Fainting Irish incident. In late December, he decided to do so on a national television program hosted by Joe Williams.

The coach and the New York sportswriter worked out Leahy's statement beforehand, essentially a non-apology for a strategy that football men had long used: "All coaches can recount scores of similar instances. We all know that, under the rules, it is perfectly legal." As Leahy later told his biographer, Father Joyce learned about the coach's impending statement before the broadcast and suggested that he not make it. The ND vice president believed that the coach's comments would only exacerbate an already difficult situation, escalating the criticism of Leahy and Notre Dame. The coach deferred to his boss, undoubtedly avoiding another wave of denunciations; however, the controversy would not die. The following week, at the NCAA Football Rules Committee meeting, after years of silence on this issue, the members publicly condemned the stopping-the-clock strategy as "dishonest, unsportsmanlike, and contrary to the spirit of the rules." By implication, they censured its most famous proponent, Frank Leahy.

Because the tactic was even older than the NCAA, the association's sudden shock and outrage seemed as phony as the swoons of the "designated fainters."

Yet, because the committee invoked the traditional ideals, many sportswriters and fans congratulated the association for its statement, allowing the NCAA to seize the classical high ground on this issue from the Fighting Irish. Few observers placed the association's action within the context of its dispute with Notre Dame on television broadcasting and other policy questions. Instead, they continued to attack Frank Leahy and his school.

After the NCAA rebuke, the coach spoke to a few close friends, including Arch Ward, about whether he should resign his ND position. The men in the Golden Dome learned of his deliberations, and, as Leahy's biographer later explained, "No one rose to stop him. Nobody truly wanted to fire him, but it was made explicit that if he quit, it might be the best thing." In addition, because of the state of his health and because, as Father Hesburgh noted, "he had eight young children under college age," and the opportunity of earning a high income in corporate America, most of Leahy's friends advised him to resign. He did so on January 31, 1954, citing his health and doctors' orders.

Joe Williams wrote a long column about Leahy's decision, arguing that "if the fake injuries clamor hadn't taken on such a harsh edge, I believe he would have preferred to stay and work at" his beloved Notre Dame. Thus ended the Notre Dame career of the school's second most illustrious football coach, a head man with an .855 winning percentage and, considering the difficulty of his teams' schedules, a record that surpassed Rockne's .881, which had been built on a fair number of "patsy" opponents.

But Frank Leahy did not go quietly into the ex-coaches' night. In early 1954 and in later years, he spoke out often and loudly about conditions in college sports, attacking his and Notre Dame's enemies with a candor that he could never exhibit while working for the university and under the restraints of the Golden Dome.

■　■　■

Feigned injuries have been part of football since Walter Camp invented the first down more than than 70 years ago . . . "Be sure," Rock used to tell us, "that the man who fakes the injury has the most capable replacement" [because under the old one-platoon rules he could not soon return to the game]. Other coaches have told their players the same thing. Just ask any coach or player you know, at the college, high school, or even grade school level. Yet, you probably never heard about a feigned injury until our Iowa game . . .

—Frank Leahy with Tim Cohane, *Look* magazine,
March 1954.

In "Farewell to Notre Dame," subheaded "The Great Irish Coach Says Good-bye to Football with a Blast at the Big Ten, the NCAA, College Presidents, and His Critics," Frank Leahy demolished various myths about college sports and also blasted a chunk out of the St. Knute statue. Yet he upheld other traditional virtues, like "Much as I hate to lose, when I did lose, I never squealed and I never alibied. Rock taught me that and I never forgot it." Frank Merriwell could not have stated it better.

In this period, *Look* magazine wanted to follow its main competitors into revisionist coverage of big-time college sports, but its sports editor, Tim Cohane, preferred another way: to combine classicism with revisionism to try to please all readers, not just those inclined toward one mode or the other. He had supervised such traditional pieces as the photo spread on Johnny Lattner, and also some revisionist exposés, but he favored mixed-form. Shortly before working on the Leahy piece, he had published an article about intentional injuries in the college game; after detailing the systemic nature of the problem, including "The most notorious case . . . the slugging of Johnny Bright," he concluded with a paean to college football as "character building" and how "character building must emphasize clean play." Mixed-form tried to have it all ways, and he applied this formula to Frank Leahy's "Farewell to Notre Dame."

Tim Cohane knew the coach well from their years together at Fordham in the 1930s, so Leahy felt comfortable discussing his true feelings about college sports with him, and the writer presented the coach's sharp criticisms as well as his sentimentality. The *Look* reader would have recognized such familiar passages as "Our football tradition was built on victory under Knute Rockne, the greatest coach who ever lived. I felt myself that I should try to maintain that tradition." Nevertheless, the revelation of Rockne's instructions on the stop-the-clock strategy must have shocked many readers. As importantly, the comment about the public's ignorance of the widespread "feigned injury" tactic revealed the gulf between traditional sports journalism and football reality, between what appeared on the sports pages and what actually occurred at all levels of school athletics.

In this article, Leahy also revealed a recent incident that probably few readers knew about: "Notre Dame was censured publicly by the NCAA last summer for trying out prospective" football players. Reacting to the new one-platoon rule and the need for authentic two-way players, many coaches had started testing prospects in tryouts, and Leahy felt that he had to keep up with the opposition. When ND authorities discovered the tryouts, they reprimanded him severely. Because these "auditions" so went against the pristine Fighting Irish image, the sporting press relegated the news to the back pages on a low-circulation summer day, when many readers were on vacation. Ironically, by calling attention to the "censure" in a heavily promoted feature in a national magazine, Leahy probably did more damage to Notre Dame's reputation than had the NCAA's action.

The former coach then quoted Father Joyce's opinion that the tryouts were "a minor offense which was decisively handled on the university level. There are many areas of really serious abuses toward which the NCAA could have much more profitably turned its attention." Leahy then discussed the underside of big-time intercollegiate athletics, focusing on "the tendering of money and gifts to football players under the table, and the notable lack of concern with the kind of education a player is getting off the field." Like the revisionist critics, he scoffed at the NCAA's reformist claims: "Instead of concentrating on these real abuses, the NCAA wastes its time outlawing or frowning upon things that are not essentially evil," mainly because it is not serious about cleaning up college sports.

Leahy also analyzed the NCAA's power structure, controlled "principally by some of the representatives from a block of the most affluent members of the Big Ten Conference," Michigan, Ohio State, Illinois, Minnesota, and Wisconsin: "These righteous personalities frequently commit football sins more grievous by far than tryouts. Yet they have sought to steer the policies not only of their own conference but of the NCAA, and have in considerable measure succeeded."

Big Ten leaders responded to this article by calling Leahy "a sore loser" because the NCAA had exposed his tryouts. But the Big Ten conference could not keep the lid on its own corruption and, within a few years, the revisionist press was featuring it. *Look* magazine, for instance, published a series by Pulitzer Prize–winning news reporter Clark Mollenhoff, "Football Scandal Hits the Big Ten" and "The Big Ten's Secret Report," revealing the cheating by the athletic programs on Frank Leahy's list, as well as those of other Big Ten schools.

Nonetheless, after all of his criticisms in "Farewell to Notre Dame," the coach concluded on a positive note: "To all the coaches I worked with or under, to all the lads I coached, I owe a debt of gratitude I can never repay for making it possible for me to be the head coach at my old school and to be successful there."

Not only did this end Frank Leahy's coaching career (he never coached again), but also his reputation as a classical mentor, nurtured during his career by many sportswriters, including a younger Tim Cohane (see Chapter 7). In reality, the traditional portrayal never fit Leahy well—he was too obsessive and too austere—and he felt more comfortable in the postwar chief executive role. Leahy was at his best in his football tower, totally on top of his program, or in all-night sessions with a movie projector, analyzing football game films frame by frame. Years later, when asked to recall typical scenes of Frank Leahy at work, Moose Krause began with the film marathons, declaring that the coach's "total—and I mean *total*—dedication was the secret to his winning."

■ ■ ■

In the autumn of 1953, Casey Stengel of the New York Yankees, the manager of the most dominant club in baseball history, meeting Frank Leahy at a banquet, informed him: "Frank, you know what I tell the Yankees when we get in a tough spot, I tell 'em that we're the Notre Dame of baseball—and that does it." In a sense, this marked the summit of Fighting Irish football, the highest point in the program's historic trajectory, even higher than Rockne had achieved. Neither Stengel nor Leahy recognized this point of apogee, which is so clear in retrospect, but the events of 1953 began the decline from the peak, then the mediocre Notre Dame teams during the following decade accelerated it. Most important, the sport of football started to change dramatically, making it impossible for future coaches to replicate Frank Leahy's accomplishment.

In 1953, the word "football" in a headline indicated the college game alone; most fans considered it the true game, with professional ball a secondary diversion, always requiring the prefaces "pro" or "NFL" before "football." In his *Look* article, Frank Leahy worried that the men "who control the NCAA" will "reduce the quality of the game and its attractiveness—[while] the pros are doing everything to make their game more attractive." Leahy believed that the NFL, with its two platoons and razzle-dazzle, would eventually surpass the college game in popularity. At the end of the 1950s, as his forecast began to come true, headline writers shifted permanently to the term "college football."

By the time another Fighting Irish team won a national championship (1966), college football shared the spotlight with the pro game, and when Notre Dame won its next championship (1973), the NFL had passed the college game, its Super Bowl becoming the country's premier sporting event. Thus, no future edition of the Fighting Irish or any other college team could ever stand astride the sport of football as Leahy's Lads did in the postwar period, and none could capture the same massive attention and adulation of American sports fans and the media.

As significant, no future university athletic program could exist as far above the college sports world as did the Fighting Irish in postwar America, an exemplar for the media and the fans in this dark time for intercollegiate athletics. The events of 1953, particularly the Fainting Irish incident, began the descent from this summit, ending the almost uniform coverage of Notre Dame football as the embodiment of the classical ideal. To be sure, many publications, like the *Chicago Tribune,* continued in this mode for another decade, but others began to move away from it in 1953, never to return.

■　■　■

I never understood why the NCAA gave us so much trouble back then [1953]. Cripes, we stood for what they preached—a clean athletic program with real students in it. Probably the arguments over television [broadcasting] had lots to do with it . . . also Frank was involved in the coaches' opposition to one-platoon, and never hesitated to yell at the NCAA about it . . .

> Coming down on us for the tryouts like they [the NCAA] did was ridiculous. I think they did it because they wanted to take over our clean image and make people believe that the NCAA, and the NCAA alone, stood for reform and purity in college sports . . .
>
> —Edward "Moose" Krause, 1991.

Just as the NCAA, because of its quarrels with Notre Dame, never acknowledged that school's crucial contribution to the image of college sports in the postwar era, Frank Leahy underestimated the importance of the association's policies, particularly its restoration of one-platoon football. In his "Farewell to Football," the coach argued that moving the college game closer to the pros—allowing tryouts, two platoons, and other practices—would solve the problems in intercollegiate football. However, because of the success and popularity of the Fighting Irish, he did not comprehend the perilous condition of the majority of college football programs in this period, or the widespread public skepticism toward the entire enterprise, which was being fed in part by revisionist articles and films. Walter Byers of the NCAA understood the situation better, and, with public relations as his priority, he supported rule changes that aligned with his publicity objectives, endorsing one-platoon football in part because of its link to the classical past.

Finally, Frank Leahy was a football coach, a brilliant one but a man who forever saw the college sports world from a coach's narrow perspective. Walter Byers was a PR man, much less concerned with on-field and on-court play than with public attitudes toward the games and their producers: the NCAA and its member colleges and universities as a totality. At times, Byers acted as if guided by the Japanese aphorism that "the protruding nail gets hammered down," regarding Notre Dame in need of a good thumping. Moose Krause mentioned that, in this period, "the NCAA and their Big Ten friends talked about 'knocking the golden halo off the Golden Dome,' " and Byers, in a section of his memoir entitled "Notre Dame's Golden Halo," boasts of his success in this endeavor.

As for the positive aspects of his policy, Byers insisted that intercollegiate athletics had to promote the "amateur ideal," and shun—not move toward— the professional sports model. He devoted his talent and energy to this policy, probably pleased that he could condemn Notre Dame for acting like a pro sports club by holding tryouts, and glad that Frank Leahy, a vociferous critic of NCAA policies, had departed intercollegiate athletics.

■   ■   ■

In 1953, college football rested in stable, albeit weak, condition, but college basketball had only recently left the trauma ward and was still trying to recover from the fixing scandals and subsequent investigations and trials. To restore college basketball to health was the NCAA's most difficult and pressing task. How the association succeeded in doing this, and within a short period of time, is the final chapter in this account of the most critical period in college sports history, a story that not only reveals the symbiosis between athletic departments and the media but also outlines the future of sports journalism and of NCAA-dominated intercollegiate athletics.

49

Saving College Basketball and Creating Mixed-Form Sportswriting

In one very important way, the basketball scandal and the resulting trials and attention benefited the NCAA. Unable to penalize violators of its Sanity Code, the NCAA used the widespread outrage and public pressure for more penalties on the schools involved to sanction Kentucky and Bradley. Consequently, the NCAA emerged from the scandal as the generally recognized enforcer of amateurism in intercollegiate sports, a position it had been trying to attain since the end of World War II.

—Economic historian Paul Lawrence, 1987.

NCAA Infractions Case No. 1 concerned the University of Kentucky, but the 1952 indictment focused on "illegal outside aid" to Wildcat players during recruiting and while in school, not on dumping games or shaving points. In addition, even though the NCAA possessed Judge Saul Streit's court record with its evidence of coach Adolph Rupp's "consorting with bookmaker Ed Curd," the association did not discipline the Baron of the Bluegrass. Fortunately for the NCAA at this time, the commissioner of the Southeastern Conference conceived the strategy of punishing Rupp indirectly by forcing the Wildcats to sit out a season of SEC play. Walter Byers backed this plan with a boycott proposal, asking all NCAA members not to play Kentucky during the year of the SEC's ban. UK officials, finally aware of the punitive mood in the country toward the schools involved in the fixes, reluctantly agreed to the one season shutdown, and Case No. 1 ended.

In his memoirs, Walter Byers commented that the Kentucky "decision to accept the penalty erased the haunting failure of the Sanity Code. It gave a new and needed legitimacy to the NCAA's fledgling effort to police big-time college sports." When the association added Bradley and CCNY to its closed-case list, its PR campaign gained momentum, even though none of the punishments fit the enormity of the crimes, and all of the coaches "walked."

From these initial NCAA cases, an increasingly elaborate enforcement mechanism sprang up, often operating as a police force beholden to no one except the executive director of the association, and always ineffective in rooting out systemic corruption in big-time college sports. But that goal was never on its agenda. Rather, as Walter Byers intended, the *presence* of the NCAA police helped convince the public that the association controlled big-time college sports and that athletic programs, coaches, and "student-athletes" adhered to NCAA rules. If the association could not produce real law and order, at least it could create its appearance.

Aiding the NCAA in the 1950s were the sports media, beginning with the campaign by sports editors and writers to resuscitate college basketball after the 1951 fix revelations.

■　■　■

ALL-AMERICAN BASKETBALL PREVIEW

Rebounding from the Nearly Disastrous Blow Leveled at It by Fix Disclosure, the College Game Is Out to Redeem Itself. Here Are the Brightest Stars, the Boys Who Will Be Carrying the Burden in the Sport's Hour of Trial.

—*Sport* magazine title and subhead, December 1951.

For this journal's annual college basketball preview—the most important one in the country at the time—the editors asked baseball and basketball announcer Curt Gowdy to outline the coming season. The tie-in with radio and TV was not accidental, broadcasters needing the survival of college basketball almost as much as the sporting press did. *Sport* and Gowdy decided to confront the obvious problem with a traditional solution: "Baseball made a comeback after the infamous Black Sox mess of 1919 largely with the help of Babe Ruth's colorful heroics. Basketball will need the same kind of help from some of its outstanding stars." Unfortunately for Gowdy's promotional efforts, the player he selected as the leading star for the coming season was Kentucky's Bill Spivey, who was soon implicated in the fixes. And throughout that year, as the Kentucky and Bradley scandals unfolded fully, college basketball struggled at the gate and on the floor.

For its "All-American Basketball Preview" for 1952–53, *Sport* had Bud Palmer, a TV announcer with an Ivy League background and style, offer his forecast, the subhead announcing, "If Individual Brilliance Is Any Indication of a Sport's Health, Then the College Game Is Really on the Upswing. Here Are the Players Most Likely to Grab Headlines." With fingers crossed, Palmer plunged into his predictions, naming Cliff Hagan of Kentucky as his brightest star—only to see this player cited in the NCAA's Case No. 1 for accepting, as a recruit, illegal payments from his university. Thus, the attempts to promote players in traditional terms—Palmer described Hagan as "the Owensboro [Kentucky] wonder boy . . . staking his claim to greatness," etc.—often crashed into the reality of intercollegiate athletics. As a result of this problem, *Sport* tried a new solution: a mix of genre forms, sometimes within one piece but more often within a whole issue.

In 1952, *Sport* began carrying revisionist articles every month, but it carefully balanced these with classic pieces. When the magazine published Jimmy Breslin's "Kentucky Apologizes for Nothing" (see page 341), it also ran "Gola Has Everything" and "Dixie's Wild About Pettit," standard profiles of All-American players Tom Gola (Lasalle) and Bob Pettit (LSU). Similarly, in October 1952, when it carried Gene Filipski's "Railroaded Out of West Point," it featured an enthusiastic "All-American Football Preview," as well as old-fashioned portraits of individual All-America candidates.

In their back-page "Time Out," the editors attempted to justify the regular inclusion of revisionist articles: "We try not to sensationalize for the sake of a quick circulation gain, and we try not to knock anybody just for the sake of stirring up some excitement. When we criticize, we do our best to make the criticism constructive." Yet, the revisionist pieces mainly destroyed: Breslin assaulted the premises of big-time college basketball; Filipski the myth of the cadet-athlete, Hugh "The King" McElhenny, the student-athlete pieties, and so on. With its mixed-form "Lineup" (table of contents), *Sport* started to develop a split personality, probably confusing readers more than pleasing them. Fortunately for college basketball, the magazine promoted more often than it attacked, not only with classical pieces but, even more powerfully, with positive iconography.

Sport's readers loved the magazine's photos of athletes, particularly its pioneering color shots of players in action or posing for the camera. The editors so emphasized this element that on each "Lineup" page, they placed a box, "Color Portraits," listing that month's posed color shots. For the 1952–53 "All-American Basketball Preview" issue, *Sport* featured Cliff Hagan, Tom Gola, and other "basketballers," the pictures accentuating the clean-cut, crew-cut All-American look. The photographers also cleverly obscured the elongated and awkward appearance of the biggest players, instead posing them in arched-back defensive postures, their bodies seeming less out of proportion to the normal human form. With this ploy, *Sport* intended to counter the longtime characterization of basketball as a "goon game," a description that even Arthur Daley contributed to with a famous article in the *New York Times Magazine* in 1952, "Real Goon Game."

But the main image that *Sport* and other proponents of college basketball wanted to erase were the player-fixers hanging their heads while being booked into various police stations. Aiding the magazines in this campaign were the college basketball game programs, particularly those produced by the Don Spencer Agency in New York. In the aftermath of the scandals, the best Spencer artists created the graphic equivalents of *Sport*'s handsome young men with crew cuts, idealizing them even more than the photographers could. Players on the basketball covers always appeared totally coordinated, and in a typical Lon Keller drawing of tall rebounders rising above the crowd to contest a ball, the bodies of the biggest men are as perfectly proportioned as those of their shorter teammates. (In fact, because basketball was a relatively new sport and many players did not start playing the game until after sudden growth spurts, uncoordinated giants were the norm, not the exception as in later generations.)

The most significant element of the Spencer Agency basketball covers, however, was the singularity of their subject matter: they only depicted players on the court. Unlike the football program illustrations of this period with their depictions of student-athletes, co-ed supporters, and all the rest, as well as the tie-ins to popular culture, the basketball programs concentrated solely on the game and the players. The focus was so universal that it indicates a public relations effort to counter the many press photos of the player-fixers in civilian clothes, handcuffed to policemen or involved in other shocking off-court activities.

The programs also carried pro-NCAA articles inside, as well as the standard stories on current players and past heroes of the sport. Often, the same writers who did classical pieces for *Sport* reproduced them for the Spencer packages, and like the basketball covers the articles concentrated only on the game, never discussing off-court matters. In addition, unlike the football programs, the basketball publications often contained photo essays of players in action as well as the coach instructing the team in a time-out huddle, or in the locker room. Again, the message was clear: college basketball players lived entirely within their sport; the game enveloped them, shutting out all outside forces and, most important, not permitting any contact with professional gamblers.

Undoubtedly, all of this propaganda helped Walter Byers and his association revive college basketball, but the NCAA also aided the sport in other ways. In 1950, it had decided to change the format and location of its men's basketball tournament, transforming it from a Madison Square Garden competition with a field of eight to one played in arenas around the country with 16 entries. Ironically, even with the obvious gambling problems at the Garden, the NCAA had departed for financial, not ethical, reasons: it considered the rent too high. Then, as a way of promoting its event at the expense of the older and more important National Invitational Tournament, the NCAA forced schools to enter either its tourney or the NIT, not both. After the scandals broke, the NCAA incorporated the new format into its PR campaign to rejuvenate college basketball, emphasizing the association's "back-to-campus" approach (early-round games occurred in campus arenas, which often came rent-free) and the sport's "All-American roots." Final rounds were played in arenas—with low rent—in regional cities.

■   ■   ■

The 6-9 Indiana high school phenom [Clyde Lovellette, arrived on the Indiana University campus in September 1948] . . . Several days before Lovellette was to enroll as a freshman at Indiana, he mentioned to [IU coach Branch] McCracken that he would like to go home to Terre Haute [an hour away] to pick up some clothes that he forgot.

"Go right ahead, son," said McCracken, "but hurry back."

That was the last McCracken heard of Lovellette until a wire service story reported ten days later that the precocious youngster [had] enrolled at Kansas. In subsequent years, Lovellette achieved All-American status and led the Jayhawks to the NCAA title in 1952.

—Sports journalist Ken Rappoport, 1979.

In the 1990s, some old-time basketball fans in Bloomington, Indiana, still talk about this theft of talent from under the nose of Branch McCracken and the money that changed hands to convince Lovellette to switch his college address. Most old-timers also agree that the amount, although sizable, was "chump change" compared to what "Phog" Allen, Lovellette's Kansas coach, later came up with to entice the greatest high school basketball prospect of the 1950s, Wilt Chamberlain, from urban Philadelphia to rural Lawrence, Kansas. But the Lovellette story did not appear in the press in the late 1940s, and a decade later, when revisionist magazine writers focused on the Chamberlain tale, college basketball was booming again, and reporters could no longer shock fans with accounts of under-the-table payments.

For all of his chicanery, Forrest "Phog" Allen played a crucial role in the 1950s revival of his sport. As a young man at the University of Kansas, Allen had played for the legendary inventor of basketball, James Naismith; subsequently, Phog headed the Jayhawk program for decades, becoming one of the most prominent and vocal American basketball coaches. He spoke out early and frequently about the gamblers flocking to the sport: unlike deals for recruits, which he considered normal business, he regarded widespread betting as a gateway to the bribery of players and a monumental danger to basketball. Events proved him correct and, characteristically, he both gloated and continued to recruit ruthlessly and build powerhouse teams. His 1952 edition was so good that, at a most opportune time for his sport, he won the NCAA tournament.

The press loved the Kansas story, the program's ties to the origins of the game, and the "aw-shucks" mannerisms of Lovellette and his teammates. When the 1952 tourney came down to the final game in Seattle between the Jayhawks and the St. John's (New York) Redmen, most reporters rooted for "the country boys" against "the Madison Square Garden club." Although St. John's had avoided the fixing scandal—some sports historians claim that Cardinal Spellman of New York prevailed upon New York district attorney Frank Hogan to spare the school—many writers portrayed the Redmen as tainted by their Garden home court, and they glorified the Jayhawks' win.

The following year, Indiana University helped Kansas keep the "Heartland Story" going. Led by six-foot-nine center Don Schlundt, the Hoosiers swept through the season. (Before Schlundt's freshman year, Branch McCracken had avoided another September snatching by bringing the high school star to IU months early and enrolling him in summer school.) For the media in 1953, the NCAA tourney final game in Kansas City produced the perfect matchup, Indiana versus Kansas—proof for many reporters and fans that thanks to schools in the "heart of America," college basketball had banished the gambling bogeymen. Indiana won, but its victory was secondary to the championship game's symbolic importance in the revival of the sport.

■　■　■

> Today the public has largely forgotten the details of a scandal it wanted very much to forget in the first place. College basketball is doing business as usual, just as if it had never been torn by a scandal a few years ago. The sports pages are filled with box scores and game action pictures, instead of the names of college boys who made the police blotters and the photos of guilty young men in the courthouse.
>
> —*Sport* editor Jack Zanger, February 1954.

Sport pointed to the increasing health of the college game, and to the crucial role of the press in the rehab process: sportswriters, with their stream of standard features, photos, game stories, and stats had convinced most fans that all was well in the "Land of the Tall Trees." This "snow job" was not difficult because, as Zanger wrote, basketball fans yearned to believe the best about their favorite college sport and wanted to concentrate on current games, not past fixes. When the rooters returned to Madison Square Garden in great numbers, *Newsweek* described them less kindly than *Sport* had, beginning its article, "Basketball Bounces Back," with "The gambler who knowingly played against a crooked roulette wheel 'because it was the only wheel in town,' has nothing on the die-hard U.S. basketball fan," who returns to his adored sport despite the continuing presence of gamblers in Madison Square Garden and many other arenas.

And the fans kept coming. College basketball attendance accelerated throughout the 1950s, with such stars and teams as Bill Russell's University of San Francisco Dons, Wilt Chamberlain's Jayhawks, and Oscar Robertson's Cincinnati Bearcats adding to the sport's popularity. By 1958, *Business Week* headlined, "College Basketball Helps Pay the Bills," explaining, "College basketball got a left-handed compliment last week" when thieves stole the receipts of the Stanford-Utah game; "It's a sign that basketball is accepted as big-time business . . . Not too many years ago, the better type of burglar ignored college fieldhouses as having nothing worth stealing. Now, neither college presidents nor burglars can afford to overlook the sport as a source of cash." Compared to college football with its immense squads and expenses, basketball was a low-cost, high-profit enterprise, and, at this time, many schools entered the big-time basketball business, attempting to ride the sport's wave of popularity and make money at the gate as well as from the expanding television coverage.

This momentum took college basketball into the fixing scandals of the late 1950s and early 1960s, an episode that involved many more players and teams than the events of the early 1950s. Professional gamblers had never left the sport. As one expert noted, "The fixing of games started again (if indeed it had ever ended) as early as 1957 . . . and by every indication, the [gamblers'] job of recruiting players [to fix games] had, if anything, become less arduous." But this time the media and the fans did not respond with the same shock and dismay as in 1951. The national magazines ran revisionist articles, first warning about the fixes—Jimmy Breslin, with his underworld contacts, did a famous piece—and then denouncing them. The sporting press summarized the details, but mainly played down the story. And the fans never turned away from the sport as many had, temporarily, a decade before. Therefore, forty years later, very few college basketball devotees can name any of the schools or players involved in the fixes of the late 1950s and early 1960s, and the vast majority of fans remain unaware of them, while the 1951 scandal remains in the collective sports memory alongside the 1919 Black Sox fix as one of the all-time perfidious acts.

Why did the second series of college basketball fixes pass like a summer cloudburst, inconvenient but giving way to the rainbow of 1960s expansion of the sport and the era of the great UCLA championship teams? The reason, in part, was the NCAA's deft handling of the situation, calling for severe punishments for the miscreants, urging member institutions to cast out the guilty and even those suspected of guilt—thus Iowa sent Connie Hawkins to temporary oblivion—but, in reality, exercising massive damage control and dispensing wrist slaps to the schools involved. The media never analyzed the NCAA's actions, and the fans continued to believe in the association's ability to control intercollegiate athletics. However, even more fundamentally, fan attitudes toward college sports had started to shift during the 1950s, affecting their reactions to the scandals and the ongoing corruption in intercollegiate athletics.

Entering the 1950s, most fans still embraced intercollegiate athletics in a somewhat naive and innocent manner; the following years of newspaper headlines and stories about the fixes and other illegalities, as well as the revisionist attacks on the entire enterprise, ended their innocence. Many fans initially reacted to the scandals by turning away from college sports, and basketball and football attendance dropped in the early 1950s, but this phenomenon proved transitory. Most fans loved the games and their favorite teams far too much to drop them forever or to endorse the revisionist conclusions that big-time intercollegiate athletics should be abolished or de-emphasized. Instead, many fans began to develop the mindset described by George Orwell in *1984* as "doublethink": they believed in contradictory ideas simultaneously, acknowledging the systemic dysfunction of intercollegiate athletics while maintaining that their favorite athletic programs worked well and deserved their support. Recent college graduates and current undergraduates were especially prone to doublethink. Encountering college sports firsthand, they relished "inside stories" about how the jocks on their campus received special financial and academic deals, but when those jocks took the court or field, they cheered wildly for them.

Not all rooters moved to a doublethink mode. A generational divide developed among sports enthusiasts; younger fans adopted doublethink first, accepting college sports corruption as the norm while embracing their favorite teams and athletes, but older Americans tended to believe single-mindedly in the classical ideal, insisting that all college sports teams, including their own, observe it strictly. The split also occurred along regional and even individual school lines. Supporters of athletic programs that openly cheated and got caught explained that "everyone does it," and this cynical view never prevented them from treating their own coaches and athletes as traditional heroes. Doublethink prevailed in such conferences as the SEC, Southwest, and Pacific Coast; on the other hand, universities adhering more closely to the traditional values kept and attracted fans who saw the old-time precepts in a single-minded manner. Among these was Penn State, with Rip Engle and then Joe Paterno (Saint JoPa) heading its football program.

■   ■   ■

The perfect media companions for fan doublethink were mixed-form treatments of intercollegiate athletics. In the 1950s, *Sport* pioneered many of the techniques but never achieved a satisfactory and pleasing format. However, because increasing numbers of fans wanted this approach to college sports, not surprisingly, a new magazine started to meet this demand: *Sports Illustrated*.

Launched in 1954, *SI* spent a number of years trying to find the right formula. At first, it presented classical and revisionist pieces side by side, but then, in the early 1960s, it hired the bright young men, Dan Jenkins, Frank Deford, and John Underwood, who perfected a new kind of sportswriting. They began to produce mixed-form articles, not potpourris as Tim Cohane of *Look* had done but pieces where the authors played the classical and revisionist scales simultaneously, demonstrating traditional reverence and hip skepticism within the same narrative, pleasing many readers and infuriating others, but always calling attention to themselves and their magazine. This breakthrough resulted in large circulation gains for *SI*, and made mixed-form dominant in sports journalism, where it remains ubiquitous to this day. This mode's most famous and typical early piece was *SI's* "Tie One for the Gipper" article.

■ ■ ■

Cheer, cheer for Old Notre Dame,
Equal *the echoes,* deadlock *her name,*
Draw *a volley cheer on high,*
Level *the thunder from the sky.*
What though the odds be even *or small?*
Old Notre Dame will tie *over all,*
While her loyal sons are marching,
Onward to victory.

—*Sports Illustrated* writer Dan Jenkins, November 1966.

Late in the 1966 college football season, two unbeaten powerhouses, Notre Dame and Michigan State, resting Number One and Two atop all the polls, played a regularly scheduled game in East Lansing, Michigan, a contest that the media quickly turned into the "Game of the Decade"—if not of the century. The extremely hard-fought match ended in a 10-10 tie, both coaches—ND's Ara Parseghian and MSU's Duffy Daugherty—becoming conservative at the end, and Parseghian, with a battered lineup of mainly substitutes, deciding in the final minute not to risk a desperation pass to try to score, instead ordering his team to run out the clock. The TV commentators complimented Ara for his "smart move," and the Sunday papers described the "intensely fought struggle," the few scoring plays, the injuries, the fumbles, and the unsatisfactory outcome, some quoting the cliché that "a tie is like kissing your sister."

As with the Fainting Irish incident of 1953, the intervention of a national magazine, again from the Time-Life stable, turned the game into one of the most famous in college football history, forever labeled "Tie One for the

Gipper." Dan Jenkins led his story in *Sports Illustrated* with "Old Notre Dame will tie over all. Sing it out, guys. That is not exactly what the march says, of course, but that is how the big game ends every time you replay it. And that is how millions of cranky college football fans will remember it," especially after this writer imposed his narrative upon it and, as one observer noted, "set the agenda for the ages." Jenkins could have told the story of this game in many other ways—other writers did—but his choice of "Tie One for the Gipper" struck a responsive chord in millions of college sports fans, rendering his narrative more famous than any other game story of the 1960s, as well as most of other decades. Films of the game reveal how Jenkins manipulated his account.

When Jenkins's article appeared, it angered some readers, particularly Notre Dame rooters, but delighted many others, not simply the anti-Irish contingent but people who felt that the author had "got it exactly right." His lead was pure revisionism: he literally *revised* the words of the most famous college fight song, a paean to the classical ideal. In addition, he turned the climactic line in the best-known scene in *Knute Rockne—All-American* "Upside Down"—which is the title *SI* gave his story. Holding the Fighting Irish to their classical history, he mocked Parseghian's team for falling short and simultaneously mocked the tradition. Subsequently lost in the myths about this article and the reaction to it were the other parts of the piece, many of them classical and essential to its success.

If Dan Jenkins had merely continued the revisionist opening, most readers would have dismissed his work as a cynical lampoon of Notre Dame football, but he succeeded because he balanced his jeers with very traditional tropes, convincing readers of his authority, and moving them to his point of view. He began the section on the main ND scoring drive by describing quarterback Coley O'Brien, not a well-known sub, coming on for injured All-American candidate Terry Hanratty. Next, "on a marvelously executed play, O'Brien, a young man who required two insulin shots a day for diabetes, shot a 34 yard spiral to [Bob] Gladieux for a touchdown in the second quarter. Gladieux was cutting behind a defender right at the goalpost and never broke stride." The glorifying narrative and the overcoming-adversity trope were hallowed sportswriting elements, neatly linked here to O'Brien's underdog status.

Jenkins continued his blend of forms throughout and, for his concluding three paragraphs, he did a classical description of Michigan State repelling ND's final field-goal attempt, then a revisionist glimpse of Parseghian in the locker room, and finally, a cleverly ambiguous last sentence, neither optimistic and sunny as classicism prescribed, nor cynical and bleak according to the revisionist formula, merely open-ended and having-it-all-ways in true mixed-form style: "A pretty Michigan State co-ed going through the tunnel [out of the stadium] looked blankly at her boy friend, 'Damn,' she said, 'Damn, damn, damn.' " Jenkins played with the lack of closure in this game, at times claiming to dislike it, but also reveling in it and, in the end, using it as a symbol of the era and its war without apparent closure.

At the time and subsequently, not everyone shared Jenkins's viewpoint. A few weeks after the game, Notre Dame president Hesburgh, upholding the classical tradition, wrote a reply to Jenkins's article, entitled "The True Meaning of the Game." *SI* ran it under a flashy subhead: "Now, with the U.S. still simmering over the tie game with Michigan State, Father Hesburgh" reveals his views. The ND president began by praising Ara Parseghian for the "great and even fantastic . . . football season" just completed, and he dismissed the complaints about the tie by congratulating the coach and the team who "played hard against the best, and solidified a proud Notre Dame tradition of doing everything with style, spirit, and excellence."

Then, after striking more classical notes on the recent season "with all its very real excitement, effort, hope, youthful optimism and ultimate success— the national championship," which had recently been awarded to the Fighting Irish, Father Hesburgh attacked those "who, in a seemingly superior intellectual fashion, depreciate, denigrate, and deplore" these accomplishments. While never naming Dan Jenkins and *Sports Illustrated,* this criticism summed up the conservative position on revisionist and mixed-form assaults on college sports. The intellectual arrogance of the *SI* writer, with his mockery of Notre Dame's most honored traditions, undoubtedly bothered Father Hesburgh, and although he was too polite and politic to sling mud at *SI,* he worded his putdown carefully and succinctly.

In many ways, Dan Jenkins's article and Father Hesburgh's response summed up the essence of American college sports from the mid-1950s on, the separate roads taken by the different groups of fans and their media companions from that historical point to the present day. The adherents of the classical tradition, those cheering the teams as well as those describing the games, have maintained their view of big-time college sports through all of the decades; the revisionists have never stopped lambasting the entire endeavor, turning up the volume during periods of scandals; and the lovers of mixed-form and their media cohorts have thrived, growing ever larger in number, their mix of hip skepticism and classical sentimentality becoming the dominant mode by the end of the century.

The media stories about college sports, the fan attitudes, and the shape of the enterprise were all created in the America of the 1940s and 1950s, and will remain with us for the foreseeable future.

Conclusion
The View from the
End of the Century

Intercollegiate athletics have existed on American campuses for well over one hundred years. However, the explosion of television entertainment during the last two decades of the century has amplified the size and importance of college sports to an unprecedented degree. In the 1980s, with the breakup of the NCAA's monopoly on TV rights and the emergence of ESPN and other cable networks, the electronic media began to hype college sports in high-tech and innovative ways. The wall-to-wall televising of college basketball and football games and the frenetic merchandising of college sports paraphernalia provided a synergy between the media and university athletic departments, expanding both and engrossing sports fans and undergraduate students as never before.

Many university officials permitted or encouraged the increasing commercialization of their schools' athletic programs in the futile hope that the added revenue would offset their athletic departments' chronic annual deficits. In fact, because the TV networks insist that athletic programs provide them with the best possible sports product to televise, most schools entered an athletics arms race, spending more money than ever before on the recruiting and retention of intercollegiate athletes. Such expenditures, including immensely expensive training facilities, produced even greater deficits. This economic absurdity exists within the context of massive public and private cutbacks to higher education, and a shortage of funds to hire faculty and staff as well as to maintain many basic university services and even the physical plant. Some schools with large enough endowments have managed to avoid these problems, but most have not.

The expansion of big-time college sports affects many areas of university life, one of the most obvious being scholarships. Since 1980, at most schools in NCAA Division I-A, athletic scholarships have increased by almost 900 percent, while, at many of these institutions, academic merit scholarships have decreased. The debate of the 1940s and 1950s on whether athletic scholarships should exist now seems as antiquated as the controversy over right-to-work laws. The only current argument on athletic scholarships concerns their size and perks: is the stratosphere the limit, or the ionosphere? In fact, many big-time sports schools spend much more on grants for jocks than on academic merit scholarships. According to the most recent *Chronicle of Higher Education* study on this topic, Duke University awarded $4 million annually to its 550 intercollegiate athletes, but only $400,000 in academic merit grants for its 5,900 other undergraduates; the nearby University of North Carolina at Chapel Hill gave almost $3.2 million a year to 690 athletes, and $636,000 in academic merit scholarships for its almost 15,000 other students.

Colleges and universities claim to be in the education business; however, when they fund athletic scholarships so much more lavishly than academic ones, they send a contradictory signal. They indicate that they place a higher priority on sports than education, and they also tell prospective students, particularly those from minority groups, that because the main chance of obtaining a free college education is through sports, they should first develop their athletic skills and then their academic ones.

Although the proponents of big-time college sports see its effects on higher education and on student life as positive or benign—a view that originated in *Knute Rockne—All-American* and other media portrayals during the classical period—they never support their position with any research. The few studies done in this area, as well as the data already collected for my next book on the impact of big-time college sports on undergraduate education, indicate many negative effects from college sports. A decade ago, Ernest Boyer, the head of the Carnegie Foundation, concluded from his organization's research that, on college campuses, "the cynicism that stems from the abuses in [intercollegiate] athletics infects the rest of student life, from promoting academic dishonesty to the loss of individual ideals. We find it disturbing that students who admit to cheating often excuse their conduct as being set by the college example . . . [of] athletic dishonesty." My research, as well as much anecdotal evidence, indicates that this situation has become worse at the end of the twentieth century.

In their attitudes toward big-time college sports, a majority of undergraduates, particularly at large state universities, exhibit a doublethink mentality, an unstable combination of cynicism and sentimentality that began in the 1950s and has increased every decade since. Many students understand the unresolvable problems in college sports, illustrating their perception with stories on how athletes at their schools cheated academically or received outrageous perks. Yet these students also claim to "love college sports" and boast of attending every game to which they can obtain tickets (a majority of seats are sold to boosters and alumni), watching all other games on TV, usually with classmates at a sports bar, and organizing their extremely active social lives around their school's sports activities.

Students also exhibit doublethink on many other college sports issues, including "special admits" for jocks: many schools use baseline SAT/ACT numbers when considering regular applicants for admission, e.g., an SAT total of 1300 at UCLA; but these universities enroll athletes with SAT and ACT scores far below those of normally admitted students, e.g., in the 850 and lower range at UCLA. To the statement "Athletic scholarship winners should meet the same college entrance requirements as regular students," a large majority of undergraduate respondents (83 percent) agreed or strongly agreed. Yet, many of these same students approved of the "Prop 48 Casualties" at their schools—athletes with SAT scores below 850—and happily cheered for them when they suited up for the varsity.

To the statement "Regular students should have the same access to academic assistance as athletic scholarship winners—i.e., free unlimited tutoring, enhanced test files, etc. . . . ," 87 percent assented, some out of egalitarianism, others wanting the same advantages for themselves. "Enhanced test files" is a euphemism for copies of exams supplied to the athletic department by instructors beforehand so that tutors can prepare the athletes for the actual tests. That some faculty members cooperate in this deception is one of the disgraces of Big-time Sports U; that it has become a common and accepted practice indicates how far intercollegiate athletics has come from the West Point "Cribbing Scandal" of 1951—the "enhanced test files" provided by Blaik's tutors to the athletes resulted in the expulsion of ninety Cadets and outraged millions of Americans.

A favorite argument of the proponents of big-time college sports is that at huge, impersonal institutions, it provides a central rallying point, bringing all elements of the university together in true community. On occasion, particularly when a school's team wins a national championship, this appears true; however, in a deeper sense, because of the idiosyncratic and artificial nature of the event—the necessity of sweeping through an entire season and/or tournament, and the immense amount of media attention—if Big-time Sports U can only develop these random, occasional communities, then it offers a sad commentary on its achievements.

Historically, colleges and universities have built communities on shared ideals, discourse, study, and goals among their members. Sometimes these communities were fragile and dissolved, but often they coalesced, providing their participants with extremely valuable experiences. Some schools, particularly those with adequate funding and a faculty commitment to undergraduate education, still foster these college communities, most notably, religiously based schools and smaller secular colleges. But mammoth public institutions too often create Big-time Sports U and its superficial coming together of fans in a stadium, arena, or bar for a few hours' duration.

Another favorite argument of the proponents of big-time college sports, one that began long ago, is that intercollegiate athletics generates wonderful free publicity for colleges and universities, imprinting the name of a school upon the public's consciousness. Indeed, this can occur, but with many hidden costs to higher education (see below). More to the point, as the institutions involved in the 1940s and 1950s scandals discovered, and many others have learned since, the publicity from college sports is a two-edged sword, ready to swing back at a university when an athletic program causes negative news, creating ugly headlines about player and/or coach misconduct, seriously injuring a school's reputation as well as its investment in intercollegiate athletics. To cite a recent case, simply one on a list of never-ending examples, in the fall of 1997, officials at the little-known University of Central Florida gloried in the national and regional publicity produced by their football team's almost-upset of the mighty University of Nebraska Cornhuskers. A few weeks later, the media blared reports of a "phone card scam" perpetrated by some of the UCF players from their locker room in Lincoln, Nebraska, and then covered up by the head coach. The University of Central Florida bled profusely from this wound, and many years will pass before the public will remember the school for something other than the phone card scam.

For all of their questionable arguments, the proponents of college sports long ago won the debate on de-emphasis, and they have grown their enterprise to gargantuan proportions. In the 1950s, many faculty members wanted to de-emphasize big-time intercollegiate athletics because they believed that it consumed too much of their students' time and energy, distracting them from serious studies. The worst-case scenarios of these advocates of de-emphasis cannot compare to the 1990s situation at Big-time Sports U: college sports and its attendant beer-and-circus atmosphere occupy the center of student life, with education on the periphery.

For many undergraduates at these schools, college sports engrosses them from the application process to graduation. A number of studies indicate that an important reason that regular students (non-athletes) select a particular university is the fame of the school's big-time intercollegiate athletics program, and many universities emphasize this aspect of their institution in the brochures they send to potential applicants. In my research survey, 62 percent of the undergraduates rated the prominence of a school's big-time college sports program as a "very important" factor in their choice of a university. In addition, to the question "How well informed were you about the intercollegiate athletic programs of the schools to which you applied," 69 percent responded, "Very well informed." On the other hand, in response to "How well informed were you about the academic programs of the schools to which you applied," only 14 percent answered, "Very well informed."

Students know so much about big-time intercollegiate athletics because of the media attention paid to it, but schools collaborate by constantly publicizing their college sports products. Members of the media operate, as they always have, out of self-interest: they want to boost ratings, sell newspapers and magazines, keep and expand their jobs. However, some big-time sports universities, particularly large public ones, promote their intercollegiate athletics programs for a new and pernicious reason. Because of the massive cutbacks in funding for their academic programs, because of their inability to provide quality undergraduate education, these schools spend increasing amounts of money on their athletic departments, using big-time college sports—commercial entertainment around which undergraduates organize hyperactive social lives—to keep their students happy and distracted and the tuition dollars rolling in. In other words, *at many big-time sports universities, beer and circus has become a substitute for meaningful education.* An administrator at a Sun Belt sports school explained:

> We certainly can't give our students a quality degree—not with class size growing geometrically and our 30-to-1 faculty/student ratio—but at least we can encourage students to have fun, and identify with our teams while they're here . . .
>
> Football Saturdays are great here and so are winter basketball nights. In our Admissions Office literature, we've stopped saying that we provide a good education—our lawyers warned us that we could get sued for misrepresentation—but we sure promote our college sports teams.

This statement prompts a variety of responses, including an analysis of increasing class sizes at most public universities and actual faculty/student ratios. Many schools lower the numbers through a variety of tricks, and true ratios are much higher than reported publicly. However, this discussion and others will continue at much greater length in *Beer and Circus: The Impact of Big-time College Sports on Undergraduate Education,* to be published at the beginning of the next century.

Notes

The following notes reference all quoted material in the book and also add further explanations to some of the comments in the text. For the citations of documents in the University of Notre Dame Archives (hereafter cited as UNDA), I have followed their cataloguing code. The UNDA codes used in the footnotes to identify sources are as follows:

> CJWC for John W. Cavanaugh, C.S.C., Personal Papers
> UPWC for University President John W. Cavanaugh, 1905–1919
> UPOH for University President John F. O'Hara, 1934–1940
> UPHO for University President J. Hugh O'Donnell, 1940–1946
> UPCC for University President John J. Cavanaugh, 1946–1952
> UPHS for University President Theodore M. Hesburgh, 1952–1987
> UVOC for University Vice President John J. Cavanaugh, 1940–1946
> UVMR for University Vice President John H. Murphy, 1946–1952
> UVHS for University Executive Vice President Theodore M. Hesburgh, 1949–1952
> UABM for University Athletic Business Manager, ca. 1900–1940
> UADR for University Athletic Department Records, ca. 1909–1929
> UASI for University Athletic Department Sports Information Office
> UORL for University Oral Interviews
> PATH for Printed Material from the University Athletic Department
> PNDP for Notre Dame Printed Collection

Thus, the source of the first citation in the text to UNDA material is the letter from Knute Rockne to Herbert R. Mayes about Horatio Alger's books, dated 11/17/27, and found in (UADR 15/38)—the first number is a box in the UADR files, and the second is the folder within the box that contains the cited document.

In addition, some UNDA citations concern scrapbook entries listed under PATH; an unusual but important reference source for this book are the scrapbooks about intercollegiate athletics contributed to the University of Notre Dame by anonymous fans and subsequently collected in UNDA. During the 1940s and 1950s, many people kept scrapbooks on many subjects (it was a popular hobby); unfortunately, the custom was to scissors-and-paste the items, attempting to fit as many as possible per page, with no attention paid to the sources or even the datelines of the articles. Indeed, to save space, the compilers carefully cut out the top parts—titles, authors, and datelines; they also did not paginate their scrapbooks. Nevertheless, for researchers, many of these scrapbooks provide a wonderful source: the compilers often had a good eye for the most noteworthy news items about their subject, and they relentlessly clipped these items from their daily papers. In an age before comprehensive newspaper indexes and computer databases, these scrapbooks supply researchers with the next best thing, useful clippings on various subjects. The scrapbooks on college sports in the Notre Dame Archives proved extremely valuable to my research for this book and I used them extensively.

I have attempted whenever possible from internal evidence, e.g., comments about a specific football game, event, or controversy, to estimate the dates. In addition, from the print typefaces of the items, I have tried to identify specific newspapers and, from internal writing styles, to guess at wire services or individual authors. UNDA has catalogued the scrapbooks, and I provide the UNDA identification tag, for example, for the first citation in the text from a scrapbook, an Associated Press item from April 1944, see (PATH "Notre Dame Scrapbook, 1941 through 1944"). Thus, if any reader wishes to find an item cited in the text and/or peruse the scrapbooks, I recommend a visit to the University of Notre Dame Archives.

Finally, the references to speeches and resolutions at NCAA annual conventions need an explanation. Every year, the NCAA published a booklet entitled *Yearbook of the National Collegiate Athletic Association and Proceedings of the _____* [the number of the] *Annual Convention at _____* [the place and date of the convention]. Rather than use this cumbersome title, I refer to NCAA convention minutes as *Yearbook*. However, nothing is ever simple and straightforward with the NCAA: the association placed the minutes of a convention in the *Yearbook* for the year *before* the convention in the title of the *Yearbook*—e.g., the 1948 convention held in New York City on January 9–10, 1948, is in the 1947 *Yearbook*, not in the 1948 one, even though the latter lists the 1948 Convention in its full title! In the footnotes below, I reference quotations from speeches at specific conventions, and the cited page numbers are in the *Yearbook* for the year *before* that convention.

The notes below follow the order of material presented in each chapter of the book. However, when a document is clearly cited within the main text, particularly magazines and their datelines, I do not repeat it in the notes. Finally, unless otherwise noted, the text is my interpretation of the primary and secondary sources; in no way is the University of Notre Dame Archives or any other possessor of primary and secondary material responsible for my particular interpretation. If readers disagree with an interpretation, please write to me at English Department, BH-442, Indiana University, Bloomington, IN 47405; do not complain to the archivists at Notre Dame or any of the other archives cited in the book.

Introduction

Almost all of the material in the Introduction is explained in the text of the book, and referenced in the notes for the appropriate chapters. However, a number of quotations do not appear elsewhere in the book and are referenced here. In addition, I must thank Jeff Sagarin, computer rankings analyst for *USA Today* and other newspapers, for the phrase "all the fine young men." It does not occur directly in NCAA literature but it nicely sums up the association's propaganda on student-athletes.

For a full discussion of Grantland Rice and his creation of the "Four Horsemen" passage, see Chapter 21, "The Four Horsemen: Grantland Rice vs. Reality," in my book, *Shake Down the Thunder: The Creation of Notre Dame Football*, New York, 1993. Rice's "odd turn of evolution" sentence is in *Sports Golden Age*, edited by Allison Danzig and Peter Brandwein, New York, 1948, p. 6; the "Four Horsemen" lead appeared in the *New York Herald-Tribune*, 10/19/24. Robert Lipsyte's comment is in his *SportsWorld*, New York, 1975, p. 170; Lipsyte added, "Without the aid and abetment of sportswriters . . . college football would never have been able to grow into America's grandest monument to national hypocrisy." Elmer Layden's remarks were in his memoir, *It Was a Different Game: The Elmer Layden Story*, with Ed Snyder, Englewood Cliffs, New Jersey, 1969, pp. 4–5. According to a recent Rice biographer, Peter Fountain, the sportswriter composed his most famous verse in 1908 for a Vanderbilt alumni magazine, and placed it at the end of a poem titled "The Alumnus"; see Peter Fountain, *Sportswriter: The Life and Times of Grantland Rice*, New York, 1993, pp. 93–96.

Columbia University coach Lou Little mocked Rice's sentiments during World War II; see Ch. 9 in the text and the notes to it for the full references. Sportswriter Fred Russell wrote about the postwar money twist on the verse in Ch. 39; and Iowa coach Forest Evashevski used it for the Fainting Irish, and Rice added his comment, Ch. 48. The *Saturday Evening Post* article "Jim Tatum of the Tarheels" by Mal Mallette, 11/2/57, is the first time a prominent mainstream journal published the "Winning is the only thing" line. The writer noted that "Tatum has responded" with this line before, indicating that the coach had used the line before 1957. Lombardi biographer Michael O'Brien maintained that the coach never uttered the line, instead saying in a 1962 interview, "Winning isn't everything but wanting to win is," see *Vince: A Personal Biography of Vince Lombardi,* New York, 1987, p. 187. Other sources attribute the line to coach Red Sanders but without clear documentation.

The best explanations of the classical Hollywood cinema are Thomas Schatz's *Hollywood Genres: Formulas, Filmmaking, and the Studio System,* Philadelphia, 1981; and his *The Genius of the System: Hollywood Filmmaking in the Studio Era,* New York, 1988. Also important is the essay by Thomas Sobchack, "Genre Film: A Classical Experience," *Literature/Film Quarterly,* Summer 1975, anthologized in *Film Genre Reader,* edited by Barry Keith Grant, Austin, Texas, 1986.

1. Knute Rockne Becomes Myth

Margaret Thorp's pioneering work is *America at the Movies,* New York, 1939. John Clellon Holmes discussed the movies in "15 cents Before 6: P.M.: The Wonderful Movies of 'The Thirties,' " *Harper's,* 12/65. The interviews with Edward "Moose" Krause, longtime athletic director at the University of Notre Dame occurred during August 1991, with follow-up telephone calls that fall and in 1992; John Kryk's interviews with Krause occurred in August 1990.

David Gergen made the comment on the American public embracing Reagan as a "heroic character," reported by Steven V. Roberts in the *New York Times,* 3/2/88 (because of the many editions a newspaper goes through daily, I will not attempt to give page numbers for newspaper articles). Howell Raines of the *New York Times* wrote about "Mr. Reagan's dying words in the film," 5/18/81. The president began this talk with, "First, Knute Rockne as a boy came to America with his parents from Norway." The quote from Michael Steele appeared in his *Knute Rockne: A Bio-Bibliography,* Westport, Connecticut, 1983, p. 137.

On page 6 of the text, Rockne commented about the Alger books to Herbert R. Mayes, 11/17/27 (UADR 15/38). The best study of athlete-heroes is Michael Oriard's *Dreaming of Heroes: American Sports Fiction, 1868–1980,* Chicago, 1982; the quote on the Merriwell stories appears on p. 48, and the one on the NCAA on p. 36. Oriard quoted Patten on "a clean mind in a clean and healthy body" on p. 61. Bronislav Malinowski, one of the founders of anthropology, offered his basic definitions of myths in *Myth in Primitive Psychology,* New York, 1926, p. 10f.

The cited *Knute Rockne—All-American* shooting script is in (UABM *Knute Rockne—All-American* Series, 3/11/40 script). The dialogue quotes are from the script and the film—they are usually identical except where noted in my text. Bonnie Rockne's lawyer, Vitus G. Jones, wrote to Warner Brothers about the themes in the film, 6/12/39; he listed the scholarly attributes that Bonnie wanted in the picture in a letter to Warners, 2/16/40 (UABM *Knute Rockne—All American* Series, Vitus G. Jones folder). Warners tried to accommodate her and asked Notre Dame for more information on former chemistry professor Nieuwland; the studio subsequently added the scene where Father Callahan and Rockne discuss whether the recent graduate should become a chemist or a football coach. For a full discussion of the making of *Knute Rockne—All-American,* see my book *Shake Down the Thunder: The Creation of Notre Dame Football,* Henry Holt & Co., New York, 1993, Chapters 36 and 37, and the long explanatory endnotes.

President John W. Cavanaugh wrote a letter of recommendation to University of Kansas athletic director W. O. Hamilton, 1/30/15 (UPWC 41/Knute Rockne folder). Rockne's undergraduate roommate at Notre Dame was Charles "Gus" Dorais, and he described Rockne's personality in a letter to former ND president John W. Cavanaugh, 6/12/31 (CJWC *Autobiography of Knute Rockne Series/* Statement of Charles Dorais folder). Also according to Dorais in this letter, Rockne earned some money by boxing at "smokers in South Bend and . . . Kalamazoo." Jesse Harper wrote about Rockne's hiring as Notre Dame assistant coach to Arthur Haley, 4/21/40 (UABM *Knute Rockne—All American* Series, "H" folder). The *National Review* article, "The Best Conservative Movies," by Spencer Warren, appeared 10/24/94.

In *Shake Down the Thunder* (op. cit.), I concentrated on the details of the production of the Rockne movie—the contracts, etc.—and I did not explore the full meaning of that movie for Americans in this period, or for the University of Notre Dame and its administrators. Fortunately, after publishing that book, I was able to continue my research on the film and see it from many different points of view, presented in depth here, and also to revise some of my earlier judgments.

2. George Gipp Becomes Myth

Bonnie Rockne's lawyer wrote to Warner Brothers about the "inspiration to young men" angle, 2/16/40 (UABM *Knute Rockne—All American* Series, Vitus G. Jones folder). The comments on the "classical narrative film" and its editing appear in *Film Theory: An Introduction,* Robert Lapsley and Michael Westlake, New York, 1988, p. 189. A detailed discussion of George Gipp's life, death, and famous last words is in Chapters 15, 26, and 28 in *Shake Down the Thunder* (op. cit.). Rockne's press assistant, Francis Wallace, quoted the coach-as-character-builder remark often, e.g., in *The Notre Dame Story,* New York, 1949, p. 121.

On page 20 of the text, Hal Wallis of Warners told Vice President John J. Cavanaugh of Notre Dame about the audience reception of *Knute Rockne—All-American,* 7/12/40 (UVOC 8/57). *U.S. News & World Report* did a "Special Report: 1940 America," by Lewis Lord and Jeannye Thornton fifty years later, 8/27/90, quoting *New York Daily News* columnist Ed Sullivan (later a TV host) on Reagan's triumph in *Knute Rockne—All-American.* Theologian Michael Novak treated sports as religion in *The Joy of Sports,* Basic Books, New York, 1976. Pat Buchanan, described in the article as "an aide," commented on Reagan's "going home" to Notre Dame in the *New York Times,* 3/9/88. That newspaper discussed Reagan's last official act—the salute to the Notre Dame national championship team of 1988—on 1/19/89. The quotes from his speech can be found there and, for the full text, in "Public Papers of the Presidents," 1/18/89, in the Lexis/Nexis database.

Moe Aranson told his story about Gipp's fatal illness in an interview for *Shake Down the Thunder* (op. cit.), 6/24/91. Jim Beach quoted Gipp's friend Grover Malone's version of the fatal illness in his article, "Gipp," *Fireside Book of Sports,* ed. Jack Newcombe, New York, 1964. Ronald Reagan's comments about the Gipp role appeared in *Where's the Rest of Me?,* with Richard G. Hubler, New York, 1965, p. 94f. The historian Garry Wills noted Reagan as Rockne as well as the Gipper in *Reagan's America: Innocents at Home,* New York, 1987, p. 123, also in Wills's "Frontline" portrait of Reagan for PBS, "The Real Life of Ronald Reagan," 1989. Another excellent albeit tendentious study of Reagan's film and political careers is Stephen Vaughan's *Ronald Reagan in Hollywood: Movies and Politics,* Cambridge, England, 1994.

3. Hollywood and the Critics of College Sports

The Carnegie report on college sports—usually given that title by the press at the time and subsequently—has the official title of *Bulletin 23 of the Carnegie Foundation for the Advancement of Higher Education,* New York, 1929. Henry S. Pritchett wrote his comments in the Preface, p. xi. The report, its predecessors, and successors are discussed at length in *Shake Down the Thunder* (op. cit.), particularly in Chapters 25 and 27. Paul Gallico offered his *mea culpa* in *The Golden People,* Garden City, New York, p. 27; in addition, the interviews with Gallico and other 1920s writers in *No Cheering in the Press Box,* collected and edited by Jerome Holtzman, New York, 1974, are wonderfully informative. The *New York Herald-Tribune* carried W. O. McGeehan's observation about "the average reader," 10/22/24.

Scripts of Marx Brothers movies differ so widely from the on-screen impromptu dialogue that the text here is transcribed from the film *Horse Feathers* (1932). Many books on the Marx Brothers exist, the best is by my late friend Paul D. Zimmerman and Burt Goldblatt, *The Marx Brothers at the Movies,* New York, 1968. The 1990s documentary on football movies was called *Football Movies* and made for ESPN by Ellen M. Krass, 127th Street Productions, Inc., 1993. Jeffrey H. Wallenfeldt wrote the extremely useful *Sports Movies: A Guide to Nearly 500 Films Focusing on Sports,* for CineBooks, Inc., Evanston, Illinois, 1989; the quote on *Touchdown* is on p. 131.

The citations for the Francis Wallace novels mentioned in the text are as follows: *Stadium,* New York, 1931; *O'Reilly of Notre Dame,* New York, 1932; and *Huddle,* New York, 1931. *Huddle* is related to *The Spirit of Notre Dame* (1931), and the University of Notre Dame's role in it is discussed in *Shake Down the Thunder* (op. cit.), Chapter 28. The historian who commented on "football players actually attending class" in *The Spirit of Notre Dame* was Wiley Umphlett, *The Movies*

Go to College: Hollywood and the World of the College Life Film, Rutherford, New Jersey, 1984, p. 28; his comment on *Navy Blue and Gold* is on p. 88. An informative entry on that film is in *James Stewart: A Bio-Bibliography,* Westport, Conn., 1992; Capra's comment is on p. 62. *USA Today* had a feature article on *Gone with the Wind's* phenomenal box office success; correcting its receipts for inflation during its various releases places it at $859 million, 8/19/96. Significantly, all of the top all-time films are classical genre movies: *E.T.* (3); *Ten Commandments* (4); *Sound of Music* (5). In the spring of 1998, *Titanic* was approaching *GWTW* in domestic sales and classical genre tropes but had not yet passed it.

Robert Hutchins offered his comments in his article, "Gate Receipts and Glory," in the *Saturday Evening Post,* 12/12/38. Paul Gallico made his in *Farewell to Sport,* New York, 1938, p. 208. The Associated Press report on Rockne's opposition to reform appeared in the *New York Times,* 12/17/30. Robert Buckner, the main scriptwriter on *Knute Rockne—All-American,* discussed the congressional committee–like scene in a letter to Arthur Haley of Notre Dame, 4/26/39 (UABM *Knute Rockne—All American* Series, Robert Buckner folder). In this letter, he acknowledged the dramatic license in his creation of the scene; see pp. 607–8 in *Shake Down the Thunder* (op. cit.). The *Variety* review of *Knute Rockne—All-American* appeared on 10/9/40; and the *New York Times's* on 10/21/40. Former president Gerald Ford offered his comments during the 1993 ESPN documentary (op. cit.).

4. Hollywood and *Knute Rockne—All-American*

Thomas Schatz's comment is in his *Hollywood Genres* (op. cit.), p. 19. Louis Giannetti discussed the stages and qualities of classical genre films in *Understanding Movies,* Upper Saddle River, New Jersey (7th edition), p. 348; and Thomas Sobchack explained the conservative nature of classical genre in his essay, "Genre Film: A Classical Experience" (op. cit.), p. 112. Schatz commented on the socializing function of genre films at length in *Old Hollywood/New Hollywood: Ritual, Art, and Industry,* Ann Arbor, Michigan, 1983, p. 44f.

Harvey Marc Zucker and Lawrence J. Babich compiled *Sports Films: A Complete Reference,* Jefferson, North Carolina, 1987; the quote on *Knute Rockne—All-American* appears on p. 145; they also quote from the billboard for *Smith of Minnesota,* p. 182. Donald Gray made his comment in an interview for this book, 4/12/91. The passage from Arch Ward's *Frank Leahy and the Fighting Irish: The Story of Notre Dame Football,* New York, 1944, is on p. 3. Dave Condon wrote about the ghostwriting of the Leahy book in his essay, "A Time for Greatness," in *Many Autumns Ago: The Frank Leahy Era at Boston College,* ed. Mike Bynum, Birmingham, Alabama, 1988, p. 15; Ward's biographer, Thomas B. Littleton, in *Arch: A Promoter, Not a Poet, The Story of Arch Ward,* Ames, Iowa, 1990, noted that Ward hired Condon after the latter left Notre Dame in 1944 and, from 1947 on, Condon ghostwrote many of Ward's "Wake of the News" columns, p. 200. Thomas Schatz discussed the effect of films upon viewers in his chapter "Narrative Strategies in the Classical Hollywood Cinema," *Old Hollywood/New Hollywood* (op. cit.), p. 45.

5. College Sports as Classical Genre

Thomas Sobchack's essay, "Genre Film: A Classical Experience" (op. cit.), applies directly to the classical form of college sports; his comment in the text is on p. 102. Similarly, many of Thomas Schatz's concepts in *Hollywood Genres* (op. cit.) also apply, particularly his section on "Plot Structures," p. 29f. The story of the 1940 Cornell-Dartmouth game is in John McCallum, *Ivy League Football Since 1872,* New York, 1977, pp. 145–47; the quoted telegrams are on p. 146. A portrait of Carl Snavely is in *Great College Coaches of the Twenties and Thirties* by Tim Cohane, New Rochelle, New York, 1973, pp. 179–84. An excellent documentary film, *More Than a Game,* also focused in part on this game and the Colorado "Fifth Down" game of 1990; the film was an Independent Image Production for BBC-TV, 1993 (the Arts & Entertainment network showed it in this country in 1994). The quote from Colorado head coach Bill McCartney is from that film as are many of the comments of the Cornell football players; in addition, David Wickham, executive producer of the film, related other material and quotes from players in an interview, 6/6/92.

Thomas Sobchack's comments on "classical characters" are in his essay, "Genre Film: A Classical Experience" (op. cit.), p. 108. Sports columnist Red Smith's comments are in *No Cheering in the Press*

Box, collected and edited by Jerome Holtzman, New York, 1974, p. 259; also in that book, Richard Vidmer remembers Grantland Rice's sincerity, p. 109; and Smith discusses sportswriting as propaganda, p. 259.

6. The Fighting Irish as Classical Ideal

The University of Notre Dame sports publicity handout on Rockne's life is in (UABM *Knute Rockne—All American* Series, Publicity folder). Father Charles Carey kindly talked with me on 11/24/96; I must thank Father John Conley for arranging the interview. Detailed discussions of and references for the following are in *Shake Down the Thunder* (op. cit.): for Notre Dame in the 1920s, Chapters 16 through 27; W. O. McGeehan's trip to Notre Dame, p. 290; Father John O'Hara's work in the 1930s, Chapters 34 and 35.

On page 58 of the text, ND vice president John J. Cavanaugh wrote to Fred Digby, sports editor of the *New Orleans Item* and a member of the Sugar Bowl committee, on 11/26/41 (UVOC 5/35). Vice President Cavanaugh pointed out the endowment figures in a press release, 3/28/41 (UVOC 6/6). Father O'Hara's connection between football and religion is discussed and referenced in Chapter 19 of *Shake Down the Thunder* (op. cit.). My interviews with Gordon Graham, longtime sports editor of the *Lafayette (Indiana) Journal & Courier*, were done during the spring of 1961 for my senior project at Purdue with Prof. Mark Rowen. As a true pack rat, I kept all of my notes from my undergraduate career, including the ones from the Graham interviews (this triumph of pack-rattism adds weight to my long-standing argument with my wife concerning the cleaning of attics, garages, basements, etc., and the throwing out of old papers).

The following material is in Thomas B. Littleton's biography of Arch Ward (op. cit.): the comment about the Notre Dame Stadium pressbox, p. x; Arch Ward's admiration of sports heroes, p. xiii and p. 78; Father Hesburgh's eulogy for Ward, p. 199; Ward's relationship with his alma mater, p. 30; and Ward's clout at Notre Dame, p. 64. With the backing of the *Chicago Tribune*, Ward was a tireless promoter but not an original thinker; he always claimed to be the "inventor" of his events, particularly the Major League Baseball All-Star game. In fact, in the late 1920s, the Negro Baseball Leagues started staging midsummer All-Star games, and their early 1930s contests in Chicago's Comiskey Park, covered by the *Tribune*, drew over 50,000 fans per game and obviously inspired Ward to apply the concept to the whites-only major leagues. Ward never gave the Negro Leagues credit. His official Curriculum Vitae listed, "1: Originated the All-Star baseball game" (UASI 7/12), and contemporaries supported his claim: Tom Meany's bio piece on Ward for *Collier's* magazine, 8/12/50, was called "Arch Dreams Up the Dream Games." Moreover, many sports historians still support his claim, e.g., Benjamin Rader, *In Its Own Image: How Television Has Transformed Sports*, New York, 1984, p. 20. Few incidents illustrate the racism of American sports better than this episode: an African American invention and huge numbers of black fans simply did not count.

Father O'Hara wrote to Grantland Rice, 10/25/34 (UPOH 55/Rh-Rog folder), and O'Hara's note on sportswriters was sent to Joseph Greeley, 2/26/34 (UVOH 2/23). ND vice president John J. Cavanaugh wrote to Grantland Rice, 12/17/41 (UVOC 5/37). Arch Ward's self-description "as head coach at Notre Dame" was in the *Notre Dame Alumnus*, 1–2/37, p. 117. Frank Leahy sent his note about taking the Wards to the Chez Paree to ND vice president John J. Cavanaugh, 2/18/42 (5/12); the ND coach wrote in praise of Warren Brown to Rex Smith, 11/13/41 (UVOC 5/11).

Francis Wallace listed his fellow sportswriter alumni on the ND "network" in *Notre Dame Story* (op. cit.), p. 47 and pp. 154–55; and Elmer Layden in his memoir (op. cit.) paid homage to the Chicago and New York sportswriting friends of Notre Dame, p. 173. Red Smith's comments are in the *Red Smith Reader*, edited by Dave Anderson, New York, 1982, p. 261. Robert Lipsyte described the relationship of Arthur Daley to Grantland Rice in *SportsWorld* (op. cit.), p. 181; and Robert Daley told the story of his father and JFK in *Sports of the Times: The Arthur Daley Years*, New York, 1975, p. 332.

On page 65 of the text, Big Ten commissioner John L. Griffith wrote to Notre Dame vice president John J. Cavanaugh, 12/9/41 (UPHO 86/36); and Arch Ward wrote to Griffith, 12/10/41 (UVOC 4/53). Ward's comments on Big Ten irregularities were in his *Chicago Tribune* columns on 11/22/41, 12/4/41, and 12/6/41; William Fox's comments appeared in the *Indianapolis (Indiana) News* on 9/5/41 and 11/28/41; and Francis Wallace's in the *Saturday Evening Post*, 9/20/41. In their September pieces, Fox also said of a Hoosier athlete (Tom Harmon of Gary) that he "is supposed to have received $5,000 in the bank and a guaranteed degree," and Wallace repeated a version of this.

On page 67 of the text, the memo of the conference between President J. Hugh O'Donnell and Frank Leahy, 8/3/42, is in (UVOC 5/12).

7. "Rockne Picked Him": Frank Leahy

Leo Lowenthal's "Rise of Biography as a Popular Literary Type" appeared in *American Social Patterns,* ed. William Petersen, Garden City, New York, 1956, pp. 63–118. Lowenthal, one of the first scholars to study popular culture, wrote the essay in 1944. Tim Cohane's "Rockne Picked Him" was in the *Saturday Evening Post,* 10/18/41. For the interview with Father Charles Carey see previous citation; Mike Holovak discussed the Lou Montgomery episode in *Violence Every Sunday: The Story of a Professional Football Coach,* New York, 1967, p. 31. Wells Twombley wrote *Shake Down the Thunder: The Official Biography of Frank Leahy,* Radnor, Pennsylvania, 1974; the quotes in the text are on p. 142. Rockne's attention to his "boys" is discussed frequently and referenced in my book *Shake Down the Thunder,* particularly in Chapter 24 (the reasons for the similar titles and my homage to Wells Twombley are in the Preface to my book).

On page 73 of the text, ND vice president John J. Cavanaugh discussed his monitoring of Leahy's career as an assistant coach to Crowley in an "Oral Memoir" (UORL 2/2), 1973, p. 210. In 1941, some reporters discovered that Cavanaugh, while on the West Coast on university business the previous December, had met Buck Shaw privately—the two men talked in a car during a rainstorm—and these reporters and later sports historians described this meeting with the appropriate Hollywood tropes. But the ND vice president had concluded that "Buck was already coming down the other side of the mountain" in terms of age and coaching ability, and that he "preferred Frank anyway," p. 214 (above cit.). The private communication from Chet Grant to Vice President John J. Cavanaugh, 1/5/41, is in (UPHO 88/19a). The dispute with Boston College over Leahy's acceptance of the Notre Dame job is in Michael J. Ryan to ND president J. Hugh O'Donnell, 2/16/41 (UVOC 5/10); Rev. Maurice Dullea to the Very Rev. Albert S. Cousineau, 4/22/41 (UVOC 5/33); President J. Hugh O'Donnell to the Very Rev. Albert S. Cousineau, 5/16/41 (UVOC 5/10); and Father John J. Cavanaugh's "Oral Memoir," (UORL 2/2), 1973, pp. 215–16.

Arch Ward's comments on Leahy's "homecoming" at Notre Dame are in Gene Schoor, *A Treasury of Notre Dame Football,* New York, 1962, pp. 134 and 141. *Chicago Times* sportswriter J. Ray Hunt's article appeared 11/26/41. Leahy's maxim on "perfection" is in Twombley's biography of the coach (op. cit.), p. 220; and Leahy's daily schedule is on p. 219. Many eyewitnesses attested to Leahy's early morning and full day schedules, among others his trainer at Notre Dame in 1941, Eugene "Scrapiron" Young, in his book, *With Rockne at Notre Dame,* p. 238. For a discussion of St. Louis University coach Eddie Cochems's pioneer work with the forward pass and Jesse Harper's innovations, see the discussion and references in my *Shake Down the Thunder* (op. cit.), p. 39f.

On page 76 of the text, for the ticket requests for the 1941 Army–Notre Dame game, see Pat O'Brien to Vice President John J. Cavanaugh, 10/24/41, and the telegraphed reply, 10/25/41 (UVOC 6/27); Cavanaugh's note to Joseph P. Kennedy, 10/17/41, is also in (UVOC 6/27). President J. Hugh O'Donnell wrote to Ambrose O'Connell, Assistant Postmaster General of the United States, about the latter's "endorsement of Frank Leahy," 9/12/41 (UPHO 88/22). A portion of Leahy's schedule in New York appears in the *Notre Dame Alumnus,* 12/41, and in (UVOC 6/27).

8. The Golden Age of Sports Radio

The first quote is from Benjamin Rader, *In Its Own Image* (op. cit.), p. 30. For the history of broadcasting, in addition to Rader's work, the following are very useful: Erik Barnouw's three-volume *The Golden Web: A History of Broadcasting in the United States,* New York, 1966–70; *Sports Broadcasting* by John R. Catsis, Chicago, 1996; and the chapter, "Sports and the Mass Media," in *Social Aspects of Sport* by Eldon E. Snyder and Elmer A. Spreitzer, Englewood Cliffs, New Jersey, 1983. Many other works on this subject exist, but the above provide the essential information.

Ronald Reagan's comments on "a little band of [radio] pioneers" are in *Where's the Rest of Me?* (op. cit.), p. 54. Garry Wills's book on Reagan (op. cit.) has an important section, "Part Three: Radio," that details Reagan's sports broadcasting career; particularly informative is Chapter 13, "Journalist," on Reagan's attitudes toward his radio work. Wills's remarks on sports broadcasters' lack of objectivity are on p. 117, and radio audiences' appreciation of the fables on pp. 119–20. Ring Lardner's comment about Graham MacNamee was carried by the Bell Syndicate in many newspapers, 10/7/24; Red Barber, *The Broadcasters,* New York, 1970, p. 32, tells the story about Ted Husing and Judge Landis, and Husing and the Orange Bowl, pp. 33–34. Barber was one of the most modest and honest radio announcers of the period, and had a long, celebrated career.

In *Sportscasting* by Karl Klages, Logan, Utah, no date, the author—the sports information director at Utah State—outlined the telegraph code for football games, p. 102. Tim Cohane related the story of the early failure to popularize the "Seven Blocks of Granite" nickname in his *Great College Football Coaches of the Twenties and Thirties,* (op. cit.), p. 49. James T. Van Hoy studied college football broadcasters in his master's thesis, *A Personal and Professional Profile of Major College Football Broadcasters: A Direct Mail Survey,* at the University of Tennessee, 1977. The legend of Michigan's Bob Ufer lives on; "a life-size cutout" of Bob rode in the 1998 Rose Bowl Parade (*Detroit News,* 1/12/98), and a CD of some of his broadcast highlights went on sale in late 1997. Fortunately, Purdue's Johnny Decamp seems long forgotten.

Bill Stern collected his radio broadcasts in a number of anthologies; the 1944 story on the "whispering" Golden Dome is in *My Favorite Sports Stories,* New York, 1946, p. 71. Stern wrote about his work in his memoir, *A Taste of Ashes: An Autobiography of Bill Stern with Oscar Fraley,* New York, 1959; the comments on his techniques and listeners are on pp. 103–4. The John Crosby quotes on Bill Stern are from Crosby's column in the *New York Herald-Tribune,* 11/24/49. Rader (op. cit.) made the comment on the "values and aspirations that shaped the lives of millions of Americans," p. 8.

On page 85 of the text, the secretary of the Notre Dame Faculty Board in Control of Athletics wrote to Frank C. Barton, 5/15/37 (UVOC 6/52). President O'Hara's estimate of the loss from refusing to sell the broadcasting rights was in an article in the *South Bend News-Times,* 5/18/37. The *Chicago Tribune's* WGN radio station broadcast the Nebraska–Notre Dame game, 11/15/24. For Rockne's reluctance to play Catholic schools, see my *Shake Down the Thunder* (op. cit.), pp. 99, 129, 150, 188, and 256. Johnny Lujack described the effect of the radio broadcasts on his decision to attend Notre Dame in *The Glory of Notre Dame,* ed. Fred Katz, New York, 1971, p. 1. Garry Wills (op. cit.) remarked on "sportscasters" losing their "equanimity," p. 117.

9. Snafus

Grantland Rice's comments appeared in his "Football Forecast" for *Collier's* magazine, 9/26/42, p. 90. Rube Samuelson in *The Rose Bowl Game,* Garden City, New York, 1951, had an informative chapter, "Rose Bowl Finds a Home in North Carolina," on the post–Pearl Harbor events and the 1942 game, p. 182f. Bill Cromartie and Jody Brown discussed the beginnings of World War II in *The Glamor Game,* Nashville, 1989, p. 120; in addition, on that page is the quote "The Show Must Go On." For the wartime football schedules—and lack of same—see *Major College Football: Record of Scores: 1869–1982,* compiled by Terry Bender and Lawrence W. Stiles, Bryn Mawr, Pennsylvania, 1983.

Francis Wallace discussed athletic scholarships in his "Pigskin Preview" for the *Saturday Evening Post,* 9/19/42; he also quoted Commander Thomas Hamilton's advice to football coaches to join the Naval program in that article. Allen L. Sack and Ellen Staurowsky trace the background and evolution of athletic scholarships in *College Athletes for Hire: The Evolution and Legacy of the NCAA's Amateur Myth,* New York, in press (1998). Father J. Hugh O'Donnell, the president of Notre Dame, made his comments on athletic scholarships at the 1940 Notre Dame football banquet, a few months after the release of *Knute Rockne—All-American; the Notre Dame Alumni Magazine,* 1–2/41, has the text quoted here. The Associated Press carried many stories on the athletic scholarship controversy in early 1941, including the "free country" quote from University of Kentucky official W. D. Funkhouser, 2/18/41, in the *New York Times,* among other papers. Bill Fay's article on Angelo Bertelli, "Football Bombadier," appeared in *Collier's* magazine, 10/17/42.

The "Confidential Report" of the Cavanaugh and Leahy visit to West Point, 1/1/42, is in the United States Military Academy Library Special Collections; the quote appears on p. 8 of the full report, and a summary of it is in General Maxwell Taylor's Superintendent's Papers, 1946; Lujack's explanation of the controversy is in *The Glory of Notre Dame* (op. cit.), p. 1. Football coach Lou Little made his remarks in a *Saturday Evening Post* article, "Sport for Sport's Sake Is Now Out," 10/17/42, and in the *New York Times,* 1/17/43. John R. Tunis's article, "Sports Return to 1900," was in *Harper's Magazine,* 5/43. For the Notre Dame–Michigan wartime games, John Kryk's book, *Natural Enemies: The Notre Dame–Michigan Football Feud,* Kansas City, 1994, provides excellent details, Chapter 10, p. 139f. Jim Costin in the *South Bend Tribune* commented on the radio broadcasts of the 1942 game, 11/12/42. Los Angeles sportswriter Rube Samuelson (op. cit.) discussed the 1943 bowl games, p. 191f.

The first printed reference to the Duke of Wellington saying, "The Battle of Waterloo was won on the playing fields of Eton" appeared many years after his death; see *Bartlett's Familiar Quotations,* Boston, 1980, p. 421. In fact, neither organized games nor playing fields existed at Eton at the time of the Battle of Waterloo; the panelists on the British Broadcasting Corporation radio program *My Word* discussed this on 3/7/98 (broadcast in the United States by National Public Radio). Robert J. Higgs has an interesting chapter on "Sports and War" in his *Sports: A Reference Guide,* Westport, Connecticut, p. 169; he also mentions the subject throughout his *God in the Stadium: Sports and Religion in America,* Lexington, Kentucky, 1995. The article from the program of the 1942 Notre Dame–Great Lakes Naval Station game referred to in the text was by Lt. Commander J. Russell Cook.

10. Programs as Propaganda

Notre Dame vice president Richard W. Conklin made his comment in an interview, 3/12/91. All of the college football programs discussed in this chapter and subsequent ones for games at Notre Dame Stadium are in the University of Notre Dame Archives (PATH collection); all of the other programs are in the Joyce Sports Research Collection at the University of Notre Dame. Both depositories have the programs catalogued according to year and, for the Joyce Collection, school as well; their cataloguing systems make it very easy for researchers to find specific program covers, advertisements, and articles.

Nothing exists in print about the Don Spencer Agency—except for the programs themselves. However, by reading them carefully, and also from various documents in the University of Notre Dame Archives, particularly the letters to and from Spencer, I arrived at the conclusions in this chapter. Similarly, nothing exists in print on the Spencer illustrators; however, by comparing their styles to such leaders in their profession as Norman Rockwell, I could trace H. Alonzo Keller's imitations of Rockwell, and the other Spencer artists' use of Rockwell and other *Saturday Evening Post* illustrators. Particularly useful for these endeavors were the following books: *The Saturday Evening Post Norman Rockwell Book,* Indianapolis, 1977, no author or editor; and *332 Magazine Covers/Norman Rockwell,* ed. Christopher Finch, New York, 1979. Case College is the forerunner of part of Case-Western Reserve University in Cleveland, Ohio.

On page 104 of the text, Notre Dame vice president John H. Murphy made his comments about the programs as souvenirs to Frank E. Cane, 4/22/49 (UVMR 1/23). For a discussion of John Huston's problems with the *Battle of San Pietro* (1944) and his other wartime documentaries, see John McCarty's *The Films of John Huston,* Secaucus, New Jersey, 1987. Many studies of cigarette advertising exist, although none mention the ubiquitous ads in the football game programs in the 1940s and 1950s. The standard works on the subject are Thomas Whiteside, *Selling Death: Cigarette Advertising and Public Health,* New York, 1971; Gerard S. Petrone, *Tobacco Advertising: The Great Seduction,* Atglen, Pennsylvania, 1996; and Richard Kluger's *Ashes to Ashes: America's Hundred-Year Cigarette War, the Public Health, and the Unabashed Triumph of Philip Morris,* New York, 1996.

On page 108 of the text, for the 1942 Army–Notre Dame game, broadcast coordinator Colman O'Shaughnessy wrote to Notre Dame president J. Hugh O'Donnell, 10/21/42 (UPHO 94/15). J. Edgar Hoover's remarks were in the *Notre Dame Alumnus* magazine, 5–6/42.

11. The Military vs. College Sports

For the first quote, an Associated Press item from April 1944, see (PATH "Notre Dame Scrapbook, 1941 through 1944"). Ray Eliot's comment is in John McCallum, *Big Ten Football Since 1895,* Radnor, Pennsylvania, 1976; this book provides an excellent summary of wartime football in the Big Ten. For useful overviews of the situation nationally, see Douglas A. Noverr and Lawrence E. Ziewacz, *The Games They Played: Sports in American History, 1865–1980,* Chicago, 1983; and Tom Perrin, *Football: A College History,* Jefferson, North Carolina, 1987; the Faurot split-T story is on p. 215 of the latter book. During World War II, the Navy had a very different policy than the Army concerning elite sports teams: the Navy encouraged its enlistees at schools with naval training programs to play intercollegiate athletics; the Army, with personnel at over 200 schools for its training courses, did not encourage its trainees to participate in college sports. In addition, at strictly military facilities, the Army gave local base commanders the option of promoting elite teams, whereas the Navy made high-level squads at all of its naval aviation stations a priority. Thus, at universities with Army programs, college sports withered and/or disappeared during the war; at some Army bases, excellent teams emerged; at higher education institutions offering naval training, like Michigan, Purdue, Northwestern, college teams flourished; and at the Great Lakes Naval Station, the Pre-Flight schools at the universities of Iowa and North Carolina and at St. Mary's College in northern California, some of the best squads in the country suited up.

John McCallum, in *Big Ten* (op. cit.), discusses team hopping on pp. 73–74; and the quote from a fan appears in (PATH "Notre Dame Scrapbook, 1941 through 1944"), the typeface appears to be that of the *Pittsburgh (Pennsylvania) Post-Gazette* and the year 1943. Grantland Rice made his comments in his article "The All-America Team," *Collier's*, 12/18/43. Arch Ward's column on freshmen eligibility appeared in the *Chicago Tribune*, 5/14/45; ND vice president John J. Cavanaugh gave his opinion on the question to Hugh Devore, 5/14/45 (UVOC 5/16). The AP had an article on the Big Six permitting athletic grants for the first time on 12/10/44, carried by the *New York Times*, among other papers. McCallum, *Big Ten* (op. cit.), quotes Crisler on two-platoon, and Bierman's failure, p. 74; Grantland Rice's summary of the season appeared in the article cited directly above. Dr. E. E. Litkenhous's "Final Grid Ratings" for 1943 is in (PATH "Notre Dame Scrapbook, 1941 through 1944"). See Samuelson (op. cit.) for the details on the 1944 Rose Bowl game, p. 198f; and for the Edward "Moose" Krause interview, see (op. cit.). Notre Dame had a naval training facility on its campus; thousands of men came to the campus, among them some outstanding football players. ND administrators did not allow head coach Frank Leahy to aggressively recruit players from other schools, but he did pick up some naval trainees from the Minnesota Gophers and an All-American from Illinois, Julie Rykovich. In addition, a number of the best members of his 1942 team passed naval officers' tests, enabling them to enter the training program on their own campus and remain on the team.

For the anti-Catholicism of Michigan's longtime coach and AD, Fielding Yost, see my *Shake Down the Thunder* (op. cit.), index entry for Yost. Concerning the excitement created by the 1943 Notre Dame–Michigan game, ND vice president John J. Cavanaugh wrote to Robert Cahill, ND athletic department employee, in the Navy at the time, 10/6/43 (UVOC 5/22). Twombley (op. cit.), p. 222, mentions Leahy's suspicions about the call-up of Bertelli. Francis Wallace in *Notre Dame: From Rockne to Parseghian*, New York, 1966, p. 95, has the *42nd Street* storyline; many newspapers used it at the time, see (PATH "Notre Dame Scrapbook, 1941 through 1944"). Twombley (op. cit.) has the summary of the media's portrayal of Leahy's enlistment, p. 238; he also discusses Leahy's work in the Navy on that page. The *Chicago Herald-American* ran a large photo of Leahy being sworn in under the headline "Gold Domer Becomes Gold Striper," 5/2/44, and the *Chicago Tribune* carried a photo of Leahy in his new Navy uniform, 5/19/44, along with fulsome praise by Arch Ward in his column.

On page 116 of the text, the letter from Notre Dame president J. Hugh O'Donnell to Local Selective Board No. 113, Middlesex County, Newton Center, Massachusetts, 12/1/43, is in (UVOC 5/12)—Leahy registered for the draft while coaching at Boston College. Twombley (op. cit.) also discusses Leahy's work in the Navy on p. 238.

12. Hollywood Reconstructs College Sports

Bill Stern discussed his movies for Columbia and Metro Goldwyn Mayer in his memoir, *A Taste of Ashes* (op. cit.), p. 78; a surprising number of Stern's films still exist in catalogues devoted to 16-millimeter films as well as in various collections, including that of the Library of Congress (hereafter referred to as LOC). Many authors have written about Hollywood during the World War II period: Thomas Schatz's recent work *Boom and Bust: The American Cinema in the 1940s*, New York, 1997, discusses the film industry in detail, and his *Hollywood Genres: Formulas, Filmmaking, and the Studio System* (op. cit.), the war film genre; Robert Sklar in *Movie Made America: A Cultural History of American Movies*, New York, 1994, has an excellent chapter entitled "Hollywood at War for America and at War with Itself"; also, Thomas Doherty in *Projections of War: Hollywood, American Culture, and World War II*, New York, 1993, discusses many individual films and trends in terms of the social history of the period. Surprisingly, none of these authors link war movies to sports, although Doherty makes a reference to sports metaphors in some of the films, p. 110.

The comment by theater manager John Krier about World War II moviegoers appeared in *USA Today*, "The Real Box Office Champs," by Andy Seiler, 8/19/96. Another movie that helped remythologize World War I was Warners's *The Fighting 69th* (1940), starring Pat O'Brien, about New York City's "Irish" regiment in World War I; it also focused on a group-hero more than other films of the time. In his *Dementia Pigskin,* New York, 1951, Francis Wallace discussed how "The Rockne picture . . . was made by Bob Fellows, one of the dyed-in-the-pigskin goobers [fanatics]," and Fellows's other film work, p. 159.

The quotes in the text are from a videotape of *The Iron Major,* when it was presented on the American Movie Classics Channel, October 1991; the LOC does not possess the film. Bill Stern's anecdote about Cavanaugh appeared on the air shortly after the film's release and was collected in his *My Favorite Sports Stories* (op. cit.), p. 53; the biographical information on Cavanaugh is from *Great College Coaches,* by Tim Cohane (op. cit.), pp. 42–49. Considering that Cohane knew the coach at Fordham, his information is probably accurate. The *Indianapolis News* critic found O'Brien's performance "too reminiscent of his work as Knute Rockne," 11/10/43, but the *Indianapolis Star* critic compared the film favorably to *Pride of the Yankees,* 11/10/43. The voice-over narrator of ESPN's *Football Movies* (op. cit.) made the comments on the importance of *Knute Rockne—All-American;* a number of books discuss Warners's business activities; the best of them are Neal Roddick's *A New Deal in Entertainment,* British Film Institute, London, United Kingdom, and Thomas Schatz's recent book, *Boom and Bust* (op. cit.).

Moose Krause made his comments in an interview (op. cit.); his joining the Marine Corps, rather than taking an easy job in the Navy, gave an indication of his character. The article on Shaughnessy's book is in *Time,* 10/11/43. Many other articles on the war-and-football-strategy theme appeared in this period, one of the most interesting in the *Michigan Alumnus Quarterly Review,* 10/45, by Col. John R. Lovell and Clinton B. Conger; they concluded that America was winning the war because "Our Fighting Forces of today are made up of tens of thousands of men who know football as they know their right hand, who can grasp the principles of modern warfare on that basis with an advantage given to no other nation in the world."

13. War/Football Movies

Many authors discuss the war film genre: Kathryn Kane, *Visions of War: Hollywood Combat Films of World War II,* Ann Arbor, Michigan, 1982, also provides an excellent "Appendix: Credits and Plot Synopsis of Films," and much of the cited material—dates, casts, etc.—in this chapter is from that source. Also useful were the sections of Thomas Schatz's *Genius of the System* (op. cit.) on "The War Film" and "The Collective Hero"; Jeanine Basinger's *The World War II Combat Film: Anatomy of a Genre,* New York, 1986; and *Celluloid Wars: A Guide to Film and the American Experience of War* by Frank J. Wetta and Stephen J. Curley, New York, 1992. Again, none of these books see the experience of sports as central to these films; apparently, like many intellectuals, these *cinéastes* disdain sports and, unlike a majority of Americans, ignore its place at the center of popular culture.

See Richard Tregaskis's *Guadalcanal Diary,* New York, 1943, for a different opening than the film's. *The Notre Dame Football Media Guide,* 1997 edition, lists every player who played in an ND varsity football game. No Donnellys appear, including under all possible alternate spellings. Bosley Crowther of the *New York Times* reviewed *Guadalcanal Diary* on 11/18/43; the quote from Thomas Sobchack's essay (op. cit.) appears on p. 110. The quote on the ethnic backgrounds of the 1943 Notre Dame team appeared in the *Pittsburgh (Pennsylvania) Press,* November 1943 (PATH "Notre Dame Scrapbook 1941 through 1944"). Also see the scrapbooks for the other articles on the team. The players' hometowns are listed on the "Official 1943 Notre Dame Football Roster" in *The Notre Dame Football Scrapbook,* ed. by Richard M. Cohen, Jordan A. Deutsch, and David Neft, Indianapolis, 1977, p. 109. This book, assembled to look like a 1940s scrapbook, contains some useful articles and information but, like the original scrapbooks, no datelines or authors on the clipped newspaper items. Longtime Big Ten commissioner Kenneth L. "Tug" Wilson described the 1930s Golden Gophers in his *The Big Ten* with Jerry Brondfield, Englewood Cliffs, New Jersey, 1967, p. 180. Grantland Rice's "Collier's All-America Team" appeared in that magazine, 12/16/44; his "Postgrad All-Americas—Pacific Chapter" followed his "All-America" piece. Francis Wallace's tribute to African American players was in his "Pigskin Preview" in the *Saturday Evening Post,* 9/19/42; Ronald Reagan's story about "a Negro sailor" at Pearl Harbor comes from Lou Cannon, *Reagan,* New York, 1982, p. 20.

Lawrence Howard Suid was the editor of the published screenplay, *Air Force,* Madison, Wisconsin, 1983; the quotes in my text are from that screenplay and the film itself. Coach John Robinson made his comments in the ESPN film, *Football Movies* (op. cit.). Fred Digby's article, "Rock in These Days," appeared in many programs, including the Georgia Tech–Notre Dame game, 10/2/43. Commander William R. "Killer" Kane's article, "Football Pays Off," appeared in the 1945 NCAA *Official Football Guide,* New York, 1945, pp. 41–43.

14. Football Becomes the Black Knights and Colonel Blaik

The Chesterfield cigarette ad with the MacArthur verse appeared in the football game programs of the schools using the Spencer Agency's services in 1943, and also in many magazines. In a special program for the Notre Dame–Army game in 1944, the head of athletics at the Academy, Lt. Col. Frank M. Greene, articulated the West Point sentiment on the verse: "No statement better expresses the value of sports training as preparation for combat leadership than General MacArthur's famous words," 11/11/44. All of MacArthur's biographers discuss his promotion of athletics as superintendent at West Point, and his composition of the famous lines about sports and war. The most exhaustive discussion occurs in Volume I of D. Clayton James's massive *The Years of MacArthur,* Houghton Mifflin, Boston, 1970; this author also discusses MacArthur's affection for Earl Blaik. Stephen E. Ambrose in *Duty Honor Country: A History of West Point,* Baltimore, 1966, offers a succinct history of the Academy and insights into MacArthur's various roles there. Jim Beach and Daniel Moore, *Army vs. Notre Dame: The Big Game 1913–1947,* New York, 1948, also discuss the Academy's long history of bending the rules on player eligibility. See the indexes of these books for the multiple references to the above topics.

The letter from General Robert Eichelberger to Colonel Earl "Red" Blaik, dated 7/5/42, is in *The Red Blaik Story,* New Rochelle, New York, 1974, pp. 180–81; that book also contains the first version of Blaik's memoirs, *You Have to Pay the Price,* New York, 1960, with Tim Cohane; all page citations here from Blaik's memoirs are from the 1974 edition. Cohane has a chapter in his *Great College Football Coaches* (op. cit.) on Blaik's pre-Army coaching career, pp. 34–41; Eichelberger's quote on "the finest bunch of losers" is in Blaik's memoir (op. cit.), p. 169. Stanley Woodward commented on Blaik's "idol of idols" in "Football's Greatest Father-Son Act," *Saturday Evening Post,* 10/7/50. Blaik frequently compared football to war, constantly remarking, "You have to pay the price"; one of Blaik's assistants, Vince Lombardi, ingested the motto, see *Vince* (op. cit.), p. 89f. *Army vs. Navy: Seventy Years of Football Rivalry* by Jack Clary, New York, 1965, describes Army's football decline in the 1930s, and its revival in the 1940s, as well as FDR's role in the process, pp. 103 and 141. The editors of *Sport* magazine also mentioned "Army's policy" of using football as "an advertisement," in their Letters to the Editor section, 2/48.

Grantland Rice's remarks on Army and Navy were in his "Collier's All-America Team" article in that magazine, 12/16/44; Francis Wallace's comments on athletes taking "refuge in the service schools" was in his "Football's Black Market" in the *Saturday Evening Post,* 11/9/46. Jack Newcombe in "Navy's Skipper in Civvies," *Sport* magazine, 11/55, commented on "Army's unofficial [recruiting] bureau"; John McCallum, in *Big Ten* (op. cit.), called Blaik the "ogre," p. 75; Ed Linn, in "Mr. Inside and Mr. Outside," *Sport* magazine, 12/55, offered an excellent account of Army's wartime recruiting, particularly of Blanchard and Davis. This article contains the quote from Davis about the senatorial appointments for himself and his twin; the material on Blanchard's recruitment, as well as that of Shorty McWilliams, Barney Poole, and Tex Coulter, among others; and the joke about "On Brave Old Army Team." A retrospective account of the Army team was provided to me by Jim Beach, co-author of the excellent history of the Notre Dame–Army game (op. cit.) and a sportswriter in New York for much of the 1940s and 1950s. In a long telephone interview on 11/6/96, Beach supplied many details on Blaik's recruiting and his teams, and the comments quoted here about Blanchard.

The McWilliams case, with the quote from West Point superintendent Maxwell Taylor, was in *Time,* 9/9/46. The exchange in the Letters to the Editor column of *Sport* magazine occurred 1/48; a surprising source for the details on Blanchard's father, including his tramp athlete days, is Blaik's memoir (op. cit.), p. 192f. In that book, Blaik also commented about driving himself and everyone else, p. 176; the importance of beating Notre Dame in 1944, p. 201; and the practices between his first two units as the best football he ever saw, p. 195f. John McCallum in *Big Ten* (op. cit.) described

Blaik's scrimmages, p. 75; Red Smith's post-game lament appeared in the *Philadelphia Record*, 11/12/44; and the comments on "Army showed no mercy" are in Cohen (op. cit.), article titled "Army 59; Notre Dame 0"; Arch Ward's "A courageous team from Notre Dame" was in the *Chicago Tribune*, 11/11/44; the United Press remarked on "three of West Point's favorite sons" in a dispatch, 11/11/44, carried by many papers, including the *Indianapolis Star*. Mrs. Joseph Reilly remembered Army's "lack of sportsmanship" in a letter to the editor of *Sport* magazine, 1/48; and Blaik, in his memoir (op. cit.), showed his lack of graciousness, p. 199.

On page 145 of the text, Notre Dame vice president John J. Cavanaugh wrote to Arch Ward, 11/14/44 (UVOC 101/3). In Wilson, *Big Ten* (op. cit.), Crisler related how he played Army in the 1944 game, p. 274; Thomas Littleton (op. cit.) noted Ward's reaction to the 1944 and '45 ND-Army games, p. xi. During this period, the military fed many articles on athlete-heroes to magazines like *Senior Scholastic*, which was aimed at high school students; the Army not only extolled athletes in combat but also praised outstanding West Point football players. A typical wartime paean to Blanchard and Davis appeared in *Youth Scholastic*, 11/45, with multiple copies distributed to every junior high and high school in the country: "What are you going to do when he [Blanchard] charges at you? Simple—take to the nearest air-raid shelter . . . His buddy, Glenn Davis, travels faster than sound," like a jet plane . . . "In front of these guns stands the Army line . . . they eat iron [tank] bolts for breakfast," etc. The author mixes sports and military metaphors constantly, reinforcing the total connection between the two activities.

15. The Wartime Irish and Rockne's Other Heirs

Notre Dame vice president John J. Cavanaugh wrote to Joseph P. Kennedy, 10/11/43, and Kennedy replied, 10/16/43 (both letters in UVOC 6/48). One of the October 1945 football programs listing the Notre Dame war dead was the home game against Dartmouth, 10/13/45. The *Esquire* magazine article, "McKeever into Leahy's Shoes," by J. Ray Hunt, appeared 10/44; Arthur Daley's *New York Times* column, "Successor to Rockne," ran on 4/22/44; and Vice President Cavanaugh's letter about "the value of Coaches Leahy and McKeever" was sent to Rev. James McKenna, 1/10/44 (UVOC 5/3).

Syndicated columnist Joe Williams, *New York Telegram*, 10/9/44, related the story of the letter from a GI, and McKeever's plea before the 1944 Navy game; Dave Condon told the story of McKeever's locker-room talk before the Army game, and his recruiting at the University of San Francisco in the *Chicago Tribune*, 9/18/74; Arthur Daley made his post-game comments in the *New York Times*, 12/12/44, and his prediction on McKeever's future, 12/20/44; and the *Chicago Times*'s Warren Brown nominated McKeever for "Coach of the Year," 12/5/44. Arch Murray and George Trevor wrote about McKeever's problems at Cornell in "The Coach They Didn't Want," *Saturday Evening Post*, 11/18/50. Red Smith, rarely given to such acerbic comments, discussed McKeever's motivation in the *New York Herald-Tribune*, 2/25/48. Dave Condon (op. cit.) told the story of how, during a recruiting trip to Chicago for LSU, McKeever pursued one phenom who had zero interest in going south, and he refused to look at another prospect whom friends kept telling him about: Johnny Lattner, future Heisman Trophy winner. Subsequently, McKeever drifted through various small businesses in the Southwest and died in 1974.

For a description of freshman football at Notre Dame when McKeever and Devore played in the early 1930s, see Chapter 28 of my book, *Shake Down the Thunder* (op. cit.); also see the index of that work for the many entries on Joe Byrne Jr. *New York Mirror* sportswriter Ralph Cannon wrote about Devore, 9/29/45; Tom Meany published the *Saturday Evening Post* feature, "Devore Likes His T, But—Notre Dame's New Coach," 11/10/45, and Meany also discussed this coach's reputation as a "Serious Man" (his caps). On page 152 of the text, Devore wrote "that I am a 4F coach or they are 4F players" to ND vice president John J. Cavanaugh, 7/27/45 (UVOC 5/16). In the same letter, Devore also responded at length about a recruiting tip that Cavanaugh had passed on to him about a high school player in Montreal, Canada, indicating Devore's deep knowledge of the Notre Dame football system as well as the extent of the ND recruiting network. (A Canadian priest had recommended Ralph Touhy to Cavanaugh; in the end, Touhy, unknown to other American schools, never came south but instead turned professional, becoming one of the youngest and best players in the Canadian Football League.) Cavanaugh had sent Devore the note from the priest in Montreal on 7/22/45 (UVOC 5/16).

Arthur Daley wrote that Devore "gave the Bonnies the best teams they ever had" in the *New York Times*, 2/9/50, and how he would revive NYU's football fortunes. However, the school soon dropped the sport, and Devore went to the NFL Green Bay Packers, next to the University of Dayton, then to a stint as head coach of the Philadelphia Eagles; after returning to ND in the late 1950s–early 1960s, he went to the pros with the Houston Oilers, completing his career with them, and devoting his final years to his son, who suffered from a major seizure disorder. Notre Dame honored him as "The Oldest Living Irish Football Coach" at the Purdue-ND game, 9/29/90.

During the first generation of TV sports, the fact that viewers could see the action for themselves inhibited many commentators from the imaginary laterals of radio broadcasts. Announcers mainly added factual material to the pictures. But, by the 1960s and the arrival of Roone Arledge at ABC-TV and his emphasis on pagentry and color, announcers began spinning various classical narratives.

16. The End of the Notre Dame–Army Annuals

Francis Wallace's comments were in his "Pigskin Preview" for the *Saturday Evening Post*, 9/21/46. Notre Dame "ticket manager" M. Robert Cahill sent out a form letter about the four-seat allotment during the spring of 1946; a letter went to Judge Ernest L. Hammer, 5/17/46 (UPHO 107/21); Hammer protested to Cahill in the most vociferous terms, 6/5/46 (UPHO 107/21). An article in (PATH "Notre Dame Scrapbook, 1946") entitled "$400,000 in Army Ticket Orders Refunded by N.D.," and one in the *Sporting News* by J. G. Taylor Spink, 11/4/46, "U.S. Stirred by Battle of Grid Giants," described the ticket history of the game; another article, "The Coming Trouble" (PATH "Notre Dame Scrapbook, 1946"), probably Associated Press, discussed the 750,000 who wanted tickets and the turndowns of important church and military officials (the compiler of the 1946 scrapbook left some of the titles on the stories). The *New York Times*'s Arthur Daley made the Frankenstein analogy a number of times, including 1/1/47; Dan Daniel of Scripps-Howard offered the Frankenstein quote in the text, 1/1/47; John Rendel of the *New York Times,* reporting on the termination of the series, 1/1/47, noted how the schools had become "considerably upset over" the ticket scalping. ND vice president John H. Murphy wrote to the Honorable Vincent A. Carroll, a Philadelphia judge: "Even though, as you truly observe, no stigma can be attached to the University proper for what is being done by some of its students or alumni, still the scalping of tickets does not set well with the public. There is no one who regrets such a situation more than the administration here at Notre Dame" 3/10/47 (UVMR 1/29).

At the time and subsequently, many members of the media proclaimed the game as the "Battle of the Century," among them the author of "The Coming Trouble" (op. cit.); Robert Leckie in *The Story of Football,* New York, 1965, discussed "The Battle of the Century" phenomenon, p. 146. J.W.L. of the *New Yorker* magazine wrote about the 1946 Army–Notre Dame game in "Mid-Autumn Madness," 11/16/46; Ken Rappaport, in *Wake Up the Echoes,* Huntsville, Alabama, 1975, discussed the jeering of the Cadets, as " 'You draft-dodging sons of bitches,' " p. 267; and an article, "Kaydets March Forth," described the street scenes (PATH "Notre Dame Scrapbook, 1946"). The United Press article of 1/1/47 on the end of the series, carried by many papers, including the *South Bend Tribune,* noted, "When the [1946] game ended in a scoreless tie, the gamblers won all bets on the ½ point margin"; and the AP article on the same topic, 1/1/47, estimated the betting as at least 10 percent of the national total, $100 million. By the mid-1940s, point-spread betting had migrated from basketball to football gambling, but it did not totally dominate until later in the decade; for the 1946 Army–Notre Dame game, bookies gave the "half-point pick-'em bet," and also 6-5 on either team—again, a tie gave all the money to the "house."

In an article titled "On Being Pushed Around" (PATH "Notre Dame Scrapbook, 1946"), the author described the treatment of the midwestern writers, including Bill Fox of the *Indianapolis News;* Whitney Martin of the AP discussed how "sports writers publicize" college football, carried by many papers, including the *South Bend Tribune,* 1/2/47. Arthur Daley commented on "our American way of life" in the *New York Times,* 11/10/46; and Red Smith's post-game remarks were in the *New York Herald-Tribune,* 11/10/46. As early as 1945, when Del Webb and Dan Topping purchased the New York Yankees baseball team and the stadium, their representative, Larry MacPhail, protested the nature of the arrangements for the Army–Notre Dame game, also stating the Yankees' intention of taking control of the game after the 1946 contest, when the current contract ended. See MacPhail's letter to Hugh Devore, interim Notre Dame athletic director, 11/2/45 (UVOC 5/16). Arch Ward proposed moving the game to Soldier Field in Chicago in the *Chicago Tribune,* 12/12/46, and also in letters to ND administrators. Jim Costin, the sports editor of the *South Bend Tribune,* wrote, "Why not bring the game out here every other year? I mean to Notre Dame Stadium, not to Soldier Field in Chicago" (PATH "Notre Dame Scrapbook, 1946"), no date.

George Gipe, in *The Great American Sports Book: A Casual but Voluminous Look at American Spectator Sports from the Civil War to the Present Time,* Garden City, New York, 1978, described the NFL playoff fix attempt, pp. 122–23; this strange, quirky book has an excellent chapter on "Fixes" that describes many little-known events in detail. Harry Wismer interviewed FBI director J. Edgar Hoover in December 1946, published in *Sport* magazine, 1/47. The "hundred-million-dollar stratosphere" is from an AP story on "Army-Irish Break," 1/1/47 (PATH "Notre Dame Scrapbook, 1946"). On page 161 of the text, Frank Leahy and Father John H. Murphy discussed the gambling situation, 2/6/47 (UVMR 1/26).

The headlines in the *New York Telegram & Sun* and the *San Francisco Call-Bulletin* appeared on 1/1/47, as did Arthur Daley's column about the meaning of "the classic Army–Notre Dame" games. Rube Samuelson (op. cit.) discusses Army's negotiations with the Rose Bowl Committee, p. 209f. During this period, because the University of Chicago had dropped out of the Big Ten, the conference was really the Big Nine, and some sportswriters referred to it that way. Others called it the Western Conference, its original nickname at the turn of the century; however, with the country having moved much farther west by the 1940s, this nickname was fading. Throughout this period, many writers and fans continued to refer to the league as the Big Ten; moreover, Michigan State petitioned to join and was accepted, soon making it a true Big Ten. The name is so ingrained that when the conference added Penn State in the late 1980s, it kept the Big Ten name, even though it is now the Big Eleven. With the above precedents, and to avoid confusing readers, I use the Big Ten name for the late 1940s–early 1950s period when, officially, it had only nine members.

Stanley Woodward, in "The Inside Story of the Notre Dame–Army Break," *Sport* magazine, 11/47, discussed West Point's national ambitions; he also provided the quote on "money and unpleasantness," and the comment on "5,000 vicious letters." See the index of my *Shake Down the Thunder* (op. cit.) for material on the Big Ten's 1920s break with the Rose Bowl, and Notre Dame's longtime policy on bowl games. Shirley Povich of the *Washington Post* mocked Army's desire for "a trip to the Rose Bowl," 1/6/47. Dan Daniel of Scripps-Howard analyzed the finances of the Army–Notre Dame game, 1/1/47; General Maxwell Taylor wrote to General Dwight Eisenhower, 10/21/46 (Superintendent's Correspondence, United States Military Academy Library Special Collections).

Arthur Daley wrote about Notre Dame's reaction to the break, 1/1/47; the AP item about the deluge of "telephone calls for tickets" for the 1947 game appeared in many papers, including the *South Bend Tribune,* 1/1/47. Earl Blaik's comments on the vitriol from Fighting Irish fans are in his first memoir (op. cit.), pp. 238–39. James A. Blackwell, in *On Brave Old Army Team: The Cheating Scandal That Rocked the Nation, West Point, 1951,* Novato, California, 1996, discusses Blaik's dislike for ending the series, p. 178. This author also describes Taylor's muddled policy, p. 173; Taylor recognized the dangers of Blaik's win-at-all-costs approach and wanted to gain control of it, but "did not want to destroy the football program" in the process; Taylor's solution, totally illogical but one followed by many other university executives over the years, "was to elevate the status of all other varsity sports at the academy to approach that of the football squad . . . The tutoring program would be expanded to any cadet engaged in intercollegiate athletics." The main result of Taylor's policy was to widen the cheating ring and, in the end, to catch many non-football players in the scandal; in particular, Army's excellent hockey team was devastated by the expulsions, see Chapter 35. For his part, Taylor, in his memoir *Swords and Ploughshares,* New York, 1972, is appropriately ambiguous about West Point intercollegiate athletics, as well as most other events in his career, particularly his crucial role in the Vietnam War.

17. The Black Market and the Birth of the Modern NCAA

Stanley Woodward's comments were in "Is College Football on the Level?" *Sport* magazine, 11/46; the other quotes from Woodward in this chapter are also from this article. For background on postwar higher education, see Frederick Rudolph, *The American College and University: A History,* New York, 1962, and Calvin Lee, *The Campus Scene: 1900–1970,* New York, 1970. Francis Wallace commented on "the black market" in *From Rockne to Parseghian* (op. cit.), p. 102, and on the "top dollar offers," including those in Shorty McWilliams's move from West Point to Mississippi State, in his arti-

cle, "Football's Black Market," *Saturday Evening Post,* 11/9/46. *Time* magazine revealed how Oklahoma had "spent $200,000 to get a good team," 10/14/46; *Collier's* did a feature on Young, 11/23/46,
mentioning also that UCLA "alumni offered him a $12,000 home, $100 in cash for every football and
track contest in which he participated, and the usual free tuition and books." Illinois was more clever
and included a full ride to Young's twin sister, Claudine, in their final package.

Paul "Bear" Bryant and John Underwood told the story of Bryant's hiring at Maryland in *Bear: The
Hard Life and Good Times of Alabama's Coach Bryant,* Boston, 1975, p. 86f; Bryant's comment on "a
double scholarship" is on p. 86. The story on how Bryant's "young men double-timed to the registrar's
office," is in Bernard Fay, "Dixie's No. 1 Gridnapper," *Collier's* magazine, 9/23/50. Paul F. Douglas's
quote was in *Time,* 10/14/46. NCAA official historian Jack Falla wrote *NCAA: The Voice of College
Sports,* Mission, Kansas, 1981. The quoted passage on the July 22–23, 1946, meeting is on p. 132.
Official histories, because they cover up unpleasant facts and attempt to build positive images, tend
to be poorly written; however, this book marks a nadir in the genre. As a result, I have edited some
quoted passages to make them intelligible—frankly, I saw no alternative, although frequently I had to
guess at meanings (I encourage the reader to follow the page references and make his/her own
guesses). If this book truly represents the NCAA, then that association is in worse trouble than its critics imagine.

The *New York Times* carried an AP report of Tug Wilson's opening speech, 7/23/46; the *Chicago
Tribune* also covered this meeting, 7/23/46 through 7/26/46. In his book, *The Big Ten* (op. cit.), Wilson described the conference's recruiting problems, p. 258f; Wilson succeeded Major John Griffith as
Big Ten commissioner in 1945—the younger man found Griffith dead on the office floor. In his comment on the "Era of Field Houses and Indoor Facilities," p. 259, Wilson did not mention that many
of the Big Ten stadiums also expanded in the postwar era, Michigan going from 72,000 to 97,500, Purdue from 13,5000 to 51,000, and Michigan State, on the cusp of Big Ten membership and as part of
its qualifying criteria, from 14,000 to 47,000. Obviously, these expansions cost these schools a large
amount of money and placed extra pressure on their athletic departments to put paying customers in
the new seats, a feat accomplished mainly by winning teams. In addition, most athletic departments
lost money annually, and had to move money from their General Operating Funds into intercollegiate
athletic programs to cover the latter's deficits (for a full explanation of this phenomenon, see my book,
College Sports Inc.: The Athletic Department vs. the University, New York, 1990).

Paul Lawrence, an economic historian, commented on the 1946 meeting in *Unsportsmanlike
Conduct: The National Collegiate Athletic Association and the Business of College Football,* New
York, 1987, p. 41f. Lawrence also argued convincingly that if the postwar inflationary market and auc-
tions for players continued, expenses would spiral totally out of control, thus the most important
members of the NCAA sought cartel control. Samuelson (op. cit.) provides an excellent summary on
the 1946 Big Ten and Pacific Coast Conference Rose Bowl pact in his chapter, "Shotgun Marriage,"
p. 209f; he quotes Wilson on p. 211. In addition to Stanley Woodward's comments on Tulsa in *Sport*
magazine, 11/46, Bob Boerg outlined that school's rise to football fame in "Oil Makes the Hurricane
Roar," the *Saturday Evening Post,* 11/24/45.

The comments of Jack Falla (op. cit.) on the 1946 meeting are on pp. 131–32; Wilson's comments
to the press are in the *New York Times,* 7/23/46, and 7/24/46; his quote "a boy will choose a school for
its educational value" is in Samuelson (op. cit.), p. 211; the AP lead, "Twenty of the nation's college
conferences," was in the *New York Times,* 7/24/46. The *Chicago Tribune's* Arch Ward made his comments on 7/22/46 and 7/27/46; also, at this time, that paper discussed the case of Perry Moss, an outstanding backfielder who transferred from Tulsa to Illinois during the summer of 1946 and qualified
at the Big Ten school with a quick round of summer courses: "In those twenty-six days, Moss showed
outstanding scholastic aptitude by passing three courses" normally requiring a full semester of work
for each, and "he didn't pick any snaps either . . . [he took] Advanced Football . . . Camping and Outdoor Leadership . . . [and] Theory of Coaching," quoted from the *Tribune* in Wallace, "The Black
Market" (op. cit.).

18. The NCAA's "Principle of Amateurism"

The Associated Press, the *New York Times,* and the *Chicago Tribune* covered the 1947 NCAA Convention particularly well, often providing quotes from meetings not in the NCAA's official minutes
for the convention; hence, I have used these sources for the material in this chapter. The NCAA's

Principles for the Conduct of Intercollegiate Athletics appeared in the *Times* on 1/7/47, as did the headline, "Firm Stand . . . ," and Allison Danzig's comments. Paul Lawrence (op. cit.) commented on the NCAA's cartel aims, p. 41; the *Chicago Tribune* discussed the opposition to the "Purity Code," 1/9/47 and 1/8/47; the AP quoted Dr. Funkhouser, 1/10/47, in the *Chicago Tribune,* among many papers.

The AP quote from an NCAA insider on how "the code should be enforced" was in the *Chicago Tribune,* 1/5/47; Wilson began advocating "ostracization" at the July 1946 meeting, *Chicago Tribune,* 7/23/46, and tried to convince the NCAA of that tactic throughout 1947. For *Sport* magazine's editorial, "Wanted: The Landis Spirit," see 3/47. The *Chicago Tribune* headline on the NCAA and the bowls, and the coverage of the NCAA debate on that issue, appeared 1/9/47. The best explanations of the bowls in this period were provided by Dan Parker in *Sport,* "My Case Against the Bowls," 11/48; and by William Fay in *Collier's,* "Bowl Games," 1/3/49; and fan Emil Tagliabue wrote a letter to the editor of *Sport* about the bowls, 1/49. Samuelson (op. cit.) discussed the California real estate aspect of the Rose Bowl, p. 214, and the 1947 ticket situation, p. 216; Shirley Povich in the *Washington Post,* 1/6/47, commented on the "juicy ticket scandals."

Tug Wilson in *Big Ten* (op. cit.), p. 228f, discussed the Rose Bowl pact and his idea for the split of the Big Ten team's payout. With Michigan State's official admission, it became a twelve-way split, but, as the Big Nine in 1947, it was only an eleven-way split at that time. The share to the commissioner's office enabled Wilson to increase his staff, including hiring Walter Byers. Samuelson (op. cit.) mentioned the Big Ten team's financial loses, p. 230. Dr. Morrill's objections to bowl games were in the *Chicago Tribune,* 1/9/47; and the exchange between Minnesota official Chester R. Doan and Dan Parker in *Sport* magazine, 12/47. The AP carried Dr. Morrill's warning on gambling, 1/8/47, with the *Chicago Tribune* printing long excerpts of the speech. The legal name of the Minneapolis Syndicate was Athletics Publications Inc., but gamblers and the sporting press usually called it by the former name; for a good description of its work, see Dan Parker's *Sport* magazine article, "Inside Story of Basketball Betting," 2/47. NCAA president Karl Leib argued for keeping the men's basketball tourney in Madison Square Garden, *Chicago Tribune,* 1/7/47, and a year later he reported on the financial success of that move, *New York Times,* 1/11/48, quoted here. The *Washington Post*'s Shirley Povich commented on the gambling situation, 1/7/47.

19. Notre Dame Reacts to the NCAA's "Purity Code"

The entire text of Notre Dame president John J. Cavanaugh's speech at the annual football banquet, 1/13/47, was printed in the *Notre Dame Alumnus* magazine, 1–2/47, under the title, "Reformers Protest Too Much." The *South Bend Tribune,* 1/15/47, also printed much of the text, interspersed with sports editor Jim Costin's gloss on it, including on "the pious hypocrites" of the Big Ten. The AP and UP circulated articles on the speech, and many papers picked them up; in addition, Catholic weeklies also ran excerpts, the *Los Angeles Tidings* commented on "the story of a coach named Leahy and a priest named Cavanaugh who occupied headlines throughout the nation during the week of Jan. 12–19," 1947.

For an example of Big Ten "wondering" about Notre Dame, see the exchange between Commissioner Griffith and Arch Ward in Chapter 6. Sports editor Fred Digby of the *New Orleans Item* discussed the Sugar Bowl's bid for the Fighting Irish, 12/12/46, and quoted Grantland Rice's support for the idea.

The minutes of the Notre Dame Faculty Board in Control of Athletics noted a letter from University of Illinois athletic director Doug Mills informing ND that "the Notre Dame–Illinois football relationship would not be renewed after 1946," 1/14/46 (UVOC 5/5). Michigan led the Big Ten opposition to scheduling football games with ND; see the discussion in John Kryk's book (op. cit.), p. 153f; Kryk also points out that Michigan so dominated the conference scheduling that "from 1943 to 1958, Michigan played Indiana 15 times, *all* in Ann Arbor," p. 169. Purdue, however, continued its historic in-state rivalry with ND; Iowa, in spite of Dr. Karl Leib's objections, also continued to play the Irish because football coach Eddie Anderson was a Notre Dame grad; indeed, the cover of the program for the ND visit to Iowa in 1946 featured Anderson and his two main assistants, Joe Sheeketski and Frank Carrideo, also ND grads. *Chicago Times* sports editor and columnist Gene Kessler quoted the unidentified Big Ten insider, 1/5/47. Boston columnist Dave Egan drew the parallel between the careers of Leahy and Cavanaugh in the *Boston Sunday Advertiser,* 1/19/47.

On page 189 and following of the text, ND vice president John H. Murphy wrote to Stanley March about the "boys that are recommended to N.D.," about Father Cavanaugh's daring "to make that speech," about the school's rigid academic requirements, including the "77% average—70% is passing," and about the "discipline here," 2/7/47 (UVMR 1/21). Wells Twombley (op. cit.) quoted Leahy's use of religion in recruiting, and the sportswriters' joke, p. 18. Bill Furlong discussed the members of the 1947 ND squad subsequently in professional football in "*Sport's* Greatest Teams: Lujack, Leahy, and Notre Dame," *Sport*, 11/65, reprinted as "The Year South Bend Had a 'Pro' Team," *The Glory of Notre Dame*, ed. Fred Katz (op. cit.), pp. 73–82. Paul Zimmerman in *Sports Illustrated*, 11/24/97, examined this team at length and explained that "Forty-three Notre Dame players from either '46 or '47 (or both) played in the NFL or the rival AAFC" (the *SI* article also had excellent photos of this team and era, thanks to Charles Lamb of the University of Notre Dame Archives). Having seen Vince Scott play for the Hamilton Tiger-Cats, I can vouch for the ability of this player who sat on Leahy's bench.

Red Grange commented about Notre Dame recruiting in the *Chicago Tribune*, 11/21/49; and Gene Kessler quoted the Big Ten insider (op. cit.). The *Chicago Times* discussed George Ratterman's expulsion from Notre Dame, 12/14/47, as did Ratterman in his *Confessions of a Gypsy Quarterback*, with Robert G. Deindorfer, New York, 1962, pp. 26–27. Leahy was considering moving Lujack to halfback in 1947 before Ratterman was expelled. For the Gordon Graham interview (op. cit.). Finally, I know that the term "blue-chip prospect" was not used in the late 1940s. But the concept certainly existed in the immediate postwar era, and rather than supply laborious phrases to denote the concept, I prefer to use the shorthand and highly descriptive term. American English evolves, in part, for this purpose. The information on Purdue Boilermakers in the pros was supplied by the Purdue University sports information department, 4/20/98.

20. Sports Media Confusion

Sport claimed a circulation of 600,000 in an editorial, 9/48, and projecting the magazine's growth to 7/49, 700,000 seems probable. Grantland Rice's article, "I Remember Rockne," appeared in *Sport*, 9/47; as he aged, Rice acquired the nickname "Granny." Bill Brandt's article on Gipp was in *Sport*, 11/46; in 1917, Gipp broke his leg in the game against Morningside College (Iowa), the week after the Army match. He did not return to the Notre Dame campus until the following September, and his academic transcript for 1917–18 is blank; Gipp spent the year living in the best hotel in South Bend and working as a professional pool shark and card player, see my *Shake Down the Thunder* (op. cit.), p. 107f.

Jack Sher's "Book Special," "Lujack, Leahy, and Notre Dame," was in *Sport*, 10/47; Ed Stanton wrote "Tripucka—Waiting in the Wings," for the 9/48 issue of that magazine; and fan Thomas Moseley complained about excessive attention to the Fighting Irish in a letter to the editor of *Sport*, 1/50. Bill Rives's portrait of Doak Walker was featured in *Sport*, 11/48; for a portrait of Bobby Layne, see Bob St. John's *Heart of a Lion: The Wild and Woolly Life of Bobby Layne*, Dallas, 1991. Bill Stern's piece on coaches' halftime talks, "Win This One for the Old Man," appeared in *Sport*, 12/47; the discussion of Rockne and "keying up" athletes in the locker room is in my *Shake Down the Thunder* (op. cit.), p. 280; also see that book's index entry on "Rockne, locker-room talks," for other commentary on this topic. Bill Stern's "Incident over Kansas" appeared in *Sport*, 4/48.

21. More Media Confusion—but Not About Frank Leahy

The *Sport* magazine articles on Charlie "Choo-Choo" Justice were "Justice Triumphs," by Garrison Wilton, 10/47; "The Truth About Charlie Justice—a *Sport* Profile," by Lewis Burton, 11/49; and "The Untold Story of Charlie Justice," by Al Costello, 12/54. Frank Deford's *Everybody's All-American*, New York, 1981, subsequently went through a number of paperback editions and the 1989 movie; Deford, as a writer employing fiction to portray a football hero, uses the facts of the Justice story and also departs from them in major ways. William Friday, the head of the University of North Carolina system in the 1980s, would not allow the movie to be filmed on the Chapel Hill campus, explaining that it "would be unfair to Justice and might tarnish UNC's reputation" (*Business–North Carolina*, April 1988). Thus the movie is set at Louisiana State University.

Al Stump's *Sport* magazine piece on Lynn "Pappy" Waldorf appeared in 1/49; Leo Katcher in "What's Wrong with West Coast Football," 9/49, had revealed various aspects of the corruption in the

PCC, including at Berkeley. During the 1950s, national magazines revealed much more, particularly the recruiting violations committed by Cal's "Southern Seas Club"—see Tim Cohane, "College Football's Greatest Folly," *Look*, 11/15/55; and Al Stump's revisionist return to the scene of his previous whitewash, "Ronnie Knox: A Football Case History," *Sport* magazine, 11/55. For all that, in recent years, "Pappy" Waldorf's players erected a statue of him on the Cal campus.

The *Time* magazine cover story on Frank Leahy appeared on 10/14/46; the *Collier's* piece by John Groth, 11/2/46; the *Redbook* article by Francis Wallace, "Mr. Leahy's Winning Ways," 7/47. In fact, although Wallace's piece is positive, he treated Leahy much more negatively in other portraits, particularly in his book, *Knute Rockne*, New York, 1960, where he started a section, "Frank Leahy—*The Robot*," (his emphasis) p. 275.

22. Reporters Cover College Sports and Notre Dame's Charlie Callahan Covers Them

The Al Stump article was in the *Saturday Evening Post*, 11/26/49; for the NCAA's mandate on changing SPD to SID, see Chapter 46; *Sport's* "Editors' Note" appeared 11/48; and Shirley Povich of the *Washington Post* wrote about the SPD puffery versus the betting lines, 1/7/47.

On page 215 of the text, Bill Stern wrote a letter of recommendation for Callahan to President J. Hugh O'Donnell, 12/5/45; and Bob Considine to O'Donnell, 12/3/45 (UPHO 107/9). Frank Leahy wrote to ND vice president John H. Murphy about the ticket requests from the media, 8/9/47 (UVMR 1/26); Charlie Callahan wrote to Vice President Murphy about the CBS radio program, "We the People," 10/17/47, and Murphy answered Callahan, 10/20/47, both letters in (UVMR 1/36). Callahan discussed his negotiations with *Life* with Murphy, 10/15/48 (UMVR 1/36). For discussion of the probable Kentucky fix against Notre Dame, see the footnotes for Chapter 34. Callahan wrote about the St. Mary's–USF game, 10/8/50 (the game was played on a Sunday); he did not mention that St. Mary's was losing large amounts of money in big-time football, and, in fact, the school dropped the sport at the end of the 1950 season. Callahan mentioned the circulation of *OSV* to Pete Brandwein of the *New York Times*, 11/2/51 (UASI 3/29); Callahan also described *OSV* as "a paper which is obtainable on a table in the rear of just about any Catholic Church in America," *OSV*, 9/5/54, and because the Church supported it, its circulation did not fluctuate. Concerning Callahan's work as a stringer for various wire services, he mentioned to Gordon Macker, *Los Angeles Daily News*, "I was covering myself that afternoon for UP [United Press] and INS [International News Service]." 1/16/47 (UVMR 1/21).

On page 219 of the text, Callahan wrote to Lillian Genn, 6/28/48 (UASI 2/97); he wrote to *Argosy* in-house writer Pat Mitchell about the latter's article under Leahy's byline, 8/3/48 (UASI 2/97); and Lillian Genn sent the check and a note to Callahan, 9/20/48 (UASI 2/97). The *Argosy* piece under Leahy's byline appeared 10/48; for Rockne's activities as ND assistant coach, and the improbability of him making a scouting trip to Nebraska, see my *Shake Down the Thunder* (op. cit.), p. 57f. The *Sport* article, "My Football Secrets by Frank Leahy," appeared 10/48; "The Truth About My Future by Frank Leahy," 8/49; and for the interview with Father Carey (op. cit.).

In Terry Brennan's first year as Notre Dame head coach, Dave Condon of the *Chicago Tribune* ghostwrote a piece for Brennan for the *Tribune's* Sunday magazine, but Charlie Callahan informed the "apparition" that when the new Notre Dame head coach read the article, Brennan said "that it doesn't sound like him, and he doesn't want his by-line on it," no date but internal evidence and follow-up letter indicates summer 1954 (UASI 5/72). Pat Patten, editor of the *Chicago Tribune* Sunday magazine, subsequently informed Callahan that "as to the Terry Brennan piece, we took off the by-line and made it By Dave Condon," 9/7/54 (UASI 5/72).

On page 221 of the text, Notre Dame vice president John H. Murphy wrote to Arthur Daley, 2/2/49 (UVMR 1/24); and Leahy wrote to Murphy about the note to Daley, 2/14/49 (UVMR 1/25). Arch Ward complained to Notre Dame president John J. Cavanaugh about the line in the *Chicago Sun-Times*, 8/17/48 (UVMR 3/14); Jerome Holtzman's article appeared 8/16/48; and Vice President John H. Murphy replied to Arch Ward, 8/24/48 (UVMR), also concluding, "I know that we need not fear clips like that in the *Chicago Tribune* sports section." ND alumnus William C. Fay wrote to Notre Dame president John J. Cavanaugh, 2/24/47 (UVMR 1/36).

On page 223 of the text, the copy of Jim Costin's letter to Bernie Masterson, and Costin's covering letter of apology to Notre Dame vice president John J. Cavanaugh, 3/27/46, are in (UVOC 5/40);

details on the break with Nebraska are in my *Shake Down the Thunder* (op. cit.), pp. 200–203. Costin's apologies to Col. Earl J. Blaik, 3/26/46, and to Capt. Thomas Hamilton, 3/27/46 are in (UVOC 5/40); President J. Hugh O'Donnell's vituperative note about Costin to Vice President John J. Cavanaugh, no date, is in (UVOC 5/40). Vice President Murphy's comment on "old Father John Cavanaugh" is in a letter to Edwin C. Varley, 2/13/47 (UVMR 1/24). Notre Dame professor of history Robert Burns remarked on the difference between Presidents Cavanaugh and "Pepper" O'Donnell in an interview, 11/11/91.

23. The NCAA's "Sanity Code" Crashes into the Power Blocs

Francis Wallace's "Pigskin Preview" was in the *Saturday Evening Post*, 9/13/47; his comment on the "easily broken" code is also in that article. Jack Falla (op. cit.) spins the NCAA's 1948 position, pp. 133–34; *Sport* published Bill Stern's loud "No" to "Should College Athletes Be Paid?" in 4/47, and Wismer's reply the following month; Wismer broadcast a portion of his essay on May 12, 1947 (LOC holdings). The *New York Times* headlines and subheads on the NCAA convention appeared 1/11/48; the AP comment in the *Chicago Tribune*, among other papers, 1/9/48; and Karl Leib's remark on "compliance" is in the *New York Times*, 1/9/48. Paul Lawrence (op. cit.) discusses the three members of the Compliance Committee, p. 42; see the index entries of this book for discussions of Prof. Ralph W. Aigler of Michigan, James H. Stewart of the Southwest Conference, and Tufts AD Clarence P. Houston. Karl Leib's reelection as NCAA president was in the *New York Times*, 1/11/48, and Walter Byers's comments are in his memoir, written with Charles Hammer, *Unsportsmanlike Conduct: Exploiting College Athletes*, Ann Arbor, Michigan, 1995, p. 5.

The quotes from Branch Rickey's speech are taken from the *New York Times*, 1/10/48, and from the NCAA's minutes; see the 1947 *Yearbook*. In this era, college baseball thrived, but because major league baseball did not have a player draft, clubs signed prospects when they found them, often bidding against each other for the best "Bonus Babies," frequently going onto campuses and snatching underclassmen, sometimes in midseason. For an article on college baseball in this period, see Johnny Winkin's "They Teach Big-League Baseball at Duke," *Sport*, 6/48, including the information that, at games of big-time programs, "if you look in the stands, you'll find scouts from virtually every club in the major leagues."

The *New York Times*, 1/10/48, quoted from the speech of Dr. George Zook, president of the American Council on Education, but the NCAA Minutes ignored his talk. The Compliance Committee met in Tug Wilson's office in Chicago; see the *New York Times* and the *Chicago Tribune*, 4/17/48. Francis Wallace's "Pigskin Preview" for 1948 appeared in the *Saturday Evening Post*, 9/18/48; one of his correspondents called the new NCAA rule, " 'The Insanity Code.' " In his 1949 "Preview," done for *Collier's*, 9/24/49, Wallace dissected the escalating "subsidization front (financial payment to athletes)"; also "the matter of commercialized gambling" on college football games, concluding, "There were no reports of 'fixes,' but 21 of my advisers [contacts around the country] thought the situation menacing."

Allen L. Sack and Ellen Staurowsky in *College Athletes for Hire* (op. cit.) outline a meeting of the Southern, Southeastern, and Southwest conferences in May 1949 to discuss "outright secession from the NCAA." However, this plan was a nonstarter, particularly in light of the NCAA's emerging cartel control of bowl games—schools in these groups loved bowl games—as well as the association's other benefits. Ed Danforth in "The South vs. the Sanity Code," *Sport* magazine, 11/49, discussed events on the eve of the 1950 Convention. University of Virginia president Colgate Darden Jr., a former governor of the state, articulated his position many times, including at press conferences reported by the AP on 8/9/48 and 7/27/49, but, most eloquently, and quoted here on clock-winding jobs, to the *Washington Post* on the eve of the 1950 NCAA Convention, 1/13/50. NCAA president Karl Leib told the *Washington Post*, 1/10/50, that schools like UVA "should step down a notch"; and that newspaper carried UVA football coach Art Guepe's attack on Leib, 1/13/50 (Guepe lived up to his name—the French word for hornet).

The *New York Times* headlines and subheads on the 1949 NCAA convention appeared 1/7/49, as well as Leib's remark, "We have sent private detectives into the field to investigate institutions allegedly not complying [with the code]. Most of the allegations [against these schools] were untrue or greatly exaggerated." Considering the rampant corruption in college sports at this time, these detectives must have been the original gang-that-couldn't-see-straight. Both the NCAA Official Minutes of this convention and the *New York Times,* 1/8/49, contain the debate on television. Jimmy Powers did the *Sport* article, "The Case Against the Bowls," 1/51; he was behind the curve on the "ticket gouges"—the NCAA had started to control them—but correct about the segregation at the bowls located in southern and southwestern states. Even though many northern universities had integrated their teams, the bowls requested that African American players stay home, and many of these institutions agreed with this stipulation. Shirley Povich commented on the bowls in the *Washington Post,* 1/11/50; the *New York Times* carried the NCAA "bowl report," 1/9/49; and Paul Lawrence (op. cit.), pp. 90–91, interpreted the NCAA's move.

24. Curly Byrd Exposes NCAA Hypocrisy

Tim Cohane wrote "How Maryland Became a Football Power" for *Look,* 11/2/54; in the postscandal period, magazines finally investigated corrupt intercollegiate athletics programs, *Look* running this article as its cover piece (for the shift by the national magazines to revisionist approaches, see Chapter 47). H. C. "Curly" Byrd's classic college sports rhetoric appeared in a season-long article, "The Man Behind the Guns at Maryland," in his school's 1949 football game programs, e.g., the West Virginia vs. Maryland game, 11/24/49, p. 10. Paul "Bear" Bryant with John Underwood (op. cit.) related his break with Byrd and Maryland, pp. 90–91; former University of Oklahoma president George Lynn Cross discussed Big Jim Tatum's payments to players after the 1947 Gator Bowl, and the coach's departure from OU, in *President's Can't Punt,* Norman, Oklahoma, 1977, pp. 54–56. Tatum began wearing ten-gallon hats during his Oklahoma days, and continued at Maryland, and then in his return to the University of North Carolina at Chapel Hill (where he began his coaching career); a *Saturday Evening Post* article, "Jim Tatum of the Tarheels" (op. cit.), described and quoted him, including the famous "winning" quip. That article also quoted Tatum's Maryland assistant Jack Hennemier on recruiting techniques, and the Middle States Accreditation Committee's criticisms of the University of Maryland; Cohane's *Collier's* piece (op. cit.) discussed the Terrapins' success in western Pennsylvania.

The Associated Press report on Curly Byrd's comments on the eve of the 1950 NCAA convention was published by many papers, including the *Washington Post,* 1/14/50; the AP also carried Byrd's attack on the Big Ten at the convention, see the *Chicago Tribune,* 1/15/50. The quotes from the 1950 NCAA convention are from newspaper accounts and from the NCAA's official minutes (*Yearbook*); the quotes differ at times, and I have used the most coherent version (the *Yearbook* notes that "the stenotype reporter who transcribed the proceedings of the Business Session, January 14, was not able to record all of the business that transpired"; some parts reported in the press but not in the NCAA minutes concern Byrd's criticisms of the Big Ten schools and NCAA leadership!).

Part of what propelled Curly Byrd to the leadership of the opposition to the "Sanity Code" and coalesced a large number of schools behind him was the arrogance of Big Ten/NCAA officials. Byrd's ally, the president of the University of Virginia, told the press that before the 1950 convention, he had "proposed an amendment to the constitution calling for above board athletic scholarships but this somehow got lost" by the NCAA. Tug Wilson and Karl Leib "expressed no knowledge of it" whatsoever—even though UVA had sent copies to them as well as to every member school. Then, at the 1950 convention in New York, when the UVA president tried to present his views to "a joint meeting of the NCAA's executive committee, council, and compliance committee," they allowed him "less than one minute" to speak, *Washington Post,* 1/13/50.

Charles Grutzner of the *New York Times* wrote about the Ohio State situation in "Athletic Problem Handicaps Schools," 3/20/51, and he also interviewed Professor Ralph Aigler of Michigan for that article. In addition, Aigler acknowledged that, at his school, "the boy with athletic ability was regarded as a greater asset to the university than a non-athlete"; his comments on the two Wolverine hockey players appeared in a United Press piece, "Holier Than Thou Big Ten Leading 'Sanity Witch Hunt,' " by Oscar Fraley, which was carried by many papers, including the *South Bend Tribune,* 1/24/50. The *New York Times* discussed General Dwight Eisenhower's no-show, 1/14/50; and Arthur Daley's criticisms ran in that paper, 1/17/50. The *Chicago Tribune* had the comments from the NCAA leadership on the expulsion vote, 1/14/50, and from their opponents, 1/12/50; from LSU AD T. P. "Red" Heard, 1/14/50; and on Karl Leib's dubious electoral trick, 1/15/50. Paul Lawrence (op. cit.), p. 47, explains that many pro-"Sanity Code" votes came from "small colleges [who] supported the Sanity Code because it placed severe restrictions on the financial aid a school could provide [athletes], thus conserving the limited resources" for intercollegiate athletics possessed by these schools. Also many schools in or near cities, particularly in the North, supported the code because they could work out "job plans" for their jocks. Thus money, not idealism, drove almost all schools on all sides of issues in the NCAA during this formative period.

The *New York Times* described Curly Byrd's postvote speech, 1/15/50, and the *Washington Post* carried Willett's replacement of Leib as association president, and Byrd's ascension to a vice presidency, 1/15/50. The NCAA's Jack Falla (op. cit.) commented on the "severe penalty," p. 134; I have unscrambled Falla's verb tenses here to try to clarify his meaning. Walter Byers, in his autobiography (op. cit.), discussed his train ride home after the 1950 convention on pp. 53–55.

25. Notre Dame Responds to the New NCAA

Notre Dame vice president John H. Murphy made his comments to *Chicago Times* writer Jack McPhaul, 11/12/47; Murphy suggested to Notre Dame president John J. Cavanaugh that the latter write to Tug Wilson, no date but from internal evidence, almost certainly early 1948 (UVMR 1/19). The Notre Dame Faculty Board in Control of Athletics, in a "Regular Meeting," 10/7/49 (UVHS 3/12), reviewed ND's position on the "Sanity Code"; Vice President Murphy discussed the 77 percent requirement in a letter to Stanley March, 2/7/47, and in letters to Dave De Long, 11/9/46, and to Morton L. Booth, 12/19/47 (all in UVMR 1/21). Francis Wallace in his *Redbook* article (op. cit.) noted, "After the last Army game, representatives from every New York paper who descended on the campus for the week were surprised to find all doors open and no restrictions on their activities," and, during this period, many reporters examined the academic records of the intercollegiate athletes and observed their living conditions. *Sport* magazine writer Ed Fitzgerald went to South Bend in 1947, and found that Johnny "Lujack has no classy convertible, no lavish apartment off the campus, no open expense accounts [downtown] . . . no bundle of cash in his pocket," but lived in the dorms as a regular student; see "Glamour? Spell It L-u-j-a-c-k," 10/47, reprinted in *The Glory of Notre Dame* (op. cit.).

On page 244 of the text, Vice President John H. Murphy wrote to Charles F. Quinn Jr. about ND's antitransfer rule, 9/10/48, and Murphy told Michael Paul Smith whom a football recruit should contact, 2/1/49, both letters in (UVMR 1/37). Notre Dame made a very few exceptions to the rule: lineman George Connor had played at Holy Cross in Massachusetts, gone to Notre Dame for naval training, and then after the war wanted to return to ND; Frank Leahy prevailed upon the Golden Dome to accept Connor, pleading his special circumstances. The chair of the Sugar Bowl committee, Frank V. Schaub, wrote to Executive Vice President Theodore M. Hesburgh about ND participation in the 1950 game, 11/9/49, and Hesburgh answered Schaub, 11/22/49, both letters in (UVHS 3/41). Father Hesburgh mentioned ND's financial situation to F. W. Coffing, 12/16/49 (UVHS 3/41). The *Notre Dame Alumnus*, 1–2/49, published the school's most recent annual financial statement; one year later, 1–2/50, that magazine had an article about the 1949 football banquet, including excerpts from Father Hesburgh's remarks and a photo of Dr. Karl Leib. Hesburgh articulated the core of his formulation on ND football to the Rev. Michael L. Doyle, 11/29/49 (UVHS 3/23). Leo Fischer in the *Chicago American*, 12/13/49, also printed some excerpts from the banquet speech and called the speaker "Fred A."

At the 1949 football dinner, Father Hesburgh discussed ND's rejection of the "de-emphasis" position; some schools, notably Johns Hopkins and a number of small Catholic colleges, had embraced "total de-emphasis," i.e., free admission to all games, no recruiting of athletes, and football costs paid by the student players (see John Kieran's article "College Football for Free!" in *Sport*, 10/49). For ND administrators, this approach was inimical to their university's long football history, and, as important, de-emphasis would nullify the deep cultural significance of the Fighting Irish for the school's alumni, fans, and Catholic America. Significantly, in all of his subsequent public statements on de-emphasis, Father Hesburgh never deviated from his original formulation in his banquet speech: "There will be no 'de-emphasis' of Notre Dame football because the sport [here] is not emphasized beyond reason." During his many subsequent years as a top ND administrator, many people accused him of de-emphasizing Fighting Irish football, but he always denied it, repeating a version of his 1949 statement.

For a discussion of Catholic higher education in America, see the index entry in my *Shake Down the Thunder* under that topic; also see under "Notre Dame, divergences from Catholic higher education." The quote from the head of Boston College, the Rev. Maurice Dullea, was in the *New York*

Times, 1/15/50; Theodore R. Smits, general sports editor, the Associated Press, wrote to Notre Dame president John J. Cavanaugh, 1/9/50 (UVHS 3/23). The NCAA's *Yearbook* for the 1951 Convention has the speech of Tufts AD Clarence Houston, p. 151; and the *New York Times,* 1/13/51, ran the account of the opposition's joy at the death of the code.

26. Fan Confusion—"Block That Two-Platoon System"

Stanley Frank wrote "Saturday Afternoon Meat Grinders" for *Collier's,* 10/1/49; the quotes from Jimmy Phelan and Gene Rossides are from that article. For a discussion of the ongoing selling of players for visiting team "Guarantees," see Chapter 3 in my *College Sports Inc.* (op. cit.). Rube Samuelson (op. cit.) described Crisler's strategy in the 1948 Rose Bowl game, p. 221; Colonel Earl Blaik in his memoirs (op. cit.) gave his impressions of two-platoon, p. 209; and Joe Doyle discussed Frank Leahy's first use of it in the late 1940s in *Fighting Irish: A Century of Notre Dame Football,* Charlottesville, Virginia, 1987, pp. 123–24. The comments about Marty Brill's coaching were in "Pigskin Progress Stuns Brill" by Dana Mozley, *South Bend Tribune,* no date but internal evidence indicates summer 1946 (PATH "Notre Dame Scrapbook, 1946"). The *Sport* magazine pro-and-con debate— "Is Free Substitution Bad for Football?"—between Harry Wismer and Bill Stern appeared in 10/48.

Fred Russell commented on two-platoon in his "Pigskin Preview" for the *Saturday Evening Post,* 9/24/49 (Francis Wallace had moved his to *Collier's*). The *Post* ran the editorial, "Football's Dirty Linen Sometimes Shows," 10/23/48, and, in the same issue, the Mary Stuhldreher article, "Football Fans Aren't Human"; the quotes from the University of Wisconsin student newspaper appeared in her article. *Newsweek* also covered the Stuhldreher controversy, 11/1/48.

The *Saturday Evening Post* article, "Football's Strangest Fan," by Stanley Frank, appeared 10/30/48; under the pen name, Louis Henry Baker, Dr. Levy published such books as *Do You Know Your Football?,* New York, 1946, and *Football: Facts and Figures,* New York, in editions from 1945 through 1949. I have tried to track down his now priceless collection of clippings, photos, and books in the hope that some library acquired it, but to no avail. If any reader knows anything about this, please let me know.

27. Leahy's Lads Capture the Spotlight

The AP pre-game report on the Illinois–Notre Dame game appeared 9/25/46 (PATH "Notre Dame Football Scrapbook, 1947"); this scrapbook compiler left many titles and dates but no logos of the originating newspapers. Paul E. Neville of the *South Bend Tribune,* 9/29/46, wrote the account of the halftime show. The Notre Dame Faculty Board in Control of Athletics recorded the letter from University of Illinois AD Doug Mills, 1/14/46 (UVOC 5/5); for the interview with Moose Krause (op. cit.); Francis Wallace's comments on "the American public" and on Jack Chevigny are in his *The Notre Dame Story,* New York, 1949, pages 68–69 and 73. Bill Stern also told the Chevigny from-football-to-Iwo-Jima story frequently on the radio, and in his *My Favorite Sport Stories,* 1948 edition, pp. 60–61. In Wallace's comments on the meaning of Notre Dame, at times his personal feelings as a ND alumnus overwhelm his professional journalist's skepticism, and he lapses into public relations work for his alma mater. ND opponents probably regard all of Wallace's writings about ND as propaganda, while some Fighting Irish fans might consider them scripture; however, the truth seems to reside somewhere between. When he wrote about Notre Dame, Francis Wallace provided a mixture of insider's knowledge and insight along with large dollops of PR posing as objective prose.

On page 257 of the text, sportswriter Robert W. Towner wrote about the "Telegraph lines leading out of South Bend" in the *South Bend Tribune,* 11/7/47; the *Notre Dame Alumnus,* 1–2/49, termed the pressbox "the Headline Helicopter," adding, "Women not permitted—probably never will be. It's an old rule" (proving, once again, "Never say never"—it's an older rule). Also in the *South Bend Tribune,* 11/6/47, was the article, "230,000 Fans to See Irish"; many of the TV sets were in local bars, and Dave Berkman in "Long Before Arledge, Sports & TV: 1937–1947," *Journal of Popular Culture,* Fall 1988, discussed this phenomenon, p. 55f. Francis Wallace in *The Notre Dame Story* (op. cit.) mentioned the ND ticket situation in the late 1940s, p. 33.

Grantland Rice's article "Are They Freezing Out Notre Dame?" appeared in *Sport* magazine, 1/49, and he discussed ND football scheduling as well as the futility of the Big Ten hostility to the Catholic school; Rice quoted the unnamed Big Ten president in that piece. For further information on the types of Notre Dame fans, please follow the index entries in my *Shake Down the Thunder* (op. cit.) under "Notre Dame du lac" for "Notre Dame Family," and under "Notre Dame football" for "fans." In an article entitled "Notre Dame—The School Nobody Knows," in the 1946 programs for Notre Dame home football games, John Hinkel put the number of living ND alumni at 20,000 and on-campus students at 4,500. Adding another 1,000 for the postwar vet bulge, and the remainder for members of the ND faculty and staff and C.S.C. members on campus, the total moves to about 30,000 in 1949. Ruth Furman sent a letter to the editor of *Sport* magazine about "the Subway Alumni Ladies Auxiliary," 3/49.

On page 261 of the text, Notre Dame AD Frank Leahy wrote to Vice President John H. Murphy, 5/21/47, about the offer to play in Boston; and Murphy replied, 5/23/47, both letters in (UVMR 1/26). The famous mayor of Boston, James M. Curley, had also requested that Notre Dame play in his city, and he received a negative reply; see Curley's letter to Vice President Murphy, 2/20/47 (UVMR 1/29). In this period, Notre Dame grad Edwin O'Connor wrote the best-selling lightly fictionalized portrait of Curley, *The Last Hurrah*, Boston, 1956. For Rockne's reluctance to play Catholic schools, see my *Shake Down the Thunder* (op. cit.), pp. 99, 129, 150, 188, and 256.

In the late 1940s, ND wanted to be more than "Catholic America's Team," but it never ignored or alienated its longtime fan base. Not only did Charlie Callahan play an important role in this endeavor as a columnist for *Our Sunday Visitor*, but he coordinated the multitude of requests from Catholic groups for Notre Dame game films. In the pre-TV era, one of the few ways for many Fighting Irish fans to see their favorites in action was in 16-millimeter highlight films screened in church basements or other public places. After each football season, Callahan and Leahy compiled a highlight film, then made multiple copies and shipped them all over the United States. Father Murphy noted that "within a week after the [1946] season closed last Fall, there were some 1,300 of these requests on hand," and the number grew almost exponentially after that; see Murphy's letter to William P. Condon, 8/19/47 (UVMR 1/30). In addition, Notre Dame alumni groups requested films, an executive of one writing Murphy, "Our main interest [with the football films], as always, is the possibility of serving the hundreds of local Holy Name, Catholic Action, Knights of Columbus, Foresters, Squires, and Catholic Boy Scout organizations," as well as parochial schools in our region; Robert P. Lonergam to Murphy, 3/4/48 (UVMR 1/30).

On page 262 of the text, Father John H. Murphy wrote to President John J. Cavanaugh about the alumnus who wanted to start a fan magazine, undated but most probably 8/46; Murphy conveyed ND's rejection to alumnus D. T. Broderick Jr., 8/29/46; and Murphy wrote again to Cavanaugh about this issue, 7/12/49; all three letters are in (UVMR 1/23). On page 262 of the text, the ND player from Boys Town, Nebraska, was Leonard Kroll, see Cohen (op. cit.), p. 124; Father Hesburgh wrote to Bob Addie of the *Washington Post* about the latter's comments on a Jewish recruit, 12/9/49 (UVHS 3/17); Addie's column had appeared, 11/8/49. For Murphy's memo to Hesburgh concerning the "All-Catholic All-American Football Team," 12/29/49, see (UVHS 3/36); and for Murphy's letter about the "Irish partisans" to Col. R. Ernest Dupuy, 11/11/49, see (UVHS 3/23). Francis Wallace wrote to ND president John J. Cavanaugh, 3/29/48, about the theme of his forthcoming book (UPCC 22/19). Father Hesburgh commented about Notre Dame's academic standing in the late 1940s in his memoir, *God, Country, Notre Dame,* New York, 1990, pp. 63–71; ND vice president Richard Conklin spoke about the trip to Seattle in an interview (op. cit.); and the photograph of Father Hesburgh at a banquet in Seattle is in the *Notre Dame Alumnus,* 11–12/1949. Also in his memoir (op. cit.), Hesburgh discussed his dispute with Leahy before and during the Seattle trip, pp. 79–80; in addition, Hesburgh's memoir contains an excellent portrait of Notre Dame in the late 1940s and early 1950s, and of Father John J. Cavanaugh and his ND presidency.

28. Images of College Sports from Hollywood and Elsewhere

Bosley Crowther reviewed *Good News* for the *New York Times,* 12/5/47; he also wrote an interesting book about MGM, *The Lion's Share: The Story of an Entertainment Empire,* New York, 1957; the best late-century work on that studio, wonderfully illustrated, is *MGM—When the Lion Roars,* by Peter Hay with Woolsey Ackerman, Atlanta, Georgia, 1991. For a useful book on 20th Century Fox, see *Twentieth Century-Fox: A Corporate and Financial History* by Aubrey Solomon, Metuchen, New Jersey, 1988; for the evolution of films like *Father Was a Fullback* into TV sitcoms, see the chapters on TV in Douglas T. Miller and Marion Nowak, *The Fifties: The Way We Really Were*, New York, 1975; Fred MacMurray, who played the father, went on to similar roles in a number of TV sitcoms. The title of this film is a misnomer—Father is a coach—but the studio probably used it because of its alliterative catchiness.

The following reviews are from the *New York Times:* Bosley Crowther's review of *Father Was a Fullback*, 10/13/49; Thomas Pryor on *Yes Sir, That's My Baby*, 11/11/49; and Howard Thompson on *Peggy*, 7/21/50. The head writer of *Peggy*, George Slavin, was a college football fan who attended many USC and UCLA games, and the script suggests his love of classical college sports; the *New York Times'* Charles Grutzner discussed Janowicz's OSU deal, 3/20/51. *Sport* magazine ran a feature, "Janowicz on the Auction Block," that outlined the player's recruiting saga, 11/49, quoting Janowicz about the deals that various schools offered above the "job plan" and athletic scholarships, including packages worth thousands of dollars a month, free cars, and signing bonuses. After Janowicz's Rose Bowl season, Stanley Frank of the *Saturday Evening Post* detailed his academic, financial, and other problems in "The Woes of an All-American," 11/17/51.

The United Press report on Johnny Lujack's potential movie career was by Virginia Macpherson, and appeared in many newspapers, including the *South Bend Tribune*, 1/10/48; Glenn Davis's criticism of his film was in the same article. The quotes from Hollywood celebrities are from an article "I Like the Trojans—Lana" by Bob Hunter in (PATH "Notre Dame Football Scrapbook, 1947"); because it is on a page with clippings from Los Angeles papers, I assume that it also came from one of them; in addition, internal evidence dates it from the first week in December 1947. *The Glamor Game* (op. cit.), in its chapters on the late-1940s Fighting Irish visits to L.A., describes the glitter surrounding the games, as well as the over 100,000 spectators in the Los Angeles Coliseum for both the 1947 and 1948 contests. Many actors proclaimed their loyalty to Notre Dame in this period but Bing Crosby was particularly fervent; in a letter to Barry Fitzgerald, Bing Crosby's co-star in the Academy Award–winning film *Going My Way*, ND alumni official F. M. Messick termed Crosby, "Notre Dame's greatest friend," 11/28/47 (UMVR 1/22). Pat O'Brien discussed his relationship with the Rockne role and Notre Dame throughout his memoir, *The Wind at My Back: The Life and Times of Pat O'Brien*, Garden City, New York, 1964.

One of Bill Stern's favorite Rockne stories, used for many broadcasts in the late 1940s and printed in his *My Favorite Sports Stories*, 1948 edition, was titled, "The Bald Eagle Who Flew High," linking Rockne to the American national symbol. A late 1940s comic book, *Sport Stars: The Life of Knute Rockne*, used "The Bald Eagle of Notre Dame" as its subtitle, and gave the highlights of the coach's life according to the Warners's movie version, see (PNDP 3320); as with many comic books, exact publishing dates and origins are obscure. For the syndicated newspaper articles by Father John A. O'Brien, see (PATH "Notre Dame Football Scrapbook, 1947"); O'Brien ran the Newman Foundation at the University of Illinois in the 1920s and 1930s, and was more intellectual and liberal than most priests of his generation, not only in obtaining a secular Ph.D. but also with his early and active participation in the National Conference of Christians and Jews.

The United Press pre-game story on the 1946 ND-Army contest appeared in many newspapers, including the *South Bend Tribune*, 11/9/46; many of Bill Stern's broadcasts are in the LOC holdings, and reprinted in his anthologies (op. cit.); Hollywood made a variety of sports films in this period, including bringing Ronald Reagan back to star as Grover Cleveland Alexander in *The Winning Team*, Warners, 1952. That movie owed more to *Jim Thorpe—All-American* (see pp. 423–26), than the Rockne saga; nevertheless Reagan helped the film achieve its happy ending. Reagan also starred in two college movies made in 1952 with college sports subthemes: in both *She's Working Her Way Through College* and *Bedtime for Bonzo*, he played a professor who comes to appreciate big-time college football, even to helping his prize chimp, Bonzo, quarterback the school's team. When Reagan began his political career in the 1960s, opponents mocked these movies; however, they overlooked the fact that the majority of Americans liked them and appreciated Reagan's good-hearted, classical portrayals.

29. Postwar Programs as Propaganda

All of the football game programs discussed in this chapter are in the University of Notre Dame Archives PATH collection and the Joyce Sports Collection; for cataloguing information see the note at the top of Chapter 10 above. Frank Leahy's comments about the game programs for 1947 are in his report to Vice President Murphy, 9/16/47 (UVMR 1/26). From my survey of the football game programs in the Joyce Collection—by far the largest known holding of them—I estimate that, during the post–World War II years, approximately 80 percent of all schools in big-time college football bought their game programs through Spencer, and the other 20 percent from smaller companies, primarily a San Francisco firm that serviced West Coast universities; a few schools, like Purdue University, worked with a local designer (as a result, Purdue's programs were far inferior to the Spencer products). The year 1949 marked the post-war peak in college football attendance when, according to the NCAA's statistics, 19,651,995 fans attended games. Dividing this number by Spencer's 80 percent market share results in 15,721,596 potential customers. Many did not buy programs, of course, and many fans attended more than one game, and saw and/or bought more than one Spencer cover. However, to state that millions of football fans were influenced by the Spencer covers seems an accurate, if modest, assertion. Moreover, because Hollywood films, the mainstream press, and radio deeply influenced the cover artists and other producers of the programs, this media symbiosis ensured that the classical view of college sports surrounded any American interested in the subject.

The *Life* magazine cover on Johnny Lujack appeared 9/29/47, and the one on Doak Walker 9/27/48. Notre Dame vice president John H. Murphy wrote to alumnus Frank E. Cane about the articles inside the programs, 4/22/49 (UVMR 1/23). Sportswriter Cal Small wrote "Number Please!—'47 Rule Changes Liberalize Substitution"; for a copy of it see the program for the Pitt visit to Notre Dame, 10/4/47. The articles on Notre Dame players, including Ray Espenan and Leon Hart, appeared in ND programs throughout the 1949 season, as did the article "Notre Dame . . . 'Upon the Moveless Rock.' " The 1950 ND home game program for the Purdue visit, 10/7/50, carried the article on the school's cancer research, "Again Meeting a Challenge Head-On."

In this period, the game programs of most schools never hinted that the institution possessed faculty members and classrooms, only athletic teams and fun activities connected to college sports events. Each fall, the USC programs printed many articles about "Trojan Activities" and "Trojan Homecoming," and many photos of the festivities as well as the prominent entertainers who performed at USC campus events, but never a word on the University of Southern California as an academic institution, or even a suggestion that there was a university there (maybe there wasn't).

30. The Rise and Odor of College Basketball

New York Post sports columnist Leonard Cohen's comments appeared 3/9/46. College basketball suffers from a lack of good histories on its early decades; the following are the best of a mediocre lot, all too superficial, idiosyncratic, and/or official: John McCallum, *College Basketball, U.S.A., Since 1892*, New York, 1972; Ken Rappoport, *The Classic: The History of the NCAA Basketball Championship*, Mission, Kansas, 1979; Zander Hollander, *The Modern Encyclopedia of Basketball*, New York, 1973, and subsequent editions; and Neil Isaacs, *All the Moves: A History of College Basketball*, Philadelphia, 1975. In the Isaacs book, despite some useful anecdotes, the author's ego consumes the narrative, but this is the same writer who discussed "sportfucking" as an *organized* athletic activity (see his *Jock Culture U.S.A.*, New York, 1978, pp. 26, 149–51).

The above books outline Ned Irish's role in promoting college basketball, but more information is in "Basketball's Big Wheel" by Stanley Frank, *Saturday Evening Post*, 1/15/49. The Randy Roberts and James S. Olson quote is from *Winning Is the Only Thing: Sports in America Since 1945*, Baltimore, 1989, and is on p. 81; both Stanley Cohen in *The Game They Played*, New York, 1977, pp. 60–63, and Charles Rosen in *Scandals of '51: How the Gamblers Almost Killed College Basketball*, New York, 1978, p. 29, discuss Utah's Vidal Peterson and the bribe attempt, as well as the Brooklyn College fix of 1945. George Gipe (op. cit.) supplied the Phog Allen quote, p. 121–22, and the one from Harold Olson, the coach at Ohio State and also a NCAA official at the time, p. 121.

On page 288 of the text, Notre Dame AD Frank Leahy wrote to Vice President John J. Cavanaugh about expanding the school's basketball program, 7/13/46 (UVHS 3/5). The Minutes of a Special Meeting of the [Notre Dame] Faculty Board in Control of Athletics, 8/31/45 (UVOC 5/5), contain the decision to avoid Madison Square Garden, and the request by NYU professor Philip Badger to reconsider this move. Sportswriters commented on Notre Dame's motivations; columnist Joe Williams of the *New York Telegram* remarked that "when the Brooklyn College scandal broke . . . the good padres [at ND] voted against any more New York engagements," no date (PATH "Notre Dame Basketball Scrapbook"). *Newsweek*'s story on the 1946 ND-NYU game appeared 2/11/46. Notre Dame vice president John H. Murphy turned down the invitation to the NCAA tournament in a letter to NCAA official and University of Illinois AD Douglas R. Mills, 3/12/47 (UMVR 1/29). A number of books provide details on the early decades of Notre Dame basketball: *Hooping It Up: The Complete History of Notre Dame Basketball* by Tim Neely, Notre Dame, Indiana, 1985; and *A Frame of Mind Game: A Story of Notre Dame Basketball* by Gene Sullivan, Chicago, 1971. In addition, *With Rockne at Notre Dame*, New York, 1951, by longtime ND athletic trainer Eugene "Scrapiron" Young, has a chapter on the school's early basketball coach, George Keogan. After Keogan's death in 1943, and before entering the service, Moose Krause coached the ND basketball team in 1943–44; the *Notre Dame Alumnus* has an article on the transition from Keogan to Krause, 1–2/43. Krause returned as head basketball coach in 1946, continuing in that position, in addition to his football and athletic department duties, until 1951. Notre Dame aided other Catholic college basketball programs with visits, including Marquette, DePaul, Detroit, Loyola of Chicago, Canisius, John Carroll (of Cleveland), and even St. Mary's of northern California. Because basketball was not ND's primary sport, competition in it with fellow Catholic schools did not spark the same fan intensity as would have occurred in football; nevertheless, some of the rivalries, notably the home-and-home annual series with Marquette and DePaul, became very spirited as opponents tried to upset ND.

John Carmichael's article on Kevin O'Shea appeared in *Sport*, 2/48; Gordon Graham's comments were made in an interview (op. cit.); Hank Iba's *Collier's* "Basketball Forecast" appeared 12/21/46; and Harry B. Wilson did the *Saturday Evening Post* story on basketball at St. Louis University, "They Took the Back Door to the Big Time," 2/25/50. Bob Broeg and Bob Morrison of *Sport* wrote the profile "Easy Ed of the Billikens," 1/49; and that magazine had Bob Cousy share the billing in "Kaftan, Cousy, and the Crusaders," by Harold Kaese, 3/48. John McCallum in *College Basketball, U.S.A.* (op. cit.) discussed the Holy Cross facilities situation, p. 80.

Marty Glickman pioneered basketball play-by-play announcing in New York, as well as many other innovations in his profession. Before the 1945–46 season, few games were broadcast; that year, Glickman recalled, "I had to sell the people at WHN on the concept of doing basketball," *Long Island (New York) Newsday*, 3/29/91. Glickman also commented at length about the Madison Square Garden scene during this period in the recent HBO documentary, *City Dump: The Story of the CCNY 1951 Basketball Scandal*, 1998. Finally, Furman Bisher profiled North Carolina State's Everett Case in *Collier's*, 1/31/48.

31. College Basketball Starts to Implode

The quote from Neil Isaacs's *All the Moves* (op. cit.) is on p. 104. Many books on the Catskill Mountain resorts exist: *A Summer World: The Attempt to Build a Jewish Eden in the Catskills from the Days of the Ghetto to the Rise and Decline of the Borscht Belt* by Stefan Kanfer, New York, 1989, is an interesting social history; and, of the many nostalgia books on the subject, *It Happened in the Catskills: An Oral History in the Words of Busboys, Bellhops, Guests, Proprietors, Comedians, Agents, and Others Who Lived It*, by Harvey Frommer, San Diego, California, 1996, stands out, mainly for the photos. The recent HBO documentary, *City Dump* (op. cit.), also had a good section on the Catskills, including excellent home movies. Kanfer discussed the basketball fixing in the mountains, as did Stanley Cohen (op. cit.), and Charles Rosen (op. cit.). Much of the Catskill wagering consisted of betting pools—the winner picked the total points scored in the game and won the pool. Professional gamblers would offer the players half the pot if they would make sure that the game ended on the correct total; thus, learning to "shave" for an exact total of, say, 163 points, required real teamwork and skill. Stefan Kanfer (op. cit.) commented on the transition from "the Mountain courts" to "one of the greatest scandals," p. 103.

The quote from Moose Krause is from the interview (op. cit.); also in Krause's memoir, with Stephen Singular, *Notre Dame's Greatest Coaches: Rockne, Leahy, Parseghian, and Holtz*, New York, 1993, he discussed Toots Shor's, p. 61. Dan Parker's *Sport* magazine article, "Inside Story of Basketball Betting," 2/47, contained the quotes from Phog Allen. The *Saturday Evening Post* article on Ned Irish by Stanley Frank (op. cit.) had the information on Irish's empire, the betting at MSG, and the Minneapolis Syndicate. In 1947–48, the NCAA epitomized the college sports establishment's hypocrisy by keeping the men's basketball tourney in the Garden, *Chicago Tribune*, 1/7/47, and *New York Times*, 1/11/48. Charles Rosen (op. cit.) quoted Ike Gellis, p. 111; and Stanley Cohen (op. cit.) wrote about what "every kid in the streets of New York knew," p. 62. Interestingly, the recent HBO film *City Dump* (op. cit.), with Cohen as its advisor, played down this aspect of the story and presented a more dramatic from-innocence-to-shock at the 1951 revelations scenario. Rosen has the story of the "irate bettor," p. 69, and the writers playing "the ponies," p. 111; former CCNY star Floyd Layne made his comments about the sportswriters in a *Sport* magazine article, "Don't I Deserve Another Chance," 9/52; and Gordon Graham's pungent comment was made in an interview (op. cit.).

Even though events overtook Max Kase and his assistants, he won a Pulitzer Prize for his follow-up articles after the initial arrests. In an early analysis of the scandal, the *Saturday Evening Post* ran an editorial, "Let's Not Duck the Real Issue in Sports Mess," 3/24/51, and it included the sports media on its list of culprits: "The sportswriters who might have been expected to evaluate this phenomenon critically, were so intoxicated by their new sense of importance—so vitiated by their allegiance to [Ned] Irish [and his Garden basketball productions]—that, far from questioning, they joined enthusiastically in the general hoorah."

32. Scandal/Scoundrel Time: Players Confess, Coaches Escape

The quote from Charles Rosen is from pages 4–5 of his book (op. cit.); the *New York Times* carried the article on the arrests of the former Manhattan College players, 1/18/51. At the time and subsequently, many experts claimed that the arrest totals were far below the number of actual fixes, see Cohen (op. cit.), p. 225–26, and Rosen, p. 131; in an editorial, 9/17/51, *Life* magazine noted that the fixes "involved many other teams and players whose names have never been published because prosecuting attorneys preferred to ignore the facts rather than wound local pride." Arthur Daley's column on Junius Kellogg appeared 1/18/51; Daley's separation from the Broadway sporting crowd not only resulted from his stature as "Sports of the Times" columnist but, as his son Robert Daley noted in his "Afterword" to a collection of his father's columns (op. cit.), the sportswriter spent his time either working on his column and other articles for the *Times*—he had a monstrous word count to feed every day—or with his family and friends. His son commented that "he was ingenuous in many ways," p. 333, and, like some innocent fans, probably he first learned about the fixes when he read about them in the newspapers.

The *New York Times* put the initial arrests of CCNY players on its front page, 2/19/51, and a large photo of the players being booked. The iconography of the arrest photos connected directly to the frequent shots of gangsters and other criminals being arrested, and averting their faces, even covering them with hats or coats—indeed, in the *Times* photo, professional gambler Salvatore Sollazzo, booked with the players, performs that ritual. That college athletes were photographed in this way truly shocked 1950s fans and was without precedent. Arthur Daley's column on the first CCNY arrests appeared 2/19/51; in this period, many people decried the moral decline in American society—an ironic counterpoint to those persons decrying the same thing in the 1990s and pointing to the 1950s as "a moral era."

The *New York Times* front-paged the "3 More Athletes" headline and article, 3/28/51; Arthur Daley did his column on Rockne, 3/30/51, and, in his passages on Rockne as inspiration-to-boys, Daley echoed the on-screen dedication at the beginning of the film *Knute Rockne—All-American:* "Knute Rockne was a great and vital force in moulding the spirit of modern America through the millions of young men and boys who loved and respected him and who today are living by the high standards he taught." Daley's paper ran the articles on the shooting of Billy Rockne and its aftermath, 1/22/51, 1/23/51, and 1/26/51; for more details on Billy's life, see my *Shake Down the Thunder* (op. cit.), pp. 466 and 605.

Yale coach Howard Hobson wrote "How to Stop Those Basketball Scandals" for *Collier's*, 12/29/51; an unnamed CCNY player remarked about the "time-honored tradition" in Rosen (op. cit.), p. 68; Norm Mager commented about double-fixes in a *New York Times* piece by Robert Lipsyte, 5/20/94. Stanley Frank's piece on Holman and the Master's controlling style, "Easy Doesn't Do It," appeared in *Collier's*, 2/18/50. In the late 1940s, Sam Winograd became "graduate manager of athletics," a sort of AD, but he still basically worked for Holman, purchasing equipment for the basketball program, etc. Rosen (op. cit.) had the story about Holman's veto of articles by Bobby Sand, p. 56, and the quote on "forging transcripts," and how Holman "wanted . . . ballplayers," p. 60; the *New York Times* carried the New York Board of Education report on Holman's CCNY transgressions, 8/28/54. Rosen discussed Sand's anger at the fixing, and Holman's nonreactions, p. 72, as well as Sand's disclosure to a CCNY administrator, p. 105. *Long Island (New York) Newsday,* 3/4/88, carried the comments on how administrators ignored the warnings; the *New York Times* quoted CCNY president Harry Wright, 3/29/50, and that paper enthused about CCNY's triumph on the same day.

Rosen (op. cit.) quoted Ed Roman, p. 243, and Floyd Layne, p. 253; the *Sport* magazine "Man of the Year in Sport" article appeared 12/50. Rosen discussed the "Original Celtics" methods, p. 15: a veteran player from this period described how clubs would visit towns, "beat the yokels by a narrow margin, then we'd get some bets down, play them again, and kill them. We'd collect our money and get the hell out of town. The Original Celtics were doing the same kind of thing when Nat was playing with them. Only we didn't call it point shaving. We called it survival." In addition, Holman spent his summers in the Catskills where he owned a profitable summer camp, and he often attended hotel basketball games. However, in the wake of the scandal, he condemned the "hotel teams [as] schools of crime"; Stefan Kanfer (op. cit.) commented: "Many summers of [crooked] resort basketball had gone by without a word from him [Holman], but now he provided a new version of Captain Louis in *Casablanca,* who was 'shocked, shocked to find gambling going on' in Rick's casino," p. 218–19. Moreover, Holman's assistant Sam Winograd, according to Rosen (op. cit.), "spent his summers at Young's Gap Hotel in Parksville, New York, where he not only ran the betting pool but distributed the winnings," and networked with professional gamblers, p. 55.

Ira Berkow's obituary of Holman appeared in the *New York Times* Sunday Magazine, 12/31/95; even Rosen (op. cit.) and Cohen (op. cit.) do not connect the dots on Holman's guilt; moreover, the HBO documentary *City Dump* (op. cit.) ignored Holman's real role in the event. Significantly, Sherman White, one of the convicted LIU fixers, told the *New York Times*'s Dave Anderson: " 'HBO wanted me [to be on the program], but I told them no.' " According to Anderson, "White, who had viewed a tape of that documentary, said 'It doesn't tell the truth about the whole thing. There were a lot of people involved besides the ballplayers. Nobody has addressed what was the coach's responsibility,' " 3/22/98. Rosen (op. cit.) had the quotes on Holman's coaching style, pp. 52 and 66; the films of Holman's CCNY teams in action indicate a highly disciplined system; interestingly, Holman allowed his team to warm up in an individual, disorganized manner but, in an age when not all coaches and teams watched endless film of opponents, Holman might have encouraged these warmups as a psychological device to lull the opposition into not expecting an organized offense and defense.

The *Collier's* article by Furman Bisher on Everett Case (op. cit.) explains that coach's use of "Racehorse Basketball"; in a letter to the *San Francisco Examiner,* 1/12/97, former Indiana high school player Bruce Parker reminisced about the old days in his sport, and offered an excellent definition: "Racehorse basketball, we called it. Grab the rebound, let it fly to your out man, and race like a horse to the other end. Shoot, score, then race like a horse to the other [defensive] end." George Gipe (op. cit.) has the Adolph Rupp response to the CCNY arrests, p. 124; the *Saturday Evening Post* editorial appeared 3/24/51; and *Commonweal* suggested total "De-emphasis" of college sports (the title of its editorial), 12/28/51. The *New York Times* obituary for Holman, and the New York Board of Education report are referenced above; David Halberstam discussed the state dinner and the quiz programs in *The Fifties,* New York, 1993, pp. 645–47. The TV producers either coached the contestants directly by telling them the answers beforehand (*21* did this with Charles Van Doren), or indirectly—during practice sessions, they learned the contestant's strengths and weaknesses, and pitched the questions accordingly. *The $64,000 Question* used the latter method, the producers discovering that Marine Captain Richard McCutcheon "knew French cuisine rather than Italian or British," and they asked him "questions [on air] remarkably similar to the ones answered correctly in the rehearsal," p. 647.

Many works discuss the early years of sports on TV, among the more informative are Donald Parente's Ph.D. dissertation at the University of Illinois, "A History of Sports and Television," 1972, and Ron Powers's *Supertube: The Rise of Television Sports,* New York, 1984.

33. Coach Bee vs. Author Bee: The Death of the Frank Merriwell Hero

The quote from *Winning Is the Only Thing* by Randy Roberts and James S. Olson (op. cit.) is on p. 80; the description of Chip Hilton is from a long appreciation of the Bee novels by author Howard Owen, *Raleigh (North Carolina) News & Observer,* 4/7/96. Clair Bee's books became so popular that one publisher, A. S. Barnes, brought out the instructional works under the imprint, "The Clair Bee Basketball Library," and another, Grosset & Dunlap, published the fiction as "The Chip Hilton Sports

Series." Rockwell's speech to the football team is in *Touchdown Pass*, New York, 1948, pp. 5–6; for the Rockne speech, see the shooting script and film *Knute Rockne—All-American*, 1940 (op. cit.); the wording of the film version is slightly different than the shooting script, and I have used a coherent, combined version here. Bee's description of Rock quoted here is in *Championship Ball*, New York, 1948, p. 48; Rock's pronouncement on "courage" is also in that book, p. 79; Chip's retrospective comment on being "one of the luckiest fellows in the world" came in *Hardcourt Upset*, New York, 1958, pp. 54–55; and the summary of his college career, as well as the statement that "Chip Hilton wasn't a loafer," is in *Backboard Fever*, New York, 1953, p. 157.

The *Sport* magazine article "Basketball's Busiest Bee," by Milton Gross, appeared 2/51; Cohen (op. cit.) cited court documents concerning Bee's 300 percent rise in salary, p. 202, and he also described Eddie Gard's work in the Catskills, pp. 99–100; Stefan Kanfer (op. cit.) wrote about how Sollazzo and Gard "traversed the Mountain roads," p. 213. Clair Bee gave Rock's warning on "outside ball playing" in *Championship Ball* (op. cit.), pp. 79–80; although Rock warns a team of high school players, in fact, the hotels did employ some high school stars on summer teams, the most famous being Wilt Chamberlain in the 1950s. Rosen (op. cit.) outlined Bee's cheating in the 1930s, pp. 18–20, and discussed Bee's tryout camps, pp. 34–35; Sherman White also described the camps in "The Basketball Fix Ruined My Life," *Sport* magazine, 7/51. Bee offered the standard coaches' argument on athletic scholarships in "Basketball's Busiest Bee" (op. cit.); Chip Hilton long disdained athletic scholarships, articulating his criticism here in *Buzzer Basket*, New York, 1962, p. 49; interestingly, Coach Bee supported athletic scholarships *before and after* the scandals, and Author Bee opposed them *before and after*, offering more evidence for the split personality theory in the text.

New York General Sessions Court Judge Saul Streit excoriated Clair Bee in sentencing the CCNY and LIU player-fixers and their gambler contacts, 11/20/51; I was unable to obtain a complete transcript of his judgment, however, the *New York Times* for the above date printed long excerpts, and Richard I. Miller included even longer excerpts in *The Truth About Big-time Football*, New York, 1953, pp. 68–73 (this book is as much about corruption in college basketball as in football). Jack McCallum's article on Chip Hilton, "A Hero for All Times," appeared in *Sports Illustrated*, 1/7/80; McCallum suggests that readers of Clair Bee's fiction try to recall specific scenes and so, from my own recollection of the Chip Hilton novels, I chose the "wave of gratitude" scene from the end of *Championship Ball* (op. cit.), p. 209.

Mike Douchant quoted Indiana University men's basketball coach Bob Knight in *Encyclopedia of College Basketball*, New York, 1995, p. 56. The United Press International obituary of Bee, 5/21/83, quoted 1940s college basketball star Leo Marsten on Bee's basketball acumen and "genius"; former North Carolina coach Frank McGuire made similar comments to Sam Goldaper of the *New York Times* for the latter's obituary of Bee, 5/21/83. The *Collier's* piece that spotlighted Bee's scouting was "Settled Out of Court" by Arch Murray and Hy Turkin, 12/20/47; the passage about Rock's off-court analysis is in *Backboard Fever* (op. cit.), p. 100; and the *Sport* magazine article was "Basketball's Busiest Bee" (op. cit.). Stanley Cohen (op. cit.) wrote the line about "a greased chute to oblivion," p. 76; Rosen (op. cit.) quoted the bookie about "a crazy time," p. 116, as well as Bee on the loss to Arizona, p. 117, and the jeering fans, p. 114. A letter from Associated Press writer Hugh Fullerton to Notre Dame's Charlie Callahan captured the craziness of the time: Fullerton relayed the joke from "a correspondent in Syracuse who wanted to know if I'd heard about the 'triple dump': both teams and the referee fixed and the result was the first scoreless tie in basketball history," 1/24/51 (UASI 2/102).

Sherman White described his problems in learning to fix in "The Basketball Fix Ruined My Life" (op. cit.); the *New York Times* put the arrest of the LIU stars on the front page, 2/20/51; Clair Bee's article in the *Saturday Evening Post*, "as told to" the ubiquitous Stanley Frank, was titled, "I Know Why They Sold Out to the Gamblers," 2/2/52. Ira Berkow's comments about Bee's "intensity" appeared in the *New York Times*, 3/12/81. Bee's NBA coaching stint with the Baltimore Bullets was described by Irv Goodman in *Sport* magazine, "The Busiest Bee in Baltimore," 1/54; the author in a preface described himself as "a friend" of the coach's, and the article was typical of the media's gentle postscandal treatment of the coach. Rosen (op. cit.) quoted Sherman White's father, p. 127; for Judge Streit's comments, see above references, and Bee's rejoinder in the *Saturday Evening Post* (op. cit.); and Heywood Hale Broun commented in the HBO special, *City Dump* (op. cit.). Finally, in the February 1951 *Sport* magazine article on Bee (op. cit.), on newsstands a few weeks before the LIU arrests, the coach made an interesting admission: "To tell the truth, I've been having some trouble getting to sleep lately. I figure if I'm going to stay awake, I might as well use the time" writing fiction.

34. The Fixes Play in Peoria and Find an Old Kentucky Home

Charles Rosen (op. cit.) quoted NYU coach Howard Cann, p. 125; for the extent of the fixing, see the opening footnotes for Chapter 22; Rosen described the Toledo fixes, pp. 150–53, with the quote on the gamblers, p. 150, and Gerry Bush's explanation, as well as the *Toledo Blade* quote, on p. 153. The *Sport* magazine article, "Gene Melchiorre—Little Man, Big Star," 3/51, was by Jack Rosenberg; an equally sanguine story on the love of people in Peoria for the Bradley Braves, "They're Balmy over Basketball," by Bill Fay, appeared in *Collier's*, 1/13/51. That piece described President Owen's role in promoting the team, as did Rosen, p. 156; the best informed comments on Owen came from Judge Saul Streit in his judgment on the Bradley fixers, quoted in Richard I. Miller (op. cit.), pp. 204–05.

After the fix revelations, *Look* magazine published Gene Melchiorre's *mea culpa*, "How I Fell for the Basketball Bribers," as told to Tim Cohane, 1/13/53; Melchiorre discussed his service ball and Bradley deals there, as well as in Rosen, p. 155f, who interviewed him for his book. Melchiorre told Rosen how the "fixes were going on for years," p. 198; Cohen (op. cit.) quoted the Bradley president about shunning Madison Square Garden, p. 173, and continuing the program, p. 177, and he paraphrased DA Hogan's indictment, p. 174; and Judge Streit condemned Owen's "subsidization" etc., see Miller (op. cit.), pp. 204–05. Because Bradley won so many games in this period—it finished atop the AP Poll in 1949–50—Gene Melchiorre was inducted into the Bradley University Hall of Fame in 1979.

John Thelin in *Games Colleges Play: Scandal and Reform in Intercollegiate Athletics*, Baltimore, 1994, analyzed and quoted the Griffenhagan Report, pp. 118–19. The Kentucky trial in New York City was separate from the other fixing trials, and Judge Streit rendered his judgment in that case in late April 1952; the *New York Times* carried the story and excerpts from the verdict, 4/30/52, and Richard I. Miller (op. cit.) quoted excerpts, pp. 28–29. Thelin commented on UK's rise to athletic prominence, p. 116, and he offered the Rupp-Rockne parallel, p. 117. Ken Rappoport in *The Classic* (op. cit.) both quoted and commented upon Baron Rupp on winning, p. 63; Tom Siler in "Football's Jittery Genius," the *Saturday Evening Post*, 11/3/51, did the honors for the Bear. Bryant, in his memoir, *Bear* (op. cit.), told the story about Rupp and the faculty group, pp. 119–20; they had adjoining offices in the athletic department for a brief period, not all of Bryant's years at UK. The story of Rupp's course in "Advanced Basketball" was in "The Crafty Wizard of Lexington" by Collie Small, *Saturday Evening Post*, 2/15/47, as were the comments about his growing wealth and importance. H. L. Maisin did "Old Rupp and Ready" for *Senior Scholastic*, 2/2/48.

Bryant discussed his "social position" in Kentucky in his memoir (op. cit.), p. 116, and his contract, p. 117; and A. H. Hardman, sports editor of the *Charleston (West Virginia) Gazette*, wrote about Bear's treatment of high school coaches, 12/9/51. The comment about the NCAA receiving "17 complaints" was in "Football's Jittery Genius" (op. cit.); and Walter Byers in his memoir (op. cit.), discussed Bryant's Kentucky "violations" and the association's ignoring of them, pp. 61–62. Gregory Sojka's comment on Rupp is in the *Biographical Dictionary of American Sports: Basketball and Other Indoor Sports*, Westport, Connecticut, 1989, pp. 255–58; John Thelin (op. cit.) also remarked that "Rupp's basketball teams were considered to be the most disciplined, best-conditioned squads in the nation, known for teamwork and defensive play," p. 121. The story about Rupp's cattle-call tryout and Bill Spivey was in Spivey's obituary by Mark Coomes, the *Louisville Courier-Journal*, 5/10/95; the quoted witness was Ralph Beard, and Spivey himself told a sanitized version of it to *Sport* magazine, 1/51, in "Seven Feet, All Spivey," by Fred Russell. Spivey was also implicated in the fixes—he always denied any involvement—and led a sad life after UK.

Charles Rosen (op. cit.) described Rupp's basketball tactics, p. 168; many authors have praised The Fabulous Five, including Rappoport (op. cit.), pp. 61–67; *Sport* magazine's article about the Indianapolis Olympians, "The Great Basketball Experiment," by Jim Dailey, 1/50, mentioned the "newly formed" NBA; H. L. Maisin in *Scholastic*, 11/30/49, also discussed the Olympians and the "new National Basketball Association . . . a combination of the two major pro leagues—the Basketball Association of America and the National Basketball League." Rappoport in *The Classic* (op. cit.) mentioned Rupp's admiration for the Fabulous Five, p. 61, and retiring their uniforms, p. 67; and Bob Richelson did "The Grozas Are Great" for *Sport*, 12/48. Yale coach Harold Hobson (op. cit.) saw the Kentucky NIT loss to Loyola and offered an excellent analysis: Groza, the UK center, "stationed himself on defense *directly behind* Jack Kerris, Loyola's center; orthodox strategy called for the defensive player to take a position *alongside* of or *in front* of Kerris to intercept passes heading into the pivot" (Hobson's emphasis; he wrote before the UK players went on trial, and *Collier's* edited Groza's name to "one of the players indicted in the scandals," but because Groza was the UK center and he guarded Kerris, he obviously fit the large basketball shoes). In addition, the Loyola center picked up four fouls, but Groza did not call for the ball on offense, nor did his teammates pass it to him.

Sport changed its attitude on intercollegiate athletics (see Chapter 49 here), and Jimmy Breslin wrote the revisionist "Kentucky Apologizes for Nothing" for the magazine, 3/53; Judge Streit discussed Groza's payments from Owen Campbell's liquor-distributing company, the New York Times, 4/30/52; the Sport profile, "Ralph Beard: Basketball's Big Shot" by Ed Fitzgerald, appeared 3/49; and Dave Kindred of the Washington Post wrote about Beard, 1/17/81. Stanley Cohen discussed the "gambler's catechism," p. 183; he also included Joe Louis on his list, forgetting that the Brown Bomber lost a number of fights as well as his championship in this period. Judge Streit's comments about Englisis are in Miller (op. cit.), p. 28; Rosen discussed the fixing by the Fabulous Five's successors, pp. 186–87; and Rupp related his use of game films to Bill Fay of Collier's for an article entitled "Inside Sports," 3/12/49.

Stanley Cohen (op. cit.) indicated that in this period, Kentucky was "fixing games . . . in every part of the country they visited" and, according to legal records, the Wildcats "conspired with gamblers in more than one fourth of the games they played during the 1948–49 season," pp. 184–85. However, the full "degree of their involvement would never be known because the state of Kentucky had no law against the bribing of amateur athletes. And so the players were not obliged to answer a single question once they left the jurisdiction of New York"; thus their admissions of "one fourth" fixed games was far too low. Moreover, in the New York depositions and trials, no one asked the Kentucky players about such games as their road loss to Notre Dame on 2/2/48; however, considering the excellence of this Kentucky team, the loss to ND was surprising—except if the fix was in. And, in many ways, this was a perfect game to fix: the volume of money on Notre Dame was usually much greater than on almost any other school—Notre Dame's large number of fans always bet on their beloved Fighting Irish whether they had a chance to win or beat the spread or not; thus, extra money from those in the know about the fix would be harder for the bookies to detect than for many other fixed games.

Not surprisingly, a number of authors loyal to Rupp and UK basketball support his denials: see Adolph Rupp as I Knew Him, Lexington, Kentucky, 1979, by Harry Lancaster, his longtime assistant coach, "as told to Cawood Ledford," even longer time UK basketball announcer; also Rappoport in his official NCAA book backed Rupp's innocence (op. cit.), as do the authors of other works written specifically for Wildcat fans. Furman Bisher in "The Life and Battles of Adolph Rupp," Sport, 3/59, presented a more balanced portrait, including the comments of Groza and Barnstable; Rosen dug a bit deeper and quoted Barnstable more specifically: "I missed a shot late in the St. Louis game and, when it was over, Rupp gave me the devil. He said that my miss had cost his friend, Burgess Carey, five hundred dollars," p. 187.

Judge Streit (op. cit.) discussed Rupp's association with Ed Curd at great length (Streit devoted 18 pages of his 63-page verdict on the Kentucky fixes to Rupp); in the Prohibition Era speakeasy tradition, the Mafia's open ownership and patronage of "The Copa" apparently made it more exciting for its customers. Rosen discussed the lawsuit by Lexington lawyer J. A. Edge, p. 207; Gordon Graham made his comments in an interview (op. cit.); and Judge Streit (op. cit.) obviously considered Rupp guilty. The Associated Press reported UK's official reaction, published by many papers, including the New York Times, 5/7/52; for Jimmy Breslin's first Sport story on UK, see above citation, and his "The Baron Is Out to Get Even" appeared in Sport, 1/54. Bear Bryant discussed his departure from UK in his memoir (op. cit.), pp. 118 and 121; Bill Rives in "Bear Bryant Is Asking for It," Sport, 9/54, mentioned the NCAA scrutiny; and Walter Byers in his memoir (op. cit.) commented on Bryant's cheating at Texas A&M, pp. 118–21. Bryant broke Amos Alonzo Stagg's record of total victories in 1981, but Joe Paterno broke Bryant's record in 1997.

35. Football Becomes the Postwar Scandal and Colonel Blaik

Historian Stephen E. Ambrose's quote is in his Duty Honor Country (op. cit.), p. 318; the New York Times's front-page coverage of the Army football scandal appeared 8/4/51, and the quote from Army Chief of Staff General J. Lawton Collins is in the front-page story. For a discussion of how Blaik presented his squad as "The Nation's Team," see Chapter 14 here; Moose Krause's eloquent comments came in an interview (op. cit.); the New York Times, 8/4/51, explained the history of the code, its many clauses, and quoted Eisenhower on its meaning; Ambrose (op. cit.) also discussed it, p. 278f. James A. Blackwell in *On Brave Old Army Team* (op. cit.) detailed the genesis of the cribbing and its many intricacies in "Part Three: Bad Boys," p. 165f; in the narrative here, instead of using West Point's jargon—e.g., "writ" for exam—I have translated it into standard terminology.

Arthur Daley, on vacation when the scandal broke, wrote his column for the *New York Times*, 8/12/51, and *The Christian Century* used it, 8/29/51—this weekly provided material for the Sunday sermons of many Protestant ministers throughout the country. Hanson Baldwin, the winner of Pulitzer Prizes for military reporting, did a special series for the *New York Times* on the aftermath of the West Point scandal, 1/14 and 1/15/52; the quote in the text appeared the second day, as did Baldwin's comment that West Point "is a tax-supported institution . . . and many citizens feel a proprietary interest in it" as well as in its football team. After the scandal broke, some reporters investigated Blaik's recruiting and admissions system: the AP had information on the "all-expenses-paid" visits and the "easy appointment to the Academy" on 8/9/51, published in many newspapers, including the *New York Times*. Gene Filipski wrote about Blaik's recruiting visit and subsequent treatment of him in "Railroaded Out of West Point," *Sport*, 10/52; Filipski also admitted that "Cadet uniforms and the picture [Blaik] painted of life at West Point had a glamor that swayed me."

The *Time* article on Blaik's "cram school" and ability "to wangle appointments" appeared 8/20/51; *Newsweek* mentioned the "Congressmen [who] recalled visits from a West Point representative," and one member's protest of West Point priorities, 8/20/51. The *New York Times*, 8/10/51, explained how the loophole in admissions worked: because the act of Congress that established appointments to the service academies contained a provision allowing members of Congress final discretion in appointments, members could go beyond the usual academic and character ratings and base appointments on athletic ability. That same issue of the *Times* contained a story about Blaik's main recruiting aide in Washington, D.C., Col. Lawrence "Biff" Jones, a former Army football hero and coach during the Rockne era. Jones admitted that "he had urged many members of Congress to appoint outstanding football players to the Point. He said he had acted on behalf of Col. Earl Blaik, head coach at the Academy." Sports editor A. L. Hardman of the *Charleston (West Virginia) Gazette* detailed the story of West Virginia Senator Harley Kilgore and high school football star Bob Orders, 11/28/51.

General Carl Spaatz criticized West Point intercollegiate athletics in *Newsweek*, 8/20/51; Colonel Earl Blaik's main written comments on the scandal came in his memoirs, *You Have to Pay the Price* (op. cit.)—an unintendedly ironic title considering his unwillingness to do so as a result of the scandal—and *The Red Blaik Story* (op. cit.); the latter book reprints his chapter, "The Ninety Scapegoats," on the scandal, and then offers "The West Point Scandal Reexamined." For an interesting view of Vince Lombardi while still an assistant to Blaik, see Stanley Woodward's "Football's Greatest Father-and-Son Act," the *Saturday Evening Post*, 10/7/50; although the son of the title is Blaik's, Woodward also interviewed Lombardi for this piece. Michael O'Brien in *Vince* (op. cit.) discussed Lombardi's reaction to the scandal, pp. 100–3; for a discussion of "Winning isn't everything," see the notes for the Introduction above. The comments on the "wide disparity in football talent between" Army and Navy are in "Navy's Skipper in Civvies" by Jack Newcombe, *Sport*, 11/55; John Lardner wrote "My Case Against Sport" for *American Magazine*, 10/51; General Spaatz's comments were in *Newsweek* (op. cit.); and Blaik excoriated his critics at the time and forever after, particularly those within the Army and "on the Post," terming them "a vindictive few" who "relished [the] opportunity to whet their blood-axes," *Red Blaik Story* (op. cit.), p. 290.

Gene Filipski explained how he became involved in the cheating in his *Sport* article (op. cit.). Stanley Woodward wrote the classic profile of Blaik, "The Man Behind the Army Team," for *Sport*, 11/50; Blaik's acknowledgment of his workaholism is in his collected memoirs (op. cit.), p. 176; in the quoted passage and many others, Blaik portrayed himself as a victim of governmental and public ingratitude. In "Army Coach Red Blaik Says: The Pro Game Isn't Football," 10/28/50, Stanley Woodward offered more details on the coach's total-control approach; ironically, part of Blaik's dislike of the pros was that "they don't work at" football hard enough, and "they only work at the development of a team for a couple of months in the fall," as opposed to his 365-days-a-year approach! The pros would soon change, in part because Blaik's assistant Vince Lombardi moved to the NFL.

James A. Blackwell (op. cit.) analyzed the "cheating ring," p. 236; for his comments on how the "cribbing system" escalated, on "the poop," and on the academic coaches' rationalizations, see pp. 178–79. Filipski (op. cit.) discussed the "benefits" received by the tutors. Most New York newspapers, wire services, and weekly magazines carried Blaik's news conference at Mama Leone's; the

New York Times covered it most extensively, 8/10/51, including with a large front-page photo, and the quotes in the text are from its reports on the event. The story about the West Point math instructor was told to me by a West Point graduate of the 1950s in an interview for this book; he claimed that "faculty members did speak to Blaik about the cribbing while it was going on . . . I heard about a math instructor who got upset when Al Pollard, one of Blaik's stars but very thick between the ears, started getting perfect scores on his math quizzes. The player didn't have a clue about the concepts, and he [the instructor] went to Blaik personally with the evidence. Blaik looked at it and proceeded to kick him out of his office . . . Because he [Blaik] was the most powerful man on the Post, and the instructor wanted to keep his job, he got cold feet and let Pollard pass. This wasn't the only time that a faculty member got into it with Blaik about the cheating, and these incidents were the talk of the Post at the time." The speaker subsequently had a long and meritorious Army career; he also enjoys attending West Point reunions, and spoke on condition that his remarks were strictly off the record. I dislike off-the-record comments and have used only one other in this book; however, I quote this one because the tutors' cheating help to Pollard and some of the latter's surprisingly perfect scores are confirmed by Blackwell, p. 287. For the postmortem West Point report, also see Blackwell, p. 334f.

From the war years on, the classical profiles of Blaik elevated him to the pantheon of American coaches; by deifying the Army coach, Stanley Woodward, the most respected sports editor in America, violated his basic rule of journalism: "Don't God Up"—treat like gods—"Athletes and Coaches." He often stated this dictum to Red Smith and other sportswriters, but because Blaik granted Woodward unique access, the journalist suspended his "sports atheism" when covering the West Point coach. For the interviews with Jim Beach and Moose Krause, see citations above; even journalistic skeptics like Jim Beach and Francis Wallace chose public silence in covering Blaik's role in the cribbing scandal.

Many of the expelled football players went on to play at other schools—e.g., the entire offensive line at Kansas State, and Gene Filipski at Villanova—but Joseph P. Kennedy, insisting upon public anonymity but known to the schools involved, offered to sponsor any expelled cadet who wanted to transfer to the University of Notre Dame, needed financial aid, and could meet ND admissions standards. Kennedy acted in part because he hoped that his gesture would improve Army–Notre Dame relations. President Cavanaugh agreed to the Kennedy gift—on the condition that the athletes *never* play varsity sports for ND. Thirteen expelled cadets accepted the offer, met the terms, and enrolled at Notre Dame. Earl Blaik wrote a thank-you note about the above to Cavanaugh, and the latter replied, 9/7/51 (UPCC 10/6); in addition, the president of Vanderbilt, Harvie Branscomb, asked Cavanaugh about the terms of Notre Dame's admission of the expelled cadets, 9/29/51, and the ND official explained them, also mentioning his school's rule against "allowing transfer students who have competed in intercollegiate varsity athletics at another institution to engage in" them at Notre Dame, 10/8/51, both letters in (UPCC 10/6).

An anonymous book reviewer in *Publishers Weekly*, 5/20/96, commented on Blackwell's not connecting the dots on Blaik; the *Time* magazine remarks appeared, 8/20/51; Blaik's discussion in his memoir (op. cit.) is on p. 295; and the *New York Times*, 8/10/51, reported on the cheering reporters at Leone's, as well as Blaik's promotion of big-time college sports. Stephen Ambrose (op. cit.) summed up the effect of the scandal on West Point, p. 321; Francis Wallace commented on the 1951 Army team in his "Pigskin Preview" for *Collier's*, 9/15/51; the *Washington Post* quoted President Ronald Reagan's salutation to Blaik, 5/13/86; *The Sporting News* carried the obituary cited in the text, 5/22/89; and Blackwell (op. cit.) discussed how the United States Military Academy has never permitted any "new athletic building or the football stadium to be named after Red Blaik," p. 406.

36. ND President Cavanaugh and the ACE Try to Reform College Sports

The *Life* editorial appeared, 9/17/51; the *Saturday Evening Post* one, 9/8/51; readers wrote to *Life* about the editorial, 10/1/51; the *Sport* magazine editorial was in the 10/51 issue; Red Smith's column on the jail sentences appeared in many newspapers, including the *Washington Post*, 11/21/51; and Grantland Rice's "Open Letter to a College President" was in *Sport*, 5/50. The six-part series in the *New York Times* by Charles Grutzner ran from 3/18/51 through 3/23/51; the remarks by A. Whitney

Griswold appeared the first day, and the comments about Notre Dame, the fourth day. The *South Bend Tribune* carried the complete text of ND president John J. Cavanaugh's speech in December 1950 (PATH "Notre Dame Football Scrapbook, 1950"); the ND president sent a standard letter to thirteen college presidents, the one to Robert G. Sproul, 2/2/51 (UVHS 3/48). The chancellor of the University of Pittsburgh, R. H. Fitzgerald, answered Cavanaugh's letter, 2/19/51 (UVHS 3/48); and Herman B. Wells sent his reply, 2/6/51 (UVHS 3/48).

Tug Wilson (op. cit.) provided a full account of the repeated cheating of Indiana University head football coach Phil Dickens and his staff in the 1950s, pp. 299–315. Because of the almost total lack of institutional control over Dickens for a number of years, the Big Ten and the NCAA penalized IU very severely: not only was its football team barred from TV for four years but in addition all of its teams and athletes were barred from NCAA championship competition for four years.

University of Iowa president Virgil M. Hancher wrote to Father John J. Cavanaugh, 2/23/51 (UVHS 3/48). Other equivocal replies came from USC president Fred D. Fagg, 2/14/51, and SMU president Umphrey Lee, 2/22/51, both letters in (UVHS 3/48). President G. L. Cross of Oklahoma University, more concerned about his boosters and alumni than were his colleagues at SMU and USC, replied positively to Cavanaugh's proposal, 2/15/51 (UVHS 3/48); see Cross's memoir, *Presidents Can't Punt* (op. cit.), for his ongoing conflicts with his school's fanatic football supporters. The *New York Times* published a feature article on the need for reform, 11/25/51, also praising Father Cavanaugh's position in it. Judge Streit's sentencing of the basketball fixers appeared in that newspaper, 11/20/51; and *Time* magazine covered the William and Mary scandal, 9/24/51.

On page 363 of the text, Notre Dame president John J. Cavanaugh wrote to Reverend Celestin J. Steiner, S.J., about the ACE "establishing a committee," 10/31/51 (UPCC 8/26). The *New York Times* put the ACE announcement on the front page, 11/10/51; Miller and Nowak (op. cit.) discussed the main religious groups in 1950s American society, p. 84f; in the early 1950s, no major political party would consider a Catholic as a candidate for the U.S. presidency or even the vice presidency—this began to break down in 1956 when JFK came close to the VP nomination. *Sport* magazine, in "Michigan State Construction Job" by Tommy Devine, 12/53, summed up the criticism of Hannah's appointment. The *New York Times* detailed the questionable practices at SMU and the University of Washington, 3/23/51; Richard I. Miller (op. cit.) discussed the athletic programs of the other ACE presidents, pp. 202–3; and President Frederick Hovde of Purdue University wrote to Father Cavanaugh about the usefulness of an "external force," 3/10/51 (UVHS 3/48). Concerning my assertion that late 1951 marked the only time in the twentieth century when systemic change in college sports was possible: I am aware that, in 1905, President Theodore Roosevelt called some university presidents to the White House and demanded that they change college football; this prompted the rewriting of various on-field rules but it did not alter the recruiting of "tramp athletes," the subsidizing of players, and so on, i.e., it did not change an already corrupt system, it only decreased on-field violence.

For the full reference to the *Sport* article, "Michigan State Construction Job," see above; Walter Byers's comments on Hannah's "athletic bootstrapping" are in his memoir (op. cit.), pp. 41–43; and Stanley Frank in "The Big Ten's Surprise Package," the *Saturday Evening Post*, 10/14/50, quoted Hannah's "show window" metaphor. For a laudatory view of Hannah, see Paul L. Dressel's *College to University: The Hannah Years at Michigan State*, East Lansing, Michigan, 1987. Tug Wilson (op. cit.) discussed the Michigan State cheating, pp. 277–85, the quotes in the text are from those pages; the University of Michigan pushed the investigation, accusing MSU of using the state's county agricultural agents, almost all MSU grads, as football scouts and recruiters.

The *New York Times* article on the beginning of the ACE presidents inquiry appeared, 11/20/51; that paper carried the panel's major deliberations as well as the Streit story, and the AP dispatch about the NCAA, 11/21/51; for the association's "12-Point Code," see Falla's official history of the NCAA (op. cit.), pp. 135–36. Interestingly, Falla indicated that the Council drew up the twelve points on August 29, 1951—if correct, why did it wait until the first day of the ACE meeting to announce the code publicly? The NCAA history also never mentioned the ACE initiative, giving all the credit for ending the crisis and scandals to the NCAA; the historians of Orwell's Oceania in *1984* never did a better job of rewriting the record, and turning various people and groups into "unpersons."

Bert McGrane, secretary-treasurer of the Football Writers Association of America, described Walter Byers's plea to sportswriters in the FWAA Newsletter, no volume or edition number, Des Moines, Iowa, 11/26/51. An AP dispatch carried by the *New York Times* discussed Byers's appearance at the next meeting of the ACE presidents panel, and that group's negative response to the NCAA twelve-point program, 12/13/51; John Thelin (op. cit.) commented on the college presidents wanting the ACE to be separate from the NCAA, p. 109. The *New York Times* covered Lloyd Jordan's appearance before the ACE panel, 12/13/51; the ACE Minutes contain his full remarks as well as Western Reserve president John S. Millis's objection (American Council on Education Archives, Records of Special Committee on Athletic Policy, 1951, Box 6). Morris Siegal of the *Washington Post* wrote about the presidents' argument in favor of de-emphasis, 1/7/52; concerning my comment on "boys from early ages," I must remind readers that intercollegiate athletics for women did not exist in this era; women's club teams played their counterparts from other schools, but national women's intercollegiate athletics was still a number of years away. The *Commonweal* editorial appeared 12/28/51. Finally, I must thank Professor John Thelin (op. cit.) for his pioneering research on the ACE presidents' initiative; although I interpret the ACE records differently than he did, I am in his debt for directing me to them.

37. The NCAA Finds an ACE Traitor and Subverts Reform

The *Washington Post* headline and article on the ACE proposals appeared 12/14/51; Fred Digby, sports editor of the *New Orleans Item*, condemned Hannah's hypocrisy, 12/15/51; Digby, on the board of the Sugar Bowl, anticipated the ban proposal and also wrote about the situation in *Catholic Action of the South*, 11/29/51. MSU was a provisional member of the Big Ten at the time—it did not become a full member until the 1953 season—thus its excellent Spartan team could not go to the Rose Bowl and wanted to accept another bowl bid; the conference, because of its exclusive pact with the Rose Bowl, turned down this request. Tennessee's General Robert Neyland made his comments to an AP reporter, and the *Washington Post* carried the story, 12/14/51; Neyland was a general in the reserves. The article about the AP poll of "sportswriters and sportscasters" was in the *Washington Post*, 12/11/51; the AP article on Bill McColl was also in the *Washington Post*, 12/14/51, and the AP story on the SEC presidents meeting appeared in that paper, 12/15/51; the *Post* had predicted that in the SEC "generally about eight of the 12 college presidents can be expected to vote the way their athletic directors recommend," 12/14/51, but that number proved too low. The *New York Times* carried the United Press report about the accrediting agencies and the ACE explanations, 12/14/51; the *Chicago Tribune* quoted Dr. Arthur S. Adams, the head of the ACE, 1/7/52; the newspaper headline, "Accrediting Groups Offer Help," ran in the *New York Times*, 1/7/52. For background on the accreditation movement in American higher education, see Fred F. Harcleroad, *Accreditation, History, Process, and Problems*, Washington, D.C., 1980; and Kenneth Young, et al., *Understanding Accreditation*, San Francisco, 1983.

The *Chicago Tribune*'s comment on the NCAA's loss of power to the ACE appeared 1/6/52; the *Washington Post*'s headlines and articles were in its 1/8/52 edition; for an excellent discussion of the problems in the Pacific Coast Conference, see John Thelin (op. cit.), pp. 128–54; the story about the Boston Braves player was told by Bill Sullivan to Notre Dame president John J. Cavanaugh, 1/30/50 (UVHS 3/51), as was Sullivan's remark about "the morals of honest persons." Sullivan, an aide to Frank Leahy at Boston College, worked for the Braves in this period, stayed in pro sports and later founded the New England Patriots. The *New York Times* ran the headline "NCAA Plans . . . ," 1/8/52, as well as the article with Willett's admission on the "Sanity Code" implementation. The *Washington Post* had Maryland football coach Jim Tatum's condemnation of the ACE presidents, as well as Curly Byrd's forked-tongued remarks, 1/13/51.

Louisiana State athletic director T. P. "Red" Heard sounded off to the AP, published by many newspapers, including the *Chicago Tribune*, 1/11/52; that same day, a *Tribune* reporter got the anti-ACE quotes from AD Tom Hamilton of Pitt and SEC commissioner Bernie Moore. For Griswold's and other Ivy League presidents' dislike of the NCAA, and the Ivy League's de-emphasis, see John McCallum's long chapter in *Ivy League Football* (op. cit.), pp. 160–94, and John Thelin's *The Cultivation of Ivy*, Cambridge, Massachusetts, 1976, pp. 30–35; in addition, on the day of the first ACE hearing, Griswold announced a step toward de-emphasis in a *New York Times* article headlined "Yale Reveals Decision to Abandon Spring Football Practice," 11/14/51. ND president John Cavanaugh had a parallel agenda plus the fact that at this convention he was also fighting the impending NCAA TV monopoly; see Chapters 39 and 40 here.

The *Washington Post* headlined "No Compromise with NCAA," as well as John Hannah's declaration, 1/11/52; for Hannah's note to NCAA president Hugh Willett, and a similar one to Walter Byers, see (American Council on Education Archives, Records of Special Committee on Athletic Policy, 1951, Box 6). The *Washington Post* reported the closed door meeting between Hannah and the NCAA officials, 1/11/52. The *New York Times* carried Willett's reassurances, 1/11/52; that paper had the headline "NCAA Maps . . . ," as well as the NCAA's perfunctory PR resolution, and Allison Danzig's interpretation on 1/13/51. The *Chicago Tribune* reported on Willett's triumphal conclusions, 1/13/52, and on the North Central Accrediting Agency's agreement with the ACE presidents, 1/8/52; in the latter article, sportswriter Wilfred Smith noted, overoptimistically, that the accrediting agency's "plan for control of intercollegiate athletics . . . is so drastic that it must spur the NCAA to action" on reform.

Pressure on Hannah not only came from the rabid Spartan Foundation but also from his powerful football coach, Clarence "Biggie" Munn. In a speech at this time, Biggie declared that "I would rather have my son be a football player than a Phi Beta Kappa. You learn democracy and Americanism in the game of football," and, by implication, not in Phi Beta Kappa! Richard I. Miller (op. cit.) quoted Munn's pronouncement, p. 34; for a profile of Munn in this period, see Bill Fay's article in *Collier's*, "King of the Football Forest," 9/17/52. Jack Falla's official NCAA history (op. cit.) carried the self-congratulation about the 1952 legislation, p. 136; and the *New York Times's* Arthur Daley did his column, 1/15/52, featuring a large photo of Hannah. The main columnist for the AP, Hugh Fullerton Jr., had a more thoughtful postconvention piece, published by many papers, including the *Washington Post*, 1/14/52.

38. ND President Cavanaugh Reacts to the ACE Failure

Arch Ward's criticisms of the NCAA appeared in the *Chicago Tribune*, 1/14/52; Joe Doyle's article about Notre Dame's reaction to the ACE proposal was in the *South Bend Tribune*, 2/52 (PATH "Notre Dame Basketball Scrapbook, 1951–53"); and the AP ran an article about the continuation of the Rose Bowl game despite the NCAA's supposed interest in banning bowl games, the *Washington Post*, 1/12/52.

On page 378 of the text, Frank Leahy wrote to Executive Vice President Theodore M. Hesburgh about spring practice, 2/5/52 (UVHS 3/6), and Hesburgh replied, 2/8/52 (UVHS 3/6). The *New York Times* discussed the Griswold-Cavanaugh alliance in its report on the first meeting of the ACE presidents, 11/14/51; the minutes of the panel's meetings show the Yale–Notre Dame agreement on almost every issue, particularly their insistence on banning bowl games (American Council on Education Archives, Records of Special Committee on Athletic Policy, 1951, Box 6). Walter Byers, who should have appreciated all that Hannah did for his association but disliked him personally, described Hannah's technique in his memoir (op. cit.), p. 43. For histories on the 1952 events in the Ivy League, see the references above to McCallum, *Ivy League Football*, and Thelin, *Cultivation of Ivy*. The *New York Times* article, "Ivy League De-emphasizes," with NCAA president Hugh Willet's response appeared 2/19/52.

On page 380 of the text, Notre Dame president John J. Cavanaugh gave his confidential opinion about the ACE panel to Joe Williams, *New York World Telegram*, 3/31/52 (UPCC 8/28); the ND president offered his pessimistic assessment of big-time college sports to Reverend Celestin J. Steiner, S.J., 10/31/51 (UPCC 8/26). Francis Wallace mocked the hypocrisy of the majority of ACE presidents in his "Pigskin Preview" for *Collier's*, 8/30/52; the president of Brigham Young University, Ernest L. Wilkinson, wrote the words quoted in the text, 5/8/52; his and other presidential letters are in (American Council on Education Archives, Records of Special Committee on Athletic Policy, 1951, Box 6). Tug Wilson (op. cit.) discussed MSU's probation, p. 284; and Walter Byers (op. cit.) outlined the aftermath at MSU, p. 45, as well as his condemnation of the hypocrisy of presidents who serve on panels like the ACE's, pp. 47–48. *Sport's* article, "Michigan State Construction Job" (op. cit.), provided the summary of the ACE-Hannah episode, 12/53; and Fred Russell in his "Pigskin Preview" for the *Saturday Evening Post* offered the pessimistic retrospective, 9/11/54. Finally, Paul Lawrence connected the NCAA's 1952 triumph to its increasing cartel status, pp. 51–52; even a conservative sports historian like Benjamin Rader agrees with the cartel analysis, see the section, "The NCAA Becomes a Cartel," in his *American Sports: From the Age of Folk Games to the Age of*

Televised Sports, Englewood Cliffs, New Jersey, 1990, p. 267f. In addition, the University of Chicago Press, a leading publisher of economic treatises, brought out *The National Collegiate Athletic Association: A Study in Cartel Behavior*, by economists Arthur A. Fleisher, Brian L. Goff, and Robert D. Tollison, in 1992.

39. The NCAA Battles Notre Dame on TV Rights: Opening Round

Notre Dame executive vice president Theodore M. Hesburgh enclosed his summary of the televising of Fighting Irish games in a letter to T. B. Payseur, athletic director of Northwestern University, 12/22/49 (UVHS 3/51). Edward "Moose" Krause, Notre Dame AD at the time, made his remarks about radio in an article he wrote for the INS (International News Service), n.d. (PATH "Notre Dame Football Scrapbook, 1951–53"). In addition to Notre Dame's radio policy of accommodating all national broadcasters for reasonable fees, Joe Boland, a Rockne-era ND player and an assistant coach under Elmer Layden, started "The Irish Football Network" out of WSBT, South Bend, Indiana, in 1947. Charging minimal rates, Boland, who also did the announcing, put together about forty stations by 1951; his network grew considerably after that until, in 1956, it evolved into Mutual Radio's coverage of Fighting Irish games; see *Joe Boland—Notre Dame Man*, ed. Peg Boland, Hammond, Indiana, 1962, pp. 100–103. Notre Dame vice president John H. Murphy explained his school's "decision to televise our football games over as wide a network as possible" to J. A. Holmes, 5/23/50 (UVHS 3/58); Murphy also outlined the policy on newsreel films to executive vice president Theodore M. Hesburgh, 11/9/49 (UVHS 3/57). The AP discussed the television payouts to Notre Dame in the late 1940s, n.d. (PATH "Notre Dame Football Scrapbook, 1951–53"); Fred Russell, in his "Pigskin Preview" for the *Saturday Evening Post*, had the $160,000 figure for the 1950 season, 9/9/50; the 1950 payout was for the four games at Notre Dame Stadium and the game against Navy in Cleveland. Moose Krause's comments about "sidelight stories" came in a press release under Krause's name, and also signed by Charlie Callahan, sent to Larry Wolters, television editor of the *Chicago Tribune*, 9/6/50 (UASI 2/12); Krause's comment about the lower bid from Dumont, and his remarks about the halftime promos came in an interview (op. cit.).

On page 385 of the text, Dumont executive Leslie G. Arries wrote about the "half-time interviews" in a letter to ND executive vice president Theodore M. Hesburgh, 1/19/50 (UVHS 3/58). Father John H. Murphy, ND vice president for public relations at the time, explained the halftime films on "the non-athletic features of the University" to Purdue University president Frederick L. Hovde, 8/4/50 (UVHS 3/61) because the Boilermakers were scheduled to play at Notre Dame on 10/7/50 (they ended the Fighting Irish undefeated streak that day). The Dumont Television Network press release is dated 9/22/50, and in (UASI 2/12). The Notre Dame film synopses are in a document titled "Suggestions Concerning Television Programming—1950," n.d. (UASI 2/12); the quoted shooting script is titled, "Under the Golden Dome, Script No. 1," and is in (UVHS 3/61). Frank Leahy's comments on "83% of all the television sets in the country" were in a Dumont Television Network press release draft sent to Charlie Callahan by Gerald Lyons, 10/7/50 (UASI 2/12). AP writer Hugh Fullerton Jr. wrote about the conflict between Notre Dame and the Big Ten, 5/20/50, which was carried by many papers, including the *Washington Post;* and Fred Russell, in his 1950 "Pigskin Preview" (op. cit.), used Grantland Rice's famous stanza, 9/9/50.

On page 387 of the text, for the letter from Tug Wilson to Notre Dame vice president Theodore M. Hesburgh, 3/31/50, see (UVHS 3/58). Northwestern AD Ted Payseur made his comments at the 1950 NCAA Convention, see its minutes in the *Yearbook*, p. 119–20; Bert Bell's comments were in a *Sports Illustrated* column by Lyall Smith, 10/4/54; Ken Rappoport quoted Dutch Lonberg in *The Classic* (op. cit.), p. 59; Michigan AD Fritz Crisler's comments came at the 1951 NCAA Convention, see the *Yearbook*, p. 124; and Father Hesburgh often made his "public service" argument, including in an AP interview, n.d. but probably early 1951 (PATH "Notre Dame Football Scrapbook, 1951–53"), and at the NCAA Convention a year later, *Yearbook*, p. 145. The NORC report appeared in the Minutes of the 1951 Convention, *Yearbook*, p. 145f; the NCAA and the NORC survey also claimed that in 1950, football attendance had actually increased by "9.3 percent in areas without televised games" and, forever after, the association based much of its argument on this single statistic. However, again NORC and the NCAA did not consider any other possible factors in their equation. The conferences with the greatest attendance increase from the 1947–48 baseline were the Southwest (39 percent), and the Big

Seven (23 percent). Economically, because of the continuing prosperity in the oil business, these areas avoided the economic dip of the late 1940s and early 1950; also, these schools benefited from the many new highways in their region, and, as importantly, the quality of play at Oklahoma, Texas, SMU, and most other conference members jumped significantly in this period; even Rice and TCU had nationally ranked teams. Finally, if the NORC/NCAA claim of increased attendance in areas without TV had been valid, then the conference in the region with the fewest TV stations, TV sets, and televised games in America should have shown a large increase—however, the Mountain Conference (forerunner to the WAC) had a 15 percent decrease, mainly because of the economic slowdown, poor roads, poor teams, and such factors.

Benjamin Rader in *In Its Own Image* (op. cit.) discussed the "stunned delegates," p. 70, as well as "the Great Sports Slump," p. 33; and Paul Lawrence (op. cit.) commented upon the importance of "this resolution" for the NCAA, p. 77. When football attendance finally increased, the NCAA attributed the growth solely to its restrictive TV policy; see Falla (op. cit.), pp. 110–11. Amherst professor Albert E. Lumley wrote "The Intercollegiate Athletics Scandals" for the *American Scholar*, spring 1952; Penn AD Francis T. Murray spoke at every NCAA Convention from 1949 through 1953 about the association's TV policy; in 1951 he pointed out that NORC failed to factor in the unusually bad weather for many Saturdays in many locations during the 1950 season and, in many cases, attendance fell below tickets sold, but NORC only considered the former number; see *Yearbook*, p. 197–99.

For the 1951 resolution by NCAA Television Committee chair Thomas Hamilton, see the *Yearbook*, p. 203; and for Father Hesburgh's criticism of the delegates, as well as his warning on ND's future course of action, see the same source, pp. 144–45. Wilfred Smith in the *Chicago Tribune* wrote about the resolution, and Moose Krause's reaction, 1/13/51. New York television executive Edgar Kobak sent a summary of "our several hours of conversation on the subject of Notre Dame Football and television" to ND president John J. Cavanaugh, 2/19/51 (UVHS 3/60). The comments of Moose Krause about the money lost when ND accepted the NCAA's TV policy appeared in an INS (International News Service) article headlined "Notre Dame Lost Million, Moose Claims," n.d. but, from internal evidence, definitely 1953 (PATH "Notre Dame Football Scrapbook, 1951–53").

On page 392 of the text, ND president Cavanaugh's comments about "educational programs" came in his letter to fellow university presidents (op. cit.), e.g. to Chancellor Robert Sproul of the University of California, 2/2/51 (UVHS 3/48). The superintendent of the Naval Academy, Vice Admiral H. W. Hill, responded, "I was very much impressed by the educational program which you [at Notre Dame] were conducting last year in connection with your pre-game broadcasts," and said that he intended to institute similar ones for Navy football telecasts, 2/10/51 (UVHS 3/48). Moose Krause's comments about Father Cavanaugh's sense of the NCAA's demise came in an interview (op. cit.); the ND president's invocation of the NCAA constitution appeared in many newspapers, including in an editorial in the *Fort Worth (Texas) Star-Telegram*, 6/21/51; and Charlie Callahan printed the full text of Cavanaugh's statement in *OSV*, 7/1/51. Jack Falla's official NCAA history (op. cit.) explained the association's postconvention reversal on the TV blackout policy, p. 103. Because of the increasing public protests about the NCAA's restrictive TV policy, some college presidents believed, according to Purdue's Frederick Hovde, that "regardless of what we [presidents] would like to do about it, the problem will be solved by the American public. Already the legislatures of three of our Midwest states have had bills introduced to force the state-supported universities to televise their athletic contests," Hovde to Cavanaugh, 3/10/51 (UVHS 3/48). These presidents, like many others, underestimated the tenacity of NCAA officials and their ability to triumph over all opponents.

Beano Cook was quoted by Tim Layden in the *Boston Globe*, 9/2/90, about Notre Dame's first TV contract; in addition, Cook remarked that "the NCAA was organized in the early 1950s to obtain control of television for the specific purpose of preventing Notre Dame from being seen coast to coast." Paul Lawrence (op. cit.) commented on the "division of the marketplace," and discussed the Penn protest, pp. 78–79; many schools, in addition to their NCAA-induced fears of televising games, blamed their attendance woes on the Notre Dame TV network, regarding a "yes" vote as a way to abolish it. The *Billboard* magazine article appeared 5/26/51.

On page 394 of the text, for the letter from Fred L. Steers to Father Hesburgh about the phone conversation with Tug Wilson, 6/15/51, see (UVHS 3/60). In addition to Lawrence's discussion of Penn's capitulation (op. cit.), p. 78, see Francis Wallace's comments in his "Pigskin Preview" for *Collier's*, 9/15/51. ND president John J. Cavanaugh's remarks about his school's having "nothing whatsoever to say about the televising of the football games" came in a letter to Galvin Hudson, 9/14/51

(UPCC 10/6). The *Washington Post* ran a headline, "Public Demands Notre Dame and Michigan State Game TV Here," 11/8/51; and the *Post* explained the background of the situation in various articles that day, quoted politicians, and also placed Shirley Povich's column above the fold.

On page 396 of the text, Father Hesburgh wrote to Robert D. McAuliffe about the blackout in South Bend, 11/12/51 (UVHS 3/60); Moose Krause commented on the "dancing lightbulbs" in an interview (op. cit.); the usually mellow Mr. Krause became vituperative when remembering the fight with the NCAA over the first TV contract. The *New York Times* ran an AP article on Penn's challenge at the coming 1952 convention, 11/20/51; for a discussion of the 1984 United States Supreme Court decision, see my *College Sports Inc.* (op. cit.), pp. 49–52, and the *Chronicle of Higher Education,* 3/28/84 and 7/5/84—the latter article contains the full text of the decision. For a capsule presentation of the arguments in the early 1950s, see the *Sport* magazine pro-and-con debate between Arch Ward, representing the Notre Dame position, "We Want Football on TV," 11/52, and Asa Bushnell, NCAA official and Walter Byers's main ally on the TV Committee, "Our Side of the TV Battle," 3/53.

40. The NCAA Battles Notre Dame on TV Rights: TKO

Paul Lawrence's comments about Notre Dame and Penn losing to the NCAA are in his book (op. cit.), p. 83; Moose Krause's witty remarks were in the *New York Times,* 1/4/53; and Jack Falla's official NCAA history (op. cit.) gave the party line on the 1952 TV decisions, pp. 103–8, with the spin on the NORC figures, p. 108. Because Falla faithfully reproduces the NCAA position of the time, for once his constant use of the present tense works rhetorically and gives the reader a you-are-there sense of listening to the NCAA's early-1950s propaganda. Allison Danzig of the *New York Times* reported Francis T. Murray's speech, 1/10/52; for Murray's full text on the U.S. Attorney, see the NCAA *Yearbook* for the 1952 Convention, p. 172; also in the latter source are Joseph Rauh's reply, pp. 175–77, and Professor Ralph Aigler's reassurances, p. 179. Allison Danzig of the *New York Times* reported and commented on Murray's amendment, 1/11/52.

On page 400 of the text, for the letter from Associated Press writer Hugh Fullerton Jr. to Charlie Callahan about the NCAA TV Committee meeting, 4/23/52, see (UASI 4/5). The 1952 NCAA convention had set up a mail ballot referendum to vote on the final form of the plan; Byers maneuvered the 1952 TV plan, and subsequent ones, into a take-it-or-leave-it proposition: either accept what the committee offered—with some goodies for most members—or return to step one and redo the entire policy. Because the committee offered the plan in June 1952, three months before the opening game, the member schools overwhelmingly approved it in a referendum vote. For the 1952 plan, see Falla (op. cit.), pp. 103–8; and for ND president Cavanaugh's protest to Walter Byers, 6/10/51 (UVHS 3/53). Walter Byers, in his autobiography (op. cit.), claims that Fritz Crisler backed the share-the-wealth plan, and that Notre Dame fought it out of greed and foolishness, pp. 81–83; but considering Crisler's frequent public statements about his desire to make money for his own and other Big Ten athletic departments, to claim his patronage of it seems far-fetched. More likely here, as elsewhere in his book, Byers underplays his own Machiavellian talents and triumphs.

Notre Dame AD Moose Krause's condemnation of the TV policy came in a speech to the "Tuesday Quarterback Club" of South Bend, Indiana, *South Bend Tribune,* 10/22/52. For more information on the University of Notre Dame's independence, see the index entry of "history" under "Notre Dame du Lac" in my *Shake Down the Thunder* (op. cit.). The *Notre Dame Alumnus* article, "Father Hesburgh New President of Notre Dame," 8–9/52, explained the changes in the ND administration. Executive Vice President Joyce's statement on the NCAA share-the-TV-wealth plan appeared in the *South Bend Tribune,* 11/26/52; that newspaper also ran the headline, "Irish Won't Defy NCAA Stand on TV," and the article, n.d. but from internal evidence 12/52, (PATH "Notre Dame Football Scrapbook, 1952"); that article also mentioned the rumor by *Chicago Daily News* reporter Jack Ryan. Francis Wallace discussed the long-simmering plan to form "a TV League" in his "Pigskin Preview" for *Collier's,* 7/18/53.

Jack Falla's official NCAA history (op. cit.) gave the NORC figures for the 1952 season, and the tortured rationale, p. 108; the *South Bend Tribune* quoted the full *Chicago Herald-American* poll in an article, n.d. but from internal evidence the first week in 1953 (PATH "Notre Dame Football Scrapbook, 1953"); Penn AD Francis T. Murray put it in the NCAA record during the 1953 Convention, *Yearbook,* p. 176. The *South Bend Tribune* printed the full text of President Hesburgh's open letter to the 1953 NCAA Convention delegates, n.d. but, from internal evidence, the first week in 1953 (PATH "Notre Dame Football Scrapbook, 1953"). For Father Joyce's initial speech at the 1953 NCAA Convention, see the *Yearbook,* pp. 187–89, and for his comments in the formal debate, pp. 228–33. The NCAA leadership's concession to Notre Dame on theater TV seemed typically hypocritical: considering the popularity of the Fighting Irish, substantial theater attendance for their games in certain cities had to have an impact on the gate receipts of teams playing nearby at the same time—another instance of the NCAA's convenient memory lapses on its only-television-ruins-attendance line. Beano Cook later explained that "the heavy population of Irish Catholics in major cities in the East and Midwest . . . assured a huge following" for any Notre Dame TV network and, in its absence, the theater TV games, *Boston Globe* (op. cit.). Richard I. Miller (op. cit.) predicted "the days of free TV football are numbered," p. 138; and Francis Wallace in his 1953 "Pigskin Preview" (op. cit.) explained Notre Dame's current TV situation.

41. Hollywood and College Sports in the Early 1950s

The scenes and dialogue in the films discussed in this chapter are based on the prints of the movies held by the Library of Congress, not to 16-millimeter prints still in existence or videotape copies. In viewing various versions of these films, I noticed that some of the 16mm and videotape copies contain less footage and shorter running times than the Library of Congress prints. Beginning in the early 1950s, after a studio completed a film, it sent a print to the Library of Congress in Washington, D.C.; thus, these prints are, as close as possible, the definitive versions. The corrupt 16mm and videotape copies resulted from editing for television presentation at some point in their histories, either for reasons of censorship or, more frequently, time constraints, possibly even some copyright issues—as with the famous edited versions of *Knute Rockne—All-American,* which were missing the "Win One for the Gipper" speech and some other scenes. Hence, for scholarly reasons, I refer to the Library of Congress prints unless otherwise noted.

The quote from Douglas T. Miller and Marion Nowak (op. cit.) appeared at the beginning of their excellent chapter, "Hollywood in Transition," p. 315f; because television was a medium that entered people's living rooms, early programming was heavily self-censored and perpetuated Hollywood classical film values. Jeanine Basinger, in *The World War II Combat Film* (op. cit.), discussed Samuel Fuller's Korean War films, p. 181; and Barbara Klinger, in "Cinema/Ideology/Criticism Revisited: The Progressive Genre," anthologized in the *Film Genre Reader* (op. cit.), defined the world view of revisionist films, pp. 80–81.

George Gipe (op. cit.) summarized the reviewers' reaction to the cynicism in *Saturday's Hero,* as well as its box office success "nurtured by a variety of sports scandals," p. 264. The *Variety* review appeared 8/22/51; reviewers at the time and subsequently did not see *Saturday's Hero* or other sports film in terms of Hollywood's genre cinema, but, of course, these films existed very much within that tradition. John Crosby, the radio and TV critic of the *New York Herald-Tribune,* commented on the old-time football movies, 11/30/51; Wiley Lee Umphlett (op. cit.) discussed the "atypically bleak ending" of *Saturday's Hero,* p. 101; and Bosley Crowther's *New York Times* review appeared 9/12/51. That newspaper outlined Millard Lampell's writing career and his work on *Saturday's Hero,* as well as the anti-Communist picketing, in an article by Murray Schumach, "Studio Buys Film by 'Subversives,' " 2/9/60.

On page 415 of the text, a copy of the Columbia Pictures publicity release for *Saturday's Hero,* titled "Exclusive in Your Area," is in Charlie Callahan's files in the Notre Dame Archives, circa 1951 (UASI 3/54); the comments from Callahan, Leahy, and Woodward are also in the file. In addition, the publicity release noted that West Point allowed a screening, ironically at the service academy "a few hours after the [cribbing] scandal broke." Apparently, Army assistant coaches "Doc Blanchard and Arnold Tucker, All-Americans, were too flabbergasted to offer praise or criticism."

New York Times film reviewer Oscar Godbout discussed *The Basketball Fix,* 9/14/51; the *Variety* review appeared 9/19/51; and film historian Leslie Halliwell described John Ireland in *The Filmgoer's Companion,* 3rd edition, New York, 1970, p. 511. A. W. Weiler reviewed *Trouble Along the Way* for the *New York Times,* 5/7/53; according to the Arts & Entertainment TV biography of John Wayne, 3/28/98, he had become the "Number One box office star" the year before. The *Variety* review appeared 3/18/53; Thomas Schatz explained the mixed-form phenomenon in *Hollywood Genres* (op. cit.), p. 35; and Wiley Umphlett commented on the new type ending of *Trouble Along the Way,*

p. 102. Neither Schatz nor any other film scholar uses the term "mixed-form" (I take the credit or the blame for inventing it), nor do the critics explore the concept in detail—yet it is crucial to understanding media representations of college sports.

42. Mixed-Form Films Become the Norm

Social critic Reuel Denney commented about college football in a collection of essays, *The Astonished Muse*, New Brunswick, New Jersey, 1957, p. 102; the quotation here is from "The Decline of Lyric Sport," which, from internal evidence, appears to have been written in 1953. Denney's best-known work is his collaboration on the 1950s best-seller, *The Lonely Crowd*, New Haven, Connecticut, 1950, with David Reisman and Nathan Glazer. David Halbertstam in *The Fifties* (op. cit.) described the work of advertising wizard Rosser Reeves in shaping the 1952 presidential campaign of General Eisenhower, p. 224f. Frank Gifford, in his memoir *The Whole Ten Yards*, New York, 1993, discussed his work on both *Saturday's Hero* and *The All-American*, pp. 68–70; Cotton Warburton, a leading Hollywood film editor during the 1940s and 1950s, helped out his USC buddies on this picture, but because he was under contract to another studio at the time, his name did not appear on the credit list.

The *Variety* review of *The All-American* appeared 3/23/53; and Wiley Umphlett (op. cit.) discussed its "rah-rah" elements, pp. 101–2; Mamie Van Doren played the blonde sexpot. *New York Times* film critic A. H. Weiler reviewed *Jim Thorpe—All-American*, 8/25/51, and the *Variety* review appeared 6/20/51. The ending trope of helping-out-the-kids is still used in mixed-form films, including *Blue Chips* (1994), written by the current master of mixed-form sports films, Ron Shelton.

Jack Newcombe wrote an outstanding book about Jim Thorpe, his Carlisle contemporaries, and Glenn "Pop" Warner, *The Best of the Athletic Boys: The White Man's Impact on Jim Thorpe*, Garden City, New York, 1975; his "Epilogue" sums up Warner's downfall at Carlisle, and the quote about Welch is on p. 242. Newcombe also discussed Thorpe's playing summer baseball on p. 98f; "the direct cash bonuses to the regular football players," p. 120; and Pop's less than outraged reaction to the Olympic Committee's stripping Thorpe of his medals, p. 208f. Rockne made his comment about Warner "changing legal names to Indian names" in *The Autobiography of Knute Rockne*, ghosted by John B. Kennedy, *Collier's*, six installments from 11/1/30 through 12/6/30; the discussion of Warner appeared 11/8/30. In 1914, a congressional committee investigated Carlisle; Warner did not like the reforms that it imposed upon the school or the criticisms of his methods and, in February 1915, he moved on to Pitt; see Tom Perrin (op. cit.), p. 83. The *Washington Post* did an obituary of the founder of Pop Warner football, Joseph J. Tomlin, and explained the genesis and growth of his creation, 5/19/88. To reinforce Warner's probity in *Jim Thorpe*, the producers cast Charles Bickford as the coach; film historian Leslie Halliwell (op. cit.) described Bickford as "one of the great Hollywood *dependables*, he effortlessly projected men of rugged and thoughtful sincerity," p. 112. The filmmakers privilege Pop Warner from the opening frame with a shot of him towering above the banquet dais, appearing omnipotent and, when he becomes the Voice-of-God narrator of the film, omniscient. Who could believe that Pop Warner had cheated at Carlisle and all the other stops in his coaching career?

43. The Temporary Return of Classical Football Films

The *Variety* reviewer considered Crazylegs Hirsch as "likable and credible," 9/30/53; *Sport* magazine printed a film publicity photo of Hirsch embracing co-star Joan Vohs, 1/54; and actor Lloyd Nolan, a younger version of Charles Bickford, played Hirsch's coach, Win Brockmeyer.

Wiley Umphlett (op. cit.) commented on *The Long Gray Line* as "The last of the [school] 'spirit' movies," p. 97, and on its "old-fashioned" quality, p. 96. Tag Gallagher's book, *John Ford: The Man and His Films*, Berkeley, California, 1986, is the most comprehensive work on the director, and the quote here is on p. 324, as is the comment on Maher's memoir as an "almost unreadable collection"; also useful, particularly for its excellent photos of *The Long Gray Line*, is J. A. Place's *The Non-Western Films of John Ford*, Secaucus, New Jersey, 1979. However, neither of these writers, nor any other Ford critics, mention the "Cribbing Scandal" subtext of the film. Producer Jerry Wald discussed the film's genesis in a *New York Times* article, 6/20/54, and the problems of film production, including dealing with the U.S. military, in "Movies in America," in the *American Forum*, 8/26/56.

Variety found the Ford film "frankly sentimental" etc., 2/9/55. In the scenes with President Eisenhower, the audience only sees the back of Ike's head at his desk in the Oval Office; in this era, the president of the United States did not appear in commercial Hollywood movies, no matter how flattering to him or his beliefs, and an actor playing the highly recognizable president would have been distracting, hence the rear shot. However, an actor does play the young Ike in the film.

For a full description of the first Notre Dame–Army game, see Chapter 6 in my *Shake Down the Thunder* (op. cit.), pp. 37–42; the comments and footnotes on the genesis of the forward pass are also in that chapter. The 1913 Notre Dame student newspaper, the *Scholastic,* collected its issues into one volume; for the mock headline, "Darwin's Original" et al., see p. 79. Marty Maher, in his memoir *Bringing Up the Brass: My 55 Years at West Point,* written with Nardi Reeder Campion, New York, 1951, discussed the first ND–Army game in the chapter, "The Irish of Notre Dame," and his specific comment on Rockne is on p. 149. In *The Long Gray Line,* John Ford does not even allow Charlie Daly to coach Army, but he assigns that duty to the Ward Bond character, Col. Herman J. Koehler, Master of the Sword, and Marty's boss. But again, this misconstrues John Ford's intention, his lack of interest in documentary-like realism, and his fascination with an ideal world. On a winter day, for example, when Marty enters his house, he does not brush real snow from his coat, but huge white flakes of an obviously synthetic material, invoking a surrealistic winter snowier than any ever experienced.

44. Fan Pleasure: The Return of One-Platoon

New York Times columnist Arthur Daley praised the return of one-platoon, 1/9/53; Fred Russell in his "Pigskin Preview" for the *Saturday Evening Post,* 9/15/51, discussed the PCC opposition to unlimited substitution; Richard I. Miller (op. cit.) analyzed the situations of the schools dropping out of big-time football, p. 4f; and the Rev. Hunter Guthrie, S.J., president of Georgetown, gave the reasons for his school's departure in the *Saturday Evening Post,* 10/13/51. *Newsweek* summed up the efforts by small colleges within the NCAA to abolish unlimited substitution, 1/26/53; Allison Danzig of the *New York Times* reported on the coaches' vote, 1/8/53; the *Times* also carried an AP report on the meeting of the NCAA Football Rules Committee in St. Petersburg, Florida, 1/13/53, and the quotes from the members.

The *New York Times* front-page article on the return to one-platoon, along with the photos and quotes appeared 1/15/53; Grantland Rice lauded the rule change in an AP report, n.d. but, from internal evidence 1/53 (PATH "Notre Dame Football Scrapbook, 1953"), and repeated his comments in his "Football Forecast" for *Look* magazine, 9/22/53. The *Sport* editorial appeared 11/53; Arthur Daley (op. cit.) invoked the fans in his 1/9/53 column and, a week later, 1/16/53, repeated his exultation over the rule change. Columbia's Lou Little endorsed the change and Ohio State's Woody Hayes condemned it in a *New York Times* article, 1/15/53; *Life* magazine ran a major photo spread on the Army-Navy game. "Big Game's Big Look," 12/6/54; and even the increasingly revisionist *Saturday Evening Post* liked the service academies enough to do "Football's Biggest Show," 11/26/55. But the major magazines did not neglect the new Air Force Academy when it entered big-time college sports: *Life* did "Air Force Falcons Soar into the Big Time," 12/8/58; and *Look,* "Football Falcons Will Fly High," 11/10/59.

Michigan State coach Clarence "Biggie" Munn sounded off to Bill Fay for his article, "Will the Fans Go for One-Platoon Football This Fall?" in *Collier's,* 9/4/53; Richard I. Miller (op. cit.), commented about the "average fan" on p. 108; Red Grange stated his liking for unlimited substitution in many newspaper and radio interviews at this time; however, his fullest articulation of his position occurred in "I Couldn't Make the Varsity Today," with Bill Fay, *Collier's,* 11/25/52. Fred Russell, in his "Pigskin Preview" for the *Saturday Evening Post,* predicted that many coaches will "employ Rock's 'shock-troops' idea" and stated, "Seldom has any sport undergone such a drastic revision," 9/12/53. For Rockne's use of shock troops, see the entries in the index of my *Shake Down the Thunder* (op. cit.) under Rockne's "coaching techniques." For Grantland Rice's 1953 "Forecast," see *Look,* 9/22/53; Francis Wallace in his 1954 "Preview" for *Collier's* discussed the NCAA Football Rules Committee's shift, 9/17/54; Tom Perrin (op. cit.) explained Hayes's technique and influence, and the dullness of the game in this period, pp. 265–71; and John McCallum in his history of the Big Ten (op. cit.) quoted Herman Hickman on the "third platoon," p. 102. Richard I. Miller (op. cit.) made his impossibly optimistic prediction about the future of college sports, p. 119.

45. Programs as Propaganda—When Needed Most

For Walter Byers's comments about his invention of the term "student-athlete," see his memoir (op. cit.), pp. 69–70; Byers scrambles his chronology, presenting the punchline about his creation of the term *before* the events that prompted it; the story makes more sense in cause-and-effect order, and I have done it that way here. For a discussion of potential IRS definitions of athletic scholarships, see *College Sports Inc.* (op. cit.), pp. 204–5; Howard Levine, the editor of "The Third Annual Directory of Sports Information Directors," sent his bulletin to Charlie Callahan, 1/13/55 (UASI 7/48). The Notre Dame publicist advised colleagues about mutating "the dope book" into the public "preview guide"; see his letter exchange with Navy publicist John Cox, 3/4/54, and 4/15/54 (UASI 5/75).

For the discussion of the cataloguing of the football program covers, see the footnotes above, particularly for Chapters 10 and 29; the cover with the QB submerged by textbooks is in the illustrations of this book. The poem "Profs and Players" appeared in the newsletter of the Football Writers Association of America, 7/29/52; Bert McGrane of the *Des Moines Register* was the longtime secretary-treasurer of the FWAA, and wrote the newsletters in the 1950s, always beginning with what he termed a "pome," purposely misspelling "poem" as part of his folk humor. McGrane did not put a volume or issue number on the newsletters, considering them casual handouts for his fellow football writers. However, this ad hoc approach bolsters their credibility as evidence on how sportswriters discussed college sports in private, away from the public print. McGrane sent out the "Heck of a half-back" "pome," 9/23/52.

On page 449 of the text, Charlie Callahan sent his "brief report" of the college sports publicists' meeting to Moose Krause, 2/5/51 (USIA 3/10); in that report, Callahan also noted the conclusion about "a good cover" selling programs. In the 1950s Americans became aware of the power of Madison Avenue; one of the surprise best-sellers was Vance Packard's *Hidden Persuaders*, New York, 1957. Father Edmund Joyce supplied me with the complete text of his speech about the findings of his research into Notre Dame graduation statistics, he delivered the speech on 12/9/54. John Cackley described the genesis of the survey in his article, "The Notre Dame Athlete," in the *Notre Dame Alumnus*, 1–2/1955. Many years later, looking back on the first survey, Father Joyce mentioned that *Sports Illustrated* eventually ran a story about it—two years later (9/24/56 and 10/1/56)—and "they were so skeptical about the results of my survey that they spent a lot of time and money in contacting players . . . What they discovered corroborated the accuracy of the original survey" (letter from Father Edmund Joyce to Murray Sperber, 9/12/95).

The *Life* article, "Big Game of the Year," on the Notre Dame–Army contest appeared 10/20/58; John T. Brady, in *The Heisman: A Symbol of Excellence,* New York, 1984, quoted Dawkins's frequent comment on a "Cadet first and a football player second," p. 116. For a copy of Charles Loftus's paean, see the program of the Oklahoma–Notre Dame game, 11/8/52. Bob Fendell discussed the plans of the Hall of Fame in "They'll Live at Dear Old Rutgers," *Sport,* 4/52, and the following year, the NCAA accepted the "Hall of Fame game" proposal and started to implement it. Chester J. LaRoche's attack on Conant and Commager came in the 1/26/61 "Minutes of Executive Committee Meeting" of the National Football Foundation and Hall of Fame, held at the Racquet & Tennis Club in Manhattan, New York; LaRoche's attack on the University of Chicago and General MacArthur's reply are in the 4/19/61 minutes of that group.

46. College Sports Publicists and Sportswriters: Symbiosis Squared

New York Times sportswriter Pete Brandwein wrote to Charlie Callahan, 11/2/51 (UASI 3/29); and Callahan replied, 11/8/51 (UASI 3/29); for an indication of Allison Danzig's acceptance of NCAA "spins" and handouts, see his work at the 1952 NCAA Convention, p. 380. Richard I. Miller (op. cit.) commented about sports media, p. 192; Joan Konner, dean emeritus, Columbia University, discussed the "blurring of distinctions" in a letter to *Rolling Stone* magazine, 12/11/97; and ND sports information director Roger Valdiserri offered his insights in an interview, 3/13/91. The *ACPRA [American College Public Relations Association] News Letter,* Vol. II, No. 8, published the material on "football trips," 9/15/54; sports publicists formed a group within ACPRA before they set up their own organization, CoSIDA. Fred Stabley, MSU sports publicist, wrote the directive, "Michigan State Press and Radio Outlets for Football—1952," to Charlie Callahan, 9/4/52 (UASI 4/86). University of

Pittsburgh sports publicist Bob Wycoff sent "Who to See in Pittsburgh" to Charlie Callahan, 8/17/54 (UASI 5/69), and the comments about George Kiseda and John Golightly are in it. The Pitt tip sheet was particularly good at making distinctions among writers and discussing their different approaches, e.g., for the *Post-Gazette,* "columnist Al Abrams . . . is sports editor and conducts a daily column. He probably won't use as much as Smith and Keck [columnists on rival papers] but he'll be receptive nevertheless."

On page 461 of the text, Carroll H. "Beano" Cook wrote to Charlie Callahan about the perils of an Ivy League education, 7/17/60 (UASI 13/97). Charlie Callahan sent "a couple of items for The Wake" to Arch Ward, 9/10/50 (UASI 2/6); Callahan followed with the Paul Reynolds item to Ward, 8/20/52 (UASI 4/99), and the Jack Mayo one to George Strickler, subbing for Ward, 5/15/52 (UASI 4/20); Strickler added the "81% average in Engineering" when he printed the item (PATH "Notre Dame Football Scrapbook, 1951–53"). The football ticket "comp list" mentioned in the text is in a University of Notre Dame "Audit of Athletic Department Receipts for 1955 Football Season Presented to Father Jerome J. Wilson, Vice President of Business Affairs," 3/19/56. Frank Leahy turned down Bill Fox's request to sit on the ND bench, 10/10/51 (UASI 3/01), and sent a carbon copy to Charlie Callahan. The story about the head-to-toe Ohio State scarlet-and-gray outfits of *Columbus (Ohio) Dispatch* sports editor and columnist Paul Horning was told to me by Tim Sullivan of the *Cincinnati Inquirer,* 9/21/95. Ed Linn, in the *Sport* article "Fordham's Fight to Save Football," quoted the remarks of university president Father Robert Gannon, 10/53; the *Saturday Evening Post* article by Georgetown president Hunter Guthrie (op. cit.) is discussed at length in Chapter 47; Dean R. F. Patterson of the University of South Dakota condemned sportswriters in a letter to the *Saturday Evening Post,* 11/24/51.

On page 465 of the text, Stanley Woodward first wrote to Charlie Callahan about featuring Bob Williams, 3/21/50 (UASI 1/83); Woodward made the specific requests to Callahan, 3/28/50 (UASI 1/83); and Callahan replied to Woodward, offering his suggestions, 4/10/50 (UASI 1/83). The best account of Woodward's work for and departure from the *New York Herald Tribune* is in Richard Kluger's history of that paper, *The Paper: The Life and Death of the New York Herald Tribune,* New York, 1986; see multiple index entries for Woodward. The edition of *Stanley Woodward's Football Guide* with Bob Williams on the cover and the photos and captions inside appeared 8/50. For Al Pollard's academic problems, see the notes on this issue for Chapter 35 above. *Sport* magazine did a full profile of Bob Williams, 10/50, and mentioned his 83 percent average as a liberal arts major.

The *Time* magazine cover article on Dick Kazmaier appeared 11/19/51; John T. Brady (op. cit.) has the final Heisman vote for 1951, p. 98; concerning Kazmaier as the least qualified Heisman victor, even Jay Berwanger of the University of Chicago, an outstanding back in the tough Big Ten of 1934, had much better football credentials. Kazmaier showed no interest in playing NFL football, announcing before the draft that he planned to attend Harvard Business School; whether he could have played in the NFL will never be known but, considering the roughness of play and the players' macho code and contempt for Ivy Leaguers, it is doubtful that Kazmaier would have triumphed. The *Sport* feature "Mighty McElhenny," by Emmett Watson, appeared 12/51; all of the quotes from McElhenny are in that article except for the comment about "the first college player to take a cut in salary to play pro football," John Thelin (op. cit.), p. 132. Considering the NFL's low pay scale for many years, probably earlier college stars could have claimed similar pay cuts.

The *New York Times* featured the award of Associated Press "Male Athlete of the Year" to Kazmaier, along with a large photo of the player, 1/6/52. John T. Brady (op. cit.) discussed the Oklahoma campaign for Billy Vessels, p. 100; and former Maryland player Joe Petruzzo, with Al Silverman, told how "I've Been Through the Football Mill," 7/52. Bill Libby in *Heroes of the Heisman Trophy,* New York, 1973, quoted Leon Hart about Charlie Callahan's key role in Hart's Heisman, p. 112; John T. Brady (op. cit.) had the Lattner/Gipper story, p. 104; and William Barry Furlong wrote "The Bashful Terror of Notre Dame" for the *Saturday Evening Post,* 11/14/53. Jimmy Breslin's praise of Lattner appeared in *True* magazine, 9/53; and the *Look* photo spread appeared 12/1/53. Subsequently in the 1950s, Charlie Callahan helped Paul Hornung win a Heisman with a 2-8 ND team. Most sports historians regard this as a remarkable achievement, the only trophy won by a player on a losing squad. Yet, for Callahan, probably the Hornung campaign was easier than the Lattner one: by Hornung's senior year, the sports publicist had established him as "the Golden Boy," and the gifted athlete more than lived up to his reputation on offense, defense, and kicking, including field goals. In his Heisman season, he was second in the country in total offense with 1,337 yards, and second on the Fighting

Irish in tackles with 55. Hornung always gave full credit for his trophy to the ND sports publicist, and as John T. Brady (op. cit.) noted, "Callahan skillfully kept the Golden Boy in front of the nation's sportswriters," and the player did the rest, p. 110.

47. Magazines Discover Revisionism

Allen Jackson's *Atlantic Monthly* piece is referenced in the main text; Harold W. Stoke's article appeared in that magazine, 3/54. The week after Father Guthrie's piece (op. cit.) in the *Saturday Evening Post*, that magazine ran Blair Cherry's, 10/20/51 and, the following year, Fred Russell's "Football's Wildest Rivalry," 11/22/52. Jeff Cravath's confession appeared in *Collier's*, 10/30/53. In the discussion of these magazine articles, when I indicate that a periodical sought revisionist pieces from writers, I am using the term as an efficient way of labeling the product. I do not mean to suggest that the editors sat around and said, "We need more revisionist articles," and then instructed a writer to send them "a revisionist piece" on, say, Florida college football. However, editors did discuss the need for "hard-hitting exposés," that "differed from the same old tired stuff," i.e., classical pieces, and they instructed writers to produce this.

The *Life* photo essay on the USC-Cal game appeared 10/29/51; and Frank Gifford discussed this game and the *Life* feature on it in his memoirs (op. cit.), pp. 61–62. For a discussion of *Life*'s methods, see Wendy Kozol, *Life's America: Family and Nation in Postwar Photojournalism*, Philadelphia, 1994. The *Life* photo spread on the Johnny Bright incident ran 11/5/51; in this period, Oklahoma State was still called Oklahoma A&M, but to avoid confusion, I use the Oklahoma State name here. The *Life* piece on the toothless Fighting Irish appeared 9/29/52; and columnist Dan Foskett attacked the magazine's "Shoddy Slur," n.d. but from internal evidence, 10/52 (PATH "Notre Dame Football Scrapbook, 1952"). *Life* apologized, 10/13/52, and ran the photo spread on the MSU–Notre Dame game, 11/24/52. Time-Life editors, taking their cue from their bosses, Henry and Clare Booth Luce, were notorious grudge keepers, never forgetting an insult or slight, and returning the favor whenever possible, no matter how long it took (see *Luce: His Time, Life, and Fortune* by John Kobler, Garden City, New York, 1968). I could not find internal Time-Life discussion on the Fainting Irish incident, but it seems reasonable that, after eating so much crow with the tooth episode in 1952, that the following year, *Life* editors jumped on the events of the ND-Iowa game. Even though the Luces themselves, particularly Clare, liked the University of Notre Dame, by 1953 they were preoccupied with other activities, Clare angling full-time for an ambassadorship; however, after the 1952–53 football incidents, possibly Time-Life editors felt that they had achieved "pay-back" and/or the Luces intervened, and subsequently both magazines featured Notre Dame more positively, putting Father Hesburgh on their covers a number of times in the following decade, and promoting him and his university.

48. The Fainting Irish and the End of Frank Leahy's Notre Dame Career

Joe Williams wrote a retrospective column about the Fainting Irish incident and Leahy's resignation in the *New York World Telegram & Sun*, 2/3/54. The AP report of the ND-Iowa game, appearing in hundreds of Sunday papers, emphasized the great comeback, and although mentioning Varrichione's questionable time-out before the half, it did not mention the final swoons to save the game in the last minute. Similarly, the UP report mentioned Varrichione but took the stoppages in the final minute as actual injuries, 11/22/53 (PATH "Notre Dame Football Scrapbook, 1953"). Allison Danzig of the *New York Times* praised the Notre Dame comeback and put a classical spin on "some of the slickest clock-stopping of the year. You can't beat the Fighting Irish for resourcefulness and preparedness for any and all eventualities and emergencies. It takes some briefing [by the coach] and some self-possession for a team to react as instantly and instinctively in the shadow of disaster as did the men in green," 11/23/53. *Life* was the only national magazine to place and keep the item on the national agenda, 11/23/53 and 12/7/53. Wells Twombley in his *Shake Down the Thunder* (op. cit.) commented that it was "Monday before anybody realized," etc., p. 278.

The AP reported Grantland Rice's comments, 11/24/53 (PATH "Notre Dame Football Scrapbook, 1953"); Cal Hubbard offered his comment to the *Chicago Daily News*, 11/25/53; and Alex Karras, with Herb Gluck, related his recruiting by Iowa in *Even Big Guys Cry*, New York, 1977, pp. 77–79.

Joe Williams's comments about a "unique tribute" to Notre Dame appeared in his column in the *New York World Telegram & Sun*, 1/5/54. Robert L. Burns, sports editor of the *St Louis Globe-Democrat*, discussed Notre Dame and Caesar's wife, n.d. but from internal evidence, 11/53 (PATH "Notre Dame Football Scrapbook, 1953"). John A. Andresen wrote to President Theodore M. Hesburgh, 11/23/53; the letter is in the University of Notre Dame Athletic Department files, "Frank Leahy Section," as is the letter from J. D. Kelley of Helena, Montana, to Frank Leahy, 11/24/53. Wells Twombley (op. cit.) discussed Leahy's non-apology, Father Joyce's advice about the broadcast, and Leahy's decision to resign, pp. 284–85; and Father Hesburgh in his memoir (op. cit.) also commented on Leahy's resignation, p. 84. Joe Williams's column about Leahy's reluctance to resign appeared in the *New York World Telegram & Sun*, 2/5/54; Leahy's article with Tim Cohane ran in *Look*, 3/23/54, and Cohane's "Gridiron Muckerism," 12/29/53. Clark Mollenhoff's articles appeared in *Look*, 8/21/56 and 10/30/56.

Moose Krause commented on Leahy's film marathons and the NCAA censure in an interview (op. cit.); Stephen Singular (op. cit.) quoted Krause on the film sessions, "He'd [Leahy] go to nine o'clock, ten o'clock, eleven o'clock, midnight. I'd go home . . . and eat dinner and then have to come back and watch more film with him," p. 68. The AP carried Casey Stengel's remarks, 12/18/53, published in many papers including the *Elkhart (Indiana) Truth*. The section of Walter Byers's memoir entitled "Notre Dame's Golden Halo" is on p. 83.

49. Saving College Basketball and Creating Mixed-Form Sportswriting

Paul Lawrence (op. cit.) commented on how the basketball fixing scandals helped the NCAA's Enforcement Division, p. 53; and Walter Byers (op. cit.) discussed the Kentucky decision, pp. 56–61, the quote in the text is on p. 61. The *Sport* magazine "Basketball Previews" are referenced in the text except for the date of the 1952–53 one, 1/53; the *Sport* articles and editorials are referenced in the notes above; and the date of Arthur Daley's *New York Times Magazine* article, "Real Goon Game," was 12/21/52. One indication of the public perception of basketball players appeared in the *Sport* article on Notre Dame's Kevin O'Shea (op. cit.); author John Carmichael described Shea: "He's tall, but not tall enough to be a freak. He's well-built, in a rangy way. He doesn't give the impression of bulk at all."

The college basketball programs are in the same depositories at the University of Notre Dame as the football ones (see the notes in Chapter 10 above). However, the Spencer Agency had fewer subscribers to its basketball publications than to its football packages, somewhat balanced by West Coast schools taking the basketball programs but not the football ones. Some colleges and universities did their own programs, employing local artists and printers; nevertheless, as college basketball recovered in the 1950s, because the Spencer Agency could deliver the national advertisers and their dollars, the big-time basketball schools increasingly subscribed to them, and others began to follow.

Sport ran an unsigned article in its new "TV Section" titled "NCAA Tournament Expands," 4/51; as NCAA official and old-time coach Dutch Lonborg explained (op. cit.), the motivation was money, not avoidance of Madison Square Garden; only later did Byers put a PR spin on it. Ken Rappoport in *The Classic* (op. cit.) told the story of the Kansas recruit-napping of Lovellette, p. 86; Ed Burkholder did a profile, "Phog Allen—Windbag or Prophet?" for *Sport*, 4/52; Wilt Chamberlain discussed his recruiting adventures and decision to go to Kansas in his memoir, *A View from Above*, New York, 1991; announcer Marty Glickman told Stanley Cohen (op. cit.) about the Cardinal Spellman, DA Hogan, and St. John's connection, p. 155. *Sport* featured the star of Indiana's NCAA championship team, Don Schlundt, in "Indiana's Sleeping Giant" by Angelo Angelopolus, 3/54; and Jack Zanger's article was titled "The Basketball Fixers—Three Years After," 2/54. The *Newsweek* article appeared 3/24/52, and the *Business Week* one 1/4/58. Stanley Cohen (op. cit.) described the late 1950s and early 1960s scandals, pp. 226–33; according to Cohen, the final "tally showed that at least fifty players from twenty-seven colleges had been involved in fixing games in fifty-one cities and twenty-two states. There were other players and former players who had acted as go-betweens, still others who declined bribes but failed to report them. By any measure it was a scandal more than twice the size of the first. It was next to impossible to calculate the number of games that had been fixed or tampered with, and the coast-to-coast network involved literally dozens of gamblers," p. 227; he also points out that the *Modern Encyclopedia of Basketball* (op. cit.) devotes over 3,000 words to the first scandal and only two sentences to the later one. Jimmy Breslin wrote "Is Basketball Heading for Another Scandal" for *Sport*, 1/58, but he left the reader with little doubt that it was.

A recent book, *The Franchise: A History of Sports Illustrated Magazine,* by Michael MacCambridge, New York, 1997, provides an inside account of the genesis and evolution of that magazine, as well as the personalities of its editors and star writers; he also discusses Dan Jenkins's "Tie One for the Gipper" game, pp. 146–48. Jenkins's article appeared in *SI,* 11/19/66, and he reworded it slightly for his chapter on this game in *Saturday's America,* Boston, 1970; Father Hesburgh's article was in *SI,* 12/12/66.

In fact, Jenkins did not originate the "Tie One for the Gipper" phrase: Jim Murray, who had left *SI* for the *Los Angeles Times,* had a hand in the authorship, but because his was still a regional newspaper, Murray's use of the phrase did not attain wide circulation. Jenkins did write, "What the Fighting Irish did, was they tied one for the Gipper," but only when the Jenkins's piece appeared in *SI* did this nickname and point of view become commonplace. Tom Pagna, Ara Parseghian's close friend and assistant coach, explained in *Notre Dame's Era of Ara,* Huntsville, Alabama, 1976, that immediately after the game, "When the press came in, no one mentioned playing for a tie. They knew they had seen a great game, one that Notre Dame had fought valiantly to win. But in the days to come, spurred by a story in a national magazine [*SI*], the venom" began, and "detractors accused Ara of being 'gutless,' " etc., pp. 120–21. In Mike Celizic's *The Biggest Game of Them All,* New York, 1992, a book devoted entirely to this contest, the author elaborates on the above circumstances, supplies quotes from the game stories in various newspapers, and is the source of the "set the agenda" quote here, pp. 294–95.

Conclusion: The View from the End of the Century

Douglas Lederman did the *Chronicle of Higher Education* study on academic merit scholarships versus athletic scholarships, 3/30/94; Ernest L. Boyer in *The Undergraduate Experience in America,* New York, 1987, commented on student cynicism, p. 184. I plan to publish the results of my survey in my next book, tentatively titled *Beer and Circus: The Impact of Big-time College Sports on Undergraduate Education,* Henry Holt, New York. The Sun Belt university official spoke off the record for obvious reasons—to protect his job; his is only the second off-the-record comment in this entire book.

Bibliography

The bibliography consists of frequently cited works in the text, and books on the background of college sports that were particularly useful for this study.

Photographs

For the use of the photographs in this book, I am indebted to the University of Notre Dame Archives, and to Charles Lamb for his time and effort in helping me select them; in addition, for the use of the non–Notre Dame football game program covers, I must thank the Joyce Sports Research Collection at the University of Notre Dame and its excellent curator, George Rugg. The photo of Grantland Rice is from the Special Collections of Vanderbilt University; curator Strawberry Luck facilitated my use of it.

Bibliography

Ambrose, Stephen E. *Duty Honor Country: A History of West Point.* Baltimore, 1966.

Barber, Red. *The Broadcasters.* New York, 1970.

Basinger, Jeanine. *The World War II Combat Film: Anatomy of a Genre.* New York, 1986.

Beach, Jim, and Daniel Moore. *Army vs. Notre Dame: The Big Game 1913–1947,* New York, 1948.

Bender, Terry, and Lawrence W. Stiles. *Major College Football: Record of Scores: 1869–1982,* Bryn Mawr, Pa., 1983.

Blackwell, James A. *On Brave Old Army Team: The Cheating Scandal That Rocked the Nation, West Point, 1951.* Novato, Calif., 1996.

Blaik, Earl "Red." *The Red Blaik Story.* New Rochelle, N.Y., 1974; also containing Blaik's first memoir, *You Have to Pay the Price,* written with Tim Cohane, New York, 1960.

Brady, John T. *The Heisman: A Symbol of Excellence.* New York, 1984.

Bryant, Paul "Bear," and John Underwood. *Bear: The Hard Life and Good Times of Alabama's Coach Bryant.* Boston, 1975.

Byers, Walter, with Charles Hammer. *Unsportsmanlike Conduct: Exploiting College Athletes,* Ann Arbor, Mich., 1995.

Celizic, Mike. *The Biggest Game of Them All.* New York, 1992.

Cohane, Tim. *Great College Coaches of the Twenties and Thirties.* New Rochelle, N.Y., 1973.

Cohen, Richard M., et al., eds. *The Notre Dame Football Scrapbook.* Indianapolis, 1977.

Cohen, Stanley. *The Game They Played.* New York, 1977.

Cromartie, Bill, and Jody Brown. *The Glamor Game.* Nashville, Tenn., 1989.

Daley, Arthur. *Sports of the Times: The Arthur Daley Years.* New York, 1975.

Deford, Frank. *Everybody's All-American.* New York, 1981.

Douchant, Mike, ed. *Encyclopedia of College Basketball.* New York, 1995.

Doyle, Joe. *Fighting Irish: A Century of Notre Dame Football.* Charlottesville, Va., 1987.

Falla, Jack. *NCAA: The Voice of College Sports.* Mission, Kans., 1981.

Gallagher, Tag. *John Ford: The Man and His Films,* Berkeley, Calif., 1986.

Gifford, Frank, and Harry Waters. *The Whole Ten Yards.* New York, 1993.

Gipe, George. *The Great American Sports Book: A Casual but Voluminous Look at American Spectator Sports from the Civil War to the Present Time.* Garden City, N.Y., 1978.

Grant, Barry Keith, ed. *Film Genre Reader.* Austin, Tex., 1986.

Halberstam, David. *The Fifties.* New York, 1993.

Hesburgh, the Rev. Theodore M. *God, Country, Notre Dame.* New York, 1990.

Hollander, Zander, ed. *The Modern Encyclopedia of Basketball.* New York, 1973, and subsequent editions.

Holtzman, Jerome, ed. *No Cheering in the Press Box.* New York, 1974.

Isaacs, Neil. *All the Moves: A History of College Basketball.* Philadelphia, 1975.

Kane, Kathryn. *Visions of War: Hollywood Combat Films of World War II.* Ann Arbor, Mich., 1982.

Kanfer, Stefan. *A Summer World: The Attempt to Build a Jewish Eden in the Catskills from the Days of the Ghetto to the Rise and Decline of the Borscht Belt.* New York, 1989.

Katz, Fred, ed. *The Glory of Notre Dame.* New York, 1971.

Kluger, Richard. *Ashes to Ashes: America's Hundred-Year Cigarette War, the Public Health, and the Unabashed Triumph of Philip Morris.* New York, 1996.

———. *The Paper: The Life and Death of the New York Herald Tribune.* New York, 1986.

Kozol, Wendy. *Life's America: Family and Nation in Postwar Photojournalism.* Philadelphia, 1994.

Krause, Edward "Moose," with Stephen Singular. *Notre Dame's Greatest Coaches: Rockne, Leahy, Parseghian, and Holtz.* New York, 1993.

Kryk, John. *Natural Enemies: The Notre Dame–Michigan Football Feud.* Kansas City, Mo., 1994.

Lawrence, Paul. *Unsportsmanlike Conduct: The National Collegiate Athletic Association and the Business of College Football.* New York, 1987.

Lipsyte, Robert. *SportsWorld.* New York, 1975.

Littleton, Thomas B. *Arch: A Promoter, Not a Poet, The Story of Arch Ward.* Ames, Iowa, 1990.

MacCambridge, Michael. *The Franchise: A History of Sports Illustrated Magazine.* New York, 1997.

McCallum, John. *Big Ten Football Since 1895.* Radnor, Pa., 1976.

———. *Ivy League Football Since 1872.* New York, 1977.

———. *College Basketball, U.S.A., Since 1892.* New York, 1972.

Miller, Douglas T., and Marion Nowak. *The Fifties: The Way We Really Were.* New York, 1975.

Miller, Richard I. *The Truth About Big-Time Football.* New York, 1953.

Neely, Tim. *Hooping It Up: The Complete History of Notre Dame Basketball.* Notre Dame, Ind., 1985.

Newcombe, Jack. *The Best of the Athletic Boys: The White Man's Impact on Jim Thorpe.* Garden City, N.Y., 1975.

Novak, Michael. *The Joy of Sports.* New York, 1976.

Noverr, Douglas A., and Lawrence E. Ziewacz. *The Games They Played: Sports in American History, 1865–1980.* Chicago, 1983.

Oriard, Michael. *Dreaming of Heroes: American Sports Fiction, 1868–1980.* Chicago, 1982.

Perrin, Tom. *Football: A College History.* Jefferson, N.C., 1987.

Rader, Benjamin. *In Its Own Image: How Television Has Transformed Sports,* New York, 1984.

Rappoport, Ken. *The Classic: The History of the NCAA Basketball Championship,* Mission, Kans., 1979.

Roberts, Randy, and James S. Olson. *Winning Is the Only Thing: Sports in America Since 1945.* Baltimore, 1989.

Rosen, Leonard. *Scandals of '51: How the Gamblers Almost Killed College Basketball.* New York, 1978.

Sack, Allen L., and Ellen Staurowsky. *College Athletes for Hire: The Evolution and Legacy of the NCAA's Amateur Myth,* New York, 1998.

Samuelson, Rube. *The Rose Bowl Game.* Garden City, N.Y., 1951.

Schatz, Thomas. *Boom and Bust: The American Cinema in the 1940s.* New York, 1997.

———. *The Genius of the System: Hollywood Filmmaking in the Studio Era.* New York, 1988.

———. *Hollywood Genres: Formulas, Filmmaking, and the Studio System.* Philadelphia, 1981.

Sperber, Murray. *College Sports Inc.: The Athletic Department vs. the University.* New York, 1990.

———. *Shake Down the Thunder: The Creation of Notre Dame Football.* New York, 1993.

Stern, Bill. *My Favorite Sports Stories.* New York, 1946 and 1948.

Stern, Bill, with Oscar Fraley. *A Taste of Ashes: An Autobiography of Bill Stern.* New York, 1959.

Thelin, John. *Games Colleges Play: Scandal and Reform in Intercollegiate Athletics.* Baltimore, 1994.

———. *The Cultivation of Ivy.* Cambridge, Mass., 1976.

Twombley, Wells. *Shake Down the Thunder: The Official Biography of Frank Leahy.* Radnor, Pa., 1974.

Umphlett, Wiley. *The Movies Go to College: Hollywood and the World of the College Life Film.* Rutherford, N.J., 1984.

Wallace, Francis. *Notre Dame: From Rockne to Parseghian.* New York, 1966.

———. *The Notre Dame Story.* New York, 1949.

Wallenfeldt, Jeffrey H. *Sports Movies: A Guide to Nearly 500 Films Focusing on Sports.* Evanston, Ill., 1989.

Ward, Arch. *Frank Leahy and the Fighting Irish: The Story of Notre Dame Football.* New York, 1944.

Wills, Garry. *Reagan's America: Innocents at Home.* New York, 1987.

Wilson, Kenneth L. "Tug," with Jerry Brondfield. *The Big Ten,* Englewood Cliffs, N.J., 1967.

Zucker, Harvey Marc, and Lawrence J. Babich. *Sports Films: A Complete Reference.* Jefferson, N.C., 1987.

Index